Great Ideas/ Grand Schemes

Political Ideologies in the Nineteenth and Twentieth Centuries

Paul Schumaker
The University of Kansas

Dwight C. Kiel
The University of Central Florida

Thomas W. Heilke
The University of Kansas

The McGraw-Hill Companies, Inc.

New York St. Louis San Francisco Auckland Bogotá Caracas Lisbon London Madrid Mexico City Milan Montreal New Delhi San Juan Singapore Sydney Tokyo Toronto

To our parents and their parents and their parents
and our children and their children and their children

This book was set in Palatino by ComCom, Inc.
The editors were Lyn Uhl and Fred H. Burns;
the production supervisor was Kathryn Porzio.
The cover was designed by Merrill Haber.
R. R. Donnelley & Sons Company was printer and binder.

GREAT IDEAS/GRAND SCHEMES
Political Ideologies in the Nineteenth and Twentieth Centuries

This book is printed on acid-free paper.

2 3 4 5 6 7 8 9 0 DOC DOC 9 0 9 8 7 6

ISBN 0-07-055519-2

Library of Congress Cataloging-in-Publication Data

Schumaker, Paul.
Great ideas/grand schemes: political ideologies in the nineteenth and twentieth centuries / Paul Schumaker, Dwight C. Kiel, Thomas W. Heilke.
p. cm.
Includes bibliographical references and index.
ISBN 0-07-055519-2
1. Political science—History. 2. Right and left (Political science)—History. 3. Ideology—History. I. Kiel, Dwight C. II. Heilke, Thomas W., (date). III. Title.
JA83.S364 1996
320.5—dc20 95–23060

About the Authors

PAUL SCHUMAKER is professor of political science and distinguished lecturer of western civilization at the University of Kansas. He received his Ph.D. from the University of Wisconsin—Madison in 1973. His research on political movements and protest, democratic processes, and gender differences in political influence have appeared in such journals as the *Journal of Politics* and the *American Journal of Political Science.* His most recent book, *Critical Pluralism, Democratic Performance, and Community Power* was published by the University Press of Kansas in 1991. His current research examines how urban officials view and apply various principles of distributive justice.

DWIGHT C. KIEL is associate professor of political science at the University of Central Florida. He received his Ph.D. from the University of Massachusetts—Amherst in 1984. He has won several teaching awards, including the Burlington Outstanding Educator Award. His publications have examined competing perspectives on human reason during the Enlightenment. His most recent article, which appeared in the *American Review of Politics,* examines language and environmental issues.

THOMAS W. HEILKE is assistant professor of political science at the University of Kansas. He received his Ph.D. in political science from Duke University in 1990. Professor Heilke has published articles in *The Review of Politics and Political Theory* and is author of a book, *Voegelin on the Idea of Race: An Analysis of Modern European Racism* (LSU, 1990). He is completing a study of Friedrich Nietzsche's political education, and is presently engaged in an analysis of Anabaptist thought.

Contents

Part Four
NASCENT IDEOLOGIES

CONCLUSIONS

Preface

How should we organize our political communities—especially our economies and governments? Who should govern? What are our rights and obligations as citizens? For what purposes should governmental authority be employed? How should various goods be distributed in a just society? How much social change is needed, and how is such change best achieved? These are among the "great issues" and "perennial questions" of politics. To think clearly about these questions, students need to understand "the great ideas" that have been proposed as answers to them. To think deeply about these questions, students also need to address the philosophical foundations of the proposed answers. What conceptions of the universe, society, human nature, and political knowledge itself do particular "great ideas" presuppose? Thinking about the great issues of politics, the great ideas that have been provided as answers to these issues, and the philosophical foundations of these ideas is the central focus of political theory and philosophy.

As teachers of political theory and philosophy, we have found that examining various ideologies is an excellent way to engage students in thinking about these questions. A political ideology is a "grand scheme" for understanding and evaluating political life. An ideology provides answers to each of the great political issues. An ideology contains (either explicitly or implicitly) assumptions about the universe, society, human nature, and political knowledge. Moreover, the ideas of an ideology are—or at least should be—systematically interrelated. Because the ideas of an ideology cover the most fundamental issues about politics and because these ideas are coherently structured, they provide people with "big pictures" of how political communities work and what more ideal communities might look like.

Political ideologies provide useful introductions to the great issues of politics, because students are familiar with ideologies. They know that their political leaders have particular ideological commitments, and they sense that the commentaries that they read or hear reflect particular ideological biases. Students believe—rightfully so—that ideologies make a difference in "the real world," because the policies that governments pursue reflect prominent ideological orientations and because the emergence of new ideologies can result in important social changes. Recognizing that ideologies are important, students want to understand them better.

A better understanding of political ideologies is important to the broader curricula of most political science—and other social science—departments. Many courses and books on politics, society, and economics introduce concepts and theories drawn from various ideological perspectives. Institutional arrangements, policy choices, and both historical and current events are typically analyzed from competing ideological viewpoints. The underlying assumption behind such analyses is that students already understand the distinctions between a variety of ideologies fairly well. In our experience, this assumption is often ill-founded. For example, students usually fail to differentiate between classical liberalism and contemporary liberalism or between Marxism, communism, and democratic socialism. To achieve more clear and focused discourse throughout the political science and social science curricula, attention needs to be given to the ideological foundations of various political ideas.

The ideological landscape is always changing—and perhaps never so dramatically as in recent years. The collapse of the Soviet Union is usually thought to signal the demise of Marxism and communism as attractive ideologies. Are these ideologies, or parts of them, still relevant to world politics? The Reagan-Bush era seems to have produced a profound shift in the ideological outlooks of many Americans, as liberalism seems to have lost much of its public appeal. Can contemporary liberals effect coherent and attractive modifications to liberalism's unpopular image of endorsing big bureaucratic government and requiring higher taxes? Various emergent ideologies—such diverse types as religious fundamentalism, environmentalism, and feminism—have gained increasing public attention. Are these newer outlooks really full-blown ideologies, and do they have attractions that might allow them to have the kind of influence over political life in the twenty-first century that communism, liberalism, and conservatism have had in the twentieth century? This text has been written, in part, to describe the changing ideological landscape and to address questions prompted by ideological transformations.

Pedagogically, the most important difference between this text and other texts that analyze ideologies is our use of a single conceptual framework for describing each ideology. Seeking to provide well-organized presentations of each ideology that facilitate comparative analyses among ideologies, we have imagined asking the proponents of each ideology to provide their ideas in response to twelve very general questions:

Problems What are the political, economic, and social problems that most need to be addressed?

Goals What are the most important political, economic, and social goals to be achieved?

Structure How are political communities organized, and how should they be organized?

Citizenship What should be the rights and responsibilities of citizens?

Rulers Who governs society, and who should govern society?

Authority For what purposes is governmental authority used, and for what purposes should it be used and not used?

Justice How are social goods distributed, and how should they be distributed?

Change How much change is needed, and how is such change best achieved?

Human nature What are the fundamental characteristics of human nature?

Society What are the fundamental characteristics of society?

Ontology What is ultimate reality, and what are the ultimate causes of change in the world?

Epistemology Can reliable knowledge about the "good" political life be attained, and how can such knowledge best be acquired or approached?

In this text, we consider twelve ideologies. For each ideology, we provide a section that describes how proponents of the ideology answer each of these questions. Such a framework facilitates direct comparisons for analyzing and evaluating the ideas of competing ideologies. Such a framework reminds students that ideologies contain interconnected principles and that such principles are based on particular philosophical foundations. We believe that student understanding and analysis is promoted by comparing the ideas of competing ideologies, by showing how the appealing principles of an ideology may be logically connected to other, perhaps less appealing, ideas in the ideology, and by exploring the philosophical foundations of these ideas.

In addition, we present various ideologies in a manner that reflects their historical development. In Part 1, we describe the main ideologies of the nineteenth century, beginning with the first ideology, classical liberalism (or democratic capitalism). Traditional conservatism, anarchism, and Marxism are then presented as responses to—and alternatives to—classical liberalism. In Part 2, we describe the main totalitarian ideologies of the twentieth century: communism, nazism, and fascism. (Nazism and fascism are presented in one chapter that emphasizes their commonalities while acknowledging their differences.) In Part 3, we describe the main democratic ideologies of the twentieth century. Here we consider how the minimal-government principles of classical liberalism were transformed into the strong-state principles of contemporary liberalism. We consider how the revolutionary ideology of Marxism was revised into the evolutionary outlook that characterizes democratic socialism. We also consider how contemporary conservatives have sought to reconcile and conserve both classical liberal and traditional conservative ideas, and to defend these ideas against the onslaught of the more state-centered ideologies that have been prominent in the twentieth century. In Part 4, we describe three "nascent" ideologies that have become increasingly prominent: religious fundamentalism, environmentalism, and feminism.

At the end of this century, many alternative voices have emerged to present counterpoints to the ideologies described in Parts 1, 2, and 3. Libertarianism and communitarianism are widely discussed among political theorists and philosophers and have become increasingly popular, especially on American college campuses. Black separatism has emerged as an expression of the political views of many African Americans. Liberation theology is a powerful voice for change in Latin America. Various nationalist movements have (re)emerged around the globe, each with its own distinct principles. Among these newer voices, we focus on fundamentalism, environmentalism, and feminism, because they seem to offer the most distinct sets of ideas setting them apart from other ideologies. Jewish, Christian, and Islamic fundamentalists remind us of the extensiveness of human faith in God's omniscience and omnipotence, and of the consequent attractions of political outlooks that challenge those ideologies that suppose that humans can understand and control the world in a manner that is indifferent to God's will. Environmentalists remind us that humans are simply one of many species to inhabit the earth and that other ideologies have been excessively human-centered, and concerned merely with justifying the exploitation of the natural environment for human purposes. Feminists remind us that other ideologies have been male-centered; these androcentric ideologies have been developed largely by men and have, perhaps, failed to express adequately the concerns of women.

Despite the importance of fundamentalism, environmentalism, and feminism, we do not treat these viewpoints with the same depth of analysis that we employ in our treatment of the other ideologies. Huge bodies of literature have recently emerged within each of these perspectives that we have only begun to assimilate. From our limited exposure to these texts, it is our judgment that there exists too much disagreement about political principles and insufficient attention to philosophical foundations within fundamentalism, environmentalism, and feminism for these perspectives to be considered fully developed ideologies. This is not to claim that there are no important theoretical and philosophical writings within or about these perspectives. To the contrary, we believe that the existence of such writings qualifies these perspectives as "nascent" ideologies and provides the foundations for their eventual establishment as "full-fledged" ideologies. Thus, we think it is very possible that fundamentalism, environmentalism, and/or feminism are more than social movements that will be integrated within existing ideologies—as some scholars have contended—but are emerging as distinct ideological alternatives. By presenting some of the ideas of fundamentalism, environmentalism, and feminism within the same framework that seems to serve well in describing the "full-fledged" ideologies, we hope to encourage the further articulation of their ideas in ways that facilitate their development and analysis as ideologies.

We would also like to point out a few conventions that we have adopted in this text. Most importantly, we present each ideology from the perspective of its proponents. Ideological thought is frequently characterized negatively, and texts on ideologies often devote much attention to criticizing the ideas they are describing. We agree that ideological thinking can involve distortions and other difficulties, and we think that all ideologies have limitations. Nevertheless, we believe that, before students can effectively evaluate an ideology and its ideas, such ideas must be understood, and the first step in understanding an ideology is to enter into its worldview. There is no doubt that students should evaluate each ideology. Thus, in Chapter 1, we provide criteria that are useful in the evaluation process, and we provide evaluative comments and questions at the conclusion of our discussion of each ideology. In addition, we sometimes use footnotes to point to difficulties with certain ideas and to present sources that criticize these ideas. However, these devices are intended to prompt students to think for themselves, not to encourage students to substitute our evaluations for theirs.

Another convention that we have employed is to provide "sidebars." For each ideology we first provide a sidebar listing important contributors to the ideological tradition, along with their major writings. Our intent is not to give an exhaustive bibliography, but rather to indicate the people for whom we presume to speak in our presentation of the ideology. Other sidebars are intended to make elaborations and connections of ideas that do not fit well within our framework but that are both important and interesting.

A final convention is that we use boldfaced type to highlight certain terms that represent important ideas within each ideological tradition and that identify concepts that should be grasped by all students of political theory and political science. A glossary at the end of the text provides short definitions of these terms, but we have found it important to stress to our students that the ideas represented by these terms cannot be well-understood by memorizing short definitions but only by comprehending their significance within the broader system of ideas contained by the ideologies.

We have accumulated many debts in the process of writing this book. Our greatest debts are to all those men and women who have contributed to the "great conversation" and whose ideas are reflected—it is hoped reasonably accurately—in the text. We are indebted to our teachers, especially those who have most sparked our interest in and understanding of political theory and philosophy: Lester McAlister, Booth Fowler, and Eldon Fields; Jeff Sedgwick and Lewis Mainzer; Barry Cooper, Thomas Flanagan, Michael Gillespie, and Anthony Parel. We are indebted to our students, whose questions have stimulated us to deepen our own understanding, and whose comments have often provided useful insights. We are especially indebted to our wives—Jean Schumaker, Charlene Stinard, and Tara Heilke—who have supported us in many ways throughout this project. They and many others have commented on all or part of this text. We would like to acknowledge the following people for their helpful suggestions: David Brichoux, Cryss Brunner, Deborah Gerner, Peter Gustafson, Marisa Kelly, Rob Kurfirst, and Nicholas Paley. We would also like to acknowledge the following reviewers who made helpful suggestions: Clarke Cochran, Texas Tech University; Gill Evans, University of Tennessee–Knoxville; William Garner, University of Southern Illinois; Michael

Gibbons, University of South Florida; Ellen Grigsby, University of New Mexico; Michael Hervey, Colorado State University; Murray Jardine, Louisiana State University; Tim Martinez, Northern Arizona University; Susan Matarese, University of Louisville; Walter Mead, Illinois State University; John Nelson, University of Iowa; Patrick O'Meara, Indiana University; and Leslie Thiele, University of Florida.

Paul Schumaker

Dwight C. Kiel

Thomas W. Heilke

CHAPTER 1

Political Ideas, Theories, and Ideologies

Cruise through the channels of your TV and you see lots of "talking heads" offering up analyses of the state of the nation. Scan your radio dial and you hear dozens of talk show hosts, callers, and guests spouting opinions on the ills of society, economics, and government. Glance at the newspapers and magazines and you encounter commentaries and editorials interpreting current events from various viewpoints. Take a class, not just in political science, but in any liberal arts discipline, and soon enough your professor will start discussing the human condition and community life. Do any of these things—or many other activities—and you will encounter a bewildering array of political ideas.

While there are many ideas about politics, not all are equally important. Many ideas concern fleeting political events, issues, or personalities, but *great ideas* concern more enduring questions about political communities. Great political ideas describe and explain how people live together in peace and prosperity, or they suggest how people can better achieve peace and prosperity. These ideas tell us how our communities are structured, or how they ought to be organized. They identify the (perhaps hidden) rulers of society, or those who ought to govern in a better (or ideal) world. They indicate how governments use and abuse their powers, and suggest when governmental authority should be used. They state the liberties and obligations of citizens, and propose extensions of or restrictions to their rights and duties. They describe how various social goods—like wealth, power, and status—are distributed, and make claims about the just distribution of such goods.

The TV and radio talk shows, the newspaper commentaries and editorials, and contemporary liberal arts curricula all reveal widespread disagreement—not only among ordinary citizens but also among supposed experts—over great political ideas. People have different ideas about how to achieve peace and prosperity. They have different ideas about who should rule. They disagree about the meaning and requirements of authority, liberty, justice, and other political ideas. Or, at least, they seem to disagree.

Perhaps the greatest political idea is that agreement on the great ideas about politics is possible. For thousands of years, people have dreamed of a world of political truth—a world having certain knowledge about how to order and govern communities in ways that provide peace, prosperity, and justice, and that fulfill other human aspirations. The ancient Greeks—especially Socrates (ca. 470–399 B.C.E.), Plato (ca. 427–346 B.C.E.), and Aristotle (384–322 B.C.E.)—gave birth to political philosophy as the discipline concerned with conducting the search for political truth. Ensuing human history has seen "the great thinkers" propose various approximations of political truth. For many who have thought deeply about the search for political truth, this quest has been—and must always be—a failure.[1] For many, the dream of acquiring certain political knowledge, or even of attaining widespread agreement about which great ideas are best, has been dashed.

But perhaps this is a premature judgment. Perhaps the disagreement over political ideas that is evident in the media (or in liberal arts education and curricula) exaggerates our differing opinions while concealing some fundamental, deeper truths on which humans everywhere increasingly agree. Perhaps politicians unnecessarily create "false choices and artificial polarization" in an attempt to gain temporary partisan advantages.[2] Perhaps fundamental truths about political life have been discovered and historical processes are unfolding in ways that are bringing about universal recognition of these ideas and their gradual implementation everywhere.[3]

To understand the great ideas of politics and to consider whether it is possible to agree about these ideas, it is necessary to step back from the talk show debates, the media's preoccupation with current events, and the apparent skepticism about achieving political truth that dominates American education. It is necessary to consider the very nature of politics and to study political theory.

Politics

"Politics" is normally defined in a manner that presupposes the answer to our question of whether it is possible to attain agreement about great political ideas. According to a leading political philosopher:

> Politics concerns itself only with those realms where truth is not—or is not *yet*—known. We do not vote for the best polio vaccine or conduct surveys on the ideal space shuttle, nor has Boolean algebra been subjected to electoral testing. But Laetrile and genetic engineering, while they belong formally to the domain of science, have aroused sufficient conflict among scientists to throw them into the political domain—and rightly so. Where consensus stops, politics starts.[4]

[1]See, for example, Judith Shklar, *After Utopia: The Decline of Political Faith* (Princeton: Princeton University Press, 1957).
[2]E. J. Dione, *Why Americans Hate Politics* (New York: Simon and Schuster, 1991), p. 15.
[3]Francis Fukuyama, *The End of History of the Last Man* (New York: Avon Books, 1992).
[4]Benjamin Barber, *Strong Democracy* (Berkeley: University of California Press), p. 139.

According to this description, politics is that human activity that deals with conflicting ideas about how people should be organized in community life. When people disagree—as they usually do—about the benefits they hope to achieve from their social cooperation, they are engaged in politics. When people disagree—as they usually do—about how to distribute among members of the community the benefits and burdens of their cooperation, they are engaged in politics. In short, this definition suggests that politics occurs whenever people disagree about how communities should be governed.

But there are other ideas about the nature of politics. According to an eminent political scientist, "Politics is the steering sector of society" and "deals inescapably with the collective self-control of human beings—their joint power over their own fate."[5] In a similar vein, it has been suggested that politics involves "cooperation among disparate community elements to attain some publicly significant result."[6] In such conceptions, politics is less about conflicting ideas than it is about achieving common goals. From this perspective, politics involves attaining social agreement that certain ideas are "good" or "right" and then organizing the community in such a way as to produce the outcomes envisioned by these good ideas.

We think politics should be defined in a way that encompasses both of these images of politics, in a way that does not exclude either of them. Politics is best understood as involving situations where community members are considering a common course of action and resolve their potential or existing disagreements about their goals and means of achieving these goals in various ways.[7] They may resort to violence, war, or coercion; some people may overpower others, forcing the weak to abide by the ideas of the strong. They may employ propaganda; some people may manipulate information and ideas in ways that achieve widespread compliance with their ideas through development of a "false" consensus that would not be obtainable if others had fuller information and unrestricted access to competing ideas. They may agree to employ certain procedures for resolving any disagreements that arise; they could flip a coin, put the issue to a vote, take the issue to court, or use any other procedure they believe is a legitimate method of resolving their disagreement. Or they can try to resolve their disputes by coming to agreement; they might engage in collaborative efforts to "work through" conflicting ideas, to get to common ground, to approach consensus, and to arrive at ideas that all regard as "right" for the community.[8]

Such a conception of politics is useful for those studying great ideas about

[5]Karl Deutsch, "On Political Theory and Political Action," *American Political Science Review* 65 (Mar. 1971), p. 18.

[6]Clarence Stone, *Regime Politics* (Lawrence: University Press of Kansas, 1989), p. 227.

[7]Our description of politics is probably closest to that of Bertrand de Jouvenal, who suggested, "We should regard as 'political' every systematic effort, performed at any place in the social field, to move other men in pursuit of some design cherished by the mover." See his *The Pure Theory of Politics* (Cambridge: Cambridge University Press, 1963).

[8]These methods of resolving political conflict are neither exhaustive nor mutually exclusive. When controversy arises in a community, the disputants are likely to employ propaganda and may use

community life. It recognizes that there is frequent disagreement over such ideas, but it leaves open the issue of whether such disagreement is inevitable and insurmountable. Such a conception of politics is also useful because it recognizes that politics is a feature of all communities. Because people are organized into many types of communities—because they are members of families and neighborhoods, churches and synagogues, corporations and unions, athletic teams and musical guilds, social sororities and fraternities, and many other types of associations—they often find themselves encountering the great ideas of politics even when they are not acting as citizens of their respective towns, states, and nations.

Political Theory

Political theory describes, explains, and evaluates human life as it is lived in community with others, and it predicts future patterns of community life. Political theory also advocates (and criticizes) certain ideals or values about how humans ought to live in community with others and prescribes methods for attaining (or avoiding) these ideals or values. Political theory encompasses all of the conflicting ideas of the "great" (and less great) thinkers about how our various communities are governed and how they should be governed. Because everyone has ideas about the governance of the communities to which they belong, everyone is, to some degree, a political theorist. But at least two qualities are found in the ideas of serious political thinkers or theorists.

First, the ideas of theorists are expressed as *generalizations*. Nontheorists often focus on concrete and specific cases. For example, they might express the notion that, say, Smith is a powerful person in the community and describe the ways he attained and used his power. Such descriptions can be fascinating and illuminating, because of the particular nuances and unique features of power that are revealed by the case of Smith. Political theorists, however, typically generalize across cases. By observing the characteristics of the most powerful persons in various communities and thinking about the sources and implications of different distributions of power, theorists might express more general ideas like "the powerful tend to be men," or "the greater power of men than women in communities is due to the different socialization experiences of boys and girls in childhood," or "communities are best governed when power is distributed equally between men and women." Theorists believe such generalizations make comprehensible the basic patterns of human life that underlie concrete cases. Theorists maintain that generalizations are necessary to explain differences among cases, to predict the outcomes of various cases, and to prescribe the best outcomes in most cases.[9]

Second, compared to most people, political theorists are more deeply

---

coercion or threaten violence; the disputants may also seek to achieve a genuine consensus before finally putting the issue to a vote.

[9]More technically, political scientists differentiate between *nomothetic* and *ideograhic* ideas. "Nomothetic" statements contain generalizations, while "ideographic" statements focus on concrete cases. While political theorists focus on nomothetic ideas, they usually recognize the importance of ideo-

concerned about the bases and **validity** of their ideas. Theorists usually present their ideas with a measure of tentativeness and humility that one political theorist calls "humane uncertainty."[10] They often suppose that the questions they address about peace, prosperity, justice, and other great ideas have true answers in the eyes of God or from some other ideal, all-knowing, unbiased, or transcendent perspective. But recognizing their humanity, they acknowledge the limits of their knowledge and the potential biases in their perceptions and analyses. According to the French philosopher Simone Weil, theorists check the validity of their ideas by regularly employing as methods of investigation a search for the contrary to their ideas and an examination of the validity of these contrary ideas. According to the Austrian-born British philosopher and educator Karl Popper, theorists check the validity of their ideas by employing scientific methods that consider empirical evidence concerning ideas, that filter out various biases to thinking, and that allow others to examine the procedures used to test their ideas. Theorists ask about the underlying assumptions that must be accepted if one is to support their ideas, and reflect on the usefulness and validity of these assumptions. Theorists look for counter-arguments to their ideas and consider the persuasiveness of these arguments. Theorists seek to find examples that are contrary to their generalizations and thus provide known limits to these generalizations. Being highly reflective about the validity of ideas, theorists conduct an open-ended and tentative search for what is true in political life and what is good in political life.[11]

While all political theory provides generalizations and is self-reflective about the validity of expressed ideas, there are important differences among various forms of political theory. Two important differentiations that are often made about political theory concern its purposes and scope.

Political theory that seeks to *describe, explain,* and *predict* political life is known as **empirical theory**.[12] Political theory that *advocates* and *justifies* certain "values" or "ends" concerning how political life should be in a closer-to-ideal

---

graphic ideas drawn from biographies, case studies, and analyses of particular policy issues, for example. Such studies are often the basis for developing nomothetic ideas and sometimes the basis for testing their validity. See Adam Przeworski and Henry Teune, *The Logic of Comparative Social Inquiry* (New York: Wiley Interscience, 1970), pp. 5–8, and Harry Eckstein, "Case Study and Theory in Political Science," in *Handbook of Political Science,* vol. 7, edited by Fred I. Greenstein and Nelson Polsby (Reading, Mass.: Addison-Wesley, 1975).

[10]Glenn Tinder, *Political Thinking: The Perennial Questions,* 5th ed. (New York: HarperCollins, 1991), pp. 225–238.

[11]Most philosophers of science recognize the tentativeness of all ideas, whether these ideas concern the natural world or the social world. See Thomas Kuhn, *The Structure of Scientific Revolutions* (Chicago: University of Chicago Press, 1962).

[12]Valid generalizations relating two phenomena in the observable world provide both explanations and predictions. Consider, for example, the generalization that the spread of democracy is associated with a decline of war. This generalization (potentially) explains the decline of war as due to the spread of democracy (because of a deeper theory that the growing demand for "equal recognition" implies support both for democratic procedures and for nonaggression against other communities). This generalization seems to predict a lessening of war as regimes having democratic values and institutions continue to replace nondemocratic regimes throughout the world.

world, that *criticizes* the values or ends of political life as it is lived, or that *prescribes* "means" or methods for moving political life away from deficient values and toward advocated ends is known as **normative theory**. While empirical theory deals with how the political world *is*, normative theory deals with how the political world *ought to be*. Because scientific methods can be used to test the validity of descriptions and explanations about political reality, the generalizations that survive such examinations are often referred to as "scientific" political theory. In contrast, normative theory contains political principles about preferred or ideal political conditions. Scientific evidence may play a role in defending or justifying normative principles; however, such evidence is never sufficient to indicate their validity, because certain value judgments are always involved in normative ideas. While the distinction between empirical and normative theory is important, the effort of some political analysts to achieve completely empirical or scientific theories of politics has been controversial and perhaps tragic.[13] Perhaps the most interesting and important great political ideas are *evaluative* and contain both empirical and normative elements. A common evaluative idea is, for example, that political power among various interests should, ideally, be relatively equal in a democracy, but that certain interests are, in fact, much more powerful than others, requiring that certain reforms be pursued to achieve a more democratic community. Empirical analysis may provide descriptions and explanations of political life that offend our moral sensitivities and political values, leading to normative ideas about how political life ought to be instead and prescriptions for how to move toward such ideals. Or, normative standards can be asserted and defended, and then empirical analyses can reveal the gaps between what is and what ought to be in political life, and empirical theories can offer explanations for this gap and prescriptions for narrowing it.[14]

Political theories range in scope from the relatively narrow to the extremely broad. Generalizations of limited scope and without a well-developed theoretical basis are sometimes regarded as *lower-range theories*. For example, the generalization that "women are more likely than men to vote for the Democratic party" is supported by a significant amount of empirical evidence, but unless the generalization has a theoretical basis that explains such a tendency, it remains at the lower range of theoretical comprehensiveness. Such generalizations have some value to understanding political life, but they are not among the "great ideas" about politics.

Midrange theories often focus on the "great ideas" of politics, but these theories analyze only one (or, at most, a few) of these great ideas. For example, such theories may attempt to explain observable differences among communities, leaders, and citizens on various specific and important variables—such as why some countries are more democratic than others, some leaders

[13]See David Ricci, *The Tragedy of Political Science: Politics, Scholarship, and Democracy* (New Haven: Yale University Press, 1984).

[14]For a leading example of political theory that blends empirical and normative ideas, see Robert Dahl, *Democracy and Its Critics* (New Haven: Yale University Press, 1989).

more effective than others, and some citizens more active in politics than others. Midrange theories might also advocate particular political practices—such as enhancing democracy or encouraging nationalism. Because ideas about democracy and nationalism are sometimes regarded as more-comprehensive theories of politics—as ideologies—it is useful to consider why such ideas should instead be regarded as midrange theories.

Democracy involves a commitment to political equality, to the idea that the interests of each member of the community matter, and matter equally. To the extent that the people of a society provide equal political rights to each other and regard everyone as equally capable of rendering effective political judgments, they have democratic principles. While democratic ideals are among the most potent forces in politics today, support for democratic ideals does not constitute a comprehensive political worldview. Holding democratic principles does not necessarily lead to other political principles and beliefs. One can hold democratic principles and believe that current inequalities in economic wealth are either justified or illegitimate. One can hold democratic principles and believe that governmental authority should be weak or strong. Being committed to democratic principles gives one very little substantive guidance about current political issues, as the democrat has only procedural norms—for example, that current issues should be resolved on the basis of such democratic procedures as majority rule—to decide what policies are best. When theorists advocate or criticize democracy, their focus is usually on a single "great idea" and they contribute to midrange theories of democracy.

Nationalism is a system of beliefs and values claiming that a group of people sharing an ethnic and cultural identity—such as the Lithuanians in the former Soviet Union, the Serbs in what was formerly Yugoslavia, the French Canadians, the Basques in Spain, or African-Americans in the United States—have the right to form an independent state. Like democracy, nationalism is one of the most important ideas in politics, but it is not a comprehensive political worldview because nationalists do not share other great ideas. Nationalist movements can be fundamentally fascist (as Serbian nationalism appears to be), conservative (as is Islamic nationalism), liberal (as the separatist movement in Quebec has been), or socialist (as many nationalist movements in Africa have been). Rather than viewing nationalism as an ideology, it should be regarded as a goal that is combined with the goals of other ideologies to generate various forms of nationalism. When people advocate (or criticize) the goal of having various nationalities form independent states, they are contributing to midrange theories of nationalism.

Beyond lower-range and midrange theories, *grand theories* attempt to address a broad range of political issues by systematically interrelating many great ideas. One approach to grand theories is the construction of paradigms. **Paradigms** seek to describe and explain the most important features of the political world as it exists. Through the application of a single set of interrelated concepts, such "frameworks" as systems theory or group theory seek to explain the outcomes of the great issues of politics—such as how and why governmental authority is used, how power and other social goods are distributed, why citizens participate, and when political change occurs. Such paradigms aspire to be scientific, empirical, and value-free, providing no evaluations of the political world and making no arguments about how the political world ought to be structured and to function.[15]

In contrast, **utopias** attempt to provide comprehensive responses to the question, "What does a good political society look like?" They provide integrated responses to the great normative issues of politics. They indicate who should rule, how authority should be used, how social goods should be distributed, and how citizens should behave. Since at least 1516, when Thomas More (1478–1535) wrote his great speculative social treatise, *Utopia,* utopias have been prominent in the history of political thought. Subsequent speculative utopias—ranging from Francis Bacon's *New Atlantis* (1624) to Theodor Hertzka's *Freeland* (1891) to B. F. Skinner's *Walden Two* (1948)—have generated both great excitement and great ridicule. Since the word "utopia" means "nowhere," utopias are often scorned as presenting completely unrealistic visions of political life.[16] Utopias are also criticized for presenting normative ideas without a rigorous defense of these ideas as they relate to competing ideas and political values, and for supposing that the ideals they describe are universally applicable for all cultures and all unknown futures. Nevertheless, utopias are valuable contributions to the world of political ideas because they provide visions of social possibilities that can open our minds to alternatives beyond existing, or expected future, conditions.

Ideologies

The most comprehensive grand theories of politics are **ideologies**. Ideologies provide logically related empirical statements about historical and present realities of social, economic, and political life, *and* they provide a coherent system of ideals or values about how societies, economies, and governments ought to be structured and perform in the near future. By performing the descriptive and explanatory functions of paradigms and the normative and visionary functions of utopias, ideologies are the truly "grand schemes" of political ideas. In addition to their comprehensive scope, ideologies have at least three other features that make them attractive tools for understanding the great ideas of politics.

First, political ideologies are directly relevant to the actual practices of politics. It is sometimes thought that political *philosophy* searches for political truth in a manner that is little concerned with direct practical applications. While we doubt that political philosophy is irrelevant to political practices, the immediate relevance of many works in political philosophy is not always apparent.

[15]During the 1960s and 1970s, grand scientific theories of politics were much more prominent in political science than they are currently. One of the most recent assessments of such theories is provided by Gabriel A. Almond in *A Discipline Divided: Schools and Sects in Political Science* (Newbury Park, Calif.: Sage, 1990).

[16]Frank E. Manuel and Fritzie P. Manuel, *Utopian Thought in the Western World* (Cambridge: Belknap Press of Harvard University Press, 1979), p. 1.

In contrast, political ideologies directly influence many political, economic, and social practices. Ideologies often prompt citizens to support or oppose political regimes. Some ideologies have enabled certain regimes to remain in power for years, decades, and even centuries. For example, liberalism (as it is broadly defined and understood) has helped sustain the U.S. Constitutional based regime for over two hundred years. Other ideologies have helped bring down old regimes. For example, Marxist-Leninism (or Bolshevism) contributed to the Russian Revolution of 1917. Ideologies have led to important changes in economic institutions and practices, as well. For example, democratic socialism played an enormous role in the creation of social welfare states in western Europe during the twentieth century, and contemporary conservatism has led to significant reductions recently in the amount of economic regulation that exists in Britain and the United States. Ideologies have also changed our social institutions and practices. For example, feminism has begun to transform the lives of men and women, enhancing educational and occupational opportunities for women, curtailing sexual harassment in the workplace, and making more equal the child-raising responsibilities of mothers and of fathers. Environmentalism has prompted many of us to reexamine and change such habits as putting chemicals on our lawns and throwing empty cans in the trash. Such examples could be cited endlessly, but these are sufficient to establish the basic point that the ideas of ideologies affect our politics and everyday lives in profound ways. Because we can better understand and evaluate ideas when we have concrete examples of their applications, this applied feature of ideologies makes them particularly useful for the study of great ideas.

Second, the study of ideologies can provide an intellectual history of the ideas that have influenced the development of political life during the past two hundred years. The study of ideologies helps to understand, or place in context, the contributions of widely recognized "great thinkers"—like John Locke, Edmund Burke, Karl Marx, and John Stuart Mill—while also pointing to the importance of other writers and activists who have yet to be recognized as part of the "canon" of political thought. All ideologies look back upon important contributions to political philosophy for inspiration, guidance, and intellectual authority, and they usually have "sacred texts" that provide the philosophical foundations for their ideas. The study of ideologies may help to reveal how the ideas of various philosophers influence the world of politics by being incorporated into ideologies that are then used to determine political goals and actions.

Third, the intellectual impetus for the creation of ideologies was to ground politics in true ideas. At the end of the eighteenth century the concept of "ideology" was invented to refer to a new "science of ideas" that would sort out "true knowledge" from opinion, myth, custom, and superstition.[17] Thus, "ideo-

[17]See Earnest Kennedy, *Destuitt de Tracy and the Origins of Ideology: A Philosophe in the Age of Revolution* (Philadelphia: American Philosophical Society, 1978). The origins of ideological thinking are discussed below in the section on "A Brief History of Ideology."

logues" have been among the most committed and diligent aspirants to resolving the seemingly endless debate that people have had over the great ideas. The proponents of certain ideologies—such as classical liberalism and Marxism—claim to provide universal truths about how political communities are and should be governed. Proponents of other ideologies—such as traditional conservatives and contemporary liberals—deny the existence of universal truth, yet develop coherent systems of great ideas that they believe are better than those of their ideological competitors. Perhaps the greatest "great idea"—than there are (or can be) true ideas about politics, or at least that some ideas are clearly better than their competitors—can be assessed by examining the leading ideologies of the nineteenth and twentieth centuries.

The claims that ideologies provide a useful approach to the study of the great ideas of politics and that ideologies provide a basis for considering the possibility of attaining "political truth" may seem preposterous, given the understanding of ideologies held by certain students of ideologies and by many ordinary citizens. Some scholars who study ideology argue that we should employ a "negative," or "critical," conception of ideologies. For such scholars, ideologies are the biased and distorted ideas of particular interests and, as such, are far removed from political truth.[18] Conceived negatively, or critically, ideologies are said to have a large number of undesirable characteristics:[19]

1. They provide ideas reflecting people's private interests rather than more universal, public interests. More specifically, ideologies are the "weapons of the ruling class"—ideas that allow the most powerful members of society to maintain their domination over everyone else.
2. They oversimplify and thus distort reality.
3. They conceal the way the sociopolitical world really works, camouflaging who most gains and who most loses from particular practices and programs.
4. They are mere rationalizations to justify programs that people hope will work, even when there is a lack of evidence to sustain these hopes.
5. They induce people to sacrifice the present for unachievable utopian goals.
6. They promote closed and rigid thinking that is resistant to new information.
7. They are based more on emotion than on reason.
8. They are based on paranoia, or irrational fears about the motivations and powers of some "evil" opponents, leading to *(a)* simplistic evaluations contrasting the forces of evil ("them") against the forces of good ("us"), *(b)*

[18]The case for employing the negative or critical conception of ideology is most forcefully made by John B. Thompson, *Studies in the Theory of Ideology* (Cambridge, England: Polity Press, 1984).
[19]An extended list of negative characteristics of ideologies is provided by Robert Putnam, "Studying Elite Political Culture: The Case of Ideology," *American Political Science Review* 65 (Sept. 1971), p. 655. The shortcomings of defining ideology in terms of these negative qualities are discussed by M. Seliger in *Ideology and Politics* (New York: Free Press, 1976), pp. 25–88.

intolerance of everyone who does not believe precisely as "we" do, and (c) an unwillingness to bargain and compromise with "them."

9. They assert a moral and political absolutism, dogmatically insisting on certain principles and behaviors and demanding conformity to their "truths."
10. They are extremist in that they reject the established political, social, and economic institutions and the stable benefits provided by these institutions.

While these negative characteristics form a mighty indictment against ideological thinking, it is unclear that all ideologies possess these characteristics. Simply because some ideologies exhibit some of these pejorative qualities, it does not follow that these qualities are present in all ideologies.

In our judgment, it is best to begin the study of ideologies by simply viewing them as systems of interrelated beliefs and values about social, economic, and political life. We believe that the ideas of each ideology must first be understood, and that one's understanding of each ideology is enhanced by entering into the worldview of the proponents of each ideology. Accordingly, we describe the beliefs and values of various ideologies in ways that reflect the ideas of their proponents.

By describing ideologies in ways that reflect the ideas of their proponents, we do not mean to imply that each or any ideology should be received positively and without criticism. Because ideologies are developed to influence politics, their proponents are likely to be less self-reflective about the truth of their claims than are political theorists and philosophers. Compared to philosophers, ideologues (now defined as people who are committed to particular ideologies) are less concerned with the bases and validity of their ideas. Socialization, rather than sustained philosophical reflection, is likely to be the basis of their (and our!) beliefs and values. Our families and friends, our schools and churches, and the media are only some of the socializing agents that induce us to accept particular ideologies without having thought very deeply about their validity. Ideologues often want to accept and assert the principles that define their worldview, suspend the search for more adequate principles, and get on with the business of implementing their principles.

Because ideologies may contain ideas that are not the result of deep reflection, those who hold a critical conception of ideologies make an important point by urging us to question the validity of all ideologies. Some ideologies may simply camouflage particular class interests. Other ideologies may be based on a paranoid worldview. Still other ideologies may invite or encourage people to make unreasonable sacrifices in the present for utopian future goals. Skepticism about the claims of each ideology is always in order, and students of ideology should be on guard for their negative features. For the most part, however, we leave the evaluations of each ideology for class discussions and to individual judgments, contenting ourselves with brief conclusions about the accomplishments and limitations of each ideology.

Before presenting particular ideologies, there are several additional introductory matters to be addressed in this chapter. First, we present the origins of ideologies and a brief overview of their history. Second, we conclude from this overview that the initial intent of the science of ideology—to discover "certain truth" about good governance—has failed, as ideological diversity has increased rather than diminished over time. We then explore the implications of this diversity for the evaluation of various ideological perspectives. Third, we present a model or framework for the description of various ideologies. This section is important because it presents the "great issues" that all ideologies must address, and it discusses how ideological thought must interconnect the answers to these great issues. In short, this section begins to "flesh out" our conception of ideology as a system of interrelated beliefs and values that answers the great questions of politics and social life. Fourth, we consider the functions and importance of ideologies. A brief summary then provides concluding comments about the characteristics of ideologies and their roles in political theory and in understanding the great ideas of politics.

A BRIEF HISTORY OF IDEOLOGIES

In 1797, a group of philosophers, the **Ideologues**, led by Antoine Louis Claude Destutt de Tracy (1754–1836), founded the Institut de France to develop and disseminate true knowledge about the governing of nations. In general, the Ideologues sought to examine critically the traditional ideas and institutions that had governed the conduct and policies of the *ancien regime* (the "old regime") of France and of other European monarchies from the point of view of "universal reason" and to develop the new, more rational ideas of governance proposed by the intellectual leaders of the Enlightenment and the political leaders of the French Revolution (which had begun in 1789). De Tracy and the Ideologues are minor figures in the history of political thought, because they simply continued the program that had become prominent since the scientific revolution which swept Europe during the sixteenth and seventeenth centuries. Just as Copernicus, Galileo, and Newton had discovered natural laws governing the physical universe, Thomas Hobbes (1588–1679), John Locke (1632–1704), Adam Smith (1723–1790), and other social theorists had proposed natural laws governing society, economics, and politics. Although de Tracy and the Ideologues did not contribute important new ideas to this emerging science of politics, they coined the word "ideology" and ushered in the "Age of Ideology," as the period comprising the nineteenth and early twentieth centuries is often called.[20]

For de Tracy, the term "*idea*-logy" referred to "the science of ideas," and the task of ideology was to discover the sources or bases of our ideas about social, economic, and political life. The science of ideology employed an empirical epistemology that had been employed in social thought by René Descartes

[20]See, for example, Henry Aiken, *The Age of Ideology: The Nineteenth Century Philosophers* (New York: George Braziller, 1957).

(1596–1650), Hobbes, and Locke. In his *Essay on Human Understanding,* for example, Locke maintained that humans have no innate ideas and that all ideas are derived from our perceptions of and experiences with concrete material reality. Employing this epistemology, de Tracy claimed that the ideas that dominated Europe prior to the French Revolution—ideas such as the divine right of kings—were based on the biased perceptions and particular experiences of the privileged classes: the monarchy, the aristocracy, and the clergy. Because these ideas were not based on universal human perceptions and experiences, they had no universal validity or truth. In contrast, the ideas of the new science of politics were based on the natural needs of everyone to protect his or her life and liberties and the universal recognition that this required what are now regarded as liberal democratic governments. In short, de Tracy believed that the science of ideology would show that the principles of classical liberalism were true. Such a science would end the maladies of government based on arbitrary power and of endless disagreement about the true principles of good government.[21]

The Ideologues' goal of establishing true political ideas was, of course, an ancient dream, dating back to the birth of political philosophy among the ancient Greeks. De Tracy thought the science of ideas—ideology—would succeed at discovering political truth where others had failed because of the advances in human understanding that had occurred during *the Enlightenment,* an intellectual movement that began in the eighteenth century with advocates throughout Europe but centered in France and England. Enlightenment philosophers sought to free humans from ignorance and superstition and to promote progress leading to a more perfect life on earth. Building on the work of Hobbes and Locke, they believed that scientific epistemologies (or understandings of the basis of knowledge) had given rise to new ontologies (theories about the nature of the universe), psychologies (theories about human nature), and sociologies (theories about the origins and nature of societies) from which true political principles could be derived.

The political principles produced by this enterprise have come to be regarded as *classical liberalism.* Classical liberals believed that the physical universe, human behavior, and social life were governed by natural, not divine, laws. Human behavior could be explained in terms of the pursuit of pleasure and the avoidance of pain. Society, which was viewed as simply a collection of individuals and their interactions, was governed by the natural laws of the marketplace. Humans who are free to pursue their own happiness enter into mutually beneficial economic and political exchanges. Social progress occurs as a result of natural human interaction, because such free exchanges make each person better off. For classical liberals, such social laws implied certain

[21]De Tracy's ideas were published in 1817 in *Elements of Ideology.* A translation and edited volume of *Elements* is provided by John Morris (Detroit: Center for Public Health, 1973). The origins of ideology are discussed in H.M. Drucker, *The Political Uses of Ideology* (London: Macmillan Press, 1974), pp. 3–12, and in David McLellan, *Ideology* (Minneapolis: University of Minnesota Press, 1986), pp. 1–10.

political principles. Capitalism, an economic system of open competition in a free market, works best when governments do not intervene in economic affairs. Wealth is distributed by the laws of free exchange, and governments should not redistribute wealth. Laws should be made by democratically elected representatives, because electoral accountability encourages rulers to provide for the happiness of citizens in exchange for their votes. Thus, classical liberals, whose ideas are systematically described in Chapter 2, became advocates of *democratic capitalism.*

The ideas of classical liberalism were not universally accepted. Those who are now regarded as *traditional conservatives* believed that there was great merit in the maintenance of the *Ancien Regime* and they feared that (liberal) ideology incited revolutionary change. The "father of traditional conservatism," Edmund Burke (1729–1797), argued that reason and science could not comprehend such matters as God, human spirituality, and moral consciousness, much less the intricate and holistic aspects of society. Burke believed that traditional ontologies, psychologies, and sociologies provided better guidance for the governing of nations than did the so-called scientific constructions of these matters provided by classical liberals. Likewise, the American conservative, John Adams (1735–1826), rejected liberal ideology as "the science of Idiocy. And a very profound, abstruse, and mysterious science it is. . . . It is the bathos, the theory, the art, the skill of diving and sinking government. It was taught at the school of folly."[22] Traditional conservatives, of course, denied that they had an "ideology," but they did have a systematic set of beliefs and values about God, human nature, societies, and governmental authority. These ideas, which are elaborated in Chapter 3, date back to the Middle Ages and dominated Europe until capitalists displaced the landed aristocracy as the predominant class during the industrial revolution.

In addition to being attacked from "the right" by traditional conservatives, liberal ideology was attacked from "the left" by anarchists and other, more radical voices for the working class and the poor.[23] The main idea of **anarchism**, an ideology that became prominent in the latter half of the nineteenth century, is that existing institutions—governments, factories, churches, schools, and so forth—are coercive intrusions that unnecessarily limit individual freedom. Governments, for example, corrupt the social and cooperative instincts within human nature and undermine harmonious natural societies. Anarchists thus have called for the destruction of these institutions and for their replacement with decentralized, voluntary associations. The ideas of anarchism are presented more fully in Chapter 4.

Clearly the most acerbic critic of capitalism and representative democracy was Karl Marx (1818–1883), who developed a two-pronged attack on liberal

[22]From the marginal notes of Adams's *Discourses on Divila,* 1813. The notes are reprinted in their entirety in *The Portable Conservative Reader*, edited by Russell Kirk (New York: Penguin, 1982), p. 66.

[23]The use of the terms "Right," "Left," and "Center" as political designators is derived from the seating arrangements in the National Assembly that governed France during its revolutionary period, as conservatives sat to the right, moderates sat in the center, and radicals sat to the left.

ideology. First, he argued that the science of ideology was a mistaken preoccupation. The human condition was not directly affected to any significant degree by our ideas. Instead, the human condition was determined by economic forces and the social and class relations that flowed out of economic developments. Second, Marx regarded liberalism as propaganda, as a mask for the interests of industrial capitalists, rather than as a true set of principles for effective government. Among his followers, Marx is regarded as the founder of a science of political economy, not as an advocate of an ideology. This science sought to analyze the deficiencies of capitalist economies and the fraudulent nature of liberal democracies. It also sought to uncover the "laws of history," showing how economic changes produced associated changes in human behavior, society, and politics, and it provided a theory of revolution predicting the demise of democratic capitalism and the eventual emergence of a communist society. While Marx denied that he was developing an ideology containing principles for how to govern societies, his ideas provide a coherent set of political beliefs and values that can be characterized as the ideology of *Marxism*. This ideology is described in Chapter 5.

Marxism split into two main branches at the end of the nineteenth century. One branch was democratic socialism, which will be considered shortly. The second branch was bolshevism, or Leninism, which initiated the transformation of Marxism into what has become known as **communism**, one of the most potent ideologies of the twentieth century. When the Bolshevik party, under the leadership of Vladimir Ilyich Lenin (1870–1924), seized power during the Russian Revolution of 1917, "communism" took on a new meaning. Previously, "communism" referred to a vague future ideal—to a more free, equal, and cooperative society that could replace liberal regimes after the Marxist revolution or after anarchists demolished existing governments. But Lenin declared himself a Marxist and initiated the process of transforming Marxism from a protest ideology into a governing ideology. In the Soviet Union (and later in Eastern Europe, China, Cuba, and other developing nations), the Communist party ruled, drawing extensively on Marxist-Leninist ideology (or, in other countries, on revisions to Marxist-Leninism introduced by Tito (1892–1980), Mao (1893–1976), Castro (1926–   ), and other communist leaders). The major revision to Marxism introduced by these leaders was the idea that communism could be created in underdeveloped, or poorly industrialized, societies. Despite Marx's assertions that capitalism had to be strongly developed in a society before a revolution could occur and that ideal communism could thrive only in affluent societies having the industrial capacities to satisfy everyone's material needs, communist parties acquired governing power in underdeveloped societies. Thus, communist states had to develop their economies through extensive state planning and investment in state-owned industries. In the process, they demanded economic sacrifices on the part of their citizens and stifled dissent. As will be developed in Chapter 6, communist ideology justified such sacrifices and political suppression as a temporary, but necessary, means of achieving communist ideals.

When these planned economies began to falter in recent years, support for communist regimes and ideology declined. With the fall of communism in the former Soviet Union and eastern Europe, many analysts have proclaimed the "end of ideology."[24] By this they mean that the main ideological debate during the latter half of the twentieth century—that between capitalism and communism[25]—is over, and capitalism has won. But this claim ignores the continuing role of communism as a governing ideology in such places as China, North Korea, and Cuba. It ignores the continuing importance of Marxism as a protest ideology against the deficiencies of capitalism. It overlooks the significant ideological differences that remain between social democratic, liberal, and conservative parties that compete for power through democratic elections in societies having free-market economies. And it ignores the continuing appeal of other authoritarian ideologies—such as (neo)fascism.

During the first half of the century, the **Nazis** and the **Fascists** (particularly in Germany and Italy) presented an enormous challenge to democratic capitalism. Rather than emphasizing economic freedom and political equality, they sought national power and world domination, and they thought that national strength was advanced by giving absolute authority to the Fuehrer (Adolf Hitler, 1889–1945) and Il Duce (Benito Mussolini, 1883–1945). While there are some important differences between German nazism and Italian fascism, both rejected the individualism of liberalism and the egalitarianism of communism. Believing that the nation is more real and important than its individual members, the Nazis and the Fascists defended the totalitarian state. They maintained that state authority should control all aspects of social, economic, religious, and family life and that the good of the nation is grasped intuitively by an absolute leader—the Fuehrer or Il Duce—who could legitimately demand complete obedience of his subjects in order to achieve national objectives. These and other aspects of nazism and fascism will be described in Chapter 7.

Despite the importance of communism, nazism, and fascism, the twentieth century has been characterized by an increase in the number of democratic nations, where citizens control governmental officials through contested, fair, free, and frequent elections. Prior to 1900, only six countries met criteria that enabled them to be characterized as democratic, but thirty-seven countries met such criteria by 1979, and the 1980s and 1990s have witnessed a further emergence of democratic regimes.[26] Democratization has had important implications for ideologies, because contested elections provide incentives for those political parties seeking office to attract voters through the use of ideology. While parties have expressed many principles, three main ideologies have achieved preeminence in western democracies in this century: contemporary

[24]The most well-known such proclamation has been issued by Francis Fukuyama, "The End of History?," *The National Interest* 16 (summer 1989). As we shall see in the concluding chapter, Fukuyama and other interpreters of the passing of the "cold war" are only the most recent analysts to proclaim the "end of ideology."

[25]A good introduction to the theoretical issues of this debate is provided in *The Main Debate: Communism versus Capitalism*, edited by Tibor R. Machan (New York: Random House, 1987).

[26]Robert Dahl, *Democracy and Its Critics*, pp. 234–239.

liberalism, democratic socialism, and contemporary conservatism.[27] Unlike classical liberals and Marxists, proponents of these ideologies do not ordinarily claim that their principles constitute the true science of politics. Unlike communists and fascists, proponents of these ideologies tolerate dissent. Acknowledging that they must win democratic elections in order to govern according to their political principles, contemporary liberals, democratic socialists, and contemporary conservatives have a shared commitment to constitutional government and representative democracy that supersedes their disagreements over other ideas.

Contemporary liberalism evolved from classical liberalism when liberals began to realize that government could promote liberty as well as reduce it. While classical liberals assumed that the free-market system and minimal government maximized individual freedom and happiness, contemporary liberals uncovered many of the problems of pure capitalism, and they called for a strong state to provide stable economic growth and more equal economic opportunities for all citizens. Additionally, contemporary liberals have sought a variety of political reforms to equalize the distribution of political power and have generally sought to solve a variety of social problems—such as racial and sexual discrimination—through a more expanded use of governmental authority than classical liberals envisioned. Contemporary liberalism is described in Chapter 8.

Democratic socialists are often regarded as revisionist Marxists. While providing a more radical critique of capitalism than that offered by contemporary liberals, democratic socialists reject the Marxist idea that revolution is necessary to solve the problems of capitalism. As early as the 1880s, the German Revisionists and English Fabians argued that the widespread appeal of socialist ideas among the working class and the poor could enable socialist parties to win democratic elections and use governmental power to achieve such Marxist goals as ending the alienation and exploitation that arise from the private ownership of the means of production. Democratic socialists have also stressed more immediate goals: higher wages, shorter hours, better working conditions, and more social-welfare programs. In short, they have embraced an ideology that calls for a more equal and communal society through governmental policies that improve the plight of the lower classes. Democratic socialism will be described in Chapter 9.

Given the gravitation to the left by contemporary liberals, persons with classical liberal principles have entered into an uneasy alliance with those who hold traditional conservative principles and those who are fearful of the "socialist-communist menace" to frame a **contemporary conservative** viewpoint. Borrowing from classical liberals the idea that individualism and individual rights are strangled by government, such conservatives want a return to free exchange in the marketplace and thus propose less governmental intervention in the economic and social-welfare realms. Drawing upon the traditional conservative belief in a natural hierarchy among humans, they reject the

[27]According to Bernard Crick, a well-known British political theorist, these ideologies are "friends" of pluralistic democracy. See Crick's *In Defence of Politics* (New York: Penguin Books, 1962).

egalitarianism that celebrates the capacities of "the masses" to govern themselves and that underlies the redistributive policies of contemporary liberal and socialist "big governments." In general, contemporary conservatives are skeptical that governments can achieve progress toward liberal and socialist goals, believing instead that governmental efforts to solve all social and economic problems normally backfire and unravel the delicate social fabric. As we shall see in Chapter 10, contemporary conservatives believe that more realistic assessments of human nature, social possibilities, and governmental power are necessary to avoid the excessively optimistic expectations engendered by contemporary liberalism and democratic socialism.

Other ideologies have also emerged during the past two hundred years, and there is evidence that new ideologies coming into prominence may play increasingly important roles in the twenty-first century. For example, political movements with deep roots in religion—such as Islamic, Jewish, and Christian **fundamentalism**—have attracted widespread support in recent years. "Green" parties, proposing a radical reorientation in understanding the role of humans in relationship to other species and the earth's ecological system, have emerged in several western democracies, and **environmentalism** has brought a wide variety of new issues to the governments of all countries. **Feminism** has not only given greater emphasis to the idea of "equality between men and women," but also to the idea that political change to achieve such equality must take place in the most "private" human association—in the family—as well as in the "public" associations of state and nation. The emergence of such ideas suggests that ideologies are continuously in the process of formation, transformation, and decline. In Chapters 11, 12, and 13, we briefly explore these nascent ideologies that may have an important impact on the next century.

EVALUATING VARIOUS IDEOLOGIES

Although the concept of ideology was invented by de Tracy to develop a science of ideas that would separate political truths from mere opinion and thus to provide philosophical foundations for incontestable political principles, this short history of ideology reveals that de Tracy's hopes have been dashed. Instead of producing philosophical and political consensus behind one set of political beliefs and values, a wide variety of political ideologies have emerged, each providing philosophical defenses for alternative political principles and providing the ideational bases for competing political practices.

The inability of the science of ideology to generate political truth has given rise to a new conception of the study of ideology, a conception most fully elaborated by Karl Mannheim in his *Ideology and Utopia,* first published in 1929. While de Tracy believed that the study of the sources of our ideas would enable scholars to determine which ideas are universally true or valid, Mannheim believed that such a study would reveal that all political ideas and viewpoints contained only partial glimpses of the truth. For Mannheim, historical and social conditions influence what we regard as true political principles. For example, the social position of the English aristocracy in the eighteenth century may have prompted them to regard traditional conservatism as irrefutable, just as the social position of American capitalists in the nineteenth century influenced them to accept classical liberalism. Mannheim proposed that the study of ideologies, which he called the "sociology of knowledge," should largely be an "empirical investigation through description and structural analysis of the ways in which social relationships, in fact, influence thought."[28] Unlike de Tracy, Mannheim made no claim that such investigations would enable students of ideologies to achieve an Archimedean viewpoint—a privileged position beyond any ideological perspective, enabling purely objective knowledge. Because no one can completely escape his or her historical and social situations, no one can judge the ultimate validity of competing ideologies.

While such an understanding of ideologies approaches relativism (i.e., the idea that truth is relative to each person), Mannheim did not conclude that all ideologies are equally valid. Instead, he suggested that "there are criteria for rightness and wrongness" when comparing alternative ideologies. For example, he argued that "pre-eminence is given to that perspective which gives evidence of the greatest comprehensiveness and the greatest fruitfulness in dealing with empirical matters"[29] and to those ideas that are most effective in terms of achieving their intended effects in the real world of politics. Most scholars have accepted Mannheim's basic approach to the evaluation of competing ideologies. No longer do students of ideologies ask, "Which ideology is most valid?" Instead, they ask, "How should an ideology be evaluated (in comparison with other ideologies)?" The difference between these questions may seem minor, but they represent fundamentally different ways of thinking about ideologies. To ask which ideology is most valid implies that some ideology could be valid or true, and it implies that there is some objective, nonpolitical standard against which each ideology should be compared in order to determine its validity. But to ask for methods of evaluating various ideologies is to recognize that all ideologies have their merits and deficiencies, that no ideology is absolutely valid or true, and that our overall evaluations of various ideologies are subject to our best judgments—judgments that we must make to avoid the problems of relativism and, indeed, nihilism.

But how should we judge various ideologies? Are Mannheim's criteria—comprehensiveness, empirical fruitfulness, and effectiveness—the only criteria to be used when evaluating an ideology? We know of no definitive list of criteria, and we doubt that such a list can be compiled, because new or additional considerations can always be brought to bear on the evaluation of ideologies. We also doubt that various criteria can be ranked or weighed. Given such difficulties, evaluations of various ideologies can employ a variety of intellectual and political criteria.

[28]Karl Mannheim, *Ideology and Utopia* (London: Routledge and Kegan, 1936), p. 239.
[29]Mannheim, *Ideology and Utopia*, p. 254.

Among the criteria that can be used to evaluate the intellectual attractiveness of an ideology are

1. *Comprehensiveness* Does the ideology address and provide useful answers to a broad array of fundamental political, social, and economic questions?
2. *Coherence* Does the ideology contain clear ideas that are internally consistent, or does it contain internal contradictions?
3. *Empirical validity* Does the ideology contain generalizations that can be tested empirically, and are the observable facts consistent with these generalizations?
4. *Critical insightfulness* Does the ideology unmask myths and debunk erroneous conventional understandings of political, social, and economic life, giving us new insights into how the political process really works and how it might more ideally work?

Among the criteria that can be used to evaluate the political attractiveness of various ideologies are

1. *Historical impact* Has the ideology shaped the course of world history and the development of various political systems in positive (or negative) ways?
2. *Public appeal* How broad or extensive is support for an ideology and how deep or intense is the commitment of supporters of an ideology to its principles?
3. *Compatibility with political ideals* Does the ideology further (or retard) such political ideals as freedom, justice, and democracy?
4. *Compatibility with ethical ideals* Does the ideology advance (or undermine) such ethical ideals as preserving self-respect, furthering individual creativity and moral development, promoting reverence for others, and living in harmony with God and/or nature?

Evaluating various ideologies in terms of such criteria is both an individual and a collective task. Each student (and each citizen) can judge for herself the comprehensiveness, the coherence, the historical impact, and the compatibility of an ideology with her political and ethical ideals. But these judgments should also be discussed and argued with others. A central political activity is to proclaim and defend one's political principles or ideology publicly. Successfully persuading others to accept your political principles or ideology is an exercise of political power. Converting others to one's ideological perspective is a very potent political act—more potent than persuading them to support a particular candidate or policy position—because the ideologies that people adopt influence many of their subsequent actions. But when arguing the merits of various ideologies with others, one must listen to the arguments of others as well as proclaim one's own position. To be closed to their arguments—to refuse to amend one's own beliefs and values even when one cannot defend them from the counterarguments of others—is to be ideological in the negative, or pejorative, sense of the word.

A FRAMEWORK FOR DESCRIBING VARIOUS IDEOLOGIES

Before evaluating ideologies, we require a clear understanding of their principles and the philosophical and political bases of these principles. Because the principles of an ideology are often evaluated and analyzed in comparison with those of other ideologies, it is particularly useful to have a common framework for describing various ideologies. Figure 1-1 provides such a framework. It directs attention to the philosophical bases of each ideology by asking about their assumptions regarding human nature, society, the universe, and knowledge. It directs attention to the political contexts, or bases, that give rise to various political principles by asking about the social problems that each ideology hopes to resolve and the goals each ideology seeks to achieve. It directs attention to six "perennial questions" or "great issues" in politics and invites us to describe the substantive political principles of various ideologies in response to these great issues. The arrows in the framework remind us that ideologies are sets of *interconnected* principles and that such principles are derived from particular political and philosophical bases. Additionally, the framework stresses that ideological principles affect the everyday world of politics by influencing the political organizations, leaders, and policies we support and the political actions we take.

Figure 1-1. A Framework for Analyzing Ideologies.

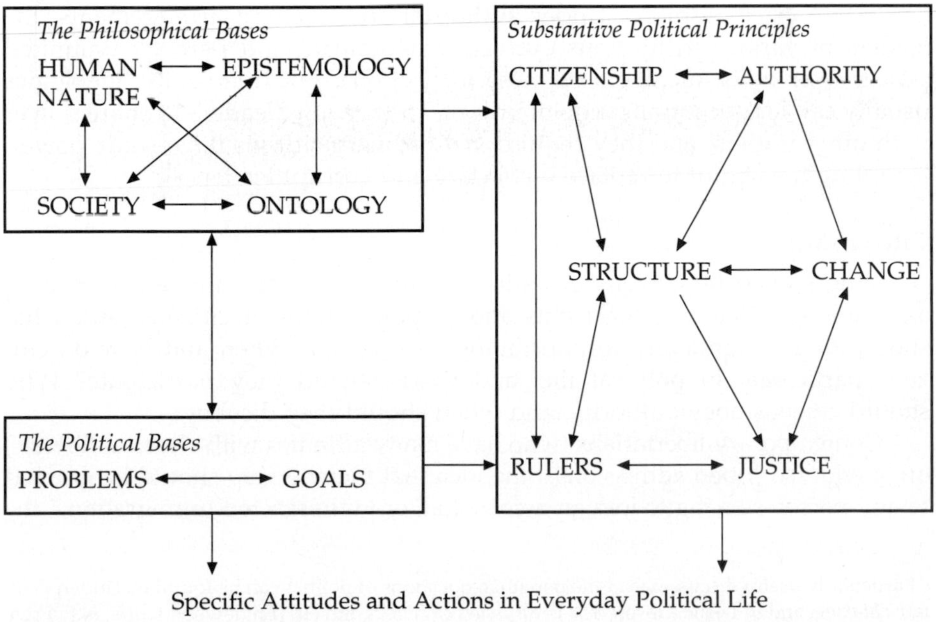

The Philosophical Bases
HUMAN NATURE ⟷ EPISTEMOLOGY
SOCIETY ⟷ ONTOLOGY

Substantive Political Principles
CITIZENSHIP ⟷ AUTHORITY
STRUCTURE ⟷ CHANGE
RULERS ⟷ JUSTICE

The Political Bases
PROBLEMS ⟷ GOALS

Specific Attitudes and Actions in Everyday Political Life

Substantive Political Principles

As shown in Figure 1-1, ideologies have *substantive political principles* that address perennial questions in six main areas.[30] Here, we briefly state these questions and indicate the range of answers to them as provided by some ideologies.

Structure

How are communities organized, and how should they be structured? To what extent should institutions be organized in a centralized (or decentralized) manner? To what extent and by what means should those with institutional power be constrained?

Perhaps the most fundamental question regarding the structure of society involves the role of public and private institutions. In "statist" societies, political parties or governments play a dominant role in organizing and controlling people. Communism gives controlling power to the Communist party. National socialism gave such power to the Nazi party. Fascism, in the case of Italy, gave such power to the Italian state. **Totalitarianism** refers to all ideologies that proclaim that giving such institutions "total control" over society is necessary to bring about massive beneficial transformations in society and to redeem human nature or to "remake" humans in more desirable ways. In "free" societies, institutions such as families, churches, and private enterprises play greater roles in structuring community life. **Social pluralism** refers to the belief—central to classical and contemporary liberalism, traditional and contemporary conservatism, and democratic socialism—that such "private" associations should be relatively autonomous and free from state control.

Both public and private institutions can be organized in either centralized or decentralized fashions. Under **authoritarian** structural arrangements, the leaders of various institutions exercise predominant and perhaps unlimited power over other members of these institutions. But democratic ideologies usually call for decentralization of power. They require leaders to share power with other leaders, and they require that ordinary citizens have some power, including the ability to replace ineffective and corrupt leaders.

Citizenship

Who should be citizens of national communities and members of other associations? What are the rights and responsibilities of citizens, and what should be the rights and responsibilities of citizens? When and how do citizens participate in political life, and when should they participate? Why should citizens obey authority, and when should they disobey?

Contemporary libertarians (who have many affinities with classical liberals) often endorse "open admissions," the idea that membership should be granted to any person seeking to join an association, or "unrestricted immigration," the

[30]Particularly useful discussions of the perennial questions of politics can be found in Tinder, *Political Thinking,* and in Leslie Lipson, *The Great Issues of Politics,* 8th ed. (Englewood Cliffs, N.J.: Prentice-Hall, 1989).

idea that anyone should be able, at his own initiative, to become a citizen of any community or nation. Contemporary liberals believe that the existing citizens of a nation should be able to limit immigration, but they hold relatively inclusive citizenship principles, welcoming a large and diverse number of immigrants into the nation and extending full citizenship to those members of the community (especially women and racial minorities) who previously suffered various forms of treatment as second-class citizens. In contrast, ideologies with racist and nativist beliefs (like nazism) have restricted citizenship to the "racially (or ethnically) pure" and those who will perpetuate native cultural traits.

Ideologies differ greatly on the rights that accompany citizenship. Classical liberals thought that political communities should only protect the natural rights of citizens—their rights to life, liberty, and property. But contemporary liberals and democratic socialists believe that citizen (or welfare) rights should steadily expand, with children acquiring the right to an education, the elderly acquiring the right to pensions, the poor attaining rights to nutrition and to housing, and everyone entitled to health care. Other ideologies stress citizen responsibilities and duties over citizen rights. For example, traditional conservatives emphasize that all citizens, no matter how high or low their rank, have the responsibility to perform the customary tasks that accompany their roles. But nazism and fascism have even stronger conceptions of duty, proclaiming that the highest human virtue is displayed through the absolute obedience of citizens to political leaders.

Rulers

Who governs, and who should govern? How should rulers be selected, and by what means are they accountable to others?

Several ideologies hold the principle of **guardianship**. They claim that society is best ruled by a few especially competent and virtuous leaders. Traditional conservatives believe in the existence of a natural aristocracy—men who are by birth and/or upbringing especially well-qualified to govern—and they resist many democratic reforms threatening such elites. Marxists and communists believe in the (temporary) necessity of a "dictatorship of the proletariat" (an intellectual vanguard comprising those who understand the true interests of the working class), and fascists and nazis believe in the capacities of great leaders to understand the real needs of nations and to mobilize populations to achieve these national goals. In contrast, the principles of participatory democracy—that everyone is capable of understanding his own interest and/or the public interest and that political power should thus be distributed equally to all—are associated with populist ideologies, including, to some extent, democratic socialism. However, most ideologies embrace some form of representative democracy, under which citizens choose their rulers and hold them accountable by requiring their periodic reelection.

Authority

What are the legitimate powers of and the limits on the powers of those who rule various communities, especially those who have governmental authority? What authority should rulers have? Should governmental authority be used to regulate the economy and legislate morality, and how extensive should governmental authority be in such areas?

No ideology is as critical of authority as anarchism. Anarchists believe that all authority—whether it be the authority of political rulers, property owners, teachers, or religious leaders, for example—is illegitimate. In contrast, more authoritarian ideologues believe that the authority of those who rule various communities should be expandable to include whatever is necessary to accomplish the goals of the community, even that of suppressing dissent from those who question these goals. Most other ideologies call for limited applications of political authority, particularly in certain areas. For example, classical liberals have held that governmental authority should simply be used to protect the natural rights of its citizens, especially securing their lives, liberties, and property from violation by other members of the community. Contemporary liberals endorse significant governmental interventions in economic life, while contemporary conservatives are more likely to call for governmental regulations that limit problematic lifestyles and moral choices.

Justice

How are social goods distributed, and how should they be distributed? By what agencies, procedures, and criteria should various goods be allocated? What kinds of public policies are just and/or in the public interest?

Social goods are those things—like money, status, education and power—that we all want, but that are relatively scarce and can be achieved or attained only in association with others. The common perception that several ideologies call for the equal distribution of such goods is mistaken. Marx thought that a communist revolution would lead, in the short run, to the distribution of income according to the amount of labor one performed (rather than the then-existing situation where the working class was exploited and received only a subsistence wage instead of the full value of its labor). He hoped that, in the more distant future, material goods could be distributed on the basis of need, but he never thought that labor or need would be equal across humans, and thus he never thought that incomes, money, or material goods should be distributed equally. Nevertheless, Marxist conceptions of justice clearly stress more equality than, for example, conservative conceptions of justice. Conservatives believe different individuals make very unequal contributions to society—based on their very unequal abilities and virtues—and that such unequal contributions merit proportionately unequal rewards. Democratic socialists and contemporary liberals have more intermediate positions on this issue, seeking more equal, communal provisions of certain goods (like education and public health services), while tolerating market-generated inequalities of wealth.

Change

How much change is needed, and how can this change be best achieved? Responses to these questions depend largely on the responses to the previous ones: the greater the gap between the beliefs about the existing system and the ideals about the "good" society, the greater is the desired change. Status quo ideologies, such as traditional conservatism, assert that political ideals have generally been realized and that change is unneeded. Reformist ideologies, such as contemporary liberalism, assert that gaps between ideals and perceived practices can be reduced by incremental and evolutionary changes in policies, rulers, and structures. Revolutionary ideologies, such as Marxism, assert that gaps between ideals and perceived practices can be closed only by extensive economic, political, social, and/or cultural transformations.

The Philosophical Bases

The political principles of each ideology are based upon certain *philosophical foundations.* Either explicitly or implicitly, the proponents of each ideology hold certain assumptions about human nature, society, the universe, and knowledge.

Human Nature

What are people's primary motivations? Are people self-interested or community-regarding? What are people's capacities? How rational are people? In what ways are people equal and unequal? Is there an essential human nature, or are people infinitely malleable?[31]

Classical liberals assume that there is an essential human nature; people are naturally and equally self-interested, and they employ human reason to maximize their pleasure and minimize their pain. Given such a conception of human nature, classical liberals believe that political principles should emphasize individual liberty within a capitalist society and under a limited government. Traditional conservatives believe that humans are very different in their capacities for reason and in their other abilities and virtues, but that the qualities we are born with are not particularly malleable. The worst instincts of people can be controlled by traditional authority, but governmental authority cannot remake people into some more utopian ideal. In contrast, Marxists and anarchists believe that social institutions, such as capitalism and government, have corrupted human nature. Their political principles call for the abolition of such institutions, because they believe more socially positive and cooperative potentialities in human nature would consequently (re)emerge.

Society

What are the fundamental elements of society? Is society just a collection of individuals, or does society have a prior existence that defines the individuals constituting it? Are considerations of class, racial, ethnic, or religious differences (or some other kind of group differences) essential to understanding the nature of society?

[31]Insofar as "human nature" is used to refer to some human "essence," the idea of infinite human malleability suggests the absence of any "human nature." Nevertheless, we think it useful to consider various theories about human malleability under the rubric of "human nature."

Non Sequitur

© 1994, Washington Post Writers Group. Reprinted with permission.

Traditional conservatives assume that societies are "organic wholes." All societies have unique histories, customs, institutions, and a unique set of hierarchical roles that precedes and helps define individuals. Because these societies are the supreme inheritance of the people who live within them, political principles must be fashioned for their maintenance. In contrast, classical liberals assume that societies are simply the result of a social contract among individuals to further the interests of individuals. For classical liberals, political principles must serve the good of the various individuals constituting society, not the good of society above and beyond that of its members. Marx declared that the most fundamental quality of any society was its class structure, and Marxists, communists, and democratic socialists have all derived their fundamental political beliefs and values from their characterizations of the class structure of society. While contemporary liberals recognize that societies are divided by conflicting class interests, they de-emphasize class structure by recognizing a bewildering array of social divisions. For contemporary liberals, societies are characterized by many categories of individuals and groups, and they embrace political principles that seek the widest possible accommodation of diverse group interests.

Ontology

How does the world work? What is ultimate reality? Is "being" fundamentally material, ideational, or spiritual? Is the world in a process of "becoming," and what are the ultimate causes of change in the world?

For classical liberals, we live in a material world; even humans are simply "matter in motion" and, as such, they act according to the laws of nature. By governing ourselves according to political principles that recognize the self-interested aspects of human nature and the individualistic elements of society, we make continuous human progress. Marxists agree that we live in a material world that unfolds according to natural laws, but while liberals believe that historical progress is determined by individuals pursuing their own interests, Marxists believe that history is economically determined. In a world of economic scarcity and exploitation, humans are not really free to pursue their happiness but must attend to their material needs. Thus, economic necessity and the economic institutions and processes that we adopt to satisfy our economic needs decisively influence other aspects of our lives, including our political principles. In contrast to liberals and Marxists, both traditional and contemporary conservatives believe that there is more to the universe than just the material world. God is our maker, and there are spiritual aspects to humans and societies that cannot be ignored. Ignoring our spiritual and religious foundations and attempting to recreate society according to some scheme of secular reason is, for conservatives, sheer human folly. Nazis and fascists also reject the materialist ontologies of liberals and Marxists, but rather than seeing history as guided by divine will, they believe history can be directed by human will. While most people lack strong wills and vision, certain leaders intuitively grasp a nation's destiny. Thus, exercising their will and mobilizing the masses to follow their will, a "Fuehrer" or a "Duce" determines history.

Epistemology

Is it possible to know, absolutely, the practices and ideals of politics? If there are objective or interpersonal truths about politics, how is such knowledge obtained? If all knowledge is subjective, what kinds of evidence and arguments are the most appropriate basis for political beliefs and norms?

As we have already indicated, the Ideologues believed that true principles of governance could be found, and classical liberalism emerged as their understanding of such truths. For classical liberals, an ultimate criterion for judging the validity of political institutions, practices, and policies became their utility: those arrangements that produce the greater good for the greater number are deemed correct. However, traditional conservatives doubt that utilitarianism can justify liberal institutions. For such conservatives, existing institutions have latent benefits that can be (unjustifiably) ignored in utilitarian calculations. Thus, to know the best political principles and practices, conservatives believe we should consult tradition—the collective wisdom of the ages.

Marx took an entirely different epistemological approach. Rather than attempting to demonstrate the desirability of his principles (by reference to utility, tradition, or any standard), he sought to show the inevitability of a communist society. The laws of political economy could be known through the scientific study of history, and the application of these laws showed that a communist revolution would occur as specific economic conditions emerged. While Marx found truth in a scientific understanding of history, his communist followers often found truth to reside in the authority of Marx—or in reinterpretations of Marx supplied by leading Marxist theoreticians. Contemporary democratic ideologies—socialism, liberalism, and conservatism—all deny that absolute truth is possible, but they each hold to a conception of science to support their principles. For contemporary liberals, social science is a pragmatic enterprise, a continuing attempt to improve the human condition through experimentation. For democratic socialists, social science can provide damning descriptions and explanations of existing conditions—especially inequalities in the distribution of wealth and power—produced by liberal and conservative regimes. For contemporary conservatives, social science is a "debunking" enterprise that can show the failures of socialist policies to equalize economic conditions and of liberal policies to eliminate other social problems.

The Political Bases

Ideologies justify and defend their political principles by drawing on alternative psychologies, sociologies, ontologies, and epistemologies; but ideologies are not simply intellectual systems. Ideologies are born not of abstract philosophy but of concrete political, social, and economic problems and aspirations. Thus we include two more categories concerning the *political bases* of ideologies in our conceptual framework: (1) the problems they seek to eliminate and (2) the goals they hope to achieve.

Problems

What do proponents of an ideology view as the most pressing political, social, and economic problems confronting their political communities?

The political basis for the foundation of classical liberalism was to overcome various problems confronting Europe as it abandoned its feudal and medieval past, such as the static social structure which curtailed social mobility, the numerous restrictions on economic activity imposed by the church and the governments, and the political absolutism of monarchies. Marxism, in turn, was born as one response to the ills of the capitalist societies that emerged under classical liberalism; it focused on the control of productive property by a small number of capitalists, the capitalists' capacity to exploit labor, the alienation produced by capitalism, and the "false consciousness" of workers who failed to understand that capitalism undermined their real needs. Nazism and fascism arose as yet other responses to the ills of capitalism, focusing on the excessive individualism within liberal societies, the subordination of all values to material considerations, and the absence of a sense of belonging in most members of such societies. Contemporary liberalism, too, arose in response to problems of nineteenth-century liberal society, as it sought to have governments address a wide range of "market failures" (such as the recurrence of business cycles resulting in periodic recessions and depressions and the emergence and persistence of pockets of poverty). For contemporary conservatives, liberal reforms meant to address such problems created more problems than they solved. The principles of contemporary conservatives seek to address the difficulties of excessive governmental planning and regulation, the rise of a "new class" of intellectuals and bureaucrats who seek to impose their ideas of what's best for society on society, and a cultural "permissiveness" that undermines the development of character and virtue in citizens.

Goals

What are the political, social, and economic goals whose realization is most important to each ideology?

Proponents of each ideology seek to achieve numerous goals, and almost every conceivable human goal is sought by some ideology. Some ideologies focus on the character of societies and national entities as a whole. The primary goal of nazism was to bring about the development, expansion, and dominance of an Aryan German nation, while the parallel goal of Italian fascism was to recover the grandeur of the Roman Empire for a modern Italy. Conservatives, too, have emphasized collective goals, as traditional conservatives have stressed the importance of maintaining the social order and contemporary conservatives have stressed the importance of maintaining military supremacy. In contrast to these collective orientations, both classical and contemporary liberals (and anarchists, too) have emphasized individualistic goals; they want to preserve and protect various freedoms and rights of individuals, and they stress creating the conditions wherein individuals can achieve their various life plans. Still other ideologies focus on achieving equality among various types of people—for example, Marxists and social democrats want to reduce class differences and many feminists focus on reducing gender differences.

In subsequent chapters, we will begin our more detailed discussion of each ideology by considering its political bases. Understanding the problems that ideologies address and the goals they seek to attain provides an important introduction to each ideology, because ideologies are primarily political constructions. Their purpose is to affect—and mostly change—the existing world. When discussing the older ideologies (such as classical liberalism and Marxism), we then follow our treatment of the political bases with a presentation of their philosophical foundations, because the founders of these ideologies were self-consciously philosophical; they sought to base their political principles on elaborate philosophical considerations. However, when discussing the newer ideologies that are predominant in democratic and pluralistic societies, we follow our discussion of the political bases with descriptions of substantive political principles. The philosophical bases of these ideologies are presented at the end of our discussions of these ideologies, because philosophical assumptions played lesser roles in their development. Contemporary liberals, democratic socialists, and contemporary conservatives focus on developing substantive political principles that they believe can maximize the political support necessary to govern in democratic societies where, as a rule, voters are not well trained in philosophical matters. For these ideologies, philosophical considerations are largely the preoccupation of political philosophers and theorists who try to infer the assumptions about human nature, society, ontology, and epistemology that underlie given political principles. Just as there is some variation in the order in which we present the political bases, the philosophical bases, and the substantive political principles of each ideology, so also there is some variation in the order in which we present the component concepts within each of these three categories. We do this because different philosophical assumptions and different political principles animate the various ideologies, and thus the relative importance of each component in each category is different for each ideology. For example, bringing about political change in an evolutionary manner is the central organizing principle of democratic socialism; to understand this ideology, it is important to present principles regarding change before discussing other substantive political principles. But for both classical and contemporary liberals, considerations about change depend on the extent to which their other substantive principles regarding authority, justice, rulers, and so forth, have been realized. Hence, for such ideologies, it is better to conclude, rather than begin, our discussion of substantive political principles by considering principles of change.

Interrelationships and Applications

Beyond calling for descriptions of the political and philosophical bases of ideologies and of their basic political principles, the framework presented in Figure 1-1 indicates that all ideologies contain *interrelated beliefs and values.* Individuals can hold ideas in response to all of the questions included in the twelve categories depicted in Figure 1-1, but if their ideas are not highly interrelated, they cannot be said to hold an ideology.

Suppose two persons share the following beliefs. Their most important political goal is to maximize individual freedom. They agree that the greatest problem in society is that the actions of governments constitute significant obstacles to freedom. As a result, they easily agree on the principle that governmental authority should be limited. But suppose that they hold different principles regarding justice. The first person is perfectly content with the inequalities of income that occur within a free-market system; she believes that justice is best served by allowing free exchanges in the marketplace and by having governments merely assure that everyone has the right to buy, sell, trade, work, and invest as they wish. Up to this point in her thinking, at least, this person is ideological, as her goals, perceptions about problems, and principles about governmental authority and justice seem perfectly consistent. By contrast, suppose that the second person is unhappy about the inequalities of income that occur within a free-market system; he believes that justice can only be served when incomes are more equal and that governments must redistribute income to achieve this equality. His principles that governmental authority must be limited (to reduce its capacity to threaten freedom) and that governmental authority should be strengthened (to achieve more economic equality) appear to be contradictory. By failing to have a logically consistent belief system, he fails to have an ideology, by definition. Before concluding that this example is a bit contrived, that few people could hold such internally conflicting values, reflect on the fact that many Americans want both more services from government and lower taxes. Also reflect on the fact that thus far in our example we have only described ideas regarding four issues and we have given very simple responses to them. As more complex responses are provided to all twelve issues, it becomes increasingly difficult to have internally consistent responses over a full range of beliefs and values. Political scientists who study the belief systems of American citizens have found that only a small percentage of people have consistent belief systems, leading them to complain about the "ideological innocence" of Americans.[32]

However, the preceding example should not lead to the mistaken understanding that political ideas over a full range of issues must be interrelated in a prespecified way in order to be ideological. Let us continue to examine the beliefs and values of our apparent ideologue. Suppose that in addition to holding principles calling for limited government and market-based distributions of income, she also is dubious about "strong democracy." She believes that it would be a mistake to give too much power to citizens, because most citizens might be tempted to use governmental power to override market-based income distributions. She fears that the poor, the working class, and the lower-middle class (the majority, with below-average incomes) may want various governmental programs that benefit them but also want to escape paying for these benefits by imposing highly progressive taxes on the rich. Because her fears about "too much democracy" seem consistent with her other beliefs, we would have no basis for claiming she failed to have a coherent ideology; in fact, we would probably claim that she is a fairly typical contemporary conservative. Now suppose that another person shares her beliefs about limited governmental authority and market-based justice, but he believes that demands for big government and redistribution come not from average citizens but from liberal intellectuals and bureaucrats; he thinks that most citizens share his disdain for big government and for income redistribution and that empowering citizens—that is, developing a more populist or democratic political process—is the key to dismantling the liberal welfare state. While his principles about rulers and democracy differ from those of our typical contemporary conservative, they seem to be coherent. Perhaps he, too, is a contemporary conservative, as the issue of how much power to provide citizens may be an unresolved issue within conservatism. Perhaps he is a different type of conservative—for example, a member of the "New Right."[33] In either case, there would be no logical basis for denying that he has a coherent ideology.

This example and our conclusions from it help to show that ideologies are not as rigid as they are often portrayed, or as closed and static as may be suggested by the descriptions of each ideology that we construct from our model. In the real world, there may be few exemplars of each ideology as described in subsequent chapters. Even major contributors to an ideological tradition—both philosophers and politicians—may have certain ideas on certain issues that depart from particular characterizations of ideologies. Most people do not force their ideas to conform to some description of an ideology. Instead, peo-

[32]Donald Kinder, "Diversity and Complexity in American Public Opinion," in *Political Science: The State of the Discipline,* edited by Ada Finifter (Washington D.C.: American Political Science Association, 1983), pp. 391–401.

[33]Many commentators argue that the populism of the New Right creates such hostility between them and contemporary conservatives that their ideological distinctiveness must be emphasized. See Alan Crawford, *Thunder on the Right* (New York: Pantheon, 1980) and Kevin Phillips, *Post-Conservative America* (New York: Vintage, 1983).

ple come to hold what they regard as consistent beliefs and values across an array of issues, and people with relatively similar beliefs and values are regarded (by their comrades, by their adversaries, and by scholars who are simply trying to understand belief systems) as members of a particular ideological camp. In other words, living ideologies do not have fixed and tightly controlled borders. To belong to an ideological camp, a person does not have to pass some litmus test regarding his ideas. Indeed, because ideologies are political, the leaders of ideological movements want to increase the number of people who identify with the ideology, and they welcome those whose beliefs are "close enough." This inclusion leads to debates within ideologies, modifications in the dominant beliefs within ideologies, and, sometimes, ideological schisms.

In addition to containing logically interrelated beliefs and values, Figure 1-1 allows us to infer another defining element of ideologies: their political principles guide the attitudes and actions of people in concrete, everyday political life. For example, because a liberal believes strongly in individual rights, she probably believes that the rights of criminal suspects should be protected, and she is likely to be horrified by the treatment of Rodney King by the Los Angeles police. In contrast, because a conservative believes strongly in the need for social stability, he is likely to value the role of the police in providing stability and security, and he is more willing to give a wide berth to the police as they go about their difficult and dangerous job. He is also likely to have more sympathy for the Los Angeles police in the King incident than the liberal does. In short, the extent to which people are ideological depends not only on the extent to which they have interrelated principles but also on the extent to which they base their policy preferences, their concrete acts of participation and their support for particular political leaders on their principles.[34]

While the concrete attitudes and actions of ideologues are affected by their principles, it is a mistake to believe that their principles *determine* such attitudes and actions. Consider the thinking of contemporary conservatives on the abortion issue. They may believe social stability and the long-term viability of the political community depend on citizens' sharing certain fundamental values, and such beliefs may prompt them to believe that governments have a legitimate role in promoting certain positions on moral issues. If conservatives also believe that the federal government should restrict abortions, we might be tempted to claim that they deduced their opposition to abortion from their principles about governments' legitimate role in regulating morality. However, it is doubtful that conservative thinking is purely deductive on the matter. First, conservatives also believe that federal governments are too powerful in relationship to state governments, and the application of this principle would seem to imply that the abortion issue should be decided at the state level. Thus, two conservatives could hold identical principles and reach diametrically opposed policy preferences regarding federal abortion restrictions, depending on whether they give priority to the principle that government ought to regulate morality or to the principle that the role of the federal gov-

[34]Mark Peffley and Jon Hurwitz, "A Hierarchical Model of Attitude Constraint," *American Journal of Political Science* 29 (1985), pp. 871–890.

ernment ought to be reduced. In short, conservative principles—like the principles of any ideology—can provide conflicting guidance on concrete issues, with the result that such principles fail to determine policy preferences.[35] Second, the actions and attitudes of people, even those people holding strong ideological positions, are not solely determined by principles *within* the ideology. No doubt, people's attitudes about abortion are shaped by their beliefs about the status of the fetus as a full human being at various stages of pregnancy, and such beliefs are not central to any political ideology. And, of course, people's attitudes about abortion can also be shaped by a variety of personal experiences (e.g., whether they have had unwanted pregnancies, their church affiliations, and the attitudes of their parents and spouses) which are quite removed from ideologies. Thus, rather than saying that ideological principles determine attitudes and actions in the everyday world, it is probably more accurate to say that ideological principles and concrete attitudes and actions interact in complex, reciprocal ways. For example, people's attitudes about abortion may be more fundamental and prior to their ideological position on government's proper role in regulating morality. Wise political thinkers constantly reexamine their principles in light of concrete cases.

THE FUNCTIONS OF IDEOLOGIES

Ideologies play an important role in shaping people's ideas about politics. For the most part, those who have studied ideologies focus on the functions that acceptance of a particular ideology serves for individuals, groups, and communities; in this section, we first consider the nature of such functions. But, in addition, we propose that the comparative study of different ideologies can enable individuals and communities to develop more well-considered and nuanced political ideas than they could attain by merely accepting a particular ideology.

Particular ideologies are embraced and employed for psychological, social, and political purposes. Once ideologies are accepted, they perform important functions for individuals, for groups that seek to mobilize for political action, and for entire political systems.

Ideologies help to define individual identities. Part of the answer to the question of "who am I?" is provided when I respond that "I am someone who believes that the political world works as specified by liberalism (or conservatism or any other ideology)" and "I am someone who holds the ideals of a liberal (or a conservative or any other ideological proponent)." While many persons dislike identifying themselves by an ideological label (because of the negative connotations of being an ideologue), our personal identity is incomplete unless we hold and acknowledge certain political beliefs and ideals. Indeed, our identity is delineated ever more clearly as our thinking about the

[35]For an extended discussion of how conflicting principles limit the impact of ideology, see Paul Schumaker, *Critical Pluralism, Democratic Performance, and Community Power* (Lawrence, University Press of Kansas, 1991), pp. 130–134.

big issues of politics becomes more developed, as our political principles become more comprehensive, as we achieve more logical consistency among these principles, and as we become aware of the philosophical assumptions that these principles presuppose.

Ideologies also serve several other functions for individuals. First, they help orient people toward political life, providing concepts and propositions that describe and explain how societies, economies, and governments work, and they provide political ideals that help people evaluate social, economic, and political institutions and issues, giving guidance about what issues are important and what positions on issues should be defended.[36] Second, ideologies can have a cathartic effect on individuals, draining off emotional tensions by "identifying" the sources of their personal and social problems. For example, ideologies create symbolic enemies such as Jews (in nazism), capitalists (in Marxism) and the "New Class" (in contemporary conservatism). By identifying such "enemies" as the source of problems, individuals can look beyond their own failures and shortcomings.[37] Third, ideologies sustain the morale of individuals. For example, liberal ideas about equal opportunity and the possibility of upward social and economic mobility have no doubt given many small businesspeople the belief that they can "make it" if they are hardworking and productive within the free-enterprise system. And Marxist ideals enabled many citizens in the Soviet Union and China to endure various short-term hardships in the hopes that these sacrifices would enable the emergence of a utopian communist society in the not-too-distant future.[38]

Ideologies are also important in bringing people together for collective action, serving as a kind of "social cement" that binds together a social group or class. There are several ways in which ideologies help organize collectivities and sustain their solidarity in pursuit of social goals. First, ideologies create a basis for collective action by identifying particular strains or problems burdening all members of the group; they define the "fatal flaw in the world" that can only be corrected by the sustained efforts of the group. Second, ideologies articulate common goals as the basis for their collective action and a strategy for achieving these goals. Third, ideologies provide a common language that facilitates communication and agreement among the social group. And, fourth, ideologies provide a basis for justifying or legitimating the claims of the group to the broader community, enabling group members to believe that their goals not only serve their group interest but also reflect the common aspiration of everyone in the community to attain economic prosperity, justice, democracy, and so forth.

Finally, ideologies serve important functions not only for individuals and groups but also for the community as a whole. When the principles of partic-

[36]Louis Althusser is perhaps the foremost theorist stressing the way ideology defines what people think. See his "Ideology and Ideological State Apparatuses," in *Lenin and Philosophy* (London: Monthly Review Press, 1972) and *Essays in Ideology* (London: Verso Press, 1984).

[37]As Eric Voegelin and others have pointed out, this function may be more psychopathic than cathartic.

[38]Of course, such beliefs may be at least partially misguided and thus dysfunctional as well.

ular ideologies are widely held throughout society, they define its **political culture.** In America, for example, liberal principles upholding the importance of individualism, freedom from arbitrary authority, and justice as equal opportunity seem to dominate our political culture.[39] In contrast, more conservative principles stressing the importance of national solidarity, social cooperation across classes, and benevolent paternalism seem to dominate Japanese culture.[40] The cultural values that predominate in societies serve several important functions. First, they provide a broad compass establishing the general direction and outer boundaries of institutional reforms and public policy. Demands by groups or initiatives by policy makers that conflict with such cultural norms are unlikely to be regarded as legitimate or to get a full hearing. As a consequence, culturally dominant ideological principles provide significant continuity or stability to the political practices of a community. Second, such principles serve to legitimate existing institutions and the authorities who occupy positions in these institutions. Thus, the commitment of most Americans to a liberal political tradition[41] contributes to their support for democratic political institutions and affirms their belief that duly elected (or appointed) officials have the right to exercise authority, even though the public may complain about the particular actions of their particular political executives, legislators, and judges. Finally, culturally dominant ideological principles provide standards enabling people within a society to evaluate and criticize conditions that seem to violate the norms established by the ideological tradition. Again, the commitment of most Americans to a liberal political tradition has provided broad support for the ideal of equal opportunity, prompting critical assessments of barriers for minorities, women, and other groups subjected to discrimination. In short, culturally dominant ideological principles provide the bases for an internal critique of social and political practices. They compel people to examine their practices not against the alien standards and ideals of another ideological or cultural tradition, but rather against the standards and ideals that the society embraces as its own.

Ideologies contribute to individuals' understandings of themselves and their political, social, and economic worlds. They facilitate the mobilization of people facing similar problems and having similar goals into political organizations and movements. And they contribute to the development of political cultures that legitimate existing institutions, give guidance to appropriate public policies, and enable critical assessments of practices that violate culturally dominant ideological principles. While particular ideologies serve these functions for individuals, groups, and communities, the comparative analysis of competing ideologies may help individuals and communities to develop better political ideas. We conclude this section with a brief discussion of how examination of the conflicting ideas of different ideologies can help in the development of more sophisticated and valid ideas.

[39]Robert Bellah et al., *Habits of the Heart* (New York: Harper and Row, 1985).
[40]Chie Nakane, *Japanese Society* (Berkeley: University of California Press, 1970).
[41]Louis Hartz, *The Liberal Tradition in America* (New York: Harcourt, Brace, and World, 1955).

First, we believe that comparing the competing descriptions and explanations of political life that are provided by different ideologies can contribute to the development of better empirical theories of politics. For example, Marxist ideology suggests that power is concentrated in the "ruling class"—those capitalists who own the means of production but seldom hold political office. In contrast, liberal ideology suggests that power is dispersed among many individuals and groups within society, and that the most powerful people are governmental officials, who are accountable and responsive to ordinary citizens. Identification of these competing ideas suggests an important research question—"who governs?," or "who really rules?"[42] While some scientific purists have suggested that scientific investigations should be completely uncontaminated by ideological matters, we think that analysis of ideologies can redirect research in political science away from rather trivial questions and back to bigger questions—like the distribution of power—and toward the scientific analysis of the competing "hypotheses" provided by these ideologies. In other words, the validity of the descriptions and explanations provided by ideologies can and should be questioned and subjected to appropriate scientific analysis. Of course, such scientific analysis might not be straightforward, as ideological commitments may influence the methods that researchers use and the evidence that they marshal on behalf of their hypotheses. But science is a cumulative enterprise in which competing methods and evidence are subject to rigorous examination and reworking, leading in the long run to better ideas than those initially provided by ideologies. In the concluding chapter, we will revisit the Marxist and the liberal responses to the question, "who governs?," (as well as other rival hypotheses derived from comparing the ideas of various ideologies) to see how going "beyond ideologies" can lead to the development of better descriptions and explanations of political life.

In addition to facilitating better descriptions and explanations, the comparative analysis of ideologies can help people develop more informed and thoughtful political ideals and principles. If one begins with the assumptions that no ideology is "true" and that all ideologies command our attention, then the comparative study of various ideologies can be a useful introduction to political philosophy—understood here as the search for better forms of political community. The study of competing ideologies challenges us to reexamine closely the principles and ideals we already hold, to consider the validity of alternative ideals, and thus to engage in the philosophical search for better ideals. Suppose, for example, that you hold the principle of "laissez faire"—that is, that governments ought not interfere in economic life. Through the study of ideologies, you will discover that this idea is central to classical liberalism (a fact that may surprise those who identify laissez faire with contemporary conservatism). You will also learn that the principle of laissez faire is based on certain ontological, psychological, sociological, and epistemologi-

[42]For a liberal and a Marxist analysis of these questions, see Robert Dahl in *Who Governs?* (New Haven: Yale University Press, 1961) and G. William Domhoff in *Who Really Rules?* (Santa Monica, Calif.: Goodyear Publishing, 1978).

cal assumptions. Perhaps you will find some of these assumptions (such as the idea that society is simply a marketplace of individuals pursuing their own interests in interaction with others) to be inadequate or distasteful, prompting you to question your allegiance to laissez faire. Through the study of ideologies, you will also discover that the idea of laissez faire is logically connected to other (classical liberal) principles—such as principles of justice that regard extensive inequalities of wealth as legitimate. If you question the justice of inequalities of wealth generated by the marketplace, you might also be prompted to question your allegiance to laissez faire. Through the study of ideologies, you will encounter principles diametrically opposed to laissez faire—principles that call for a strong state that regulates economic activities in various ways. Perhaps the reasons that other ideologies provide for a strong state prompt you to see the limitations of laissez faire and undertake a search for other principles regarding the proper relationship between the state and the economy. Our point here is not to refute the principle of laissez faire. The study of ideologies will require those who hold strong-state political principles to go through a similar process of discovery, reexamination, and, perhaps, reformulation. Our point is that a serious analysis of ideologies requires us to locate our ideas within ideological traditions, to consider the (perhaps questionable) philosophical assumptions that underlie our principles, to consider how our political principles are logically connected to other political principles (some of which we may reject), and to compare our ideas with competing ideas from other ideologies.

Perhaps such a reexamination of your political ideas will lead to a reaffirmation of these ideas and to a confident assertion of a particular ideological identity. Perhaps such a reexamination will lead to the adoption of new principles and an assertion of a newfound political identity. Perhaps such a reexamination will lead to a more complex outcome wherein some of your old ideas are reaffirmed, some of your old ideas are discarded and replaced by new ideas, and some issues linger unresolved in your mind. Perhaps such a reexamination will lead you to believe your ideas fall somewhere between various ideological traditions or that your ideas are quite distinct from the ideological traditions that we have explored. We think that truly thoughtful students of politics will resist any final ideological resting point for their ideas. They will discover that their ideas may change as social, economic, and political conditions change or as new understandings about the bases and implications of these ideas become more apparent. They will also discover the need for greater complexity in their assessments of political matters. For example, some people have come to hold what appear to be competing and inconsistent principles of justice, only to discover that particular egalitarian principles are appropriate for certain kinds of cases and spheres of life, while particular inegalitarian principles are appropriate for other circumstances and spheres of life.[43] We believe that such changes, discoveries, and complexities are part of

[43]Jennifer Hochschild, *What's Fair?* (Cambridge: Harvard University Press, 1981), and Michael Walzer, *Spheres of Justice* (New York: Basic Books, 1983).

an important and intellectually exciting process that occurs when men and women engage in a continuing search for better ideas and principles to govern their political, social, and economic lives. We believe that the study of political ideologies need not lead to the dogmatic acceptance or rejection of particular ideological principles, but rather can open the door to the search for better political ideas, which is the essence of political philosophy.

SUMMARY AND CONCLUSIONS

The comparative study of ideologies provides an excellent introduction to the great ideas of politics, to political theory, and to philosophy. The past two centuries has witnessed the emergence of a variety of provocative and appealing ideologies—and some utterly distasteful and even murderous ones as well. By organizing descriptions of these ideologies around such concepts as justice, citizenship, and authority, competing great ideas of politics can be analyzed and evaluated. The following chapters provide descriptions of the great ideas of each ideology in a way that, we hope, will facilitate such analysis and evaluation, and open the door to even more clear and creative thinking about how political communities are governed and how they should be governed.

This chapter has located political ideologies in relationship to political theory. Earlier in this chapter, we encountered a "critical conception of ideology" that suggested that political ideologies undermine the development of better political ideas, that they retard the evolution of political theory. While acknowledging that ideologies can have a negative impact on political thinking, we think that ideologies can also be functional. Having previously listed the pejorative characteristics that accompany a negative conception of ideology, we are now able to provide another—more positive—list of the qualities that characterize all ideologies:

1. Ideologies interpret existing social, economic, and political conditions, describing and explaining the problems within the contemporary context.
2. Ideologies present ostensibly realizable ideals—statements of goals that their advocates typically claim can be achieved within a generation.
3. Ideologies advocate a set of abstract principles and concrete actions as a means of achieving these goals.
4. These abstract principles address the great issues of politics, providing answers to such questions as "When is the use of governmental authority legitimate?," "How should social goods be distributed?," and "Who should rule?"
5. Ideological principles have, either explicitly or implicitly, particular philosophical foundations, as all ideologies make certain assumptions about human nature, society, the universe, and the sources of knowledge.
6. Ideologies contain coherent and systematic beliefs and values; their philosophical bases and political principles are logically interrelated.
7. Ideologies are formulated and articulated in their own literary traditions that provide their philosophical bases and that define and defend their political principles. Accordingly, each ideology has its own "sacred literature."
8. While the philosophical underpinnings of ideologies may be complex and little understood by the public, their analyses of current problems, their goals, and their political principles can be simply stated and, thus, readily grasped by the public

(or, at least, the informed public). Indeed, the central purpose of ideologies is to generate widespread support for particular political objectives.

9. Ideologies, nevertheless, may remain complex, because they address a wide range of abstract issues about human life. Such complexity leads to disagreements and debate within ideological camps, and the resolutions of these debates lead to transformations of ideas within ideologies.
10. Ideological principles influence the attitudes and actions of people in concrete political life. But people's concrete experiences in political life also influence their ideological principles, allowing for some change and evolution in their abstract beliefs and values.

Classical liberalism was the first ideology. Its basic ideas are deeply rooted in American (and European) institutions and culture, and there is some evidence that these ideas are increasingly being absorbed by political communities throughout the world. Nevertheless, the historical and philosophical foundations of these ideas and the more subtle principles logically associated with these main ideas are not always clearly understood (and continue to be debatable). It is to the ideas of classical liberalism that we turn first.

PART ONE

Ideologies of the Nineteenth Century

Capital as such is not evil; it is its wrong use that is evil. Capital in some form or other will always be needed.

—Mohandas Gandhi

The effect of liberty to individuals is that they may do what they please; we ought to see what it will please them to do, before we risk congratulations.

—Edmund Burke

I am truly free only when all human beings, men and women, are equally free. The freedom of other men, far from negating or limiting my freedom, is, on the contrary, its necessary premise and confirmation.

—Mikhail Bakunin

Capital is dead labor, which vampire-like, lives only by sucking living labor, and lives the more, the more labor it sucks.

—Karl Marx

Ask anyone committed to Marxist analysis how many angels on the head of a pin, and you will be asked in return to never mind the angels, tell me who controls the production of pins.

—Joan Didion

CHAPTER 2

Classical Liberalism

Liberalism has fallen on hard times, as even those politicians who hold liberal values and support liberal policies avoid labeling themselves "liberals." Most citizens and students apparently wish to distance themselves from any identification with the dreaded "L-word." Such resistance to liberalism invites analysis because liberal ideas—or at least the ideas of classical liberalism—are sewn into the fabric of American government and culture. When liberalism emerged as the first ideology two centuries ago, it endorsed many ideas that are widely accepted today. Classical liberals believe that individuals should enjoy extensive social, political, and economic liberties. They assert that although natural rights are distributed equally to all citizens, the unequal distribution of many social goods, including property and wealth, is not unjust. Classical liberals want the powers of governments to be limited, divided, and subject to the consent of their citizens. They argue that revolutions—like the American Revolution—may be justified if governments abuse their powers and curtail individual liberties and rights.

Many liberal ideas originated several centuries before the term "liberalism" was coined in 1810 by the *Liberales* in the Spanish legislature. To understand how classical liberalism emerged as a coherent ideology, we examine the following developments. First, we explore the problems that concerned "men of liberal temperament"—especially Englishmen and Frenchmen—during the sixteenth through eighteenth centuries.[1] Second, we briefly specify the political goals of leading Enlightenment thinkers during the eighteenth century. Third, the philosophical assumptions of classical liberalism are presented. Fourth, we discuss the political principles that emerged to justify capitalism in

[1]Male nouns and pronouns are used here and subsequently in this chapter because most classical liberals thought and wrote in terms of a male-centered society. Of course, some liberals recognized that liberal assumptions implied equal rights for women. Two feminist classics within the liberal tradition are Mary Wollestonecraft's *A Vindication of the Rights of Women,* published in 1792, and John Stuart Mill's *The Subjection of Women,* published in 1869. Mill's longtime companion, Harriot Taylor, played an important role in the development of this book, but whether she is properly a coauthor continues to be debated.

increasingly democratic societies. Sidebar 2-1 identifies some of the major contributors to classical liberalism and their principal writings.

In subsequent chapters, we will see that the ideas of classical liberalism have been both partially abandoned by contemporary liberals and partially absorbed by adherents of other political ideologies. Indeed, libertarians and contemporary conservatives often argue that they are the true heirs of the liberal tradition, and that contemporary liberals are no longer committed to individualism and limited government. For now, it is important to recognize that classical liberalism describes beliefs and values that were dominant in western Europe (especially England and France) and the United States during the nineteenth century and that are still widely held today. People currently holding these views are seldom regarded as liberals, however, as contemporary liberalism has emerged as a separate, though related, ideology.

THE POLITICAL BASES

Problems

Classical liberalism slowly emerged as a response to a variety of problems confronting Europe as it abandoned its feudal and medieval past and embraced

Sidebar 2-1

Some Classical Liberals and Their Main Writings

John Locke (1632–1704)
- *Letter Concerning Toleration* (1689)
- *Two Treatises of Government* (1690)
- *Essay on Human Understanding* (1690)

Charles-Louis de Secondat, baron de Montesquieu (1689–1755)
- *The Spirit of Laws* (1750)

Voltaire (Francois-Marie Arouet) (1694–1778)
- *Lettres Philosophiques* (1734)

Adam Smith (1723–1790)
- *The Wealth of Nations* (1776)

Jeremy Bentham (1748–1832)
- *Fragment on Government* (1776)
- *Introduction to Principles of Morals and Legislation* (1789)

Thomas Paine (1737–1809)
- *The Rights of Man* (1791)

James Madison (1751–1836)
- *The Federalist Papers* (1787–1788), with John Jay and Alexander Hamilton

James Mill (1773–1836)
- *Essay on Government* (1820)

John Stuart Mill (1806–1873)
- *Principles of Political Economy* (1848)
- *On Liberty* (1859)
- *Considerations on Representative Government* (1861)
- *Utilitarianism* (1861)
- *The Subjection of Women* (1869), with Harriet Taylor

Friedrich Hayek (1899–1992)
- *The Road to Serfdom* (1944)
- *The Constitution of Liberty* (1960)

modernity. Particularly eager to have Europe escape its past and become a progressive, scientific, and industrial society were economic entrepreneurs and traders, proponents of more political rights and freedoms, and the intellectuals of the Enlightenment. Several features of European society during the Middle Ages impeded the development of modern societies emphasizing commercial activity, political liberty, and scientific progress.

First was the problem of a static social structure. During the Middle Ages, people inherited an **ascribed** (or fixed) **social status**. Four classes of people—the clergy, the nobility, the bourgeoisie, and the serfs—could be readily identified. Two or three percent of the population consisted of members of the clergy of the Catholic Church, whose prominence and special privileges were indicated by their recognition as the First Estate in the parliamentary structures that emerged during the late Middle Ages throughout Europe. Another two percent of the population was the nobility or landed aristocracy. In the feudal societies of the Middle Ages, the nobility was responsible for providing law and order and caring for the material welfare of those beneath them. As urbanization and guild manufacturing developed and as monarchies centralized political power, the nobility lost most of its economic functions, but it retained social and political prominence as the Second Estate. Most people were commoners. Some commoners, who became known as the "bourgeoisie," engaged in commerce in the emerging medieval towns. In time, these free commoners gained certain rights, such as representation as the Third Estate in the parliaments. Most commoners remained peasants or agricultural laborers. These serfs were unfree, unrepresented politically, and bound by law and custom to the land they worked or the lords whom they served. People were born into these various ranks in society, and they had little chance to advance to higher levels. The clergy and nobility enjoyed special rights. Even as late as the eighteenth century in France, the nobility were exempt from most taxes and had almost exclusive rights to hold governmental and religious offices. Such privileges were greatly resented by commoners, and the system of ascribed status deprived the emerging capitalist industrial order of mobile wealth and labor. Liberals wanted greater social mobility, giving individuals opportunities to move beyond the class into which they were born.

A second problem concerned the *restrictions on economic activity* that were imposed by the Catholic Church and many European governments (monarchies) during the late Middle Ages. Among the rules and regulations governing economic activity, especially the production and exchange of goods, were the following:

1. Prohibitions against usury (charging any interest on lent money)
2. The establishment of "just prices" (or the practice of permitting local religious officials to set the prices of goods at a level which limited profits)
3. Prohibitions against advertising
4. Prohibitions against working by candlelight
5. Limitations on the number of apprentices employed by craftsmen

6. Control over inventions in order to prevent inventors from gaining competitive advantages from their discoveries
7. Prohibitions against competing with royal monopolies

Some of these restrictions were not always enforced rigorously, but they proved a formidable barrier to the creation of a free market. Classical liberals joined commercial and craft interests in attacking these barriers to freedom in the marketplace, as these restrictions were designed to limit what classical liberals would later celebrate: competition in the market.

A third problem concerning those of liberal temperament was the scope and power of government. Initially, the decentralized nature of feudal society hindered economic development, and the merchant class welcomed the emergence of such nation-states as England, France, and Spain and the centralization of power in the monarchies of these nations. Such centralized governments provided traders greater security from robbers as they transported goods to distant markets, and they facilitated economic transactions by replacing complex and diverse local rules and regulations with common laws, measurements, and currency. But as the authority of these monarchies increased during the sixteenth and seventeenth centuries, so too did the problem of **political absolutism**. Kings gathered for themselves the powers that were previously dispersed among members of the First and Second Estates (the church and the aristocracy), placed themselves above the law, practiced censorship and inquisition into private affairs, gave patronage to favored industries (such as the French tapestry works), and imposed taxes and oppressive regulations on the rising middle class. Louis XIV of France may have declared *"L'etat c'est moi"* (the state is me), but his absolute rule was regarded as rapacious government by leading philosophers of the Enlightenment. Liberals sought to curb such political tyranny and the abuses of concentrated political power.

A fourth problem was the primacy of religion and the associated demand for religious conformity. The Middle Ages were characterized by the domination of the Catholic Church, which encouraged people to orient their goals toward spiritual salvation. Practicing Christian virtue and saving one's soul were considered much more important than such worldly concerns as attaining a natural and scientific account of the universe or producing economic goods and making a profit. During the sixteenth century, the Protestant Reformation challenged the domination of the Catholic Church by declaring that religious belief was a private affair between the individual and God and that the clergy had no special authority to interpret and declare God's will. The Reformation also helped instill the "Protestant Ethic." This ethic suggested that hard work, productivity, and the accumulation of goods and capital were virtues enhancing one's private enjoyment, contributing to the greater glory of God, and identifying those with spiritual excellence. Protestantism helped reorient people toward secular life, but it did not solve the problem of religious intolerance. Both because of religious conviction and because of a desire to strengthen support for their regimes, the monarchies of the era often required subjects to conform to particular religious doctrines and suppressed heretics. This resulted in a series of civil wars (sometimes between Protestants and Catholics and sometimes between different Protestant sects) in Germany, France, and England. Persons of liberal temperament, like England's John Locke (1632–1704), called for religious toleration and a wall of **separation between the church and the state**. They argued that in the interest of maintaining social stability the church must concern itself solely with spiritual salvation and the state must concern itself solely with citizens' secular interests, such as their liberty and their property.

The religious wars exemplified a more fundamental problem: the need to protect the most basic human rights, such as each individual's life and liberty. Thomas Hobbes (1588–1679) emphasized that each individual's security and possessions were threatened by the actions of other individuals. To overcome social disorder (or anarchy) and to deter individuals from harming each other, a sovereign government was needed to define and protect proper rights. However, Thomas Paine (1737–1809) argued that oppressive governments were themselves the greatest threat to individual rights. To secure individual liberty, societies must constrain arbitrary and rapacious government. Believing that the British had succeeded in restraining government, John Stuart Mill (1806–1873) argued that the greatest threat to individual liberty was public opinion. For Mill, individual liberty could only be secure when government protected and fostered individualism from the views of the majority. Given such diverse views, it can be said that the greatest problem for classical liberals was to construct a government that secured individual liberty without, at the same time, encroaching on individual rights.

Goals

This discussion of the problems that concerned liberals suggests that classical liberals have been—and remain—primarily concerned with enhancing individual liberty, promoting capitalism, establishing constitutional democracies, and developing a scientific understanding of human behavior and social life. Securing liberty is probably the primary liberal goal, as classical liberals value both capitalism and constitutional democracy, in large part because they enhance liberty. The new science of politics envisioned by liberals during the eighteenth and nineteenth centuries would contribute to liberty by providing an intellectual foundation for individual rights, capitalism, and constitutional democracy.

Classical liberals have a particular conception of liberty, one that departs from the ancient, Christian, and republican notions of liberty that had previously dominated western thought. In ancient Greece, liberty involved the acquisition of such classical virtues as wisdom, courage, and moderation. In Christendom, liberty involved knowing and acting according to the will of God. In the republican tradition, liberty involved political participation and acquiring the civic virtues of citizenship. For liberals, ancient Greek, Christian, and republican virtues might be pleasant and laudable sentiments, but they did not define the essence of liberty. Hobbes provided the **liberal conception of liberty** when he declared that "a freedman is he that in those things which by his strength and wit he is able to do is not hindered to do what he has a will to."[2] In general, the liberal conception of liberty emphasizes three things. First, liberty is not acquired by the striving of individuals but is, instead, given to each person at birth; it is a natural right of everyone. Second, the value of liberty is that it enables each individual to choose and pursue his own ends. Liberals assume that each person wants happiness—that he wants to maximize pleasure and minimize pain, but they recognize that each person has a different conception of happiness because everyone experiences pleasure and pain in different ways. Only the individual can define his own good, and liberty involves the right to pursue a self-defined conception of happiness. Third, liberals recognize that while everyone is born with an equal right to pursue his own happiness, such liberty can and should be constrained. Most generally, liberals understand that complete natural liberty results in a state of disorder. To be part of society, people must give up some liberty. The classical liberal conception of how far liberty should extend was provided by John Stuart Mill: "The only freedom that deserves the name is that of pursuing our own good in our own way, so long as we do not attempt to deprive others of theirs or impede their efforts to obtain it."[3] Such a formulation is intended to give individuals an absolute right to think and worship as they wish and to act on their own inclinations within a private sphere. But absolute liberty ends when individuals encounter other people. People are not free to harm others or infringe on others' rights. People are not free to renege on their agreements and contracts with others. The purpose of law is to specify precisely the limits on individual liberty, and government exists to enact and enforce laws restricting individual liberty in the public sphere.

Developing **capitalism** or an economy based on the principles of a free market, is a second liberal goal, one related to the goal of enhancing individual liberty. Important freedoms sought by liberals include the freedom to make contracts with other people, the freedom to acquire, exchange, and maintain private property, the freedom to sell one's labor for the highest wage one can secure, and the freedom to invest one's capital in those areas having the greatest potential for profit. In short, liberals want the liberty to trade, work, invest, produce, and consume in a free market. They want a society where people have the capacities and motivation to produce material abundance. They want economic progress, a steady enhancement in the wealth of nations. Economic freedoms are seen as important prerequisites for producing material abundance, for such freedoms allow persons to maximize their economic interests. Economic liberty permits each individual to increase his economic prosperity, and society as a whole becomes more prosperous. According to liberals, cap-

[2]Thomas Hobbes, *Leviathan* (Indianapolis: Bobbs-Merrill Liberal Arts Library, 1958 [1651]), p. 171.
[3]John Stuart Mill, *On Liberty*, edited by Elizabeth Rapaport (Indianapolis: Hackett Publishing, 1978 [1859]), p. 12.

italist economies do more, though, than create prosperous domestic conditions. Classical liberals argue that if countries practice capitalism and free trade, then international tranquillity is promoted. At the very least, the economic causes of wars among nations can be removed.

Developing **constitutional democracies** is a third liberal goal, and this goal is related to enhancing individual freedom and economic progress. During the seventeenth, eighteenth, and nineteenth centuries, liberals wanted to replace monarchies and aristocracies with democratic governments. Monarchies concentrated power in royal families, which often used their power to restrict individual liberties and to pursue mercantilist economic practices which discouraged free trade. Aristocracies concentrated power among the landed nobility, who regarded capitalist freedoms as threats to their traditional privileges. In contrast, the early liberal theorists argued that democratic governments would protect individual rights and economic freedoms in order to obtain the consent of the governed. In seeking democratic governments, liberals have not endorsed the highly participatory democracies practiced in ancient Greece or advocated by radicals such as Jean-Jacques Rousseau (1712–1778). Instead, liberals want the kind of representative democracies that protect the rights of citizens, even if citizens do not actively participate in governmental affairs beyond voting for representatives in periodic elections. To the extent that citizens can minimize their political involvement, they are free to pursue their economic interests as producers and consumers in a capitalist society. Constitutional restrictions, including provisions that governmental leaders stand for election, are regarded by liberals as the means by which democratic governments can be prevented from infringing on individual rights and intervening in the capitalist economy.

Most generally, classical liberals have sought to develop a *science of politics* which affirms these goals. Traditional beliefs, religious dogma, and metaphysical speculation have contributed to unnecessary restrictions on individual freedom, to archaic economic practices, and to the justification of political absolutism. Liberals hope to eliminate these "idols of the mind," and base political, social, and economic thought on rational deductions from minimal assumptions about the natural world. To understand the liberal science of politics, we must consider their philosophical foundations: their assumptions about ultimate reality (ontology), human nature, the nature of society, and knowledge itself.

THE PHILOSOPHICAL BASES

Ontology

In medieval Europe, it was generally assumed that God constitutes ultimate reality. God had created the world, and his will determines the course of human history. These assumptions about how the world works obviously empowered religious authorities, especially the leaders of the Catholic Church, who claimed to know God's will and his divine laws. Many classical liberals, like John Locke, were devout Christians who never questioned God's existence, but the founders of liberalism often embraced **deism**—the view that God created the universe and the laws governing the universe but no longer exercises any influence over it. According to deist assumptions, God created a material world that works according to precise laws—a world of mechanical and mathematical regularity. After creating a well-ordered and perfect world, God "retired." Deists reject the medieval assumption that God actively intervenes in the world, arguing that it was absurd to think that God would alter the perfect natural order that He had created and set in motion. Deism was an important liberal assumption, because it allowed liberals to view the world in completely naturalistic terms. Science could be used to observe nature and discover the regularity and order that God had created. If God's laws are completely reflected in nature and if God does not exercise his sovereignty over the universe except through the working of natural laws, the roles of religious dogma and religious authority in political life could be eliminated. For example, deism laid to rest the idea of the divine right of kings—that God bestowed and thus legitimated monarchical power.

In order to understand the material world that God created but no longer controlled, liberals developed the idea of the "**state of nature**," a hypothetical situation of cultural, social, and political nothingness. Envision a world without cultural heritages providing ideas about God, virtue, justice, and human potentialities. Envision a world without social structures (like churches, schools, or even families). Envision a world without political institutions (like the military, the police, the courts, and other civil authorities). If we envision a world without cultural preconceptions and without social and political institutions, what remains? The founders of liberalism believed that what remains in an unadorned state of nature is simply matter in motion. Their doctrine of **ontological materialism** holds that the world is composed of physical objects set in motion, and thus subject to change, according to natural laws of causation. While philosophers have often posited the existence of ultimate realities greater than that of the material world—such as Platonic forms, Aristotelian teleological causes, and the Divine Spirit—liberals view such ultimate realities as mere metaphysical speculation. Such speculation impedes human understanding of the obvious reality presented to us in the material world.

By setting aside metaphysical concepts, history can be understood as a natural process. Liberals have thus been receptive to the theory of Charles Darwin (1809–1882) that the evolution of life can be explained by the process of natural selection. Human history can also be understood as a result of natural human motivations and capacities, rather than as a result of God's will. Many nineteenth-century liberals thus embraced the theory of Herbert Spencer (1820–1903) that human evolution depends on the playing out of unchecked forces of human competition. According to Spencer, human progress requires the "survival of the fittest," where those humans best adapted to the environment prosper and multiply, and the weak and unfit become extinct.

By eliminating religious and metaphysical concepts that impeded a scientific and natural understanding of the physical world and history, the idea of the state of nature was important for the origins of liberalism. But, more important, the idea of the state of nature facilitated a liberal understanding of human nature and civil society.

Human Nature

Classical liberals assume that humans, like the rest of nature, are essentially "matter in motion." As material beings, humans are ontologically estranged from each other. They are physically separate beings lacking any sort of spiritual unity. Humans are also psychologically estranged from one another. They are primarily concerned with the preservation of their own lives and with their own happiness. In short, in the state of nature, humans are self-interested. Their primary motivation is to achieve as much pleasure and to avoid as much pain as possible. According to C. B. Macpherson, the liberal "model of man" is as a *"maximizer of utilities."*[4] Liberals do not regard human self-interest as a sign of moral depravity. On the contrary, liberals believe that some of the more inhumane episodes in human history—such as those evidenced by the butchery of war—could have been avoided if people had been more interested in their own preservation and happiness. Liberals do, however, regard the uncontrolled pursuit of self-interest as a social problem. The tendency of humans to put their interests ahead of others means that individuals must be constrained in their pursuit of happiness. And political and economic institutions must be devised which channel self-interest in ways that benefit others in society.

Humans have various qualities that help them maximize their utility. They have, of course, their bodies. With their bodies they can labor, removing from nature those goods like food that are necessary for their survival. And through physical labor they can transform nature, providing for basic needs (as when they weave clothing from cotton and build shelter from timber) and pleasures (as when they craft precious jewelry from minerals like diamonds and gold).

Humans also have such senses as sight and hearing, which enable them to perceive the external world. According to Locke, our senses receive sensual experience from the environment. Such sensations impress themselves on the human mind, which records these perceptions (as on a *tabula rasa,* or blank slate) and then classifies and relates these perceptions to one another, forming concepts, establishing ideational relationships, and deriving abstract theoretical knowledge about the world. Humans are thus endowed with **instrumental reason,** understood as the capacity of the mind to arrive at useful ideas on the basis of sensations and reflection on these sensations. A concrete though mundane example of the liberal conception of reason might be as follows: The

[4]C. B. Macpherson, *The Life and Times of Liberal Democracy* (New York: Oxford University Press, 1977), p. 24.

solitary individual perceives occasional rumblings in his stomach, which in time he classifies as hunger and associates with pain. He also perceives a number of similar red juicy objects growing in the fields, which he classifies as strawberries and which he learns are pleasant tasting and satisfy his hunger. The application of reason thus yields for the individual the useful generalization that the picking and eating of strawberries reduces the pain of hunger and provides a pleasant tasting sensation.[5]

This liberal conception of human reason differs from most previous conceptions of reason. In ancient Greek thought, for example, reason was thought to be capable of producing ultimate knowledge. Reason enabled people to know what is good or virtuous for all humans. "Right reason" enabled people to know the appropriate goals or ends of life. But in liberal thought, human reason cannot deliver ultimate knowledge. It can only give us efficient knowledge. Reason enables each person to know the means by which he gains pleasure and avoids pain. Reason informs individuals about efficient and effective means to their own ends. But reason cannot tell humans whether their ends are good or virtuous. In short, while the ancient Greeks viewed reason as a human capacity to restrain or overcome human desires and appetites in order to attain some knowable higher good or virtue, liberals view human reason as a resource to help fulfill human desires and appetites, which are the only goods recognized by the individual.

Classical liberals believe that humans are equal in some respects and unequal in others. They accept **equality of being**. Each human is equally human, everyone is "matter in motion," everyone exists (at least in the state of nature) in the same estranged condition, everyone is fundamentally self-interested, and everyone's happiness is equally important. "Equality of being" means that each individual can rightfully claim that his life, liberty, and happiness is as important as the life, liberty, and happiness of any other individual. The "categorical imperative" of Immanuel Kant (1724–1804) gave moral expression to the liberal idea of equality of being. No one ought to use another person merely as a means to his own happiness. No one is justified in sacrificing the life, liberty, and happiness of others to achieve his own well-being. Everyone must act according to rules that apply equally to all.

In addition to endorsing equality of being, liberals believe that people also have certain equal, minimal capabilities. As Hobbes noted, for example, everyone is equally capable of causing others physical harm. And Locke's understanding of human rationality implies that all people are fundamentally equal in their ability to learn, because learning is ultimately grounded in experiences that are available to everyone.

Nevertheless, it is a great oversimplification to claim that liberals think humans are equal. Liberals understand that humans have very different goals and very different conceptions of happiness. They recognize that people have different physical and mental endowments and different propensities to make

[5]For a discussion of instrumental reason, see Thomas Spragens, *The Irony of Liberal Reason* (Chicago: University of Chicago Press, 1981).

use of these endowments. For example, Adam Smith (1723–1790) argued that social arrangements, especially the division of labor, where individuals specialize in particular activities, enhances differences in human talents that must be recognized in constructing economic and political principles. As another example, John Stuart Mill understood that the extent to which people have developed their intellectual capacities is unequal. Indeed, his view that people are different in their capacity to reach informed political judgments led him to reject the democratic ideal of "one man, one vote" and to endorse a scheme of plural voting that would give more political power to the more educated. These examples illustrate that classical liberals understand that human physical and mental capacities are neither equal nor fixed. Differences in human capabilities have always been recognized by liberals. Indeed, as liberalism matured, its advocates thought that a liberal (and democratic) society provides a fertile context where each individual can develop his own capacities and powers to the fullest extent possible, but that the level of such development is naturally unequal in different individuals.

Society

For classical liberals, societies arise from agreements among individuals to band together in order to escape the loneliness, disorder, and inconveniences that occur in the state of nature. Liberals recognize that humans are bound to one another in many types of societies. The most basic of these is conjugal society, which is based on a "voluntary compact between man and woman."[6] The most inclusive of these is political or civil society, which is based on a **social contract** in which individuals consent to limit the liberties they would enjoy in the state of nature in order "to join and unite in a community, for their comfortable, safe, and peaceable living amongst one another, in a secure enjoyment of their properties and a greater security against any that are not of it."[7]

There are several important features of this liberal conception of political society. First, while societies do not exist in the state of nature, they arise from the state of nature through natural processes. Hobbes viewed the state of nature as a "state of war." He argued that men in the state of nature desired the same things, which they could not each enjoy, thus creating perpetual conflict. In such a condition, men would live in "continual fear and danger of violent death, and the life of man (would be) solitary, poor, nasty, brutish, and short."[8] To escape this condition and to achieve the goals of peace and security, rational men would naturally conclude that they should make a covenant, or social contract, with other men in which each person would agree not to infringe on the life, liberty, and possessions of others. Such an agreement (and the designation of a sovereign power to enforce the agreement) creates a commonwealth—or civil society. Locke viewed the state of nature in less conflic-

[6]John Locke, *The Second Treatise of Government* (New York: Mentor, 1960 [1690]), p. 362.
[7]Locke, *Second Treatise*, p. 375.
[8]Hobbes, *Leviathan*, p. 100.

Sidebar 2-2

The Liberal Critique of the Patriarchal Family and State

In *The Second Treatise of Government,* Locke argued that it was a mistake to rely on the family as a model for government. Locke was attacking such absolutist thinkers as Robert Filmer, the author of *Patriarcha; or the Natural Power of Kings* (1680). Filmer held that the monarch was the father of the country and that members of society were the children. These children (and their mother) must obey their father, the monarch. By declaring that the family was based on a voluntary agreement between a man and a woman, Locke criticized the traditional norm of the patriarchal family (and suggested that divorce was permissible). Locke also criticized this "family model" of political authority by arguing that the contemporary Englishman owes his father what he owes the Crown: respect, but not unquestioned obedience.

Locke's contemporaries were receptive to his argument because it was consistent with emerging understandings of individuality, happiness, and responsibility. As Lawrence Stone has noted in his *The Family, Sex and Marriage: In England 1500–1800,* before 1550, marriage was dominated by the interests of the family. Children married on the instructions of their parents. After 1550, the practice of allowing children one veto over their parents' choice emerged. By the 1650s, parents had only a single, often ineffective, veto over their children's choices. These developments are signs of the increasing importance of individualism.

Filmer was relying on an outdated model for his metaphor. Locke was the spokesman for those who recognized neither Filmer's description of a family nor his analysis of political authority. For classical liberals, authority required the consent of "mature" Englishmen.

tual terms than Hobbes, but he agreed that people would seek to escape it by entering into agreements, thus forming a civil society. Locke maintained that individuals in the state of nature comprehend an important law of nature: "no one ought to harm another in his life, liberty, or possessions."[9] Nevertheless, he recognized that some people would violate this law of nature, giving injured parties the right to defend themselves and to punish offenders. While the laws of nature specify that the degree of punishment should be proportionate to the transgression and merely be sufficient to deter transgressions, injured parties would not be impartial judges of these matters. They would be partial to their own interests and vindictive toward the accused. The state of nature is thus "inconvenient," because there is no impartial power to adjudicate alleged infringements of rights. To overcome such inconveniences in the state of nature, people may "resign to the public" their power to punish offenders for infringing upon their rights.[10] When people agree to such an arrangement, civil society is created. In short, political societies arise because of the desire to escape the insecurity or inconveniences of the state of nature.

[9]Locke, *Second Treatise,* p. 311.
[10]Locke, *Second Treatise,* p. 367.

Second, the society established by these natural processes can best be conceived of as an aggregation of the individuals composing it and their interactions. While the ancient and medieval world attributed to society an existence and properties beyond the individuals that constitute it, liberals rejected such an "inflated" conception of society. Society was not an entity created by God. It was created by man. Society did not define the individual and give him an identity. Rather, individuals defined society and gave it an identity. In short, classical liberals viewed society simply as a marketplace comprised of individuals pursuing their interests, often in interaction with each other, and constrained only by the need to respect the rights of other individuals.

Third, this **individualist image of society** suggests that classical liberals put the rights and needs of individuals before any considerations regarding society as a whole. In the ancient and medieval worlds, it was thought that individuals should yield to the claims of society. In contrast, liberals assumed that society could not make certain claims upon the individual. It could not, for example, ask the individual to die for the good of society or to refrain from exploiting natural resources for the good of the environment. Indeed, the liberal conception of society implied that all societal claims on the individual had to be framed in terms of the needs of other individuals within society, not society itself. If the greater good of most members of society is served by compelling an individual to act in a certain way, such as being drafted into the army, such infringements on individual liberties might be justified. But individuals cannot be compelled to do things against their will simply to serve the needs of "the country," where the country is conceived of as an emergent entity with needs beyond those of its present members.

Finally, the creation of liberal societies implies very little about the institutions of those societies. For Locke, majority rule is the only institutional arrangement implied by the existence of society. Each political society must establish institutions to enact, administer, and enforce laws providing for the peaceful resolution of conflict. It must authorize a particular government to carry out these functions, and if a particular government abuses its powers, it can be dissolved by society. Since members of society may disagree about what kind of government to authorize and when a government should be dissolved, these social decisions must be made by majority rule of its members.

In sum, classical liberals have a "weak" conception of society. Society is merely a collection of individuals who sometimes interact with each other to further their economic interests. Political societies arise out of a social contract among individuals. Hence, political societies have no emergent properties beyond those of its members. They are limited in terms of the claims they can make on their members. Their main function is to authorize some government to provide security for their individual members.

Epistemology

Classical liberals doubt that modes of behavior prescribed by tradition or by religion correctly define the "good life." They are skeptical that existing institutional arrangements are conducive to achieving the good society. Traditionally prescribed modes of behavior and institutional arrangements are regarded as mere prejudices and opinions rather than as being objectively correct. However, classical liberals have not been skeptical about the possibility of arriving at objective truths about the good life, the good society, and the good state. They believe in the possibility of a science of politics—a science rooted in the methodology of the French mathematician and philosopher, René Descartes (1596–1650).[11]

The **Cartesian method** involves doubting the truth of all propositions except those clear and distinct ideas that are self-evident. Self-evident ideas form the building blocks of more complex ideas derived or deduced from them. Because ultimate knowledge about politics involves the good life, the good society, and the good state, Cartesian liberals must begin with a clear and distinct conception of the good. Propositions about what is good for everyone can hardly be considered self-evident, however, given the differences in the goals, capacities, and circumstances of individuals. Each individual must define for himself his own conception of good.

For each individual, the good is known through **utilitarian** analysis. The basic clear and distinct idea of the good for liberals is that whatever causes an individual pleasure is the good to him and that whatever causes an individual pain is the bad to him. The good for each individual is that which provides him "utility"—defined as the sensation of pleasure minus the sensation of pain.

There were two implications of utilitarianism as the basis for knowing the good. First, since only the individual can experience his own pleasure and pain, only the individual can know his own good. This led liberals to advocate **tolerance** of different conceptions of the good life held by various individuals and to deny that government or any other authority has a legitimate role in promoting, much less imposing, particular conceptions of the good or virtuous life. Second, because only the individual can know his own good, each individual has a right to pursue his own good as he sees fit. For early liberals, the **natural rights** to life, liberty, and the pursuit of happiness were immediate deductions from the self-evident truth that only individuals know their own good. And by further deduction, at least for early liberals, those social and political arrangements that secure and maximize these natural rights are good.

The doctrine of natural rights did not long survive, however, as an essential part of liberal epistemology. David Hume (1711–1776) argued that the human mind can only know what it perceives and that the perceptions of all individuals are unique. Thus people could only know their perceptions of nature and not nature itself. Because there could be no universal understanding of nature, there could be no universal understanding of human rights (or duties) dictated by nature. Liberals, thus, turned to more complex and sophisticated versions of utilitarianism in the work of Jeremy Bentham (1748–1832) and John Stuart Mill.

[11]For an excellent discussion of the debt that liberalism owes to Descartes, see Benjamin Barber, *Strong Democracy* (Berkeley: University of California Press, 1984), pp. 46–66.

The major contribution of Bentham was to develop utilitarianism as a method for analyzing the goodness of laws and governmental policies. As we have seen, the earlier utilitarianism of Locke supported the ideas that only the individual can know his own good and that governments should infringe on individual rights only as much as necessary to protect the rights of other individuals. While this formulation supports the general minimalist tendencies of a good government, it does not indicate whether a particular law or policy serves the public interest—that is, whether it is consistent with the greater good of the greater number. As industrialization developed, liberals discovered that governmental policies of noninterference in the economic realm (of allowing everyone to have maximal economic liberties) protect the privileges of the wealthy and harm the poor. For example, if governments failed to provide public schools, the wealthy could use their economic liberty and resources to purchase private education (and the economic benefits accompanying such education) for their sons (and daughters), while the poor (being unable to afford a private education) would be forced to use their more limited economic liberty to send their children into the workplace. From the immediate perspective of the individuals involved, the utility of the wealthy may be well served by their purchasing private education, and the utility of the poor may be well served by their sending their children into the workplace. But to reform-minded liberals like Bentham, it was at least arguable that governmental provision of public schools would best serve the public interest.

Bentham did not argue that the public interest exists apart from the individuals constituting society. Instead, the public interest is simply the aggregate of the utilities of the individuals in society. In our example, the government should estimate the pleasures and pains for each individual that would be derived from providing public schools. Public schools would be good public policy if the aggregate amount of utility accruing to all individuals from such public schools exceeded the aggregate amount of utility that would occur if no public schools were provided. The calculation of aggregate utility is complicated. Such factors as the intensity, duration, and certainty of induced pleasures and pains must be weighed for all individuals, as must the different susceptibilities or sensitivities to the pleasures and pains of different individuals. The complexity of this **felicific calculus** for determining the public good of policy options led Bentham to acknowledge that "It is not to be expected that this process should be strictly pursued previously to every moral judgment, or to every legislative or judicial operation. It may, however, always be kept in view."[12] By keeping the pleasures and pains of all citizens in mind when enacting laws and policies, Bentham believed that governments would reform themselves by gradually eliminating laws that are burdensome to individuals and by enacting laws that enable a steady increase in the material happiness of most citizens.

While proclaiming his support of Bentham's utilitarian method, John Stu-

[12]Jeremy Bentham, *An Introduction to the Principles of Morals and Legislation,* edited by Wilfred Harrison (Oxford: Basil Blackwell, 1967 [1789]), p. 153.

art Mill introduced fundamental revisions to it. Essentially, Mill thought that Bentham's conception of pleasure was overly sensual and material. For Bentham, drinking a beer can provide more utility than reading a good book if it produces a pleasant sensation for the individual. To correct this possibility, Mill argued that some pleasures—especially intellectual ones—are objectively superior to others: "It is better to be a human being dissatisfied than a pig satisfied; better to be Socrates dissatisfied than a fool satisfied."[13] Mill modified utilitarianism in three ways so that it could better justify a more intellectual, spiritual, and idealistic society, and the governmental policies promoting such a society. First, he argued that there are objective qualitative differences among pleasures, and that intellectual activity enhances the value of a pleasure. Second, he argued that the object of a good life is a pleasurable existence rather than immediate pleasurable sensations. If the attainment of an immediate pleasant feeling increases the risk of significant future losses, the value of such immediate pleasures must be discounted. Third, he suggested that individuals might secure a more pleasurable existence if they contributed to the public good rather than maximizing immediate personal happiness. For example, if people are required to pay taxes to increase the education, health, and welfare of other members of society, the loss of utility from the pain of taxes can, in the long run, be compensated for ultimately by living in a better society as a direct consequence. In short, Mill argued for **enlightened self-interest**. The good life is one where individuals maximize their intellectual and spiritual pleasures and minimize their pains over the course of a lifetime and where people recognize the pleasure of living in a society where other individuals are likewise satisfied. The good state is one having laws and policies that stimulate such a good life for all individuals within society.

The application of Bentham's utilitarian calculus and, especially, Mill's "enlightened" modifications of that calculus to the analysis of public policies led liberals in due course to support positive governmental actions to improve the lives of citizens. But positive, strong government is a feature of contemporary liberalism. Classical liberals endorsed minimal government throughout most of the nineteenth century. Most liberals—including Bentham and, to a lesser extent John Stuart Mill—believed that utilitarian considerations justified a government whose authority is largely confined to providing security for individuals.

SUBSTANTIVE POLITICAL PRINCIPLES

Authority

While individuals have an unlimited natural right to pursue their own happiness in the state of nature, classical liberals understand that individuals are driven to give up absolute freedom and enter civil society in order to attain security. A critical question for members of civil society is, By what means can

[13]John Stuart Mill, *Utilitarianism* (New York: Bobbs-Merrill, 1957 [1861]), p. 14.

we secure our rights to life, liberties, and properties from being infringed upon by other individuals? John Locke and other classical liberals assumed that government is the proper remedy to the insecurity and inconveniences of the state of nature. Governmental authority should be used to establish laws protecting individual rights and to administer and enforce these laws. To understand why liberals assume that government should play these roles, it is useful to consider how contemporary **libertarians** respond to this question. Libertarians are in many respects the true heirs of the Lockean liberal tradition, but they do not easily grant that government is the proper remedy for the inconveniences of the state of nature. Libertarians, such as Robert Nozick,[14] claim that before creating a government to police society and adjudicate conflicts among individuals within it, it is desirable to explore more voluntary arrangements for securing individual rights.

In a state of nature (i.e., in a world without government), security could be provided through the entirely voluntary actions of individual "customers" seeking security and the "producers" of such security, called "protective agencies." In exchange for customer fees, protective agencies—perhaps organizations like the "Pinkertons" or the Mafia—could provide a type of "police" protection to deter others from violating the rights of customers, apprehend and punish those who violated customers' rights, and seek just compensation from offenders for those customers whose rights are violated. While many such protective agencies might initially be formed, the logic of providing security would, in time, lead to the existence of a **dominant protective agency**. People would, of course, have conflicting views over who violated whose rights, and everyone would want to be protected by the strongest protective agency—the one having the capacity to impose its views of the conflict on all parties. In short, as people in the state of nature pursued their interest in security in a totally free and voluntary manner, they would logically form and support an organization that would evolve to resemble a "minimal" state. People would grant the dominant protective agency the largely uncontested power to protect members of society and to resolve conflicts among them.

Still, the dominant protective agency is not a government, for two reasons. First, its capacity to protect, adjudicate, and compensate is based on its power, not on its legitimate authority. While a government exists only when people believe it has legitimacy or the moral right to rule, the dominant protective association rules by virtue of its superior coercive capacity and physical power. Second, a dominant protective agency serves only its paying customers. Those individuals living within the territory ruled by the dominant protective agency can be apprehended and punished by it, but they cannot expect to receive its protection. These deficiencies in strictly voluntary arrangements for providing security prompt libertarians to concede Locke's assumption that government is the proper remedy for the inconveniences of the state of nature. For liberals, a dominant protective agency becomes a government when it acquires legitimacy and when it serves everyone in its territory.

[14]Robert Nozick, *Anarchy, State, and Utopia* (New York: Basic Books, 1974), pp. 10–28.

Sidebar 2-3

Libertarianism

The ideas of classical liberalism have been partially incorporated in many contemporary ideologies, but perhaps are most pervasive in libertarianism. American libertarians trace their ideas to such classical liberals as John Locke, Thomas Paine, and Herbert Spencer. They have also been influenced by the novelist-philosopher, Ayn Rand (1905–1982)—whose works include *The Fountainhead* (1943), *Atlas Shrugged* (1957), *The Virtue of Selfishness* (1961), and *Capitalism: The Unknown Ideal* (1966)—and by such noteworthy free-market economists as Friedrich von Hayek and Milton Friedman. Robert Nozick's *Anarchy, State, and Utopia*, published in 1974, has helped libertarianism gain considerable academic respectability. As we will see in Chapter 10, libertarian ideas constitute part of contemporary conservatism, but pure libertarians have been reluctant to dilute their ideology by forming alliances with "statist conservatives" or the Republican party. These libertarians have formed their own political party, and their candidates for the Presidency have received one or two percent of the vote in recent elections.

Libertarians emphasize a rugged, perhaps strident, individualism. Each individual is unique. Each individual has rights, especially property rights, that cannot be violated. Each individual is responsible for his or her own life and the choices he or she makes. Each person must be self-reliant, looking to no one else or to no institutions for security or assistance. This emphasis on individualism make libertarians advocates of free markets in all goods. Since individuals are responsible for their own behavior, any state-imposed restrictions on drugs, pornography, prostitution, or other "vices" should be repealed.

As illustrated by liberal support for public education and libertarian opposition to the public school system, libertarians are more antistatist than are classical liberals. While classical liberals want limited governments that do little more than protect people's rights, they view such governments in a fairly benevolent manner; republican institutions and democratic elections can ensure that governments are agents of the people. Libertarians also want governmental authority restricted to the protection of people's rights, but they have no faith that republican institutions and democratic elections can tame or control governments. Governmental authorities always abuse their power, both because they are self-interested and corrupt and because their altruistic intentions to secure "social justice" and to serve the public interest are inherently misguided. For example, libertarians assert that compassion for the poor has prompted contemporary liberals to develop a welfare state that is financed by illegitimate seizures of property, in the form of progressive taxes, and that denies the poor the opportunity to develop self-reliance. As another example, libertarians assert that a fetish for "national security" prompted U.S. officials to engage in the Vietnam War, even though these officials violated the rights of many young men by drafting them to serve in an undeclared war that did not serve their interests and that undermined their moral convictions.

Libertarian emphasis on individualism and the "virtues of selfishness" has prompted charges that theirs is an ideology without morality. Libertarians respond, however, that morality should not be confused with altruism. Ayn Rand's "objectivist" philosophy claims that current moral decay is rooted in the contemporary tendency to equate morality with altruism. Because humans are really unprepared to sacrifice themselves for others, libertarians conclude that altruistic morality is something that may be given lip service, but which would be foolish to actually practice. In contrast to futile altruistic moralities, libertarians argue that a truly moral person simply respects the rights of others, pursues the virtues that improve his or her life, and does nothing that discourages others from becoming similarly self-reliant.

An agency acquires the legitimacy of a government when members of civil society, by majority vote, establish it and authorize it through a second kind of social contract. While the first social contract is among individuals in the state of nature to form civil society, the second social contract is between civil society and the designated government. This contract gives government the legitimate authority to use its powers to provide security in ways designated in the contract (while requiring citizens to obey governmental authority as long as the government acts within the scope of its powers). The important point is that governmental authority is legitimate because it is derived from a social contract, while the power of a dominant protective agency lacks legitimacy because it is derived from a series of contracts with individual customers.

A dominant protective agency attains the scope of a government only when it provides its services to everyone within society. In order to cover the costs of those people within society who cannot afford to pay for its protective services, a government is (mildly) redistributive. It adopts a tax structure that extracts the necessary resources from the more wealthy members of society to cover the costs of providing security for the poor. But providing equal security for all is the extent of governmental redistribution.

Classical liberals thus support **limited government**. Most classical liberals thought that governmental authority should be used to perform only the following functions:

1. To provide national defense, making individuals secure from the threat of invasion from people outside their society and from other governments
2. To enact and enforce civil laws requiring individuals to live up to private agreements and economic contracts
3. To enact criminal laws protecting the lives, liberties, and property of all members of society from potential offenders
4. To punish violators of civil and criminal laws with sufficient regularity and severity so as to deter the breaking of private contracts and of criminal laws

5. To provide public education and those public works—like roads, canals, safe water, and sewers—that are necessary for business and public safety but cannot be provided through free enterprise.

While the authority of the minimal state is limited to performing these functions, it is a mistake to assume that classical liberals therefore want a weak state.[15] Liberals like Voltaire (1694–1778), Montesquieu (1689–1755), and Kant argued that central governments must be stronger than those social forces—like religious majorities or local strongmen—that might limit individual rights. In his famous *Federalist No. 10*, defending the American Constitution, James Madison (1751–1836) argued that the central government had to be strong enough to protect citizens from the tyrannical acts of the factions that often dominate localities. Governments based on liberal principles have proven to be enormously powerful, as illustrated by the capacity of the English government to rule over a vast empire in the nineteenth and early twentieth centuries. Indeed, liberals believe that a government whose authority is limited to specific functions can best enlist citizen cooperation and contributions of private wealth in the pursuit of large-scale national objectives. In short, classical liberals want a government whose authority is limited to specific functions so that it has the necessary power to perform these functions effectively.

To prevent governments from acting in a tyrannical fashion, classical liberals stress that governmental authority should not be used in the following ways:

1. To constrain freedom of thought and expression
2. To restrain self-regarding actions, even if these acts are harmful to the individual who does them or are considered immoral by most members of society
3. To regulate economic activity beyond enforcing contracts
4. To redistribute income and wealth (except minimally, as necessary to provide fundamental public safety, public works and public education)

Central to classical liberalism is the principle that no government should "prescribe opinions" to its citizens or "determine what doctrines or what arguments they should be allowed to hear."[16] No government should enforce or restrict religious beliefs or suppress political opinions, no matter how offensive these beliefs might be to most citizens or how critical these opinions might be of governmental officials. While early liberals regarded liberty of thought and of discussion as natural rights, derived from the idea that only the individual could know his own good, Immanuel Kant and John Stuart Mill provided utilitarian defenses for governmental noninterference in the *freedoms of conscience, speech, and the press.* According to Kant, governments should not stifle freedom of the press, because by so doing they would lose access to vital information

[15]Stephen Holmes, "The Liberal Idea," *The American Prospect* 7 (fall 1991), pp. 84–85.
[16]Mill, *On Liberty*, p. 15.

needed for effective governance. According to Mill, governments (and societies in general) must abide all ideas, even the most noxious ones, because tolerance fosters human progress and the discovery of truth. Opinions that governments might be tempted to suppress could be true or partially true, and even if such opinions were false, their suppression would deprive people of "the clearer perception and livelier impression of truth produced by its collision with error."[17] Furthermore, according to Mill, "mental development is cramped and reason cowed by the fear of heresy."[18] Only a general policy of governmental nonintervention in the exercise of the freedoms of thought and expression allows the kinds of intellectual experimentation that produces human progress.

Classical liberals like Mill argue that individuals should be allowed to act on their beliefs, as long as these acts do not harm others. While governments should restrain individuals from harming others, governments should not interfere with the self-regarding acts of individuals. Liberals partition human life into two spheres. The private sphere concerns that part of life wherein "a person's conduct affects the interests of no persons besides himself." In this sphere, "there would be perfect freedom, legal and social, to do the action and stand the consequences."[19] The public sphere concerns the part of life in which a person's conduct may injure others or wherein certain actions by individuals are required to defend society and its institutions. For the most part, the **public and private spheres of life** are distinct and separate. Liberal governments can legitimately intervene and limit individuality only when individual actions clearly fall into the public sphere. Because of dominant religious and moral sentiments, governments are often urged to regulate such "private amusements" as dancing and public games, to prohibit the consumption of "fermented drinks," to close businesses and public facilities on the Sabbath, or to regulate marriage practices (such as prohibiting the Mormon practice of polygamy). According to Mill, "the intrusively pious members of society (and their government should be told) to mind their own business."[20]

Governments had, of course, long regulated economic activities which were regarded as immoral (such as usury) or contrary to the public interest (such as purchasing foreign goods). But classical liberals oppose all restrictions on free trade (such as setting limitations on profits, placing tariffs on foreign goods, and establishing production standards for manufacturers), arguing that

[17]Mill, *On Liberty,* p. 16.

[18]Mill, *On Liberty,* p. 32.

[19]Mill, *On Liberty,* pp. 73–74.

[20]Mill, *On Liberty,* p. 85. Despite the belief of classical liberals that governmental authority ought not be used to legislate morality, it does not follow that such liberals were uninterested in morality or in promoting the virtue of citizens. They believed that citizens should exhibit such virtues as self-denial, civility, industry, and truthfulness in order for liberal institutions to function well. However, they believed that enlightened individuals, in their roles as private citizens, and such nongovernmental institutions as churches—not government—should promote such virtues. See William Galston, "Liberalism and Public Morality," pp. 129–150 in *Liberals on Liberalism,* edited by Alfonso J. Damico (Totowa, NJ: Rowman and Littlefield, 1986).

the best way for a society to become economically productive and wealthy is to permit people to pursue their private interests. Among those who contributed to the liberal rejection of governmental restraints on trade were Bernard Mandeville (1670–1733), the French "Physiocrats"—including Francois Quesnay (1694–1774) and Jacques Turgot (1727–1781), and Adam Smith. Mandeville contributed *The Fable of the Bees,* a tale of the disastrous consequences of efforts by reformers to make a hive of bees work for the good of others rather than for their own gain. The story suggested that the bees were better off before the reforms, when they were motivated by greed. The Physiocrats, members of the first systematic school of political economy, produced an economic theory showing the productivity of free enterprise (or an economy unregulated by government), and they contributed the slogan "**Laissez faire, laissez passer**" (let it be, leave it alone). Adam Smith, a very influential Scottish moral philosopher and economist, argued that when people are allowed to pursue their own economic gain, unconstrained by governmental regulations, an "invisible hand" creates social harmony and improves the condition of everyone. In *The Wealth of Nations* (1776), the bible of economic theory for classical liberals, Smith protested numerous state interventions in commerce, agriculture, and manufacturing.

Finally, classical liberals oppose all governmental interference with the property rights of individuals. They reject the idea that government should redistribute wealth by seizing the property of the wealthy or imposing extensive taxes on them in order to provide for the needs of the poor. When listing the limitations on state power, Locke stated that "The Supreme Power cannot take from any man any part of his property without his own consent."[21] The Physiocrats and Adam Smith argued that if men are permitted to accumulate great wealth, they will reinvest that wealth in enterprises so that society as a whole becomes wealthier. In order to gain a good reputation among other men, the wealthy will also contribute to charity. Thus, by permitting the unequal accumulation of wealth, classical liberals believe that the condition of the poor will ultimately be improved (through a process which contemporary economists call "trickle-down economics"). Social Darwinists took an even more strident position against governmental redistribution. For example, Herbert Spencer argued that social progress depends on competition among individuals and that efforts to alleviate suffering among the poor interfered with the natural process of eliminating the weak and unfit from the species. Thus, Spencer rejected the idea that governments should enact "poor laws" to reduce economic hardship. Governments should not "administer charity . . . adjust the prices of food . . . vaccinate children . . . or see that small dwellings are supplied with water."[22] In short, classical liberals argue that governments should do nothing to interfere with the unequal distribution of economic

[21]Locke, *Second Treatise,* p. 406.

[22]Herbert Spencer, *The Man Versus The State* (Caldwell, Idaho: Caxton Press, 1940 [1892]), pp. 79–120. See also Spencer's "The Survival of the Fittest," in his *Social Statics* (New York: D. Appleton, 1851).

resources that result from a competitive market. Government should only ensure that everyone competes fairly and freely. The principle that governments should not redistribute wealth is consistent with the more basic idea of classical liberals that any increase in the role of the government results in a decrease in individual liberty.

Justice

The U.S. Declaration of Independence, a preeminent liberal document, declares, "That all men are created equal; that they are endowed by their Creator with certain unalienable rights; that among these are life, liberty, and the pursuit of happiness." Some have assumed that classical liberals therefore hold egalitarian principles of justice, but such an assumption is greatly mistaken. Such liberals are only narrowly egalitarian. Formally, they hold that everyone has equal rights to life, liberty, and property, but these equal, formal rights do not imply that individuals should enjoy equal amounts of economic resources or other social goods (like education, social prestige, or political power).

John Locke's **labor theory of value** illustrates how equal, formal rights lead to unequal but just distributions of economic resources, according to liberal ideology. According to Locke, the earth and its material resources have been given to humans to own in common. At the same time, each individual enjoys equal ownership of his own body and mind. Everyone thus has an equal liberty to use his body and mind—i.e., to labor—as he wishes. By mixing his labor with nature, the individual creates value that did not previously exist. For example, a forest has little value until someone chops down the trees, produces lumber, and then builds a home with the lumber.[23] By creating value through his labor, the individual attains a property right to those aspects of nature on which he has labored. Thus, each person has an equal property right, because each has an equal opportunity to give nature value through his labor, but people deserve different amounts of private property because of the differences in the quantity and quality of labor that they expend. Locke added two provisos to the amount of property that people can extract from nature and thus possess through their labor: (1) they must leave enough for others, and (2) they must not allow the goods they appropriate from nature to spoil. But Locke assumed that if people are assured the fruits of their labor, they will labor more diligently, multiplying the goods that are available for others. He realized that the invention of money enabled people to exchange their perishable goods for more durable forms of wealth. In short, Locke's labor theory of value justified unequal distributions of wealth among individuals who have equal formal rights.

As economic theory developed from its Lockean foundations during the eighteenth and nineteenth centuries, classical liberals embraced the more general principle of **market justice**: people should be rewarded according to their

[23]Locke maintained that about ninety-nine percent of the value of material goods comes from the labor that goes into them. See *Second Treatise*, p. 338.

Sidebar 2-4

Property, Talents, and Freedom

For Locke and many classical liberals, property meant more than money and tangible goods. One's property also included one's talents, faculties, and ideas. The protection of one's property from others included the ability to express these intangible properties.

Classical liberals sought protection of their intangible property by demanding various freedoms of expression, such as the rights to free speech and a free press. They sought constitutional restrictions against governmental tendencies or attempts to silence citizens, and they asked governments to prohibit other organizations (e.g., churches) from exercising authority over speech and other forms of communication.

In the nineteenth century, classical liberals battled over the issue of protecting ideas. Some claimed that governments should issue patents to protect the value of the ideas of creative individuals. Others argued that patents created unfair monopolies. By the end of the nineteenth century, western industrial countries had put into place a fairly comprehensive patent system that created a market for the ideas of individuals.

For classical liberals, the demand for life, liberty, and property included a call for the freedom to express the talents and ideas of individuals. The pursuit of happiness by individuals was dependent upon this expansive understanding of property.

contributions in the marketplace. Classical liberals believe that economic goods (money and commodities) are the primary social resources to be distributed, economic goods should be distributed through the workings of a free market (rather than by some other agency such as government), and the market will allocate rewards according to its own intrinsic laws. Several laws of the marketplace determine the distribution of economic rewards. First, the free choices of individuals influence the value and thus the price of commodities and labor. People will be able to command higher wages for those forms of labor that are most in demand by others. Second, the scarcity of goods or services influences prices. People will be able to command higher wages for those forms of labor that are in limited supply. Third, if workers are self-interested, instrumentally rational, and have economic mobility (i.e., there are no artificial barriers to entrance into the marketplace), they will move into those areas where there is high demand and scarce supply. The **laws of supply and demand** establish an equilibrium of fair prices and wages. For example, if lawyers are making huge salaries relative to those of teachers, students will flock to law schools, thereby increasing the supply of lawyers, increasing competition among them, and reducing their salaries. Fourth, if investors are self-interested, are instrumentally rational, and have market mobility, they will remove their capital from those areas of production where they suffer economic losses and move their capital to those areas where they perceive opportunities for profits to be—where demand is predicted to be high but production is currently scarce. For example, if demand for automobiles declines, reducing the profits of those who have invested in the auto industry, these investors will search out better investment opportunities (say, for example, in solar energy). If they correctly predict that existing production of solar energy is inadequate to satisfy consumer demand, these investors may reap extensive profits by moving into the area. By increasing the supply of a highly demanded good, the investors have been economically productive, and their contribution to the marketplace justifies their profits. In short, the laws of the marketplace reward those who take their labor and invest their capital in those areas of the marketplace where they increase the supply of goods that are scarce but highly demanded by others. Market justice occurs when people are rewarded commensurate with the extent to which they contribute to the supply of demanded goods.[24]

Robert Nozick's **entitlement theory** has recently clarified and extended liberal principles of market justice.[25] According to Nozick, we need not ask whether the distribution of wealth is justified on the basis of some measure of people's contribution to the marketplace. If there was nothing unjust in the historical processes that have given rise to an existing distribution of wealth, the distribution is just. Consider inheritances, for example. A straightforward application of the principle of market justice would suggest that it would be unjust for some people to acquire a significant inheritance, as they could become very rich without having made any contribution to the market. But classical liberals have always assumed that people have the right to bequeath their property to others. Nozick's entitlement theory claims that inheritances are perfectly justified. He reasons that inherited wealth arises from a just historical process that in no way infringes on the rights of others.

The entitlement theory also acknowledges that unequal wealth can be justly derived from any process of free exchange among individuals. To demonstrate this, Nozick presented his famous Wilt Chamberlain example. In this example, we are asked to imagine a situation in which everyone in society starts with an equal income, but everyone (except Wilt) voluntarily deposits a quarter at the turnstile at the entrance to the gym in exchange for the pleasure of watching Wilt stuff balls into a basket. Through these voluntary exchanges, Wilt becomes enormously wealthy and everyone else becomes a little poorer. Nozick argues that to avoid such inequalities, government would have to "forbid capitalist acts between consenting adults."[26] In short, if

[24]For a further discussion of market justice, see Robert Kuenne, *Economic Justice in American Society* (Princeton: Princeton University Press, 1993), pp. 30–32. While classical liberals believe that the free market provides the best process of distributing income and wealth, they usually refrain from claiming that the resulting distributions are "just." For example, Friedrich von Hayek argues that the concept of justice should refer only to those laws of right conduct governing the processes by which people compete and cooperate when producing and distributing goods. According to Hayek, creating concepts of "economic justice" or "social justice" to evaluate the distributions that result from free markets reflects "naive thinking" because markets serve other beneficial purposes—such as directing human activity in ways that are socially desirable—other than to provide people with their "just deserts." See F. A. Hayek, *Law, Legislation, and Liberty*,Vol. 2: *The Mirage of Social Justice* (London: Routledge, 1982).

[25]Nozick, *Anarchy, State, and Utopia*, pp. 149–182.

[26]Nozick, *Anarchy, State, and Utopia*, p. 163.

people are given the freedom to exchange goods and services as they wish, the results will be unequal but just distributions of economic goods. Both classical liberals and contemporary libertarians, like Nozick, argue that inequalities, even huge inequalities, are just because they are the inevitable results of giving individuals the freedom to labor, invest, and exchange as they wish.

Structure

Classical liberals want governments that are strong enough to provide security for their citizens, but they do not want governments to infringe on rights to life, liberties, and property. Classical liberals want governments that can adjudicate economic disputes and provide the basic infrastructures (such as roads and harbors) necessary to an industrial society, but they do not want governments that regulate the economy and redistribute wealth. Liberals thus have had to address the problem of how to structure governments so that they perform their necessary functions without abusing their powers. Their solution to the problem involves establishing constitutional restraints on government, dividing and balancing governmental power, and providing political accountability.[27]

According to classical liberals, governments are formed by social contracts between the government and its citizens. A central part of such contracts is a **constitution** containing specific, written rules regarding the operations of government. Just as bylaws organize and regulate the activities of many organizations such as businesses, churches, and academic departments, constitutions organize and restrain the activities of governments. They do so in four ways: First, constitutions specify in general terms what governments can and cannot do. The U.S. Constitution, for example, specifies that the national government can collect taxes, coin money, and declare war, but that it cannot establish a state religion, infringe on the right of people to keep and bear arms, or infringe on other liberties as specified in the Bill of Rights. Second, constitutions establish structures (such as the Presidency, Congress, and the federal judiciary) for enacting and implementing the authorized policies. Third, constitutions specify how governmental positions are to be filled and how occupants can be removed from these offices. Fourth, constitutions specify extraordinary procedures for amending the constitution—such as Article 5 of the U.S. Constitution requiring that three-fourths of the states must ratify each proposed amendment in order for it to become effective. While classical liberals view these constitutional provisions as important devices for blocking certain governmental abuses of powers, they face the problem of ensuring that governments adhere to constitutional limitations. In America, the practice of judicial

[27]In this section, we emphasize American governmental structures, which were influenced by republican ideals as well as liberal ideals. Most British liberals believed that existing parliamentary institutions need not be abandoned to achieve liberal ideas. However, constitutionalism and divided government seem to be more effective barriers to governmental abuses of power than are parliamentary arrangements.

review—which enables the courts to declare legislative and administrative acts unconstitutional—may strengthen constitutional restraints, but, in general, governments are prompted to abide by constitutional limitations out of fear of loss of legitimacy. If a government ignores constitutional constraints, liberals argue, its citizens may believe that the social contract has been violated and withdraw their consent to be governed by it.

Many liberal constitutions specify a specific organizational arrangement—**the separation of powers**—as a means of constraining governmental power. Although the idea of dividing governmental power among various institutions is ancient ("mixed regimes" were defended in Plato's *Laws* and Aristotle's *Politics*), the French political philosopher Baron de Montesquieu is credited with transforming this doctrine into a device for limiting government and preserving individual liberty. By insisting that legislative, executive, and judicial powers be distinguished and relegated to different institutions, by providing that positions within these different institutions be held by different people who may represent different interests or perspectives, and by giving each institution devices for resisting encroachments and usurpations of powers by officials in other institutions, the power of all governmental officials is limited and checked. An **independent judiciary** is strongly endorsed to ensure that legislators and executives cannot suppress their political opponents through political trials. **Bicameral legislatures**—requiring that laws be passed by two legislative bodies representing different interests—are recommended for limiting the capacity of popularly elected legislatures to enact laws that infringe on personal liberties, unduly regulate the economy, or redistribute wealth. And **federalism**—which distributes power among national, provincial, and local governments—is encouraged as another institutional arrangement for dividing governmental authority.

Providing procedures of **accountability** is another liberal means of preventing abuses of governmental power. A prominent example of such accountability is the liberal practice of civilian control of the military. By having the President serve as Commander in Chief of the armed forces and by investing Congress with the power to declare war, the liberal founders of America hoped to restrain military power and ensure that it would only be employed to secure or protect citizens' rights.

A more general method of providing accountability is having governmental officials stand for reelection. According to Madison, "a dependence on the people" is "the primary control on government, more important than even the separation of powers." Classical liberals do not envision elections as a means of discovering "the will of the people" that is, of dictating what governments should do in a positive sense. Liberals do not intend elections to be a means for forcing government to be responsive to the views of most citizens, who might have "a rage for paper money, for the abolition of debts, for an equal division of property, or for any other improper and or wicked project."[28]

[28]James Madison, "Number Ten," in *The Federalist Papers,* compiled and edited by Isaac Kramnick (New York: Penguin, 1987 [1788]), p. 128.

Instead, elections are intended to give citizens an opportunity to petition officials about their grievances and punish officials for misconduct. The founders of liberalism thus created a variety of institutional arrangements for allowing citizens to replace officials who abuse their power while preventing citizens from using elections to install representatives who simply transform public sentiment into public policy. Indirect methods of election (such as the American electoral college) and staggered terms of office (such as for U.S. senators) are typical methods for reducing the likelihood that elections will result in policies responsive to majority sentiment. By providing some officials (such as federal judges) with lifetime tenure and giving them the capacity to overturn legislative policies, elections are further limited to the function of providing accountability to the public.

Rulers

According to classical liberals, democratic elections not only provide accountability, they also authorize the winners to rule for their terms of office. Winning a democratic election gives representatives more authority to govern (or legitimate power) than other members of society possess. By endorsing **representative democracy**, liberals do not want to concentrate all political power in the hands of legislators and directly elected executives (such as the President). They want citizens and nonelected experts to share in the distribution of power. But liberals have always assumed the preeminent position of representatives.

For liberals, the power of representatives resides in their capacity to enact legislation. In this capacity, representatives should not be mere "instructed delegates" who decide issues on the basis of dominant public opinion. Nor should representatives be "trustees" who decide issues on the basis of their independent judgments about the good of society. Instead, liberals expect representatives to decide policy issues on the basis of expert recommendations, public discussion, debate, and bargaining among various affected interests. In order for effective and fair policies to emerge, liberals believe that all legitimate interests should be represented in the policy-making process. Thus, liberals have focused considerable attention on the question of representation.

Liberals have not always demanded adequate representation, at least, not according to today's standards. Believing that the role of government was to protect property, nascent liberals thought that only property holders had a legitimate interest in government. Thus, John Locke argued that only property owners needed to be represented in government, and most early liberals supported property qualifications for those wishing to hold elected office. But as liberalism matured in the nineteenth century, liberals became increasingly concerned with the representativeness of governmental officials. In *Considerations on Representative Government*, for example, John Stuart Mill expressed the idea that to secure the rights and interests of every person, it is important that every person be represented in government. Fearful that majority rule could leave minorities with no representatives at all, he argued for **proportional repre-**

sentation. Rather than having the majority select representatives from geographical districts, he called for a scheme that assured that each interest be represented according to its proportion of the total vote.

Mill's endorsement of proportional representation did not become a central tenet of classical liberalism, but it does illustrate the liberal concern with increasing representativeness of elected officials. Most liberals were content to increase representativeness by extending the franchise. Bentham, for example, understood that representative governments are supposed to maximize the utilities of all citizens and that citizens are the best judges of their own happiness. Consequently, he (toward the end of his life) endorsed the universal franchise as the most appropriate means of ensuring the expression and representation of all interests. James Mill (1773–1836), a close associate of Bentham and the father of John Stuart Mill, argued that "one person, one vote" was the best means to protect all citizens from abuses of government and to ensure that all interests were represented, but fearing that some people are too ill-informed and irrational to use their vote wisely, he retreated to a position of advocating "adult male suffrage," which permitted the continued disenfranchisement—and underrepresentation—of women, men under 40 years of age, and the poorest one-third of society. His son, John Stuart Mill, endorsed a far more extended franchise—including female suffrage—but he excluded the illiterate and the poor who were recipients of governmental relief. Furthermore, he favored a scheme of weighted voting which would give multiple ballots to the most educated. Thus, while classical liberals want a greater representation of interests among elected officials, their fear that the poor and the working class will be represented in greater numbers than the more well-to-do (but smaller) classes has tempered their commitment to exact or proportional representation. They fear that if legislators mirror the demography and interests of the nation, they will produce "class legislation"—laws which trample the property rights of the wealthy, redistribute economic goods to the poor, and ruin capitalism.

By endorsing representative democracy, classical liberals have thus sought a much broader distribution of power than that which existed in the ancient regimes of Europe, but they have always stopped short of calling for a populist democracy that would give direct and equal power to all citizens. They endorse **popular sovereignty** in the sense that they believe that political power is derived from the consent of the governed and can revert back to the citizenry if it is abused. But they do not want citizens to participate directly in policy making, and (as discussed under the "Structure" heading) they seek to structure elections in ways that prevent popular majorities from imposing their will on the policy-making process. The idea of the "**tyranny of the majority**"—best expressed by Alexis de Tocqueville (1805–1859) in *Democracy in America*—is central to the liberal tradition. Liberals fear that minority rights to hold property, to exercise freedom of conscience, and to act freely in the private realm can easily be violated by unlimited majority rule by citizens. James Madison argued that minority rights must be guaranteed in order to secure minority compliance with electoral results. If elections permit majorities to enact legislation curtailing minority rights, outvoted minorities may resort to violence whenever they lose an election. Thus, to provide universal security and peace, classical liberals argue that majority rule must yield to minority rights.

Illustrative of liberalism's aversion to populism is John Stuart Mill's call for "skilled democracy": a three-tiered scheme regarding the distribution of political power. At the top would be a governing elite, nonelected experts who should craft legislation based on utilitarian analysis. In the intermediate position would be elected representatives, who should oversee the elite, accepting or rejecting their proposals. At the bottom would be ordinary citizens, who should in turn oversee the decisions of their representatives, using the electoral process to remove any representatives who should approve proposals that violate the rights of the citizenry. In short, liberals like the younger Mill are content to remove citizens two steps from direct governing power.

Citizenship

For the most part, classical liberals think that limiting direct participation in government is a benefit—not a deprivation—for citizens. Their original goal was to create a government that would protect the rights of citizens and, to a limited extent, respond to their wishes without requiring extensive involvement of citizens in government. Hoping to enlarge the private sphere of life so that citizens can devote their energies to economic production and consumption and other means of satisfying personal interests, most liberals want to limit the extent of citizen participation and obligation in the public realm. They want government of and for the people, but not government by the people.

Liberal government is "of the people" in the sense that its authority is derived, by means of the social contract, from the consent of each citizen. Government is "for the people" in the sense that government exists to protect the rights of each citizen to his life, liberty, and property, as specified by the social contract. But government is "by the people" in only a limited sense, in that citizen participation is to be confined to selecting representatives. Such participation is regarded by liberals as sufficient to ensure that representatives act as guardians of citizen rights and interests. James Mill understood that representatives, like all people, naturally pursue their own selfish interests. Having representatives stand for reelection ensures that the primary interest of representatives in retaining their power prompts them to make policy decisions that coincide with the rights and interests of the citizens to whom they are responsible. All that citizens must do is monitor the policies of representatives and cast their ballots on the basis of whether or not these representatives further or reduce their rights. The institution of frequent elections, the presence of a free press informing citizens about the actions of their representatives, and the provision of a secret ballot allowing citizens to express their true opinions are sufficient to induce representatives to protect citizen rights and to respond to citizen interests.

Classical liberals thus favor limited citizenship in two senses. First, they have been willing to limit the scope of citizenship. As we have seen, Locke thought ownership of property by residents was a necessary prerequisite to the right to vote; James Mill was willing to exclude women, the poor, and the young from the ranks of the enfranchised; and John Stuart Mill was willing to exclude welfare recipients and the illiterate from the ranks of the enfranchised. Second, classical liberals are satisfied with limiting governmental participation among citizens to voting in periodic elections for representatives.

Despite these limitations on citizen participation, classical liberals insist that everyone within a liberal society must obey the laws of their governments. Even those citizens who are deprived of voting rights must obey because they receive the benefits of governments and because they have, at least tacitly, consented to obey their governments. When discussing the role of liberal governments, we have seen that such governments exist to be the "nightwatchmen" for everyone—to protect everyone's rights whether or not they have property, whether or not they pay taxes, whether they are man or woman, young or old. And as Locke suggested, everyone who enjoys the security of government—all residents of the territory ruled by a government—"doth thereby give his tacit consent, and is as far obligated to obedience to the laws of government."[29] For liberals, the social contract is an implied agreement between all residents and their government—an agreement which obligates all residents. The obligation to obey is not very burdensome, however, because the laws of liberal governments are limited to those necessary to protect everyone's rights. If the laws of governments are limited and just, citizens will not have to compromise their consciences or refrain from self-regarding acts in order to obey government.

What if a liberal government exceeds its legitimate powers and creates unjust laws? For classical liberals, there are three main options for citizens who believe that their government has acted unjustly. First, they can vote against the representatives who created the unjust laws, hoping that most citizens share their views and that new representatives will eliminate the offending laws. Second, citizens can leave the jurisdiction of that government—a viable option for those who believe that governments are infringing on their rights, but whose views are persistently in the minority. Third, if the majority of citizens believe that they have endured a "long train of abuses,"[30] they can, by majority vote of all members of society, dissolve their government and create another that will better protect their rights.

Change

The idea that citizens can dissolve their governments suggests that liberalism is a revolutionary ideology, but this is somewhat misleading. Under some conditions, liberals may seek to overthrow existing political regimes, but under other conditions they call for reform, maintenance of the status quo, and even

[29]Locke, *Second Treatise,* p. 392.
[30]Locke, *Second Treatise,* p. 463.

reactionary change. A more general statement about the attitude of liberals toward change is that they want economic, intellectual, and moral progress. Governments that fail to provide the conditions for such progress should be dissolved or reformed. Governments that do provide the conditions for such progress should, of course, be maintained.

Liberals believe that economic progress occurs through capitalism. If individuals are given property rights and economic freedoms, they will make choices to maximize their economic well-being, the economy as a whole will become more productive, and nations will become wealthier and wealthier. Government can best facilitate economic progress by ensuring economic freedoms, protecting property rights, enforcing contractual obligations, and refraining from interfering in the marketplace.

Liberals believe that intellectual progress occurs when people are freed from religious dogma and political absolutism and pursue knowledge through scientific reasoning. According to the Marquis de Condorcet (1743–1794), increases in scientific understanding (which have occurred throughout history, but were especially evident during the Enlightenment) result in technological advances, improved industrial and agricultural productivity, medical innovations, and an overall increase in citizens' physical well-being. Additionally, new principles of social organization and cultural possibilities (such as more effective methods of educating children or producing products) are constantly being discovered, becoming part of the cumulative inheritance of humans, and thus ensuring that each generation is more advanced intellectually than its predecessors. Liberals like Condorcet thus focus on achieving an "open society"

Sidebar 2-5

Reform and Progress

The word "reform" (*re*-form) was not always associated with progress. In the classical tradition and in the Middle Ages, "to reform" was to return to the original condition. Reform is necessary because things of this world decay and degenerate over time. Thus, reform was a conserving and cleansing act. This understanding of reform survived well into the sixteenth century. For example, rather than viewing the Reformation as an attempt to create a new or improved version of the church, Martin Luther regarded his break with the Catholic Church as a return to the values of St. Augustine.

Early in the seventeenth century, English Puritans began to use the term "reform" in its more modern political sense. They rejected the traditional and organic political metaphor for the state, the "body politic," and replaced it with the metaphor of the "ship of state." This ship could be modified and improved, since it was the creation of men, not a body designed by God. Reform became linked to the ideas of improvement and progress.

Classical liberals would accept the metaphor of the "**ship of state**," and they would connect reform with progress. Government and society became arenas for experimentation in the quest for constant improvement.

where there is intellectual freedom to discover knowledge that is useful for improving human life and where these new truths are freely transmitted to all citizens. The role of government in fostering human improvement is minimal but crucial. Government provides a stable and secure context in which intellectuals can make scientific discoveries and educate the public about these discoveries.

Liberals also believe that moral progress is possible and is furthered by citizen involvement in the democratic process. According to John Stuart Mill, democratic institutions draw citizens into the public realm, give them an interest in public issues, stimulate them to become knowledgeable about social matters, and encourage them to make better and more fair political judgments. Mill believed that by giving people the right to vote for representatives and permitting them to participate in local political arenas, people would progress from being irrational, uninformed, and self-regarding individuals to becoming rational, informed, public-spirited citizens.

In short, classical liberals seek social progress. They believe that economic progress is furthered by ensuring property rights and economic freedom. They believe that intellectual progress is furthered by ensuring intellectual freedom to attain scientific knowledge. And they believe that moral progress is furthered by providing basic political freedoms and opportunities for political participation. Liberal attitudes about maintaining, reforming, or dissolving existing governments are dependent on the performance of these governments in securing the conditions of social progress.

Political revolution is justified if governments inhibit social progress by limiting intellectual, religious, economic, or political freedoms. John Locke wrote that governments could be dissolved if they violated property rights or other freedoms. Thus he supported the Glorious Revolution in England because it eliminated the threat that a Catholic monarchic dynasty posed to religious freedom. Thomas Paine defended both the American and French Revolutions because the existing regimes had failed to provide adequate political freedoms and democratic representation. While classical liberals defended the most significant political revolutions of the seventeenth and eighteenth centuries, their commitment to revolution in general is limited. Locke, for example, regarded his defense of the right of citizens to dissolve government as a means of deterring revolution rather than as an invitation to rebellion: "This power in the people of providing for their safety anew by a new legislature when their legislators have acted contrary to their trust by invading their property, is the best fence against rebellion, and the probablest means to hinder it."[31] In other words, by acknowledging that citizens have the right to rebel when governments abuse their power, and by recognizing that citizens will rebel against abusive government, Locke hoped to convince legislators that their best hope of forestalling political revolution was to secure rather than abuse the rights of their citizens. Moreover, even radical liberal theorists, like Paine, are silent on how aggrieved citizens might go about fomenting a revo-

[31]Locke, *Second Treatise*, p. 464.

lution. The image of revolutionary action that emerges from Locke and Paine is that all members of society should assemble and decide to remove or retain their government by majority vote. There is no manning of the barricades here.

If the economy is basically organized around capitalist principles, if a constitutional democracy exists, but if laws and practices remain that depart from liberal ideals, liberals advocate **political reform**. During the beginning and middle of the nineteenth century, Jeremy Bentham and James Mill were the intellectual leaders of the "philosophical radicals" who hoped to reform the British legal and electoral systems. Bentham focused on codifying and rationalizing British law. He sought to replace those laws that secured the privileges of the traditional aristocracy and were inconsistent with utilitarian principles with laws which were consistent with these principles. The Benthamites—including economist David Ricardo and legal theorist John Austin—pushed reform in such areas as criminal justice, education, public health, and foreign trade. James Mill focused on reforming the electoral system by increasing the extent of the franchise and the frequency of elections.

John Stuart Mill argued that legislative reforms could increase and equalize the liberties of citizens generally. By suggesting that the role of government extends beyond that of safeguarding people's rights to that of creating conditions that make life more humane and by suggesting that government can redistribute the wealth generated by the market economy, Mill advocated reforms that had been anathema to earlier classical liberals, and thereby opened the door to the reform of liberalism itself. As the nineteenth century gave way to the twentieth century, liberals advocated numerous economic and political reforms that betrayed their earlier principles of minimal government and market justice, and contemporary liberalism emerged as a distinct political ideology—"welfare-state liberalism."

As "welfare-state liberals" proposed numerous economic regulations (such as those regarding child labor and the monopolistic practices of industry) and as socialists came to prominence advocating various welfare policies and legislation empowering labor unions, classical liberals came to be regarded as "conservatives" for opposing these economic reforms. Because their principles of minimal government and market justice were used to justify the continuance of an unregulated capitalist economy, classical liberalism became a *status quo ideology* during the first part of the twentieth century throughout much of Europe and in the United States.

Today, of course, most industrial societies have governments that extensively regulate the economy and redistribute wealth through welfare policies. They have created "welfare rights" that infringe on the "property rights" so important to classical liberals. Perhaps one of the most prominent social movements today is composed of classical liberals who call themselves "conservatives" and libertarians who call for economic deregulation and the dismantling of the welfare state. By seeking to eliminate welfare rights and to return to a political economy that conforms to the principles of classical liberalism, this movement can appropriately be regarded as a proponent of **reactionary** change. But, of course, such classical liberals would respond that only a return to these earlier principles can promote an environment of economic, intellectual, and political freedom that will revitalize the economy, unleash the intellectual energies of individuals, ensure political rights, and thus promote human progress.

SUMMARY AND CONCLUSIONS

Classical liberalism was the first systematic ideology, and it remains a powerful voice not only in the United States and Western Europe but in Eastern Europe and the former Soviet republics. Classical liberals argue that their enduring influence is due to their having created a science of politics providing universally valid principles of political economy based on appropriate philosophical assumptions. By assuming a natural world in which humans are utility maximizers and in which society is simply an aggregation of self-interested individuals, they have deduced "objective" standards for evaluating the goodness of political institutions: To what extent do these institutions protect the natural rights of citizens? To what extent do these institutions provide for the greatest good of the greatest number?

A minimal government is needed to protect natural rights, and capitalism is needed to maximize economic utility. Constitutional government and representative democracy limit governmental power and protect the rights and interests of citizens. In order to turn their energies to private and, often, economic concerns, citizens need only participate in the periodic selection of their representatives and obey minimal governmental laws. Human progress is secured by allowing individuals to pursue their own happiness as they see fit, as is possible within a free society, a capitalist economy, and a constitutional democracy.

The principles of classical liberalism have brought many social, economic, and political benefits to those countries in North America and Europe where they have been applied. Societies which provide the opportunity for social mobility have replaced societies based on fixed social status. Religious intolerance and religious wars have, for the most part, subsided. Absolutist governments have given way to constitutional democracies. Political liberties—such as freedom of the press and freedom of speech—are widely permitted. Capitalism has produced enormous material wealth. And individuals enjoy an extensive private sphere in which to think, act, and live according to their own wishes.

But classical liberalism has not been without its detractors, as we shall see when we explore alternative ideologies in subsequent chapters. Perhaps the philosophical assumptions of liberalism are inadequate. Is the material world our only world, and what are the political implications of beliefs in divinity? Are humans only utility maximizers, or is there something more noble in the human spirit? Are societies only an aggregation of individuals, or do they exist prior to individuals, imposing social roles and obligations on everyone? Do people really have natural rights? Is utilitarianism an adequate guide for evaluating the merit of political practices and policies?

When liberal assumptions about these questions are rejected, numerous criticisms of liberal principles emerge. Perhaps governments should do more than secure individual rights—perhaps they should regulate morality and the economy. Perhaps market justice is unfair to those who fail in the marketplace. Perhaps limited and divided government diminishes the capacity of political authority to achieve the public good. Perhaps representative democracy is unable to provide strong national leadership or ample opportunities for citizen participation in government. And perhaps liberal principles have excused citizens from taking an active role in public life and exercising more social responsibilities. While classical liberals can become ideologues who are blind to the limitations of their philosophical assumptions and political principles, liberalism is an inherently tolerant and open-minded political outlook. True liberals engage in continuous internal debate and have developed a variety of "liberalisms" to accommodate their evolving political differences.[32]

[32]See, for example, John Gray, *Liberalisms: Essays in Political Philosophy* (London: Routledge, 1989).

CHAPTER 3

Traditional Conservatism

Traditional conservatism is a political outlook formulated by those who sought to protect customary ways of life against the liberal (and sometimes radical) ideas that emerged in western Europe during and after the eighteenth century. Traditional conservatives think that the liberal celebration of individualism is misguided, because it undermines traditional social units such as the family, the church, the guild, and the local community. They argue that the growth of capitalist economies encourages individuals to take self-interested rather than public-regarding actions, and that it encourages innovation and competitiveness to a degree that undermines social order. For traditional conservatives, strong political and religious authority—located in the monarchs, the landed aristocracy, and religious leaders—is necessary for social stability and to guide society toward the public good. Most generally, they believe that traditions and conventions of societies serve as more prudent guidelines for individual, social, and political conduct than do the scientific theories of political liberals and the utopian ideas of radicals.

Between the Middle Ages and the late 1700s, most Europeans assumed that social solidarity was more important than individual rights, that governments must create social harmony, that societies should be governed by natural leaders, and that traditions must be respected. Nevertheless, these ideas began to be challenged by several developments at the dawn of modernity. The Renaissance (particularly in France and Italy during the fifteenth and sixteenth centuries) had emphasized intellectual and artistic creativity and humanism. It had questioned traditional ideas about political authority and had pried open some space for individualism. The Protestant Reformation, a religious upheaval that broke the monopoly of the Catholic Church during the sixteenth century, had initiated resistance to religious authority and had voiced new understandings about individualism, equality, and participation in government. The scientific revolution that occurred in Britain and western Europe from about 1550 to 1650, gave rise to more natural understandings of both the social and the physical worlds, and it suggested that humans could know, control, and change the world on the basis on their empirical investigations and rational deductions regarding it. The Enlightenment, a philosophical movement that was centered in France during the eighteenth century, had attacked traditional and religious beliefs as enemies of rationality and had placed the individual at center stage, as both a source of knowledge and as a unit of inquiry. The industrial revolution had begun and gave rise to demands for economic freedom, especially the freedom to trade in a manner unrestricted by religious, governmental, and customary regulations. Each of these attacks on tradition had evoked criticisms from "conservatives" who feared instability and disorder from these developments. Nevertheless, these conservative criticisms and impulses required a defining moment to emerge as a full-blown ideology.

The **French Revolution** provided such a defining moment. In 1789, the absolutist state of King Louis XVI was overthrown, and a National Assembly established the principles for a new order with its *Declaration of the Rights of Man and of the Citizen.* By 1791, a new constitution established a constitutional monarchy and extended citizen rights to tax-paying property holders. In the period from 1792 to 1793, radical politicians abolished the monarchy and executed the king and queen. The French Republic was born. In theory, this regime was to act on the basis of the national will, as known by majority vote, and was to cast aside all traditions in favor of rational principles of government. But resistance to this regime led to the suspension of constitutional government and the creation of a provisional regime. This provisional regime initiated the "Reign of Terror" to suppress enemies of the revolution and to achieve a "Republic of Virtue," wherein popular education would mold ethical citizens. The most radical events and phases of the French Revolution had run their course by 1795, when one of the revolution's principal leaders, Robespierre, was executed. However, these events in France and the threat that such

Sidebar 3-1

Some Traditional Conservatives and Their Main Writings

Edmund Burke (1729–1797)
Reflections on the Revolution in France (1790)
An Appeal from the New to the Old Whigs (1791)

Joseph de Maistre (1753–1821)
Considerations on France (1797)

Henry Adams (1838–1918)
History of the United States of America (1889)
Democracy: An American Novel (1880)

Emile Durkheim (1858–1917)
Suicide (1897)

José Ortega y Gasset (1883–1955)
The Revolt of the Masses (1930)

Michael Oakeshott (1901–1990)
Rationalism in Politics and Other Essays (1962)

Russell Kirk (1918–   )
A Program for Conservatives (1954)

revolutionary events would be repeated elsewhere in Europe were sufficient to give rise to traditional conservatism articulated as a set of counterrevolutionary principles. Indeed, by 1790, the basic ideas of traditional conservatism were set forth in *Reflections on the Revolution in France* by the central and guiding figure in conservative thought, the Irish intellectual Edmund Burke (1729–1797), who served as a member of the British Parliament for thirty years.

During the nineteenth and twentieth centuries, traditional conservatives accepted some new developments in politics and economics. They accepted certain aspects of democratization, such as increasing the number of elected officials and enlarging the franchise, but they never forgot the need for strong political authorities. They accepted certain aspects of capitalism, but they never celebrated capitalism (as did classical liberals), because they feared that the economic liberties of individuals posed moral dangers to the good society. Resisting the rapid social, economic, and political changes of the nineteenth and twentieth centuries, traditional conservatives sought to protect the world against this avalanche of change. When protection proved impossible, as was often the case, traditional conservatives fought to slow down the modernization of society.

The number of self-proclaimed traditional conservatives has declined in the twentieth century, but many of their ideas continue to be embraced by people who believe that human rationality and individualism have been unduly celebrated in the contemporary world and that traditional values and virtues have been unduly neglected. To some extent, the ideas of traditional conservatives are expressed by contemporary conservatives, but traditional conservatism and contemporary conservatism have sufficient differences to merit consideration as separate ideologies. Traditional conservatism continues to provide imporant political insights and interesting perspectives that are inadequately captured by the views of most people who call themselves "conservatives" today.

THE POLITICAL BASES

Problems

Most generally, traditional conservatives feared liberal and radical innovations. The human propensity to resist change and to clutch the old and habitual routines is not new and is certainly not uniquely modern. Criticisms of change accompanied by reverence for traditional practices had long been common in western Europe. The Renaissance, the Reformation, the scientific revolution, and the Enlightenment all had their opponents. The French Revolution, however, inspired more than a "typical" conservative reaction. Because the French Revolution combined the most radical assaults on the old order with a methodical ruthlessness, it drove conservative commentators to focus their criticisms and to elaborate their perspectives into a more coherent view that served as the foundation for traditional conservative ideology.

Edmund Burke summarized the traditional conservative reaction to the revolution in his *Reflections on the Revolution in France.* For Burke, the French Revolution revealed the dangerous consequences of basing politics on abstract rights, of guiding political reforms according to Enlightenment concepts of rationality, and of rejecting established authority. An examination of these three central problems in the context of the French Revolution exposes a number of related concerns shared by traditional conservatives.

The rallying cry of the French Revolution, *"Liberté, Egalité, Fraternité,"* drew upon liberal and Enlightenment thought in demanding **abstract rights** for all Frenchmen. *The Declaration of the Rights of Man* had included as civil rights such abstractions as "liberty, property, security, and resistance to oppression." While such abstract rights sound appealing, it is unclear what they signify in practice. Does everyone have unlimited liberty to do what they wish? If someone has the right to own property, doesn't that imply that others do not have a right to that property? Can one feel secure if others have unlimited liberties, or license, which infringe on one's rights and property? The abstract right to equality was even more troubling. Even if all citizens should have equal freedom from arbitrary arrest or equal freedom of speech, does this mean that everyone should be complete political, social, and economic equals? Should political power be equally apportioned between the wise and the foolish, or between the virtuous and the corrupt? Should economic wealth be equally distributed between the industrious and the lazy?

Burke argued that the demand for such abstract rights as equality and fraternity ignored the historical development of rights, which were different in each country. Each national political community developed its own unique differentiation of rights and obligations over a long period. Rights were not universal; they were historically grounded in specific events and in specific groups. Burke claimed liberal and radical demands for abstract rights ignored the historical dimension of rights, and encouraged tampering with structures and practices that had met the test of time.

The demand for liberty, equality, and fraternity in the French Revolution also led to assaults on traditional groups and associations in France. The revolutionaries viewed the aristocracy, the church, and the guilds as barriers to abstract rights. Traditional conservatives argued that such institutions tie people together, moderate behavior, and differentiate responsibilities. Without these institutions, citizens will forget their obligations to others and will ignore the different roles that different citizens must play for society to function properly.

Burke warned, *before* the Terror began in France, that the pursuit of abstract rights in the absence of traditional associations would promote violence when these abstract rights were not realized in practice. Traditional groups buffer individuals from abuses of social and political power. These mediating institutions must be maintained not only to moderate the behavior of individuals, but to protect citizens from the power of the state.

The demand for abstract rights, such as equality, can serve to foster demands to redistribute land and money. Traditional conservatives viewed the redistribution of the lands of the church and the nobility during the revolution as a further assault on traditional groups and on the traditional hierarchy. Traditional conservatives did not object when land was held for long tenures by only a few (noble) families. The estate of the noble tied the family to the land and cultivated a love and admiration for the land. Land was not simply a commodity, but had value far beyond any price established in the market. This explains, in part, the uneasiness with which traditional conservatives have supported market economies and capitalist practices. In capitalist countries, land becomes a commodity to be bought and sold, often only for future profit. Speculation on land—land often bought and then sold without the owners ever having seen the plot—severs the nearly sacred connection which traditional conservatives believed could exist between land and owner.

Traditional conservatives also rejected socialist arguments for the redistribution of wealth, because redistribution, too, attacks the natural hierarchies that have developed in societies. Personal property must be protected, not because property ownership is a natural and abstract right, but because the protection of property provides social stability. Inequality of wealth is acceptable. Inequality is made less painful, according to traditional conservatives, by the doctrine of "***Noblesse Oblige***" (nobility obligates). Elites must practice the art of charity out of an inculcated sense of compassion and obligation. Working through and with traditional groups, elites are obligated to look after the less fortunate. While traditional conservatives have rejected socialist rationales for redistribution, they are uncomfortable with the extreme economic inequalities and the irresponsibility of elites in capitalist economies. In capitalist economies, everyone has the legal right to own as much property as can be acquired through "free" exchanges with others. However, this "formal and abstract equality" of everyone in a capitalist economy creates very unequal results. For traditional conservatives the undesirable results include undue poverty, excessive social mobility, and socially neglectful elites. The antidote to these problems is not, however, the provision of abstract welfare rights for the poor. Instead, traditional conservatives seek to reinvoke in elites the sense of responsibility to the poor contained in the concept of *Noblesse Oblige*. When capitalism produced in elites a sense of rugged individualism that thwarted their sense of responsibility, traditional conservative politicians have occasionally, and reluctantly, used government to provide some benefits to the poor. These benefits were not, however, based on abstract rights of citizens to material necessities, but rather on the hopes of diffusing revolutionary social movements and of promoting social stability.

Traditional conservatives are uncomfortable with the consequences of putting abstract rights into being. Capitalism relies on abstract individual economic liberties and equalities. Such rights create neglectful elites, and encourage the pursuit of self-interest by all in society. The pursuit of self-interest is a problem for traditional conservatives, because people pursue interests without attention to the consequences for society and for the community. Self-interested individuals are prone to neglect their social responsibilities and to divest themselves of the social ties that would bind them to the community. Of course, traditional conservatives do not want to replace capitalist economies with socialist ones; they prefer, instead, feudal economies, where different localities provide different economic rights and engender different responsibilities for the landed nobility, for the serfs, for the emerging craftsmen and traders in urban centers (the bourgeoisie), and for other sectors of society. Such an economic order would produce social order, according to traditional conservatives, because it encourages public-regarding action rather than self-interested behavior. While the economic rights of capitalism may stimulate innovation, competition, profit making, and social mobility, traditional conservatives believe that the consequences of such rights undermine the traditional fabric of society, produce relentless and distressing change, and uproot individuals from their traditional and secure places in the feudal economy.

For traditional conservatives, politics based on abstract rights promotes individualism at the expense of historical understanding, at the expense of mitigating institutions, and at the expense of the bonds that hold society together.

A second set of problems for traditional conservatives was generated by the deployment of Enlightenment rationality as a guide for social and political reforms.[1] As we saw in the last chapter, classical liberals believed that rational individuals could look inward to discover those courses of action that best served their interest by maximizing their pleasure and minimizing their pain. They believed that rational societies could thereby discover those political reforms that best served the greater good of the greater number of persons in society. Traditional conservatives rejected Enlightenment claims that pure reason could serve as a guide for individual choices and for political changes. Although Burke thought that people should, of course, use their capacity to reason, he thought that human reason was always influenced, clouded, and informed by **prejudice** derived from long-standing habits, human emotions, and social attachments. According to Burke, everyone is a creature of habit, with emotions and attachments that do not allow the pure use of reason. Humans are not isolated calculating machines. We have bodies, we have passions, we have histories, we have social bonds that shape our world. We must act in a world that never provides all of the information perfect reason demands. For Burke, the inevitable role that prejudice plays in our thinking is not a liability, as presupposed by Enlightenment philosophers. Instead, by providing valuable orientation and proper perspective, prejudice aids reason.

Just as humans are not calculating machines, neither is society simply a contraption to be easily altered, fixed, or improved. For traditional conservatives, societies are best understood as organic entities. Traditional conservatives prefer to talk about the "body politic" rather than using such classical liberal terms for society as "the ship of state" or "a delicate watch." These latter terms suggest that society can be improved by well-trained social engineers. It may be possible and necessary to improve society, but such improvements must, for traditional conservatives, be made slowly and carefully.

[1]Edmund Burke, *Reflections on the Revolution in France* (New York: Liberal Arts Library Press, 1955 [1790]), pp. 99–100.

Careless hacking away at the body politic will surely lead to unintended consequences that may prove far worse than the offending condition. The confidence with which the French revolutionaries approached reform struck Burke as dangerous *hubris*. The body politic is a complex organism that eludes human mastery. Drastic interventions will almost always be counterproductive and may lead to the death of the body. Social reform is not comparable to the fixing of a machine, but to the careful tending of a living entity.

A third set of problems for traditional conservatives involved the rejection of traditional authority, especially that of the government and of the church. In his *Reflections on the Revolution in France*, Burke expressed his dismay over the composition of those who constituted the National Assembly. For the most part, they were undistinguished, untalented, and without evident virtue. Most importantly, ". . . of any practical experience in the state, not one man was to be found. The best were only men of theory."[2] For Burke, governing requires practical wisdom, or "prudence." Only men of experience *and* historical knowledge can exercise good political judgment; prudence cannot be reduced to simple theories and mathematical formulas. Those who have acquired good judgment, wisdom, and virtue constitute a natural aristocracy. It is foolhardy to remove such men from office and entrust political authority to representatives of various interests within society or to liberal theoreticians who claim to know the best course of action on the basis of abstract principles and rights.

For traditional conservatives, it was also foolhardy to undermine religious authority. Even traditional conservatives who were ardent Anglicans, like Burke, viewed with horror the attacks on the Catholic Church during the French Revolution. Traditional conservatives defended **established religions** as essential social institutions.[3] The authority of a single religion supports the state by promoting social harmony, establishing a set of common religious practices, and reinforcing morality. Traditional conservatives viewed demands for religious freedom and for a separation of church and state as dangerous steps toward social decay.[4]

Goals

Given the traditional conservatives' view of social and political problems, it might seem as if the only goals they seek are the protection of the status quo and a longing for the "good old days" of the Middle Ages. There is certainly

[2]Burke, *Reflections on the Revolution in France*, p. 46.

[3]Burke, *Reflections on the Revolution in France*, pp. 102–120.

[4]In the twentieth century, traditional conservatives have accepted religious toleration and some separation of church and state. The role of churches as social institutions is still applauded by most traditional conservatives. However, the religious views of twentieth-century traditional conservatives range from the devoutly religious to the ardently atheistic. The views of most traditional conservatives, of course, would fall in a narrower range—from advocacy of some public commitment to religious institutions to public indifference to religion. For a more detailed discussion of the various views on religion held by traditional conservatives, see Robert Nisbet, *Conservatism: Dream and Reality* (Minneapolis: University of Minnesota Press, 1986), pp. 68–74.

a nostalgia for the Middle Ages in much of the traditional conservative literature,[5] but the emphasis on the status quo should be understood as a means of seeking to cultivate a deep *respect for tradition* and convention. Traditions are the product of the accumulated knowledge of previous generations. They provide social bonds of common practices and understandings. Conventions provide similar social bonds and give life a predictable rhythm. During the seventeenth and eighteenth centuries, such traditions and conventions had been threatened by scientific thought, by liberal innovations, and by radical aspirations. Traditional conservatives doubted that these understandings could match the social wisdom embodied in traditional practices which have withstood the test of time. By restoring respect for traditions and conventions, traditional conservatives sought to bestow on individuals and communities the wisdom of the ages and restrain the vexations that occur through the pursuit of every (sometimes fleeting) scientific theory and radical belief.

Despite the emphasis on restoring respect for tradition, traditional conservatives have not simply been reactionary; they have articulated a number of goals that have too often remained unattained in historical societies and unreflected in traditional ways of life. First, traditional conservatives have sought a well-ordered and peaceful community; its laws and rules of conduct should be clear and should be a reflection of the current beliefs in society. Law should not lead the public, but follow it. Governing should be a "specific and limited activity . . . enabling people to pursue the activities of their own choice with minimum frustration."[6] The government should pay special attention to the reduction of friction and clashes among groups. Rather than worrying about perfecting society, it should concentrate on reducing passions and minimizing conflict. Government should avoid grand theories and dreams of utopia, and instead rely on rituals and established practices to guide it in a *common sense* approach to politics.

Second, traditional conservatives want to preserve and develop a variety of voluntary organizations within society. These fulfill many of the functions once performed by the mitigating institutions of the old regime (e.g., trade guilds, merchant clubs, local parishes, and extended families). Voluntary organizations such as churches, community groups, charity organizations, and schools provide shelter for the individual and an attachment to society through association with familiar and local people. Voluntary associations remind citizens of their social life, shake them out of a narrow, self-interested perspective, and provide opportunities for them to practice their social obligations and responsibilities in a supportive environment. Voluntary organizations also mediate the relationship between the national government and the people, reducing the need for governmental intrusion into private life and lessening the power that governments might have over otherwise resourceless persons.

[5]See Nisbet, *Conservatism,* pp. 2–11.

[6]See Michael Oakeshott, "On Being Conservative," in his *Rationalism in Politics and Other Essays* (New York: Basic Books, 1962), p. 184.

Third, traditional conservatives want to cultivate and nourish individual character and excellence. They seek the development of citizens with a strong civic commitment. They see this commitment as a necessary counterweight to the pursuit of self-interest in capitalist economies. Individuals need to be aware of their connections with others and need to realize social solidarity by acting cooperatively within a variety of local organizations. Traditional conservatives promote individual excellence not only because it will contribute to the betterment of society, but because excellence is threatened by both capitalism and socialism, and thus must be reinforced. Capitalism threatens to reduce excellence to whatever the market will bear, and socialism threatens excellence by celebrating the average person.[7] High culture should not descend to the masses, but rather, individuals with talent should ascend to the heights of culture.

Fourth, traditional conservatives encourage individuals to engage in activities that are noninstrumental. Michael Oakeshott has argued that modern individuals too often limit their activities to those which provide rewards, awards, and profit.[8] A conservative disposition is cultivated and human happiness is expressed best in activities and relationships that are enjoyed for themselves, without concern for future benefits. Friendship is one of the obvious relationships in which a consideration of prospects of future gain need not play a part in enjoyment of the company. Leisure activities also may be enjoyed without concern for the "success" of the activity. In noninstrumental activity, one can draw pleasure from the familiar and cultivate the cooperative citizenry traditional conservatives desire.

In promoting these goals, traditional conservatives have asserted the importance of *social cooperation.* They have fought against excessive individualism in politics, science, economics, and religion. They sought to maintain the political community against reforms that assumed that government was the result of a "mere contract" among equal individuals. They sought to retain allegiance to social traditions that were viewed with skepticism by those who believed that science could produce new and better understandings of the world by focusing on the individual as the proper unit of analysis of social issues. They sought to remind people that there is more to life than economic productivity and the accumulation of wealth as instruments of individual fulfillment. And they defended established religions against the modern claim that religion is a purely personal and private matter. They thus suggested that excessive individualism creates levels of friction and conflict that threaten a well-ordered and peaceful community. They suggested that society is more important than the individual, and that society must be ordered in a manner that promotes individual responsibility to the community. The creation and maintenance of mitigating institutions attach the individual in a concrete, rather than abstract, way to society and thus provide a "rooted individualism" whereby citizens have a sense of belonging to something bigger than them-

[7]See José Ortega y Gasset, *The Revolt of the Masses* (New York: W. W. Norton, 1957 [1930]).
[8]Oakeshott, "On Being Conservative," pp. 175–178.

Sidebar 3-2

Communitarianism

During the 1980s—sometimes called the "decade of greed"—some American intellectuals and activists coined the term "communitarianism" to encourage the development of a new public philosophy. In the view of communitarians, contemporary Americans give too much emphasis to self-interested individualism and insufficient attention to community life and the public good, understood as something more than the sum of individual interests. In the view of communitarians, we overemphasize individual rights and inadequately discharge those obligations necessary for cohesive communities. By criticizing political and economic individualism and defending community values, traditional conservatives helped lay the foundations for communitarian perspectives.

Many ideologies have communitarian moments, but scholars who call themselves communitarians have generally fallen into two camps. The older camp, the "left communitarians," criticize liberal individualism for failing to promote the public good, ignoring economic inequalities, and neglecting the ways in which individuals are embedded within community life. These communitarians—including Michael J. Sandel, Charles Taylor, and Alasdair MacIntyre—insist that liberal claims that individuals should be free to define their own good and that governments should be neutral with regard to different conceptions of the good undermine the moral development of individuals and social progress. For these communitarians, the liberal conception of the public good—as the summation of individual interests—is simply "too thin"; they argue that a broader social understanding of "the good" is necessary to provide important guidance to governmental efforts to improve society. They view the state and individuals as having mutual obligations, including obligations to redress the inequalities generated by capitalism. Left communitarians believe that the liberal picture of individuals as being prior to the community—of knowing their own good prior to the social contract—misses the ways in which individual opportunities, choices, and self-understandings are constituted by the community and existing social values. By assuming that individuals are self-determined, liberals overlook the ways in which individuals are embedded in the social relations of communities. The great danger of liberal individualism is that it cannot generate allegiances to values necessary for the survival of healthy political communities, especially the values of obligation, compassion, and sacrifice.

The other contemporary camp that labels itself communitarian is not concerned with economic inequalities or the embeddedness of individuals. Rather, these "right communitarians"—such as Amitai Etzioni and Daniel Bell—claim that the most serious liberal threat to community is the growth of individual legal rights. Etzioni, a noted sociologist and one of the founders of right communitarianism, argues that the protection of individual civil liberties has endangered the rights of the community. Such groups as the American Civil Liberties Union (ACLU) protect individual rights, especially the rights of the accused, without regard for the safety of the community. For right communitarians, the rights of individuals need to be weighed against the consequences for the community. Citizens must understand that social obligations (especially to promote public order) are just as important as individual rights.

selves and of being committed to something more important than their immediate self-interest.

THE PHILOSOPHICAL BASES

Ontology

Two different views of ontology have been forwarded by traditional conservatives. The first view, generally held by nineteenth-century traditional conservatives, is that there exists a "**Great Chain of Being**." God is at the top of this chain, and God's will creates, but does not wholly determine, reality. Humans, who are much lower on this chain, can only see imperfectly the will of God. In between God and humans, helping humans improve their imperfect knowledge, is society. Society offers insight because it contains the collective reservoir of human knowledge developed through trial and error over a long period of time. This social knowledge is superior to the insights of any one person or even one group of people, because it combines the insights of all previous generations. This social knowledge is also less prone to the human afflictions of pride, passion, and folly than any one individual or group. Social knowledge is not perfectly attuned to God's will, but it is much closer to it than are the insights or knowledge available to any individual. This is why traditional conservatives rely on tradition and custom as the best guides for human activity.

This idea of a Great Chain of Being also includes the idea of the connectedness of all members of a society. The connection is not just among all those living, it includes the connection among the dead, the living, and those yet to be born. The living are connected to the dead, because the dead have bequeathed their social knowledge to the living. Both the living and the dead have an obligation to future citizens, because they are part of the ongoing history of the (living) society.

The second view of ontology, held by some twentieth-century traditional conservatives and expressed most forcefully by Michael Oakeshott, is that conservatism does not need to be concerned with ontology. In this view, conservatism does not rest on philosophical foundations, and it need make no reference to God or religion to sustain its arguments. Conservatism is a disposition to enjoy things as they are for themselves and is a belief that governance should be a limited activity.[9] Religious beliefs may improve morality, and religious organizations may be useful as mediating institutions in society, but conservative dispositions and beliefs need not rely on any ontological claims.

Despite the differences in these two views, they both share the fundamental conviction that human knowledge is limited, is always marked by prejudice, and is always prone to distortion by the passions. For both, ultimate reality is never grasped, but only dimly perceived.

[9]See Oakeshott, "On Being Conservative," pp. 182–84.

Human Nature

Traditional conservatives do not accept the classical liberal view of human nature. To traditional conservatives, humans are not simply material beings motivated by the pursuit of pleasure and the avoidance of pain. Instead, humans are spiritual beings who are tied to one another and linked to God in the Great Chain of Being. Humans are motivated by spiritual considerations and by the principles, by the rights and obligations, and by the sentiments cultivated in their society. Self-interest cannot explain the choices humans make, nor can self-interest serve as the guide for wise choices within the community. Human *prudence* must be guided by the lessons learned in a well-ordered society that structures choices through custom and tradition.

Human nature, according to traditional conservatives, is neither fundamentally good nor fundamentally evil. All humans have the potential for goodness, but the propensity for evil can easily overcome the potential for good. The propensity for evil is increased when self-interest is encouraged and when humans must rely on reason without the guidance of the customs and traditions of a well-ordered society. Even in such a society, humans are still prone to vices and still subject to human frailties. However, a well-ordered society can provide humans with a reasonably good life in which all make contributions to the public good and in which all feel integrated into the community. Society cannot create perfect humans, but it can create an environment in which the propensity for evil will be reduced and the bonds among citizens will be nourished.

As indicated above in the section on ontology, traditional conservatives believe that human reason and rationality are limited. Humans are not capable of full recognition of their best interests. The use of reason is always influenced by human passion and attachments. Human reason is never pure, and is always prejudiced, because human reason must be mixed with emotions and habits. Human reason is always limited, because the world, as well as each society, is too complex and interconnected for any human to grasp fully.

This view of limited reason, however, does not lead traditional conservatives to abandon the use of reason. Reason must be employed carefully and with attention to the specific details of the case at hand. It is possible to derive generalizations from the study of specific cases; but traditional conservatives are suspicious of great theories and grand schemes. They do not believe that a "science of politics" or a "science of man" is possible. They do not believe that social actions and human behavior can be explained mathematically. Thus, the best use of reason is a common sense approach that relies on experience and a focus on the concrete and specific. Neither the utilitarian calculations of classical liberals nor the utopian plans of socialists take into account the limits of human reason and the complexity of human motivations.

The limited reason available to each individual limits the potential for human autonomy. The liberal idea that each person should be the source of his own truths about how to live misunderstands the human condition.

Humans need society to shape their behavior and to promote their commonsense by providing customs, traditions, and stability. Human goals must be socially defined, so that individuals recognize their place in society, their role in the Great Chain of Being, and the meaningfulness of their existence.

Traditional conservatives argue that liberalism promotes an isolated individualism. "Freed" from the bonds of custom and from the stability of traditional authority, individuals in liberal societies pursue individual pleasure, but cannot discover a meaningful existence. Liberal societies engender an alienated self—a self that has no place, no companions, no purpose. Emile Durkheim called this alienation of self "anomie," and in his book *Suicide* he argued that the breakdown of traditional authority and the rise of individualism in Europe was accompanied by an increased incidence of suicide.[10]

The cure for isolated individualism is not to be found in abstract claims about human equality. Traditional conservatives argue that people vary greatly in their talents and abilities. The well-ordered society takes advantage of these concrete differences among people by positioning people in social roles on the basis of the different characteristics of citizens. Society works best when the respective roles, privileges, and responsibilities of various citizens or groups of citizens are differentiated. Each individual makes different, but important, contributions to society. Working at different tasks, but all working together for the good of society, provides citizens with a sense of belonging to a larger and more meaningful entity.

Society

By 1790, liberal thinkers had developed the idea that society was simply a human construction. As we saw in the last chapter, classical liberals believed that society originated when a group of individuals created a social contract to set aside certain natural liberties in order to enjoy the benefits of civil society, and they believed that society was simply the sum of the individuals that constituted it. This conception of society was rejected by Burke, who expressed the earlier, medieval conception of society. Society is more than a contract that can be dissolved by unhappy individuals. Society is more than the sum of its parts. In a famous section of *Reflections on the Revolution in France,* entitled, "Society is a Permanent Contract," Burke declared:

> Society is indeed a contract. Subordinate contracts for objects of mere occasional interest may be dissolved at pleasure—but the state ought not to be considered as nothing better than a partnership agreement in a trade of pepper and coffee, calico, or tobacco, or some other low concern, to be taken up for a little temporary interest, and to be dissolved by the fancy of the parties. It is to be looked on with other reverence because it is not a partnership in things subservient only to the gross animal existence of a temporary and perishable nature. It is a partnership in all science; a partnership in all art; a partnership

[10]Emile Durkheim, *Suicide: A Study in Sociology,* edited by George Simpson (New York: The Free Press, 1966 [1897]), esp. pp. 241–360.

> in every virtue and in all perfection. As the ends of such a partnership cannot be obtained in many generations, it becomes a partnership not only between those who are living, those who are dead, and those who are to be born. Each contract of each particular state is but a clause in the great primeval contract of eternal society, linking the lower with the higher natures, connecting the visible and invisible world, according to a fixed compact sanctioned by the inviolable oath which holds all physical and all moral natures, each in their appointed place.[11]

Society is not just a contract, then, but a living entity that has a past and a future. Societies can grow, change, and mature. Traditional conservatives reject the mechanistic metaphors for society used by liberals and prefer organic metaphors, such as the "body politic."

This **organic conception of society** is central to traditional conservative thought. An organic society is necessarily hierarchical and highly interdependent. Just as a body has certain organs that are more important than other tissues, the body politic has people and groups who are more important than others in the society. All members of the society contribute to the health of the body politic, but given the unequal distribution of human abilities, some members' contributions are more important than others. Thus, society is class-based. Traditional conservatives in the eighteenth century sought to maintain the class distinctions that prevailed in medieval society which gave more privileges (and responsibilities) to the royalty, the landed aristocracy, and the clergy, than were given to the urban bourgeoisie, the serfs or peasants who worked the land, and the laborers in the factories of the emerging capitalist economy. While allegiance to a feudal class structure has receded among traditional conservatives, there remains an understanding that class distinctions are important. The doctor, the judge, and the politician are more important than the farmer, the plumber, and the chimney sweep. However, the latter group is also essential for a healthy society and its contributions must be acknowledged. Everyone has a role to fulfill and a duty to perform that role conscientiously.

This view of society as a highly complex and interdependent organism is opposed to the classical liberal claim that individual choices generally have few spillover effects or social consequences. Traditional conservatives argue that the interconnections among all members of a society make many individual choices socially important. Everyone must fulfill his particular role, and everyone must be protected from choices unhealthy for himself and the society. Attempts to redefine roles and responsibilities can destroy the natural harmony of the body politic and lead to dire, unintended consequences. Social reformers ignore the complex interdependencies in society and can produce results that are far from those expected. Like medical treatment of a human body, the cure for a minor ailment to the body politic may cause serious injury or disease unanticipated by the physician. Thus, traditional conservatives are wary of all interventions in the roles and structures in society. These roles and

[11]Burke, *Reflections on the Revolution in France*, p. 110.

structures have developed over a long period of time to produce the arrangements now practiced, and they should not be tampered with lightly. As noted above, society is a reservoir of social knowledge that exceeds the insights of any one person or group.

Members of society must be protected from themselves, as well as from social reformers. Society has an obligation, as Burke stated, to promote virtue and perfection. Individuals and groups can make bad choices, especially when guided by self-interest and the passions, and society has a responsibility to protect errant members from themselves. Society requires that the wills of individuals be controlled, and their passions brought into subjection.[12]

The maintenance and creation of mediating institutions in society is one of the ways in which inclinations can be thwarted and passions subjugated. Churches, voluntary associations, neighborhoods, and families are groups which provide direct and specific connections to others and promote indirect connections to the state. In local organizations, one can see one's actions *for others* and *with others* in detail and to completion. Such groups minimize the need for state intervention in society and provide a sense of belonging for members of these groups. This emphasis on the importance of mediating institutions in society makes clear that the organic society cherished by traditional conservatives is also a pluralistic society—a society where diverse associations as well as diverse individuals and classes play important roles.

The mediating institutions provide people with multiple and varied connections to society. They are a protection against the dangers of anomie associated with liberal individualism. In the twentieth century, traditional conservatives argue that the spread of liberal anomie has created populations highly susceptible to fascism.[13] Fascism, which offers a "thick" notion of community based on national glory, appeals to people who have lost a sense of direction and who view their lives as meaningless. But this fascist appeal to national glory envisions a unitary organic society, rather than the pluralist organic society championed by traditional conservatives. In a fascist society, everyone identifies with the national leader and national purposes, as opposed to a traditional conservative society, where people identify with the many, various particular institutions and groups among which they live their everyday lives. For traditional conservatives, mediating institutions are an essential means of connecting people to society. These institutions also protect people from the isolated individualism of liberalism and from the dangerous nationalistic appeals of fascism.

Traditional conservatives do not reject individual freedom in the quest for an organic society, but they insist that the individual be rooted in society and that freedom be exercised within the limits of the rights *and* responsibilities that accompany the (varied) roles performed by members of the society. Soci-

[12]Burke, *Reflections on the Revolution in France,* p. 68.

[13]See Nisbet, *Conservatism,* pp. 35–38. This analysis draws on the insights of Hannah Arendt [see *The Origins of Totalitarianism* (New York and London: Harcourt, Brace, Jovanovich, 1951)]. Arendt is not a traditional conservative.

ety thus precedes the individual, and individual egoism must be constrained in order to maintain society.

Epistemology

As noted earlier, traditional conservatives reject the idea that truth can be known by rational inquiry. As indicated in the discussion of society, the best guide to proper thought and action is a reliance on the conventions and traditions developed within specific societies. The reliance on convention is necessary, because neither faith nor reason is a sufficient guide to the truth. Faith is insufficient because, although God is truth, God's knowledge and will are not immediately discernable by humans. Science, as it was developed by early Enlightenment figures, is also inadequate, because science rests on extravagant claims about causality and underestimates the power of passion, prejudice, and habit.

Given the traditional conservative view of society as a highly complex organic entity, it is not surprising that traditional conservatives think that human understanding of causal relations is limited. Even a minor change in one area of society may lead to large and unexpected changes throughout the organism. Of course, Enlightenment philosophers can acknowledge that the complexity of the organism impedes causal understanding but still maintain that causal sequences and distant consequences can be understood through the increasingly sophisticated knowledge that science provides.

The counterresponse by traditional conservatives to this Enlightenment optimism was developed by drawing on the insights of David Hume (1711–1776), a thinker whose ideas influenced conservatives as well as some economic liberals, including Adam Smith (see below, "The Scottish Enlightenment"). Hume argued that we cannot "know" the things in this world. Rather, we can only know our ideas about things in this world. For example, when we claim that B is caused by A, what we are really claiming is that our idea of B is connected (or conjoined) to our idea of A. Because we cannot know the world, we cannot even claim that causal relations actually exist. Through our experiences, we see that there are connections between our ideas that regularly occur, but these connections are between our ideas and cannot be assumed to be causal. The connections we make about things are really just connections we make in our minds, and are not necessarily explanations of the external world. We talk as if cause and effect existed, when there are really only conjoined ideas in our minds. We do have a habit of conjoining ideas, but this is a habit, not an insight by reason into external reality. Indeed, this habit of conjoining ideas is a product of experience and custom, and our ideas are always shaped by prejudices, customs, habits, and passions.

Reason alone, then, is not a guide to truth. We must rely on the customs, traditions, and conventions of our society. The search for truth must rely on our experiences, our knowledge of history, and a commonsense approach to each particular issue. Grand theories of Enlightenment reformers are thus mis-

Sidebar 3-3

The Scottish Enlightenment

In the eighteenth century, a school of thought dubbed the "Scottish Enlightenment" emerged, which provided important foundations for both classical liberalism and traditional conservatism. The Scottish thinkers who were part of this intellectual movement had varied interests, but they all recognized David Hume (1711–1776) as the central influence on their scholarly enquiries. Adam Ferguson (1723–1816), Thomas Reid (1710–1796), Adam Smith (1723–1790), and many others acknowledged their indebtedness to Hume, even on points of disagreement. Hume shaped the course of the Scottish Enlightenment by pursuing an empirical science, but he argued that such a science must recognize both reason *and* passion in the study of humans *in* society.

The inclusion of the passions, the sentiments, "the moral senses," in the human sciences in the Scottish Enlightenment led to some conservative ideas that were not experienced by other Enlightenment movements. If reason was limited and the "moral senses" were of importance, then more attention must be paid to such influences on humans as habit, social customs, and social institutions. Habits, customs, and institutions shape behavior and limit human reason.

The views of the Scottish Enlightenment on the limits of reason, the importance of habit and tradition within each society, and the roles of institutions in acquiring a store of historical knowledge provide some theoretical foundations for the beliefs held by traditional conservatives. For example, Burke's view that human reason is always prejudiced can, obviously, be supported and extended by the analyses of Hume and his fellow Scots. Traditional conservatives seeking a philosophical and theoretical source to support their views on human knowledge have often turned to ideas developed during the Scottish Enlightenment, especially those developed by Hume in *A Treatise of Human Nature* (1739).

The Scottish Enlightenment, though, was also shaped by assumptions and goals that diverged sharply from those of traditional conservatives. Scottish Enlightenment thinkers, unlike traditional conservatives, were generally optimistic about human progress, and the ability of the sciences to help shape that progress. Furthermore, they believed that a science of humans in society was possible, and that such a science would be much more rigorous than just "prudent" thinking (some even claimed that this science could be reduced completely to mathematical explanations). They insisted that this science of humans must study more than reason. It must include an understanding of sentiments and habits, and of conventions and institutions. These inclusions would not make the human sciences unrealizable, but rather would make them more accurate. This confidence in progress and science was especially evident in the works of that "great foe" of traditional conservatism, Adam Smith. Smith's view of self-interest as the *predictable* combination of reason and sentiment allowed him to develop economic theories in *The Wealth of Nations* (1776) that would become central to classical liberal demands for freedom from state intervention and for the rights of individuals in general.

guided, and are neglectful of the knowledge accumulated within specific societies.

SUBSTANTIVE POLITICAL PRINCIPLES

Authority

Traditional conservatives reject an activist government that constantly implements grand schemes for the improvement of society, but they also reject the very limited role of governmental authority advocated by economic liberals. Government, as the head of the body politic, has important roles to fulfill. Traditional conservatives, once again looking back fondly on the Middle Ages, argue that governments must use their authority to perform six functions.

First, government must promote harmony in society by reducing the friction among individuals and among groups. The government should not be just an "umpire"—a favorite metaphor for economic liberals—because an umpire makes rulings after collisions have taken place. Government should be active in reducing collisions and conflicts among members of the society. Government must be willing to persuade, cajole, reward, and punish members in order to promote social unity. Good government "conducts" members of society as if the members were all part of a large and diverse orchestra. Members of this "social orchestra" should willingly sacrifice self-interest and give deference to the government in the quest for social harmony.

Second, the government can promote social harmony by promoting mediating institutions within the society. One of the most important mediating institutions is the church. Traditional conservatives, with few exceptions, are untroubled by government support for religion, and view churches as one of the most important institutions within the society. Churches serve society by inculcating morals, by providing for the needy, and by reminding members of their places within the Great Chain of Being. Government creation, maintenance, and expansion of voluntary groups is a serious and ongoing responsibility that must be taken seriously and practiced carefully.

Third, government must protect traditional norms and conventional rights. The rights to be protected are not "abstract rights" derived from natural law. Rather, they are those that have emerged over time from the specific legal and institutional arrangements that are unique to each country. Different individuals and different groups have different rights and responsibilities, which must be respected and protected. Elites may have more rights that need to be protected, but they should also have commensurate obligations, and the government needs to make sure that such obligations are met.

Market economies pose a threat to traditional norms and conventional rights and obligations because they sever the bond between lord and serf and replace it with a contract between owner and worker. The worker is "free" to sell his labor to the highest bidder, but the worker finds himself now bound to an employer who feels no obligation to the worker other than that incurred by the monetary connection sealed by the contract. The treatment of workers in market economies is troubling for traditional conservatives, because it reflects poorly on a society that should look after its own, and because it detaches the worker from an organic connection to the society. Thus, while traditional conservatives have supported market economies, they are uncomfortable with the way workers are treated and they fear the loss of stable social roles that have bound together the body politic.

The fourth role, then, of government must be to protect society from the changes in condition, behavior, and attitude that result from market practices. By the nineteenth century, most traditional conservatives had accepted many of the ideas and outcomes of market practices, including the role of contracts and the commoditization of land. However, conservatives were not willing to accept a laissez faire approach to the economy nor to endorse the self-interest and unrestrained competition promoted in market economies. Traditional conservatives have advocated intervention in the market when the market produces extreme inequalities and the mistreatment of workers. For example, in the late nineteenth century, conservative politicians in England and Germany supported legislation that aided the poor and protected the rights of workers. In England, Benjamin Disraeli (1804–1881), a conservative prime minister, revised the labor laws to recognize some rights for workers and supported legislation that attempted to provide for public housing, public health care, and pure air and water. Otto von Bismarck (1815–1898), an empire builder and domestic conservative during his reign as First Chancellor of the German Empire, established accident insurance for workers, pension plans for the elderly, and health care programs for all. These policies also reduced the friction caused by socialists' emphasizing the class divisions and social upheaval caused by capitalist development. In the quest for social harmony, government must limit the dislocations and the friction created by competition in a market economy.

Traditional conservatives will also intervene in the market when individual decisions in the market foster immoral or imprudent behavior. Members of society are not free to choose their vices or to provide the means for others to indulge such vices. Traditional conservatives thus reject the claim that buyers and sellers always know best their wants and interests. The government has a role in determining which goods and services are made available to the public. Thus, traditional conservatives usually believe that governmental authority can be legitimately used to forbid gambling, prostitution, pornography, and the use of alcohol and drugs.

Fifth, then, the government has a responsibility to maintain and nurture public morality. The rights to free exchange and to free speech should be limited in the interest of public morality. Each society has developed its own moral principles and standards, and these must be safeguarded by the governments of each country. Regulation of expression and behavior is appropriate, because all members of the society have a responsibility to the greater whole that is society. Individual choices are not limited in their impact, but have an influence on the entire society.

Sixth, the government has a role in furthering the public good and reminding citizens of their role in this endeavor. In particular, the government must not allow the market and the liberal values of self-interest and competition, which the market encourages, to create citizens who are selfish, self-centered, and zealously competitive. By reducing conflict in society, by promoting mediating institutions that bind people together, by guarding traditional rights, by protecting society from the dislocations created by market economies, and by preserving public morality, government can enhance the public good and nurture the development of citizens who look beyond personal interest to the public good.

The roles ascribed to government by traditional conservatives may seem to create a large and constantly intrusive government. It certainly creates a government more active, visible, and authoritative than the "umpire" or "night watchman" governments advocated by economic liberals. A traditional conservative government, however, will rely heavily on the contributions of mediating institutions to aid it in the performance of these roles; thus, the visibility of the government is cloaked by the many voluntary associations in society. The intrusiveness of government will be diminished by the care with which any changes in society will be introduced and by an approach that seeks to guard and defend that which exists.

Justice

Justice, for traditional conservatives, is not equality, nor is it some transcendental claim based on abstract rights. Justice is the enforcement of rights and obligations that have developed within the traditions, institutions, and conventions of a society. Hence, justice is different in different societies.

One characteristic of traditional conservative justice is that those who enjoy increased rights and privileges have increased obligations and responsibilities. Rights and obligations are commensurate. The specifics of these rights and obligations are different in each country. Two examples illustrate this idea of **commensurate rights and obligations**.

The first example is from medieval France. In Paris, the law held that it was legal for paupers and traveling serfs to sleep under the bridges at night. It was, however, illegal for royalty, no matter their condition, to sleep under the bridges. Royalty had so many privileges that it would be inappropriate for them to displace the poor in one of these places of refuge. In a society with different rights and distinct roles for members of society, justice is served by treating different people differently.

The second example comes from twentieth-century Britain. In World War II, British Army officers were almost always sons of the elite. They attended the best schools, and when they became officers they were given rights and privileges far superior to those afforded the common soldier. It was understood that these rights and privileges entailed commensurate obligations and dangers. The "bomb squads," which were developed to defuse German bombs that landed in England but did not detonate, were composed of both officers and common soldiers. When an unexploded bomb was discovered, it was the responsibility of the common soldiers to transport gear, secure the area, and to expose the bomb for defusing. Once these operations were complete, the common soldiers exited the danger area, and the officers took on the task of defusing the bombs. Mortality rates on the bomb squads were high, and officers were almost always the only troops killed. Officers did not complain, nor did they attempt to have the bomb squads reorganized so that the "less important" soldiers might bear the dangers. The officers accepted the convention that their greater rights and privileges must be matched by the greater risk undertaken by placing themselves in the line of fire.

Nineteenth- and twentieth-century traditional conservatives hold slightly dissimilar views on the just distribution of goods in society. Burke, representing the nineteenth-century view, held **ascriptive principles of justice**.[14] He maintained that goods should be distributed on the basis of such traits as race, gender, and class, according to the specific cultural differentiations among people developed in each society.

Twentieth-century traditional conservatives have argued that the distribution of goods in society should be based on the talents and abilities of the members of that society.[15] Citizens possessing such traits as intelligence, perseverance, prudence, and beauty, for example, should be awarded a greater share of goods than those who lack such traits. Goods are thus to be awarded on the basis of mental, physical, and moral qualities.

Despite the dissimilarity of these two views, they do share affinities. Both views reject the equal distribution of goods. Both views reject the "unpatterned" results of the just distribution that classical liberals celebrate.[16] Classical liberals believe that talent *and* luck contribute to the distribution of goods in a market economy. The combinations of talent and luck that lead to economic success or failure cannot be predicted and thus there will be no final pattern of just distribution that is desirable or that can be predicted. Both traditional conservative views assume that there is a desirable pattern of justice, although that pattern will be different in different countries. Ideally, the two traditional conservative views could be reconciled, because the natural hierarchy of Burke's ascriptive approach to just distribution would correspond to the differences in talents and abilities. Simply put, elites would be born into their positions, but they would also deserve those positions because of their talents.

Once again we see that although traditional conservatives generally accept features of a market economy, they are uncomfortable with some of the results

[14]For a discussion of the ascriptive norm of distributive justice, see Jennifer Hochschild, *What's Fair?* (Cambridge: Harvard University Press, 1981), pp. 70–75.

[15]Russell Kirk, *A Program for Conservatives* (Chicago: Henry Regnery, 1954), pp. 164–192.

[16]A discussion of "patterned" versus "unpatterned" distribution is presented by Robert Nozick in *Anarchy, State, and Utopia* (New York: Basic Books, 1974), esp. pp. 149–182.

of that economy. The social mobility and unpatterned results that emerge in a market economy are not quite compatible with the views on just distribution that traditional conservatives hold. Justice may require the intervention of government to insure that distribution does not undermine the natural hierarchies necessary in a good traditional conservative society.

Structure

There is no one preferred structure of government for traditional conservatives. Each society has its own unique traditions and conventions, and these will lead to unique structures of government.

In general, though, traditional conservatives have supported "republican" structural arrangements rather than "authoritarian" or "democratic" arrangements. Authoritarian structures are too far removed from the people. Democratic structures are too close to the people. Authoritarian structures create governments that neglect the needs of society while serving only the needs of those who govern. Democratic structures pander to the whims and passions of the many. This pandering undermines stability and causes government to neglect its commitment to the public good. Traditional conservatives thus favor **republican structures** having the following characteristics. First, there should be "mixed" governmental structures where the interests of the various elements of a pluralist society are balanced and blended so that no faction within society can corruptly pursue its own interest and generate unnecessary conflict in the body politic. In such a mixed system, some persons and classes may lead, but all elements within society have an opportunity to concur that the policies produced are for the good of society as a whole. Second, although the public has some role in government—principally holding leaders accountable through elections—the role of the public is limited. The public should not be too powerful, because authority should rest with leaders who are competent to govern. Governmental structures should protect such leaders from the passions of the electorate.

Twentieth-century traditional conservatives have been critical of attempts to make U.S. institutions more democratic. While often hostile to the decisions of the Supreme Court, they accept the idea that judges should be appointed and not elected. They also have been critical of the Seventeenth Amendment to the U.S. Constitution, which changed the method for selecting senators. They preferred the older method of state legislatures' selecting senators, rather than the new method of relying on the popular vote. Such devices as the electoral college in Presidential elections they deem perfectly appropriate. Indirect elections, appointed positions, and long terms of office are all seen as acceptable, because they remove officials from the passions of the governed.

Given these views on the structures of government, it might seem as if traditional conservatives would be very comfortable with the views and ideas of the founders of the U.S. Constitution. However, traditional conservatives view the founders as having set up a system that excessively limited the government's power—especially the government's power to enforce morality and conventional norms. Traditional conservatives accept higher levels of government activity than those envisioned by the "liberal" founders. In addition, Burke (and others) viewed written constitutions as unnecessary and even repugnant, because they furthered the idea that society was a mere contract. A state is not created by a contract, but is a living and inherited tradition. When Burke spoke of the British Constitution, he included all acts of parliament, the common law, and the traditions and informal norms that define political power and its limits. A constitution in this perspective is not a document, but a living set of conventions.

Rulers

Historically, traditional conservatives have defended monarchies. They have accepted parliamentary supremacy and the move toward more democratic institutions, but they retain a nostalgia for the Crown and for elitist rule.

Traditional conservatives maintain there is a **natural aristocracy** in society, and society is best served when these people of high station and birth are in positions of leadership. Only these "aristocrats" have the virtue, competence, and prudence to govern wisely.

Most members of society should not exercise political authority. The role of the people is to control the improper use of authority, especially if that authority is used to attack tradition. Government is not by the people, but only for the people. Burke wrote:

> . . . no legislator, at any period of the world, has willingly placed the seat of active power in the hands of the multitude; because there it admits of no control, no regulation, no steady direction whatsoever. The people are the natural control on authority; but to exercise and to control together is contradictory and impossible.[17]

This view that the people are too passionate, inconsistent, and incompetent to rule and that there is a natural aristocracy that should rule creates the foundation for Burke's famous theory of **virtual representation**. Burke rejected the liberal claim that elected leaders should be agents (or *delegates*) of their constituents and thus responsive to their constituents' preferences. Burke argued instead that both elected and nonnelected rulers have an obligation to the long-term interests of the society. They should be custodians of the national interest, not errand boys representing the short-term passions of their constituents. Leaders under the theory of virtual representation are **trustees** of the national interest, and their duty is to rule paternalistically and prudently. They must stay above the fracas and fray of partial and passionate interests as they pursue the public good.

[17]Edmund Burke, "An Appeal from the New to the Old Whigs," in *The Political Philosophy of Edmund Burke*, edited by Iain Hampshire-Monk (London: Longman, 1987 [1791]), p. 242.

Citizenship

The traditional conservative emphasis on the obligations and duties of members of the society leads to a view of citizenship that is much less rights-oriented, and much more passive, than the view held by classical liberals. The good citizen is simply a law-abiding traditionalist who accepts his particular role within the society.

The level of citizen participation in any society is to be determined by the traditions and conventions of each society; it is not something that can be determined by appealing to (abstract) natural rights. In societies with a tradition of elections, citizen voting is a perfectly acceptable level of participation. If a society offers other alternatives for participation, such as jury duty, then these forms of participation are also acceptable as long as they are part of the given society's historical tradition.

Traditional conservatives do not accept the argument that public participation in itself improves the moral development of citizens. Some democratic theorists have argued that only by taking part in public life can citizens improve their decision-making abilities and their ethical judgment. Such claims lead these theorists to demand ever-increasing participatory roles for citizens. Traditional conservatives view such arguments as, at best, naive. Burke wrote:

> The mind is brought far more easily to acquiesce in the proceedings of one man, or a few, who act under a general procuration for the state, than in a vote of a victorious majority in councils in which every man has his share in deliberation. For there the beaten party are exasperated and soured by the previous contention, and mortified by the conclusive defeat.[18]

Burke admits that, in some countries, citizens have learned to live with majority rule, but this is a slow process and not necessarily appropriate for all countries. Most citizens are incapable of achieving the virtue, competence, and prudence necessary for public participation, and many citizens are quite rightly focused on their personal and local concerns rather than on the national good. If citizens feel a need to participate in group activities, there are plenty of opportunities available in the many voluntary associations in the society.

Most citizens will have few obligations to participate in politics. Their obligations, instead, will be (1) to accept traditionally constituted government institutions, (2) to obey the laws of the land, and (3) to perform their allocated roles in society to the best of their abilities. For most citizens, then, the guides to behavior are obedience, duty, and hard work. Elites, of course, have these obligations, as well as obligations to perform public service and to be actively involved in politics. Their role is to promote the national good and, if necessary, to practice benevolence towards the least fortunate in society.

Obedience is warranted from citizens because everyone is part of this larger, living entity that is society. Obedience is not the result of "signing" a

[18]Burke, "An Appeal from the New to the Old Whigs," p. 246.

social contract. The social-contract perspective encourages citizens to question their loyalty and obedience to a society. Indeed, under social-contract theory, a citizen denied equal rights has good reason to be disobedient. Remember, though, that for traditional conservatives the bonds of society are much more than a mere contract. Civil disobedience is thus almost always rejected as a legitimate response from citizens, because traditional conservatives fear the loss of social stability that such disobedience might engender.

The only time that disobedience and radical action are justified is when the political system violates the traditional rights which have developed within a country. Burke opposed the French Revolution because it was based on abstract claims. He supported, however, the American colonists in their revolution, because he argued that they were simply demanding their traditional rights. The colonists were, according to Burke, legitimate heirs to British traditions, and they must be treated accordingly by Britain. The failure of Britain to respect the traditional rights of the colonists justified the disobedient and rebellious acts of the American revolutionaries.[19]

Change

Traditional conservatives wish to conserve the traditions and practices of their societies. They do recognize, however, that change is sometimes necessary and that states must be prepared for social changes. Indeed, Burke proclaimed, in the middle of his attack on the French Revolution:

> A state without the means of change is without the means of its conservation. Without such means it might even risque the loss of that part of the constitution which it wished the most religiously to preserve.[20]

Change must not be based, though, on abstract rights or on a mechanical conception of society. Change must be *correction*. If a society begins to degenerate, or if it faces new circumstances, it must seek change that fits within the bounds of its traditions and that salvages the best of those conventions that are still healthy. Careful change will lead to **organic evolution**, which will not disrupt social stability. Careful maintenance and proper attention to any ills in society will prevent the need for more radical surgery. A body politic that practices preventive medicine can forego drastic medical interventions.

The corrective approach to change does not mean that every ailment deserves an immediate cure. Tampering with as complex an organism as society is always dangerous, and such tampering must employ prudence to make sure that the cure is not worse than the disease. Reform and change, claim traditional conservatives, too often replace existing social evils with other, potentially more dangerous, social evils.

Traditional conservatives have articulated three principles (or preferences)

[19]*Burke's Politics: Selected Writings and Speeches of Edmund Burke on Reform, Revolution and War*, edited by Ross J. Hoffman and Paul Levack (New York: Alfred A. Knopf, 1967), pp. 46–112.
[20]Burke, *Reflections on the Revolution in France*, p. 24.

in regard to change. First, there is a conservative preference to avoid change entirely. The past should be respected, and tradition should be revered. Change always entails a loss of the familiar, with no guarantee that the loss will be offset by new gains. The modern fascination for innovation, for the new, and for the ideal is not shared by traditional conservatives. Well-established routines, time-honored conventions, and familiar surroundings are imperative components of the proper environment for living the good life.

Second, changes that are necessary should be put into place gradually and should be aimed at solving limited and specific problems. Innovation should resemble growth in an organism, rather than wholesale remodeling of a machine. Change will always have unexpected costs and unanticipated consequences; thus, change must be gradual and contained so that if it does go awry, the costs will be limited and the consequences manageable.

Third, changes in the law should reflect changes in public opinion and understanding. Traditional conservatives oppose the use of law to try to change public views or to alter traditional behaviors. Laws should try to follow public norms rather than try to shape public norms. Traditional conservatives have not been sympathetic to feminism nor to "liberation" movements in general. They see such reforms as attempts to "engineer" a new society. Moreover, such reforms fail to acknowledge that differentiation and difference are necessary for the organic and unequal society traditional conservatives seek.

SUMMARY AND CONCLUSIONS

The twentieth century, of course, has not been a favorite century for traditional conservatives. This has been the case even in societies that have resisted socialist and fascist ideologies. Democratic values have encouraged a variety of reforms aimed at greater social equality. Furthermore, democracies in their quest for change have relied increasingly on bureaucracies to provide such change. Bureaucracies treat everyone the same, destroying the possibility for individual excellence. Even the art of war has become a science of killing, leading Winston Churchill to comment, "War, which used to be cruel and magnificent, has now become cruel and squalid."

Capitalism also undermines traditional conservative values, because it rewards innovation and provides opportunities for social mobility. Capitalism encourages a utilitarian perspective that robs the world of intrinsic worth and an egoism that shatters community life.

Liberalism has generated demands for laws designed to change cultural norms. Some liberal societies have passed laws and enforced court rulings that have protected minorities against majoritarian wishes *and* traditional norms. In the United States, the courts, much to the dismay of traditional conservatives, have been willing to make decisions that shape public norms and ignore traditional conventions.

In the face of these onslaughts on their values, twentieth-century traditional conservatives have advocated a personal commitment to a conservative temperament more than they have championed a systematic political agenda. Michael Oakeshott's description of this temperament reveals the distance between traditional conservatism and the other ideologies we will examine in this text:

> The man of conservative temperament believes that a known good is not lightly to be surrendered for an unknown better. He is not in love with what is dangerous and difficult; he is unadventurous; he has no impulse to sail uncharted seas; for him there is no magic in being lost, bewildered or shipwrecked. If he is forced to navigate the unknown, he sees virtue in heaving the lead every inch of the way. What others plausibly identify as timidity, he recognizes in himself as rational prudence; what others interpret as inactivity, he recognizes as a disposition to enjoy rather than to exploit. He is cautious, and he is disposed to indicate his assent or dissent, not in absolute, but in graduated terms. He eyes the situation in terms of its propensity to disrupt the familiarity of the features of his world.[21]

[21]Oakeshott, "On Being Conservative," pp. 172–173.

CHAPTER 4

Anarchism

Although anarchists are often regarded today as unprincipled terrorists, many adherents to anarchism have, on the contrary, held many principles that have attracted persons (like Henry David Thoreau, Leo Tolstoy, and Mohandas Gandhi) who have been deeply committed to justice, freedom and nonviolence. The following ideas are central to anarchism: It is possible for individuals to live freely, unconstrained by man-made laws; only natural constraints should limit human freedom. Most existing institutions—especially governments—repress human freedom; the displacement of such institutions is the most urgent political task. The new social order should be highly decentralized, voluntary, and communal. In such an order, the injustices that arise from traditional authority and the ownership of private property can be replaced by a new ethic of justice prompting individuals to treat each other with dignity and respect and to attend to the needs of one another.

The term "anarchism" is derived from the Greek word *"anarchos,"* which means "without a ruler." Thus, the central idea of anarchism is that it is possible for humans to live together in social communities which do not have any rulers or any governing institutions. Emma Goldman (1869–1940) provided the following definition of anarchism:

> *Anarchism* The philosophy of a new social order based on liberty unrestricted by man-made law; the theory that all forms of government rest on violence and are therefore wrong and harmful, as well as unnecessary.[1]

There are many precursors to anarchism in the history of political thought.[2] In ancient Greece, the Cynics disliked authority and espoused with-

[1]Emma Goldman, "Anarchism: What It Really Stands For," in *Anarchism and Other Essays* (New York: Dover Publications, 1969 [1911]), p. 50. Goldman was the most prominent of many women involved in the anarchist movement. See Margaret S. Marsh, *Anarchist Women, 1870–1920* (Philadelphia: Temple University Press, 1981).

[2]For a discussion of the precursors of anarchism, see George Woodcock, *Anarchism: A History of Libertarian Ideas and Movements* (Cleveland: World Publishing, 1962), pp. 37–59.

drawal from conventional political institutions. Renaissance philosophers exalted the individual and a natural social order. Various millenarian movements—like some Anabaptists—sought a communal existence while denouncing all earthly authority. And some classical liberals—like Thomas Paine—had a dislike and distrust of government approaching that entertained by anarchists. But such attitudes did not constitute a coherent anarchist ideology. People can exalt individual freedom and distrust government while still believing that some authority is nevertheless necessary to attain social order. Anarchists went beyond these attitudes and developed a coherent set of ideas that insist that social order is possible without any government authority.

Nevertheless, anarchism is not as systematic an ideology as classical liberalism or Marxism. Indeed, anarchists have libertarian attitudes that resist dogma and systematic theory. Persons having quite different political outlooks have been regarded as important contributors to anarchist thought. Thus, there is a highly individualistic strand of anarchism—exemplified in the writings of William Godwin (1756–1836) and Max Stirner (1806–1856), and there is a collectivist strand of anarchism—exemplified in the writings of Mikhail Bakunin (1814–1876) and Peter Kropotkin (1842–1921).[3] In this chapter, we look beyond some of the differences among anarchists and attempt to delineate a coherent general theory of anarchism based on the predominant assumptions and principles of those who are usually identified as anarchists.

The term "anarchism" first appeared in modern political thought during the French Revolution and was used to characterize disparagingly the *Enragés*, an unorganized but like-minded group of revolutionaries who rejected the structures of governmental authority developed by the Jacobins and who urged the development of communes (rather than democratic government) as the means of alleviating the suffering of the poor. At approximately the same time (in 1793), the first important anarchist treatise appeared—William Godwin's *Enquiry Concerning Political Justice.* But Godwin did not call himself an anarchist; indeed, he seemed to see his ideas as simply a logical extension, or radicalization, of the ideas of classical liberalism. It was not until 1840 that the term "anarchism" was proudly embraced by Pierre Proudhon (1809–1865), who recognized that the Greek word *"anarchos"* implied a deep criticism of authority without, at the same time, advocating disorder. For Proudhon, "Order is the genus: Government is the species,"[4] meaning that social order

[3]As Robert Booth Fowler points out in "The Anarchist Tradition of Political Thought" (*Western Political Quarterly*, Dec. 1973, p. 743), most analyses of anarchism have stressed the differences between individualist and collectivist anarchists, but other classification schemes for distinguishing among anarchists have been proposed. For example, James Joll emphasized the important difference between religious and rationalist anarchists in his study *The Anarchists* (New York: Grosset and Dunlop, 1964), p. 27. In his *In Defense of Anarchism* (New York: Harper and Row, 1970), Robert Paul Wolff distinguishes between his "philosophical anarchism" (which urges individuals to disobey government authority when its commands conflict with their own moral judgments) and political anarchism (which stresses actions aimed at destroying existing institutions).

[4]Proudhon, *The General Idea of the Revolution in the Nineteenth Century,* translated by John B. Robinson (New York: Haskell House Publishers, 1923 [1851]), p. 129.

could be attained in more ways than by government authority—indeed, governmental authority was perhaps the most ineffective and unjust means of attaining order. Nevertheless, most followers of Proudhon preferred to call themselves "mutualists," a term that implied that order could be attained, not by governmental authority, but by the mutual cooperation of free individuals. It was not until the 1870s that the term "anarchism" was fully embraced by followers of Mikhail Bakunin, who wished to distinguish themselves from Marxists. At the end of the nineteenth century, anarchists competed with Marxists for leadership in the revolutionary movements against liberalism and its institutions of capitalism and representative democracy. Although Marxist ideas have been more influential than those of anarchists throughout the twentieth century, anarchism is nevertheless an important political ideology.

Historically, anarchism has often provided the ideological impulse behind prominent social movements. On the European continent, at the end of the nineteenth century, anarchism was a significant force among the working class, as anarchists urged labor unions to go beyond the struggle for better wages and working conditions and to employ the "general strike" as a weapon for ultimately destroying capitalism and the state. In America, at the beginning of the twentieth century, the Wobblies (the Industrial Workers of the World) adopted many anarchist ideas and played a vital role in organizing

Sidebar 4-1

Some Contributors to Anarchism and Their Main Writings

William Godwin (1756–1836)
Enquiry Concerning Political Justice (1793)

Max Stirner (Johann Kaspar Schmidt) (1806–1856)
The Ego and His Own (1843)

Pierre Proudhon (1809–1865)
"What Is Property?" Or an Inquiry into the Principles of Right and Government (1840)
The General Idea of the Revolution in the Nineteenth Century (1851)

Alexander Herzen (1812–1870)
From the Other Shore (1850)

Mikhail Bakunin (1814–1876)
Statism and Anarchy (1874)

Henry David Thoreau (1817–1862)
On The Duty of Civil Disobedience (1849)
Walden or Life in the Woods (1854)

Leo Tolstoy (1828–1910)
The Kingdom of God Is within You (1905)

Peter Kropotkin (1842–1921)
Conquest of Bread (1892)
Memoirs of a Revolutionist (1899)
Mutual Aid: A Factor in Evolution (1907)

Emma Goldman (1869–1940)
"Anarchism: What It Really Stands For" (1911)

Paul Goodman (1911–   )
Communitas (1960)

Robert Paul Wolff
In Defense of Anarchism (1970)

Sidebar 4-2

The New Left on American Campuses During the 1960s

During the 1960s and early 1970s, the New Left was a prominent part of the intellectual and political climate of many American universities. Many current students have thus been raised by parents and are being taught by professors who were involved in or were sympathetic to the New Left. Although the New Left was a broad social movement, its organizational center was the Students for a Democratic Society (SDS), and its manifesto was the *Port Huron Statement,* written by Tom Hayden in 1962. While some ideas of the New Left were drawn from Marxism and democratic socialism, anarchistic ideas were especially prominent. Just as historical anarchists had done earlier, the New Left emphasized critical analyses and "negative thinking"; they sought to illuminate the problems of capitalism, militarism, and representative democracy; and they questioned the legitimacy of all authority, such as that of political leaders, the police, teachers, and parents. The goals of the New Left were largely to end perceived injustices—for example, to eliminate the practice of "in loco parentis" (where universities assumed such parental responsibilities over students as imposing curfews and regulating dormitory life); to reduce or eliminate racial discrimination; to abolish the military draft; and to end the Vietnam War. The intellectual gurus of the New Left, such as Herbert Marcuse (1898–1979) and Paul Goodman (1911–), spoke in anarchistic terms about the "total domination" of modern culture, economics, and government over the individual. The New Left urged students to "question authority," to criticize conventional ideas, and to experiment with alternative lifestyles and social arrangements. Some supporters of the New Left "dropped out" of conventional society and founded rural communes in which they could pursue more natural and simple lives. Some urged disruptive "direct action" tactics. Some engaged in violence. But, just as anarchists of the nineteenth century had done, the New Left (and its supporters) disagreed on the moral legitimacy of disruption or violence, and many preferred the "flower power" of the Hippies, who simply sought to show the possibility of a more liberated, equal, and communal life to those addicted to money, power, and status. Some scholars believe that the New Left faded because of its successes; when universities eliminated most student codes and when the draft and the Vietnam War ended, the New Left lost its most prominent issues. But others believe that the "anarchistic" disruptive and violent tactics associated with the movement "turned-off" many supporters and precipitated its decline.

miners, loggers, and other unskilled workers.[5] In Russia, anarchists played a significant role in the mass uprisings that destroyed the Provisional Government in 1917 and resisted the regime of "state capitalism" established by the Bolsheviks. Anarchists were a major force in the Spanish Civil War of 1934 to 1939, and succeeded in controlling much of eastern Spain for several years. In Italy and Germany, anarchists were adamant in their opposition to fascism and

[5]American radicalism may be more closely linked to the ideas of anarchists than to those of Marxists. See David de Leon, *The American Anarchist* (Baltimore: Johns Hopkins University Press, 1971).

nazism. Anarchists like Georges Bataille were involved in the French Resistance because they despised the Nazis' "thick" notion of the state, their cult of leadership and hierarchy, and their emaciated sense of citizen responsibility. During the 1960s and early 1970s, anarchist thought was prominent among the radical students of the "New Left" in both the United States and France. During the 1980s and 1990s, libertarian thought has drawn heavily upon the individualistic strand of anarchism.[6] In general, whenever there is widespread discontent with government and when cultural values stress the importance of unfettered individualism and voluntary associations, the principles of anarchism are attractive.

Anarchism is also important because it challenges the validity of almost every important political theory and the answers that other ideologies give to the great issues of politics. Why ask, What are the proper functions of governmental authority? if all governmental authority is illegitimate? Why ask, Who should rule? if no one should rule? Why ask, Why should citizens obey? if citizens should disobey? Unless we can reject anarchism's central idea that all states are illegitimate, we cannot go on to ask, What kinds of states are best?

THE POLITICAL BASES

Problems

Anarchism provides radical critiques of the prominent institutions and cultural values of modern society. Anarchists reject the idea that social problems are rooted in such natural limitations as scarcity of resources or in such human frailties as egotism or ignorance. Instead, anarchists contend that social problems are rooted in the institutions and values that constitute conventional society. Anarchists seek to eliminate these institutions and values in order that better—that is, more natural—institutions and values can emerge. According to Goldman, anarchism "is merely clearing the soil from weeds and sagebrush, that it may eventually bear healthy fruit."[7]

Conventional institutions unnecessarily coerce and dominate everyone. Religion is based on the idea that individuals are incapable of governing themselves and that they must submit to divine authority. By making God everything and demanding human subjugation to his will, religion dominates the human mind and humiliates and degrades the human soul.[8] Schools imprison the young, and teachers are the students' "oppressors and despots."[9] Rather than helping students become creative and critical—and thus, autonomous—thinkers, schools emphasize rote memory, demand conformity to dominant

[6]See, for example, Murray N. Rothbard, "Society without a State," in *Anarchism: Nomos XIX*, edited by J. Roland Pennock and John Chapman (New York: New York University Press, 1978).
[7]Goldman, *Anarchism and Other Essays*, p. 50.
[8]Goldman, *Anarchism and Other Essays*, p. 53
[9]Bakunin, *The Political Philosophy of Bakunin: Scientific Anarchism*, compiled and edited by G. P. Maximoff (New York: Free Press of Glencoe, 1953), p. 335.

cultural values and norms, and stress acceptance of the status quo. Because schools fix in our minds the errors of conventional society, people must unlearn a great deal before they can become wise.[10] Families are institutions of paternal authority and—especially for women anarchists—family life extends the oppression of women and forces women into roles of economic dependence.

Under capitalism, large-scale economic enterprises had emerged that make workers dependent on those who own and manage these enterprises, thus facilitating the exploitation of workers and providing them unfree, robotlike existences. Moreover, by stimulating people to want consumer goods (for example, through advertising), capitalists induce people to embrace their servitude, accepting long, arduous, and dirty toil to gain paltry wages in order to afford desired, but unneeded, products.

In the minds of most anarchists, the ownership of private property became a major problem with the development of capitalism. According to Proudhon, "**Property is robbery**."[11] While most anarchists find no fault in allowing workers to own the products of their own labor, they reject the accumulation of property by individuals when the value of that property has been enhanced by the labor of others. Anarchists recognize that most property has been given value by the contributions of many workers and that such property must be regarded as "social property" rather than private property. When individuals expropriate social property as their private property, they do so on the basis of their power or domination over others, not on any moral basis of right.

Most anarchists are highly critical of existing religious, educational, social, and economic institutions, and anarchists are united in their disdain for the state or government. Governments are instruments of violence and coercion, that force people to obey laws that are not of their making, that undermine peoples' true conscience, and that deprive people of their freedom. Governments inhibit moral progress. While moral responsibility is fostered when individuals act on the basis of their considered judgments about the course of action that produces superior goodness for everyone involved, governments force individuals to act on the basis of law. The laws that governments enforce through their coercive power generally uphold the domination of some people over others. Governmental power protects those who have illegitimately acquired property from those who have been denied property. For anarchists, the repressive institutions of government include the police, the judges, the prisons, and the guillotines (or other instruments of state-sanctioned execution).[12] The police engage in constant surveillance of our thoughts and actions. The courts convict innocent men of so-called crimes that violate the *property rights* of the rich, who use their property to exploit and enslave the average

[10]William Godwin, *Enquiry Concerning Political Justice* (Middlesex, England: Penguin Classics, 1985 [1793]), pp. 612–618.
[11]Proudhon, "What is Property?" translated by B. R. Tucker (London: William Reeves, n.d. [1840]).
[12]Witnessing a public execution by guillotine was apparently a defining moment in the emergence of Tolstoy's anarchism. See Woodcock, *Anarchism*, p. 224.

citizen. The prisons and guillotines deprive the innocent victims of a repressive society of their freedom and their lives. Moreover, governments are the instruments of war. It is through the coercive power of armies that one political community seeks to dominate other political communities.

The common problem with all of these conventional institutions is that they provide some people with the power and resources to dominate others. The unequal distribution of power is an ultimate source of social problems, because power enslaves, enrages, and degrades those who are subject to it.[13] All institutions that allow one person or group to dominate another are unnatural and unjust.

In addition to focusing on the problems of conventional institutions, anarchists point to the repressiveness of the entire culture of liberal societies. High society—encompassing fashion, cuisine, artistic display, and so forth—is particularly artificial; the ostentation of high society creates false senses of superiority (among those who participate in it) and inferiority (among those who don't). Liberal values—the need to obey laws, the emphasis on upward social mobility, and the equating of the accumulation of goods with the good life—surround the individual and entrap him. Even the most worthy of liberal ideals—such as democracy and equality—are external and abstract prescriptions that artificially constrict the internally generated feelings and judgments of people; they repress true self-expression.

All of these institutions and conventions create an enslaving environment, or "system of domination," in which the authentic, natural, and free individual cannot flourish. People are enslaved by the artificial power of institutions that demand conformity to conventional, rather than natural, life processes.

Goals

Anarchists do not provide a clearly defined blueprint for a future utopia because they recognize that many types of utopias can be envisioned and that humans will be better able to evaluate the goodness of alternative utopias in the future, once they have overcome their present prejudices and have come to know better their (evolving) needs and preferences. To adopt exhaustive plans for the future now would enslave humans. If humans are to be genuinely free, they must be free from the dogma of any preconceived utopia. For anarchists, moreover, the ideal society is not one that conforms to a fixed picture, but one that is in perpetual motion. The ideal society is one that is kept alive and changing by continual criticism of itself. The goals of anarchists must, therefore, be broadly and loosely defined.

According to Alexander Herzen (1812–1870), humans must "leap to the other shore."[14] The shore of our present, conventional existence is cluttered

[13]Goldman, "Anarchism: What It Really Stands For," p. 54.

[14]Alexander Herzen, *From the Other Shore,* translated by Moura Budberg (London: Weidenfeld and Nicolson, 1956). The articles in it were mostly written between 1848 and 1849, and the book first appeared (in German) in 1850.

with repressive institutions that deny human freedom, that fail to provide true social order, and that encourage humans to pursue false values. The other shore—that to which we must leap—is one that allows for individual liberty, that creates social order based on natural cooperation among individuals, and that encourages humans to embrace simple and natural lifestyles.

Anarchists cherish liberty in almost all its forms. Indeed, their conception of liberty is so broad and deep that some anarchists find existing conceptions of freedom to be inadequate expressions of their goals in this area. Max Stirner, for example, coined the term *"ownness"* to discuss the radical liberty sought by anarchists.[15] For Stirner, the individual should completely own himself and should use all his powers to make the world around him his own. Such a person is a truly authentic self. He is aware or conscious of his own true needs; what he wills is internally generated by his heart and soul, and no external force influences his will. Knowing his internally defined needs, he uses all the resources at his command to fulfil these needs. *Authenticity* is another term often used by anarchists to describe the kind of freedom they seek. Believing most people live unfree "lives of quiet desperation," Henry David Thoreau (1817–1862) urged that "everyone mind his own business, and endeavor to be what he was made."[16] According to these anarchists, being completely true to the feelings in one's heart and to one's inner voice and ignoring the demands and requirements of conventional society is essential to living an authentic and free life.

While other anarchists often regard such concepts as ownness and authenticity as antisocial, they nevertheless seek extensive individual freedom in many forms. First, they seek the negative liberty, or "freedom from hindrances," that classical liberals believe man possessed in the state of nature. Anarchists believe that classical liberals have too readily renounced such natural liberty by agreeing to obey the laws of government. Second, anarchists seek the "freedom to choose" the types of work they do, the places they live, the enjoyments they pursue, and the people with whom they associate. By calling for the "sovereignty of human choice,"[17] anarchists anticipated the demand for "positive liberty" of contemporary liberals. Third, anarchists seek **moral autonomy**. Believing that all humans possess the capacity to make rational and appropriate ethical judgments concerning their conduct and its effects on others, anarchists believe that no individual should surrender to any higher power—such as governmental authority—his capacity to develop his own moral code and make his own moral decisions on the basis of that code. Anarchists reject concerns that to provide individuals with such freedoms would undermine social order. They recognize natural constraints on freedom.

[15]Max Stirner, *The Ego and His Own,* translated by S. T. Bylington (London: Jonathan Cape, 1921 [1843]).

[16] Thoreau, *Walden or Life in the Woods* (New York: Collier, 1962 [1854]), p. 230. Because Thoreau often resigned himself to the necessity for limited role of government and its "inevitable functions," it is questionable whether he should be classified as a pure anarchist. Nevertheless, he articulated many principles, including authenticity, that anarchists embrace.

[17]Woodcock, *Anarchism,* p. 33.

Nature teaches humans living in free and equal association with each other that the freedoms and needs of others must be respected. Thus, anarchists do not call for complete freedom—or license—to do anything one wants. Individual choices must conform to those necessary constraints that nature imposes on humans who seek to live cooperatively with one another.

Anarchists thus seek to form **natural communities**. They believe that conventional communities have sought to achieve social order by limiting individual freedom, but that natural communities can achieve social order without endangering liberty. Anarchists agree that the organic communities championed by traditional conservatives deny individual liberty by demanding conformity to the guidance of conventional authority and tradition. Anarchists also agree that the civil societies championed by classical liberals are based on fictitious social contracts in which individuals are required to renounce their liberties in order to secure a false sense of security provided by governmental authority. Such conservative and liberal communities are counterfeit. The security they provide is insubstantial, because it is imposed on individuals who will skirt the decrees and laws of such authority when they think their unruly acts will remain undetected. Crime and strife characterize communities whose order is governmentally imposed. In contrast, real order can occur among individuals whose associations are based on genuine mutuality. When individuals freely choose to associate with each other, when they agree among themselve to respect one another's liberties and needs, when community and social order are based on a series of continual, bilateral face-to-face understandings rather than on a tacit social contract, then individuals share a genuine and natural sense of community, and they are least likely to harm one another. Thus, rather than seeking disorder and chaos, anarchists seek a much more deeply rooted and more natural community than conventional societies provide.

Finally, anarchists champion simpler and more natural lifestyles than conventional societies promote. Some commentators have found a "**cult of the primitive**" among anarchists.[18] Anarchists often contrast simple, natural rural life with complex, conventional urban life. They admire peasants, who live simply and peacefully. Anarchists often have an ascetic attitude that sees little value in acquiring material luxuries. While Marxists regard the unequal distribution of wealth as a problem but generally aspire to a society where everyone has access to wealth, anarchists see wealth—or at least excessive wealth—as a problem for everyone. The wealthy are victims of their own state of luxury because they become enslaved by their material goods and the need to maintain these goods. Thoreau exemplified the anarchist's attitude toward abandoning luxury by the simple and natural life he chose to live at Walden Pond. For Thoreau, an individual was most free when he dispensed with all unnecessary material possessions. Proudhon, too, urged living in comparative poverty and having only one's minimal needs satisfied. When we live simply, we free ourselves from the bondage of satisfying our sensual pleasures and

[18]Woodcock, *Anarchism*, p. 190.

appetites and are able to spiritualize our lives.[19] When Kropotkin asked for more luxury for the working class, he was not asking for more material goods, but for the leisure to pursue the more spiritually fulfilling delights provided by art, science, and philosophy.

THE PHILOSOPHICAL BASES

Ontology

Like classical liberals, anarchists believe that the natural world is ultimate reality. However, anarchists believe that liberals have misunderstood the natural world. While liberals equate the natural world with material reality, anarchists view nature in much broader terms. God, the earth, the plants and animals that live on the earth, energy, social life, and simple values are all natural and, thus, important aspects of reality.

While God does not play a central role in the ontology of most anarchists, the God of such religious anarchists as Tolstoy is a natural, rather than supernatural, God. Tolstoy's God does not reside outside of humans or nature but rather resides within all living beings. Such a **pantheistic** God does not control nature or dominate human beings, he is a vital natural force within humans connecting man to man and man to nature. Such a natural force means that the consciousness of each person is but part of a larger collective consciousness.

The earth and all life on earth is not simply matter, but an interplay of matter and energy, and matter and energy obey certain *natural laws,* such as the laws of thermodynamics. The laws of thermodynamics maintain, for example, that matter and energy can neither be created nor destroyed, but only transformed, and that all transformations consume matter and energy in a process called "entropy." While liberals have suggested that humans can endlessly exploit nature because of its unlimited bounty and that material progress could thus continue indefinitely, anarchists understand that the laws of nature impose restraints on humans. Humans can try to defy natural constraints by developing energy-consuming technologies to produce material affluence, but in the long run, limited resources and energy must overwhelm man in his struggle with nature and require humans to live simply, within the limits imposed by natural laws.

Nature also provides for social life. By creating a fictitious state of nature that portrays human beings as completely solitary animals and society as nonexistent, liberals have underestimated the social qualities of human beings and the possibility of a natural society. Anarchists maintain that if one looks at humans in nature, and outside of conventional society, it is clear that humans are not just a bundle of atoms pursuing their self-interest, but are also fundamentally social beings. If one looks at natural human interactions, when

[19]Woodcock, *Anarchism,* p. 28.

these actions are unconstrained by conventional authority and institutions, there can be little doubt about the existence of natural societies—societies in which individuals cooperate and help each other because of instinctual fellow feeling.[20]

In general, anarchists believe that human ideas (values and beliefs) are derived from the external environment. Ideas can be natural—if they are derived from a natural environment, or they can be artificial—if they are derived from conventional sources. Many human values and beliefs—such as the inherent desirability of material progress or the need for governmental authority—arise from convention and are rooted in the interests of those people who dominate conventional institutions. But other ideas—such as the need to respect the freedom of others and the desirability of living a simple life uncluttered by material luxuries—arise from natural instincts and rational reflection concerning natural processes. Conventional ideas are not part of ultimate reality, because they are mere reflections of artificial power relations. But *natural ideas* are an independent aspect of ultimate reality, because they exist outside of the material world and conventional society and because they can have an independent impact on the course of history.

According to Alexander Herzen, "life does not try to reach an aim," but allows for many possibilities.[21] The historical process is marked by conflict, as humans struggle against such natural forces as drought and disease, against other animals, and against each other. The outcomes of these struggles are not predetermined by natural laws. Contrary to Herbert Spencer's view that the strongest necessarily survive the struggle for existence, anarchists maintain that the characteristics of sociability or solidarity are positive resources in historical struggles. In the struggle for existence among species, humans have survived, not because they are strong, but because they have practiced cooperation or mutual aid—for example, by providing food and safety to one another and by helping one another raise progeny.[22] But if social cooperation fades, humans can lose in their struggles against nature and other species.

Anarchists also recognize struggle between humans. They believe that a desire for material accumulation and private property among some people is at the root of human conflict. To protect their wealth, the rich created institutions of domination—such as governments, industrial corporations, and churches. But such institutions offend and suppress the desire for liberty and sociability that exists naturally in human beings. The natural spark of freedom in each human leads the oppressed to struggle against domination, and the natural spark toward sociability leads humans to band together for collective action against their oppressors. Thus, struggles between the oppressors and the oppressed characterize the course of history. Whether the oppressors or the oppressed win a given struggle is indeterminate. But natural ideas, such

[20]Peter Kropotkin, *Mutual Aid: A Factor in Evolution* (New York: New York University Press, 1972 [1907]).
[21]Herzen, *From the Other Shore,* p. 107.
[22]Kropotkin, *Mutual Aid,* pp. 81–82.

as the desire for liberty, are potent, and they can enable the oppressed to succeed in destroying the institutions of domination. When this occurs, destruction is natural and good. It enables humans to be liberated from their oppression and permits natural social instincts to flower and natural society to emerge.

Human Nature

Anarchists accept many liberal assumptions about human nature. They believe, for example, that each person seeks liberty, that all people have the capacity to reason, and that all humans are equally worthy of respect and dignity. However, they regard as inadequate the liberal assumption that humans are self-regarding utility maximizers.

In general, anarchists maintain that two diametrically opposed impulses coexist in natural man. Herzen asserts, for example, that man is both an egoist and a social animal: "Kill the social sense in man—and you get a savage orangutan; kill egoism in him and he will become a tame monkey."[23] Goldman perceives both individual and social instincts in humans—"The one a most potent factor for individual endeavor, for growth, aspiration, self-realization; the other an equally potent factor for mutual helpfulness and social well-being."[24] In short, humans have both a self-interested impulse to subdue others for individual purposes and an impulse to help others. By stressing only the self-interested impulse in humanity, liberals miss the often-unconscious instinct within humans to recognize that their own happiness and well-being is dependent on the happiness and well-being of others. Peter Kropotkin is the anarchist who has most thoroughly documented this more altruistic impulse within humans (and other animals).[25] Calling this impulse **mutual aid**, he argued that it consists of more than feelings of love or sympathy toward others; it is an instinct in man that makes him respond automatically to cries for help.[26] When others are in danger, humans often risk their well-being to help them. When others suffer, humans often sacrifice some of their pleasures to aid them.

While anarchists recognize the existence of this altruistic impulse within humans, they also understand that it can be suppressed. When we are subjected to repressive conditions (like great poverty) and institutions (like government and capitalism), our selfish, antisocial instincts come to the fore. Because humans have most often lived under repressive conditions, the selfish side of human nature has been abundantly evident. As Emma Goldman asks, "When human nature is caged in a narrow space, and whipped into daily

[23]Herzen, *From the Other Shore,* pp. 139–140.

[24]Goldman, "Anarchism: What It Really Stands For," p. 51.

[25]Kropotkin, *Mutual Aid,* pp. 194–251.

[26]Other anarchists employ concepts about human altruism that are consistent with Kropotkin's concept of mutual aid. For example, Proudhon claimed that humans have an immanent sense of justice that involves aiding others in need. Tolstoy maintained that humans are motivated by Christian love.

submission, how can we speak of its potentiality?"[27] Kropotkin's investigations of the mutual aid instinct were particularly important because he showed that altruism thrived under more natural conditions. According to Kropotkin, "savages" living in a natural condition were not the self-interested aggressors depicted by Hobbes; instead savages practiced the motto "each for all." While historians have emphasized the rampages that sometimes occurred among barbarian tribes in times of great distress, they have ignored the solidarity that existed among such people in normal times. In the Middle Ages, people treated each other as brothers and sisters within decentralized guilds.[28]

According to anarchists, environmental conditions also shape other human characteristics. For example, humans sometimes appear to be lazy and unproductive, but such qualities are not inherent in humans but are, rather, the result of large-scale capitalist institutions that provide dreary work environments from which people seek to escape. In other environments, humans find satisfaction in creative work that is freely done under pleasant circumstances and that results in socially useful products.[29] Humans can also appear ignorant and unreasonable, but these qualities, too, are a result of living in an antisocial environment. The intellectual facilities of humans are strengthened when humans live in cooperative natural societies, because intelligence is developed and communicated by language (the most social of all human inventions) and it is enhanced by the accumulated experiences of one's fellow humans.

Thus, anarchists stress **human malleability**. If conditions are oppressive, the dark side of human nature will prevail. If conditions are natural and humane, the tendency of humans to exhibit mutual aid and to act justly will prevail. This does not mean that humans can be made perfect by natural conditions. But when oppressive conditions are overcome, humans can continuously improve toward perfection. Humanity's worst instincts may never disappear entirely, but they can be overshadowed by our better impulses.

Society

Anarchists reject the organic conception of society of traditional conservatives. Rather than believing that organic societies exist prior to the individuals who live within them, anarchists believe that societies emerge from the interactions of individuals. Rather than believing that individuals should conform to the traditions of such societies, anarchists believe that individuals should challenge social conventions.

Anarchists are closer to classical liberals in their assumptions about society. Like liberals, they believe that societies arise out of agreements among

[27]Goldman, "Anarchism: What It Really Stands For," p. 62.

[28]Kropotkin, *Mutual Aid*, pp. 83–193.

[29]Woodcock, *Anarchism*, p. 206. Anarchists, like Marxists, were attracted to Charles Fourier's idea that all humans find some work naturally enjoyable. Fourier was an influential "utopian socialist" during the first half of the nineteenth century. His ideas are available in Jonathan Beecher and Richard Bienvenu, *The Utopian Vision of Charles Fourier* (Boston: Beacon Press, 1971).

individuals to cooperate with and to assist one another. But anarchists reject the liberal idea that these agreements constitute a social contract to create a political society providing security through government. Such political societies are artificial because they are based on the myth of each individual's consenting to give up his or her natural liberties to attain the spurious benefits of governments. In order to entice rational individuals to enter into a social contract, liberals have depicted a state of nature that is much more conflictive and hostile than anarchists believe the natural condition of humanity to be. If people are naturally social and must seldom be restrained, the need for individuals to give up their liberty to attain security is much less defensible.

While political society is artificial, other small-scale, face-to-face voluntary societies are natural. Indeed, when artificial, centralized political societies are abolished, people will be more inclined to develop decentralized natural societies. According to Herzen, the glue that holds natural societies together is people's need for the support and assistance of one another. Left to himself or herself, each person will discover whom to love, whom to befriend, and with whom to associate.[30] A natural community (or, natural society) is one in which individuals agree, through a continual series of face-to-face encounters, to respect and to help each other. From these encounters arise norms of reciprocity and habits of sociability that are impressed into the consciousness of individuals. These norms and understandings may be augmented by a common religion, leading to the kind of religious, anarchist society envisioned by Leo Tolstoy. They may also be augmented by socialist values, leading to the type of communist, anarchist society envisioned by Peter Kropotkin. Or these norms and understanding may be little more than the recognition that others are equally self-contained individuals whose solitude and personal liberties must be respected, leading to the kind of egoist society envisioned by Max Stirner. In other words, natural societies may exhibit great solidarity (with extensive provisions for mutual assistance) or great individualism (with minimal provisions for mutual assistance), depending on the particular norms and habits of the individuals that freely constitute them.

In summary, natural societies are fundamentally different from conventional (or civil) societies, which are regulated by law and political authority. Conventional societies are ordered by coercion, while natural societies are ordered by common understandings of mutuality or communal interests. Anarchists believe that people have moral urges—both in their instinctual tendency toward mutual aid and through customs that reinforce sociability—that are strong enough to hold natural societies together in the absence of conventional authority and law.

Epistemology

The epistemological basis of anarchism is less developed and less uniform than that of the other leading ideologies of the nineteenth century. We have seen

[30]Herzen, *From the Other Shore,* p. 139.

that classical liberalism is built on a deductive Cartesian science, and in the next chapter we shall see that Marxism is built on inductive sciences regarding the laws of history and the political economy. Anarchism, however, does not have such a "scientific" basis. When G. P. Maximoff published a book called *The Political Philosophy of Bakunin: Scientific Anarchism,* a leading student of Bakunin objected, "There is no such thing as *'scientific' anarchism.*"[31] Indeed, many anarchists reject the desirability of creating a science of anarchism, for all sciences involve highly authoritative and constricted intellectual frameworks.[32] Anarchists do not want modes of inquiry and understanding restricted to a single scientific mode or to a dogmatic theory. Some anarchists even reject the very idea of truth—whether truth be based on science or any other epistemological foundation. For Stirner, belief in any truth is confining, because it makes the individual a servant to such "truths." An anarchist prefers to be a thinker of his own thoughts rather than a believer in the thoughts contained within some external intellectual system.[33]

Traditional conservatives, of course, have also rejected the idea of a science of politics, but they believe that the traditions of each society contain collective wisdom that is superior to scientific truths as guidelines for governance. Claiming that traditions merely reflect the interests of those with predominant power in society, anarchists reject the validity of such traditions as the basis for thinking about the good society and the good state.

Rather than basing their political principles on traditions or on science, anarchists base their ideas on a vision of how humans could live in a natural world, unconstrained by existing institutions. For anarchists, truth about the good society was based on

> . . . their vision of the rule of nature. The rediscovery of nature might be immensely difficult to accomplish, but they refused to waver in their hopes, and they constructed their faith on three propositions about nature: the possibility of discerning its truths; that nature was good; and that eventually every soul could know and follow nature.[34]

In attempting to discern the truths of nature, Kropotkin employed the methods of empirical science. As indicated earlier, his scientific investigations provided evidence for the existence of an instinct for mutual aid in more natural circumstances. Moreover, Kropotkin proposed that "science be devoted to considering the means by which the needs of all may be reconciled and satisfied."[35] Thus, scientific studies could both support certain anarchist assumptions and serve anarchist goals, but such studies did not make anarchism scientific. In contrast to the "scientific socialism" of Marx and Engels, anarchists

[31]Sam Dolgoff, *Bakunin on Authority* (New York: Alfred A. Knopf, 1972), p. ix.

[32]Some contemporary political theorists insist that scientific and positivist modes of inquiry unnecessarily restrict political thought. See, for example, Henry Kariel, "Creating Political Reality," *American Political Science Review* 64 (Dec. 1970).

[33]Stirner, *The Ego and His Own.*

[34]Fowler, "The Anarchist Tradition," p. 748.

[35]Woodcock, *Anarchism,* p. 204.

have not conducted careful empirical studies of the capitalist economy or of government, nor have they proposed scientific laws of historical development predicting the emergence of anarchism. For anarchists, the deficiencies of capitalism and government are clear, and the emergence of anarchism depends much more on human will and action than on the predictions of any scientific theory.

In attempting to provide principles about how people ought to act in relationship to one another in a natural society, anarchists in general—and Godwin, in particular—emphasized the role of reason. Godwin believed that nature provided a standard for eternal truth regarding moral conduct—for example, that nature commands everyone to act in such a way as to produce the public good. He also believed that if people employ their reason and deliberate among themselves, they will readily agree on the principles of right and wrong conduct. For example, Godwin believed that people would agree, after rational deliberation, that material goods be given to those who would most benefit from having them.[36] Thus, for anarchists, reason plays a major role in providing principles of justice and morality.

Despite the attention that anarchists have given to both science and rationality, their belief in the possibility of an orderly society without governmental authority is ultimately based on a particular vision of human nature and natural society. While science and rationality cannot show the truth of this vision, the vision is neither contrary to scientific evidence nor unreasonable. The idea that conventional institutions suppress the instinct for mutual aid is a reasonable hypothesis for which there is some scientific evidence. The idea that people can live orderly and secure lives free of government control is another reasonable hypothesis for which there is historical evidence. Anarchists believe that the evils of existing institutions are sufficiently evident to warrant abolishing these institutions in order to test more fully the hypothesis that a natural society provides more liberty, equality, and social harmony than do conventional societies.

SUBSTANTIVE POLITICAL PRINCIPLES

Change

Because of the radical hostility of anarchists toward the status quo—because they seek the destruction of most existing institutions and a major transformation of human values—anarchism is usually regarded as a revolutionary ideology. Nevertheless, anarchists sometimes claim that they are committed to **rebellion** rather than revolution. From this perspective, revolutionary change involves the destruction of old institutions and their replacement with new institutions. Revolution can consist of turning things around by replacing one state with another one. In contrast, "rebellion" means placing oneself in radi-

[36]Godwin, *Political Justice*, pp. 168–177.

cal opposition to existing institutions. Rebels refuse to obey conventional authority. Rebels seek the destruction of conventional modes of domination, without any provision for their replacement.

From the anarchist perspective, Marxists mistakenly seek revolution. Bakunin criticized Marx for supporting a revolution in which the working class would conquer the state rather than destroy it. As we shall see in the next chapter, Marx thought that the proletariat must seize the state's power during the revolution and use the coercive capacities of this power during a transitional period of undetermined duration. During this transitional period, the (now proletariat-controlled) state would abolish capitalism and nurture the development of an anarchistic society. Anarchists generally—and Bakunin, in particular—rejected such a scenario. Bakunin believed that the leaders of the new proletarian state would become corrupt and use state authority for their own purposes. If the apparatuses and power of the state were merely conquered rather than destroyed, the new authorities would refuse to relinquish their power even when the state had become unnecessary.[37] Anarchists thus insist that when the old state is destroyed, anarchistic arrangements involving a natural society without government must spring immediately into the void.[38] In other words, anarchists seek to destroy all organizations that control society from above—such as centralized governments and large-scale economic enterprises—so that free associations, organized from below, can arise.

Anarchists generally agree that rebellion should involve four characteristics. First, they believe that participation in the rebellion against conventional institutions must be *voluntary.* Instead of conceiving of rebellion as a mass action in which individuals are swept away by historical circumstances or are caught up in mob behavior, anarchists regard rebellion as a conscious act by each individual. Each rebel must *choose* to rebel, because each is, ultimately, morally responsible for his or her acts. Second, anarchists believe that rebellion must, consequently, be *spontaneous.* While Marxists believe that a revolution can be led by "a vanguard" that recognizes the moment when conditions are ripe for a successful revolution and that can organize the masses, anarchists reject the "claim that even the most intelligent and best-intentioned group of individuals will be capable of becoming the mind, soul and guiding and unifying will of the revolutionary movement."[39] In order for rebellion to occur voluntarily and spontaneously, anarchists perceive the need for a long period of preparation in which the desirability of destroying the old institutions is deeply etched into the consciousness of humanity.

Third, anarchists often insist that only *total* rebellions can be effective. The

[37]Bakunin, "Letter to La Liberte," in *Bakunin on Authority,* edited by Sam Dolgoff. Bakunin's criticisms of Marx were published in 1872, while Bakunin and Marx struggled for leadership of the First International Workingmen's Association.

[38]Before the split between anarchists and Marxists in the 1870s, there were some anarchists who thought that a minimal government might be appropriate following the destruction of the old state. For example, Proudhon urged anarchists to make temporary use of the state because it would remain the "mainspring of society" following a revolution.

[39]Bakunin, "Letter to La Liberte," p. 275.

French Revolution and the various uprisings in Europe in 1848 had taught anarchists that changes in government without broader social changes are of little lasting significance. In addition to destroying the old political regime, anarchists seek to overturn the existing economic system, the authority of established churches (and other such institutions), and those cultural values that promote materialism, selfishness, and the sanctioned dominance of some people over others. A total rebellion involves destroying simultaneously all conventional institutions and cultural values that allow some people to dominate others.

Fourth, anarchists maintain that once revolutionary activity begins, it should be rapidly pursued on an *international* scale. If an anarchistic society were established, it would be vulnerable to violence used against it by other states, because an anarchistic society is without the military means of defending itself. Thus, to be successful, all coercive institutions—especially all national governments—must be rapidly abolished throughout the world.

While agreeing upon these aspects of a successful rebellion, anarchists disagree about the role of *violence*. Godwin and Tolstoy were committed to nonviolence, judging acts of revolutionary violence to be as coercive as the violence of governments. Godwin claimed that force was no substitute for reason and that rebels should exhaust all means of moral persuasion before considering violence. Tolstoy also urged rebels to use reason to persuade others of the validity of anarchist views, but he urged passive resistance against authority—refusal to accept military service or pay taxes—as an appropriate method of persuasion.

Other anarchists (e.g., Bakunin) believe that violence is a necessary, if undesirable, means of resisting authority. Even the gentle Kropotkin reluctantly endorsed violence as unavoidable at certain stages in the progress of human history. Anarchists differentiate among various forms of violence and provide several justifications for specific types of violence. Sabotage and strikes can be regarded as violence against property; since capitalist claims to property are illegitimate, acts that destroy property or disrupt its employment are not unjust. Political assassinations and acts of violence that result in death to innocent people raise more difficult moral issues, because of the inherent worth of all life. But such violence can sometimes be justified, according to anarchists, if the good that results from such violence outweighs the evil. If the target of an assassination practices policies that instill terror, violence, and death on many citizens, then is not the murder of that person justified?

In general, anarchists point to several justifications for employing violence. First, employing violence may be an act of liberation for those who have long been dominated by their oppressors; by taking up arms, the oppressed can simultaneously shed their shackles and perform acts of courage and self-realization. Second, confronting oppressors through violence polarizes conflict, provoking the oppressors to overreact and use much more violence than was originally used by the rebels. Such overreactions by the oppressors often prompt uncommitted members of the public to recoil at the excesses of authorities and to side with the rebels. Third, violent destruction must simply be understood as part of a continual natural process of death and rebirth. Violence is a necessary part of the process of renewal in the natural world.

In sum, dismantling conventional institutions—whether by nonviolent or violent means—is the principal goal of anarchists. Because governments, inherently, are particularly coercive, it is important to examine more closely the anarchist arguments that there should be no political rulers and that all governmental authority is illegitimate.

Rulers

Anarchists criticize both conventional governments (such as those ruled by monarchs, aristocrats, and capitalists) and revolutionary governments (such as those ruled by a "dictatorship of the proletariat"), because all such governments create systems of rulers and the ruled, and anarchists refuse to be ruled. Proudhon captured this anarchistic sentiment when he proclaimed, "Whoever puts his hand on me to govern me is a usurper and a tyrant; I declare him my enemy."[40]

But what about democratic governments? At least ideally, democracy is a system of government in which the people rule themselves. Indeed, early anarchists like Godwin argued that democracy is superior to other forms of government, because under its ideal form every man is considered an equal and because democratic participation helps develop fellow feeling among citizens.[41] Nevertheless, subsequent anarchists stressed that even democratic governments are coercive. Even in ideal democracies where all citizens participate in making laws, the people as a collective body rule, and their laws restrict individual liberty.

Anarchists insist that each person must rule himself or herself. To be free, each person should only obey those laws of his or her own making. Two aspects of democracy undermine this imperative. First, most democracies employ representatives rather than providing for direct participation by citizens. Whenever representatives vote or enact legislation contrary to the will of their constituents, the policies or laws no longer reflect the will of the people. Yet, in representative democracy, citizens must obey even those laws that are contrary to their will. Second, most democracies employ "majority rule" in reaching decisions. This means that all those who are in the minority are ruled by those in the majority; the minority must obey laws that are not of their making. Thus, the only kind of democracy that is consistent with the anarchist principle that each person must rule himself or herself is **unanimous direct democracy**.[42] Anarchists recognize that only very small, face-to-face communities would have the ability to allow everyone to participate directly in decision making and would be likely to be successful in unanimously resolving each issue.

[40]Quoted in Woodcock, *Anarchism*, p. 34.
[41]Woodcock, *Anarchism*, p. 81.
[42]Robert Paul Wolff, *In Defense of Anarchism*, pp. 21–67.

Authority

Governments normally claim that their authority is legitimate because order and security for citizens depend on their laws and their coercive capacity to punish those criminals who violate their laws. Anarchists offer three main arguments against this claim.

First, anarchists claim that governmental laws normally favor the property rights and liberties of the rich and powerful against the needs of the poor and powerless. By protecting the oppressors from the oppressed, governmental laws make criminals of those who are victims of conventional society. According to Kropotkin:

> Three-quarters of all the acts which are brought before our courts every year have their origin, either directly or indirectly, in the present disorganized state of society with regard to the production and distribution of wealth—not in the perversity of human nature.[43]

Rather than protecting society from criminals, governmental laws force those who have been exploited by society to engage in "crimes" in order to fulfill their basic needs. If society produced the goods that were needed—rather than being organized to produce the frivolous luxuries consumed by the rich at the expense of necessary production—and if society distributed these goods in a way that reflected the efforts and needs of those who have been exploited, most crime would disappear.[44]

Second, anarchists argue that creating governments to enact laws and punish lawbreakers promotes struggles for power within societies and thus only increases social disorder. Social systems that are based on governmental laws must empower certain people—and only certain people. History shows that people will engage in great cruelty to and violence against others to become so empowered. In short, more disorder is injected into society by the struggle to secure governmental authority than is removed from society by the government in fulfilling its role of providing security.

Third, anarchists assert that governmental laws lead, in the long run, to the moral depravity of citizens and that "demoralized" citizens cannot achieve a well-ordered society. Anarchists claim that, as governmental laws become the codes of conduct in a society, individuals become less governed by moral principles. Their motivation to obey governmental laws is to avoid being punished by the state; with such motivations, individuals often violate the rights of others when they think they can do so without being detected by state authorities. More generally, when individuals believe that the state's laws define right conduct, they are unlikely to exercise their own moral judgment

[43]Peter Kropotkin, "Anarchist Communism: Its Basis and Principles," in *Revolutionary Pamphlets* (New York: Vanguard Press, 1927), pp. 68–75.

[44]Governments also fail to curb "crimes of passion," because such crimes are essentially irrational. If one person is about to beat or murder another in a fit of anger, he is unlikely to think about the punishment he will suffer at the hands of the state and be deterred by the threat of such punishment.

about what is right. But the laws of government often are unjust or are silent on issues involving moral judgment, thus providing inadequate moral guidance. When people rely on governmental laws rather than on developing and adhering to their own moral code, they are likely to perpetuate the injustices of government and to act on the basis of personal expedience, rather than in accordance with the needs of others.

The idea that governmental authority is illegitimate because it undermines human moral development has long been part of anarchist ideology, but the reason this is so has never been stated so succinctly and clearly as by Robert Paul Wolff in his *In Defense of Anarchism.* According to Wolff, there is an irreconcilable **conflict between authority and autonomy**. "Authority is the right to command, and correlatively, the right to be obeyed,"[45] and political theorists have produced many (spurious) justifications of the state's authority to issue commands and right to be obeyed. Traditional conservatives argue that obedience to the superior wisdom and virtue of those in authority produces a stable and harmonious community. Classical liberals created the idea of a social contract in which citizens grant authority to governmental leaders in return for receiving various benefits from government, such as security of their lives and property. According to Wolff, such justifications fail to address the central idea of moral philosophy: each individual must be morally autonomous. Moral autonomy is a combination of freedom and responsibility.[46] Because humans have free will, they possess the capacity to choose how to act. Because humans are endowed with reason, they possess the capacity to make responsible choices based on "a process of reflection, investigation, and deliberation about how [they] ought to act."[47] Given their intrinsic moral autonomy, humans should not simply obey authority. Yet governments constantly issue commands with which morally autonomous people disagree. Governments spend tax money for programs that some individuals conclude are morally wrong. Governments prohibit actions (such as euthanasia) that some individuals regard as morally right. Governments engage in wars or other acts of violence that some individuals believe are unjustified.[48] Given such irreconcilable conflicts between governmental authority and individual autonomy, individuals must assert their autonomy and reject governmental authority. If humans simply obey the commands of government, they forfeit the exercise of those aspects of autonomy—their free will and their capacity for moral reflection—that define their humanity.

Anarchists thus reject government authority, claiming that the only legitimate authority is that which stems naturally from society. In this regard, anarchists often distinguish between the written laws of government and the unwritten laws of society. While governmental laws are tools of domination

[45] Wolff, *In Defense of Anarchism,* p. 4.
[46] Wolff, *In Defense of Anarchism,* p. 14.
[47] Wolff, *In Defense of Anarchism,* p. 13.
[48] The classical statement of these difficulties remains Henry David Thoreau's *On the Duty of Civil Disobedience* (New York: Collier, 1962 [1849]), written to protest his arrest for failing to pay taxes which supported the Mexican-American War.

Sidebar 4-3

The Anarchism of Primitive Societies

Anarchists often point to primitive societies as evidence of the possibility of humans living securely in communities without being coerced by governmental authority. Rousseau's depiction of "the noble savage" in his *Second Discourse* prompted various anarchists to examine social life among primitive peoples untouched by the institutions and values of civilization. Rousseau rejected the common understanding that such savages lived a miserable existence. Not only did the savage enjoy great freedom, but his physical needs were easily satisfied. Moreover, the natural compassion that the savage had for others "takes the place of laws, morals, and virtue, with the advantage that no one is tempted to disobey its gentle voice." When he published *Mutual Aid* in 1907, Peter Kropotkin drew upon emerging anthropological evidence to show that some of Rousseau's speculations about the noble savage were valid. Such evidence indicated, for example, that the Fuegian tribes (on the coast of Denmark) lived peacefully together, that the Bushmen (in southwest Africa) "used to hunt in common and divided the spoil without quarreling, that they never abandoned their wounded and displayed strong affection to their comrades," and that, in general, the behavior of primitive folk is "regulated by an infinite series of unwritten rules of propriety which are the fruit of their common experience as to what is good or bad—that is, beneficial or harmful for their own tribe."* More recently, some contemporary anthropologists, such as Marshall Sahlins, have suggested that, during the Stone Age, humans lived by an ethic of sharing and mutuality, made decisions by consensus, and lived in deep communion with their fellows, their surroundings, and ultimately, the cosmos.

Consequently, critics of anarchism have had to address the possible attractiveness of primitive societies without government. For example, Robert Dahl acknowledges in *Democracy and Its Critics* that the Inuit (Eskimo) in northern Canada "achieved a tolerable existence, perhaps even a highly satisfactory life, without a state."† But Dahl gives three reasons for doubting that modern people can go back to primitive society. First, primitive peoples have been relatively few in number and these comparatively small communities have occupied vast areas, but most of the world is now densely populated and requires a much more complex regulation of people in order to prevent their infringement on each other. Second, primitive people have lived relatively solitary lives, but the lives of modern people involve "a multiplicity of interdependencies." Such interdependencies have produced many blessings that few people would be willing to abandon, but these interdependencies would be "snapped apart" without governmental regulations. Third, existing states would most likely conquer and absorb any people who attempted to return to small, autonomous, stateless groups. Indeed, in the modern world there is a high probability that any people who tried to live without a legitimate government would come to be dominated by a "small gang of wrongdoers" who would, in effect, use coercion to create a "gangster state."

*Peter Kropotkin, *Mutual Aid: A Factor in Evolution* (New York: New York University Press, 1972 [1907]), p. 110.

†Robert Dahl, *Democracy and Its Critics* (New Haven: Yale University Press, 1989), pp. 44–47.

by oppressors, **social laws** are those norms of a society that support social harmony. While governmental laws are enforced by coercion, social laws are supported by much more gentle social pressures from other members of society. While governmental laws are incompatible with moral autonomy, social laws help guide individuals in making right moral choices. By recognizing that individuals can be guided by social laws, anarchists provide a glimpse of how they would structure society to provide social order without governmental authority.

Structure

Anarchists believe that conventional social structures must be abolished so that natural structures can emerge in their place. Anarchists have been unwilling to provide precise designs of these natural structures, because they understand that people envision different utopian structures or are unsure what utopia should be like. Only by creating a set of structures and seeing how they work in practice will it be possible to know how well various structures provide liberty, order, mutual respect, and other values that are part of people's various conceptions of the good life.[49] Nevertheless, the social structures that would be acceptable to anarchists will clearly contrast with conventional structures in the following ways.

Centralism must be replaced by **decentralism**. Centralized states (and other institutions) have been organized from above, and they contain vertical relationships of authority in which those at the top issue commands that those below must obey. In contrast, decentralized institutions are organized laterally, and they contain horizontal relationships in which all members of the organization have equal power. Although different people may have different roles and responsibilities, they are neither in permanent positions of authority nor in permanent positions of subordination.

Large organizations must be replaced by small ones. The nation-state should be abolished, and replaced by primary social units that are *local*. Insofar as possible, people should know other members of the social units to which they belong, and they should have continual face-to-face interactions with them. People should understand the particular needs of their associates.

Coercive organizations must be replaced by *voluntary* ones. No one should be a member of a state or any other organization against his or her will. Each person should voluntarily associate with other persons because he or she approves of their principles and sees benefit in associating with them. At the same time, the members of any existing association should be able to choose those individuals whom they wish to admit into their association, enabling each association to maintain its solidarity by denying membership to those who disagree with its principles and who fail to contribute as much to the association as they receive from it.

Rather than emphasizing territorial associations, anarchists emphasize

[49]Robert Nozick, *Anarchy, State, and Utopia* (New York: Basic Books, 1974), pp. 312–317.

nonterritorial associations. States, of course, are organized on the basis of proximity or regionalism—that is, people living in the same area—and states have coercive police powers over everyone living in that area. However, people residing within the same area may have little substantive basis for associating with each other. Because of some collaborative economic, educational, social, or religious interests, only some people within a territory may wish to associate with one another. And those who would wish to associate because of such collaborative interests may include people who come from many different geographic locations.

Anarchists wish to destroy centralized, large-scale, coercive, and territorial social structures, and replace them immediately with decentralized, small-scale, voluntary, and nonterritorial ones. But they understand that there will be some evolution in the precise character of such institutions. Immediately after the destruction of conventional institutions, some "statist" organizations may be necessary. Proudhon, for example, called for the creation of a "people's bank." This bank would enable workers and peasants to become economically independent of the dictates of centralized industry by facilitating free exchanges between independent workers and by providing credit (at low or nominal interest rates) for those seeking to establish their own small enterprises. Godwin thought that there would also be a temporary need for local democratic assemblies, which would write laws protecting people from each other, and for juries, which would adjudicate conflicts, because, initially, humans who had been used to living under repressive institutions would act prejudicially—putting their interests ahead of those of others.

Over time, these voluntary and/or decentralized statist arrangements could be abandoned, and social life could be structured on the basis of **mutualism**. In economic life, mutualism provides for on-going associations to ensure the production and distribution of goods and services based on voluntary contractual arrangements between economically independent persons. In principle, capitalism also provides for associations based on voluntary contracts; but anarchists insist that, in practice, capitalist agreements are coercive, because the parties to them are not genuinely independent. If one party owns the land or the equipment used to produce goods, the party that owns only his or her labor is in a poor bargaining position and is thus often exploited. But if each party owns his or her own land or tools, or if such means of production are owned in common, no one is dependent on the (comparatively few) owners of private property. In this context of independence (or interdependence), parties can acknowledge that their cooperation can be mutually beneficial and they can voluntarily become associates in workplaces or syndicates in order to produce goods more efficiently. Education could also be provided on the basis of mutualism. Rather than being organized by centralized and hierarchical public and private institutions, anarchists seek voluntary, mutually agreeable, and mutually beneficial arrangements among parents, teachers, and students. In general, a vast proliferation of mutual-interest associations could be organized in which people having common intellectual, artistic, spiritual, and recreational interests could agree to provide certain benefits to one another according to whatever regulations they choose to adopt for their association.

Because mutual-interest associations would be composed of individuals having similar interests and ideals and because individuals would only join those groups having regulations which they regarded as just and necessary, there would be little conflict within such associations. But anarchists are not so unrealistic as to think that no conflict would ensue. They recognize that *social pressure* would be an important natural instrument that associations would use to ensure that individuals do not harm each other. For example, members of a workplace association who fail to act responsibly toward others could be subject to criticism, chastisement, and even ostracism. Associations could also form internal police units to detect violations of just conduct, and they could resolve disputes among members by employing mediation and arbitration.

Anarchists also recognize the need for different associations to work out appropriate agreements regarding their mutual and conflicting interests. Although Proudhon often referred to a "federal principle" that would serve as a means of structuring such interassociational relations, the term "**confederation**" seems to capture more accurately his ideals in this regard. Proudhon, Bakunin, and other anarchists envisioned the formation of different local associations into larger umbrella organizations by mutual agreement. According to Bakunin, "there may arise free unions organized from below by the free federations of communes into provinces, of provinces into nations, and of nations into the United States of Europe."[50] Nevertheless, anarchists insisted that sovereignty would be largely retained at the local level, and that the higher-level organizations would primarily coordinate cooperative activity among the local associations.[51]

Justice

Anarchists reject both traditional conservative and classical liberal conceptions of justice. Conservatives emphasize that social goods should be distributed according to the traditional rights and responsibilities that societies proscribe for the occupants of different social roles, but anarchists believe that the upper classes have used their power to acquire maximum rights and impose utmost obligations on the lower classes. Classical liberals emphasize that social goods

[50]Quoted in Woodcock, *Anarchism*, p. 163.

[51]Anarchists have never resolved the problem of conflicts among local associations. For example, what would prevent some associations from invading and seizing the assets or persons of other associations? Federal interassociational agreements could empower some central authority to protect each local association and to adjudicate conflicts among them. Because anarchists regard such central authorities as potentially coercive, they have preferred confederative agreements calling for more ad hoc and informal—and less decisive—conflict-resolution processes among the parties to disputes. Robert Nozick discusses this issue in *Anarchy, State, and Utopia* (pp. 326–331), but he is unable to propose a solution to the problem that would be compatible with anarchist ideals.

should be distributed on the basis of universal market forces, but anarchists believe that the property rights of the wealthy enable them to exploit others in market transactions. For anarchists, neither traditional societies nor capitalist economies provide natural justice. Such justice cannot be delivered by any set of institutions, nor can justice be reduced to a single precept regarding the right distribution of social goods.

Natural justice takes place when people treat each other rightly. According to Proudhon, justice is "respect, spontaneously felt and mutually guaranteed, for human dignity, in whatever person and under whatever circumstances we find it compromised, and to whatever risk its defense may expose us."[52] Godwin stressed *sincerity* as a key element in the conduct of a just person. People should be honest with one another; people should express their genuine, natural needs and emotions, avoiding all pretenses designed to provide an advantage for oneself. Proudhon stressed *reciprocity* in transactions and relations among people. Just relationships or transactions avoid exploitation in which one gains at the expense of others. Instead, a just relationship occurs when one person gives benefits to another and receives an equivalent benefit, to the betterment of both.[53] Other anarchists emphasized *generosity* or acting on one's natural sense of duty to aid and support those who are poor or whose basic needs are unfulfilled. In general, anarchists admire *impartiality*—the ability to avoid confusing one's good with the general good. According to Godwin, if a person can promote the general good by dying rather than living, justice requires that he die.[54]

Conceiving of justice as sincere, reciprocal, generous, and impartial conduct toward others may seem to be inconsistent with the strong commitment of anarchists to individualism. But it must be remembered that only a few anarchists (like Max Stirner) ignore humanity's social nature. While classical liberals regard individual freedom as the right to pursue one's own good, anarchists generally regard individual freedom as the right to decide for oneself what constitutes socially responsible conduct. As we have seen, anarchists see liberty as moral autonomy, and they argue that the morally autonomous individual must make his or her own determination about how his or her conduct can best serve the general good.

Anarchists are more egalitarian than conservatives and liberals are. According to Godwin, there is justice in "an equal distribution of the good things of life,"[55] and he provides several justifications for an equal distribution of property and material goods. First, inequality hinders intellectual growth, because it prompts humans to emphasize the accumulation of property instead

[52]Quoted in Mulford Q. Sibley, *Political Ideas and Ideologies: A History of Political Thought* (New York: Harper and Row, 1970), p. 540.
[53]Aristotle first proposed such "numerical equality" in transactions, but Proudhon's receptivity to the idea of a just relationship came from his reading of seventeenth-century Anglican clergyman, Jeremy Taylor, who called such reciprocity "commutative justice."
[54]Godwin, *Political Justice*, p. 170.
[55]Godwin, *Political Justice*, pp. 725–735.

of focusing on mental development. Second, inequality promotes a sense of involuntary dependence on others, "reducing the great mass of mankind to the rank of slaves and cattle for the service of a few." Third, inequality promotes in the wealthy an insatiable desire to satisfy material appetites, and it promotes in the poor a sense of injustice, fanning the emotions of envy and anger in the latter. Such concerns demean the human spirit of both the wealthy and the poor. Such emotions cause crime and war.

Nevertheless, anarchists do not propose that all goods should be distributed equally to everyone. Only an authoritative and coercive institution could enforce an equal distribution of goods to all members of an association. Rather than claiming that all people have a right to an equal share of social goods, anarchists believe that justice is furthered when people have an **egalitarian ethic**—when people accept the norms that everyone is, in general, equally deserving of most social goods and that the needs of everyone are equally important.

Students of anarchism often distinguish between individualistic anarchists, who suggest that goods should ordinarily be distributed according to one's deeds, and collectivist anarchists, who suggest that goods should ordinarily be distributed according to one's needs. Distribution **according to one's deeds** is Proudhon's principle for the just allocation of material goods. Proudhon (like Locke) believed that labor is the key contributor to the value of goods, that each individual has the right to that property (tools and land) necessary to make his own labor productive, and that each individual then deserves rewards proportionate to the productivity of his labor.

Distribution according to one's needs is Kropotkin's principle for the just allocation of material goods. Kropotkin believed that much of the value of social goods derives from social processes too complex to permit the fair assessment of each individual's contribution to the worth of goods. He noted, for example, that a person could build equivalent homes in St. Petersburg and Siberia, yet the home in St. Petersburg would have much more value because of the greater "social production" surrounding it—for example, the theaters and shops that others have built in St. Petersburg enhance the value of homes there. Kropotkin was more inclined to focus on urban and industrial production than was Proudhon (who envisioned more rural communities of farmers and craftsmen), and Kropotkin understood that industrial production is a collective process in which the labor of different individuals is intermixed and individual contributions become indistinct. Because of the social nature of production, Kropotkin argued that the land, tools, and factories that were used in the productive process should be owned in common. No individual has a right to ownership of the products of such social or collective productive processes; only the community as a whole may own these products. Many products must, nevertheless, be consumed by individuals; communities must therefore be composed of impartial and generous persons, who would fairly distribute such products to those people with the greatest need for them. Collectivist anarchists believe that distribution according to need is just, not because the poor person has a right to be supported by the community, but rather because individuals committed to justice have a positive duty to support the needy.

Distributions according to either deed or need are likely to be much more equal than distributions based on traditional rights or provided by the market forces of a capitalist economy. Both Proudhon and Kropotkin understood their distributive principles as prohibiting domination and exploitation. When distributions are based on deed or on need, the mass of humanity would not be subservient to those in the upper echelons of society and would no longer be in positions where they could be exploited by this elite. For anarchists, a just society is characterized by its lack of domination and exploitation, not by a particular pattern in the distribution of goods.

Indeed, different anarchistic associations could stress different distributive patterns. An individualistic association could choose principles that allow persons to own their own tools, to work individually, to retain private ownership of the goods they produced, to exchange such goods on contractual and market bases, and thus to accumulate goods roughly in proportion to their labor. A communist or collective association could choose principles that call for the common ownership of the means of production, for the communal production of goods, and for the distribution of products on the basis of need. Anarchists envision a variety of associational arrangements, and any of these arrangements can be just, as long as they are noncoercive and reflect the moral principles of the persons who are members of the associations.

Citizenship

Anarchists do not relish the condition of citizenship, because they regard citizens as subordinate members of political associations, subject to the commands of governmental authorities. Consequently, anarchists call on people to abstain from participating in government and from voting for representatives during democratic elections. Only by abstaining can the individual maintain that the acts of government are not his responsibility. By abstaining from making laws (or from participating in the process that leads to making laws), citizens strengthen their right to disobey laws.

Traditional conservatives and classical liberals believe that citizens have political obligations to obey the state, but anarchists believe that people have only moral obligations—to act justly in relation to others. According to Godwin, "every man is bound to the exertion of his facilities in the discovery of right, and to the carrying into effect all the right with which he is acquainted."[56] Rather than obeying some external authority, each person should obey the decision of his own understanding, the dictates of his own conscience.

According to Godwin, morally responsible persons have benevolent intentions; they are motivated to do good for others rather than to serve their own interests. Their actions contribute to "general happiness," understood as that

[56]Godwin, *Political Justice*, p. 207.

which actually is most beneficial and least harmful to others. And their actions produce benefits that correspond with their capabilities. According to Godwin:

> It is not enough that conduct is attended with an overbalance of good intention and beneficial results. If it appears that [a person] has scarcely produced the tenth part of that benefit, either in magnitude or extent, which he was capable of producing, it is only in a very limited sense that he can be considered as a virtuous man.[57]

Thus, for a wealthy person to be virtuous, he must not only seek to help those in need, he must actually benefit them, and he must be more generous in his assistance than are less wealthy persons. Absolutely just and virtuous people would distribute their resources—their time, their money, their support, and so forth—to those who could most benefit from their use; if someone else needs a good more than the possessor of that good needs it, justice requires that the possessor give that good to that person most in need of it.

Anarchists understand that people are unlikely to meet this absolute standard of human virtue, but the prerequisite disposition of being morally autonomous should be cultivated. Obedience to external authority undermines such cultivation of moral autonomy and its accompanying predisposition to be virtuous. Thus, rather than calling for the obedience of citizens to the state, anarchists call for the obedience of persons to individually evolved principles of moral conduct.

SUMMARY AND CONCLUSIONS

Anarchism is an important radicalization of liberalism and a precursor of Marxism. Like classical liberals, anarchists look to nature and the individual to develop political and moral principles that they believe will lead to human progress. But anarchists find nature to be more social and benevolent than classical liberals find it, and they believe that individual fulfillment derives less from the freedom to secure one's own interests than from the opportunity to implement one's vision of the public good. Such philosophical foundations lead anarchists to believe that no government is better than even a minimal government, that self-rule is better than popular rule, and that an egalitarian ethic among just men is better than the inequalities of wealth and power that occur under capitalism. Like Marxists, anarchists call for the abolition of liberal, capitalist societies. And, as we shall see in the next chapter, Marx believed that the decentralized, voluntary, and noncoercive social order sought by anarchists could be, and actually would be, achieved after a transitional period of socialism.

Anarchism has many attractions. It recognizes how traditional societies, capitalist economies, and even democratic governments can dominate and coerce individuals. It provides an inspiring vision of a future when individuals have extensive freedom, yet use that freedom to pursue just relationships with one another. It describes a simple and natural life that better supports the moral development of humanity and the eco-

[57]Godwin *Political Justice,* pp., 185–186. Aristotle provided similar prescriptions regarding virtuous conduct in his *Nicomachean Ethics.*

logical survival of the world than does our current obsession with material possessions and economic development.

Despite these appeals, anarchism has not attracted as many followers and has not had as broad a historical impact as other ideologies that we examine in this book. Perhaps there are important internal contradictions within anarchism—for example, anarchists hold nature as a standard while at the same time regarding human nature as almost infinitely malleable. Perhaps anarchists depend too heavily on the intrinsic benevolence of people, and fail to have a realistic conception of the self-interested aspect of human nature. Perhaps anarchists ignore various positive benefits that governments can provide for members of society. Perhaps governmental authority is not as incompatible with individual autonomy as anarchists assert, since citizens may normally recognize their obligations as citizens to the state, yet disobey specific governmental commands that they regard as unjust.[58] Perhaps the destruction of existing institutions, especially by means of violence, demands a more convincing, concrete alternative vision of society than anarchists provide.

In any event, anarchists remind us of the importance of examining the repressive aspects of existing social structures. They urge us to question conventional authorities, institutions, and ideas. They prompt us to expand our vision and conceive of new social orders, expanded human freedoms, and more just human relationships.

[58]See Jeffrey H. Reiman, *In Defense of Political Philosophy: A Reply to Robert Paul Wolff's "In Defense of Anarchism"* (New York: Harper Torchbacks, 1972).

CHAPTER 5

Marxism

For many Americans, Marxism embodies some foolish ideas that were embraced by communist regimes in the Soviet Union, "Red China," North Vietnam, Cuba, and elsewhere during the Cold War. In this view, Marxism is responsible for the international hostilities between "the East and the West" and for the lack of freedom for people living behind the "Iron Curtain." It justifies despotic government and relies on failed economic doctrines that undermine productivity and human initiative in an attempt to enforce a drab equality on people everywhere. Perhaps there is some truth to such a characterization of Marxism, but a less biased assessment of this ideology requires a deeper understanding of its many great ideas.

"Marxism" refers generally to the ideas proposed by Karl Marx (1818–1883). According to Marx, humans are naturally laboring beings, and all human activity is ultimately economic activity. All societies are divided, on the basis of economic activity, into ruling and subordinate classes. All societies pursue economic productivity by enforcing a division of labor that alienates humans from their potential as creatively laboring beings. These features are especially true of capitalist society, in which there are only two significant classes: a small group of capitalists, who own all the means of production, and the large mass of the proletariat, who own only their own labor and who are the more alienated of the two classes. Analysis of the laws of history and political economy reveals that capitalism is doomed and will be overthrown by the proletariat. This revolution will pave the way to a classless, communist society. Private property will be abolished, and the political state (which upholds the interests of the ruling class) will cease to be necessary and will ultimately wither away. In this society, all human beings will achieve their potential as creative laborers, and none will be alienated from their labor, from the products of their labor, or from each other.

On the basis of such ideas, Marx sought to provide an intellectual foundation to the working-class movements in Europe during the latter half of the nineteenth century. *The Manifesto of the Communist Party,* which he wrote with Friedrich Engels (1820–1895) in 1848, was an attempt to unite the work-

Sidebar 5-1

Main Writings of Marx and Engels

Karl Marx (1818–1883)
- *On the Jewish Question* (1843)
- *Economic and Philosophical Manuscripts* (1844; published in 1927)
- *The German Ideology* (1846)
- *The Manifesto of the Communist Party* (with Engels, 1848)
- *The Grundrisse* (1856–1857)
- *Contribution to the Critique of Political Economy* (1859)
- *Das Kapital, vol. I* (1867)
- *The Civil War in France* (1871)
- *Critique of the Gotha Program* (1875; formally published in 1891)
- *Das Kapital, vol. 2* (1885; edited by Engels)
- *Das Kapital, vol. 3* (1894; edited by Engels)

Friedrich Engels (1820–1895)
- *The Condition of the Working Class in England* (1845)
- *Anti-Duehring* (1878)
- *Socialism: Utopian and Scientific* (1880)
- *The Origin of the Family, Private Property, and the State* (1884)

ing classes throughout Europe and inspire them to engage in coordinated revolutionary activity at a time when revolutions were sweeping the continent. The "revolutions" of 1848, however, were uprisings of liberals and progressives, and were essentially targeted against the monarchies and the autocratic regimes of the period—not against the capitalist regimes at which Marx and Engels aimed their efforts. After the failure of these liberal revolts, Marx began extensive studies of capitalism and the problem of how to develop class consciousness among working men and women. During the 1850s, he sketched out a grand ideological system that placed capitalism into broad historical-economic perspective. The notebooks in which Marx recorded the development of his ideas at this time are called the *"Grundrisse."* It is from the outlines in the *Grundrisse* that Marx fleshed out the text he published as the first volume of *Das Kapital* in 1867. Two subsequent volumes were published posthumously under Engel's editorship in 1885 and 1894.

Marx was active in the working-class politics of his era. In 1864, he participated in founding the International Workingmen's Association, and remained active in the group until the early 1870s. He often competed with anarchists such as Mikhael Bakunin for doctrinal leadership in the association (later known as the First International). By 1872, his influence in the International had waned, after many former allies deserted him.[1]

Despite his limited political influence during his lifetime, however, Marx bequeathed to opponents of classical liberalism (or of democratic capitalism) a number of economic, sociological, political, and philosophical doctrines. Even before his death, intellectuals sympathetic to the revolutionary overthrow of capitalism began to interpret and, to some extent, alter Marx's theo-

[1]David McLellan, *Karl Marx: His Life and Thought* (New York: Harper and Row, 1973), pp. 407–411.

ries. These activities showed that they regarded his theories as an authoritative beginning point. Engels was perhaps the most enthusiastic interpreter and systematizer of Marx's frequently complex and chaotic writings; his interpretations became the credo of **orthodox Marxists**. Such Marxists maintain that capitalism is plagued with contradictions that doom it to self-destruction; they believe that a revolution against capitalism is inevitable once "conditions are ripe," and that an egalitarian, socialist order will eventually appear after the revolution. Orthodox Marxists remained influential in many communist and socialist parties in Europe throughout the twentieth century, but other critics of capitalism who believed themselves to be the true Marxists gave Marx's writings different interpretations.

Revisionist Marxists, who emerged in Germany during the 1890s, argued that Marx was not as deterministic as Engels and other orthodox Marxists claimed, and they argued that Marx had not foreseen the political, economic, and sociological changes that enabled the working class to challenge capitalism and establish socialism by nonrevolutionary means. Revisionist Marxism has evolved into democratic socialism, a distinct and powerful ideology that is the basis of many socialist parties that have successfully competed in democratic elections and governed pluralist societies throughout the twentieth century. In Chapter 9, we describe democratic socialism as a separate ideology—but it is one that has nevertheless been strongly influenced by Marx.

sidebar 5-2

Karl Marx

Karl Marx was born in 1818 to a well-to-do Jewish lawyer and his wife, both of whom had converted to Protestantism in order to circumvent the anti-Semitism of the time. Marx studied philology at the universities of Bonn and then of Berlin, where he became associated with the Young Hegelians. Upon completing his doctoral dissertation, "The Difference Between the Democritean and Epicurean Philosophies of Nature," he wrote articles for a Young Hegelian journal, and became editor of *Rheinische Zeitung*, an opposition newspaper in Cologne. There he met Friedrich Engels. The Prussian government exiled him for his radical activities, and when he continued these activities in Paris, it successfully petitioned the French government to exile him again. He moved his young family to Brussels, and then, in 1849, to London. For the next twenty years, Marx and his family lived in genteel poverty. To support himself, he wrote articles for newspapers and journals, such as the *New York Tribune* (and received considerable financial help from Engels), but he spent the greater part of his time in the British Museum, studying and writing about economics and history.

During his lifetime, Marx (often supported by Engels) engaged in frequent, vociferous debates and disputes with other socialists, but Marx remained little known outside the socialist movement in Germany until shortly before his death in 1883. Then, Marx's writings rapidly became known throughout Europe and, especially, in Russia.

Marx's writings were interpreted—and perhaps significantly modified—in yet other ways by many, including Vladimir Lenin (1870–1924), Leon Trotsky (1879–1940), Mao Zedong (1893–1976), and other revolutionary strategists who orchestrated "communist" revolutions in societies in which capitalism was nascent, but in which conditions were not ripe for true communist revolutions, according to orthodox Marxism. **Marxism-Leninism** has been influential in Russia and other parts of the former Soviet Union, in China, and in many of the developing countries throughout the present century. We discuss these interpretations of Marxism in Chapter 6, which describes communism.

Our separate treatments of Marxism in this chapter and communism in the next are based on the belief that Marxism and communism are not the same ideology. Marx is the central figure in both Marxism and communism, but whereas Marx was chiefly concerned with an analysis of the historical laws of economic development that culminate naturally in a revolution and a classless society, communists like Lenin and Mao were more concerned with how to bring about the revolution, and how to establish communist party rule once the revolution has taken place. Most Marxists have emphasized the need for an analysis and critique of capitalist society, and they have developed the "laws of history" from a study of capitalism and of the various stages of history before capitalism. Marx provided only the most basic outline of the features of a postcapitalist life, and he never intended his outline to be a guide for governing (a transitory) socialist society or for developing an ideal communist society. As Bertil Ollman suggests, Marx considered attempts to pro-

Sidebar 5-3

Friedrich Engels

Friedrich Engels was born in 1820, in Barmen, Germany, the son of a wealthy businessman. Unlike Marx, Engels received little formal philosophical training. Although he managed to attend lectures at the University of Berlin and to join the Young Hegelian radicals while serving in the Prussian Army, his father had sent him to business school to train for service in the family business. On his way to Manchester, England, to complete his business training, Engels met Marx in November 1842, in Cologne. By this time, Engels had written various articles for press journals, and in 1844 he sent "Outlines of a Critique of Political Economy" to Marx, who published it. On his return to Germany from Manchester, Engels visited Marx in Paris. Their lifelong collaboration and profound friendship dated from this meeting. Engels collaborated with Marx on several "Marxist" works, including *The Holy Family* (1845) and *The German Ideology* (1846).

Shortly after Marx moved to London, in 1849, Engels moved to Manchester to work for his father's firm. For the next twenty years he financially supported both Marx and himself. In 1870, he moved to London, remaining active in publishing Marx's works and in the international communist movement, even after Marx's death. Engels died in 1895, twelve years after Marx.

vide systematic accounts of communism to be "foolish, ineffective, and even reactionary."[2] Communism, in contrast, is chiefly concerned with life "after the revolution." While Marxism claims to be a scientific critique of present practices based on a knowledge of the laws of history and economics, communism is an ideology that focuses on the practical problems of governing. It is concerned with how the dictatorship of the proletariat should be organized, how the proletariat should govern, and how the governing Communist party can gain, maintain, and retain power and legitimacy.

Yet another interpretation of Marx has emphasized the philosophical and humanistic aspects in Marx's writings, especially those in the works of the **young Marx**. George Lukács (1885–1971) was the first Marxist intellectual to recapture Marx's appreciation—as well as his critique—of the works of George W. F. Hegel (1770–1831), the great German idealist philosopher of the Napoleonic era. Lukács's writings opened the way for a favorable intellectual reception of *The Economic and Philosophical Manuscripts,* which Marx had written in 1844, but which remained unpublished until 1927. These manuscripts reveal a philosophical and idealist strain in Marx, along with a strong Hegelian influence, that seems to undermine the claim by orthodox Marxists that Marx was strictly a scientist and a materialist.

We believe that Marxism is best understood when one recognizes the general doctrines of political economy stressed by orthodox Marxists, but interprets these doctrines in light of the philosophical and humanistic concerns of the young Marx. In short, our presentation of Marx is based on the judgment that the young Marx established many of the goals and theoretical foundations of Marxism, while the "scientifically based" laws of history and political economy that the mature Marx stressed describe the means by which these goals can and will be achieved.

THE POLITICAL BASES

Problems

Insofar as Marx attempted to provide a scientific theory of the historical processes that resulted in capitalism, we cannot say that his ideology is a response to the problems of capitalism, nor can we classify it as an effort to ameliorate those problems. Instead, Marxism must be seen as an attempt to uncover the laws of the social, economic, and political forces that led to capitalism, including those problems that would eventually lead to its collapse and to the advent of communist society. In developing this analysis, however, Marx also uncovered many of the problems of capitalism and thereby provided a body of criticism that has remained useful even for those who do not subscribe to his "science" of history. Four problems are particularly prominent.

[2]See Bertil Ollman, "Marx's Vision of Communism: A Reconstruction," in *Critique no. 8,* 1978, cited in Alec Nove, *The Economics of Feasible Socialism Revisited* (London: HarperCollins, 1991), p. 12n1.

Sidebar 5-4

Marxism Today and Neo-Marxism

The demise of communism in Eastern Europe may signify a decline of Marxism as an ideology with widespread political appeal. However, it should be remembered that Marx's ideas continue to be reflected in communism, which remains a significant governing ideology in China, Cuba, North Korea, and elsewhere. Marxism remains a significant component of various revolutionary ideologies in less-developed nations. Marxism also remains important for its influence on democratic socialism, which continues to affect electoral outcomes and policy decisions in most modern industrial states.

Among intellectuals, **neo-Marxism** remains an influential social theory. For example, the critical theory of the Frankfurt School—especially as it is presented in the writings of Max Horkheimer and Juergen Habermas—is deeply indebted to Marxist theory and has made important, though controversial, contributions to political philosophy by insisting that philosophy must be a practical activity that aims to further human emancipation by enhancing human consciousness of oppressive social and political conditions. Neo-Marxists are also prominent in the contemporary social sciences, insofar as many descriptions and explanations of contemporary life in capitalist societies incorporate Marxist concepts. Perhaps the most straightforward example of Marx's influence in contemporary social science is structural Marxism. This school takes up Marx's claim that the state is simply the "executive committee of the bourgeoisie" (or of capitalists). While previous neo-Marxists have sought to show (with little success) that political leaders typically have bourgeois backgrounds and/or values, structural Marxists emphasize the "structural embrace of the state by capitalism." According to this theory, even left-leaning politicians inevitably support "capital accumulation" and attend more to the needs of capitalists than to those of the working class, because capital accumulations ultimately increase the affluence of the working class and, thus, appease its members. In short, neo-Marxism, which uses and modifies concepts and theories from Marx, constitutes an important analytical framework for understanding contemporary social, economic, and political life.

First, capitalism produced *economic and social misery* in the working class, particularly among women and children. With the advent of capitalism, the working life of adult men became one of long hours spent on meaningless, repetitive tasks under unsafe and dreary working conditions for subsistence wages—and the plight of women and children was frequently worse. The social conditions for working-class people in nineteenth-century industrial England were particularly bleak. Factories were unsanitary, unventilated, cramped, dark, and dangerous. Workers seldom received adequate breaks for rest from the dreary rhythms of the machines, and often worked fourteen hours a day or longer, sometimes seven days a week. Factory owners justified the harsh regimen by claiming that idleness was the worst of sins. Women and children worked alongside the men, usually for even less pay. Thousands died of diseases and ailments that were contracted in the steamy, dusty, dark, and filthy conditions of the factories, or from injuries caused by dangerous machines and unsafe working conditions. Some workers rarely left the factory, and often even slept beside the machinery they operated. Children would sometimes be chained to their machines so that they would not wander. Beatings, incarceration, and other abuses were regular aspects of factory discipline for children and adults alike. Meanwhile, industrialists, successful entrepreneurs, and the remaining gentry often lived in opulence, and a small middle class kept itself solvent. These people often justified their luxurious lives by suggesting that their social and economic success could be attributed to their competitive advantages of character, stamina, and intelligence—not to fortune of birth or providence. Marx rejected such explanations, calling them an ideology that the bourgeoisie used to justify its oppressive role.

Second, capitalism had certain ethical shortcomings. In 1843, the young Marx wrote *On the Jewish Question*, in which he argued that capitalism justified the self-interested and materialist aspects of human motivation at the expense of more public-regarding and spiritual concerns. He also recognized that capitalism emphasized competition rather than cooperation among people.

Third, capitalism enhanced the alienation of human beings, a problem that we will consider in our discussion of Marxist conceptions of human nature.

Fourth, Marx was highly concerned with the disunity of the working class, which weakened the political power of this progressive and potentially revolutionary segment of society. According to Marx, most people were objectively members of the working class, because they did not own the means of production; however, these people were unaware (i.e., lacked subjective consciousness) that they were oppressed, that other members of the working class shared their oppression, and that becoming ***class-conscious*** was an essential precondition to a successful revolution against capitalism. Many factors contributed to this lack of working-class consciousness. The great poverty of the working class resulted in its preoccupation with attaining immediate, material (subsistence) needs like food and shelter, which left its members with scant time and energy to focus on larger political issues, such as understanding the role of the working class as a revolutionary force in history. The prevailing liberal ideology also diminished class consciousness, because it prompted the working class to view the world as individuals rather than as a class, to stress the equal opportunities for advancement that were formally available to individuals within the working class, and to dampen discontent with capitalism by proclaiming that the system was the key to economic progress that would benefit everyone, including the working class. Religion, "the opiate of the masses," also helped to curtail class consciousness. Not only did religious differences divide the working class, but religion turned the workers' attention away from worldly oppression and toward the hope of heavenly salvation. Although the working class was able, to some degree, to overcome these factors and become conscious of its common oppression under capitalism, it nevertheless failed to acquire a realistic understanding of how to escape this oppression. Most socialist alternatives to capitalism were, according to Marx and Engels, utopian. They involved the creation of small-scale socialist communities—such as the industrial cooperatives created by Robert Owen in New Lanark (Scotland) or New Harmony (Indiana) or the phalanxes envisioned by Charles Fourier, which provided the basis for such social experiments as Brook Farm, the utopian community established in Massachusetts. While such utopian communities might have some romantic appeal to those members of the working class who were aware of their own oppression under capitalism, they deflected the working class from understanding its role as a historical force. For Marx, the historical role of the working class was to bring about a revolution from a capitalist to a socialist system, not to break itself into little, self-sufficient communities within a larger capitalist system.

Goals

If we accept a deterministic view of Marx's ideas, then it is difficult to talk about the "goals" of Marxism, because we can say that Marx saw in the unfolding of the historical process a kind of economic determinism that made the communist revolution inevitable and the articulation of goals irrelevant. Because history would unfold of itself as it should, Marx's deterministic science did not seem to require the specification of goals as a means of propelling human beings to take political action. However, if we argue that Marx's early works seem to be less animated by this deterministic science of history, we may contend that Marx was driven by philosophical, ethical, and social objectives that seem to allow for more human intervention in the material unfolding of history. During the twentieth century, moreover, Marxists have tended to reject the notion that Marx provided a completely deterministic view of history. Instead, they use his concepts as the basis of a social critique that may hasten the coming of communism. It is at this point that communists of the activist tradition, starting with Lenin, began to part ways with orthodox Marxists, who did not anticipate a direct intervention into the historical process. Communists foresaw the need for much stronger and more immediate practical political intervention in the historical process. In this light, it is possible to speak of two kinds of goals in Marx and Marxism: ultimate goals and immediate goals.

Marx's ultimate goals were especially evident in his early writings. The first goal was to enable human beings to overcome alienated, oppressive conditions and live authentic, satisfying lives as creative laborers. This goal included the need to end the state of psychological dualism in which people found themselves existing under capitalism. They were expected to be public-regarding in public life and private-regarding in private life, even though, in liberal bourgeois society, concern for the private overwhelms the interest in the public. Marx argued that public and private life must be integrated by developing a universal human consciousness that enhances humanity's communal, public, and social nature.[3]

The second goal was to create a society in which no one is constrained by economic necessity. To achieve this end, we would have to overcome material scarcity and build an affluent economy through technological innovations, less wasteful production processes, and the benefits of collaborative, cooperative work. Such a society would also require a more equal and fair distribution of material goods.

The third goal was to create a communal society in which men and women interact as brothers and sisters. This goal implied three requisite changes in current practices. First, private property would have to be abolished and the common ownership of the means of production established. Second, the state would have to be abolished, as it was, in effect, the coercive and oppressive instrument of the owning classes. Third, no economic classes must exist. The new society would be classless.

Marx was not the first social philosopher to be concerned with achieving such goals. Various sorts of utopian schemes were already popular in classical Greek literature and in the millenarian fantasies of the early Christian era. Thomas More (1478–1535), the Diggers, Charles Dickens (1812–1870), and the utopian socialists—Claude-Henri Saint-Simon (1760–1825), Robert Owen (1771–1858), Charles Fourier (1772–1837), and Auguste Comte (1798–1857)—are among the important pre-Marxist "socialists" who outlined the shape of the perfect, egalitarian society.[4] Marx and Engels borrowed from some of these thinkers, but they were arguably the first to develop a systematic and comprehensive socialist ideology.

Marx also had immediate intellectual and practical and/or political goals. Marxism's intellectual goal was to provide an account of how the long-term goals *will* be met, rather than why they *should* be met. The normative justification for an egalitarian society had been provided by previous utopian socialists, and Marx found these arguments both insufficient and unpersuasive from a scientific point of view.[5] Intellectually, Marx sought to provide a scientific account of the historical process that had resulted in the present abysmal conditions of capitalism and to articulate the laws of social, economic, and political change that would inevitably lead to the realization of his ultimate goals. His immediate practical-political goal was to unite the working class by fostering genuine class consciousness among the proletariat. He would do so by demonstrating the single underlying cause of their misery (the abusiveness of capitalism) and by making them aware of capitalism's weaknesses and its historically inevitable demise.[6]

[3]Karl Marx, *On The Jewish Question*, in *The Marx-Engels Reader*, 2d ed., edited by Robert C. Tucker (New York: W. W. Norton Co., 1978 [1843]), pp. 31, 32, 46.

[4]For a comprehensive history of utopian thinking, see Frank E. Manuel and Fritzie Manuel, *Utopian Thought in the Western World* (Cambridge: Belknap Press of Harvard University Press, 1979).

[5]See Marx and Engels, *The Manifesto of the Communist Party*, in *The Marx-Engels Reader*, pp. 497–499.

[6]There is a curious tension between Marx's goal of promoting a socialist society and his goal of developing a science of the historical processes that will result in socialism. On the one hand, his

THE PHILOSOPHICAL BASES

Human Nature

Along with Marx's ontology of history, his understanding of human nature is perhaps the most distinctive and important philosophical foundation of his ideology. We should point out, however, that the implicit rigidity of the term "human nature" makes its use problematic when we speak of Marxism.

In Marx's view, the essence of a human being is labor. All humans have the potential to exist as **creative laborers**, but contemporary material and economic conditions prevented anyone from realizing that potential. Marx was strongly influenced in this regard by Hegel, who developed the notion that labor is the most important way in which human beings realize themselves and actualize their potential to be true human beings.[7] While other animals can only labor within their environment and extract what they need from that environment, humans can transform their environment through creative labor. When humans freely and creatively labor in this way, they achieve their full human potential. In fact, Marx states that human beings *create* themselves through labor:

> Men can be distinguished from animals by consciousness, by religion or anything else you like. They themselves begin to distinguish themselves from animals as soon as they begin to *produce* their means of subsistence, a step which is conditioned by their physical organization. By producing their means of subsistence men are indirectly producing their actual material life.[8]

In other words, our labor is what makes us human, and it is also what makes us the particular sorts of human beings that we are.

In his analysis of labor, Marx accepted Charles Fourier's assertion that labor is not inherently unpleasant. Like Fourier, he believed that humans are most happy when they are permitted to develop themselves freely and use their capacities as laborers, and he argued that only existing social structures make labor unpleasant and degrading. When social structures are oppressive, the rewards of labor are merely extrinsic or instrumental; labor is a means to acquire needed material things. In contrast, if social structures were correctly altered, labor could have intrinsic value; it could become an activity that is an end in itself. Since emerging from the prehistorical state of nature, however, humans have never been able to labor freely and creatively and thereby realize their true potential. Social structures have always been oppressive. As a result, human beings have always been alienated.

---

systematic analysis of human nature, economics, and history is an attempt to develop a science of the necessary, material unfolding of history. On the other hand, this science must be seen in the context of a set of problems that Marx sought to "solve," of which the abuses of capitalism were the most important. Whereas the term "solutions" implies activity, Marx's "science" seems to imply that we should simply wait for the material order of things to unfold, as it inevitably will, solving all human problems as it does so.

[7]Cf. Hannah Arendt, *The Human Condition* (Chicago: University of Chicago Press, 1958), p. 86 n14.

[8]Marx, *The German Ideology*, in *The Marx-Engels Reader*, p. 150.

For Marx, **alienation** was a general concept referring to the gap between humanity's potential and its actual condition.[9] The causes of human alienation, according to Marx, have been the economic or material scarcity that accompanies human existence and the division of labor that results from organized attempts to overcome this scarcity. This "division of labor" includes both the horizontal specialization among people in terms of the various tasks they perform, and the vertical arrangements of authority and subordination. Both have been essential features of every mode of production that humans have historically adopted in an effort to overcome scarcity. In order to maximize production and fulfill the community's interest in satisfying material needs, individuals have been assigned specific social, economic, and gender roles that have varied historically depending on technological developments, and they have accepted relations of authority and subordination.

According to Marx, such division of labor has contributed to four types of alienation. First, human beings have become alienated from the fruits of their labor: "The worker put his life into the object; but now his life no longer belongs to him, but to the object."[10] When humans develop a division of labor to produce things more efficiently, and when humans consequently produce things primarily for consumption, the objects produced by labor take on a life of their own. However, the objects are no longer the workers'. Instead, they pass on to those at the top of the hierarchy in the division of labor.

Second, humans have become alienated from nature. According to Marx, nature not only provides for our physical subsistence, it also provides objects upon which the laborer can creatively operate. Without such a "canvas" on which the laborer can exercise his creativity, he cannot be a full human being. "Nature provides labor with the *means of life* in the sense that labor cannot *live* without objects on which to operate."[11] According to Marx, humans and the products of human labor are originally a part of nature itself, and the fruits of one's labor are a natural extension of oneself in much the way a duck's eggs are a natural extension of itself. However, when the products of labor are viewed as things to be "owned"—especially by those at the top of the hierarchy—they become objects over and against us, rather than the natural effusion of our activities. Claiming ownership over objects implies that nature is separate from humanity and human products rather than the context within which we labor and within which we achieve self-realization through creative labor.

Third, humans have become alienated from the process of laboring itself. Humans no longer labor creatively for the intrinsic enjoyment or satisfaction of doing transforming work, or for the sake of their own self-actualization as creative laborers. Labor becomes externalized, and no longer reflects the laborer's "essential being." It is often forced labor, as in the case of slaves, serfs, and wage earners. Laborers become mere "cogs in the machine," and they

[9]Marx drew upon and altered earlier understandings of alienation. For Kant, alienation was the distance between how humans ought to live and how they do live. For Hegel, human alienation resided in a series of struggles that humans must undergo in order to attain their ultimate spiritual fulfillment.

[10]Marx, *Philosophical and Economic Manuscripts of 1844*, in *The Marx-Engels Reader*, p. 72.

[11]Marx, *Philosophical and Economic Manuscripts*, p. 72.

labor to acquire a wage. Labor no longer satisfies the immediate human need to labor creatively, but becomes only a *means* for satisfying human needs that are external to labor itself—food, shelter, clothing, and so on. In Marx's terms, labor has become "abstracted."[12]

Fourth, human beings are alienated from what Marx called their "species-being." This means both that people fail to experience themselves as members of the creatively laboring human species and that they are separated from their fellow humans. Their failure to recognize themselves as creative laborers stems from the previously identified alienations, especially from their experiencing work as a means rather than as an intrinsically rewarding end. Their separation from other humans is due to the ceaseless competition among humans for the most desirable positions in the division of labor. As competitors for better positions and for scarce goods, humans fail to see others as comrades engaged in collective actions of transforming the environment for their mutual benefit.

Cast in historical perspective, capitalist society is particularly divided and competitive, and has thereby contributed to the extreme alienation of all classes. Nevertheless, capitalist society has also provided the means of production that can allow for more authentic living—if these means are socialized. The technology of capitalism allows for great productivity and abundance, reducing the need for a division of labor to overcome material scarcity. Socializing the means of production will preclude the expropriation of the products of labor away from the laborers who produced them. In these circumstances—that is, under socialized production—laborers would begin to relate to each other as comrades rather than as competitors. In the initial stages of socialization, the workers' conception of their species-being will remain stunted because of their long exposure to the alienating effects of capitalism; hence, for a time, laborers will still require a wage as an incentive to work. But as socialist society develops and human beings begin to experience some of the joys of creative and free labor, the workers' consciousness of their species-being will increase. In time, the laborers' desire to engage in free and creative labor will surpass their desire for a wage. At this point, humans will have overcome their alienation and it will be possible to achieve a communist society.

Society

Marx claimed that "the history of all hitherto existing society is the history of class struggles." Accordingly, "freeman and slave, patrician and plebeian, lord and serf, guildmaster and journeyman—in a word, oppressor and oppressed stood in constant opposition to one another, carried on an uninterrupted, now hidden, now open, fight, a fight that each time ended, either in a revolutionary re-constitution of society at large, or in the common ruin of the contending classes."[13] This claim that all societies are characterized by *class divisions* is a rejection of the idea of traditional conservatism that society is an organic whole and of the liberal doctrine that society is a voluntary agreement among

[12]Marx, *Philosophical and Economic Manuscripts*, pp. 74–75.

[13]Marx and Engels, *The Manifesto of the Communist Party*, pp. 473–474.

individuals. According to Marx, societies are characterized by dominant and subordinate classes.

There are both objective and subjective aspects to the class structure of societies. Societies exhibit "classes in themselves" that are distinguished "objectively" on the basis of people's economic position. "Classes for themselves" are distinguished "subjectively," as when a class of people with common economic interests first perceives itself as a class, and therefore develops a class consciousness (of itself).

According to Marx, economic classes are determined objectively by economic production. The positions of human beings in the class structure of society are determined by what they produce and how they produce it, and these class positions determine much of their individual characteristics:

> As individuals express their life, so they are. What they are, therefore, coincides with their production, both with *what* they produce and with *how* they produce. The nature of individuals thus depends on the material conditions determining their production.[14]

An individual's specific laboring activity determines the way that he or she thinks about the world, nature, himself or herself, and his or her relations with others. But all people do not labor in the same way. Variations in how people labor are due to differences in what Marx called the "**forces of production**." These include both the **means of production**—namely, the physical materials and the technologies we employ to produce things—and the **modes of production**—namely, how we organize the activities of production. Additionally, Marx recognized variations in how humans distribute products. These **relations of production** include the **modes of exchange** (i.e., who gets what from whom) and the **modes of appropriation** (i.e., who owns what and the basis for their ownership). According to Marx, people are divided into social classes on the basis of their particular roles in the processes of production, exchange, and appropriation. In other words, the position that an individual has in the organization of production and the goods that he or she receives and owns determine his or her social class. Those individuals holding similar positions and receiving similar rewards belong to the same objective social class. Additionally, Marx claimed that historical changes in the forces and relations of production produce changes in the class structure of society. Whole social classes can come into being and fade from existence as a result of economic changes.

In capitalist society, there are two objectively distinguishable classes: the **bourgeoisie** and the **proletariat**. The bourgeoisie own the means of production (the land, factories, banks, and so forth, that provide the resources that allow humans to accumulate wealth). The proletariat own only their own labor and consequently have less desirable positions in the division of labor. These different economic positions enable the bourgeoisie to be the oppressors and make the proletariat the oppressed class in capitalist society. However, the proletariat may or may not recognize its own oppression. To the extent that the

[14]Marx, *The German Ideology*, p. 150.

proletariat recognizes its common oppression, its members develop class consciousness and become a class-for-themselves. Class consciousness transforms a group of people who passively occupy the same economic roles—without relating to each other as comrades—into a group of people who actively, collectively seek to transform the economic and social structure of society. Only when the proletariat acquires class consciousness does it become an active force for social change. Only when the proletariat acquires class consciousness can there be a revolution.

After the revolution, these classes will continue to exist, but the proletariat will have expropriated and socialized the means of production, and will have become the predominant class. The bourgeoisie will fade away during this period of socialism. The most powerful and wealthy of the bourgeoisie—those who have been the primary beneficiaries of the capitalist system—may cling to their old ways of perceiving the world, others, and themselves; some will be beyond redemption. Only as these people die off will the bourgeoisie disappear. However, the greatest portion of the bourgeoisie—the small business-people, shopkeepers, and lower-level professionals (or "petite bourgeoisie")—will be transformed by their new roles in the socialist economy. Thus, there will be a **classless society** within a generation or two of the revolution, because both the objective and subjective conditions that underlie class differences will have disappeared. Class conflict and the kind of dialectical change (to which we now turn) that characterized the historical epoch up until the revolution will cease.

Ontology

Marx embraced **historicism**, claiming that history is made up of major events that mark the beginnings and ends of various historical stages, and that these events are strongly influenced by material conditions and processes that are beyond human control. According to Marx, human history has progressed through two major stages. The first was a prehistorical period in which humans lived in an uncorrupted natural condition, more or less as depicted by Jean-Jacques Rousseau (1712–1778) in his description of the state of nature.[15] The second stage was a historical period in which society was organized on the basis of private property and power; at least three important eras can be identified within this historical period: the slave-holding era, the feudal era, and the capitalist era. We can envision and achieve a third, final, posthistorical period in which private property and power are eliminated.

This sort of historical speculation did not originate with Marx; it has a long history in the western tradition. In Jewish prophecy from the sixth century B.C.E. onward (Isaiah, Ezekiel, Daniel, Malachi, etc.), we find images of a world that will be transformed through the intervention of God himself. These images take on a more strident form in many of the Jewish and, later, the Christian apocalyptic writings from the first century B.C.E. onward. An Italian cleric,

[15]See Jean-Jacques Rousseau, *A Discourse on the Origin of Inequality* (first published in 1755).

Joachim of Fiore (1145–1202), was the first writer to turn such images into speculation on the unfolding of the historical process in precise epochs. Based on an idiosyncratic interpretation of biblical texts, he speculated that history could be divided into three eras. Each era was characterized by a different, ever more intimate relationship between God and human beings. In the first, the "Age of the Father," God ruled human beings and related to them by means of religious and civil laws, which he had passed down through Moses. In the second age, the "Age of the Son," God revealed His love through allowing His Son to be crucified for the sake of human redemption. The third age, the "Age of the Spirit," was about to come (in A.D. 1260). God would rule in the hearts of men, and human understanding would be complete. A great leader would reveal the beginning of this age, and he would establish a community of spiritual men with spiritual understanding. Their community would not be a hierarchy of rulers and ruled, but would be an egalitarian community in which all believers were guided by the Spirit of God. It would be a blessed age. Since its delineation by Joachim, this historical schema has been repeated endlessly, with many variations, as part of the European intellectual tradition of the subsequent six hundred years.[16] Marx's conception of progressive stages in history may be read as a recent variant in this tradition. Not God, but material forces are now the "engine" that drives history forward. Marx's analysis of the events that cause the transitions from one epoch to another is perhaps his most unique contribution to this tradition of historical speculation.

According to Marx, historical change occurs when class relationships change, and class relationships change when the ways in which human beings produce things change. The prehistoric period was a classless and rather destitute society in which everyone took care of his or her own needs by hunting, fishing, and gathering. Classes (and the historical period) emerged when people began to associate with one another in order to acquire the higher economic standard of living that could be gained by cooperation, specialization, and a division of labor. To accommodate commercial activity and trade, ancient societies developed rigid class systems, with patricians or nobles at the top, and slaves at the bottom. In between, there were classes of peasants, merchants, craftsmen, bureaucrats, and professional soldiers. When the last of these imperial systems in the West, the Roman Empire, disintegrated, trade diminished and semimilitary societies emerged in the feudal period in an effort to provide security against the northern and eastern marauders of the period. The landed nobility of the feudal period dominated the serfs or peasants, but gradual efforts to renew commercial activity reinvigorated city life and gave rise to the bourgeoisie. As feudalism declined and capitalism emerged, the bourgeoisie became owners of the means of production. The new technologies and knowledge that led to new ways of production and social organization and that destroyed feudalism included looms for cloth-weaving, the printing press, expanded shipbuilding knowledge, and the military use of gunpowder. The need of the bour-

[16]For a brief account of millenarian ideas of history inspired by Joachim's schema, see Norman Cohn, *The Pursuit of the Millennium* (New York: Oxford University Press, 1970), pp. 108–111.

geoisie for labor in their factories and warehouses created an industrial working class, the proletariat, that the bourgeoisie were able to dominate. Just as previous class structures had eventually broken down, however, the dominance of the bourgeoisie would also eventually end. The end of bourgeoisie dominance would lead to a classless society and to the posthistorical period.

The engine—or material forces—that produces these changes in social and class structures is known as **dialectical materialism**, a term coined by Engels. Engel's use of the term "dialectical" to describe historical changes reflects his (and Marx's) understanding of the ancient Greek philosophers (in particular, Socrates and Plato), who thought of dialectic as a kind of conversational debate—a conception which implies an inherent element of conflict between different conceptions of reality. In the course of a dialectical conversation, these oppositions are clarified and resolved, so that we may arrive at the truth or, at least, the approximate truth of a matter.[17] By describing all change as "dialectical," Marx asserted that all historical change occurs as the result of opposition and conflict.

Marx owes much of this interpretation of dialectic as a historical force to Hegel. In broad terms, Hegel understood human history to be produced by a movement of *Geist* (Spirit or God) in time. *Geist* actualizes itself in history in a series of social and political forms in an attempt to come to self-realization. To put it another way, history is driven by or made up of a series of conflicts of *ideas.* Each idea is embodied in a particular social or political form. Each society contains two conflicting forms—masters and slaves, patricians and plebians, lords and serfs, and so forth. Thus, feudal and capitalist societies embody and reflect different ideas. During the course of historical development, the conflicting ideas embodied in different societies become progressively better (i.e., there is less conflict) and societies approach rational perfection. History ends when *Geist* is fully self-actualized and the perfect state is realized. History ends when we fully know all there is to know and our political practices reflect our perfect knowledge. Some interpreters of Hegel have understood him to mean that states embodying the ideas of democratic liberalism have achieved such perfection.[18]

Marx took up Hegel's grand schema of the historical dialectic and inverted it:

> The mystification which dialectic suffers in Hegel's hands, by no means prevents him from being the first to present its general form of working in a comprehensive and conscious manner. With him it is standing on its head. It must be turned right side up again, if you would discover the rational kernel within the mystical shell.[19]

[17]See Stanley Rosen, *The Limits of Analysis* (New Haven: Yale University Press, 1980), pp. 7–8; and Plato, *Gorgias,* 447c, 448d, 449b–449c, 461c–462a.

[18]G.W.F. Hegel, *Phaenomenologie des Geistes* (Frankfurt: Verlag Ullstein, GmbH, 1970), p. 15. For a study of this sort of interpretation of Hegel, see Barry Cooper, *The End of History: An Essay on Modern Hegelianism* (Toronto: University of Toronto Press, 1984).

[19]Marx, "Afterword" in *Das Kapital,* cited in *The Marx-Engels Reader,* p. xxi.

According to Marx, human consciousness, the shape of human societies, and progress in history are not determined by the self-realization of Spirit, but by the material activity of humans. Marx claimed to have discovered the laws of the political economy and the laws of historical change that would allow him to analyze specific historical stages and to predict the downfall of capitalism and the "end of history." Marx argued that political economies and history work according to empirically verifiable patterns and that change arises out of conflicting material forces. *Material conditions* are the root cause of class structure, class conflict, revolution, and all other aspects of political life. This assertion is consistent with Marx's claim that the conditions of human life are, in essence, material. Human consciousness is determined by the social and material conditions of human life. Thus, while Hegel believed that history was determined by "ideas"—that is, by human beings' slowly evolving consciousness of their spiritual nature and of their ultimate union in *Geist,* Marx argued that history was determined by material conditions.[20]

In the prehistorical and historical periods, human beings confronted a hostile world of material scarcity. Under such conditions, human beings had to provide for their subsistence before they could freely choose to do anything else. This meant that economic necessity was the primary force that motivated human behavior and that economic conditions were therefore the root causes of all human phenomena—which includes everything from religions, customs, and ideologies to laws and governmental and social structures. This ontology—that the ultimate realities and root causes of human life in the historical eras are economic or material and not intellectual or spiritual—has been called **economic determinism** or *historical materialism* by orthodox Marxists, though Marx never used these terms.

The idea of economic determinism has both a static and a dynamic dimension. Statically, the **infrastructure**—Marx's term for various material, objective, or economic conditions of a particular era—determines class structure, which in turn determines the **superstructure**—Marx's term for the ideas we have about religion, morality, law, political ideology, and political institutions. We may think of this as a pyramid, with the infrastructure as the base of the pyramid, the class structure as its middle section, and the superstructure as its tip, which is held up by the rest of the pyramid. In capitalist society, for example, emerging industrial technologies and the factory system (the forces of production) require that products be produced socially or collectively, exchanged in the marketplace, and distributed in such a way as to yield a subsistence wage for the proletariat and profits for the bourgeoisie. This economic system produces a class structure in which the bourgeoisie dominate the proletariat. The bourgeoisie then use their dominant position (1) to develop religious ideas that increase the docility of the proletariat, (2) to impose the ideological hegemony of classical liberalism on the proletariat, (3) to create a set of laws that

[20]Marx was indebted to Ludwig Feuerbach (1804–1872), a German philosopher and moralist, for the idea that history is determined by material conditions, rather than by ideas. See Feuerbach's *The Essence of Christianity,* originally published in 1845.

proclaim universal protection of everyone's rights while they, in fact, merely protect the property interests of the bourgeoisie (liberal law "in its majestic equality forbids rich and poor alike to sleep under bridges"), and (4) to create institutions of representative democracy based on the myth of political equality—institutions that, in reality, respond primarily to the needs of capitalism. In short, economics, or material conditions, determine how we understand the world and our place in it. According to Marx, economics determine consciousness.

Dynamically, changes in the infrastructure or economic conditions bring about changes in the class structure of a society and, ultimately, in its superstructure (its ideology, religion, and laws), thereby bringing about changes in its politics. For example, the change from a feudal economy to a capitalist economy brought with it changes in the class structure of feudal society (the bourgeoisie became the dominant class), which resulted, in turn, in a representative democracy dominated by capitalists and in a liberal ideology that legitimated their power. When economic conditions are ripe, however, and when economic events create class consciousness among the proletariat, revolutionary changes will occur in the capitalist class structure—and, ultimately, in its politics, religion, law, and ideology. In common with all previous economic systems, the existing system of democratic capitalism is doomed, according to Marx, because of the economic forces constantly at work producing "contradictions" and conflict in it. These contradictions include, first and foremost, the tension between the social mode of production and the individualistic mode of appropriation within capitalism and the conflict of interests between the proletariat and the bourgeoisie. These contradictions within the capitalist system will exacerbate class conflict, prompting the rejection of liberal ideology and the widespread acceptance of Marxism as an alternative interpretation of the political economy. Socialism—and, finally, communism—therefore, will be the inevitable result of the material economic forces working themselves out dialectically over time.

Marxists often employ the term "thesis-antithesis-synthesis" to describe this dialectical or conflictual process of change. The present dominant conditions are the **thesis**. For example, the thesis, or dominant condition, of feudal society was an agrarian form of production wherein the social power and privileges remained in the hands of the landed nobility and the authority of the religious order kept the serfs subjected. But an **antithesis** is needed to complement the thesis—that is, to respond to its needs for fulfillment. Without an antithesis, the thesis will stagnate and decay. Accordingly, the landed nobility of feudal society required the bourgeoisie to develop a commercial society that could provide the nobility with more luxurious commodities and a richer culture. To fulfill this need required new means and modes of production (new technologies, along with systems such as factories, warehouses, corporations, and the like). In time, the bourgeoisie developed needs that put them in conflict with the needs of the nobility. For example, they wanted the serfs to be freed from their bondage to the land so that the serfs could provide the necessary manpower for the new urban industries that the bourgeoisie controlled.

They also wanted an end to the idiosyncratic local customs, units of measure, and excise taxes that were the long-established prerogative of the nobility, but that made trade across greater distances difficult.[21] Consequently, the nobility and the bourgeoisie developed irreconcilable differences that could only be resolved (according to Marxists) through such overt conflicts as the French Revolution. Marx regarded the outcomes of these conflicts as the **synthesis** of the old thesis and the challenging, antithetical groups. The synthesis provided an entirely new social order, in which the (old) antithesis—the bourgeoisie and its structures—became the (new) thesis that required a (new) antithesis—the proletariat—to provide the labor to fuel industrialization. But just as the nobility and the bourgeoisie had become conflicting forces, so did the bourgeoisie and the proletariat, and from this conflict would result a new revolution and a new, but final, synthesis, which would be the universal communist society of creative laborers. In all of this, it is important to remember that technological innovation (changes in the means of production) is what makes changes in the modes of production possible. A new antithesis is made possible by new ways of producing the material goods that people (especially the ruling class) desire. Technological progress drives change.

This doctrine of historical change (dialectical materialism) seems to presume that all change is mechanical and predetermined by material forces. But, among different types of Marxists, there is much debate regarding strict economic determinism. Most have maintained that Marx may have provided for some indeterminism (e.g., as evidenced by his notion that historical change is not completely determined by economics, but is also influenced by individuals and ideas) and for reciprocal causation (e.g., as evidenced by his notion that politics could somewhat modify economic conditions) in his ideology. How one chooses sides in this debate is in part determined by which of Marx's and Engel's texts one chooses to emphasize. One source for the "soft" interpretation of Marx is his "Introduction" to *Contribution to the Critique of Hegel's Philosophy of Right.* There, Marx wrote that "just as philosophy finds its material weapons in the proletariat, so does the proletariat find its intellectual weapons in philosophy . . . Philosophy is the head of this emancipation, and the proletariat is its heart." Those who stress the "soft" Marx claim that Engels, by systematizing Marx, made his theory more deterministic than Marx had intended. The strongest statements of economic determinism are found in Engels' *Anti-Duehring.*[22] Among neo-Marxists, Louis Althusser is the foremost proponent of economic determinism, while Nicos Poulantzas argues for a more autonomous political realm.[23] How one chooses to interpret this matter is not trivial. If one views Marx as essentially a determinist, then he is also

[21]See Robert L. Heilbroner, *The Worldly Philosophers* (New York: Simon and Schuster, 1953), pp. 12–17 and 21–23, for anecdotal accounts of these and other (often intentional) impediments to bourgeois commerce.

[22]See Heilbroner, *Worldly Philosophers,* pp. 129–130, and David McLellan, *Marxism after Marx* (Boston: Houghton Mifflin, 1979), pp. 9–17.

[23]See Robert Alford and Roger Friedland, *Powers of Theory: Capitalism, the State, and Democracy* (Cambridge: Cambridge University Press, 1985), pp. 273–278.

essentially a "scientist" of history. If, on the other hand, one views him as merely a "soft" determinist, at best, then one can see him as much more an activist political revolutionary than scientist.

Epistemology

The idea of historicism, or historical determinism, addresses Marx's epistemology as well as his ontology. While conservatives justified the structures and practices of traditional societies based on the collective wisdom of tradition, and while liberals justified democratic capitalism on the basis of utilitarianism, Marx rejected such approaches to justifying communist goals. He did not work out a scheme of an ideal communist society, nor did he provide a systematic argument delineating why such a society would be "good." He regarded all attempts to demonstrate the rationality of a socialist system as merely "metaphysical." According to Engels, "there is no end to the conflict among absolute truths" in asserting the goodness of particular economic, social, and political systems.[24] In response to this apparent tradition of metaphysical dogmatism, Marx and Engels rejected any "moral appeal" as the basis for communism. Instead, they chose to base the legitimacy of communism on a science—the correct scientific understanding of the laws of history in general and of the laws of political economy in particular. Rather than demonstrate that communism is good, Marx wanted to show that the laws of history and political economy make it inevitable. In this way, he wanted to replace utopian socialism with **scientific socialism**.[25] What Marx meant by this was that his version of socialism was the product of a scientific study of economic and historical laws, not the result of a moralistic sentiment that "this is what ought to be (although not yet in existence)." The problem with all other forms of socialism, according to Marx and Engels, is that they are all either impractical forms of utopian wishful thinking or a means by which the ruling classes continue to hold the subordinate classes in subjection. "My results," wrote Marx, "have been won by means of a wholly empirical analysis based on conscientious study of political economy."[26] This "scientific" approach to the problems of human existence in history ultimately makes Marxian epistemology the linchpin of Marxism.

Marx was not the first ideologist to seek a science of politics. Liberals, too, wanted to build an understanding of politics on science. But while they employed a Cartesian methodology that builds truths *deductively* from indubitable facts about human nature, Marx and Marxism employed an *inductive* science. They formulated certain concepts that described the world in general terms and then developed generalizations based on what they thought to be

[24]Engels, *Socialism: Utopian and Scientific,* in *The Marx-Engels Reader,* pp. 695–696.

[25]See *Socialism: Utopian and Scientific,* pp. 683–717, and *The Manifesto of the Communist Party,* pp. 491–500.

[26]*Philosophical and Economic Manuscripts,* p. 67; cf. *The Manifesto of the Communist Party,"* pp. 491–499, and *Socialism: Utopian and Scientific,* passim.

empirical observations about the relationships among these concepts.[27] Such generalizations served to describe and explain social life, and provide the basis for predictions about the future.

We have seen that Marx's science is both static and dynamic. The *dynamic* element is usually the one stressed in discussions of Marxism, but both aspects are important.[28] *Static* analysis is concerned with the interrelationships within and among various domains of life for a particular historical period. Each historical period has its own "reality," which is uniquely valuable and important and which static analysis reveals. We recall that this "reality" consists of the prevailing means and modes of production and the superstructure of intellectual, cultural, religious, and legal institutions and modes that is erected on top of them. The realities of each period are not immutable, however, and their value is only identifiable relative to a particular period in time.

According to Marx, the process of induction based on empirical observations of capitalist society confirms the following scientific propositions. There are two main classes: the bourgeoisie, who own the means of production, and the proletariat, who own only their own labor. Because the bourgeoisie are relatively wealthy and few in number, whereas the proletariat are poor and many in number, the bourgeoisie and proletariat do not confront or bargain with each other as equals, despite their formal legal equality. The unequal bargaining power of the bourgeoisie and proletariat constrains the proletariat to sell their labor for subsistence wages, which permits the bourgeoisie to extract surplus value (about which we will say more in our discussion of justice) from the proletariat. This creation of surplus value provides the bourgeoisie with profits, which, in turn, increases their capital in a seemingly endless process of accumulation. Moreover, market competition forces the bourgeoisie to reduce their production costs in order to survive economically. Consequently, they reinvest

[27]The deployment of concepts in this manner is consistent with Marx's oft-cited declaration that whereas "the philosophers have only *interpreted* the world, in various ways; the point, however, is to *change* it." (Marx, *Theses on Feuerbach,* no. 11, in *The Marx-Engels Reader,* p. 145.) Marx urged us not to investigate the world empirically to determine what is and to develop conceptual accounts based on that investigation, but to apply concepts (generated by ourselves) to the world in order to develop an understanding of the world that allows us to transform it.

The reader should note the methodological difficulties of this way of thinking about concepts and conceptual language. If concepts have theoretical relationships rather than empirical ones, they allow us to understand intellectual abstractions among phenomena, but they do not give us immediate access to the phenomena in themselves. If we understand that inductive theories are only intellectual abstractions, then we understand that we must first "operationalize" theoretical concepts in order to use them for action in the real world. While Marx's inductive theory allows him to understand political change, orthodox Marxists thought that change would come about automatically, because of the development of the theory itself. To believe that concepts give us an immediate, practical purchase on empirical reality, rather than an intellectual understanding of it, is to believe that we can perform magical operations in or on reality by invoking conceptual language as though it were an immediate tool for empirical transformation—a tool that does not require us to "operationalize" in practical, contingent terms the concepts we deploy intellectually in our theorizations. Cf. Kenneth Hoover, *Ideology and Political Life,* 2d ed. (Belmont, CA: Wadsworth Publishing, 1993), pp. 138–139.

[28]Cf. Tony Smith, *Thinking Like a Communist: State and Legitimacy in the Soviet Union, China, and Cuba* (New York: W.W. Norton, 1987), p. 54.

their profits in labor-saving technological improvements, permitting them to reduce production costs by replacing labor with machines. This competitive process continually exacerbates the misery of the proletariat, and it also reduces the ranks of the bourgeoisie, because the "losers" in the competitive drive for cost-reducing are bankrupted, and "fall down" into the ranks of the proletariat.[29] Liberal ideology (including the idea that capitalism improves the condition of everyone) and Christian beliefs (including the idea that this world is a "vale of tears" and that the poor will receive their reward in heaven) incline the proletariat and "dispossessed bourgeoisie" to accept their wretched conditions.[30]

Marx and his followers constructed similar analyses of other periods of history. The analysis of capitalism is the most important to Marxian thought, however, because the conditions of capitalism are prerequisite to the culmination of history in the communist society. By themselves, such generalizations provide unappealing descriptions of capitalism and may explain the plight of the working class, but they do not provide a basis for predicting changes in these conditions. In order to achieve predictions of change, Marx developed a dynamic science about the laws of history—namely, dialectical materialism. We considered the broader outlines of these dynamic changes in our discussion in the section on ontology. Now we are in a position to summarize Marx's more specific doctrine concerning why change from a capitalist to communist society is inevitable.

SUBSTANTIVE POLITICAL PRINCIPLES

Change

According to Marx, all societies have experienced fundamental and progressive change. Capitalist society necessarily will experience such change, too. In general, Marx assumed that this change would be revolutionary and that it would occur only when objective economic conditions were ripe, and when subjective class consciousness among the proletariat had been adequately developed. Marx, and his orthodox followers, rejected the notion that revolutions could be made before both objective and subjective conditions were ripe, and they did not believe that change could occur by political reform without a revolution. Marx thought that revolutionary change in Europe was imminent; indeed, he thought that the political turmoil in Europe in both 1848 and 1871 was the harbinger of revolutionary change.

The revolution that overthrows capitalism and inaugurates the reign of communism will occur as the following ten laws of political economy take their course:

1. As industrial society develops, there will be extensive competition among capitalists. To compete in the marketplace, capitalists must exploit the laborers, paying them only subsistence wages, thereby extracting surplus

[29]See Marx, *Manifesto of the Communist Party*, pp. 474–480.
[30]Marx, *German Ideology*, p. 159; *Manifesto of the Communist Party*, p. 489.

value, or profits, which the capitalists must, in turn, reinvest in more modern and efficient technology.

2. Some capitalist enterprises will be successful, and some will fail under these conditions of competition and modernization. The unsuccessful ones will be forced out of the marketplace, and capital and capitalist power will become ever more concentrated.
3. As successful capitalist enterprises replace workers with machines, and as more and more enterprises fail, there will be fewer employers, and more and more workers will be laid off, with many becoming permanently unemployed.
4. These unemployed workers will lack the purchasing power to buy the goods that are being produced by capitalist enterprises. Production will therefore slow down, and even more workers will become unemployed.
5. Cycles of unemployment and consequent slack demand (recessions) will recur over time. With each recession, there will be fewer and fewer successful capitalists—i.e., those who manage to weather the economic storm. The economic position of these surviving capitalists improves with the lack of competition, and their wealth will increase.
6. But, with each recession, there will also be greater and greater numbers of unsuccessful people in the marketplace. The unsuccessful bourgeois capitalists will be displaced and fall down into the ranks of the proletariat (and some of the proletariat will descend even further into an underclass, or *Lumpenproletariat*). These downwardly mobile bourgeoisie will continue to swell the ranks of the proletariat, more and more of whose members are unemployed. Marx called this downward cycle the **immiseration of the proletariat**.
7. These increasingly desperate conditions will cause the proletariat and others who are being marginalized in the economic system to question the usefulness and fairness of capitalism. Working-class consciousness will develop out of this questioning.
8. When the economy inevitably hits a severe depression and proletarian misery is particularly acute, and when the proletariat finally comes to believe that the capitalist system has outlived its usefulness, a spontaneous mass rebellion will occur. Initially, unrelated small strikes, boycotts, riots, and mass uprisings will occur. These will coalesce into more militant and unified political action. One of the following scenarios will then lead to **revolution**: a general strike may bankrupt capitalists overnight; a civil war may occur between capitalists and their agents of order (police and army) on the one side and an armed proletariat on the other; or, the bourgeoisie could be overthrown by ballots rather than bullets in a democratic election, although this scenario is unlikely.[31]

[31]There is some evidence that near the end of his life, Marx thought that the revolution could be achieved by parliamentary means in democratized societies such as England, the United States, Belgium, and the Netherlands. Cf. "Amsterdam Speech of 1872," in Karl Marx, *Selected Writings*, edited by David McClellan (Oxford: Oxford University Press, 1977), p. 594.

9. After the proletariat has seized power, a state of emergency will exist. Because the bourgeoisie will remain wedded to liberal ideology, and because their concern will be to restore their own power and wealth, the bourgeoisie may initiate a counterrevolution. To prevent this possibility, the proletariat must establish a **dictatorship of the proletariat** that will forcefully suppress the bourgeoisie, but not the members of the proletarian class.
10. The decisive proletarian defeat of the bourgeoisie will begin a period of socialism, a period of transition from capitalism to full communism in which the social and ideological remnants of capitalism disappear and are replaced with new, cooperative social arrangements and a "New Man"—one who is committed to socialist ideals of egalitarian liberty and fraternity.[32] A completely communist society will eventually emerge out of this socialist interlude as the state gradually loses any significant purpose and withers away.

Marx left the precise nature of this final, posthistorical state largely unspecified, only hinting at its utopian nature. He refused to delineate its precise organizing principles and structure. He did suggest, however, that in a completely communist society, people would no longer be constrained by economic necessity, because their planned, industrialized economy would produce the goods they needed. They would no longer make decisions on the basis of narrow self-interest, because they would be "New Men"—existing without class interests in a classless society.

Given this doctrine of social change, it is useful, when we are discussing the political principles of Marxism, to distinguish between three historical periods, as noted earlier. Marx characterized capitalist structures, rulers, authority, justice, and citizenship in certain critical terms. He suggested alternative principles to guide socialist society (the transition from capitalism to communism) and yet another set of ideals for a completely communist society. After first recalling the conditions of humans and the class structure of society in these three periods, Table 5-1 summarizes these distinctions.

Structure

Marx and Marxists are radicals in their political principles, which means that they find the root causes of human problems such as our oppressive class system and our alienation in the structure of society itself. The key to achieving Marxist goals is, therefore, to transform the structure of society. Marx provided a penetrating and critical analysis of the structure of capitalist society, and he hinted at how he believed socialist and communist societies should be structured.

The central structural element of modern bourgeois society is **capitalism,**

[32]This agenda is outlined in Marx, *Critique of the Gotha Program,* in *The Marx-Engels Reader,* pp. 525–41.

TABLE 5-1. Marxist Characterizations of Three Historical to Posthistorical Periods

	Capitalism	Socialism	Communism
Human Nature	Alienated.	Alienation is being overcome.	Community-oriented creative workers.
Society	Bourgeoisie dominate proletariat.	Proletariat dominate bourgeoisie.	Classless.
Structure	Dominance of private industry.	Dominance by centralized state.	No coercive institutions; only voluntary associations.
Rulers	Dictatorship of bourgeoisie.	Dictatorship of proletariat.	Self-management.
Authority	Government is the instrument of capitalism.	Government socializes property, plans the economy.	Government withers away.
Justice	Capitalists exploit workers.	To each according to his labor.	To each according to his need.
Citizenship	Citizens are mostly subjects.	Citizens are both participants and subjects.	Citizens are mostly participants in making their collective history.

whose central features include private ownership and control of the means of production, increasing monopolization (or concentration of the ownership and control of property), and bourgeois domination of all other aspects of society, including family life, culture, and government. Because in capitalist societies private industry dominates government, Marxists view governmental structures in capitalist societies as relatively unimportant, and they do not have much to say about what, if any, specific political institutions within capitalist society might help them achieve their goals. Even liberal democratic institutions in such societies are of little value, because they simply provide a facade behind which capitalist business organizations may continue to dominate government and the bourgeoisie may continue to deceive or appease the proletariat with talk of rights, freedom, and equality.

The relative impotence of the capitalist state—namely, its inability to exercise political authority on behalf of the common good—means that essential decisions about society, including what goods to produce and how to distribute them, are left to the apparent anarchy of the market. Thus, the most powerful institutions of capitalist society are organized to serve immediate and private interests. Such structural arrangements served positive social functions during the early industrial stage in capitalism's history, for several reasons. First, through these arrangements the bourgeoisie "pitilessly [tore] asunder the motley feudal ties that bound man to his 'natural superiors'. . . . In a word, for exploitation, veiled by religious and political illusions, it has substituted naked, shameless, direct, brutal exploitation."[33] Second, by creating "more massive and more colossal productive forces than have all preceding generations together," according to Marx, capitalist institutions enabled human beings to master nature.[34] These productive forces include material technologies (chemical applications, steam navigation, electricity, etc.), as well as the technologies of organization (bureaucracies, bookkeeping, communication, and industrial management). After the revolution, these productive forces will create the wealth of the final, communist society, but in a nonalienating fashion. Third, capitalism has created a perpetual need for innovation and change. The competition of the marketplace drives industry to become ever more efficient. This competitive imperative leads to innovations in the material technologies of production and in the technologies of organization. These changes (according to Marxist logic) lead to changes in the social relations of production, and these lead, in turn, to changes in the wider society:

> The bourgeoisie cannot exist without constantly revolutionizing the instruments of production, and thereby the relations of production, and with them the whole relations of society. Conservation of the old modes of production in unaltered form was, on the contrary, the first condition of existence for all earlier industrial classes. Constant revolutionizing of production, uninterrupted disturbance of all social conditions, everlasting uncertainty, and agitation distinguish the bourgeois epoch from all earlier ones. All fixed, fast-frozen relations, with their train of ancient and venerable prejudices and opinions, are swept away, all new-formed ones become antiquated before they can ossify. All that is solid melts into air, all that is holy is profaned . . .[35]

For this reason, Marx claims that the bourgeoisie have historically "played a most revolutionary part."[36]

Finally, the bourgeoisie, in playing its "most revolutionary part," has "simplified class antagonisms: Society as a whole is more and more splitting up into two great hostile camps, into two great classes directly facing each other: bourgeoisie and proletariat."[37]

All of these developments are positive for Marx, not because of any intrinsic moral worth, but because they hasten the coming of communism. But this also means that these developments have been overtaken, and that capitalism and its illusory democratic institutions have outlived their usefulness. Its modes of production can produce more goods than can be consumed, given

[33]Marx, *The Manifesto of the Communist Party*, p. 475.
[34]Marx, *The Manifesto of the Communist Party*, p. 477.
[35]Marx, *The Manifesto of the Communist Party*, p. 476.
[36]Marx, *The Manifesto of the Communist Party*, p. 475.
[37]Marx, *The Manifesto of the Communist Party*, p. 474.

its modes of exchange and appropriation, and it has exacerbated human alienation in every dimension. Moreover, as we have seen, capitalism is self-contradictory. On the one hand, capitalists seek profits, but on the other hand, the realities of competition make this goal increasingly difficult to achieve. The pressure of competition and profit-seeking lead to ever greater general misery even as the capitalist means and modes of production seem to promise abundance. Capitalism's waning usefulness will prompt an inevitable revolt against it that will sweep away its institutions.

After the revolution, the political economy will be dominated by a **centralized proletarian state**. Contrary to the assertions of subsequent communists, Marx thought that the communist state, and not the communist party, would be the dominant institution in the transitory socialist society. He made this clear in *The Manifesto of the Communist Party,* asserting that the party would "centralize all instruments of production in the hands of the State, *i.e.,* of the proletariat organized as the ruling class," which would end the rule of the bourgeois capitalists. As socialism matures, however, the centralized state will, in its turn, become outmoded. Having implemented a series of measures to revolutionize the mode of production—including the expropriation of several forms of private property, the quashing of counterrevolutionary forces and tendencies, and the nationalization of various industries—the state will have overseen the transition from capitalism to communism. It will no longer be needed, and will therefore "wither away." Society will then be organized on the basis of decentralized, voluntary organizations as a "vast association of the whole nation," in which "the free development of each is the condition for the free development of all" and in which class antagonisms no longer exist, so that the political power and political institutions that are "merely the organized power of one class for oppressing another" are no longer needed.[38]

Rulers

Marx asserted that capitalist society is ruled by capitalists, which, despite the existence of liberal democratic institutions, makes it a de facto "dictatorship of the bourgeoisie." Most important decisions about the production and distribution of material goods are made by capitalists in the private sphere, with little or no participation or influence by governmental officials, let alone representatives of the proletariat. Insofar as governmental officials exercise authority, they do so in response to the interests of capitalists and not those of ordinary citizens. Consequently, Marx characterized even democratically elected rulers as "the executive committee of the bourgeoisie." In this context, democratic elections fail to empower citizens, because the real power brokers of society—the capitalists—are not candidates for election, nor can they be democratically "removed from office"—or separated from ownership of the means of production. Those people seeking election, moreover, have to respond to the "economic imperatives" that foster the interests of the capital-

[38]Marx, *Manifesto of the Communist Party,* pp. 490–491.

ist class. For this reason, Marx did not think it likely that democratic elections could bring to power representatives who would serve the interests of the working class and who would use their governmental power to achieve socialist goals. It would probably require a revolution to bring such rulers to power.

According to Marx, the revolution itself could not be dominated by an intellectual vanguard. The intellectuals and leaders would play a minor role: at best, they would simply provide instruction that would help to form proletarian class consciousness. According to Engels, "Marx entirely trusted to the intellectual development of the working class, which was sure to result from combined action and mutual discussion," so that "the emancipation of the working class must be an act of the working class itself."[39] Unlike later communists, Marx embraced no "theory of substitutionism" in which proletarian class consciousness is a possession of an intellectual elite.

After the revolution, the dictatorship of the bourgeoisie would be replaced by a dictatorship of the proletariat. Marx used the term "dictatorship" to emphasize the domination of the proletariat over the bourgeoisie. However, there was to be no dictatorship *within* the proletariat. As Tony Smith has noted, Marx never mentioned a "vanguard of the proletariat" that would govern on behalf of the proletariat, nor did he conceive of one-party control of the state by leaders of the communist party. For Marx, the dictatorship of the proletariat would be, in Smith's words, "a decidedly popular affair."[40] The bourgeoisie, however, would not be included in this popular dictatorship, because truly democratic rule could only function when there were no longer class divisions that distorted political debate and prompted people to think in class rather than communal terms.

The Paris Commune (1871) seemed to provide Marx with a model for rulership in the transitory socialist society. In *The Civil War in France,* Marx outlined its characteristics. There would be freedom of speech and assembly, and open discussion and debate at the most immediate levels of neighborhood and factory. Delegates would be selected to represent citizens at meetings of higher-level state organizations, but they would act as delegates, rather than independently. They would be subject to recall if they failed to act according to their instructions—instructions that would be democratically devised. Delegates would receive few perks of office, and their salaries would be those of the average worker.[41]

As the need for the state withered away, so, too, would the need for the dictatorship of the proletariat. Power would be broadly dispersed among workers—the new creative laborers—in their decentralized workplaces and associations. There would be genuine self-management, but more importantly, an end to the conditions of class conflict and its resulting hierarchies of power, false consciousness, and human alienation. Changes in economic structures

[39]See Engels, "Preface to the 1888 English Edition" of *The Manifesto of the Communist Party,* cited in Smith, *Thinking Like a Communist,* pp. 57–58.
[40]Smith, *Thinking Like a Communist,* p. 24.
[41]Cf. Engels, "Introduction" to Marx, *The Civil War in France,* in *Marx-Engels Reader,* pp. 627–628.

would bring about a true transformation of human nature that would eliminate the need for some humans to be ruled by others.

Authority

Governmental authorities in capitalist society use their power to further the interests of the capitalist class, or bourgeoisie, and the capitalist system. They create policies that promote several measures aimed at achieving that end. These include policies that foster capital accumulation and the concentration of wealth among an increasingly smaller number of people who can invest it in ever more innovative and labor-saving technologies.[42] Other policies are directed toward averting economic stagnation and crisis. Finally, some policies are attempts to ameliorate class conflict—for example, efforts to prevent the politicization of the working class by means of social control through appeasement, including the provision of welfare and unemployment insurance. The capitalist state performs these functions of control through force, mythmaking, and cooptation.[43] The police and the court system enforce property laws; the reigning capitalist and liberal ideologies, religious beliefs, and social customs sustain the myth of freedom and property rights; and welfare policies attempt to mollify the dispossessed.

In socialist society, state power will be used to socialize the means of production.[44] The state will plan and manage economic production. Rejecting the anarchy of the market, the socialist state will rationalize production through central planning. Social needs will be determined by consensus, and the state will organize production to meet these needs. The state will begin its nationalization of the means of production with the creation of a centralized bank, socialization of the communication and transportation industries, collectivization of agriculture, and confiscation of the property of all opponents of the revolution.[45] State management of production will ensure that private interests will not take precedence over public interests. The socialist state will also crush the likely dissent and counterrevolutionary activities of the bourgeoisie, and it will play a leading role in educating people to accept the egalitarian and fraternal values of a future communist society. Later, in the communist society, the state will have only administrative functions, if any remain necessary. Its political purposes will have withered away as class conflict disappears.

Justice

Marxists have engaged in a lively debate over Marx's ideas regarding justice. Some commentators argue that Marx did not emphasize justice, that he regarded such ideas as "equal rights" and "fair distribution" as "obsolete ver-

[42]See Alford and Friedland, *Powers of Theory*, pp. 288–307.
[43]Smith, *Thinking Like a Communist*, p. 44.
[44]Marx, *Manifesto of the Communist Party*, pp. 490–491.
[45]Marx, *Manifesto of the Communist Party*, p. 490.

Born Loser reprinted by permission of NEA, Inc.

bal rubbish."[46] Other commentators argue that Marx understood that capitalism was based on injustice—on capitalists wrongly taking what rightfully belongs to the worker—and sought an alternative, more just system for distributing social goods.[47] What is clear is that Marx believed that the issue of "just distribution" was much less important than the question of fair and efficient methods of production. Whether or not it was unjust, the capitalist mode of production exploited and alienated workers. Eliminating private property by socializing the means of production is central to Marxist theories of justice.

Marxists deny that justice can be achieved by capitalist forces in capitalist society. *Exploitation* occurs under capitalism, because the bourgeoisie receive the surplus value of the goods produced by the laborers—whom they effectively control. Laborers are exploited, because they do not receive the full value of their labor. While laborers provide much of the value of the commodities that are produced in a factory and sold in the marketplace by capitalists, laborers are paid only a minimum, **subsistence wage**, an amount significantly less than the value of their contribution to these commodities.[48]

While the labor market produces some variation in the wages that workers are given, "the average price of wage-labor is the minimum wage, i.e., the quantum of the means of subsistence which is absolutely requisite to keep the labourer in bare existence as a labourer."[49] The laborer receives a minimal wage, not because the capitalist is necessarily greedy and mean-spirited, but rather because of the logic of capitalist competition. If a capitalist were to pay a worker more than a subsistence wage, his costs would rise, the price of the product would rise, and consumers would choose to purchase the cheaper goods of his competitor, who maintained minimum wages. The threat of unemployment and eventual starvation force the worker to accept this minimum wage. Each worker understands that there is a large reserve of indus-

[46]Marx, *Critique of the Gotha Program,* p. 531.

[47]This debate is summarized in Steven Lukes, *Marxism and Morality* (Oxford: Oxford University Press, 1987), pp. 48–59.

[48]It is often asserted that Marx accepted a Lockean labor theory of value—that labor alone creates value. G. A. Cohen, in *History, Labour, and Freedom: Themes from Marx* (Oxford: Oxford University Press, 1988) suggests that Marx merely claimed that workers produce *some* value for which they are not rewarded, and that this constitutes exploitation (pp. 226–227).

[49]Marx, *The Manifesto of the Communist Party,* p. 485.

trial workers who will accept subsistence wages to survive, so he must do so as well.

The capitalist, meanwhile, extracts a **surplus value**, or profits, from the labor of his workers. The workers produce goods whose value in the marketplace is greater than the costs incurred by the capitalist to produce them, because the capitalist's labor costs are only minimal, subsistence wages rather than the real value of the worker's labor. The capitalist owner of the means of production pockets the difference between the value that the worker actually produces and the subsistence wage paid to the worker. Much of this profit is then reinvested in labor-saving machinery so that the capitalist can reduce his costs of labor in the future and ensure his survival in the marketplace. Thus, the worker provides the very "surplus value" that is used to bring about his future unemployment. In this way, the capitalist system, more than the capitalist as a person, is unjust; it is capitalism as a system that exploits the working class and that causes human misery.

Nevertheless, Marx did not believe that the exploitation of labor in this way was necessarily unjust. The exchange between capitalist and worker was, in some sense, a voluntary and mutually beneficial exchange. The worker exchanged his labor for the money he needed for subsistence. For the cost of the money-wage given to the laborer, the capitalist also purchased the surplus value produced by the laborer. The power of capitalism resides in its unique ability to accumulate and deploy this surplus.[50]

Even if the exchange of labor for wages was not, for Marx, necessarily unjust, there is substantial evidence that he regarded as unjust the larger capitalist system built on the private ownership of productive property. The **abolition of private property** is central to Marxist notions of justice. While Marx had no objection to the private ownership of personal property such as clothes, shelter, furnishings, and leisure goods, he argued that capitalists had "no moral right to the private ownership and control of productive resources," which he called "capital."[51] He ridiculed the idea that the means of production had been (or could be) justly acquired by capitalists, or that capitalists deserved such productive resources because of prudent saving and reinvestment of their earned recovery or because of the unusually great risks they had taken. Instead, Marx asserted that capital had typically been accumulated by force, "by conquest, enslavement, robbery, and murder."[52]

For Marxists, abolishing private ownership of the means of production is important for several reasons. Until private property is abolished, workers will be alienated, as we described in our discussion of human nature. Until private property is abolished, unjustified inequalities in power will persist, as capitalists will retain control over workers. Inequalities in control of productive resources make the "equal rights" of classical liberals a mere formality, since

[50]Marx, *Grundrisse*, in *The Marx-Engels Reader*, p. 249.

[51]Cohen, *History, Labour, and Freedom*, p. 298.

[52]John Roemer, *Free to Lose: An Introduction to Marxist Economic Philosophy* (Cambridge: Harvard University Press, 1988), pp. 58–59.

such inequalities effectively deny those without private property the rights or opportunities to live as they wish. Until private property is abolished, a few private individuals will continue to make the key economic decisions, a problem that will be reflected in the anarchy of the marketplace. Without public control of the production process, there will be recurring cycles of economic crises that impoverish nearly everyone.

Accordingly, Marx believed that private ownership of productive property contributed heavily to economic scarcity. While industrialization provides the means through which humans could attain economic abundance, the private ownership of property instead ensures scarcity, for several reasons. It produces alienated workers who do not use their full creative capacities, but work only as much as they must to attain their subsistence. It leads to ruthless competition, and to the closure of many productive enterprises. It leads capitalists to produce luxuries for which there is market demand, rather than the commodities that average men and women need and want, but cannot afford. In short, it leads to inefficiency and to the underutilization of human and economic resources.

As a system of the private ownership of the means of production, capitalism has continued what Will Kymlicka has called the "circumstances of justice."[53] Like all previous political economies, capitalism has been characterized by scarcity, and scarcity encourages people to be preoccupied with justice—with how to distribute scarce resources fairly. Marx sought to move beyond these "circumstances of justice" to an affluent society. A truly good society would have no need for "justice" when "the springs of co-operative wealth flow more abundantly."[54] Marx believed that the "circumstances of justice" would be transcended only in the ideal communist society—after human alienation has ended, after humans have become creative workers who are motivated by the intrinsic satisfaction that work provides, and after economic scarcity has been eliminated. He did not assume that the abolition of capitalism would immediately usher in such circumstances.

During the transition to communism, goods might better be distributed by the **contribution principle**—those who contributed the most to the productive process would deserve, and receive, a greater share. In the transitionary state, there would be an "unequal right for unequal labor." While Marx regarded the idea of "to each according to his labor" as an improvement over the exploitation that occurred in capitalism and as a useful means of motivating people until they overcame their alienation, he did not regard distribution based on labor as just. He understood that unequal talents and unequal social circumstances would lead to unequal work contributions. Because inequalities such as talents and social circumstances may be unearned, distributions based on labor, which reflects such inequalities, may also be unearned (and unjust). Distributions based on labor therefore fail to treat people fairly, as equals.

Once scarcity had been eliminated, questions of distribution would no

[53]Will Kymlicka, *Contemporary Political Philosophy* (New York: Oxford Press, 1990), p. 164.
[54]Marx, *Critique of the Gotha Program*, p. 531.

longer be pressing. Society would no longer need principles of justice to resolve conflicts over the fair distribution of social goods. In his *Critique of the Gotha Program,* Marx asserted that the ideal communist society would inscribe on its banner: "From each according to his ability, to each according to his needs."[55] But this is perhaps less a principle of justice, understood as a method for distributing scarce resources, than a projection of what could happen in an affluent communist society. With scarcity no longer a consideration, people will be free to simply take what they need from the stock of abundant resources.[56]

In summary, Marxism is normally perceived as a critique of the injustices of capitalism. While Marx disapproved of the exploitation and alienation of labor under capitalism, he regarded the private ownership of productive property as the greatest evil of capitalism—an evil because it was inefficient, as well as "unjust." According to Marxists, distributions based on "labor" or "needs" may be less exploitative and thus less unjust than those that occur under capitalism, but there is little evidence that Marx believed that the maxim "to each according to his labor" or "to each according to his needs," constituted a principle of justice that would guide distributional issues in socialist and communist societies. In the affluent world that Marx anticipated—in a world freed by highly efficient industrial production from the claims of necessity and scarcity—distributional issues and the need for principles of justice would disappear.

Citizenship

Marx (and Marxists) argue that citizen participation in a capitalist democratic society is essentially symbolic and ineffectual. It is merely a formal democracy, and, as such, is part of a "legitimation system" that is intended to induce loyalty in the masses.[57] Indeed, the hallmark of the democratic state is its ability to legitimize citizen obedience. The power of the "myth" of the democratic state lies in its ability to make citizens believe that they are obeying laws of their own making—but these laws are, in fact, made by capitalists or their rep-

[55]Marx, *Critique of the Gotha Program,* p. 531.

[56]Kymlicka, *Contemporary Political Philosophy,* p. 183. Kymlicka points out that if the unrealistic assumption of complete abundance is dropped, the principle of distributing goods according to need is not very clear or helpful. The principle can be interpreted in two different ways. First, needs could be interpreted narrowly—everyone would be provided the base material necessities—minimum food, clothing, and shelter. In this interpretation, communist societies would not be significantly more egalitarian than existing welfare states. Second, needs could be interpreted much more broadly—different people would have different needs to sustain the different kinds of lives they pursue. For example, the "needs" of an artist who paints with watercolors are less than those of an architect who creates large ornate buildings, and the needs of a jogger are less than those of a person who sails yachts for recreation. When resources are scarce, we must decide whose needs to satisfy, and the principle "to each according to his needs" provides no guidance to resolving such questions.

[57]Jürgen Habermas, *Legitimation Crisis,* translated by Thomas McCarthy (Boston: Beacon Press, 1975), p. 37.

resentatives. While Marx had little to say about the major vehicles of proletarian participation—including trade unions, working-class parties, and social movements—he does not seem to have regarded them as effective means of citizen influence, except in rare circumstances. Neo-Marxists have continued to debate the potential of such vehicles.[58]

In a socialist society, citizens would have more opportunities to be involved in decisions concerning production and distribution. As we noted in our discussion of rulers, Marx suggested that workers would enjoy extensive political rights during the transition to communism. In the workplaces and neighborhoods where direct participation is possible, workers would debate and resolve issues, and they would elect and hold accountable their representatives to higher-level political institutions. Citizenship would be restricted in socialist society; former capitalists and others who continued to cling to liberal, bourgeois ideas would be denied citizenship until they no longer constituted an important reactionary force. The notion of the "dictatorship of the proletariat" clearly implies that citizenship would be limited to those who were qualified for participation in a socialist state, and that qualifying was dependent upon having overcome the exploitative attitudes and false consciousness that predominate in capitalist society. The socialist state also would impose many obligations on its citizens and command widespread obedience to its authority. Former aristocrats and capitalists would be obligated to relinquish their land and factories as the state collectivized and nationalized industry. Those with great wealth would have to pay heavy progressive income taxes, the right of inheritance would be abolished, and estates would be confiscated by the state. Those workers who disagreed with their comrades would have to submit to mediation by the dictatorship of the proletariat and obey its rule without resistance. While the burdens of obedience might appear excessive during the transitional socialist period, Marxist theory suggests that they are justified as necessary means for achieving a fully communist society.

In a communist society, citizenship would be both minimal and extensive. It would be minimal, because the state would have withered away, and members of society would no longer be citizens of a centralized state. They would no longer participate in governmental decision making and they would no longer be obligated to obey governmental authority. In another sense, citizenship would be extensive, because the members of society would participate in resolving many social issues. If the communist citizen is to "hunt in the morning, fish in the afternoon, rear cattle in the evening, [and] criticize after dinner, just as I have in mind,"[59] he or she will likely need to attend a variety of meetings to discuss and vote on issues regarding these matters.[60] He or she will need to discuss, for example, those fishes and animals that should be protected as endangered species, the appropriate fishing and hunting seasons, and

[58]Cf. Alford and Friedland, *Powers of Theory*, pp. 345–360.

[59]Marx, *The German Ideology*, p. 160.

[60]See Michael Walzer, "A Day in the Life of a Socialist Citizen," in *Obligations: Essays on Disobedience, War, and Citizenship* (Cambridge: Harvard University Press, 1970), pp. 229–238.

the weapons that humans can use to catch or shoot their prey. On such matters, communist citizens will govern themselves, and this will be a demanding and time-consuming activity. Most importantly, the nature of citizenship will be transformed from what is regarded as citizenship in liberal societies. Rather than viewing citizenship as a means of protecting his or her rights and pursuing his or her self-interests, the communist citizen is envisioned by Marxists as someone who possesses an extraordinary degree of public-spiritedness and a strong sense of responsibility. Such a citizen would disregard the liberal distinction between the public and private spheres of life. Citizens would live entirely within the public sphere, always concerned with society, understanding their own good as being intertwined with the public good. Rather than viewing citizenship as primarily an obedience to the laws of the state, the communist citizen would submit to the decisions of those who are active in resolving the issues of community life. Such submission, however, would not be problematic. If goods are abundant, and if everyone is public-spirited, the decisions of self-governing citizens will hardly be repressive, but will simply represent the (general) will of free men and women finally making their own history in accordance with their shared understanding of the good life.[61]

SUMMARY AND CONCLUSIONS

The collapse of the communist regimes of Eastern Europe and the former Soviet Union has led to a general discrediting not only of communism, but also of Marxism, which is nominally the underlying ideology of these regimes. As we shall see in the next chapter, Marx would likely have been very critical of communists' attempts to "telescope" the various stages of history to bring about the revolution (before he, relying on his science, would have considered it historically possible) in the countries of Eastern Europe, Russia, or China. Such peasant countries, Marx (and Marxists) might argue, must shed their crude communism and make the tough and long, but necessary, transition to capitalism and bourgeois democracy, before they can hope for the final transition to true communism.

However we may interpret Marxism's practical political failure at the hands of the communists, which for the time being remains manifest, this perspective also raises many theoretical questions. Is it true that labor and the material processes of production are the essence of human beings? Or is this materialist supposition suspect, just as it is in the case of liberalism? Are spiritual and intellectual phenomena only the epiphenomena of material forces, or is this an inadmissible form of reductionism? If there are more than merely material forces shaping our human nature, is it not true that Marx's hope for a future communist society becomes just one more utopian wish that is essentially a "castle in the air," as Jonathan Swift might have called it? Moreover, is it truly possible to understand the forces of history in the way that Marx claims? If so, why is Marx's class consciousness not determined by his historical situation in the way that

[61]While such an abstract vision of a self-governing citizenry may seem attractive, it obviously rests on assuming away the two problems that make for politics: the diversity of interests that make people self-regarding rather than public-regarding, and the scarcity of resources that intensifies the diversity of interests.

he claims it is for all other human beings? In other words, if our consciousness of ourselves is not transcendent, but depends entirely on our material place in history, how is Marx able to transcend the limitations of his historical-material "place" and deliver a total picture of history that overcomes the limitations of his location? These questions are serious, perhaps damning. It is also true that Marx failed to see the ability of capitalism to adapt to the complaints of the proletariat. Communists would address themselves to these adaptations and question whether the material dialectic was as straightforward as Marx and, especially, Engels seemed to think.

Yet Marxism also offers insights that may retain their utility. His analysis of the ways in which ruling classes use ideology, religion, and other intellectual forms to suppress dissent and to mollify their subjects, his insight—shared with other political thinkers—that class conflict is a perennial aspect of politics, and his examination of human alienation may be aspects of his ideology that endure beyond its demise in the rubble of the Eastern European political economy.

PART TWO

Totalitarian Ideologies of the Twentieth Century

Communists have always played an active role in the fight by colonial countries for their freedom, because the short-term objects of communism would always correspond with the long-term objects of freedom movements.

—Nelson Mandela

Let's not talk about Communism. Communism was just an idea, just pie in the sky.

—Boris Yeltsin

Left-wing movements have tended to be unisex, and asexual in their imagery. Right-wing movements, however puritanical and repressive the realities they usher in, have an erotic surface. Certainly Nazism is "sexier" than communism.

—Susan Sontag

Everything I do is done within the sight of the Fuehrer, so that my faults or mistakes are never hidden from him. I do my very best to live and act in such a manner that the Fuehrer should remain satisfied with me.

—Martin Bormann

CHAPTER 6

Communism

Marxism provided the intellectual foundations for communism, which became one of the most influential ideologies of the twentieth century. Between World War II and the collapse of the Soviet Union, the debate between communism and democratic capitalism structured much of international politics. Recent world history and the current conditions of many countries cannot be understood without grasping the ideas central to communism, summarized by the following: Worldwide imperialism—where advanced industrial societies economically dominate underdeveloped nations—constitutes a higher stage of capitalism than Marx had foreseen, and this development requires certain modifications in Marx's predictions about the processes that will bring about a communist society. Instead of revolutions occurring automatically in mature industrialized societies, revolutions must be initiated by a "vanguard" of intellectuals and activists in nascent industrial societies and in developing nations, which suffer most under imperialism. Nations that experience successful revolutions must temporarily be ruled by this vanguard—organized as a communist party—that acts on behalf of the true interests of the proletariat (and peasants) and whose duty it is to pave the way for an ideal communist society. In order to achieve economic affluence and to eliminate human alienation—accomplishments that are prerequisites for ideal communism—party leaders must nationalize private property, plan economic investment, production, and distribution, and prevent the dissemination of counterrevolutionary (capitalist or bourgeois) ideas. While communist party rule may involve some temporary sacrifices by the general population, communist ideology provides reassurance that these sacrifices are worthwhile, because they are necessary for the future achievement of an affluent, and classless society.

Modern communism is a direct descendant of Marxism. Communists rely on the basic doctrines of Karl Marx concerning dialectical materialism, human alienation, labor as the essence of human nature, the need to abolish private property, and the importance of a transforming revolution. Nevertheless, communism is sufficiently distinct from Marxism to be regarded as a separate ideology. Among the many differences between these ideologies, two stand out. First, Marxists are less politically active than communists. While Marxists do not seek to foment revolutions (because they believe capitalism will inevitably fall when conditions are ripe), communists accept the necessity of human initiative to bring about revolutions. Second, Marxism is essentially a protest ideology, while communism is often a governing ideology. Marxists are primarily concerned with criticizing capitalist societies, and their principles about socialist and communist societies are not well-developed, because Marx and his immediate followers never had to govern or to legitimate their governing principles. In contrast, communists have come to power in many societies, and they have had to transform Marxism into an ideology that legitimates their rule. Given these differences, we may think of communism as a kind of "applied Marxism." Communists have taken Marx's basic ideas as the bases of their ideology, but they have interpreted and perhaps modified Marx in various ways so as to foster their revolutionary and governing activities.

Marxism may also be less historically bounded than communism. Arising in the mid-1800s to analyze capitalism, Marxism may provide insights into the nature of capitalist societies well into the twenty-first century. In contrast, communism may be considered a distinctly twentieth-century ideology. Vladmir Ilyich Lenin (1870–1924) most fully developed a communist ideology out of the writings and thought of Marx. Lenin wrote "What Is to Be Done?" in 1902, became the leader of the Bolshevik Party in Russia in 1903, and founded the Soviet Communist state after the Russian Revolution of 1917, guiding the state in its formative years. Communist ideology has also been shaped by other twentieth-century Marxists such as Rosa Luxemburg (1879–1919), Leon Trotsky (1879–1940), Antonio Gramsci (1891–1937), Ernesto ("Che") Guevara (1928–1967), and the leaders of various parties and regimes that call themselves communists. Perhaps the most important of these leaders are:

1. Joseph Stalin (1879–1953), who became the leader of the Communist Party of the Soviet Union after Lenin's death in 1924, and who nationalized industry, collectivized agriculture, and developed a police state in pursuit of "socialism in one country," in the Soviet Union
2. Mao Zedong (1893–1976), who established the People's Republic of China in 1949 and who served as the Chinese president and chairman of the Chinese Communist Party until his death
3. Josip Broz Tito (1892–1980), who became the secretary-general of the Yugoslav Communist Party in 1937 and the prime minister of Yugoslavia in 1945, and who led a national communist regime that retained its independence from the Soviet Union throughout the cold war era
4. Ho Chi Minh (1890–1969), who was the founder of the Indochinese Communist Party in 1930, one of the main opponents of Western imperialism in Asia after World War II, and the leader of North Vietnam during its war with the United States in the 1960s

5. Fidel Castro (1926–), who led the Cuban revolution that ousted the corrupt regime of Fulgencio Batista in 1959 and who created a communist regime that continues to survive only a few miles from U.S. shores

The presence of communist regimes in the Soviet Union, Eastern Europe, China, and in other Asian, African, and Latin American countries after World War II made communism the major ideological rival to various democratic (and capitalist) ideologies during most of the second half of the twentieth century. As we approach the twenty-first century, however, the crumbling of the communist bloc and the collapse of the Soviet Union in 1989 have been widely interpreted, by most of the world, as signaling the end of communism as an attractive ideological alternative.[1]

Communism is undoubtedly in retreat. While still nominally communist, China has introduced many market reforms in recent years. Bereft of the aid of the Soviet Union, Cuba appears to be sliding toward capitalism. The most prominent communist revolutionary movement in recent years, the "Shining Path" in Peru, recently saw its leader arrested and has become less visible as a model for Latin American rebellion. Nevertheless, it may be too soon to proclaim the demise of communism. The fates of the communist regimes in China and Cuba are yet to be determined. Communist parties in Eastern Europe—such as those in Lithuania, Poland, Hungary, Romania, Ukraine, and Russia—continue to do reasonably well in popular elections. Because the citizens of for-

[1]Perhaps the two most important expressions of this view are those of Francis Fukuyama, in *The End of History and the Last Man* (New York: Avon Books, 1992), and Z (an anonymous observer of the Soviet Scene), in "To the Stalin Mausoleum," *Daedalus* (winter 1990), pp. 295–342.

Sidebar 6-1

Some Communists and their Major Writings

Vladmir Ilyich Lenin (1870–1924)
- *What Is to Be Done?* (1902)
- *Imperialism, The Highest Stage of Capitalism* (1917)
- *The State and Revolution* (1917)

Rosa Luxemburg (1879–1919)
- *The Accumulation of Capital* (1913)

Leon Trotsky (1879–1940)
- *The Defense of Terrorism* (1920)
- *History of the Russian Revolution* (1933)

Joseph Stalin (1879–1953)
- *Dialectical and Historical Materialism* (1938)
- *Economic Problems of Socialism in the USSR* (1952)

Antonio Gramsci (1891–1937)
- *The Prison Notebooks* (1929–1936)

Mao Zedong (1893–1976)
- *On Contradiction* (1937)
- *On Practice* (1937)
- *The Socialist Upsurge in China's Countryside* (1956)

Ernesto ("Che") Guevara (1928–1967)
- *Guerrilla Warfare* (1961)
- *Reminiscences of the Cuban Revolutionary War* (1968)

Mikhail Gorbachev
- *Perestroika* (1987)

mer communist countries continue to suffer many hardships as their governments begin to create free markets and implement democracy, communism remains attractive to those who recall more prosperous and stable periods in their nations' histories. In short, while communism is currently an "endangered species," it cannot be ignored or discounted. It is impossible to understand world politics in the twentieth century without understanding communism.

THE POLITICAL BASES

Problems

Communism seeks to address many of the same problems that were the context for Marx's development of a science of history: the problems of the working conditions of the proletariat; the immoral and exploitative characteristics of capitalism; human alienation; and the false consciousness of the proletariat. Of these, the most central problem for communist theory is false consciousness, but communists treat this problem differently than did Marx.

While Marx believed that the objective conditions of capitalism would, of themselves, result in the maturing of the revolutionary consciousness of the proletariat, Lenin believed that workers by themselves lack the ability to develop a proper revolutionary consciousness. He stressed that the proletariat requires leaders to guide and shape them into a coherent class having the necessary consciousness of itself as a class to initiate or to support the revolution. According to Lenin, the communist party serves this function. In short, because the proletariat does not know its true interests, the leaders of the Communist Party must act on its behalf. The possibility that communist party leaders can exercise their free human initiative in history and can act as an elite vanguard on behalf of the proletariat most clearly sets communism apart from Marxism.

Communists also confront other problems Marx did not notice or that arose after Marx's writings. First, capitalism appears to be more adaptable than Marx had predicted. According to Marx, there is a fundamental contradiction within capitalism that will eventually result in its demise. The surplus value that capitalists attain from workers allows for capital accumulation, investment, economic efficiency, and thus the production of an increasing abundance of consumer goods, but this process of capital accumulation is accompanied by the enlargement and progressive impoverishment of the working class. Because most people cannot afford the goods that capitalism produces, economic stagnation and the revolutionary overthrow of the capitalist system is, according to Marx, inevitable. By the end of the nineteenth century, however, the massive economic dislocations that Marx predicted had not occurred. In 1902, an English economist, John Atkinson Hobson (1858–1940), wrote *Imperialism: A Study,* in which he suggested the failure of Marx's theory. According to Hobson, the limited purchasing power of most citizens made it rational for capitalists to restrict production for domestic markets and to limit domestic investment. Thus, to continue to accumulate wealth, capitalists would have to sell their goods in foreign markets and discover profitable investment opportunities in less developed nations. In short, the life of capitalism could be extended by **imperialism**, which is the practice by more advanced capitalist societies of establishing economic domination over less developed nations. To ensure ready markets for their products and to facilitate investment, the imperialist nations could either acquire these countries directly and make them colonies, or they could put great economic and military pressure on the formally independent governments of these nations to ensure their subservience.

In 1913, Rosa Luxemburg, a Polish revolutionary theorist, wrote *The Accumulation of Capital,* which further explained how imperialism extended the life of capitalism. She proposed that capitalism could no longer be regarded as a closed system within particular nations; capitalism had become a worldwide phenomenon. Capitalists no longer depended on the surplus value attained from their workers to fuel capital accumulation. In worldwide capitalism, surplus value is attained from sales and profitable investments in nascent capitalist (or developing) societies. According to Luxemburg, mature capitalist societies would thrive as long as developing nations were available to be exploited.

A few years later, in 1917, Lenin wrote *Imperialism: The Highest Stage of Capitalism,* in which he agreed with and extended Luxemburg's analysis. According to Lenin, capitalism had taken on a new character. The capitalist system that Marx had analyzed was **industrial capitalism**, in which large corporations increasingly developed into monopolies, as market competition led either to bankruptcies or mergers. The capital to finance the mergers and the investments of these corporations came from the surplus value that each corporation extracted from its workers. Lenin, however, discovered a new form of capitalism that he called **finance capitalism**. In this system, financiers and bankers supplied capital to corporations, making such industrial capitalists increasingly dependent on finance capitalists, until the banks gained virtual control of industry. This new form of capitalism concentrated great power in the hands of a small group of financiers, most of whom were not associated in any way with the processes of production over which they had control.

Internationally, the concentration of financial wealth in a small number of banks in the most mature capitalist nations resulted in these few imperial powers dominating less developed nations. By exporting capital to developing nations, by investing in large operations to extract mineral and other natural resources from them, by developing profitable collaborations with the indigenous "national bourgeoisie," and by employing the poor of developing nations (at minimal wages), the imperial nations gained economic and political control over the developing nations. The large quantities of capital that were invested in the extraction of raw materials from the colonies actually meant that the developing countries' wealth was transferred back to the capitalist countries. Lenin called this new phenomenon "imperialism, or the domination of finance capital," and he considered it the "highest stage of capitalism." During Lenin's time, even liberal democracies engaged in such imperialism. British and American oil companies, for example, became active in the Middle East, and Dutch rubber companies built huge plantations in southeast Asia. Lenin recognized that colonial people often responded to capitalist imperialism with

Sidebar 6-2

Dependency Theory

Dependency theory seeks to explain why some states suffer economic and technological underdevelopment, why they seem to remain highly dependent on more dominant nations, and why they seem to experience difficulty in developing and implementing autonomous domestic policies and goals. Dependency theory sees solutions to these problems *in part* through a Marxist lens, although not all dependency theorists are Marxists. It proposes that we can understand international inequalities of wealth and power by considering international relations in terms of economic and class relations. It suggests that we should think of the world as divided between a "core" of economically dominant capitalist countries, and a "periphery" of economically less developed countries. The core countries seek—in various ways and largely for reasons of exploitation—to integrate the periphery into a world capitalist system. Dependency theorists argue that international capitalists from core countries create alliances with the most affluent elements within the class structure of peripheral countries. Dependency theorists also argue that such alliances use the governments of both core and periphery states to shape and manage economic development in the periphery according to their interests.

Dependency theory implies that the most important relationships internationally are not those of autonomous, self-interested states. Instead, it focuses on how the various economic classes of states relate to one another internationally in particular ways, and on how these relationships can account for the economic, technological, and even cultural inequalities in the international system. For example, some dependency theorists suggest that the relatively small bourgeois classes of less developed states ally themselves with the bourgeoisie of capitalist states, and that they in unison extend the exploitation of the less developed state, which is largely made up of peasant and proletarian classes. Dependency theory focuses especially on these asymmetries (or inequalities) of commerce, power, decision-making discretion, and so forth, that exist between classes of various states and within states as a result of the structures of the international economic system.

Like Marxists and communists, then, dependency theorists look to the means, modes, and relationships of economic production to account for the differences and relationships between diverse socio-economic classes of people internationally, and they suggest that economically powerful classes tend to use the political state as a tool for achieving their own ends of domestic and international domination. As these classes attempt to integrate less developed societies into the international (capitalist) system, the inequalities of technology, capital, organizational efficiencies, and industrial development between states create further inequalities, disruptions, and developmental discontinuities within states and between them.

various kinds of nationalist movements. Because they fought against capitalism, Lenin treated these nationalist movements as allies of communism.[2]

A second problem that communists have faced in the twentieth century is that not only has capitalism not collapsed from inward contradictions, but the workers in advanced capitalist societies have not become more impoverished, as Marx had also predicted. Indeed, there have been notable improvements in the working conditions and standards of living of the working classes in industrialized countries. According to Lenin, these improvements are made possible by imperialism. By achieving surplus value through the exploitation of the workers and natural resources of the developing nations, capitalists have less need to exploit their own workers back home. To defuse the revolutionary consciousness of the proletariat in advanced industrial societies, capitalists can even share their profits from the colonies with their workers at home. Imperialism also allows capitalists to permit the development of trade unions at home. **Trade unionism** undermines revolutionary consciousness, because it encourages workers to be preoccupied with improving their working conditions and attaining better wages and benefits. Accordingly, Lenin regarded trade unionism as essentially a capitalist tactic of "throwing a bone" to the proletariat, since, under capitalism, the proletariat would never receive a fair share of the proceeds from industrial production, and humans in general would continue to be alienated beings. Imperialism and trade unionism are merely ingenious ways in which the bourgeois capitalists can realize their aim of domination over the proletariat.

Third, Joseph Stalin, who was the de facto dictator of the Soviet Union after Lenin's death, saw as a central problem for the communist revolution the need to transform the underdeveloped society that he ruled into an affluent industrial society having citizens who were trained to be productive laborers within such a society. Marxists had anticipated no such problem, because Marx predicted revolutions would occur in advanced industrial societies that have both a technological base to sustain an affluent society and a skilled proletariat. The Soviet Union, however, was largely a preindustrial, agrarian society that had to undergo industrialization in order to be prepared for the coming communist society. One obstacle to industrialization in Russia and other nonindustrialized nations was the fact that they contained few proletariat. The peasants, who made up the vast majority of these populations, were unsympathetic to Marxist goals, but were instead preoccupied with obtaining ownership of the land on which they worked. The lack of an economic and technological infrastructure in these preindustrial societies was another obstacle. Consequently, the Communist Party would have to initiate economic development and its attendant material affluence through forced intervention. The state would have to limit the production of consumer goods and invest in the physical infrastructure required for industrialization. The state would also have to force peasants into the factories and onto collective farms. Under Stalin, large portions of the Soviet population were transferred from farms to urban indus-

[2]V. I. Lenin, *Imperialism: The Highest Stage of Capitalism* (New York: International Publishers, 1939 [1917]), pp. 13–14, 78–79.

trial centers. He also developed an extensive system of labor camps, which one could view as a system for training the peasants and general Soviet population in the rigor, discipline, and relative homogeneity needed for industrialized life. The inhuman conditions that British workers had to endure for several generations in the process of industrialization could be suffered by Soviet citizens in only one.[3] A full transformation to an industrial economy, if it were properly directed, could be accomplished in a much shorter time than it had taken the original industrial innovators in Britain and Germany.

Later in the twentieth century, communism faced several further strategic problems. A science of history implies a single correct answer to the questions of strategy and historical development. After World War II, however, communist regimes emerged in several different countries, including China, Cuba, Yugoslavia, and the Eastern European client states of the USSR. In each of these, the contingencies of the specific political, ethnic, historical, and economic situations led to minor or major revisions in their Marxist-Leninist doctrines. The communist regime in the USSR had originally proclaimed world leadership in matters of interpretation of Marxist and communist doctrine. However, as the Chinese and Yugoslavian regimes developed their own paths to the revolution, as communist parties in Western Europe increasingly distanced themselves from what they perceived to be Soviet self-interest, and as even Eastern European regimes differed on points of interpretation, the world communist movement began to appear more and more like a set of sectarian groups, rather than as a unitary science of history. By the 1950s, the Soviets could no longer presume to impose a worldwide interpretive hegemony on communist doctrine.

Most recently, communism has been faced with the problem of an overly centralized, bureaucratized, and closed economy, which may have been the single most important social factor in the fall of the communist regimes of Eastern Europe and the Soviet Union. Whereas the revolution was intended to eliminate the class system, communist society seemed to have become stratified into two groups: those within the party and those outside it.[4] Whereas the revolution was to bring prosperity for all, the populations of Eastern Europe and the Soviet Union have been reduced to increasing poverty, even as they see the standards of living of their wealthier West European cousins continue to rise, or at least remain stable. Whereas the revolution was supposed to create a worker's paradise, life expectancy in communist or formerly communist societies is generally lower and environmental degradation from industry much higher than in western, industrialized societies. Since the breakup of the Soviet Union, communists have increasingly recognized these problems. Perhaps the major issue confronting communism today is whether it can modify its doctrines to address these problems and, if so, how this can be done without abandoning the essential ideas of communism.

[3]See Barry Cooper, *The End of History: An Essay on Modern Hegelianism* (Toronto: University of Toronto Press, 1984), pp. 298–327.

[4]This thesis was most forcefully developed by Milovan Djilas in *The New Class: An Analysis of the Communist System* (New York: Praeger, 1957).

Goals

The goal of communism is to implement Marxism, which involves three stages. First, revolutions must occur, and communists seek to play a role in bringing about such revolutions. Second, socialist states must be established and governed by communist parties during a transitional stage toward an ideal communist society. Third, this ultimate society must eventually be realized.[5]

Unlike Marx, communists such as Lenin and Stalin did not believe that the revolution would come about by itself, even in highly industrialized countries. Its advent would require the help of intellectuals and others who understood the course of history and who could "steer" history toward communist revolutions.[6] Because capitalists could use the wealth gained by imperialistically exploiting their colonies to co-opt the proletariat and thereby defer revolutions in mature capitalist societies, Lenin and Stalin developed a strategy of depriving the capitalists of their colonies: they planted the seeds of communist revolutions throughout the third world. They believed that by mobilizing peasants in these nonindustrialized colonies, communist parties could create "premature" (or preindustrial) communist revolutions there. Once the Western bloc's capitalists lost their colonies, they would turn back to exploiting their own proletariat, which would bring about the crises that, in turn, would bring about the "necessary" revolution in the industrialized nations, as Marx had described it.

Following the "manufactured" revolutions both in industrial societies and in their former colonies, socialist states governed by the dictatorship of the proletariat must be established. In this stage, leaders, acting on behalf of the proletariat, take over the apparatus of the state, using its instruments of coercion against the capitalists to prevent a counterrevolution. Ownership of property is abolished, and every means of production is socialized. In the Soviet Union under Lenin, this meant that the representatives of the proletariat, the Communist Party, took complete control of all state institutions, all economic planning functions, the media, and most industries. All ownership was transferred to the state, which was operated by the Communist Party—the vanguard of the proletariat. These measures, so communist doctrine claims, would allow industrialization to occur in poorer nations and greater economic affluence to result in industrialized nations. Economic classes would gradually disappear, and ideal communism would ultimately emerge.

In ideal communist society, production and distribution of goods are in the hands of the community and democratically administered. The means of production is collectivized for communal purposes, and the state will have

[5]In this chapter we use the term "socialist state" to refer to the transitional state in Marxist theory that precedes ideal communism. Communists believe that the Communist Party must be dominant in such states and thus socialist states in communist systems have been less willing to tolerate opposing parties than have social democratic states (see Chapter 9). Cynics might question whether members of communist parties really sought the realization of ideal communism because this would mean they would have to give up their power and privileges.

[6]See Arthur Koestler, *Darkness at Noon*, translated by Daphne Hardy (New York: Macmillan, 1941), pp. 79–81, 125–132.

been gradually transformed from a coercive entity into an administrative one, until finally its reason for existence will have disappeared altogether. In this way, the state withers away.[7]

THE PHILOSOPHICAL BASES

Epistemology

Communists may be described as ideologues who find political truth in the theories of Marx and other Marxist ideologists. Their conception of truth is monistic, but not monolithic. This means that there is one truth, and one authoritative voice to guide policy making. This authoritative voice is Marx. When other interpreters introduce changes into the received doctrine, they do so within the broad Marxist framework and they provide interpretations of Marx to support their modifications. Thus, communists consult Marx's writings as a kind of holy writ, which serves as the authoritative guide to all political practice.

The communist understanding of truth is not monolithic, however, because Lenin, Stalin, Mao, Ho, Tito, Castro, and other communist leaders have had different interpretations of Marx, which have led to different versions of communism. These differing interpretations necessarily reflect concessions to contextual circumstances and national needs, rather than adherence to iron-clad doctrine.[8] Despite these different schools of interpretations, however, all communists strive for the same objective or scientific truth about history and present conditions that Marx did.

Ontology

The basic ontology of communism is essentially a modification of Marx's theory of **dialectical materialism**. Let us recall that Marxist ontology claims that the ultimate realities and the root causes of all characteristics of human life in history are material and economic. Economic forces of production determine the structure of social classes, religious beliefs and practices, legal systems, political ideologies, and the organization of state institutions in societies. History follows a materially determined course. According to Marxism, unavoidable economic factors would lead to class conflict and to an inevitable revolution. As communism evolved and as communists confronted practical

[7]V. I. Lenin, "The State and Revolution," in *The Lenin Anthology,* edited by Robert Tucker (New York: W. W. Norton, 1975 [1917]), pp. 379–384.

[8]Cf. Joseph Stalin, *Dialectical and Historical Materialism* (Tirana: "8 Nentori" Publishing, 1979 [1938]), pp. 26–30. It might be argued that most Marxist interpretations—such as that of Stalin—are rendered in the context of trying to justify or legitimize the rule of a particular regime. In other words, new interpretations have frequently been attempts to explain why things are not developing as Marx seems to have said they would, or to explain why repressive measures are necessary to bring about the new communist order.

problems of conducting a revolution and of governing societies, its leaders accepted the basic framework of Marx's dialectical materialism. They accepted that material factors were prompting historical developments that would culminate in communism, and they accepted the notion that revolution (rather than governmental reform) was a necessary step in the historical process leading to communism. However, communists modified Marx's position by viewing dialectical materialism as a less deterministic theory. In this section, we discuss four modifications that communists introduced into Marx's science of history.

First, communists recognized that capitalists were not merely prisoners of history, but could also act to modify economic conditions in ways that sustained capitalism and reduced the threat of revolution. Communists identified several capitalist practices that seemed to show that human initiative played a greater role in world history than is suggested by a strict interpretation of dialectical materialism. As we have already seen, capitalists developed imperialism as an adaptive system to extract wealth from colonies, "buy off" the proletariat, and sustain the capitalist system. In addition, capitalist states introduced welfare policies, unemployment insurance, universal education, and other governmental programs that attenuated the inherent contradictions of capitalism. Communists viewed such initiatives as the efforts of capitalists to keep the system going by making minor concessions to the grievances of the proletariat, while keeping the essential features of repression and domination in place. Capitalism would eventually collapse, Lenin thought, but it could be kept artificially alive for much longer than Marx had predicted. Lenin reasoned that if capitalists could take initiatives to forestall a revolution, then revolutionary leaders could take counterinitiatives to speed along the system's collapse.[9]

Second, communists acknowledged changes and variations in economic structures that Marx did not foresee. Marx had treated capitalism as a monolithic economic system. For him, all capitalist societies were essentially identical. Communists, however, argued that capitalism was a **differentiated world system** in which different capitalist societies showed important differences in economic structure and relations. These differences in economic development and historical circumstances had theoretical implications that Marx had not properly assessed in his broad historical approach. For example, at the turn of the century Russia was a semifeudal society that was not yet industrialized. Its two major classes continued to be the nobility and the peasants. To bring the revolution to czarist Russia would require different measures than would be required in Germany, which was heavily industrialized and had a large, somewhat self-conscious proletarian class. In the same way, although some parts of the United States (primarily, the northeastern states) were in an advanced state of industrialization, other states were more rural, and the country as a whole possessed a vast, open frontier whose exploitation could serve to deflect the pressures that capitalism exerted on the working classes. Prole-

[9]Lenin, *Imperialism,* p. 127.

tarian workers always had room to move out of the city, to escape their debts, and to start over on their own piece of land with little interference from government agencies. Hence, a proletarian revolution in the United States seemed unlikely. In short, the opportunities for challenging capitalism and beginning the revolution were not the same in all societies, even for industrialized societies.

Third, communists like Trotsky and Lenin developed a theory of **telescoping the revolution**. Capitalism, this theory argued, was strongest at the core—in the heavily industrialized countries like Germany, Great Britain, and the United States—and weakest at the periphery—in countries like Russia, China, and the colonies of European countries. It would be easiest, the theory went on, to "snap the chain at its weakest link"—namely, at the periphery, where capitalism had not yet fully developed and was, therefore, most vulnerable. In contradiction to Marx, who argued that the revolution would first come to the most industrialized nations and then proceed throughout the world as other nations industrialized in their turn, Trotsky argued that the revolution might be easiest to accomplish in the least industrialized nations. This argument had a threefold implication. First, the transition from feudalism to communism could be accomplished in one large step, rather than in the series of class conflicts that Marx envisioned. The revolutionary progress of history, in other words, could be "telescoped" into one long revolution, rather than being allowed to proceed as a two-step process of first a bourgeois and then a proletarian revolution with a long period of capitalism in between. Second, this process would require a **permanent revolution**, a period of time in which the Marxist revolutionaries (the vanguard) would foment a continuous revolution that would achieve the transformation from feudalism to communism in one extended step. Third, it seemed that the revolution was not a historically necessary event, one determined by precise historical and material factors, as Marx had thought. Because the revolution was not *inevitable* in the economically peripheral states (the "weakest link"), it would have to be brought about by deliberate human intervention.

Consequently, a fourth modification of Marx's thinking—Lenin's doctrine of a **vanguard of the proletariat**—implies a theory of revolutionary voluntarism that seems to be at odds with Marx's notion of a deterministic material dialectic in which the revolution unfolds, more or less necessarily, as it should. Marx believed that a group of intellectuals could speed the revolution by helping the proletariat to develop class consciousness more quickly than it would if it were left to itself. But he foresaw no other significant task for such revolutionary leaders. In contrast, Lenin argued that a small group of intellectuals—whom he called "the vanguard"—understood the "historical moment," the requirements of the revolution, and the needs of the proletariat; the vanguard could act on behalf of the proletariat and greatly hasten the coming of the revolution. To wait for historical developments to "catch up" with the historical moment would be unnecessary, and possibly foolish.[10] By giving

[10]Lenin, "What Is to Be Done?" in *The Lenin Anthology*, pp. 49–54, 72–79.

this vanguard a greater importance than Marx did, Lenin makes much more room for the role of a voluntary human will in the political realm than even a "soft determinist" interpretation of Marx allows.

In sum, Marx's theory of historical change was considerably modified by the communists. Changing economic conditions were, in fact, somewhat indeterminate, so that a successful revolution required the injection into the historical process of leadership that could guide the proletarian or even peasant masses in the proper direction and that could overcome or counter the wiles of the capitalists. Human action could shape history in ways that Marx had not considered.

Sidebar 6-3

Mao's Departure from Dialectical Materialism

The need for communist leaders to modify Marx's ontology of dialectical materialism is particularly apparent in the Chinese revolution. The revolution against the Chinese imperial regime was begun in 1911 by republican forces. The Chinese Communist Party (CCP) was founded in 1921, and at first it was allied with the republicans against the regime. But, led by Chiang Kai-shek (1887–1975), the republicans turned on their communist allies in 1927, and nearly annihilated them. Those few communists who survived fled into the countryside. These events, and a close study of the revolutionary potential of the Chinese peasantry, convinced the leader of the CCP, Mao Zedong, that the rural peasantry, not the urban proletariat, was the true revolutionary force in China. For the next ten years, the Chinese Communists suffered a series of military defeats at the hands of the republican Kuomintang. A slow reversal of fortune, aided by the outbreak of World War II, international political maneuvering, and decisive military victories, gave the Chinese Communists a final victory in 1949. Throughout this time, it was not the urban proletariat, but the rural peasantry that carried on most Marxist revolutionary activities and that gave the CCP support. Moreover, the CCP found refuge and the needed resources for its recovery and final victory not in the cities, but in the countryside. Not only was the peasantry the greatest source of support for the CCP but, according to Mao, it also presented the best locus for a revolutionary transformation:

> China's 600 million people have two remarkable peculiarities; they are, first of all, poor, secondly blank. That may seem like a bad thing, but it is really a good thing. Poor people want change, want to do things, want revolution. A clean sheet of paper has no blotches, and so the newest and most beautiful words can be written on it, the newest and most beautiful pictures can be painted on it.*

The shift from a proletarian-based to a peasant-based revolution was clearly a major departure from Marxist orthodoxy. It was even a step beyond Lenin, who allowed the peasants a role in the revolution, but who did not give them a central leadership role as Mao did.

*Quoted in Stuart R. Schram, *The Political Thought of Mao Tse-Tung*, rev. ed. (New York: Praeger, 1969), p. 352. Reprinted by permission of Armand Colin SA.

Society

Communists follow the Marxist doctrine that society is composed of classes that are struggling for predominance. Marx believed that the only remaining class struggle in capitalist societies was between the bourgeoisie and the proletariat. Communist leaders trying to initiate the revolution, however, discovered a more complex situation. In those societies that had not yet become industrialized, they found, as Marx predicted they would, a large number of classes with varying interests, few of which were concerned with any sort of revolution. The most important class in nonindustrialized societies was the peasant class. Lenin, and especially Mao, argued that peasants were an important source of revolutionary resources and an important source of resistance to the capitalists of the imperialistic, industrialized societies. Accordingly, they developed a more complex model of revolution that included a role for the peasants, who constituted the vast majorities of the populations in Russia and China. Whereas Lenin found it impossible for the proletariat in Russia to overwhelm the capitalists and to carry out the revolution without the active support of the peasantry,[11] Mao went even further and established a revolutionary doctrine that was based entirely on the peasantry. Such a shift in emphasis moved him a long distance from Marx, who had assumed that only the proletariat could lead the revolution and accomplish the transformation to communism.

But even in capitalist societies, communists discovered a more complex social structure than Marx had foreseen. In countries like Germany, Great Britain, and the United States, a sizable and complex new middle class was developing, which seemed to contradict Marx's prediction that capitalism would lead to a polarization of all people into two classes: a large mass of proletariat and a small minority of bourgeois capitalists. Instead, the growing middle class was becoming differentiated into many classes: a managerial class, a class of skilled craftsmen, a class of salaried and professional workers, a class of small businesspeople, and other classes. Marxism could not account for this development, and progress toward the revolution would therefore require the devising of new theories and strategies. In Europe, communist parties developed strategies of obtaining political power through democratic processes of electoral politics, political compromise, and promises of political reform. Rather than immediate proletarian domination, they considered the possibilities of working through popular unions, and the like.

Like Marx, the communist views the ideal society as one in which all class differences have been eliminated. It is a society in which everyone is a freely creating laborer, no longer alienated from himself or herself, his or her fellows, or the products of his or her labor. It is a society free of conflict, want, and dissatisfaction. Communists focus more than Marx did on the transitional phases needed to get to this society and on the strategies that are required to make it possible.

[11]Lenin, "Introducing the New Economic Policy," in *The Lenin Anthology*, p. 504.

Human Nature

Antonio Gramsci, an important Italian communist theoretician, wrote:

> Reflecting on it, we can see that in putting the question, "what is man," what we mean is: what can man become? That is, can man dominate his own destiny, can he "make himself," can he create his own life? We maintain therefore that man is a process and, more exactly, the process of his actions.[12]

As this quote suggests, communists believe that "human nature" is essentially malleable.[13] Like Marxists, communists see the core of human identity as the ability of human beings to produce things through labor. This ability, however, is not constant and must be brought to full and nonalienated expression through the communist revolution. People can become free and creative laborers, but only by means of a total and revolutionary transformation of society. While communists thus accept Marx's theory of alienation and his theory of revolutionary transformation, they reject his notion that this transformation occurs in a deterministic way through a necessary historical process. Communists suggest various means of transforming human nature.

The most notorious of these methods were those of Lenin and Stalin. Political intimidation, the internment of millions of Soviet citizens into forced-labor camps, and the use of surveillance by the secret police to terrorize the entire society were methods some communists believed would be useful in bringing about the transformation of human nature and human existence.

Mao's doctrine of **continuous revolution** was another attempt to bring about a revolutionary change in human motivation and identity. Continuous revolution was intended to break down political and social institutions and customs on a continual basis through a variety of policies. Perhaps the most radical (and economically disastrous) of these schemes were the Great Leap Forward, introduced in 1960, and the "Cultural Revolution," begun in 1966. The policies of these revolutionary periods disrupted ordinary life by sending factory workers and intellectuals into the fields and replacing them with farmers. Such policies were intended to break down the "chains of institutionalism," ensuring that no one would become overly complacent in his or her social niche. By reversing roles, people would acquire a broader social consciousness. People were kept in a continuous state of dislocation, so that their fundamental identities could be reshaped in accordance with requirements of the revolution.[14]

[12]Antonio Gramsci, "The Study of Philosophy," in *Selections from the Prison Notebooks of Antonio Gramsci,* edited and translated by Quinton Hoare and Geoffrey Nowell Smith (New York: International, 1971 [1929–1936]), p. 351.

[13]Insofar as the concept of "human nature" points to some "essence" of humans, claiming that human nature is malleable suggests, of course, that there is no essential (or unchanging) human nature.

[14]Since Mao's death in 1976, China has embarked on a path of comparative moderation and gradualism and has even pursued limited economic reforms to foster a free market. Perhaps such reversals suggest that the basic desires and needs of a human being are not quite what communist revolutionaries thought, and perhaps human nature is more static than they had anticipated.

A third method for transforming human consciousness as required for an ideal communist society involves the **self-managed workers' councils** in Tito's Yugoslavia. Tito resisted economic and industrial centralization, as well as centralization in the government and in the Communist Party. He shared Mao's concern about bureaucratic rigidity, but, unlike Mao, he did not propose continual disruptions of society from the center as the solution. Instead, he decentralized political control into a kind of loose federalism, and he gave economic control to worker councils at the local factory level. One rationale for these decentralized institutions was that they would promote the development of nonalienated workers. By giving workers control of their state-owned workplaces, Tito sought to reduce the alienation that occurs when workers are dominated by capitalists or by bureaucrats of the centralized state. Yugoslavian workplace democracies were founded on the premise that people would be less-alienated, creative workers if they were allowed to control themselves rather than being controlled by others.

A fourth method of creating a "new socialist man" involved the use of **charismatic leadership** in a revolutionary context. For example, on numerous occasions, Fidel Castro spoke for hours to crowds of more than one million Cubans. During these talks, he recited the abuses that American imperialists had inflicted on Cubans. Then Castro would explain how the revolution revealed the potential of Cuban citizens, including their courage, willingness to sacrifice, vision, heroism, and unity of purpose. According to the Cuban model of communism, "the path of communist consciousness leads through the struggle against imperialism."[15] Castro believed that human consciousness would be transformed when people experienced socialist programs in action. By providing free electricity, public transportation, and education, Castro believed that the communist Cuban state was forging a "socialist and communist consciousness" that allowed its citizens to live "according to truly fraternal norms, truly human norms, and [in a society] in which each man and woman will see others as his brothers and sisters. . . . Here work will never be an ordeal, but rather the most enjoyable, noblest, most creative activity of mankind."[16]

SUBSTANTIVE POLITICAL PRINCIPLES

Change

Given that communism is an essentially revolutionary ideology, change is arguably the most important political principle of communists. Like Marxists, communists accept the notion that all societies experience fundamental and progressive change. Unlike Marxists, communists do not believe that such

[15]Tony Smith, *Thinking Like a Communist* (New York: W. W. Norton, 1987), p. 151.
[16]From *Castro Speaks,* quoted in Smith, *Thinking Like a Communist,* p. 154.

change, and especially the ultimate change to a communist society, will occur only when economic and historical conditions are "ripe" or when proletarian class consciousness has been fully developed. Instead, change can be provoked by a vanguard of leaders with a proper understanding of the conditions needed for a revolution combined with the required political acumen. Since change is, therefore, no longer a product of simple historical evolution, but can and must be enacted by human agency, the question for communists becomes: How shall we bring about the revolution that establishes the communist society? Several strategies have presented themselves over time to communist ideologues and rulers. The precise characteristics of these strategies have often been a function of the character of the society within which the revolutionary is trying to produce his desired change.

Lenin's strategy for change called for organizing and training a relatively small, secret, professional, and **disciplined Bolshevik party**, led not by the proletariat, but by middle-class intellectuals like Lenin who understood the interests of the proletariat and the requirements of the revolution. When their enemies were weak, the Bolsheviks staged a political coup. When this coup succeeded, the party then centralized its power in order to initiate a gradual transformation of society through the use of instruments of terror such as labor camps, secret police, and forced mass migrations of ethnic populations.

Mao Zedong had a three-part strategy for bringing change to China. First, he emphasized that the **peasantry** would play a critical role in the revolution. This aspect of Mao's revolutionary doctrine clearly contradicted Marx, who had stressed that the revolution would be conducted by the urban proletariat rather than the peasants who lived in the countryside. Mao's emphasis on the peasantry went well beyond Lenin's recognition that the Russian peasants could sometimes be helpful to the Bolsheviks. Even more than Russia, China was without a sufficiently developed proletariat, but it had a large, alienated peasant population. Because Chinese landowners had exploited and divided these peasants for centuries, Mao believed the peasants had the motivation to take part in the revolution, and Mao had observed in them the virtues of innate goodness, self-sacrifice, courage, and shrewdness. Given these characteristics, Communist Party leaders had only to mobilize the peasants for political action.

Second, Mao believed that **guerrilla warfare** was the appropriate method of revolutionary struggle in colonial nations. While Lenin had used a small and disciplined party to seize power in a coup, Mao's doctrine of guerrilla warfare called for long-term popular effort, extensive local initiatives by the peasants, and numerous opportunistic skirmishes with the imperialist enemies and local authoritarian regimes. Guerrilla warfare had both military and social components. By declaring that "power comes from the barrel of a gun," and by teaching guerrilla soldiers to remain mobile and to engage in direct combat only when victory was assured, Mao emphasized "effective violence." Because successful guerrilla warfare depended on the support and cooperation of the local population, however, Mao's "liberation army" built extensive social networks with the peasants, gaining their allegiance so that they would provide the guerrilla soldiers with needed information, food, shelter, and new recruits.[17]

Third, Chinese communists (and some others) believed that Mao's doctrine of a "people's war" could be exported to other third world countries—like Vietnam and Cambodia—that had characteristics similar to those of China.[18] A successful export to other colonial countries would defeat capitalists on two grounds: it would undermine imperialism, and it would mean that these underdeveloped countries could "leap forward" into the revolution, sidestepping the indigenous capitalist phase that Marx thought necessary in order for a revolution to take place.

Mao's revolutionary strategy was both adopted and modified by Fidel Castro and Che Guevara, who developed the "**Cuban model**" for exporting communist revolutions to developing nations throughout Latin America, Africa, and other areas. The distinctive aspect of the Cuban model was its deemphasis of the role of the communist party. Although Castro had come to power in Cuba in 1959 through a popular insurrection, he did not declare his allegiance to Marxism-Leninism until after the Bay of Pigs incident in 1961, when American hostility pushed him into the Soviet camp. Even then, Castro and Guevara did not depend on the Communist Party to govern Cuba or to initiate revolutions elsewhere. Guevara insisted that so-called underdeveloped nations were in truth "colonial, dependent countries," and that the struggle against Western domination required communists to work within a "united, anti-imperialist front."[19] Such a front should not be controlled by a centralized party, which would prompt brutal governmental repression. Instead, revolutionaries should be composed of many spontaneous, independent, and decentralized *focos*. Such units would be small, egalitarian, and fluid, engaging the enemy in guerrilla warfare. According to Castro, such a decentralized approach to revolution would not only be more effective in defeating "Yankee imperialists," it would also reduce the danger of revolutionaries turning away from democratic principles once the revolution had succeeded.

In Western Europe, revolutionary change in accordance with the Marxist or Leninist models became increasingly unlikely as the twentieth century progressed. Antonio Gramsci was the communist theorist who provided the most important explanation for this development. According to Gramsci, **bourgeois hegemony** made a mass-based revolution unlikely. Capitalists ruled not by force, but by consent, because most citizens thoroughly embraced a bourgeois ideology that praised capitalism, legitimated liberal democracies, and justified current social institutions concerning property, family life, education, law, discipline, and culture. In other words, bourgeois hegemony meant that the processes of socialization, the institutions of education, and the means of communication all impressed on the Western European mind the values of liberal

[17]Chalmers Johnson, *Autopsy on People's War* (Berkeley: University of California Press, 1973), pp. 14–15, 29, 47–53.
[18]Johnson, *Autopsy*, pp. 22–30.
[19]*Che Guevara Speaks*, edited by George Lavan (New York: Pathfinder Press, 1983), p. 31.

democratic or capitalist societies. Gramsci also thought that it was futile and dangerous for communist parties to act as a vanguard on behalf of the proletariat—who lacked class consciousness because of this hegemony. It was dangerous because the excesses of Lenin and Stalin suggested that a successful revolutionary vanguard necessarily maintained itself in power through coercion and force. Consequently, demolishing capitalism and establishing a democratic socialist state required that an ideological revolution precede a political one. The populace had to become free of bourgeois hegemony through a slow process of reforming civil society. In this way, Gramsci modified the Marxist claim that the ideological, governmental, and social superstructures of society are entirely dependent on the economic infrastructure. He claimed that the superstructure was somewhat independent of economic forces and could be transformed by communists working within the institutions of civil society. Gramsci gave the Communist Party the new roles of teaching the population about the injustices and failings of capitalist society and of modifying the orientations of old institutions. For example, communists could be active in municipal politics, blocking local economic developments that threatened citizen interests. Communists could also attempt to democratize the workplace, get churches to speak on behalf of the poor, and encourage new cultural expressions portraying the evils of capitalism. By engaging in such activities, communists could transform the beliefs and values of the population prior to any political revolution.[20] Gramsci's ideas continue to influence communist parties in Europe, who hope to acquire power by means of popular acceptance and electoral victory rather than by means of revolution. Perhaps such ideas place contemporary "Eurocommunists" ideologically closer to democratic socialists than to the revolutionary founders of communism.

Lenin, Mao, Castro, and Gramsci each had theories of change that are predicated on a less deterministic, more voluntaristic view of the world than orthodox Marxism seems to allow. The material forces of history can be considerably manipulated by human will, even to the point that revolution is not an indigenous event that arises only in a given society with the necessary conditions for revolution. Instead, revolution can be "exported" to a given society from outside.

Structure

Like Marxists, communists believe that the root of human ills can be traced to the structure of society itself. To eradicate these ills, these structures must be transformed. Communists have more to say than Marxists about what these transformed structures will look like. The structure of communist government and revolutionary activity must be understood from both a domestic and an international perspective.

On the domestic side, the structure of communist government in most communist states can be understood as the structure of the Communist Party,

[20]See Antonio Gramsci, "Problems of Marxism," in *Selections from the Prison Notebooks,* pp. 381ff.

which controls all the organs of government. According to Lenin, the Communist Party (i.e., the vanguard of the proletariat) should be organized according to the principles of **democratic centralism**. First, all decisions should be made in free and open debates of the party congress. Second, all decisions of the party congress must be binding on all lower agencies and officials of the Communist Party and of the government. Third, no factions must be allowed within the party, and no minority parties must be permitted to secede from the party or to air their grievances in public. Fourth, all officers of the party, from the lowest membership upwards, should be elected indirectly.[21] Fifth, all decisions and instructions of the party executive officials must be binding upon all subordinated party and state organs and officers. Sixth, executive officials of the party must be authorized to purge members who do not toe the official line of the party hierarchy. In principle, this structure is democratic, because it allows for open debate and because leadership is formally accountable to the rank-and-file members. But this structure is also centralized, because decisions are made by a few leaders and enforced for the good of all.

Flowing from this Leninist doctrine, the central debate among communists concerning government structure has been centralization versus decentralization. Like Marxists, communists find the root causes of human problems, including class oppression and alienation, in the structure of society itself. The question for communists is whether this structure can best be overcome through a centralized force—the Communist Party—or by decentralized means. The latter would include associations of labor collectives not controlled by the central party organs and the use of democratic decision making at the local level. Marx believed that the political economy of postrevolutionary societies would be dominated by a centralized state that would establish the necessary conditions for the final, universal communist state. In communist experience, however, this centralization has usually produced large and inefficient bureaucracies, government waste, and poor economies. For this reason, there has been some strategic debate about the merits of such centralization as a means of structuring communist society.

The most famous of the efforts to decentralize a communist regime was **perestroika**—a term denoting economic "restructuring" that was introduced in 1987 by Soviet leader Mikhail Gorbachev. The original aim of perestroika was to reduce the power of the huge centralized Soviet bureaucracy. Rather than have the bureaucracy plan and direct all economic activity, the state would allow managers of local plants the freedom to plan production, obtain raw materials, hire workers, and establish prices. While these reforms brought some decentralization to the Soviet political economy, they were not intended, initially, to privatize it. Only when Gorbachev introduced "revolutionary perestroika" in November 1989, and professed his intentions to privatize ownership of the means of production and to pursue a liberalized free-market sys-

[21]In the Soviet Union, democratic centralism meant that members of the party elect delegates to the Party Congress, that these delegates in turn elect members of the Central Committees, and that these committeemen in turn elect members of the Presidium and Secretariat. In the Soviet Union, however, nominations for party posts came from above.

tem did the Soviets move decisively away from core communist principles.

Another structural issue confronting communists has concerned international organization. Communism, like Marxism, was intended to be a class movement that transcended ethnic and national boundaries. Indeed, Marx had considered ethnic and national boundaries to be yet another form of bourgeois organization that would disappear with the coming of communism. Accordingly, communists had formed an international organization, the Communist International, or Comintern, that debated and set policies for revolutionary activities, and the like. Karl Marx helped to organized the First International (also known as the International Workingmen's Association) in 1864. It was internally beset by factions and externally oppressed and persecuted by hostile governments. It convened six congresses over nine years before it disbanded in 1873.[22] Engels helped to establish the Second International in 1889, six years after Marx's death; it had a strong internationalist and pacific policy. In 1912, two years before the outbreak of World War I, the Second International drafted a resolution opposing working-class participation in any war. In the words of the resolution, war meant that workers were "shooting one another for the sake of the capitalists' profits, for the sake of the ambitions of dynasties, for the accomplishment of the aims of secret diplomatic treaties."[23] At the outbreak of World War I, most of the communist rank and file gave up its pacifism and supported the military endeavors of the countries of which its members were citizens. The Second International dissolved in 1914 amid its members' conflicting nationalist loyalties. The Third International began with an antiwar conference of communists in 1915, and was formally organized at its First Congress, in 1919, though not officially begun until its Second Congress, in 1920. Even though thirty-five parties joined in its founding, it was dominated by the Russian communists, who were soon to emerge victorious from the Russian civil war and complete the first successful communist revolution. As Lenin had feared, this third Comintern became a tool of Russian foreign policy. This development eventually discredited it among some non-Soviet Marxists, which also dissipated the cohesion of the international communist movement. Nevertheless, in 1939, there were nearly sixty communist parties in the Comintern. Their common membership helped to centralize the revolution, and it provided the communist parties of various nations with important ideological, financial, and organizational ties to other communist parties in their efforts to create a worldwide revolution. In 1943, however, the Soviets were more interested in national survival and defeating the Nazis, so in order to placate their Western Allies, they temporarily abandoned the doctrine of worldwide revolution, and dissolved the Third International to indicate their goodwill. After the war, the Soviets continued to try to dominate communist movements worldwide, but differences between them and Mao,

[22]See Franz Mehring, *Karl Marx: The Story of His Life*, translated by Edward Fitzgerald (Ann Arbor: University of Michigan Press, 1962), pp. 316–356, 387–500, and David McClellan, *Karl Marx: His Life and Thought* (New York: Harper and Row, 1973), pp. 360–411, for a detailed history of the First International.

[23]Edmund Wilson, *To the Finland Station* (London: Macmillan, 1972), pp. 499–500.

Tito, and other communists undermined these efforts. In short, creating and maintaining a unified international communist movement has been a major challenge for communists. International communist organizations have had only limited success in overcoming national differences and national self-interests among communist societies.

Rulers

Communists such as Stalin, Lenin, and Mao agreed with orthodox Marxists in believing that all societies are ruled by the ruling class in its own interests, and that the government that exists after the revolution develops in two distinct stages. In the first phase, government is a dictatorship of the proletariat that must eradicate every trace of capitalism or feudalism (depending on the type of society in which the revolution has taken place) and must transform the people's way of thinking into a mode of communism in which there is nonalienated, creative labor. In the second and final stage, as the population is transformed into a communist society, government will have no coercive tasks left to perform, rulers will no longer be necessary, and the state structure will "dissolve." In the ideal communist society, anarchism will be possible.

Communists departed from Marx not only in their views of how the revolution would come into being, but also regarding who would rule during and after it. Whereas Marx did not believe that the revolution could be dominated by an intellectual class that would lead the revolution, communists such as Lenin, Stalin, and Mao were leading revolutions in countries that required an intellectual vanguard.

In a similar departure from Marx's conception of how the revolution would unfold, Stalin perceived the need for a one-party state that would enforce the dictates of the revolutionary process. The coercion of masses of people that this move implied was quite contrary to Marx's anticipation of a generally popular revolution in which only a small class of bourgeoisie would be coerced in any serious way. The suppression of dissent among large numbers of people, especially in the proletariat, was not a political measure that Marx seems to have imagined in his portrayal of a largely popular revolution of the proletariat.

The logical outcome of the role of the Communist Party as a revolutionary vanguard is that its leaders become the absolute rulers of the society during its initial revolutionary stage. Once this initial stage is past and the proletariat has gained full consciousness of itself, Lenin's doctrine seems to indicate that the functions of the party are to decrease as the proletariat takes over and the state proceeds to full communism. Thus, rulership shifts over the course of the revolution from the vanguard or party to the proletariat proper and, finally, is replaced by an absence of rule, as full communism emerges and eliminates the need for the state or any other form of rule.[24]

[24]Lenin, "The State and Revolution," pp. 371–375, 383–384.

Justice

If we accept the interpretation of Marx that sees in his writings a substantive notion of justice, then we may say that communists essentially accept Marx's critique of the injustices of capitalist (or even precapitalist) societies, and that they also accept Marx's picture of the postrevolutionary, just society. Under capitalism (and earlier economic systems), workers and laborers do not receive the full value of their labor, but are compensated only enough so that they can survive. Like Marxists, communists stress the injustice of such exploitation of workers in capitalist societies. Surpassing Marxists, however, communists stress that peasants and other indigenous populations in developing countries are equally exploited by imperialists.

In the transitory, socialist stage that immediately follows the revolution, Marx suggested that workers and laborers should receive compensation in accordance with the quality and quantity of their work. Under the communist regimes of Lenin, Stalin, Mao, and Castro, the government took control of all property and all means of production. The intent was that government would pay out wages that were truly proportional to the quality and quantity of work each person performed. Rather than having the fruits of their labor seized by capitalists, workers would receive fair recompense for their labor. Nevertheless, Marx realized that the compensation workers would receive from their labor would not equal the full value of that work, but rather, must be subject to some social deductions. For example, the state would have to retain funds to replace and expand the technology used in producing goods and to pay for the "communal satisfaction of needs, such as schools, health services, etc."[25] Because such deductions would promote a future ideal society, they constituted no injustice. Communist regimes have drawn upon such Marxist ideas to extract "forced savings" from workers. While the difference between what workers contribute to production and what they receive as compensation must be regarded as exploitative surplus value when it is retained by capitalist employers, this difference should be regarded as a social contribution when it is retained by states to industrialize their weak economies and to provide for extensive welfare services.

Following this transitional period of socialism, people would willingly engage in self-actualizing and creative labor, and government would gradually wither away. It would no longer be needed as a means to ensure that all workers and laborers received fair compensation for their labor, since everyone would give to society in accordance with their talents and abilities, and each member of society would be provided for in accordance with his or her needs. Thus, the principle of justice in the final, ideal communist society would reflect Marx's dictum "from each according to his abilities to each according to his needs."[26]

To achieve such justice, communists foresee and practice extensive social

[25]Marx, *Critique of the Gotha Programme*, in *The Marx-Engels Reader*, 2d ed., edited by Robert C. Tucker (New York: W. W. Norton, 1978 [1875]), p. 529.
[26]Lenin, *The State and Revolution*, p. 379.

control over human thought and behavior.[27] Liberals, socialists, and even conservatives decry this control as harmful, ineffective, and unjust, but communists argue that to create a truly communist society, one must transform the lives and the consciousness of the people who inhabit it in fundamental ways. This includes a transformation in the way people think about the distribution of resources. Although this sort of social control and mind alteration may seem unjust at the revolutionary moment, it serves the greater good of helping to bring about the transformation into an ideal communist society, which will be so much more just than any present system can hope to be. The material abundance and human freedom that communist society ultimately offers is more than sufficient compensation for transitory social control now.[28]

Authority

Like Marxists, communists believe that state authority in liberal democratic societies is used to further the interests of capitalists. After the revolution, however, state authority will reside in the Communist Party, and this authority will be used to bring about the transition to a future ideal society in which there will no longer be a need for state authority. Such authority will not be needed in this latter world of economic affluence and transformed human beings because everyone will have come to accept the universal truth of communism, which he or she demonstrates practically in an unalienated life of creative self-realization and material prosperity.

Communists augment these Marxist ideas about state authority by developing Marx's view of the role of the state during the transition to the perfect society. Communists insist that during this period, state authority must be absolute and should be of three kinds: social, economic, and interpretive.

First, the communist state must use its authority to shape social life in a manner that will enable the realization of an ideal society. The state must exercise control of various social institutions (the family, schools, religion, and other local associations) so that they promote the development of a "new man."

Second, communist states must use their authority to industrialize their precapitalist economies, creating the affluence that ideal communism presupposes. Most communist regimes have embraced a very authoritative role for the state in achieving these goals. The prototypic example is the **collectivist Soviet state** established by Stalin in 1929 and generally retained until reforms were introduced by Gorbachev in the mid-1980s. Stalin nationalized all industrial private property; he collectivized agriculture; and he established strict, centralized, and bureaucratic control of the national economy. Central planners established Five-Year Plans that set production priorities and established

[27]On the "dictatorship of the proletariat" and the dictatorship of the Communist Party in Russia after the 1917 Revolution, see Leszek Kolakowski, *Main Currents of Marxism, vol. 2, The Golden Age*, translated by P. S. Falla (Oxford: Oxford University Press, 1978), pp. 485–491.
[28]Lenin, *The State and Revolution*, pp. 378–384.

production goals and quotas. Pay rates for various jobs were established by the state. Supervision of local industries was from above, by state *nomenklatura.* rather than from below by satisfied (or dissatisfied) customers.

Such state control of the economy has been subjected to many criticisms—such as its inability to reward innovation and effort[29]—but there is some evidence that such a planned economy did bring about economic improvements, at least for many years. Between 1960 and 1973, for example, estimates indi-

[29]Perhaps one of the best critical evaluations of the Soviet planned economy is provided by Alec Nove, *The Economics of Feasible Socialism Revisited* (New York: HarperCollins, 1991), pp. 73–126.

Sidebar 6-4

Liberation Theology

Every theistic religion must wrestle with the relationship between doctrine (beliefs about the divine, the world, human beings, and the relations of these to one another) and practice (how, given our religious beliefs, we should behave). Liberation theology, which originated among Latin American Catholic theologians in the 1950s and the 1960s, is not the first theological discourse to engage this problem, nor the first to emphasize the importance of right practice ("orthopraxis") over right doctrine ("orthodoxy"). Moreover, liberation theologians are not the first to recognize the overwhelming needs of the poor and the injustices to which they are subject.

The unique contribution of liberation theology to the Christian theological tradition, however, has been to express these concerns with language and concepts that it has consciously borrowed from Marxist analyses of society. Liberation theology speaks of the "class struggle" between rich and poor, of the "alienation" of the poor, of the need to "conscientize" the poor (or proletariat), of international "capitalist oppression" and "imperialism," and of the need for constructing—perhaps through revolutionary activity—a "new social order."

Poverty, injustice, and social responsibility are important themes in many Christian traditions, but because it has adopted a specifically Marxist analysis and vocabulary, liberation theology has come to be identified by many scholars and clergy in a variety of Christian traditions as either essentially a branch of Marxist thought, or as a doctrine so closely associated with Marxism that its Christian roots have become hidden and unimportant. Whether or not this is a fair assessment, liberation theologians have reminded Christians of the need to move beyond questions of doctrine to questions of social activity. Moreover, whether or not other Christians accept a Marxist analysis and call to action, and whether or not they accept the central claim of liberation theology that the Christian faith should be used to mobilize the poor and help them collectively to overcome their oppression, liberation theologians of Latin America, and elsewhere, have been prominent political spokesmen and activists on behalf of the poor in many developing countries in South America, Africa, and Asia and in poor European cities, and they have reminded other Christians of the importance to Christian belief and practice of a social ethic and a concern for social justice.

cate that the Soviet Union experienced an annual growth rate of 5.3 percent, a rate better than that of most capitalist societies—including the United States. In addition, the Soviets were able to increase their expenditures on fixed investments during this period, actually surpassing American investment levels by 1977. While Soviet consumption never reached American levels between 1955 and 1975, the Soviets significantly reduced the gap between American consumption and Soviet consumption.[30] Nevertheless, Soviet central planning and control did not sustain economic growth rates into the 1980s that could produce either parity with capitalist economies or the affluence required for the achievement of ideal communism. These disappointments led the citizens of communist states to begin to question the sacrifices imposed on them in the name of a future ideal society, and they began to view communist ideology's justification of these sacrifices as mere myths and lies. In this environment, communist leaders began to reevaluate their commitment to state control over the economy.

It can be argued that the degree of state control of the economy is not a central principle of communism. Prior to Gorbachev's effort to reduce state control through his perestroika reforms, other examples of communists' opting for less-extensive state involvement in the economy include the New Economic Policy (NEP) of Lenin and the self-management based Workers' Councils of Tito. Lenin's NEP was initiated in 1921, in response to extreme state control of the Soviet economy under "war communism" during the first years of Bolshevik rule. The NEP, which lasted until 1928, removed many restrictions on free trade, denationalized some smaller enterprises, and allowed greater market freedom in agriculture. Tito's Workers' Councils, mentioned earlier, allowed industrial workers to elect (and dismiss) their managers and to deliberate on all decisions of local firms—what to produce, how to distribute income, how much income should be redirected into investment, who should be hired and promoted, and so forth. Gorbachev's perestroika allowed local managers to gear production to consumer demand and to establish wage and bonus policies in ways that encouraged productivity. Whether or not communism requires extensive state economic planning or whether the state can give more autonomy to local enterprises may, therefore, be a question of interpretation.

Thus, for communists, the ability to interpret Marx is a third, and perhaps preeminent, aspect of authority. They argue that the proper interpreters of Marx on matters regarding the revolution and revolutionary practice are not political theorists, but the communist parties themselves. In economic matters, as well as in all other social concerns, the party declares what is to be done. It bases its absolutist dicta on its inerrant understanding of historical forces, which is, in turn, based on its inerrant understanding of Marx, supplemented by its insights into the details of current conditions.[31] Thus, Stalinists could

[30]Data on the success of the Soviet planned economy is provided by Charles McCoy, *Contemporary ISMS: A Political Economy Perspective* (New York: Franklin Watts, 1982), pp. 70–94. A much more critical assessment is provided by Z in, "To the Stalin Mausoleum."
[31]See Koestler, *Darkness at Noon*, pp. 67–68.

point to certain passages in Marx regarding the importance of collective ownership and central control, while Gorbachev could point to other passages in Marx (and especially Lenin) calling for more decentralization in economic decision making.[32] While Communist Party leaders of different countries might draw different conclusions from Marx, it is essential to communism that only such party leaders have interpretative authority. One task of the party is to eliminate all errant interpretations and all those who would—willfully or accidentally—derail progress toward the ideal communist society because of their failed understandings of Marxism and of present conditions and necessities.[33]

Thus, perhaps the interpretive authority of the Communist Party is more central to communism than is the social and economic authority of the state. The authority that the party claims in interpreting Marx's texts becomes evident in its absolutely authoritative statements on the course of history and what is to be done to get to the "end of history," where ideal communism will flourish. The interpretative authority of the party determines the authority that the state can properly exercise over social and economic life under different circumstances and at various points in time.[34]

Citizenship

Like Marx and Engels, communists argue that citizen participation in liberal democracy is largely symbolic and ineffectual. Formal democracy tends to legitimize the rule of the few over the many. In this sense, the word "citizen" is itself problematic for Marxists, since it is essentially a legal term, referring to one's legal obligations and rights under a specific system of rule; it is merely another form of bourgeois domination.

To get beyond bourgeois domination, communists argue that people must perform certain duties. For example, before and during the Russian Revolution, members of communist parties everywhere were expected to fulfill those obligations itemized in a list of "twenty-one conditions," of the Third International in 1921. These obligations included an absolute ideological commitment to communism; support for the principle and practice of democratic centralism, which included eliminating from the party ranks all so-called reformists, revisionists, and trade unionists; support for the USSR from all communists, regardless of their nationality; the duty to establish underground and even illegal organizations in preparation for prerevolutionary activities that included undermining and disrupting the military forces defending cap-

[32]For Gorbachev's attempt to interpret Marx and Lenin as ideologically supporting perestroika, see his "The Socialist Idea and Revolutionary Perestroika," published in *National Affairs* (Nov. 17, 1989), pp. 70–80.

[33]Lenin, " 'Left-Wing' Communism: An Infantile Disorder," in *The Lenin Anthology*, p. 609.

[34]This suggests that Gorbachev's retreat from communism was not his policy of perestroika, but that of glasnost. Perestroika was, literally, "a turning" (of the economy in some other direction), but only under "glasnost" ("openness" or "publicity") did the Soviet Communist Party relinquish its final, interpretive authority and permit open debate on social and economic issues.

italist nations (of which communists were citizens); and aid and support for revolutionary activities among people in the colonies of the imperialist powers.[35] The programs of every communist party had to be reviewed and approved by the executive committee of the Third International.[36]

At the outset of the revolution, the obligations of the citizens and their subjection to the authority of the Communist Party are paramount. As the transition into communism progresses, however, they will receive more and more freedom until they reach that point at which they will have become the autonomous, freely creating laborers that communists foresee. In the same way, there is considerably more differentiation between the characteristics of individuals at the beginning of the revolution than those at the end. Although communists have differed on this matter, the dominant paradigm for citizen participation originated with Lenin. Citizens should subordinate everything to the political organization, will, and leadership of the party in its efforts to bring about the revolution. In precapitalist societies, the peasants—who were the numerically dominant social class—were to promote revolution against capitalism and imperialism. They often could and did so in the name of nationalism, which was a kind of "intermediate ideology" that they could use on their way to achieving the ideal communist society. The more intellectually or organizationally gifted members of society—those who understood history and could therefore determine the proper path for the development of socialism and communism to take—were obliged to speak and act on behalf of the proletariat and peasantry as the elite vanguard of the revolution. This body of the gifted, the Communist Party, was to follow the objectives established by the leadership without dissent or contention. Under Stalin, for example, such blind obedience was strictly enforced, and workers lost the right to participate in the making of decisions either at the local or national level. Workers were required to work for everyone, without regard for self-interest, and they were to submit totally to Stalin's (or the party's) doctrinal and policy opinions. Under Tito, however, Yugoslav workers often had comparatively much more autonomy and decision-making discretion. The meaning of "citizenship" therefore depends somewhat on the interpretive framework of Marx that a specific communist regime adopts.

[35]An extended diatribe against these socialist "heresies," along with a thorough discussion of revolutionary principles and tactics, may be found in Lenin's " 'Left-Wing' Communism," pp. 550–618. This work was first published as a booklet and distributed to the delegates of the Second Congress of the Third Communist International in July 1920 in Moscow.

[36]Leszek Kolakowski, *Main Currents of Marxism, vol. 3, The Breakdown,* translated by P. S. Falla (Oxford: Oxford University Press, 1978), pp. 107–108. Because the Soviet Communist Party was the dominant force in the Third International, and because the revolution had, at that point, only "succeeded" in the Soviet Union, these principles tended to be heavily influenced by the Soviets, biased toward their interests, and shaped by the particular characteristics of the Russian-Soviet revolution and its aftermath. Lenin was presciently pessimistic that this influence was not in the best interests of the future of international communism. Cf. V. I. Lenin, "Foreign Communist Parties and the Russian Spirit," in *The Lenin Anthology,* pp. 626–627.

SUMMARY AND CONCLUSIONS

It is perhaps ironic that of all the ideologies studied in this text, communism has been most affected by historical developments. The ideology that most clearly identified with a "science of history" that it uses to implement its strategies has been most changed by developments in history itself.

The apparent demise of Soviet and East European communism, economic reforms in China, and a faltering Cuban economy give communism an uncertain political future. For the most part, free-market economies or the mixed economies supported by democratic socialists are replacing centralized planning. The "dictatorship of the proletariat" has been exchanged for various versions of either benevolent authoritarianism or parliamentary democracy. Communism may become an ideological relic of the very history it sought to transform. Whereas Marxism may live on in the form of various critiques of capitalism and liberal society, communism appears, for now, to have been politically and intellectually discredited. The revolution did not develop as communists hoped and foretold. Instead, tyrannical and totalitarian regimes firmly entrenched themselves, with no future society of free creativity and plenty for all in sight. In the end, we witnessed the peculiar sight of communist "conservatives"—a seemingly self-contradictory phrase—trying to retain political power in the face of popular uprisings against them.

CHAPTER 7

Fascism and Nazism

Most thoughtful people regard the events associated with the rise of German nazism and Italian fascism—the Holocaust and World War II—as signaling the darkest hour in human history. While humans have long acted toward one another in cruel and barbarous ways, the magnitude and scope of evil that these ideologies wrought on the world in general and the Jews in particular was unprecedented. Perhaps most chilling is the fact such evil could be committed by citizens of highly developed and cultured societies.

What ideas did nazism and fascism share that won the acceptance, and often the firm allegiance, of such people? Both rejected liberalism, stressing the supremacy of the collectivity over the individual. Both rejected communism, believing that Marxist notions of class conflict and injustice undermine the unity of society and retard the attainment of the common good. Both rejected democracy, arguing that it panders to human weaknesses and special interests. Both endorsed rule by authoritarian leaders who mobilize the masses on behalf of elite-defined goals. Both believed that human reason can play only a limited role in political life, and stressed that collective greatness depends on an intuitive understanding of human destiny and on energizing human emotions and will in order to unite citizens behind such goals as military conquest and national unity.

Nazism and fascism are not, however, the same ideology. Fascism celebrates the nation as the collectivity that its members should venerate and serve, while nazism celebrates the so-called "Aryan race" as the collectivity to be promoted.[1]

The origins of nazism are found in the ideas and governing practices of Adolf Hitler (1889–1945), who became influential in Germany during the 1920s

[1]Technically, the Aryan peoples are the Indo-Europeans who originate in southwestern India and Iran. Rather than celebrate such darkly complected peoples, the nazis asserted the racial superiority of the light-complected Germanic peoples who were of Scandinavian origin. But they called these peoples "Aryans," nonetheless.

and was dictator of the German Third Reich from 1933 to 1945.[2] Hitler stressed **racial struggle** (primarily between Aryans and the Jews) as the central problem of politics. Nazism proclaimed that many German problems were due to the "Jewish conspiracy"[3] and sought as a major goal the development of a superior and pure Aryan race that could bring greatness to humankind. By planning the physical annihilation of the "Jewish race" and by killing an estimated six million European Jews during the **Holocaust**, the nazis made racial genocide (of Jews, Gypsies, and others) and racial supremacy (of Aryans) the central tenets of their ideology. Other ideologies have been accused of leading to spiritual stultification, abuses of judicial power, and tyranny, but the use of nazi ideology to justify the systematic murder of large numbers of people exposes most clearly the dark side of ideological thinking.

[2]For nazis, the "First Reich" refers to the era characterized by the centralizing tendencies evinced by German kings in various Germanic territories, between the tenth and thirteenth centuries. The Second Reich was the Imperial German Empire that was shaped by the policies of Otto von Bismarck between 1871 and 1918, and that was dismantled after World War I by the Treaty of Versailles.
[3]For evidence of a Jewish conspiracy, Nazis frequently cited the *Protocols of the Elders of Zion*, an alleged record of Jewish plans to conquer the world. The *Protocols* were a forgery, fabricated in the late nineteenth century by anti-Semites to provoke popular hatred of the Jews.

Sidebar 7-1

Some Precursors and Proponents of Fascism and Nazism and Their Main Writings

PRECURSORS

Arthur Schopenhauer (1788–1860)
World as Will and Representation (1818)

Arthur de Gobineau (1816–1882)
Essay on the Inequality of Human Races (1854)

Guiseppe Mazzini (1805–1872)
The Duties of Man (1875)

Friedrich Nietzsche (1844–1900)
The Genealogy of Morals (1887)

Georges-Eugène Sorel (1847–1922)
Reflections on Violence (1906)

Vilfredo Pareto (1848–1923)
The Mind and Society (1916)

Houston Stewart Chamberlain (1855–1927)
Foundations of the Nineteenth Century (1899)

Gaetano Mosca (1858–1941)
The Ruling Class (1896)

FASCISTS

Benito Mussolini (1883–1945)
The Doctrine of Fascism (1928)

Giovanni Gentile (1875–1944)
The Philosophical Basis of Fascism (1928)

NAZIS

Adolf Hitler (1889–1945)
Mein Kampf (1925–1926)

Rudolf Huber (1903–)
Constitutional Law of the Greater German Reich (1939)

The foundations of fascism are in the ideas and governing practices of Benito Mussolini (1883–1945), who was dictator of Italy from 1922 to 1945. Fascist philosophers, such as Giovanni Gentile (1875–1944), made clear that true fascists reject the racist ideas of nazism. Rather than being racists, fascists are primarily nationalists, who put the power of the nation at the center of their principles. While a stress on the nation can have racial overtones, it does not necessarily entail a belief in racial struggle or "racial eugenics" (hereditary improvement by genetic control and manipulation of racial characteristics). Indeed, Mussolini's regime (and, for a time, the fascist regime in Hungary) treated Jews much better than did the nazis.[4]

The defeat of the German nazis and the Italian fascists at the end of World War II in 1945 discredited these ideologies in the minds of many people. Nevertheless, nazism and fascism contain ideas that have been the bases of various governing regimes and of many radical right-wing movements throughout the latter half of the twentieth century. The Spanish Fascist Party (the

[4]See Hannah Arendt, *Eichmann in Jerusalem* (New York and London: Penguin Books, 1963), pp. 138–140, 176–180; and David E. Ingersol and Richard K. Matthews, *The Philosophic Roots of Modern Ideology: Liberalism, Communism, Fascism,* 2d ed. (Englewood Cliffs, N.J.: Prentice Hall, 1991), pp. 246–247.

Doonesbury

Falange) led a rebellion against the Spanish Republic in 1936 and brought Francisco Franco to power, which he retained until his death in 1975. Argentina's Juan Perón (1895–1974) incorporated many fascist ideas into the Peronist party, which ruled Argentina from 1945 to 1955 and from 1973 to 1976. Various third-world military dictatorships—such as that of Saddam Hussein in Iraq—have also incorporated fascist principles into their regimes, although they usually avoid claiming allegiance to fascism as a whole. Until very recently, the Nationalist Party in South Africa used the racist policy of **apartheid**—the complete separation of all whites and all "coloreds"—to guarantee white minority rule and the repression of black Africans. The Serbian policy of "ethnic cleansing" in Bosnia (a republic within what was formerly greater Yugoslavia) is the most conspicuous reminder that racial goals similar to those of the nazis are alive and well in the post-cold-war era. Industrialized and democratic nations like Germany and the United States also continue to be influenced by neo-nazi organizations and movements that are able to mobilize significant numbers of people behind their racist political ideas. While we will stress Italian fascism and German nazism in this chapter, it is important to remember that the principles of these ideologies continue to play important roles in world politics.

THE POLITICAL BASES

Problems

Fascism and nazism are usually linked to a particular set of social, economic, and historical developments of the late nineteenth and early twentieth centuries. To understand the emergence of these two ideologies, let us begin with the problems they addressed during that time. Because nazism and fascism seem originally to have been nearly ad hoc responses to a particular set of historical problems, one might conclude that they will not become prominent again as ideologies, unless similar circumstances reemerge. This belief is an oversimplification, but it is useful to our understanding to consider carefully the several historical conditions that seem to have prompted the rise of fascism in Italy and nazism in Germany.

The first condition was a sense of international injustice engendered by the punitive measures of the Treaty of Versailles, signed in 1919 and ending World War I. Many Germans, in particular, believed that the treaty unfairly blamed and punished Germany for the war. Germany lost roughly one percent of its prewar arable land, ten percent of its population, all overseas colonies and other investments, and much of its military and merchant fleets. It was also forced to pay large sums for reparations to France and Great Britain. Signing the treaty at all was an unpopular measure among the German populace. The Italians, who had broken their treaty with Germany and joined the Allies in 1915, putting them on the winning side of the war, also had grievances stemming from the postwar settlement. In her secret treaty with the Allies, Italy had been promised territory in modern-day Slovenia if the Allies were victorious. After the war, however, the Allies reneged on the agreement. This decision insulted the Italians, wounded their sense of national pride, and produced in them a sense of betrayal. In short, widespread perceptions of international injustice stirred intense nationalist sentiments to which nazis and fascists could appeal.

The second historical condition was the existence of rising economic expectations combined with economic instability. Class distinctions faded among Italian and German soldiers during World War I, giving rise to a spirit of egalitarianism and raising the economic aspirations of those of lower birth, less education, and less wealth. Italians and Germans had accepted extensive economic sacrifices during the war; when the war ended, demands for economic comforts were widespread. Although, in both Italy and Germany, there were significant gains in economic productivity and the standards of living rose during the 1920s, economic problems persisted. In Italy, for example, industrialization was confined to a small number of northern cities, and the rural northern areas and the south retained a peasant economy that did not participate significantly in economic growth. Extensive budgetary deficits by Italy's liberal-democratic government necessitated higher taxes and reduced expenditures. Italy also suffered from a balance-of-payments deficit in international trade, and the Italian lira dropped significantly in value. Such problems caused widespread disillusionment and resentment among Italians, stimulated a rapid growth in trade unionism, and precipitated many labor disputes. In this climate, the middle class sought an alternative to the socialist parties on the left, while the working class sought a party that promised economic self-sufficiency for Italy. The fascists appealed to both classes.

The German economy immediately following World War I was devastated by several factors, including the need to pay reparations that were far beyond its capacity, the imposition of extensive restrictions on its international trade, and the eventual French occupation of the Ruhr region in response to Germany's failure to keep up reparations payments. The Weimar government responded by printing more money to meet expenses and, from 1922 to 1923, this policy resulted in runaway inflation. The hyperinflation wiped out savings and pensions and other bases of economic investment. By 1923, barter replaced other commercial dealings, and food riots broke out. The middle class was particularly hurt by such inflation, but workers also suffered reductions in their real wages. Although there was a temporary recovery in the mid-1920s, the worldwide depression of 1929 caused unemployment in Germany to rise to six million workers. By 1932, more than twenty-five percent of the German labor force was without employment. In this economic climate, the allegiance of German citizens to liberal democracy eroded. Economic instability and hardships seemed to reaffirm the widespread German distrust of liberal democracy and its institutions, which had not been able to secure the complete confidence or allegiance of the German people during the early years of the Weimar Republic, which lasted from 1919 to 1933. The lack of a stable liberal-democratic tradition provided a receptive audience for the authoritarian rhetoric of the nazis, who implied that Germany's economic problems could be solved by attacking the alleged source of these problems (the Jewish domination of the economy) and by instituting a program of "national socialism" involving extensive governmental control of the economy while retaining private production and enterprise.

A third problem to which fascists and nazis responded was the apparent inefficiency and ineffectiveness of parliamentary government. After World War I, Italy and Germany adopted electoral laws under which political parties obtained parliamentary seats not on the basis of single-constituency plurality voting, but on the basis of a party's proportion of the national vote. In the German Weimar Republic, parties sent one deputy to the parliament (Reichstag) for every 60,000 votes received nationally. Consequently, voters did not perceive a vote for a small party to be a "wasted" vote, and such parties proliferated in the Reichstag. In 1932, for example, thirty-eight parties appeared on the ballot, of which eighteen obtained parliamentary seats. No party in the Weimar Republic ever won an absolute majority, so that a group of parties had to be brought together to assemble a coalition large enough to form a government. Cooperation proved difficult; political infighting, petty jealousies, genuine differences of policy, and bargaining and positioning for influence continually undermined coalitions, so that governments fell frequently (there had been fifteen governments by May 1928). The spectacle of political wrangling, and the instability of any government operating under this system, which made governing with decisiveness and authority nearly impossible, did little to enhance popular confidence in parliamentary rule. In both Italy and Germany, the economic crises of the 1920s tended to polarize the electorate and its parliamentary representatives into right-wing and left-wing extremes. Such polarization did little to foster the compromise and cooperation that is needed if multiparty parliaments with no absolute majorities are to function effectively. These deficiencies and the lack of popular support enabled nazis and fascists to point to liberal democracy as faction-ridden, ineffective, and unworkable. They insisted effective government required institutions of national unity, such as a supreme leader, a one-party state, and closely coordinated domestic policies. In Italy, in fact, parliamentary government only lasted about six years. The socialist party became the largest party in November 1919 (but without an absolute majority). This electoral victory, and the disintegration of the centrist parties, confronted the conservative rulers and economic elites of Italy with the possibility of radical social and economic reforms that they did not want. In order to prevent this, they aided Mussolini's ascent to power through illegal, extraparliamentary means and with corrupt electoral practices.

A fourth problem to which nazism and fascism responded was the sense of alienation (a feeling of purposelessness or of not being attached to a community larger than oneself) from traditional social structures that modernization and industrialization had brought to many Germans and Italians. Industrialization uprooted many Germans and Italians from their rural communities, local parishes, and extended families. They found themselves immersed in large urban masses, with few group loyalties and attachments. The alienation of the urban masses, particularly under conditions of widespread unemployment, led them to search for a secure, meaningful place in the world. Nazism and fascism appealed to the desire for "higher" purposes of race or state as a way of satisfying this need for meaning, and they offered simple explanations for the ills of the world. The fascists focused on the idea that Italians could find meaning in their lives if they identified with the state and its aspirations in the world. If Italy could regain the glory and power of the Roman Empire, each Italian citizen would be glorified and empowered by Italy's restoration to world prominence. The nazis explained German alienation and the troubles of Germany by focusing on racial factors. They claimed that Jewish ownership of business—not industrialization and capitalism—was the root cause of German economic problems, and that the alienation arising from industrialization was caused by Jewish conspiracies and machinations. Jews had also contributed to public unrest by providing the intellectual foundations of Marxism and socialism—the political doctrines that preached class struggle rather than national harmony. For nazis, it was no coincidence that many left-wing agitators—such as Rosa Luxemburg, Eduard Bernstein, and Karl Marx himself—were of Jewish origin. The nazis also stressed that Germans' lack of attachment to one another was due to racial mingling. Only when the Aryan race was purified and the subversive influence of non-Aryans (primarily Jews) had been eliminated could each Aryan German take pride in belonging to a superior race of people who constituted a strong and united Germany.

While these problems of international injustice, economic instability, political ineffectiveness, and social alienation were real and provided fascists and nazis with fertile material with which to develop their ideologies, fascists and nazis were also inventive in creating the perception of problems that they were uniquely suited to address. Fascists stressed the "problem" of the lost Roman Empire to justify their aggressive nationalist policies. Nazis stressed the "problem" that Aryans had been weakened by race mingling and Jewish machinations. Why did significant numbers of Italian and German citizens accept these as problems? The political ineptness and lack of political will among the "democratic middle" (the democratic liberals and others who supported truly liberal-democratic systems of government and did not lean toward the extreme left or right) contributed to German and Italian receptivity to these concerns. Conservative and authoritarian attitudes that were skeptical of liberal and democratic institutions also enhanced the appeal of such concerns. But widespread public support did not itself propel Mussolini into power in Italy in 1922, nor Hitler to power in Germany in 1933. The fascists had won less than twenty percent of the vote in Italy in 1921; Mussolini attained power when King Victor Emmanuel III asked him to take office during a threatened general strike staged by socialists, communists, and other left-wing organizations. Hitler received less than thirty-seven percent of the vote in 1932, and while the nazis became the largest party in the German parliament after that election, they did not have an absolute majority. Preceded and followed by considerable intrigue and extraconstitutional manipulations, this election result encouraged the aged, nearly senile president Paul von Hindenburg to make Hitler the chancellor of a conservative-nationalist government on January 30, 1933. Within two months, Hitler was granted dictatorial powers, and the abbreviated tenure of the Thousand-Year Reich began.[5]

Goals

Nazis and fascists have similar goals, contributing to the perception that nazism and fascism are the same ideology in different guises. These goals follow directly from the problems they address. Most fundamentally, both nazis and fascists seek **national solidarity**—the end of competition between classes or individuals within the state, and a redirection of competitive tendencies and resources toward other states in the international system. This goal therefore demands that the energies of all citizens be channeled toward the preservation and enhancement of state power. All segments of society must be made to work in unison. This universal, enforced cooperation will assure that the interests of the greater whole are secured. Even here, however, the two ideologies are not identical. Whereas fascists generally have had no well-formulated program for fostering the strength, prestige, or expansion of the nation in the world, the nazis had a very clear program by which they could establish their version of the good society.

Mussolini, for example, had no doctrine that elaborated beforehand the precise goals of Italian foreign and domestic policy. The Italian people would come to know their goals only through struggle and action in the international arena. The survival of the fittest in this political-military struggle between nations would determine the relative merits of the nations involved. But there was no preestablished fascist vision of a set of tasks or of a utopia that would be the end product of an international struggle. In Mussolini's own words, "Our program is simple; we wish to govern Italy. They ask us for programs, but there are already too many. It is not programs that are wanting for the salvation of Italy, but men and willpower."[6]

The nazis, on the other hand, had a much more clearly defined end in mind. The goal of their foreign and domestic policy was not so much national strength as **Aryan supremacy**. It would be achieved when all other races had been subjugated by the Aryans. Subjugation would be followed by elimination, so that in the end, only Aryans—and perhaps some slaves from the subordinate races—would populate the world. Certainly the "great enemy race" of the Aryans—the Jews—would have to be destroyed. This goal of destruction was tied to a larger discourse concerning the nature of human life that was, in turn, derived from various notions of race that had been circulating in Europe since the seventeenth century. Nazis explained Germany's problems

[5]For a brief, but more thorough, analysis of this period, see David P. Conradt, *The German Polity*, 5th ed. (New York and London: Longman, 1993), pp. 1–10. See also Karl Dietrich Brader, *The German Dictatorship* (New York: Praeger, 1970).

[6]Cited in James D. Forman, *Fascism: The Meaning and the Experience of Reactionary Revolution* (New York: Dell, 1974), p. 34.

and their solutions in terms of such race "theories." We will consider the nazi race discourse more closely in the section on ontology.

At the level of public policy, the nazis made several concurrent responses to the race question and the need for national unity. The most heinous was the **Final Solution**, which called for the physical destruction of all Jews, Gypsies, and other so-called subhuman races, and for the genetic cleansing of the Aryan race itself (which would include the extermination of all physically and mentally handicapped individuals, as well as the elimination of those with any of a long list of illnesses, physical "defects," or "deviant" behaviors).[7] In the resulting Holocaust, about six million Jews, and six million other "undesirables" and opponents to the nazis, were killed. Most died under horrifying circumstances from disease, starvation, and systematic abuse in concentration camps throughout Europe. Public policies enacted before the Final Solution was decided upon at Wannsee in 1942 included the Nuremberg race laws of 1935 and government support of extensive vandalism against the Jewish community on "Kristallnacht" in November 1938. The nazis had also considered the possibility of deporting all German and European Jews to their own homeland, perhaps in Palestine or even Madagascar. In all cases, Hitler's *Gleichschaltung*—the coordination and reprogramming of all segments of society toward the purposes of the state—would ensure the strength and clear aims of the Aryan state and a sense of belonging and purpose for all its Aryan citizens.

All of these nazi policies and activities should make clear the decisive political difference between nazis and fascists: whereas the state is an end in itself for fascists, it is merely the "vessel" of the race for nazis.[8] For nazis, the state is the means to a higher end—namely, the survival and flourishing of the race, which is the highest political entity. Nazi policy was intended to preserve not merely the state, but the race.

Whether the goal of national solidarity focused simply on enhancing state power or on attaining Aryan supremacy, it also encompassed a number of other goals for both fascists and nazis. First, the achievement of national solidarity would enhance social and political order. The disputes between management and labor that resulted in work stoppages and strikes would be replaced by employer-employee cooperation. The hostilities between rural and urban areas would be replaced by collaborative efforts to build the nation as

[7]Hannah Arendt notes, "The Nazis did not think that the Germans were a master race, to whom the world belonged, but that they should be led by a master race, as should all other nations, and that this race was only on the point of being born." In a footnote to this observation, she continues: "In a decree of August 9, 1941, . . . Hitler prohibited the further use of the term 'German race,' because it would lead to the 'sacrifice of the racial idea as such in favor of a mere nationality principle, and to the destruction of important conceptual preconditions of our whole racial and folk policy.' It is obvious that the concept of a German race would have constituted an impediment to the progressive 'selection' and extermination of undesirable parts among the German population which in those very years was being planned for the future." Hannah Arendt, *The Origins of Totalitarianism* (New York and London: Harcourt, Brace, Jovanovich, 1951), p. 412.

[8]See Adolf Hitler, *Mein Kampf*, translated by Ralph Mannheim (Boston: Houghton Mifflin, 1971 [1925–26]), p. 393.

a whole. The partisan disputes and competition among special interests that accompany the disorderly democratic process would be replaced by legislators' rallying around the national objectives articulated by Hitler and Mussolini. Second, the achievement of national solidarity would result in efficiency. The trains would run on time. Economic and military goods would be produced on schedule and according to national needs. Costly disruptions in production resulting from labor stoppages and sabotage or from wasteful competition among firms would be eliminated. Third, the achievement of national solidarity implied the development of a more uplifting human ethic. The material and selfish preoccupations of individuals in liberal capitalist societies would be replaced by more communal values. Individuals would become more dutiful and responsible to others as they learned the gratification of contributing to the good of the nation or of the race, and individuals would become more heroic as they set aside their own smug and comfortable bourgeois existences and embraced the great adventures that awaited them as soldiers in pursuit of national greatness.

THE PHILOSOPHICAL BASES

Nazism and fascism were action-oriented ideologies; they focused on achieving power in the real world of politics and de-emphasized deep philosophical reflection. Nevertheless, they appropriated and reconstituted a number of ideas and symbols from various sources, including German Romanticism, French and Italian elitist theories, and European theories of race. In the following sections on the philosophical foundations of fascism and nazism, we indicate how proponents of these ideologies drew upon various philosophical, scientific, and literary ideas that were popular in Europe in the nineteenth and early twentieth centuries. Often the meanings and applications that nazis and fascists gave to these ideas departed from the intended meanings and uses of the authors. Thus, it would be a mistake to conclude that those who contributed to the philosophical foundations of nazism and fascism were themselves nazis and fascists. With this caveat in mind, let us turn to the question of how nazis and fascists think about the ultimate forces in the universe that shape world history.

Ontology

To understand nazi and fascist ontologies, it is useful to recall a crucial distinction between two ways of thinking about history—as the *res gestae* ("the totality of events"), or as the *historia rerum gestarum* ("the account, or report, of these events"). In the case of *res gestae,* history is an object of study that has an objective reality. Here we think of history as the things that have been done, as the totality of events that constitute the unfolding of the human drama. History occurs in some necessary and determinate way, and so we consider various historical events and processes to be justified, because they were necessary precursors of subsequent history. The answers to the questions, "Where do we come from?" and "Where are we going?" are found on a determinative line we call history, whose origins, dynamic, direction, and perhaps even endpoint are known. In the case of *historia rerum gestarum*, history is viewed as a story of events, and no perceived necessity for these events exists. Recounting the sequence of human events that make up the narratives of history reveals not a linear necessity to human affairs, but the indeterminacy of the human condition. In this case, we see history not as a necessary unfolding, but as a story of contingent events in which human beings have had and continue to have choices.

By viewing history as a determinative process of class struggle, orthodox Marxism exemplifies an interpretation of history as *res gestae*. Classical liberals also tend to view history in such terms, because of their focus on the material world, its conformity to the laws of nature, and the possibility of progress in that world toward solving the problems of "man's estate."[9] In contrast, by viewing history as the context within which we act willfully, fascism exemplifies an interpretation of history as *historia rerum gestarum*. Nazism is perhaps somewhere in the middle, combining a view of historical necessity with respect to race with a notion of human will with respect to what can be accomplished by human initiative in the midst of the struggle between races.

Mussolini, who had been a Marxist-Leninist until at least 1914 and was thus influenced by Lenin's "voluntaristic" theory of revolution, stressed the role of human will in affecting the course of human history. Like Lenin, Mussolini rejected the orthodox Marxist view of dialectical materialism that suggested revolutions were completely determined by social and economic conditions and instead maintained that elites could decisively influence transforming historical events. He found in the writings of Friedrich Nietzsche (1844–1900) a helpful emphasis on the role of the will in human affairs. In Mussolini's reading, Nietzsche seemed to argue that a great human being is able to transcend his immediate environment and reconstruct the world according to his will. In this reading, human will is the determinant of history. Creative human actions of great individuals determine the aesthetic and political boundaries within which human beings orient themselves and act out their desires, aspirations, and goals. Extracting from Nietzsche this emphasis on creative, willful human action, Mussolini transferred it from the sphere of the individual to that of the collective.[10] Rather than depending on the creative

[9]The liberal view is provided by René Descartes, *Discourse on Method*, translated by Donald A. Cress (Indianapolis: Hackett Publishing, 1980 [1637]), p. 33. For a discussion of the liberal view of progress in history, see Thomas A. Spragens, Jr., *The Irony of Liberal Reason* (Chicago: University of Chicago Press, 1981), esp. pp. 50–58.

[10]This transfer indicates the distance between Nietzsche and fascism. Although certain of his ideas were appropriated by the fascists, Nietzsche was neither a fascist nor a "protofascist." He looked forward to the rule of a cultural aristocracy, and he abhorred the notion of any sort of mass participation in politics. He was, moreover, sharply critical of anti-Semitism, nationalist chauvinism, and Darwinian theories of race or social competition.

individual to change history or to shape the horizons of human existence, the masses must themselves be mobilized to engage in acts of change and creation. The state would serve as the focal point of such acts. Thus, in Mussolini's theory of "voluntarism," the strong national leader must mobilize the masses, and, with their cooperation, determine—or at least shift—the course of history.

Because history can be shaped by willful human actions, fascists reject the Marxist idea that there is a predictable and determinate end to history. Nevertheless, fascists and, especially, nazis do not claim that humans are free to shape history as they wish. Circumstances constrain *how* humans can manipulate historical processes to accord with their will. According to Mussolini, "To act among men, as to act in the natural world, it is necessary to enter into the process of reality and to master the already operating forces." Thus, Mussolini's fascism did not accept a notion of "total freedom." According to Mussolini, "man could not be what he is without being a factor in the spiritual process to which he contributes, either in the family sphere or in the social sphere, in the nation or in history in general to which all nations contribute. Man without a part in history is nothing."[11] Thus, the historical process limits or at least channels the will.

For fascists, the spiritual process to which men could contribute was the realization of Italian national unity and power. For nazis, this process involved the emergence of the Aryan race as the dominant force in world history. Thus, the ontology of nazism must be sought in the discourse of race. The history of the race idea in European intellectual history is complex, but the nazi appropriation of the idea can be told briefly by summarizing three streams of race thinking.

The first is composed of broad ethnographic and historical studies that attempt to explain political and historical phenomena on the basis of vaguely defined notions of race. The principal originator of such **ethnographic studies** was Count Arthur de Gobineau (1816–1882), a French diplomat and social theorist. A "race" is understood by Gobineau and others in this tradition to be a group of people that share a common set of physical, intellectual, and spiritual characteristics—passed on through the process of reproduction—that determine the cultural, political, and historical development and possibilities of that group of people. Racial characteristics may originally have been determined by the interrelationship of climatic, genetic, and geographic factors, but they are then transmitted in sexual reproduction from generation to generation as fixed traits. In Gobineau's speculation, there existed a hierarchy of race—whites being the greatest, followed by the yellow and then the black races. Gobineau argued that racial and ethnic impurity explained the historical decline of civilizations. When an ascendant race began to mingle with others, Gobineau thought, its civilization began to decline. Most of the ethnic groups within the white race were the products of such racial mingling. Those

[11]Benito Mussolini, "The Doctrine of Fascism," in *Readings on Fascism and National Socialism* (Chicago: Swallow Press, 1952 [1928]), p. 10.

that were ethnoracially purest had the best potential for developing civilization. The greatest of these were the Teutons—Germans, Scandinavians, or English. Those that were ethnically mixed were capable only of transmitting ethnic decay, which hastened the collapse of civilization. Chief among these were the Slavs and Celts. The present decline of civilization was, therefore, the result of the superior race mingling with an inferior one. To sustain a "high" culture, the Teutons would have to keep themselves racially pure.[12]

A group of artists and intellectuals known as the **Bayreuth Circle** made Gobineau's analysis more ideologically and politically focused. The originator of the Bayreuth Circle was the composer and essayist, Richard Wagner (1813–1883). His operas emphasized the myth of the ancient, noble, and pure German as a heroic figure who transcended conventional ideas of good and evil. Wagner's aim was to use his music to initiate a renaissance of German culture. Hitler was to become particularly attracted to Wagner's work. Another figure associated with the Bayreuth Circle was Houston Stewart Chamberlain (1855–1927). He claimed that the western Aryan peoples, which included European whites other than Germans, were responsible for the intellectual and creative accomplishments of Europe, and he argued that the Jewish influence on Europe had been strongly negative.

The second stream of race thinking in Europe was most closely tied to the natural-scientific study of man, and writers in the other two streams often appealed to it for validation of their racial speculations. Central to this tradition was the theory of evolution proposed by Charles Darwin (1809–1882). Although Darwin's writings never mentioned the Jewish race, the idea that some species were "higher" on the evolutionary scale than others led to speculation that some subspecies, or races, were more evolved and intelligent than others. For example, Samuel Morton (1799–1851) had developed the pseudoscience of craniology, which maintained that there were significant correlations between race and the size of the cranium (the portion of the skull enclosing the brain) and between the size of the cranium and intelligence. According to this "science," whites were more intelligent than other races because they had the largest craniums. Such "theories" provoked a popular public response in the period leading to nazism. [13]

"**Volk**" is the central idea of the third stream of race thinking. It is

[12]Gobineau's writings attracted others, who coarsened his ideas further. For example, he was not specifically anti-Semitic, arguing that the present inferiority of the Jews was the result of mingling with black races, and not an inherent fault in the race itself. Others, however, would appropriate his racial ideas and mold them into justifications for anti-Semitism and for agendas for eugenics, race wars, and the like.

[13]There are at least two reasons for rejecting a scientific basis for racism. First, race and species must be demonstrated to be scientifically equivalent—which they are not. Second, one must also show how either the genetic material of a race or its physiological manifestations determine nonmaterial, spiritual, and intellectual characteristics of individuals and groups. Neither requirement was fulfilled by any of the race theorists on whom the nazis depended for the scientific validation of their racial mythologies. Rather than being a scientific concept, race remained a political symbol used to rally people behind a certain idea of political community.

German for "folk," or "people," and came to evoke the notion of a biologically, culturally, spiritually, and linguistically homogenous people whose aspirations are embodied in a kind of mystical nationalism that unites them against the other peoples and nations of the world. Johann Fichte (1762–1814), an early German Romantic philosopher, was among the first to use the term in a politically focused way. The widespread use of the term in the art, literature, and political rhetoric of the time, often entangled with biological and ethnographic speculation, caused "Volk" to become a commonplace of the German political vocabulary. This everyday usage enabled the nazis to employ the term at rallies and other Nazi Party events to evoke immediate feelings and images in the Germans of unity, greatness, and external threat.

The three streams of race thinking converge in national socialism to create a kind of ontology of race. Despite nazism's anti-Marxian stance, the nazi notion of a race struggle resembles the Marxist world-historical speculation of class struggle. As with the Marxist idea of class, the idea of race served the nazis as an explanation for a full range of sociopolitical phenomena. To nazis, the essence of history is the struggle for supremacy between races, a conflict that has culminated in a struggle between the "purest," "most civilized," or "highest" race, which is the so-called Aryan race, and the "subhuman" race of the Jews. Other, less world-historically significant races are included in this struggle (e.g., Slavs, Gypsies, Negroes), but the Jewish-Aryan conflict is paramount. In the midst of this struggle, the Aryan race itself must also be "purified." Genetic defectives—the mentally and physically handicapped, congenitally diseased, and so on—will also be eliminated. All is to the glory and strength of the race. This doctrine of race was rarely disseminated in such a pure, undisguised form to the German masses, nor did it play any immediate role in the national socialist seizure of power in 1933. Instead, it became the essential basis for nazi domestic and foreign policy after 1933.

Epistemology

Fascists may be said to have a simultaneously strong and weak conception of truth. On the weak side, they do not believe that there is a rational or natural basis for determining political ends or the good for man in general. Knowledge is subjective, and science, reason, measurement, or empirical observation provide only a glimpse of knowledge. The truth is known ultimately through intuition. This notion of intuition leads to the strong sense of truth. The leader's views are regarded as absolute truths. The leader intuitively knows the collective will or the shape of the collective good, which the masses are then to pursue. It is the duty of the leader to grasp the national will, to communicate this will to the masses, and to ensure that the nation fulfills its historic destiny in accordance with this will. Because the leader's intuitions about the collective will are not subject to logical or empirical disconfirmation, they must be accepted as the authoritative truth. The truth resides not in some objectively correct ideas or in nature, but in the authority of those who claim to possess the truth and in the acceptance of that claim by others. Because fascism accepts the leader's intuitions as absolute truth, it is categorized as an **authoritarian** ideology. While nazis share these doctrines about the role of the leader and his intuitive knowledge, it is clear that with respect to the world-historical struggle of races, at least, something definite and politically determinative *can* be known. The leader is responsible for intuitively guiding the race to its proper end in light of that knowledge.[14]

As with race and racism, nazi and fascist doctrines of the will and intuitionism have their origins in philosophies that are often only distantly related to the eventual shape of these ideologies. The primary source of nazi and fascist epistemology was **German Romanticism**, especially as developed in the philosophical writings of Arthur Schopenhauer (1788–1860). German Romanticism was a school of thought that can be understood in part as a reaction against what it perceived as the excessive rationalism, positivism, scientism, and utilitarianism of the eighteenth century Enlightenment. Romantics tended to emphasize the importance of the emotions, intuition, and other irrational forces in human life. Romantics claimed that these forces of the spirit are superior to science in the power and knowledge that they give us. Thus, we look to art, music, poetry, mysticism, and the like, for "true" knowledge of the world. Romanticism rejected the mechanistic view of nature propounded by Enlightenment science, and turned to organic views of both nature and society. Schopenhauer, for example, argued that positive science could only give us access to the surface appearance of things; he sought to find the true essence of all human and natural phenomena in the universal will. This notion of will was loosely based on human experiences of willing, but was translated by Schopenhauer into a conception of a universal force that incorporated all the phenomena of the universe:

[14]Unlike fascism and nazism, liberalism—and, in some interpretations, Marxism—shares Aristotle's basic concern with linking "thought and action." Put simply, a person is free and responsible when his thoughts guide his actions and his actions influence what he is thinking. He criticizes inconsistent claims or actions in himself and others, and he may learn from his own and others' mistakes. Fascism and nazism sever this link between thought and action. The leader cannot be criticized for changes in views, strategies, or principles, because his intuitive perceptions put him above ethical condemnation; he is always right. Indeed, Mussolini claimed that he was a *tempista*, a man of "great timing." He knew intuitively what to do, and when to do it. Accordingly, no ethical categories from within fascist or nazi ideology could be applied to criticize his (or the Fuehrer's) statements and actions. For a follower of either ideology, ethical reflection is neither possible nor desirable. In Aristotle's terms, followers become either slaves or young children who have no ability to reason ethically or critically about action. They merely obey the injunctions of the leader. See Aristotle, *Nichomachean Ethics*, 1135a16–1135b12; and *Politics*, 1254b2–1255a3; 1260a10–15,33. For useful commentaries, see T. H. Irwin, "Reason and Responsibility in Aristotle," in *Essays on Aristotle's Ethics*, edited by Amélie Oksenberg Rorty (Berkeley: University of California Press, 1980), pp. 117–155; and David Wiggins, "Deliberation and Practical Reason," in *Essays on Aristotle's Ethics*, pp. 221–240.

> Besides will and representation, nothing is known to us or thinkable. If we wish to attribute the greatest known reality to the material world which exists immediately only in an idea, we give it the reality which our own body has for each of us; for that is the most real thing for every one. But if we now analyze the reality of this body and its actions, beyond the fact that it is idea, we find nothing in it except the will; with this its reality is exhausted. Therefore we can nowhere find another kind of reality which we can attribute to the material world.[15]

The **intuitionism** of thinkers like Henri Bergson (1859–1941) was another important source of nazi and fascist epistemology. Bergson's philosophy was in large part a response to the scientism and positivism of the French universities of the nineteenth century. Against the scientists who claimed that it was impossible for human beings ever to know the real essences of things, and that we could only hope to measure and describe their surface appearances, Bergson countered that we could indeed "penetrate the inner core of being."[16] This penetration is not possible through intellect, which can only accomplish what the scientists and positivists claimed. Instead, we require "intuition" to tell us of the ontological, absolute world. Thus, Bergson's intuitionism can be understood as an attempt to secure recognition for the emotional and spiritual dimensions of human experience over against the positivist—and increasingly technocratic—philosophies of the nineteenth century.[17]

Both nazis and fascists adapted the mystical, mythological symbols of the Romantic philosophers and the intuitionism of philosophers like Bergson to recover the nonrational elements of human experience and to appeal to the irrational side of the human psyche. These symbols served as powerful tools for creating feelings of national or racial unity and greatness. Thus, the antiliberalism and antirationalism of the nazis and fascists were not only a part of their ideological dogmas, but an important component of their practices. The famous Nuremberg rallies of the nazis, for example, incorporated flags, lights, music, and speeches to evoke moods that overwhelmed many of the people gathered there.[18] From the Romantic revolt against the Enlightenment, the fascists and nazis acquired doctrines of the will, radical subjectivism, and emotivism that they incorporated into their own programs. Appeals to the emotions of the masses included claims (and future promises) of national supremacy, racial purity and supremacy, and the emergence of (racial) supermen. All of these themes had been present in one way or another in the writings of the Romantics.

[15]Arthur Schopenhauer, *World as Will and Representation*, translated by R. B. Haldane and J. Kemp (London: Kegan Paul, Trench, Trubner, 1883 [1818]), p. 136.

[16]Charles A. Fecher, *The Philosophy of Jacques Maritain* (New York: Greenwood Press, 1953), p. 22.

[17]Cf. Henri Bergson, *The Two Sources of Morality and Religion*, translated by R. Ashley Audra and Cloudesley Brereton (Garden City, N.Y.: Doubleday, 1954 [1935]), esp. pp. 312–317, 209ff.

[18]The description of the Nuremberg rallies by Hitler's chief architect, Albert Speer, is particularly enlightening on this point. See Albert Speer, *Inside the Third Reich: Memoirs*, translated by Richard and Clara Winston (New York: Macmillan, 1970), pp. 58–62.

Human Nature

Just as nazis and fascists emphatically rejected the rationalism of liberal epistemology, they also rejected the liberal conception of human nature. According to fascists, humans are not distinguished by their rational pursuit of self-interest, but are instead motivated by emotional appeals to their wills. Humans are not characterized by their individualism, but by their connection to collective entities such as nations and racial groups. Humans are fundamentally unequal, because some are superior and others inferior in the possession of such human virtues as strength of will, courage, and creative insight.

For fascists, the central characteristic of all humans is that they possess a *will.* Most simply, the possession of a will gives each person the capacity of choice or decision, the ability to pursue a course of action. The concept of the will as the core of human nature has a lineage extending back at least to René Descartes.[19] Classical liberals equated the individual will with individual wants or utility. Liberals believed in the rationality of the individual will; they believed each individual would choose to pursue courses of actions that could maximize his pleasures and minimize his pain. Marxists generally agreed with liberalism on this point, but focused on the economic, social, and political constraints on the exercise of human will that resulted in human alienation. Fascists sought to overcome the implications and difficulties of liberal and Marxist psychologies by recognizing that the human will was less rational, less self-interested, less utilitarian, and less constrained than their ideological rivals believed. Human will is motivated not by rational, individualistic, and utilitarian ends, as liberals argued, but by a broad range of desires and needs.

Rather than simply being motivated by the satisfaction of individual wants, the will is also motivated by the need to belong to a coherent, recognizable group that transcends the individual, by the need for collective or individual glory, and by the need for order and security. Human motivation includes not merely material gain, but courage, emotions, instincts, and a collective need for violence. The human need to belong and to have order is fulfilled in the nazi and fascist return to group values and authority that relieves individuals of the "burdens" of freedom and free choice that liberalism imposes on them. The need for violent action is fulfilled in war, which, according to Mussolini, "alone brings all human energies to their highest tension and sets a seal of nobility on the peoples who have the virtue to face it."[20] War and

[19]"In fact, I cannot complain that I have received from God an insufficiently ample and imperfect will, or free choice, because I observe that it is limited by no boundaries. . . . If I examine the faculty of memory, imagination, or any other faculty, I manifestly find none, except what in me is feeble and limited, but what in God I understand to be immense. The sole exception is the will or free choice; I observe it to be so great in me that I grasp an idea of nothing greater, to the extent that the will is principally the basis for my understanding that I bear an image and likeness of God." René Descartes, *Meditation on First Philosophy,* translated by Donald A. Cress, (Indianapolis: Hackett Publishing, 1980 [1641]), pp. 80–81.

[20]Mussolini, "The Doctrine of Fascism," p. 15.

violence also serve a unifying role. "A test [in blood]," wrote Giovanni Gentile, "only war can bring by uniting all citizens in a single thought, a single passion, a single hope, emphasizing to each individual that all have something in common, something transcending private interests."[21]

Fascists also rejected the liberal assumption that each individual is the best judge of his or her own interests, that the motivations of each individual are internally derived by looking within oneself to discover that which produces pleasure and pain. Instead, fascists believe that most people in a society are like a flock of sheep. Lacking self-actualization, the will of the herd is malleable or open to being shaped by the values and motivations, the policies and programs, selected for them by the elite. Thus, humankind is essentially bifurcated in its power of will. The inferior masses lack strong wills, and the activities they pursue are directed by others. Given the herd mentality of most people, it is best that people be directed by the leaders of the state to pursue the interests of society as a whole. The superior leaders of the state possess strong wills that can identify the needs of the collectivity and that can pursue such needs with unyielding determination and courage. Such leaders motivate the masses to act in concert on behalf of the collective will by employing emotional appeals.

Because of their emphasis on the centrality of the will in human nature, their recognition that the human will is not always rational, and their stress on the capacity to motivate people with emotional appeals, both fascism and nazism have been labeled "**ideologies of irrationality**." This label may be somewhat misleading, because much of the actual organization and focusing of national energies, especially in Nazi Germany, incorporated the most technologically rational of principles. Death camps may be irrational with respect to ethical and humanistic principles, and they are a completely inefficient source of labor, but they are technologically a relatively efficient tool for genocide and social, psychological, or medical experimentation.[22] The use of propaganda, mythology, slogans, and other emotional appeals were shown by the nazis to be a very effective and, therefore, instrumentally rational means of mobilizing the citizens of a society on behalf of national goals that were ethically irrational.

For many people, the fascist and nazi conception of human nature was an attractive alternative to the rationalistic, materialistic, and egocentric conception of human nature provided by liberals and to the seemingly vague promise of a classless, laboring society offered by Marxists. By recognizing the emotional elements within human nature, fascism suggested that people could live more authentically outside of liberal society. By recognizing that the will could be motivated by spiritual and social values beyond the material self, fascism suggested that humans could be remade or redeemed in ways that fostered

[21]Giovanni Gentile, "The Philosophical Basis of Fascism," in *Readings on Fascism and National Socialism* (Chicago: Swallow Press, 1952 [1928]), p. 48.

[22]See Arendt, *Origins of Totalitarianism*, pp. 437–459; and Jay Lifton, *The Nazi Doctors: Medical Killing and the Psychology of Genocide* (New York: Basic Books, 1986), passim.

human and cultural excellence. The notion that humans can overcome their petty economic self-interests and courageously pursue their higher possibilities in spiritual harmony with others (without having to undergo the class warfare of a communist revolution) seems appealing.

Society

For fascists, the most fundamental unit of social organization was the nation; for nazis, it was the racial group. The nation or the race is the single most important identity that its members hold. Insofar as a nation or race has a history and a culture that defines the spirit of its people, the nation or race is more than the sum of its parts. The nation or race, not the individuals that make it up, is "real." In sum, a society is defined in terms of its national or racial characteristics, which are prior to and determinative of the individuals who make up the society.

As we have repeatedly stressed, a crucial difference between fascists and nazis hinges on the question of homogeneity. Fascists generally have not been as racist and, therefore, as insistent on social homogeneity as were the nazis. Mussolini, for example, usually included all Italian citizens under the rubric of the Italian nation, and was largely unconcerned about "racial" purity. The national socialists, on the other hand, defined the nation in terms of race, and therefore went to considerable lengths to ensure the homogeneity and racial purity of the Aryan nation. Fascists have tended to be more interested in uniting people around the goals of national strength or glory, channeling the energy of all people in the nation to serve these aims. Nazis subordinated even these goals to the yet higher end of purifying the race.[23] In short, fascists reduced their conception of society to the nation, and nazis reduced their conception of society to a racial group.[24]

[23]This tendency was manifested in particularly stunning fashion when the national socialist government subordinated the increasingly desperate war effort in 1944 and 1945 to the transportation of millions of Jews and other "undesirables" to extermination camps.

[24]The focus of fascists on the nation and of nazis on the race is repellent to those committed to other ideological perspectives. Liberals believe that individuals ontologically precede societies or nations and form collectivities for their own individualistic purposes. Accordingly, liberals reject arguments that individual interests and needs should yield to superior national interests. Marxists believe that an emphasis on nation or race ignores important class differences within these collectivities; the most powerful and privileged persons within a nation and racial grouping simply use appeals to national and racial identifications to trick the powerless and poor to pursue elite-defined national and racial goals rather than their more urgent class interests. Perhaps conservatives offer the most important critique of fascism and nazism on this matter. Like fascists and nazis, traditional conservatives are collectivists and not individualists. However, traditional conservatives hold that men and women are attached not only to the nation, but to a wide variety of social entities. Conservatives view society pluralistically—as composed of many groupings, organizations, and associations. While individuals recognize themselves as part of something greater than themselves, this greater entity is not, and should not be, confined to the nation or racial grouping. Individuals find social and spiritual identification and meaning in churches, schools, business enterprises, trade unions, voluntary associations, and local communities, as well as in the larger societies emphasized by fascists and nazis.

SUBSTANTIVE POLITICAL PRINCIPLES

Authority

The term "fascist" comes from the Latin word *fasces*, a bundle of sticks wrapped around a battle-ax whose head protrudes from the top. This emblem was carried by the ancient Roman magistrates as a public symbol of their authority. For the Italian fascists, the *fasces* served as a nostalgic and emotive reminder of the glory of ancient Rome that they were trying to recover, and the tightly wrapped bundle came to symbolize the communal unity of individuals in a state that generates power and authority.

In general, the state can be characterized as a "special instrument of society for achievement of common goals."[25] Especially fascists regard state authority as the means for empowering the nation and attaining national objectives. According to Mussolini:

> The State, as conceived and enacted by fascism, is a spiritual and moral fact, since it gives concrete form to the political, juridical, and economic organization of the country. Furthermore, this organization, as it rises and develops, is a manifestation of the spirit. The State is a safeguard of interior and exterior safety, but it is also the keeper and transmitter of the spirit of the people, as it was elaborated throughout the ages, in its language, customs, and beliefs. The State is not only the present, but it is also the past and, above all, the future. The State, inasmuch as it transcends the short limits of individual lives, represents the immanent conscience of the nation.[26]

Nazis regarded the state as an instrument that the race uses in its quest for dominance and security. According to Hitler:

> The state is a means to an end. Its end lies in the preservation and advancement of a community of physically and psychically homogenous creatures. This preservation itself comprises first of all existence as a race and thereby permits the free development of all the forces dormant in this race. Of them a part will always primarily serve the preservation of physical life, and only the remaining part the promotion of a further spiritual development. Actually, the one always creates the precondition for the other.
>
> States which do not serve this purpose are misbegotten, monstrosities in fact. The fact of their existence changes this no more than the success of a gang of bandits can justify robbery.[27]

Conservatives were among the most vehement objectors against what they regarded as the fascists' and nazis' attempts to obliterate (or at least subordinate) all secondary social organizations that stand between the individual and the nation (or racial grouping). See Robert Nisbet, *Conservatism* (Minneapolis: University of Minnesota Press, 1986), pp. 49–74. The importance of intermediate associations between the state and individual is argued by William Kornhauser, *The Politics of Mass Society* (Glencoe, Ill.: Free Press, 1959).

[25]Mark O. Dickerson and Thomas Flanagan, *An Introduction to Government and Politics: A Conceptual Approach* (Toronto: Methuen Publications, 1982), p. 24.

[26]Mussolini, "The Doctrine of Fascism," pp. 236–237.

[27]Hitler, *Mein Kampf*, p. 393; cf. 386ff.

Thus, fascists and nazis believe that the state is the political manifestation of either the nation or the race. State authority should be used to express the national will and to provide the power necessary to achieve national goals. Since the goal of fascism is to create a powerful nation, the state must have the total authority necessary to achieve that end. Thus, Gentile described the state as a "**totalitarian**" entity:

> The relationship between State and citizen (not this or that citizen, but all citizens) is accordingly so intimate that the State exists only as, and in so far as, the citizen causes it to exist. Its formation therefore is the formation of a consciousness of it in individuals, in the mass. Hence the need of the Party, and of all the instruments of propaganda and education which Fascism uses to make the thought and will of the *Duce* the thought and will of the masses.[28]

The state must aspire to be the exclusive guide for national goals, which include most especially the attainment of an organic unity of society, economy, and politics. The state must exercise total and exclusive control over all aspects of social, economic, religious, and private life. Family, church, and all other political, social, and private organizations or activities fall under the purview of the state. The role of the government, then, is to ensure that the organic unity of the nation is preserved by the state at all costs. The nazi doctrine of ***Gleichschaltung***—the synchronization by the state of all private, social, and political institutions and activities toward the fulfillment of the nazi goals—articulated the same intention. The goal of racial purity, however, increases the totalitarian pressure, because its achievement requires even more state control than does that of the goal of national unity.

In short, fascist and nazi principles regarding state authority are similar and simply stated. In principle, the state must be given unlimited authority to pursue the goals of the nation or racial group. This means that the state can be dominant in economic life, planning and controlling production, consumption, and investment. The state can also be dominant in cultural life, controlling art, literature, and religion. In practice, neither the nazis nor the fascists nationalized industry; private ownership of industry remained the norm. Instead of using state authority to own industry, fascists and nazis used such authority to control the economy so that its outputs conformed to national needs.[29] Similarly, neither the nazis nor the fascists used their authority to eliminate churches, but remained satisfied with cowing religious leaders into passive acceptance of their regimes. To comprehend the totalitarian aspects of fascism and nazism, however, one must understand that state authority was potentially unlimited and total, and that any limits on the use of state authority were pragmatic concessions based on the calculation that, at least in the short term, national objectives could be attained most effectively by allowing some latitude for organizations and activities outside the state.

[28]Gentile, "The Philosophical Basis of Fascism," p. 60.

[29]As we shall see, Italian fascist corporations significantly blurred the distinction between public and private enterprise.

Justice

There is no well-defined theory of justice in either the fascist or national socialist ideologies.[30] Neither are particularly concerned with the well-being of the individual, focusing instead on the well-being or power of the collective. Maximizing national (or racial) strength precludes giving much attention to problems of distributive or retributive justice insofar as such problems affect individuals. Any sort of distribution or redistribution of resources and theorizing about the role of law in general is always done with a view to the good of the collective. If the organs of the state implement policies to maximize productivity and national power, everyone, it is thought, will benefit. Thus, problems of the fair distribution of wealth are only problems if they affect the productivity and power of the whole. Otherwise, they do not concern the state.

This is not to say that fascists and nazis did not use the rhetoric of distributive justice in their initial efforts to come to power. In Germany and Italy, nazis and fascists appealed to those segments of society that felt threatened either by economic instability or by the redistributive policies of the left-wing parties. Fascists, in particular, made redistributive pledges to many segments of society, but these could only be paid for with the booty of war. Nevertheless, concerns with distributive justice at the individual level were at all times subordinated to concerns of national unity and strength. This trend sharpened when the nazis and fascists came to power. Once in power, both parties demonstrated a decided lack of concern with workers' rights and economic fairness.[31] The fascists, for example, raised wages in certain industrial sectors, not out of a feeling of fairness, but out of a need to enhance productivity (for the good of the state). Similarly, the nazis built the Autobahn system (a network of freeways similar to the later U.S. interstates) in response to a military need, not to enhance the transportation of domestic goods or give German citizens greater mobility. The point was to be able more quickly to move military personnel and materiel, not to make public travel more convenient. Their many other public work projects and organizations all had the ultimate end of unifying society around the nazi agenda, not of enhancing individual well-being, except insofar as the individual took part in the good of the whole.

Rulers

Fascists and nazis reject democratic forms of government for a form of **elitism** in which political power is concentrated in the hands of a single ruler (e.g., Il Duce in Italy and the Fuehrer in Germany). There are three central elements to such elitism. First, it abandons the idea of electoral accountability. Second, it makes power centralized and unlimited, rather than divided and checked,

[30]Even the legal system in Nazi Germany was characterized by moral corruption and professional degradation. See Ingo Mueller, *Hitler's Justice* (Cambridge: Harvard University Press, 1991).

[31]See Eduard Tannenbaum, *The Fascist Experience: Italian Society and Culture, 1922–1945* (New York: Basic Books, 1972), pp. 89–116.

Sidebar 7-2

Adolf Hitler

Adolf Hitler was born in 1889 in the small Austrian bordertown of Braunau-am-Inn, the son of a minor customs official. He was a mediocre student, and relations with his parents were unhappy. He was orphaned by age 15. In 1906, he went to Vienna to pursue a career in architecture or painting. The city's leading art schools rejected him, and he was unqualified to study architecture, so he turned to odd jobs in construction and eventually to painting houses, hanging wallpaper, and designing postcards to support himself. In Vienna he acquired much of his worldview, including a virulent anti-Semitism and a simplistic, disjointed set of romantic and nationalistic political maxims for deciphering the world. In 1912, he left for Munich, enlisting in the German Army when war broke out in 1914. He remained at the rank of corporal, but served with distinction, twice winning the coveted Iron Cross for bravery. When the war ended, Hitler was among the many Germans who felt a deep sense of injustice and betrayal at the German surrender.

In 1920, he joined the tiny German Workers' Party, soon proving to be an effective organizer and an especially talented orator. Under his leadership, the renamed National Socialist German Workers' Party (NSDAP, or "Nazis") quickly developed a full policy platform, and its membership grew to several thousand. On November 8, 1923, Hitler attempted a coup, or "putsch," to overthrow the Bavarian government in the hopes of thereby causing the overthrow of the national government in Berlin, which would lead to the rule of the nazis. Hitler served nine months of a light prison sentence for treason, during which time he wrote the first part of his autobiographical manifesto, *Mein Kampf*. Upon his release in December 1924, Hitler renewed his activities. Nationally, the nazis held a handful of seats in the German parliament (the Reichstag) from 1924 onward; but in 1930, their allocation of seats vaulted from 12 to 107, then to 230 in 1932, and to 288 in March of 1933. In January 1933, Hitler was appointed chancellor, and, on March 23, the Reichstag granted him full dictatorial powers. The nazi dictatorship had begun.

as in democracies. Third, rather than deriving their goals and programs by consulting the people, rulers are said to derive superior knowledge about the national interest from their own intuitions. Let us consider each of these elements of fascist and nazi principles concerning leadership.

First, rulers should not be elected by competitive democratic elections, at least once a true leader is installed in office. While Mussolini and Hitler ran for office when they initially sought power, both were appointed to their positions by figureheads in crisis situations. Shortly after coming to power, both the Italian Fascist Party and the National Socialist Party in Germany acquired dictatorial powers for their leaders from subservient legislatures, and they suppressed political opposition. Insofar as elections are held under fascist or nazi regimes, they merely permit citizens to recognize and affirm the power of those who have emerged as leaders of the parties in power.

Sidebar 7-3

Benito Mussolini

Born the son of a poor blacksmith in a small Italian village, Benito Mussolini secured a formal education despite his impoverished background. He had a varied career as, among other things, a bricklayer, a schoolteacher, and the editor of the Italian socialist newspaper, *Avanti!*. A difference over policy between the Italian socialists—who supported a neutral stance in the war—and Mussolini—who supported Italy's entry into the war—cost Mussolini his editorship and his membership in the Socialist Party. He established his own newspaper, but was soon drafted and severely wounded at the front. In 1919, Mussolini founded the Fascist Party. After his party suffered three consecutive losses at the polls between 1918 and 1921, Mussolini moved from merely appealing to the disgruntled masses and the nervous capitalists (who feared a Bolshevik revolution) to planning and implementing open insurrection. On October 27, 1922, with the tacit support of conservative elites, he initiated a coup against a disorganized government and a weak monarch. On October 29, King Victor Emmanuel III, intimidated by the threatened coup, invited him to form a new government. "Il Duce" ("the leader"), as Mussolini styled himself, had become prime minister of Italy. By January 3, 1925, he was able formally to declare his dictatorship. Because of this sudden rise to power, the Italian fascists lacked a coherent, well-formulated idea of what they hoped to accomplish, and how. As a result, Italian fascism often had something of an ad hoc quality to its ideological pronouncements and programs.

Second, constitutional and institutional checks or limitations on the powers of ruling elites are weak or nonexistent. In Fascist Italy and Nazi Germany, the party controlled public opinion, education, the media, and most other groups or institutions that might resist elite edicts. All agencies of the state were placed in the hands of party members who were obedient to Il Duce or the Fuehrer at the top of the party. According to fascist ideology, the power of the leader emanates downward through hierarchies of party and state authority. Using the Italian example, in fascism (in contrast to nazism), there is no all-encompassing notion of purely delegated authority establishing the responsibilities of Mussolini's subordinates to Il Duce; while all authority is vested in Il Duce, there is some room for latitude among subordinates. In nazi ideology, the centralized and unlimited authority of the Fuehrer is specified as the **Fuehrerprinzip**, establishing one-man rule. The Fuehrer's absolute power is enforced by a hierarchical administration whose personnel are each personally responsible to the leader, and whose authority, even though formally transferred through a hierarchy, is understood as having been "delegated" directly from the leader himself.[32] This principle permits a delegated

[32]Cf. Paul Brooker, "The Nazi Fuehrerprinzip: A Weberian Analysis," in *Political Ideologies and Political Philosophies*, edited by H. B. McCullough (Toronto: Wall and Thompson, 1989), pp. 193–199.

leadership that emanates from the Fuehrer and proceeds to the most humble local level. All decisions and actions are ultimately the responsibility of the Fuehrer, whose power, even though delegated, is absolute. This form of organization tends to subvert normal authority and hierarchy, replacing it with totalitarian domination by abolishing the freedom and spontaneity of subordinates. It accomplishes this end by removing all "reliable intervening levels [between the Fuehrer and the ruled], each of which would receive its due share of authority and obedience," so that "the will of the Fuehrer can be embodied everywhere and at all times, and he himself is not tied to any hierarchy, not even the one he might have established himself."[33] A multiplicity of agencies and bureaus seems to indicate a hierarchy and stability, but in fact, this onion-like structure of continuous, overlapping layers of bureaucracy and administrative agencies magnifies the leadership principle:

> A continuous competition between offices, whose functions not only overlap but which are charged with identical tasks, gives opposition or sabotage almost no chance to become effective; a swift change of emphasis which relegates one office to the shadows and elevates another to authority can solve all problems without anybody becoming aware of the change or of the fact that opposition had existed, the additional advantage of the system being that the opposing office is likely never to learn of its defeat, since it is either not abolished at all (as in the case of the Nazi regime) or it is liquidated much later and without any apparent connection with the specific matter. This can be done all the more easily since nobody, except those few initiated, knows the exact relationship between the authorities.[34]

Thus, nazi rulership is enmeshed in a kind of fluid system of rule that enhances its totalitarian possibilities. In contrast, fascist rule lacks an all-encompassing notion of delegated authority, so that it has tended to remain bounded by hierarchies of authority that typically make it strongly authoritarian, without causing it to become totalitarian.

Third, the roles of fascist and nazi leaders are far greater than those circumscribed by the formal powers given authorities in democratic regimes. Beyond establishing a legislative agenda, administering the executive branch of government, being the military commander-in-chief, and representing the nation in foreign affairs, Il Duce or the Fuehrer is expected to know and articulate its nation's will and destiny. In fascist and nazi ideology, the leader's will is the will of the nation, or the "general will." Ideally, neither Il Duce nor the Fuehrer acts out of personal interest or whim. Instead, each is in mystical union with all people of the nation and intuitively grasps the will of all people and the national destiny. Having discovered and interpreted the will and destiny of the nation, it is their leader's role to communicate it to the people in ways that elicit their affirmation and obedience. Fascists and nazis do not claim that there is a rational or objective basis for determining that the goals, policies, and programs of Il Duce or the Fuehrer do, in fact, conform to the general will; instead, these ideologies simply assume and assert that they do. Such an

[33]Arendt, *The Origins of Totalitarianism,* p. 405.
[34]Arendt, *The Origins of Totalitarianism,* p. 404.

assumption greatly enhances the power of the Il Duce or the Fuehrer, since these ideologies provide no basis for questioning the legitimacy of the leader's directives.

These principles about rulers may seem odd to people accustomed to democratic norms, but such norms were not especially prevalent in Italy and Germany (and many other nations) when fascists and nazis came to power. Indeed, a leading school of social scientists at the beginning of the twentieth century—the **elite theorists**—was highly critical of democratic rule, and its adherents were strong proponents of elite rule. Vilfredo Pareto (1848–1923) differentiated between the gifted few and the herd, the masses that follow like sheep. Gaetano Mosca (1858–1941) examined democratic systems of government and was led to propose that these were actually states that relied upon forms of elite rule that might be relatively responsive to the wishes of the masses, but whose elites nevertheless ruled by the use of self-legitimizing myths. Robert Michels (1876–1936), a student of Mosca, continued his teacher's examinations and proposed his well-known "iron law of oligarchy," which states that all forms of organization and political rule tend to evolve into structures composed of a small group of leaders and a large group of the led. The debates between Pareto, Mosca, and Michels were antagonistic and complex, since the three did not agree on the implications of elite rule for participatory systems of government. How elites come to rule, the nature of these elites, the nature of their rule, and the desirability of such rule animated the lifelong investigations of these and other elite theorists. What the fascists and nazis took from them was rather more simple: societies are ruled by elites, and they should be. The power and glory of a nation, moreover, is dependent upon the "right" elite ruling in the proper manner.

Beyond the elite theorists, many other European intellectuals espoused ideas that helped to justify elite rule. For example, the writings of Friedrich Nietzsche were often simplistically interpreted as calling for a heroic man or the overman, whose desire to rule and creative will-to-power would put him in a position of dominating the multitude. The writings of Georges-Eugène Sorel (1847–1922) provided Mussolini, in particular, with both an appreciation for the use of myth in manipulating and motivating the masses, and an appreciation for the nobility and usefulness of violence. Sorel seemed to suggest that the ruler should govern by right of his superior ability and use mythical images and violence to enforce his rule and to direct the masses to their proper ends.

Citizenship

At the same time that they are elitist, fascists and nazis seek extensive **citizen mobilization** behind governmental programs and policies. The people of the nation need to act on behalf of national goals, but their participation is not for the sake of gaining political influence or securing their personal political and economic interest; rather, it is understood in terms of attachment, loyalty, and obedience. The interests and will of the individual are again subordinated to the interests and will of the whole.

Fascist mobilization of the masses has sometimes been understood as a kind of "democratic centralism." Rule is focused in one leader, who articulates the will and interests of the whole, but this leader mobilizes the masses to work toward achieving those interests in terms of that will. Participation in securing the goals that the leader articulates ratifies the individual's attachment to the state at the same time that the complete participation of everyone secures the external interests of the state.

For the fascist or the nazi citizen, the highest ethical value is duty, and the true freedom of the individual consists in his or her **total obedience** to state authority. The notion of obligation illuminates the meaning of citizenship in a fascist regime. Each person in a fascist society is part of a collective whole, having specific responsibilities toward the state, which is the instrument of society. Fascists do not seek to foster pluralism, individual self-expression, freedom of speech, nor the social and political institutions that must accompany these ideals. Such activities and institutions, in the fascist view, would only breed conflict within society. Instead, fascists encourage participation in rallies, party organizations, and the like, in order to develop loyalty and obedience to the state and to dampen enthusiasm for the individualistic forms of expression that liberalism is said to encourage. It is the duty of every member of the state to participate in state activities and to bind himself or herself to the goals and activities of the greater whole. Fascists seek not factional politics, but universal support for the state. This support is centered on the leader. The citizens of a national socialist or fascist state are confronted first and foremost not with a catalogue of rights that they may claim over and against the state, but with a list of duties and obligations that they have toward the state or the greater social whole.

Thus, fascists desire both liberty and citizenship participation, but these are understood in terms very different from the liberal tradition. Liberals tend to argue that *individual* liberty is the greatest human good. The state exists for the sake of securing individual rights to life, liberty, and property. Contemporary liberals may expand these rights to include others, such as rights to education, a minimum standard of living (welfare), proper housing, minimal health care, and the like. Fascists, on the other hand, argue that "liberalism denied the State in the interests of the particular individual," whereas "fascism reaffirms the State as the only true expression of the individual." Mussolini expressed the **fascist conception of liberty** in the following terms:

> If liberty is to be the attribute of the real man and not of the scarecrow invented by the individualistic Liberalism, then Fascism is for liberty. It is for the only kind of liberty that is serious—the liberty of the State and of the individual in the State. Because, for the Fascist, all is comprised in the State and nothing spiritual or human exists—much less has any value—outside the State. In this respect Fascism is a totalizing concept, and the Fascist State—the unification and synthesis of every value—interprets, develops and potentiates the whole life of the people.[35]

[35]Mussolini, "The Doctrine of Fascism," p. 10.

"Our concept of liberty," declared Alfredo Rocco, "is that the individual must be allowed to develop his personality in behalf of the state," so that "freedom therefore is due to the citizen and to classes on condition that they exercise it in the interest of society as a whole and within the limits set by social exigencies, liberty being, like any other individual right, a concession of the state."[36]

Structure

The structure of fascist and nazi governments is a logical outcome of their principles regarding authority and rulers. In order to secure state power and elite rule, fascists and nazis structure government, the economy, and society to eliminate competing centers of power.

A constitutional model of government, such as that of the United States, which is built around the idea of balancing competing groups and factions against one another, is anathema to fascists and nazis. They reject both the separation of powers and the idea of checks and balances among various institutions. As revealed in our discussion of the Fuehrerprinzip in the section on rulers, the nazis emphasized structures that enhanced the power of the Fuehrer; insofar as there were multiple institutions of power, each was controlled by central authority. Such structural arrangements ensured that governmental power was highly concentrated and centralized into a monolithic entity in which competing bases of power had been eliminated. Such **centralization** permits government to focus on the national will rather than on accommodating factional interests, and it helps the government achieve the ends determined by that will in an expeditious manner.

In Fascist Italy, Mussolini reduced intrasocietal conflict by implementing a kind of **corporatism**. The fascists formed twenty-two corporations that represented broad areas of economic activity. Sectors of the economy such as transportation, steel, textiles, and grains were each represented by their own corporation. Workers, unions, managers, and executives were all represented within the corporation corresponding to their particular industry. Finally, members of the Fascist Party were included in the governing structure of each corporation so that the corporation would be directly tied to the state. The fascists thereby had a mechanism for controlling workers and managers alike, and for maintaining a unity of purpose and activity in the economy in order to maximize productivity toward the national goals of the state. By establishing this kind of close, institutionalized cooperation, centralization promotes the collective strength and focused initiative needed to succeed in the international struggle for supremacy and glory.

The nazi emphasis on the Fuehrerprinzip as a way of structuring power in society was somewhat more successful than the fascists' emphasis on structuring the economy using the principles of corporatism.[37] By creating over-

[36]Alfredo Rocco, "The Political Doctrine of Fascism," in *Readings on Fascism and National Socialism* (Chicago: Swallow Press, 1952), p. 36.

[37]In Eduard Tannenbaum's estimation, corporatism was an abject failure in Italy. The corporations served to discipline workers, but did not seriously affect the capitalist owners, who made decisions

lapping spheres of activity and competence (rather than distinct corporations), the Fuehrer could delegate authority to those institutions which were most effective and responsive to his will. The apparent unitary hierarchy of the nazi state was contradicted by the multi-layered, permeable structure of the post-1933 German administration that we noted in the discussion of nazi rule. This structure made the nazi institutional arrangements more malleable than those obtained by the static Italian corporations, allowing the nazis to create an institutional fluidity that produced an unending mobilization. Overlapping spheres of activity and competence, coupled with the notion of a direct and personal delegation of authority from the Fuehrer, tended to undermine administrative stability, which in turn helped to keep German institutions, and society as a whole, in a continuous kind of motion. Nazis were able to transform the German polity into a highly mobilized mass movement intent on purifying the Aryan race and eradicating all others.[38]

Change

On a "left-right" ideological scale, fascists and nazis are often placed in a position somewhere in the vicinity of, but to the right of, traditional conservatives. Several common characteristics of all three ideologies may explain this apparent ideological proximity. First, traditional conservatism, fascism, and nazism all share an antipathy toward Enlightenment liberalism and individualism. Second, in word, if not in deed, nazism and fascism also claim to maintain conservative, rural, agrarian values that are threatened by urbanization and industrialization. Third, all three ideologies hold to an organic notion of society in which a communal ethic transcends individual rights and freedoms. Fourth, all three accept some form of hierarchical structure in society, based on either hereditary or mythical kinds of claims. Fifth, although all three resist socialist and communist arguments for universal redistribution of wealth, they also reject the wide disparities of wealth and, especially, the destitution of the lowest social classes that is bred by the mobility and social neglect of elites in capitalist societies. Sixth, all three have roots in romanticism, sharing an appreciation for the irrational, mythical, and emotive aspects of human existence, and emphasizing such myths as national unity and national self-determination. Seventh, traditional conservatism may contain strong nationalistic or even racist images, making it appear closely akin to fascism and national socialism. Finally, and perhaps because of these common features, some conservative political parties and politicians have historically been sympathetic to or willing to cooperate with fascists and nazis to some degree. The conservatives in Weimar Germany were instrumental in shunting aside the liberal democrats and helping the nazis to power. Similarly, conservative elements in Italy saw

---

largely as before, independent of corporatist interference. The economic aims of the fascists were never realized. (See Tannenbaum, *The Fascist Experience*, pp. 89–100). On the relative success of the nazis in restructuring the state, see Brooker, "The Nazi Fuehrerprinzip," pp. 198–199.

[38]Arendt, *The Origins of Totalitarianism*, chaps. 11–13, passim.

in Mussolini's fascists a counterweight to the threatening Bolsheviks and socialists. When the fascists, and especially the nazis, had come to power, however, conservatives soon realized that they had encouraged forces not in sympathy with their own aims.

Despite their apparent "conservative" features, fascism and nazism soon disillusion conservatives, because both are revolutionary ideologies in ways that conservatism is not. They arose in a context of serious social and political problems (as well as "manufactured" problems) that their ideologues took it upon themselves to solve. Thus, fascism is an ideology that emphasizes revolutionary action over ideological speculation or preservation of established social customs and institutions. Openly antagonistic to both communism and liberalism (and, implicitly, toward conservatism), fascism constitutes an effort to overthrow and eradicate both ideologies. Since both liberalism and communism divide and weaken society, fascists require a quick, fundamental change in the structures and aims of the liberal or socialist state in order to synchronize and organize the people, and thereby to establish the strength and power of the nation and to restore it to its rightful place of prominence in the community of nations. This goal cannot be achieved by speculation on the meaning and direction of history, as in communism, nor by gradual education and institutional reformation, as in liberalism, nor by incremental change with a steady view to the past, as in traditional conservatism. It requires immediate political—and possibly violent—action.

The most radical or revolutionary component of nazism may be its intention to effect a complete transformation of the citizens of the state. Nazis envision the creation of a new kind of man and woman, based on the image of a superior racial type. The conservative images that nazis romantically evoke are merely the tools they use to mobilize the masses toward this end. The masses are moved in a rather different direction, from conservatism to a realization of a new type of superhuman—the men and women of the Aryan race. Human nature, which is neither perfect nor static, must itself be transformed.

The methods of coming to power have varied among the Spanish and Italian fascist and the German national socialist movements. It is ironic that the nazis came to power more or less legally through elections in the Weimar Republic. In Italy, government resolve would have defeated Mussolini's modest coup, yet he was invited to become ruler by the Italian king during the crisis of a general strike in 1923. On the other hand, Franco came to power in Spain only after a bloody civil war. It is not the method of coming to power, but the fact that action is taken to do so that is important to fascists and nazis.

SUMMARY AND CONCLUSIONS

National socialism, and especially fascism, are not dead. Variants of both continue to flourish. At present, movements based on both ideologies exist in nearly all industrialized nations. Politically legitimate fascist political parties exist in Germany, France, and elsewhere. These movements remind liberals, Marxists, and adherents to variants of liberalism and Marxism not to disregard the nonrational and noneconomic dimensions of human life. Human needs for a feeling of belonging, for a sense of purpose that transcends the individual, and for a sense of glory and power will continue to make fascism and even national socialism attractive to some. Moreover, the continued existence of fascism serves as a warning to liberals, socialists, and conservatives alike of the power of chauvinism and nationalism, fear of isolation, and the need for community. Nazism continues to warn us of the power of racist thinking as a way of constituting a sense of community. Both nazism and fascism serve to remind us of the limits of liberal individualism, socialist egalitarianism, and conservative traditionalism.

PART THREE

Democratic Ideologies of the Twentieth Century

The label of liberalism is hardly a sentence to public ignominy; otherwise Bruce Springsteen would still be rehabilitating used Cadillacs in Asbury Park and Jane Fonda, for all we know, would be just another overweight housewife.

—BARBARA EHRENREICH

By concentrating on what is good in people, by appealing to their idealism and their sense of justice, and by asking them to put their faith in the future, socialists put themselves at a severe disadvantage.

—IAN MCEWAN

The word "conservative" is used by the BBC as a portmanteau word of abuse for anyone whose views differ from the insufferable, smug, sanctimonious, naive, guilt-ridden, wet, pink orthodoxy of that sunset home of the third-rate minds of that third-rate decade, the nineteen-sixties.

—NORMAN TEBBIT

When a nation's young men are conservative, its funeral bell is already rung.

—HENRY WARD BEECHER

CHAPTER 8

Contemporary Liberalism

We have seen that liberalism—at least in its classical articulation as a defense of democratic capitalism—was relentlessly criticized throughout the nineteenth and early twentieth centuries. As a result, many Europeans with a commitment to liberty and democracy sought to fuse these liberal ideals to other ideologies (such as democratic socialism) rather than to reform or recast liberalism. In America, however, liberalism remained a highly respected, if somewhat flawed, doctrine. Efforts to retain the "liberal" label and core liberal ideas while recasting the ideology to answer its critics have been, therefore, primarily an American enterprise. Such American intellectuals as John Dewey (1859–1952) and such American politicians as Franklin D. Roosevelt (1882–1945) were instrumental in redefining liberalism in the following terms. While political, social, and economic liberties are of prime importance, they are more often furthered than threatened by democratic governments. While there is no injustice in owning private property or in the inequalities of wealth that emerge under capitalism, it is desirable and fair for governments to regulate certain uses of private property and redistribute wealth. While governments must act within constitutional limitations and electoral mandates, strong and active national governments are needed to stimulate and regulate the economy and to extend liberty and equality. While social change and progress are important, they should occur through reform, not through revolution.

While classical liberalism emerged at the beginning of the industrial revolution to justify capitalism and limited government, liberals acknowledged many problems with unfettered capitalism as industrialism matured. The seeds for the emergence of "reform liberalism" were sown as early as 1848, when John Stuart Mill suggested (in *Principles of Political Economy*) that goods should be produced and exchanged according to capitalist principles, but that governments could play a role in distributing (or redistributing) these goods in a more equal manner. But it was not until the twentieth century that reform liberalism emerged as a coherent ideology committed to reforming capitalism, extending democracy, enhancing the role of government, and developing more egalitarian theories of justice.

The idea of reforming capitalism is like a two-edged sword. On the one hand, reforming capitalism involves a fundamental commitment to capitalism. Like classical liberals, contemporary liberals believe that the good life requires material prosperity that can best be attained through a capitalist economy. By promoting steady economic growth and facilitating business interests, contemporary liberals are sometimes seen as advocating "corporate liberalism."[1] On the other hand, reforming capitalism involves commitments that are often regarded as hostile to capitalism. For example, because they wish to impose regulations on businesses and to enlarge welfare rights, contemporary liberals are sometimes regarded as "welfare-state liberals." These two tendencies within contemporary liberalism have led to extensive debate and some confusion regarding its political principles, but Theodore Lowi has suggested that contemporary liberals have sought to resolve these tensions by becoming "interest-group liberals."[2] Such liberals regard the demands of most groups in society as sufficiently legitimate to warrant a positive governmental response: If businesses face bankruptcy, then liberal governments should provide subsidies that bail them out of their financial difficulties. If the wealthy need encouragement to invest in new economic enterprises, then liberal governments should provide appropriate tax incentives. If labor needs safer working conditions, liberal governments should regulate the workplace. If minorities are discriminated against, liberal governments should enact and enforce civil rights legislation. If the poor need better health care, liberal governments should improve their access to medical services. Such examples could be multiplied endlessly. While contemporary liberals seldom identify themselves as "interest-group liberals," they have evolved principles and policies that they hope appeal to corporate leaders, welfare recipients, minorities, and many other groups and interests within society.

"Reform liberalism," "corporate liberalism," "welfare-state liberalism," and "interest-group liberalism" are thus the main designations applied to contemporary liberalism to differentiate it from classical liberalism. In this chapter, we try to describe contemporary liberalism in a way that recognizes these different emphases. This requires that contemporary liberalism be viewed as more pragmatic than philosophical. Its political principles reflect the problems that liberals hope to address rather than specific philosophical assumptions about the nature of the universe, humans, society, and knowledge. Accordingly, we defer our consideration of the (often implicit) philosophical foundations of contemporary liberalism until after we have described the political bases of the ideology and its political principles.

[1]James Weinstein, *The Corporate Ideal and the Liberal State* (Boston: Beacon Press, 1966); and R. Jeffrey Lustig, *Corporate Liberalism* (Berkeley: University of California Press, 1982).

[2]Lowi is a contemporary American political scientist. In this and subsequent chapters, persons who are identified without dates of birth and death should be regarded as contemporaries. Lowi's most well-known book is *The End of Liberalism: The Second Republic of the United States* (New York: W. W. Norton, 1979).

THE POLITICAL BASES

Problems

Classical liberals were preoccupied with problems arising out of medieval life: inadequate social mobility, restrictions on economic activity, political absolutism, and religious orientation and conformity. Such problems receded in importance as capitalist economies and representative, secular democracies were developed in the industrializing nations of the West. By the end of the nineteenth century, liberals in the United States, England, and France had succeeded in eliminating the vestiges of feudalism and in establishing liberal institutions. Thus, their attention turned to resolving the problems that occur within liberal societies having capitalist economies and democratic institutions and to defending liberal societies from their external enemies.

Liberals have come to recognize that the benefits of capitalism—for example, its capacity to promote economic freedom and material prosperity—are partially offset by certain problems. If complete freedom is allowed in the marketplace, a number of **market failures** occur.[3] First, it was apparent by the end of the nineteenth century that an unregulated marketplace can result in concentrations of economic power that undermine economic competition, increasing the exploitive capability of corporate giants and reducing their incentive to become economically efficient. In America, capitalists like John D. Rockefeller (1839–1937) and J. P. Morgan (1837–1913) were able to squeeze competitors out of their industries, establishing monopolies and oligopolies which dominated such markets as oil and railroads. Second, liberals (as well as Marxists) realize that an uncontrolled market economy exhibits business cycles producing economic inefficiency and insecurity. During periods of economic growth, the price of goods often rise in an inflationary manner and the values of currencies and savings are reduced. During periods of economic stagnation—such as the worldwide depression that occurred during the 1930s—many workers become unemployed and are thrown into poverty. Third, liberals realize that the self-interested actions of participants in the marketplace often create externalities harming the broader public. The tendency of industries to reduce their costs of production by dumping their waste by-products into rivers, into the air, or underground—spoiling the environment and causing public health problems—illustrates the externality problem. Fourth, liberals understand that pure market systems are unable to provide many beneficial services—or public goods—such as national defense, education for the poor, universal immunization against contagious diseases, and mass transportation. Fifth, liberals recognize that the wealth created by a capitalist economy is not distributed to everyone. Some people—the very young, the very old, the severely handicapped, and so forth—cannot participate in a market

[3]For a further discussion of market failures, see Alan Stone, "Justifying Regulation," in *The Liberal Future in America*, edited by Philip Abbot and Michael B. Levy (Westport, Conn.: Greenwood Press, 1985), pp. 102–126.

economy. Other people who are capable of economic productivity may become unemployed during depressions and recessions. While liberals do not usually regard economic inequality as a problem, they do regard poverty as a problem.[4] When people live in poverty, they are unlikely to acquire the education and skills necessary to become productive, they are likely to be a source of other social problems (like crime), and their freedoms and opportunities for intellectual and moral development are limited. In the section on governmental authority, below, we will discuss how liberals would use the power of the state to address these market failures.

Liberals have also come to realize that the decline in the importance of ascribed social status (a major feature of feudal social systems) did not eliminate all problems of social mobility. According to classical liberals, individuals should have an equal opportunity to employ their talents and energies to advance themselves socially and economically. However, many people have been denied equal access to jobs, education, housing, and public accommodations because of their race, ethnicity, gender, sexual preferences, and so forth. During the early stages of the civil rights movement, liberals sought to eliminate explicit discriminatory laws (such as those creating racially segregated schools) and practices (such as when realtors "redline" white neighborhoods and discourage black home ownership in such areas). Formal equal opportunity has been furthered by the passage of laws forbidding such discrimination, but liberals recognize that the historical legacies of racism, sexism, and homophobia continue to constrain the upward mobility of minorities, women, and gays. Liberals also recognize that certain cultural values and traditional practices constitute subtle forms of discrimination. For example, the use of standardized tests to determine admission to universities appears to disadvantage minority students, and promoting people at work on the basis of continuous years of employment seems to discriminate against women who temporarily interrupt their careers to raise children. Thus, contemporary liberals are concerned with detecting and changing all social norms and practices that constitute significant barriers for those whose equal opportunity to achieve upward social mobility has been constrained by historical and continuing discrimination.

Although contemporary liberals have focused on such economic and social problems, they have not forgotten the main problem that concerned classical liberals: providing security for citizens. Contemporary liberals have recognized many international threats to security and have thus endorsed the state's maintenance of military power that is sufficient to deter potential aggressors. Liberals like George Kennan created the policy of containment to check communist expansion. And liberals like Robert McNamera sought a "second-strike" capability to deter nuclear attacks on liberal democracies. When liberals believed that American security and national interests were threatened by the Axis powers during World War II and by a communist regime in North Vietnam, they endorsed military action. Liberals have also recognized many domestic threats to security and have called on governments to declare war against organized crime and drug dealers and to enact gun control legislation.

[4]Paul Starr, "Liberalism After Socialism," *The American Prospect* (fall 1991), pp. 79–80.

Various market failures, various forms of discrimination, and various security threats are only the most persistent problems faced by contemporary liberals. The problems on the liberal agenda are always changing. Indeed, liberals have recognized that some of their "solutions" to the problems of previous decades have created new problems. For example, "**neoliberals**" have come to believe that there is currently a problem of excessive governmental regulation of business.[5] While some governmental regulations have reduced certain externality problems, other regulations have emerged that serve the interests of regulated industries (rather than the public interest). Additionally, the costs of implementing and ensuring compliance with many regulations have made it difficult for regulated industries to compete in the international marketplace. Neoliberals also believe that some policies to further equal opportunity can lead to other problems. For example, forced busing of schoolchildren can cause "white flight" out of school districts, leaving the formally desegregated schools to serve predominantly minority populations. Liberal perceptions about threats to security have also changed. During the course of the war in Vietnam, many liberals concluded that American democracy was more threatened by the military-industrial complex than by the threat of communism posed by the Viet Cong and North Vietnamese. The breakup of the Soviet Union and the Russian embrace of economic and political reforms have convinced many liberals that American security is less threatened by communist aggression than by the economic might of such powers as Japan and a unified Germany. As a result, American liberals today are more likely to emphasize policies to "reindustrialize" the U.S. economy than policies to arm America. However, such changes in the agenda of issues concerning liberals have had little impact on the central principles of contemporary liberalism. Most importantly, contemporary liberals have viewed strong governmental authority as essential to solving these changing problems. While classical liberals thought that barriers to economic prosperity, individual liberty, and social mobility could best be overcome by allowing people to act within a free market having minimal governmental supervision, contemporary liberals believe that such barriers can best be overcome by positive action on the part of government.

Goals

Contemporary liberals do not repudiate the goals of classical liberals, but they give somewhat different interpretations to the ideals of enhancing liberty, sustaining capitalism, promoting constitutional democracies, and creating a science of politics.

[5]Charles Peters, "The Neoliberal Manifesto," *The Washington Monthly* (May 1983). Morton Kondracke coined the term "neoliberalism" to designate a movement that emerged after the Reagan defeat of Jimmy Carter in 1980. This movement sought to reorient liberalism by moving it away from its preoccupation with solving the problems of the poor and minorities and toward solving economic problems of business. Leading neoliberal intellectuals include Lester Thurow, James Fallows, and Robert Reich. Leading neoliberal politicians include Gary Hart, Paul Tsongas, Bill Bradley, Richard Gephardt, Bruce Babbett, Albert Gore, Jr., and (arguably) Bill Clinton. See Randall Rothenberg, *The Neoliberals* (New York: Simon and Schuster, 1984).

Classical liberals sought to secure individual freedom. Believing that liberty was the right to do as one willed, they thought liberty was something that was given to people at birth but could be taken away from people by others. Coercive governments and oppressive majorities were regarded as the major threats to people's natural liberties, and classical liberals wanted to restrain such threats to liberty. According to T. H. Green (1836–1882), a British philosopher who is regarded as one of the founders of reform (or contemporary) liberalism, classical liberals were preoccupied with **negative liberty**. For them, liberty was the absence of restraint. Liberty was being left alone.

Contemporary liberals have sought what Green called **positive liberty**. Such liberty is not something given to people equally at birth, but is something that people may acquire as they mature, especially if they live in environments that facilitate the capacity to make real choices. Liberty is more than being left alone; it is the capacity to make choices that enhance one's ability to live in accordance with one's own conception of the good life. If left alone, a poor, ignorant, or ill child has few real choices. Such a child may wish to become a doctor, lawyer, or scientist, but is not really free to pursue such aspirations, given the formidable obstacles. Positive liberty occurs as these obstacles to individual choices are reduced or eliminated.[6]

[6]An important analysis of negative and positive liberty is provided by Isaiah Berlin in *Four Essays on Liberty* (London: Oxford University Press, 1969), pp. 118–172.

Sidebar 8-1

Some Contemporary Liberals and their Main Writings

T. H. Green (1836–1882)
Lectures on the Principles of Political Obligation (1879–1880)

John Dewey (1859–1952)
The Public and Its Problems (1927)
Liberalism and Social Action (1935)

John Maynard Keynes (1883–1946)
General Theory of Employment, Interest, and Money (1936)

Karl Popper*
The Open Society and Its Enemies (1945)

John Kenneth Galbraith*
The Affluent Society (1958)
Economics and the Public Purpose (1973)

Robert Dahl*
Who Governs? (1961)
Democracy and Its Critics (1989)

John Rawls*
A Theory of Justice (1971)
Political Liberalism (1993)

Martin Luther King, Jr. (1929–1968)
Why We Can't Wait (1963)

Ronald Dworkin*
Taking Rights Seriously (1977)
Law's Empire (1986)

Robert Reich*
The Next American Frontier (1983)
The Work of Nations: Preparing Ourselves for the 21st Century (1991)

*Living author.

There are four important implications of endorsing positive liberty. First, while classical liberals thought that liberties were equally distributed, contemporary liberals understand that there are differences in the amount of positive liberty that an individual can enjoy in the course of a lifetime and that there are inequalities in the amounts of positive liberty enjoyed by different individuals. Second, the amount of positive liberty that persons have depends on their intellectual, moral, and spiritual development. More mature people make choices that contribute positively to their own life plans. Third, the amount of positive liberty that people have is also dependent on their external environments. If people are surrounded by poverty, racism, disease, and other environmental constraints, freedom of choice is restricted. In such circumstances, people are likely to be preoccupied with fulfilling their minimal economic and security needs, and the choice of developing themselves intellectually, morally, and spiritually will be foreclosed to them. Fourth, by promoting the health, education, and welfare of its citizens, governments can play important roles in overcoming environmental restraints to real choices and individual development.

Contemporary liberals usually assert that societies, acting through their governments, have not only the capacity but also the obligation to further positive liberty. Such obligations are expressed as **citizen (or welfare) rights**. Rather than seeking natural rights, contemporary liberals seek a steady expansion of citizen entitlements through the mechanisms and policies of the state. Liberals assert that students have a right to an education, and many liberals claim that the education provided for poor and minority students by governments must be equal to that provided for affluent white students. Liberals assert that all citizens have the right to be protected from certain health hazards and that governments should provide such basic health services as immunizations, sanitation, and access to doctors through public health clinics; increasingly, liberals seek expansion of citizen rights in this area by calling for national health insurance. Liberals assert that the poor have a right to various forms of welfare—such as food stamps and subsidized housing—and many liberals want to expand such welfare provisions by increasing cash-transfer payments to the needy. While contemporary liberals debate among themselves the content and extensiveness of various citizen rights, they agree that governments are the appropriate vehicles by which societies can extend citizen rights in order to facilitate the positive liberty of all citizens.

Classical liberals sought to develop a mature capitalist economy in order to produce material prosperity and enhance negative liberty. Developing a capitalist economy meant unleashing people's productive capacities and allowing them to trade, work, invest, and consume as they wished, constrained only by the private and social contracts to which they had agreed. Contemporary liberals want to retain capitalism (because they, too, value prosperity and economic liberties), but they want to reform capitalism in order to minimize market failures, to spread the wealth more broadly, and to enhance the positive liberty of all citizens.

Contemporary liberals want *steady* economic growth; they want to prevent both economic stagnation and excessive or erratic growth. They recognize that economic stagnation throws people into poverty, makes them preoccupied with satisfying economic and security needs, and limits their real choices for personal development. They believe that some growth is needed in order to provide new economic opportunities and progress and to provide additional revenues for financing governmental expansion of citizen rights. And they believe that economic development is a prerequisite for the attainment of stable liberal democracies in many less-developed nations around the world.[7] However, contemporary liberals also recognize that such economic growth can become excessive and costly. Rapid economic growth involves vast changes in where and how people work. Rapid growth uproots people from their communities. It redistributes income and wealth, creating the *nouveaux riches* but also the "*nouveaux pauvres*" ("newly poor"). Indeed, there may be more losers than gainers from rapid growth, at least in relative terms. As a result, rapid growth can breed widespread social discontent, threatening social stability.[8] Unregulated rapid growth can also erode the natural environment, resulting in aesthetic losses and health dangers. Given the dangers of economic stagnation and of rapid growth, contemporary liberals hope to achieve steady, slow, managed growth through macro-level social planning rather than micromanagement of the economy. A major goal of liberal governments is to design policies that provide opportunities for and impose constraints on private individuals and firms which prompt them to make those economic choices that result in a steady economic expansion.

Classical liberals wanted to develop constitutional democracies in order to protect the citizens' economic, social, and political liberties. Contemporary liberals want to retain—and reform—constitutional democracies. Two types of reforms have been particularly sought. First, contemporary liberals have sought a steady increase in the representativeness of democracies, bringing previously excluded groups such as minorities and women to the voting booths and into governmental offices. Because liberals have become increasingly skeptical that "neutral" experts can determine those policies that best serve the public interest and justice, they have concluded that the policy-making process must be open to those of all viewpoints and interests. Achieving more representative electorates and governing bodies has been sought as a means of getting the problems of underrepresented groups on the policy agenda and of enacting policies more responsive to their needs. Second, contemporary liberals have understood that constitutional restraints on the powers of government should not prevent democracies from actively seeking to solve social and economic problems. They have denounced the "deadlock of democracy" produced by the separation of powers and divided government, and have urged strong roles for extraconstitutional organizations (like political parties) in order to integrate and lubricate government. They have urged executives, legislators, and judges to interpret constitutional constraints liber-

[7]Daniel Lerner, *The Passing of the Traditional Society* (Glencoe, Ill.: Free Press, 1959).
[8]Mancur Olson, "Rapid Growth as a Destabilizing Force," *Journal of Economic History* 23 (1963), p. 529.

ally and adopt "activist" problem-solving styles. In short, contemporary liberals have argued that constitutional limitations are intended to restrain capricious and tyrannical government, but they should not be allowed to produce weak and passive government. Because social and economic problems change with the times, constitutions must be reinterpreted over time so as to achieve the flexibility to solve contemporary problems.

Finally, contemporary liberals seek government that operates in a scientific fashion, but their understanding of scientific politics differs from that of classical liberals. Classical liberals sought a scientific theory of politics in which general principles of government were deduced from self-evident philosophical assumptions. However, contemporary liberals believe that the principles of classical liberalism—the desirability of an unregulated market, the inviolability of property rights, the prohibition against legislating morality, and so forth—are too dogmatic, and they doubt that solutions to problems can be deduced from a set of principles that are themselves deduced from assumptions about the nature of the universe, humans, society, and knowledge. No principles—not even liberal principles—can always provide appropriate guidance to policy making. Contemporary liberals prefer to apply the scientific method to analyses of social and economic problems. As suggested by John Dewey, problem solving and policy making are pragmatic sciences, and problems should be solved by "organized intelligence."[9] Innovative solutions to problems must be continually entertained by the democratic community. Reforms must be tried and tested. The best solution to a problem can only be known experimentally. What works? What policies are effective? What policies produce the most desirable consequences while having the fewest adverse affects and costs? Just as scientific inquiry should never be blocked, the door to social and policy change must never be closed. For contemporary liberals, scientific politics means having the democratic community apply its collective and evolving intelligence to changing social problems, pursuing reforms as experiments in better living, evaluating these reforms in terms of their effectiveness, and continuing this process of discovery, experimentation, and evaluation in an endless political process in pursuit of social improvement.

SUBSTANTIVE POLITICAL PRINCIPLES

Authority

Contemporary liberals agree with classical liberals that individuals must be protected from excessive governmental authority, as governmental absolutism and arbitrariness must be restrained in order to protect such individual rights

[9]John Dewey, *Liberalism and Social Action* (New York: Capricorn, 1935), p. 51. Because Dewey doubted that experts monopolized understanding of the best answers to social problems, he insisted that liberal planning and problem solving must be democratic. For discussions of Dewey's contribution to democratic liberalism, see Thomas Thorson, *The Logic of Democracy* (New York: Holt, Rinehart, and Winston, 1962); and Paul Starr, "Liberalism After Socialism," p. 76.

as the freedoms of religion, speech, and assembly. But compared to classical liberals, contemporary liberals endorse a much more expanded role for governmental authority. Governments should expand citizen rights so that everyone can maximize his or her positive liberty. Governments should enact and implement policies that provide steady, well-managed economic growth. Governments should employ the scientific method and organized intelligence to solve economic, social, environmental, and security problems.

In order to solve such problems and achieve liberal goals, governments must first ascertain what the significant social problems are and determine the gaps between liberal goals and existing conditions. To aid in problem identification, liberal governments employ a variety of **economic and social indicators**. Particular attention is given to monthly reports on the levels of unemployment, inflation, growth, and other measures of economic activity. Attention is also given to the inequalities of opportunity and condition between, for example, blacks and whites, or men and women. What percentages of black students and of white students are dropping out of school? What percentages of those earning Ph.D.s are minorities and women? Such indicators also assess changes and trends in such areas as the spread of the HIV virus and other diseases, the levels of violent crimes, and the concentrations of dangerous pollutants in the ozone layer and other aspects of environmental deterioration.[10] Implicit in the collection of all this data is the liberal view that governments should respond to adverse changes in economic, social, and environmental conditions.

Liberals do not, however, expect governments to solve indicated problems through enactment of omnipotent laws or the institution of omnipotent programs. If inflation is high, liberals seldom call for mandatory wage and price controls. If unemployment is high, liberals seldom call on government to be the employer of last resort for the unemployed. Liberals recognize that governments work within market economies and pluralist societies that vitiate the possibility and effectiveness of such authoritative approaches. Thus, liberals are satisfied with modifying the laws and circumstances under which individuals, business firms, and other groups and organizations act. Rather than imposing price controls, liberal governments seek to reduce inflationary pressures by reducing the supply of money and reducing consumer demand. Rather than requiring businesses to hire more workers or invest more money in capital improvements, liberal governments attempt to devise circumstances under which firms will choose to hire more workers and to invest because it is profitable for them to do so.[11] In short, liberals do not want governments that seek to solve problems by micromanaging and strongly controlling economic and social life. Instead, they want governments that engage in **macro-**

[10]Many of these indicators are provided by Lester R. Brown, Hal Kane, and David Malin Boodman, *Vital Signs* (Washington, D.C.: Worldwatch Institute, 1994).

[11]See Robert Reich, *The Next American Frontier* (New York: Times Books, 1983) for a discussion of neoliberal industrial policy. For example, contemporary liberals have proposed a governmentally funded "Innovation Finance Corporation" to increase the availability of capital and absorb some of the risk of investment in high-tech industries.

level planning and produce a broad framework of laws, programs, and conditions that induce individuals and organizations to act in ways that reduce problems. Like classical liberals, they want to honor the existence of a private sphere, permitting individuals to make free choices regarding their economic and social aspirations. However, unlike classical liberals, contemporary liberals believe that public authority can be employed effectively to induce people to make choices that serve to realize public goals.

Contemporary liberals increasingly recognize the difficulty of maintaining a firm distinction between the private and public spheres of life. While liberals want to preserve an extensive private sphere where individuals can pursue the good life as they understand it and where government is neutral about moral values, they also have come to recognize that some social problems can only be addressed by using governmental authority to promote certain moral positions. According to William Galston, classical liberals sought governmental neutrality on moral questions because they understood that civic peace required governmental toleration of different religious traditions and because they could assume the universal acceptance of such virtues as self-denial, industry, tolerance, and civility.[12] However, in contemporary liberal societies, such private virtues, which are necessary to maintain a liberal society, seem to be disappearing due to the rise of unlimited self-expression. As a consequence, liberal governments may find it necessary to promote certain moral values.[13]

One set of moral values long fostered by liberal authority revolves around the desirability of nondiscrimination on the basis of race, gender, and other ascriptive traits. If governments were indeed neutral, prejudiced individuals could, of course, refuse to do business with anyone they wished. However, liberals recognize that the refusal to hire women because of their sex or to sell property to blacks because of their race constitutes a significant social problem, and they have enacted and enforced laws legislating a morality of nondiscrimination.

Because liberals currently recognize such epidemic problems as pornography, drug and alcohol abuse, family breakdown, and teenage pregnancy, they debate among themselves the role of government in regulating morality. Do the increasing levels of pornography constitute a social problem requiring governmental regulation? From one liberal viewpoint, the producers and consumers of pornography are acting as consenting adults acting in the private sphere, and their actions harm no one. From another liberal viewpoint, pornography involves the exploitation of such people. Should governments prohibit or regulate the sale of drugs and alcohol? While some liberals would argue that government has no right to infringe on such private choices, most liberals endorse varying degrees of governmental control. On what is perhaps today's most passionate moral issue, many liberals seem to endorse the moderate position of instituting some governmental regulations on abortions rather

[12]William Galston, "Liberalism and Public Morality," in *Liberals on Liberalism*, edited by Alfonso J. Damico (Totowa, N.J.: Rowman and Littlefield, 1986), p. 131.

[13]Thomas Spragens, "Reconstructing Liberal Theory," in *Liberals on Liberalism*, pp. 34–53.

than the extreme of "outlawing abortions" or of permitting "abortion on demand." By endorsing laws such as those restricting abortions after the first trimester or providing for a mandatory waiting period or requiring parental consent before allowing minors to receive abortions, liberals can acknowledge their moral reservations about abortions. But liberals have similar reservations about using governmental authority to deprive individuals of their rights to make important choices on matters that fundamentally concern only the individual.[14]

While contemporary liberals have reluctantly endorsed some governmental intervention in areas concerning moral freedom, they have more enthusiastically endorsed governmental intervention in economic life. They point out that America's economic competitors (such as Japan and Germany) have succeeded by increasing, rather than reducing, governmental intervention in business.[15] Viewing various market failures as serious problems, contemporary liberals have called for a **mixed economy** in which governments augment, stimulate, and regulate the activities of firms, workers, and consumers. But just as liberals want to retain extensive moral choice for individuals, so do they want to retain extensive economic freedom. Contemporary liberals want governments to shape the free market, not abolish it.

In dealing with the problem of concentrations of economic power that undermine competition in the marketplace, liberals do not prohibit all mergers or the establishment of any monopoly. Instead, they enact laws prohibiting certain "corrupt practices" (such as price-fixing), they create **antitrust agencies** (such as exist within the U.S. Department of Justice) to scrutinize proposed mergers for their effects on competition within an industry, and they establish public agencies (usually at the state level) to regulate such natural monopolies as utilities (providing natural gas, electricity, and so forth).

Liberals have developed a variety of programs to cushion the losses and limit the insecurities that occur during the recessions and depressions that characterize a market economy, when many companies go out of business and workers become unemployed. Investors' insurance programs (such as that of the Federal Depositors Insurance Corporation, FDIC) and social insurance programs (such as unemployment insurance) have been created to protect key industries and most workers. Liberals have also been willing to provide "bailouts"—usually consisting of subsidies and low-interest loans—to major employers (like Chrysler) and defense contractors (like Lockheed) when these companies faced bankruptcy.[16]

More generally, to deal with the problems associated with business cycles, liberals employ the **fiscal policies** developed by John Maynard Keynes

[14]See Mary Ann Glendon, *Abortion and Divorce in Western Law* (Cambridge: Harvard University Press, 1987), and Richard Flathman, *Toward a Liberalism* (Ithaca, N.Y.: Cornell University Press, 1992), pp. 168–205.

[15]Lester Thurow, *The Zero Sum Society* (New York: Penguin Books, 1980).

[16]In *The End of Liberalism,* Lowi argues that liberal governments are preoccupied with reducing economic risks. He claims that such governments maintain the position that any institution that is a significant factor in the community must have its security underwritten.

(1883–1946). When economic indicators point to low levels of economic growth (and high levels of unemployment), liberals believe that the economy ought to be stimulated in either of two basic ways. First, governmental expenditures can be increased—for example, by building roads, dams, or other public works, by subsidizing corporate investments in new capital improvements, or by increasing social insurance payments to the unemployed (and liberals will debate among themselves the best ways of investing the public funds to stimulate the economy). Second, taxes can be reduced (and liberals will also debate among themselves the most effective and fair way of reducing taxes). Either increased governmental expenditures or reduced taxes are expected to "pump-prime" the economy by making additional money available to workers and employers. With more money available to them, workers and employers should increase consumption and investment. Such consumption and investment should, in turn, provide job opportunities for other workers and investment opportunities for other businesses. This continual process of increased employment, consumption, and investment is expected to produce what economists call a "multiplier effect," stimulating the economy out of recession or depression.

When economic indicators point to an "overheated economy"—one of excessive growth and inflation—Keynsian fiscal policies call for reduced governmental expenditures and/or increased taxes. Such policies should reduce consumption and investment, increase unemployment, restrain price and wage increases, and thus reduce inflation.

Keynes expected that economies would become overheated as often as they became stagnated and that governments would thus reduce expenditures and/or increase taxes as often as they increased expenditures and/or reduced taxes. Keynesian fiscal policies thus imply that the budget deficits that occur when governments stimulate depressed economies would be offset by the budget surpluses that could be attained when governments put the brakes to overstimulated economies; over time, governmental budgets would thereby balance. However, reducing governmental expenditures and increasing taxes—even in highly inflationary times—has proved difficult, as liberals believe that most governmental expenditures address important problems and that the public will inevitably resist higher taxes.

For the most part, liberals have sought to deal with the problem of **budget deficits** in three ways. First, they have sought increased governmental revenues through economic growth. As incomes rise, income taxes rise, especially if tax structures are progressive and people must pay higher proportions of their incomes in taxes as they move into higher tax brackets. And as investments rise, wealth is created in such forms as new factories and machinery, new homes, and new automobiles—all of which can be subject to such revenue-producing policies as property taxes. Second, liberals have supported the increase of taxes that target those who can most afford to pay such taxes (e.g., by increasing income tax rates on the wealthy or by imposing luxury taxes on the purchase of such things as expensive cars and yachts). Liberals have also supported increased taxes as a means of addressing other problems (e.g., by increasing gasoline taxes in order to encourage conservation and/or reduce dependence on foreign oil producers). Third, liberals have sought to reduce governmental spending in specific areas where problems are no longer pressing. Thus, during times of peace and reduced international tensions, liberals have often called for cuts in the military budget.

Liberals also believe that governmental authority should be used to deal with the problem of **externalities**. Externalities occur when people produce goods or undertake transactions in ways that are beneficial to them but that hurt (or externalize costs upon) nonparticipating third parties or the public

Sidebar 8-2

The Tax Burden in Liberal Societies

Liberal Democrats in the U.S. Congress have often been accused of pursuing policies of "tax, tax, and spend, spend." However, the unpopularity of tax increases has made liberal politicians less enthusiastic about new taxes than are liberal economists. Liberal economists support higher taxes to pay for public investments in both the physical infrastructure (e.g., roads and airports) and the social infrastructure (e.g., education and health care) and to reduce the size of the federal deficit. Such economists point out that, compared with other advanced liberal democracies, public spending and taxation is relatively low in the United States, as shown in the following table.

Taxes and Social Security Payments as a Percentage of GNP

	1976		*1986*	
	Percentage	Rank	Percentage	Rank
Denmark	48	4	63	1
Sweden	54	2	62	2
Norway	56	1	57	3
France	44	8	51	4
Netherlands	48	3	50	5
Austria	45	6	50	6
Belgium	45	7	49	7
Germany (Fed. Rep.)	46	5	45	8
Britain	39	10	44	9
Finland	42	9	44	10
Greece	30	15	41	11
Canada	36	11	39	12
Italy	28	16	38	13
Australia	32	13	37	14
Spain	23	16	35	15
Switzerland	32	12	33	16
United States	30	14	31	17
Japan	23	15	31	18

Source: *Survey of Current Affairs* 21 (Jan. 1991), p. 1. Crown copyright is reproduced with the permission of the Controller of HMSO.

at large. For example, in order to lower their costs of production (and hence make their products more attractive to consumers), industries can discharge their waste by-products into the environment. If effluent from a paper mill is dumped into a river, the costs of cleaning and treating the water may have to be borne by those living downstream. As another example, landowners in neighborhoods of single-family homes may wish to sell their properties to developers seeking to build apartments or businesses there. While such sales may be profitable for both the landowners and the developers, nearby residents are likely to believe that their property values and the quality of their neighborhoods will decline as a result. To protect the interests of those adversely affected by such externalities, liberals seek to regulate the problematic activities. Polluters may be required to cut their emissions to a certain level by a particular date. Zoning controls may be (and often have been) employed to protect neighborhoods from the harmful effects of unrestricted development. In general, liberals have endorsed many such regulations of economic activity in order to protect the health and welfare of the broader public.[17]

Contemporary liberals also want governments to address the problem that the market does not adequately provide **public goods**. A "public good" is something with benefits that are (at least, to a degree) indivisible. The classic example of a public good is national defense. National defense is "indivisible" because when some citizens are provided national defense, all are provided national defense. There is a problem in providing public goods in the marketplace without governmental involvement. Because everyone gets the benefit from the provision of public goods, whether or not he or she pays for them, it is rational for everyone to choose not to pay for them, hoping that he or she will get the benefits anyway because others will pay. In other words, when it comes to the provision of public goods, the economically self-interested person will want to be a "free rider." Because liberals assume that people are self-interested, they recognize that public goods will not be provided adequately in a pure market economy. Potential suppliers of public goods cannot attract buyers of such goods, because potential buyers hope to consume the goods as free riders. Liberals argue that the adequate provision of public goods requires that governments supply such goods and, by imposing mandatory taxes, ensure that everyone pays.

Foremost among these public goods is, of course, an adequate national defense. American liberals have endorsed military budgets of about $300 billion annually, to enable the military to employ and train over three million soldiers to protect American security interests, and to procure new weapons that are believed necessary to protect all Americans from nuclear attack and to equip American soldiers in ways that maximize their effectiveness and safety. Liberal economists like John Kenneth Galbraith also stress that there are many domestic goods and services that, although highly valued, are underproduced

[17]According to Karl Polanyi, "regulations and markets, in effect, grew up together." See Polanyi, *The Great Transformation: The Political and Economic Origins of Our Time* (Boston: Beacon Press, 1944), p. 68.

by the market, because some of their benefits are indivisible. For example, human resources need to be developed and protected through increased governmental investment in education, job training, public health, public safety, and so forth. As another example, the country's physical infrastructure needs to be enhanced and renewed through increased governmental spending on transportation systems, on housing, on waste-disposal systems, and on other capital improvements that facilitate both human development and business. As a further example, scientific and technological progress in many areas—from cures for cancer and AIDS to more efficient means of building cars—needs to be encouraged through governmental subsidies of research and development.[18]

Finally, liberals recognize the need for governments to assist those who cannot participate in the market economy. In contrast with conservatives, liberals are unlikely to believe that the poor are lazy, or that the problem of poverty could be solved if everyone would simply "get off the public dole and get a job." First, liberals argue that many of the poor cannot work or that they already work at poorly paying jobs. Many of the poor are children, or single parents (usually mothers of small children), or the handicapped or disabled. Second, liberals recognize that recessions and other problems with the economy can cause structural unemployment, throwing productive and willing workers out of jobs. Third, liberals recognize that many people are trapped in a "culture of poverty," whereby they lack appropriate role models showing the kinds of skills and traits needed to succeed in a capitalist economy. As a consequence, liberals believe that governments have a variety of responsibilities toward the poor. Welfare payments—such as Aid to Families with Dependent Children (AFDC)—must be provided to those who cannot work. Persons who lose their jobs should be provided unemployment benefits and opportunities for retraining. And the culture of poverty needs to be attacked by a variety of social reform measures that teach the poor about economic opportunities and ensure that these opportunities are genuinely available to them. Educational opportunities must be expanded and improved, particularly for the very young. The conditions of crime and disease that pervade the slums and ghettos must be eradicated and replaced by safe and sanitary housing conditions. Racial discrimination that closes the doors to blacks and other minorities must be eliminated, as must other forms of discrimination. There must be public provision of minimal needs in the areas of nutrition and shelter though such welfare programs as food stamps, free school lunches, and subsidized housing. In short, liberals believe that capitalism is partly, but not solely, responsible for the problem of poverty. Abolishing capitalism would probably increase, rather than reduce, the extent of poverty, but maintaining a purely capitalist economy would result in a failure to respond to the needs of the poor. Nor can private charity be a reliable and efficient means of responding to the needs of the poor. For the contemporary liberal, governments have extensive responsibilities toward the poor.

[18]John Kenneth Galbraith, *The Affluent Society* (Boston: Houghton Mifflin, 1958).

Justice

In 1975, Arthur M. Okun, who chaired Lyndon Johnson's Council of Economic Advisors during the development of the "great society," wrote a book, *Equality and Efficiency: The Big Tradeoff,* that captures the views of contemporary liberals regarding justice.[19] Like classical liberals, Okun stressed capitalism's efficiency. The market system encourages investors and laborers to use their resources and energies productively, and individual effort is stimulated by the unequal distribution of rewards in capitalism. The result is that capitalism produces an ever-expanding economic pie and a higher standard of living than alternative systems. Capitalism thus accords with utilitarian ideals of justice, because it increases the aggregate wealth of society and the average level of economic well-being of the individuals constituting society. Like socialists, however, Okun lamented the inequalities of wealth—the unequal slices of pie—produced by capitalism.

Okun suggested that market justice—where each person is rewarded according to his or her contribution to the marketplace—may not be fair, for various reasons. First, the unequal rewards of the marketplace are only partly a function of the efforts that individuals expend. The talents with which people are born and the skills and assets that they acquire during their lifetimes also affect their contributions to the market and their rewards in it, but it is morally problematic that those who were born with special talents or who were raised in advantageous circumstances (e.g., those whose parents could afford to send them to the best schools) deserve to be rewarded for their good fortune. Additionally, the market rewards people on the basis of the behavior and tastes of other people. A person may train for many years to become skilled in a certain field, only to discover that there are no economic rewards there, because the market is glutted with other persons having similar skills. Or a person may spend years writing a great book that fails to sell, while a pulp novelist makes a fortune in the marketplace. Given such difficulties, it is hard to claim that the market distributes material goods justly. Second, the fairness of market justice may be rejected if societies proclaim the equal worth of all citizens and believe that everyone is entitled to certain rights whatever his or her contributions to the market. In American society, for example, commitment to pure market justice is limited by certain widely held beliefs. Everyone should have a right to one vote during elections. Everyone should have equal legal rights. Perhaps everyone should have a right to a certain level of education, to minimal nutritional requirements, to adequate health care, or to other social and economic goods. In short, people within a society may choose to recognize certain common needs of all citizens and choose to modify market distributions by having their governments provide specific "citizen rights" or entitlements to everyone.

Okun recognized that there is a **trade-off between efficiency and equal-**

[19]Arthur M. Okun, *Equality and Efficiency: The Big Tradeoff* (Washington, D.C.: Brookings Institution, 1975).

ity. When governments distribute the economic pie more equally by expanding citizen rights, they simultaneously reduce the size of the pie. Redistribution is costly because "more equality" must be financed by higher tax rates on upper-income citizens, which can reduce their tendency to save and invest, which can, in turn, reduce economic growth. Redistribution is also costly because the provision of more welfare rights can reduce the incentives for the poor to work. And redistribution reduces economic efficiency, because governments must absorb administrative costs as they establish and implement welfare programs. All contemporary liberals want both efficiency (increases in aggregate wealth) and more equality (through extended welfare rights) than are provided by pure capitalism. But, Okun points out, there is no generally accepted liberal principle establishing the point at which efficiency should be traded for more equality.

Some contemporary liberals argue for the need to emphasize efficiency and to provide for an expanded economic pie. This is the position of neoliberals, who argue that economic growth is vital to other liberal goals and that liberals must thus pursue policies of economic renewal and reindustrialization. Economic growth is a necessity if there is to be meaningful equal opportunity, as it is growth that provides new and better jobs. Growth enables liberals to avoid internal strife or "civil war" between those who currently have the best jobs and those who aspire to them.[20] Growth also is a prerequisite to expansion of citizen rights, as it generates the revenues to pay for the welfare state. As Paul Tsongas said, "If the economy is expanding, we can open our hearts to the aspirations of others, since the growth can accommodate their demands."[21]

While neoliberals emphasize efficiency over more equality, they argue that their principles should not be confused with those of some contemporary conservatives—such as those in the Reagan and Bush administrations. While such conservatives want to reduce welfare spending and taxes to increase growth, neoliberals do not wish to reduce or eliminate legitimate welfare rights. Instead, they want to use economic growth to expand citizen rights into new areas, such as national health insurance, that target the most needy members of society.

Some liberals, however, want to emphasize more equality over efficiency. To use the phrase coined by Ronald Dworkin for the title of his influential book, they endorse *Taking Rights Seriously*. Beginning with the basic assumption that all people are to be treated equally—regardless of their natural or social differences—such liberals have sought to clarify the principles and policies implied by a commitment to equal treatment. A necessary, but insufficient, condition for equal treatment is **formal equal opportunity**—the right for everyone to compete for the best and most rewarding positions in society in

[20]Ronald Terchek, "The Fruits of Success and the Crisis of Liberalism," in *Liberals on Liberalism*, pp. 22–23.

[21]Paul Tsongas, *The Road from Here: Liberalism and Realities in the 1980s* (New York: Knopf, 1981), p. 129.

an environment where no one is disadvantaged in the competition because of his or her race, sex, or other ascribed characteristic. While laws and policies enforcing such nondiscrimination are important, they do not adequately provide for **fair equal opportunity**, because inequalities in natural talents and social circumstances provide undeserved advantages for some over others in the ensuing competition. A society that takes seriously its commitment to equal treatment will recognize that differences in natural endowments—in intelligence, in health, in physical attractiveness, and the like—are unearned. Such a society will also recognize that many differences in social circumstances—for example, whether one was raised amid the turmoil of the inner city or in the comfort and among the opportunities provided by a wealthy suburb—are also unearned. While such differences in natural endowments and social circumstances are inevitable and cannot be erased, a liberal society with a strong commitment to fair equal opportunity will attempt to reduce the effects of these differences on the ability of people to achieve their goals. How might this be done?

Through governmental "welfare" programs, liberal societies can provide certain essential goods and services, or **entitlements**, to everyone—regardless of their ability to pay. Basic nutritional and housing needs can be made available to all through such programs as food stamps and housing subsidies. Public schools can serve to guarantee the right to basic education to everyone. Public libraries allow everyone to have access to books and other educational resources. Public health centers can provide some basic medical care to all.

Liberal governments can—and have—expanded these public welfare provisions in several ways. First, compensatory programs can be made available to those who are disadvantaged or handicapped. Most public schools, for example, have developed special-education programs for students with physical handicaps and behavioral, learning, and developmental disabilities. Second, the level of public provision can be increased. For example, more generous food and housing subsides can be provided. Third, entitlements can be extended into new areas. In the United States, for example, the idea of publicly funded child care is being proposed by many liberals as a means of extending the real job opportunities of many women.

Of course, expanding entitlements does not enhance equality if the persons who consume these goods and services are naturally well-endowed or advantaged by their social circumstances. According to neoliberals, "means-tests" should be required to ensure that the recipients of welfare are indeed among the "truly needy."[22] They want to be sure that strict needs tests are included when developing new welfare-rights policies in such areas as national health insurance and the provision of day care.

Additionally, liberal societies can regulate access to the most desirable opportunities (such as schools and jobs) in ways that make it easier for the disadvantaged to compete for them. **Affirmative action** policies begin by encouraging schools and employers to exert greater efforts to recruit African

[22]Peters, "A Neoliberal's Manifesto."

Americans, women, and other disadvantaged groups. Stronger affirmative action policies may entail having schools and employers adopt "preferential admissions" policies, whereby lower qualification standards are used to increase admissions of members of specific disadvantaged groups. Still stronger affirmative action policies may stipulate that a certain percentage—or quota—of new positions be filled by members of disadvantaged groups. Preferential treatment and quotas have sometimes been disparaged as "reverse discrimination," because they violate the idea of formal equal opportunity—that people should not be classified by race, gender, and so forth, in ways that influence their chances for success. However, contemporary liberals often respond that such policies are necessary to achieve *fair* equal opportunity.[23] They argue that formal equal opportunity—understood as giving "equal consideration" for a desirable position to everyone with the same standardized test score—works to the advantage of those with the (undeserved) greatest natural talents or from the most advantageous social backgrounds. Such "equal consideration" results in those with lesser natural abilities or from disadvantaged backgrounds having poorer (unequal) prospects for success than their competitors. Alternatively, fair equal opportunity might mean that everyone in all socially relevant groups will have an "equal prospect" of achieving the desired position.[24] In this case, "equal prospect" means that those with lesser natural abilities or from disadvantaged social backgrounds will do as well as—though not better than—more advantaged people.

Liberals provide several justifications for supporting strong affirmative action policies—for supporting "equal prospects" over "equal consideration." First, affirmative action may be justified on utilitarian grounds, as providing an overall gain to the community. For example, there may currently be a greater need for black lawyers than white lawyers to serve the American system of justice, especially if black clients prefer to be represented by black attorneys and if blacks comprise only a small percentage of those in the legal profession. Second, affirmative action policies may not, in fact, involve reverse discrimination. White males have no right to equal consideration in the assignment of positions, even if they have outperformed their competitors on standardized tests, because a society can justly employ a variety of criteria when filling desired positions—including some prediction about how well various kinds of people will serve the public. It might decide, for example, that it is desirable to have more black teachers or policemen, and thus might make minority racial status, as well as test scores, relevant criteria in hiring decisions. As long as affirmative action criteria are employed impartially to specific cases, those who are disadvantaged by the criteria cannot complain of injustice.

[23]Ronald Dworkin, *Taking Rights Seriously* (Cambridge: Harvard University Press, 1977), pp. 223–239.

[24]Douglas Rae, *Equalities* (Cambridge: Harvard University Press, 1981), pp. 68–76.

Sidebar 8-3

John Rawls and His Liberal Theory of Justice

The most famous and controversial attempt to develop a liberal theory of justice is that made by John Rawls (1921–), a professor of philosophy at Harvard University. In his monumental work, *A Theory of Justice,* published in 1971, he defends two basic principles of justice. Rawls's first principle—the equal liberty principle—provides everyone with the most extensive system of equal basic liberties compatible with a similar system of liberties for all. Rawls's second principle—the difference principle—specifies when equality can be abridged (or when differences in primary social goods are acceptable) in order to attain efficiency (more aggregate goods). Inequalities in distributions of such social goods as money and power are permissible if opportunities to receive greater amounts of these goods are equally open to all, and when the resulting inequalities are to the advantage of the least advantaged.

The **equal liberty principle** is essential to Rawls's theory of justice and has been relatively uncontroversial. This principle specifies that all members of a liberal society are guaranteed equal political liberties (the right to vote, the right to seek office, and freedoms of speech and assembly), liberties of conscience (freedom of thought and of religion), property rights (e.g., the opportunity to acquire and hold personal property), and legal rights (e.g., freedom from arbitrary arrest, and the right to an impartial judge and jury). Notice that this principle does not necessarily allow for unlimited amounts of these liberties. For example, the right to vote does not mean that all members of society have the right to decide who will hold each public office (e.g., judges could be appointed rather than elected) or what laws should be enacted (e.g., representative democracy may be preferable to direct democracy). Instead, the equal liberty principle states that liberal societies should provide their citizens the most extensive liberties that are feasible and desirable, and when such liberties are provided—as in the case of selecting representatives to the legislature—these liberties should be provided equally to all.

Moreover, according to Rawls, the equal liberty principle takes priority over the difference principle. This means that basic equal liberties can never be sacrificed or compromised. For example, some individuals—probably the poor—may be tempted to sell their voting rights or even to sell themselves into slavery in order to acquire their minimal material needs. In order to ensure everyone's dignity, such exchanges must be banned even though they may be economically efficient and advantageous to the poor. But having banned the capacity of the poor to sell their basic liberties in order to survive, a liberal society incurs an obligation to prevent individuals from finding themselves in such desperate conditions that they would be tempted to give up their basic liberties in order to survive. The second principle is intended to achieve this goal.

The **difference principle** begins with a presumption that primary social goods—resources directly distributed by social institutions, such as income and wealth, powers and opportunities, and certain rights—are to be distributed equally unless an unequal distribution of any or all of these goods is to the advantage of the least favored. However, recognizing the trade-off between

Sidebar 8-3 (continued)

equality and efficiency, Rawls says that some departures from equal distributions are justified if they result in greater efficiencies (i.e., if they result in greater aggregate levels of primary social goods) that improve everyone's condition. For example, giving some (gifted) people a larger share of wealth in order to give them an incentive to use fully their socially useful talents and energies might ultimately help everyone and, thus, be acceptable to everyone. In short, inequalities are allowable if they add to each person's share of goods, but are disallowable if they diminish anyone's share of goods.

The difference principle specifies that in order for there to be acceptable inequalities, there must first be fair equal opportunity for all to achieve the larger shares. Formal equal opportunity is insufficient, because inequalities in natural endowments and in social circumstances unfairly privilege some individuals. An extensive system of welfare rights must be in place to ensure that everyone has equal prospects of achieving the larger shares and to ensure that the larger shares are rewards for greater-than-average efforts and responsible choices. This condition is important because it ensures that the social goods available to individuals are determined by the choices the individuals make, not by their circumstances. It is unfair for individuals to be disadvantaged or privileged by arbitrary and undeserved differences in their circumstances.

The difference principle also specifies that the resulting inequalities of primary social goods must benefit the representative person in the lowest socioeconomic class.* Although Rawls sometimes says that inequalities must be "to everyone's advantage," his concern is clearly over the fate of the poor and disadvantaged.† Policies and programs that reduce the social goods available to the advantaged while increasing the social goods available to the disadvantaged are just, because they move society toward the preferred state of equality. In contrast, policies that increase the aggregate level of social goods, that provide fair equal opportunity to all, that increase the social goods available to the advantaged, but that decrease the social goods available to the poor, are unjust, because they move society away from the preferred state of equality.

Consider, for example, the economic policies of the Reagan administration. Reagan claimed that economic growth and, hence, aggregate social goods could be enhanced by reducing the taxes on the wealthy and eliminating various welfare programs. Moreover, he claimed that everyone would have an equal opportunity to obtain greater wealth and that the poor, as well as the wealthy, would see an improvement in their economic situations. These claims make Reagan's economic policies appear compatible with Rawlsian principles. However, such policies were not created in a context of fair equal opportunity. Clearly, the poor did not have the same opportunities as the wealthy to convert tax cuts into profitable investments. Moreover, the evidence suggests that such policies did not improve or increase the shares of the least advantaged. Studies have shown that posttax income growth during the Reagan period "was limited mainly to the 20 percent of American households with the highest incomes. Households headed by poor persons from traditionally disadvantaged groups faired less

*John Rawls, *A Theory of Justice* (Cambridge: Harvard University Press, 1971), p. 78.

†Rawls, *A Theory of Justice*, p. 303.

well. The poorest black and Hispanic households actually lost 30 to 40 percent of their incomes between 1983 and 1987."*

But why should principles of justice—and thus, the social and economic policies of a society—favor the disadvantaged? In *A Theory of Justice,* Rawls employs a social contract argument to defend these liberal principles. Recall that classical liberals used the concept of a social contract to deliver humans from the state of nature into civil society and to create a government that would protect everyone's natural rights. Recognizing that the state of nature is a fiction and that individuals do not really consent to join civil society, Rawls creates an alternative to the state of nature that he calls the "original position." This is a hypothetical situation defining the ideas on which there must be consensus in order for people to conclude that their interests are served by being part of a society that bases its institutions and policies on the two principles of justice. Essentially, the "original position" specifies the foundational ideas that must be shared in order for each person to enter voluntarily into a liberal society governed by Rawlsian principles. Rather than specifying presocial conditions that individuals consent—by social contract—to leave, the "original position" specifies various liberal ideas that, if consensually held, would lead everyone to accept the equal liberty and the difference principles as the basis for their social cooperation, because everyone's interests would be served by being part of such a society. Some of the most important of these ideas are the following:

1. *Equal respect* The goals (or life plans) of each individual must be equally respected by everyone. The state must be neutral regarding the value of various life plans. Its principles and policies should not privilege certain life plans (e.g., a desire to become a doctor or lawyer) in relation to other life plans (e.g., a desire to become an artist or a surfer). Most importantly, no one's goals can be deemed insignificant or valueless and thus, no one's goals can be sacrificed for the sake of the greater good of society.

2. *Nonrisky rationality* Everyone realizes that the achievement of one's life plans will be facilitated by acquiring more social goods, and everyone also realizes that one's life plans will become endangered if one's social goods drop below a certain minimal level. While it is rational to seek more social goods, it is irrational to put oneself in a situation where it is possible to attain large increases in one's social goods only by risking the availability of those minimal social goods that are needed to achieve one's life plans.

3. *Mutual disinterestedness* Everyone is unconcerned about the social goods available to others. Being concerned with their own life plans and the social goods available to them to achieve their goals, individuals will not altruistically provide needed social goods to others. At the same time, envy will not preclude people from agreeing to the provision of larger holdings of social goods of others—as long as they recognize that providing others with such holdings does not adversely affect, and may even enhance, their own situations.

*"Growing Inequality in America's Income Distribution," *The Urban Institute Policy and Research Report* (winter-spring 1991), p. 1. The most extensive statistics about income inequalities and fairness of American society are available in *The Green Book,* published annually since 1981 by the House Ways and Means Committee. These data clearly show that the new wealth generated during the 1980s went mostly to the most privileged members of society.

Sidebar 8-3 (*continued*)

4. *The veil of ignorance* The distributions of natural talents and social advantages that affect the chances for individuals to succeed or fail in their attempts to acquire more social goods must be unknown. Everyone must be ignorant of whether they are relatively smart or healthy or energetic. No one can know whether they are born to privileged or disadvantaged social circumstances. Of course, in practice, people do have knowledge of their natural endowments and social circumstances. However, Rawls argues that everyone must ignore this knowledge and assume that it is possible that they are relatively disadvantaged in terms of natural talents and/or have been born into social circumstances that limit their opportunities.

Rawls contends that people who hold these ideas will find his two principles of justice preferable to alternative principles. For example, they will reject utilitarianism—the principle that governments should maximize the greater good for the greater number—because this principle permits some individuals and their life plans to be sacrificed for aggregate gains. They will also reject pure equality, because some inequalities can be mutually beneficial. They will accept the equal liberty and the difference principles because these principles protect the fundamental interests of each person from being sacrificed for the gains of others and from bearing the misfortunes caused by natural and social contingencies.

Of course, it can be objected that the foundational ideas that people must hold in the original position are themselves problematic. Why, for example, should people be expected to ignore their natural endowments or social circumstances in choosing principles of justice? Or why should people be expected to prefer a risk-free situation where they are guaranteed access to minimal social goods rather than preferring to gamble such a situation in the hope of winning one that provides extensive wealth, power, and so forth? Rawls's response to such criticisms is that the ideas in the "original position" are consistent with our "considered judgments" and intuitions about the good life and morality. For example, the "veil of ignorance" simply requires people to choose principles that are good for everyone, not just oneself. Without the "veil of ignorance," people will choose "principles" that benefit people in their circumstances, but the essence of principles is that they guide conduct and choices independently of opportunistic considerations of particular circumstances. While Rawls acknowledges that the idea of nonrisky rationality may not be suitable for all circumstances, he argues that it is attractive for situations such as deciding among principles of justice, because rejection of this idea of nonrisky rationality has "outcomes that one can hardly accept. The situation involves grave risks."* In 1993, Rawls published *Political Liberalism,* in which he claimed that the ideas in the "original position" are consistent with values inherent in the liberal tradition. Rawls now concedes that his theory may not be universally applicable and holds only for those liberal societies where there is a commitment to the fundamental ideas of liberty and equality. While such arguments and concessions have not silenced Rawls's critics, his theory continues to have a strong appeal for contemporary liberals, because it reconciles their desire to balance the efficiencies of capitalism with a strong sense of equality.

*Rawls, *A Theory of Justice*, p. 154.

Structure

Contemporary liberals generally accept the governmental structures and institutions that they have inherited from classical liberals. They recognize the need for constitutional restraints on government. They understand that governmental power needs to be divided. And they hope to check abuses of governmental power through various procedures of accountability. Compared to classical liberals, however, contemporary liberals want a strong state that can solve economic problems and deliver social justice. As a consequence, contemporary liberals have endorsed processes and practices that strengthen governmental institutions.

While recognizing the importance of constitutions, contemporary liberals believe it is permissible that such constitutions be amended to accommodate new moral understandings and to allow government to address new problems. For example, constitutional amendments (e.g., the Sixteenth Amendment to the U.S. Constitution, establishing the income tax) can give governments new powers to collect revenues to finance the strong state. It is also permissible for constitutions to be reinterpreted. During the New Deal, for example, liberals urged and endorsed several Supreme Court rulings permitting an expanded role of the federal government in the areas of economic regulation and redistribution. During the 1950s and 1960s, liberals supported judicial reinterpretations of the Fourteenth Amendment (the "equal rights" amendment) to desegregate schools. And, in 1973, liberals applauded when the Supreme Court ruled (in *Roe v. Wade*) that constitutional privacy rights implied that women have the right to abortions. In general, liberals have endorsed **judicial activism**—the practice whereby judges interpret vague and abstract wordings in the Constitution in a manner that expands the powers of government in economic matters and that extends the political, social, and legal rights of minorities, women, and persons accused of crimes, for examples. For liberals, the practice of actively reinterpreting the Constitution is justified because the abstract vagueness of constitutional provisions requires that constitutional language be fused with contemporary moral theories—such as that provided by John Rawls in *A Theory of Justice* (see sidebar entitled "John Rawls and His Theory of Justice")—to address new problems.[25]

One of the major areas where American liberals have reinterpreted the U.S. Constitution concerns the powers of the national government relative to state governments. Classical liberals in America assumed that the states should do most of the governing. Indeed, the Tenth Amendment to the U.S. Constitution provides that those powers not given to the national government by the Constitution "are reserved to the states respectively or to the people." During the nineteenth century, the national government exercised few powers, as the states made and enforced most of the laws regarding business and finance, property, labor, welfare, and crime.[26] However, contemporary liberals (citing

[25]Dworkin, *Taking Rights Seriously*, p. 149.
[26]Lowi, *The End of Liberalism*, p. 272.

the "elastic clause" in the Constitution giving Congress the power "to make all laws which shall be necessary and proper . . .") have sought to increase the authority of the national government for several reasons. First, modernization and globalization have made many economic problems difficult to solve at the state level. For example, states are often reluctant to impose strict environmental regulations on their industries for fear that such regulations would prompt businesses to relocate in states with more lax regulations. Only national governments (and international agreements) can impose strict regulations that leave businesses with few choices but compliance. Second, states have often been controlled by local special interests that are unresponsive to broader public concerns or minority rights. Thus, some Western states were long controlled by mining and/or agricultural interests that resisted reforms. And Southern states, of course, were controlled by conservative whites who resisted minority rights. In the liberal view, only by expanding the power of the national government could such injustices as state-supported racial discrimination be curbed. Third, national governments are much more able than state governments to expand welfare rights in a mobile, modern society.[27] The problem is that there are strong economic disincentives for states and localities to produce redistributive policies. States that create more generous welfare programs than other states can expect to attract the "wandering poor" from other states while effectively encouraging businesses and wealthy citizens to leave the state to avoid the high taxes needed to cover increasing welfare costs. In short, states face especially severe trade-offs between equality and efficiency, and their concern to enhance aggregate economic well-being makes them unreceptive to redistribution. Because national governments can limit entry of the poor of other countries through restrictive immigration laws and because the wealthy are less inclined to give up their citizenship than they are to move to low-tax states, national governments have fewer disincentives to have generous welfare-rights policies than the states do.

Despite the willingness of contemporary liberals to expand national government, it is probably a mistake to regard national supremacy—the view that the powers of state governments should be limited and made accountable to the sovereignty of national governments—as a liberal doctrine. As budget deficits have curtailed the capacity of the federal government to enhance welfare rights and provide public services, and as the executive branch has fallen into the hands of conservative administrations, liberals have increasingly turned back to the states, seeking innovative solutions to social and economic problems at that level. In short, liberal beliefs about the proper powers of national, state, and local governments are derivative rather than fundamental. Contemporary liberals are more basically concerned with using governmental power to resolve social and economic problems and to enhance social justice, and they will use the power of any level of government—national, state, or local—that is readily available for such purposes.

[27]Paul Peterson, *City Limits* (Chicago: University of Chicago Press, 1981), pp. 210–222. Also see Deborah A. Stone, "Why the States Can't Solve the Health Care Crisis," *American Prospect* (spring 1992), pp. 51–60.

Another area where American liberals have reinterpreted the Constitution concerns the distribution of powers between the executive branch and the legislative branch. While classical liberals generally supported legislative-centered government, contemporary liberals have generally supported **executive-centered and bureaucratic government**.[28] At least until conservative Republicans began to dominate the executive branch during the Reagan administration (while liberal Democrats continued to dominate Congress), liberals generally sought to strengthen the executive branch for several reasons. First, legislatures represent diverse and parochial interests and contain many veto points, making it difficult for them to pass progressive legislation solving social problems and furthering social justice. It has often been observed that liberal legislation in the areas of civil rights and welfare policies could only pass through Congress during periods when liberal Democrats had supramajorities in each house and were influenced by the prodding of liberal presidents.[29] Second, in the United States, the Chief Executive has accrued significant political powers to define the agenda of social problems and to convey his concerns to the public. Beyond the formal powers provided to them by the U.S. Constitution, presidents have acquired informal powers that, if fully employed, can facilitate the building of coalitions supporting policy initiatives on behalf of liberal goals. Third, as society has become more modern, problems have become more complex, and the expertise to address these problems appears to reside in a professional bureaucracy rather than among legislative generalists. While legislators might be able to agree that certain problems—such as environmental pollution or AIDS—require public attention and the investment of governmental resources, they seldom have the expertise to define specific policy solutions. As a result, legislative lawmaking amounts to little more than "expressing broad and noble sentiments, giving almost no direction at all but imploring executive power, administrative expertise, and interest-group wisdom to set the world to rights."[30] In short, liberals have come to depend on bureaucratic expertise to define the social and economic problems that confront society and to develop and implement specific programs addressing these problems. They recognize that presidents can use their popularity and prestige to develop coalitions supporting governmental initiatives. And they hope that legislatures will respond to these initiatives by passing broad enabling laws and by appropriating funds for such programs. By supporting such executive-centered government, liberals have come to endorse the bureaucratic state.

Despite supporting strong, executive-centered national governments, contemporary liberals are well aware that such governments can abuse their powers, and so they endorse structures and practices of accountability. In general, they believe that executive agencies should be accountable to the legislature and the legislature should be accountable to citizens. Bureaucratic programs

[28]Lowi, *The End of Liberalism*, pp. 274–279.

[29]James Sundquist, *Policies and Politics: The Eisenhower, Kennedy, and Johnson Years* (Washington, D.C.: Brookings Institution, 1968).

[30]Lowi, *The End of Liberalism*, p. 276.

should be subjected to **legislative oversight**. Legislative staffs should evaluate the legality, effectiveness, and fairness of bureaucratic actions, and legislative hearings should permit testimony from outside experts, interest groups, and citizens. Executive abuses of power—such as were commited by the Nixon administration during the Watergate scandal or by the Reagan administration during the Iran-Contra affair—can be investigated by the legislature, which should apply appropriate sanctions ranging from impeachment to the cutting off of program appropriations.

Understanding that legislators should, in turn, be accountable to citizens, contemporary liberals have endorsed a variety of reforms to enhance such accountability. For example, American liberals have sometimes criticized indirect selection methods, endorsing the popular election of senators (rather than selection by state legislatures) and the president (rather than selection by the Electoral College). Liberals have sought to devise legislative districts that apportion legislators equally based on population, to ensure that legislators are as accountable to urban voters as to rural ones. More recently, liberals have called for public financing of elections, believing that such reforms would make representatives more accountable to the general public rather than to "fat-cat" contributors. But liberals have not supported all electoral reform proposals. There is no evidence, for example, that liberals are more supportive than conservatives of term limitations on elected representatives. Indeed, there are good reasons for liberals to reject such proposals. Term limitations curtail the rights of both representatives (who can thereby be prohibited from seeking reelection to office) and voters (who can thereby be denied the right to vote for representatives who have served them effectively). And liberals have argued that term limits would hamper the development of the effective leadership needed by a strong state.

Rulers

Like classical liberals, contemporary liberals are committed to representative democracy. They believe that preeminent power should reside with elected officials, and they have sought to increase the representativeness of such officials. Indeed, they recognize that there have been significant departures from the ideals of representative democracy, divergences which necessitate political reform.

Contemporary liberals have continued the process of making the electorate more representative. While classical liberals focused on removing property qualifications, contemporary liberals have worked to extend voting rights to such groups as women, racial minorities, and younger people, among others. Moreover, contemporary liberals have shown some concern with increasing the representativeness of state and local legislatures. For example, liberals are concerned that Afro-Americans and Hispanics (as well as the poor, women, and many other groups) remain significantly underrepresented on city councils in the United States, and they have discovered that electoral institutions and practices that are prominent in American cities—at-large constituencies and nonpartisanship—tend to exacerbate such underrepresentation.[31] As a consequence, liberals often seek, and have sometimes achieved, district-based partisan elections. Because liberals recognize the increasing power of bureaucracies—both in the formulation and implementation of public policies—they have also been concerned with more equitable bureaucratic representation. For example, liberals have urged urban police departments to recruit and promote more minority and women officers.

Despite gains in the representativeness of the electorate and of public officials, liberals believe that real power remains distributed in ways that depart from democratic ideals. Compared to other groups and most citizens, business interests and people with higher incomes have always been well organized and thus in a position to disproportionately influence public officials. To balance the pressure-group system, liberals have urged the formation of new groups representing labor, consumers, the poor, minorities, women, and other relatively uninvolved and powerless citizens. But most liberals suspect that business organizations continue to have a "privileged position" among pressure groups.[32]

More specifically, liberals recognize that specialized policy arenas—often called **subgovernments**—have emerged. These subgovernments are often dominated by business organizations having large economic stakes in the area, agency officials providing policy-specific expertise, and legislative-committee members whose constituencies benefit from governmental spending in the area. The most famous of these subgovernments is the military-industrial complex composed of defense contractors, leaders in the defense department and the military, and congressmen whose districts contain military bases or defense contractors that employ many constituents. Additionally, subgovernments dealing with scientific-educational, agricultural, medical, and other interests have been identified.[33]

Contemporary liberals have ambivalent attitudes regarding such power arrangements. Subgovernments can be effective means of bringing governmental power to bear on national problems. The expertise of interest groups and bureaucrats can be employed in specialized arenas. And legislators can develop expertise in specialized policy areas while serving the interests of their constituencies. Nevertheless, contemporary liberals recognize that many interests and citizens are unable to penetrate these power arrangements. As a result,

[31]Susan Welch and Timothy Bledsoe, *Urban Reform and Its Consequences: A Study in Representation* (Chicago: University of Chicago Press, 1988), pp. 35–53.

[32]Charles E. Lindblom, *Politics and Markets* (New York: Basic Books, 1977), pp. 170–188.

[33]It has been observed that an increase in judicial activism has enabled the courts to enter into these subgovernments, transforming "triangles of power" into "policy rectangles." Indeed, some analysts insist that the emerging activism of newly organized environmental, consumer, and minority groups make obsolete such terms as "triangles of power" and "policy rectangles;" they prefer the term "policy networks," as it denotes an allowance for the participation and power of many actors in these subgovernments. While contemporary liberals normally welcome more extensive participation in subgovernments, they recognize that some legitimate interests continue to be excluded from such arenas.

the policies of subgovernments may better serve the special interests that dominate them than they do the public interest. These negative aspects of subgovernments have prompted neoliberals to try to control—though not abolish—their powers. Theodore Lowi argues that such control must begin by having legislatures practice the principles of **juridical democracy** by delegating fewer powers to these subgovernments.[34] Rather than passing vague legislation directing agencies to achieve certain goals, the rule of law must be restored. According to Lowi, legislatures must draft laws that state precisely what is to be done or what is to be forbidden, that indicate clearly who is to be affected, and that specify exactly the rewards and punishments to be utilized. Additionally, Lowi and other neoliberals believe that the policies and practices of these subgovernments must be continuously monitored to determine whether or not they are achieving specified standards and goals. Those programs that are not performing adequately should be terminated by "sunset clauses" in the enabling legislation. By reducing the discretionary powers delegated to subgovernments and by holding them more accountable to the legislature, neoliberals hope that power can be distributed in ways that more closely reflect the democratic ideal that the primary rulers in a liberal society are its elected representatives.

In summary, contemporary liberals support various reforms in order to make the distribution of power in liberal societies better correspond to the ideals of representative democracy. Believing that dominant power should reside among elected representatives, contemporary liberals seldom support reforms that would empower citizens through the institution of populist democratic procedures.[35] They believe that parliaments are better than open assemblies, because representatives are more able than citizens to adjust competing interests through compromise, oversee administrative bodies, and employ institutional devices (like party leadership) for setting an agenda that establishes priorities among issues.[36]

Citizenship

Classical liberals made citizenship contingent on competence, slowly extending citizenship rights as various classes of people were deemed qualified. Contemporary liberals have rejected competence as a criterion for citizenship, asserting that all adults who are affected by political decisions should be citizens. As noted by Robert Dahl, they have adopted the principle of maximal inclusion, as citizens, of all but the mentally defective, children, and transients.[37] Having granted citizenship to minorities and women and having lowered the age at which the young are granted various citizenship rights, the question of "who should be citizens?" in a liberal society now focuses on how

[34]Lowi, *The End of Liberalism,* pp. 295–313.
[35]William Riker, *Liberalism Against Populism* (San Francisco: W. H. Freeman, 1982).
[36]Elaine Spitz, "Citizenship and Liberal Institutions," in *Liberals on Liberalism.*
[37]Robert Dahl, *Democracy and Its Critics* (New Haven: Yale University Press, 1989), p. 119–131.

many and which "outsiders" should be granted residency and made citizens.

Classical liberals assumed that citizenship was available to those who chose to reside within the borders of a country, agreed to obey the laws of its government, and met the qualification standards that applied to long-term residents. Such "open admissions" principles, which continue to be endorsed by most libertarians,[38] are viewed with skepticism by contemporary liberals. Liberal societies have achieved levels of economic affluence and extensive welfare rights that make such societies attractive to people outside their borders. Without some restrictions on who can be citizens, liberal societies would be besieged by those seeking admission. Unrestricted immigration, where outsiders could simply choose to become citizens, raises several difficulties. First, as outsiders become residents, their willingness to work for wages below prevailing rates may reduce the economic security of existing citizens. Second, unrestricted immigration can threaten the welfare state because of the reluctance of taxpayers to maintain or extend economic entitlements if they believe that such programs will simply entice the poor from other countries to arrive on their shores in order to receive welfare. Third, open admissions can threaten the "common culture" of a society—for instance, if the dominant language were no longer the primary means of communication. Finally, unrestricted borders threaten the very idea of "national autonomy"—the concept that a basic right of every nation is to decide, according to its own values and its own procedures, who will be citizens.

As a consequence, contemporary liberals have adopted several principles dealing with admissions and criteria for citizenship.[39] First, liberals reject nativist conceptions of restricted admissions (or largely closed borders) in favor of *higher, but qualified, immigration* levels. Liberals recognize the extraordinary economic and cultural contributions to society made by immigrants, they admire the qualities of many newcomers to society, and they find morally appealing the idea of admitting the oppressed from other parts of the world. Second, liberals believe some qualifications must nevertheless be established limiting the admission of new citizens. Preference should be given to those who seek asylum from political oppression in their native lands, whose occupational skills can most contribute to the economy (and who are least likely to become dependent on welfare), whose cultures, ideologies, and languages lead to easy assimilation into society, and whose extended families include those who are already citizens. However, such criteria should not be used to exclude certain applicants on racial, ethnic, or religious grounds, as the immigration policies of a liberal society must promote diversity rather than nativist prejudices. Third, residence in a liberal society should translate as quickly as possible into citizenship. Liberals are uncomfortable with the presence within their societies of both illegal and landed immigrants (or guest workers), because

[38]See Joseph H. Carens, "Aliens and Citizens: The Case for Open Borders," *Review of Politics* 49 (spring 1987), pp. 252–254, 263–264.

[39]Paul H. Schuck, "The Great Immigration Debate," in *The American Prospect* 3 (fall 1990), pp. 100–117.

such people are relegated to a lower status within the community and have inferior rights to those of citizens. Lacking the full rights and protections of the state, such residents experience the liberal state as a repressive force. Immigrants should either be denied admission if they cannot qualify for citizenship, or they should be granted citizenship as soon as naturalization processes can be completed.

The issue of being or becoming a citizen is important to contemporary liberals for three principal reasons: citizens acquire rights; citizens incur public obligations and responsibilities; and citizens obtain opportunities for political participation. As we have discussed earlier, liberals have sought to expand citizen rights. Compared to classical liberals, contemporary liberals have given broader definitions to political liberties, legal rights, and economic entitlements, and they have tried to ensure that these rights have been extended to the lower classes, minority groups, women, and so forth. For the most part, the broader rights pursued and provided by contemporary liberals have been "private" rights. They are the equal liberties of each individual against the state (e.g., the right to privacy) or the claims of individuals upon the state (e.g., the right to consume various public goods and services). By emphasizing such private rights, contemporary liberals have remained faithful to the conception of citizenship held by classical liberals. They view citizens as individuals who devote most of their lives to economic production and consumption and to the satisfaction of their personal interests. They have sought to emphasize and enhance the private sphere of life through public protections and provisions. Accordingly, they have de-emphasized those aspects of citizenship which propel individuals more strongly into the public realm. They have de-emphasized citizen obligation and participation.

Nevertheless, contemporary liberals—perhaps liberal theorists more than liberal politicians—recognize that citizens have **political obligations** as well as rights. While some ideologies claim that citizens have "duties" (such as the duty to obey God or the Fuehrer), liberals prefer the language of obligations and responsibilities. While such ideologies conceive of duties as disconnected from rights, liberal see obligations as being intimately connected with citizen rights. Most basically, the rights that governments secure for each citizen impose obligations on other citizens to obey those laws that secure these rights. Each person's property rights impose an obligation on all other citizens to obey no-trespass laws. Each person's right to due process if accused of a crime imposes an obligation on all citizens to serve as jurors if called. The right of citizens to be secure from foreign invasion imposes military obligations on them. While liberals have supported various policies as alternative means of distributing such military obligations—including drafting young men by lot and recruiting a voluntary army financed by higher taxes—liberal commitments to equal rights imply commitments to universal responsibilities. Believing that a volunteer army merely permits the more affluent to hire the relatively disadvantaged to do their dangerous work, many neoliberals have called for a national public service program requiring all young men and women to serve in the military or in some alternative service for a few years.

The expansion of welfare rights by contemporary liberals is, at least in principle, accompanied by parallel increases in obligations on citizens to pay for welfare entitlements through higher taxes. When liberals enact new welfare programs, they simultaneously obligate citizens to pay for such programs. Citizens having welfare rights may express these rights as claims against the government (and these rights are often treated as such), but governments are merely relatively efficient and fair instruments for providing these rights and imposing corresponding tax obligations on citizens. Of course, although most citizens want rights, they don't want responsibilities—this gives liberal politicians an incentive to emphasize rights while minimizing obligations. When contemporary liberal politicians have stressed obligations, they have usually encountered hostile responses. When President Kennedy said, "Ask not what your country can do for you; ask what you can do for your country," he was chastised in the press for forgetting that government was the servant of the people. When Walter Mondale promised to raise taxes when accepting the Democratic nomination for President in 1984, he thereby virtually sealed his defeat in the general election. In summary, liberal theorists insist that the welfare state is based on an implicit social contract in which citizens define rights corresponding to their perceived basic, common needs. Citizens then develop governmental programs fulfilling these needs and obligate themselves to contribute their fair share to the costs of these programs. But, in the everyday world, liberals "have not had a well-developed public language of responsibility to match our language of rights."[40]

Increasingly, liberal theorists and politicians are searching for an improved understanding of political obligation.[41] They hope to move beyond the "thin" conception of citizenship that is widely held in liberal democracies and is exemplified by the common view that citizens fulfill their public obligation by voting and that the exercise of this "responsibility" entitles them to the most basic citizen right today: the "right to bitch" at politicians rather than contributing to the process of finding solutions to public problems.[42] Initially, this "thicker" conception of citizen responsibilities simply seeks to reestablish the intimate link between responsibilities and rights.[43] Obedience to just laws, involvement in public service, and payment of necessary taxes are responsibilities that citizens must discharge if they hope to retain the rights and benefits provided by a liberal state.

In addition, many liberal theorists sense the need for a conception of citizen responsibilities that goes beyond those obligations that are merely the flip

[40]Mary Glendon, quoted in a symposium on drafting a bill of duties entitled, "Who Owes What to Whom?" *Harper's Magazine* 282 (Feb. 1991), p. 45. For a further discussion of communitarian views regarding rights and responsibilities, see Glendon's *Rights Talk: The Impoverishment of Political Discourse* (New York: Free Press, 1991).

[41]A new journal, *The Responsive Community: Rights and Responsibilities*, has been founded to explore these matters, and liberals are prominent both on its editorial board and among its contributors.

[42]Dan Kemmis, in "Who Owes What to Whom?," p. 46.

[43]President Clinton's call for a "new covenant" during the 1992 presidential campaign is the most visible recent attempt to stress citizen responsibilities as well as rights.

side of our rights. Perhaps citizens have obligations to preserve the oceans, the earth, and spotted owls.[44] Perhaps citizens have obligations to future generations. While there are no living human rights-holders on the other side of these potential obligations, liberals recognize the need of citizens to exercise greater responsibility toward the environment and the future members of society.[45]

While many contemporary liberals seek to develop a "thicker" conception of citizen obligation, they normally reject a duty to engage in political participation. For liberals, there can be no duty to vote, because the right to vote also implies the right not to vote. Compelling citizens to vote would not ensure that they voted in an informed manner, in a way that furthered democratic or liberal outcomes. Compelling citizens to vote might prompt them to participate for the wrong reasons—to escape penalties to be imposed on nonvoters rather than to express their sense of responsibility to their fellow citizens and their commitments to the effective functioning of democratic institutions.

As long as all citizens have the right and opportunity to participate, liberals believe that democracy can function effectively and fairly even if many people choose not to participate or choose to limit their participation to voting in periodic elections. Rather than seeking highly participatory democracy, contemporary liberals are satisfied with a form of democracy that Robert Dahl calls **polyarchy**. In polyarchies, citizens are provided fundamental political rights, including the opportunity to participate, and governments are controlled by elected officials who modify their conduct so as to win elections in political competition with other candidates and parties.[46] Such arrangements are supported by liberals for several reasons. Citizens need not devote vast amounts of time to politics. Simply by voting in periodic elections, citizens acquire "indirect influence," because elections give elected officials incentives to enact policies reflecting citizen preferences and needs. Citizens need not meet Herculean, or ideal, standards. They need not be well-informed on all issues of the day; they need not have sophisticated ideologies; they need not know "the public good"; and they need not put the public good ahead of their personal interests. All that citizens need to do is to evaluate the overall performance of officials based on casual observations. Have officials abused the public trust? Have they normally responded to the preferences and needs of their constituents? Have social and economic problems dwindled or are they increasing in number or severity? Relatively unsophisticated citizens can remove elected officials who fail these tests through the device of contested elections. Thus, public officials can be controlled and held accountable for their

[44]Lawrence Tribe, "Ways Not to Think About Plastic Trees: New Foundations for Environmental Laws," *Yale Law Review* 83 (fall 1974), pp. 1314–1348.

[45]It remains an unresolved question as to whether such responsibilities can be reconciled within liberal ideology or whether such responsibilities can only be accommodated within other ideologies, such as environmentalism or conservatism. In his *A Theory of Justice* (pp. 284–293), John Rawls claimed that citizens have obligations to future generations. But Rawls insisted that current generations can no more have an obligation to sacrifice their own good for that of future generations than they can sacrifice the good of future generations to their own immediate interests.

[46]Dahl, *Democracy and Its Critics*, pp. 218–224.

performances even if only some citizens actually vote in elections and even if the voters' information about politics is limited.[47]

In addition to having the freedom to vote, citizens also have opportunities to become more directly involved in political life. They can become active in interest groups (or limit their participation to paying annual dues that enable the leaders of such groups to represent their concerns through continual interactions with public officials). They can organize or join ad hoc, issue-specific groups to make known their concerns and grievances—a particularly popular and effective mode of participation at the local level. They can also join voluntary associations that contribute to society in ways that are relatively removed from politics and public policy making.[48]

While polyarchy gives citizens the right to vote and to participate in various organizations, it also gives citizens the right to oppose government and dominant groups within society. Contemporary liberals have emphasized two modes of oppositional participation: involvement in protest movements and the practice of civil disobedience.

Contemporary liberals have been active in numerous **protest movements**—in activities of relatively unorganized collections of people who share common political values and goals. Some protest movements—such as the civil rights movement, the women's rights movement, and the gay rights movement—have simply sought to extend liberal rights to excluded groups. Other protest movements—such as the antiwar movement and the environmental movement—have sought to redirect policies away from the goals sought by the most powerful interests and groups within liberal society. Contemporary liberals have often supported protest movements because they provide vehicles for participation and influence for those citizens who are otherwise excluded from, or underrepresented in, the political process. Contemporary liberals also have supported protest movements because they raise the consciousness of political officials and of the broader public about important social problems that otherwise escape public attention. Such movements generate support for structural and policy innovations that reform public life in accordance with new moral understandings and emerging social and economic possibilities.

A particular form of political protest that is often supported by contem-

[47]V.O. Key, Jr., *The Responsible Electorate* (Cambridge: Harvard University Press, 1966).

[48]The importance of voluntary organizations in liberal society is stressed by Spitz, "Citizenship and Liberal Institutions," p. 198. Nevertheless, contemporary conservatives emphasize participation in voluntary associations more than do liberals. For conservatives, voluntarism is often viewed as a substitute for political action; for example, they view participation in private charitable associations as a means of reducing the size of the welfare state. For liberals, voluntarism can only complement political action. Liberals believe that participation in charitable organizations can be the decent thing to do when welfare provisions of the state are inadequate. But liberals also believe that charitable organizations are no substitutes for public welfare (1) because contributions to such organizations decline during hard times when the need is the greatest, (2) because such organizations often set criteria for receipt of aid that involve "helping our own kind" rather than helping the most needy, and (3) because charity fails to establish welfare rights. See Jeffrey Henig, *Public Policy and Federalism* (New York: St. Martin's Press, 1985), pp. 116–120.

porary liberals is **civil disobedience**. Civil disobedience occurs when a citizen or group of citizens publicly defies a law or policy of a government with the intention of pointing out its injustice and promoting a policy change. Acts of civil disobedience are premeditated, are understood to be illegal or of contested legality, are carried out for limited public ends, and employ carefully chosen nonviolent means.[49] The most prominent example of civil disobedience in recent American history is provided by Martin Luther King, Jr. (1929–1968) and his followers in the civil rights movement.[50] King sought limited ends by calling for the end of segregation laws but not for the overthrow of the racist regimes that created such laws. Rather than seeking some private advantage, he addressed the rights of a large but oppressed group and argued that his aims were to further justice and the common good. He employed limited means, as his direct action tactics sought to create an atmosphere of crisis without involving violence. He acknowledged that his actions violated existing laws and was prepared to accept the penalties for his disobedience, even while arguing the injustice of these laws.

While liberals believe that citizens normally have an obligation to obey the laws of government, they also regard civil disobedience as morally legitimate in a pluralistic society. Liberals recognize that citizens have multiple obligations. Sometimes their obligations to their families, to fellow members of oppressed groups, or to humanity may conflict with their obligation to obey the laws of their government. In such situations, disobeying questionable governmental laws may contribute to a good society. Existing liberal societies, of course, fail to realize perfectly their liberal principles. Within liberal societies, tyrants can acquire political power, and well-motivated public officials can create oppressive and unjust laws. A society that does not respect and, indeed encourage, such courageous acts of resistance as civil disobedience runs the danger of producing citizens who will submit to tyranny and injustice. Civil disobedience serves both to educate liberal citizens about civic virtues and moral obligations, and to inhibit and correct departures from liberal ideals.

Change

It is generally understood that "conservatism stands for conserving the inheritance" while liberalism has an "inclination toward reform or change."[51] Contemporary liberals welcome change because they have confidence that collective political action can narrow the gaps between liberal ideals and existing conditions. Economic problems can be alleviated by governmental policies. Social injustices can be corrected. More democratic distributions of power can

[49]Seminal treatments of civil disobedience are provided by Christian Bay, "Civil Disobedience: Prerequisite for Democracy in Mass Society," in *Political Theory and Social Change*, edited by David Spitz (New York: Atherton Press, 1967) and by John Rawls, *A Theory of Justice*, pp. 363–391.

[50]Martin Luther King, Jr., "Letter from Birmingham Jail," in *Why We Can't Wait* (New York: Harper and Row, 1963).

[51]Joseph Cropsey, *Political Philosophy and the Issues of Politics* (Chicago: University of Chicago Press, 1977), p. 117.

be achieved. Liberals have specific ideas about how to achieve such economic, social, and political changes.

First, contemporary liberals believe that change should occur through democratic political action. While classical liberals thought that an "invisible hand" inevitably transformed the self-interested actions of individuals into social progress, contemporary liberals believe that progress can best be achieved collectively. They believe that the future must be deliberately and socially constructed, that democratic politics provides the best forum for deliberating on future goals and the courses of action for achieving these goals, and that the power of the state must be applied in order to bring about beneficial changes.[52]

Second, change need not be revolutionary, at least for those contemporary liberals living within Western democratic societies. The basic economic, political, and social institutions of these societies should be maintained. Small, family-owned and operated businesses may have often turned into large corporations, "night watchman" states may have become strong states, and social structures may have become more heterogeneous and complex, but these aspects of modernization have evolved slowly, naturally, and, for the most part, beneficially. While such institutional arrangements sometimes engender social problems that need correction, the basic structures are sound.

If contemporary liberals have any desire for revolutionary change, it is in seeking the transformation of illiberal societies. Certainly liberals have applauded the revolutionary developments in Eastern Europe whereby communism and authoritarianism have been replaced by market economies and democratic governments. And many liberals support the overthrow of governments that violate human rights in such places as China, Iraq, or Haiti. Nevertheless, liberals are cautious in their support of revolutionary change—even in illiberal societies. They realize that liberal institutions cannot be imposed on developing nations without disrupting their unique cultures. Liberals recognize that different people—and thus different societies—have their own goals and ways of life that may not include the materialism and individualism pervading liberal societies.

Third, contemporary liberals usually want to achieve progress through reform. Occasionally, liberal reform can transform social life while preserving fundamental institutions. For example, Alexander II ordered the emancipation of the serfs in Czarist Russia and Abraham Lincoln freed American slaves even though such reforms were intended to maintain rather than change basic political institutions.[53] Perhaps leading examples of such transforming reforms in liberal societies during this century are the New Deal and the Great Society. While unconcerned with changing fundamental political institutions, Frankin D. Roosevelt's New Deal brought about extensive economic reforms by equalizing the bargaining power of business and of labor (through the Wagner Act

[52]See, for example, *The Collected Writings of John Maynard Keynes*, vol. 27, edited by Donald Moggridge (London: Macmillan, 1980), p. 260.
[53]James MacGregor Burns, *Leadership* (New York: Harper and Row, 1978), pp. 181–195.

of 1935) and by enhancing the role of the federal government in providing the citizenry security against economic deprivation. While leaving intact basic economic and political institutions, Lyndon Johnson's Great Society initiative sought far-reaching changes in race and class relations through civil rights legislation and antipoverty programs.[54] Despite conservative rhetoric about the failure of such liberal reforms, liberals insist that these laws and programs have resulted in significant progress. For example, John Schwarz argues that the liberal policies in the United States during the 1960s and 1970s significantly reduced poverty, curbed flagrant malnutrition, relieved overcrowded and substandard housing, improved educational opportunities for impoverished children, gave useful skills to thousands of otherwise unemployable persons, reversed pollution trends, and accomplished all of these gains without significantly increasing the tax burden on American citizens as a percentage of their steadily expanding incomes.[55]

Liberals are also committed to achieving incremental changes, as they understand that progress in most areas occurs by making many small adjustments over time. Even the massive changes in international politics at the end of the Cold War have not prompted most liberal politicians to call for an immediate, drastic transfer of funds from defense to domestic programs. Instead they call for incremental reductions in military expenditures over a five-to-ten-year period. Liberals are willing to seek incremental changes for several reasons. First, **incrementalism** avoids intolerable dislocations; for example, a slow build-down of the armed forces avoids flooding society with unemployed soldiers and producing massive shocks to local economies that are dependent on military expenditures. Second, incrementalism is more acceptable politically than massive reform; conflicting interests can more easily be accommodated by making changes slowly. Third, incrementalism allows for remedial actions; problems and unexpected consequences may occur as reforms are implemented, but incrementalism allows for adjustments and even reversals to deal with such difficulties.[56]

Liberals have thus sought to achieve progress through both transformational and incremental reforms rather than through revolutionary politics. Nevertheless, it can be argued that the effects of liberal reforms over an extended period can indeed be revolutionary. According to Theodore Lowi, the "First American Republic," which was based on the principles of classical liberalism, died during the 1960s, and the "Second American Republic," which is based on the principles of contemporary liberalism, has emerged as its successor.[57] The reforms of contemporary liberals have resulted in the following revolutionary transformations of American politics. The small state has given way to the strong state. Free enterprise has yielded to a regulated and mixed economy. Support for market justice—emphasizing the unequal contributions

[54]See, for example, Sidney Verba and Gary Orren, *Equality in America* (Cambridge: Harvard University Press, 1985), pp. 41–48.

[55]John Schwarz, *America's Hidden Success* (New York: W. W. Norton, 1983).

[56]The rationality of incrementalism is defended by David Braybrooke and Charles Lindblom in *A Strategy of Decision* (New York: Free Press, 1963).

[57]Lowi, *The End of Liberalism*, pp. 271–294. Lowi disapproves of these changes.

of individuals to the economy—has been partially eclipsed by support for social justice—emphasizing equalities among citizens. The separation of powers has become somewhat modified by the emergence of executive-centered government. The primacy of state governments has yielded to the dominance of national institutions. Power has become more broadly dispersed, as many interest groups and agency officials wield significant influence, as do elected officials and voters. Citizen rights have been enormously expanded, and many new vehicles have emerged for furthering opportunities for citizen participation. Liberals laud these changes because they enable governments to extend the positive liberty of citizens, solve social and economic problems, and thus bring about progress.

THE PHILOSOPHICAL BASES

Ontology

Contemporary liberals have abandoned the classical liberals' goal of achieving a universal theory of politics based on firm, incontestable, philosophical foundations. Rather than seeing liberalism as a fixed doctrine based on a true understanding of nature, they see liberalism as an evolving historical and political achievement—an inheritance of a valuable political tradition that is justified by its deeds and potentialities, not its metaphysics.[58] Contemporary liberalism can be regarded as **deontological** in a narrow sense (which we will consider below, in our discussion of epistemology) in that it postulates no knowledge of "the good" or "the good life" other than the entirely subjective understandings that individuals have of "the good." But contemporary liberals can also be considered deontological in a broader sense; they view attempts to define the true nature of the universe, humans, and societies as fruitless.

Like classical liberals, contemporary liberals view the world in natural or secular terms, as they regard ideas about God's role in the universe as serving only private, spiritual needs and as being irrelevant to the construction of political principles. But while classical liberals believe that the natural world works according to precise natural laws, contemporary liberals doubt that there is a natural order that determines social and human life. Social arrangements are not naturally ordered, but socially created. Human capacities are not defined by nature but rather are shaped by social contexts and human choices. History will not unfold according to predetermined social and natural forces but rather will be of our making. The social world now, and in the future, takes on many possibilities and is not subject to iron laws, but rather it can be modified culturally and politically.[59]

To claim that there are no iron laws of capitalism, politics, or social life is

[58]John Rawls, "Justice as Fairness: Political not Metaphysical," *Philosophy and Public Affairs* 14 (1985), pp. 223–251, and John Gray, *Liberalisms: Essays in Political Philosophy* (London: Routledge, 1989), p. 240.

[59]John Maynard Keynes, for example, saw belief in "some law of nature" that precludes human intervention as "nonsense." See *Collected Works*, vol. 9, pp. 90–91.

not to say that developments in these areas are completely contingent and unshaped by either ideational (Hegelian) or material (Marxian) forces. Contemporary liberals seem to assume that the achievement of progress will be influenced by both human values and organizational power. Liberals understand that people have many, often competing, values. The values that are strongest within individuals, groups, or societies will influence their goals—and thus, their achievements. Liberals thus understand that the maintenance and progress of liberalism requires the fostering of certain liberal values—such as the importance of individual excellence and accomplishments, a commitment to social justice, a respect for the rights of others, and a willingness to fight for liberal rights and values.[60] Liberals also understand that in order for values to have an impact, they must be backed by political power. In modern societies, significant political power resides in well-structured organizations of people and material resources. Organized power which affects historical progress may reside in governments, in corporations, in labor unions, or in other large-scale organizations.[61] In short, contemporary liberals believe that there are many possibilities for human history and that our fates depend on the values we choose to emphasize and on how power is organized. If liberal ideals are to be more fully realized, liberal values must be encouraged and political power must be effectively organized on behalf of such values.

Human Nature

Classical liberals assumed that humans have fixed and specific characteristics—people are maximizers of utility, endowed with instrumental reason, and equal in certain fundamental ways. In contrast, contemporary liberals believe that it is a mistake to assume a fixed and invariant human nature. When thinking about "human nature," contemporary liberals tend to make moral prescriptions about how humans ought to be—and how others ought to regard them—in order to thrive in a liberal society, instead of making descriptive statements about the actual motivations and qualities of human beings.

Like classical liberals, contemporary liberals believe that all humans have an essential interest in leading a good life and in having the things that a good life provides and requires, but such liberals doubt that the particulars of the life plans of humans can be specified. People can regard the good life as attaining capitalist values—such as material comfort and security—or as involving other values emphasizing emotional fulfillment, social belongingness, and public spiritedness. Different people may emphasize different goals, and individuals alter their life plans when they conclude that their current priorities are mistaken.[62] Individuals do not choose their goals in a completely autonomous and disembodied manner; they are influenced by

[60]William Galston, "Civic Education in a Liberal State," in *Liberalism and the Moral Life,* edited by Nancy L. Rosenblum (Cambridge: Harvard University Press, 1989), p. 93.
[61]The determinant power of organizations is discussed by John Kenneth Galbraith in *The New Industrial State* (New York: Signet Books, 1972).
[62]Will Kymlicka, "Liberalism and Communitarianism," *Canadian Journal of Philosophy* 118 (June 1988).

community traditions and the values of others, even by the values of people from different cultures. But these outside influences often emphasize conflicting values—especially in pluralist liberal societies. In choosing among competing values (and reconsidering one's choices), individuals define and redefine both themselves and their life plans.[63] The moral imperative is that all individuals be given opportunities to form and revise their life plans "from the inside"—with as much autonomy and as few external constraints as possible.

Contemporary liberals also believe that humans have the capacity for instrumental rationality—that humans have the potential to make economic, social, and political choices that enhance the possibility that they will achieve their life goals. But in order to be fully rational, one must understand the options that are available, one must have information about the likely consequences of pursuing various options, and one must be able to make discriminating judgments about which options best serve the full range of values that are at stake—over the long haul as well as in a more immediate time frame. The extent to which humans are fully rational varies across individuals and within individuals as they develop intellectually. The moral imperative is to foster the intellectual development of each individual. Rather than denying the rational capacity of people and having authorities paternalistically choose what's best for them, liberals insist that humans must continuously develop their capacities to reason by being given opportunities to choose for themselves.[64]

Contemporary liberal theorists also stress other human qualities that must be developed if liberal principles, institutions, and policies are to thrive. For example, in the sidebar entitled "John Rawls and His Liberal Theory of Justice," in this chapter, we pointed out that Rawls argues that people should avoid risky choices, overcome envy of justly acquired inequalities, and adopt principles of justice without regard to their own circumstances. Rawls understands that (some) humans are inclined to gamble, are envious of the greater wealth and power of others, and opportunistically choose "principles" that reflect their interests, but he suggests that these human weaknesses can be surmounted. It is thus imperative that liberal societies foster the moral development of humans.

Finally, liberals (contemporary as well as classical) accept the equality of being of each human. Despite existing differences in human values, rationality, and other capacities and talents, liberals accept the idea of **intrinsic equality**.[65] The moral imperatives of this idea are to regard conceptions of the good held by different people as being of equal value, to construct institutions as if no person is inherently superior to another, and to give equal consideration in policy making to the life plans and interests of each person.

[63]Emily Gill, "Goods, Virtues, and the Constitution of the Self," in *Liberals on Liberalism.*

[64]Dahl calls this imperative the "presumption of personal autonomy." See his *Democracy and Its Critics*, pp. 97–105.

[65]Dahl, *Democracy and Its Critics*, pp. 84–88.

Society

Classical liberals viewed society as simply an aggregation of individuals and their interactions. Contemporary liberals believe that this view of society failed to recognize the social forces that influence individuals and bind them together. Contemporary liberals believe that societies are ongoing associations of various groups of people who attempt to live peacefully and tolerantly alongside each other, and that such groups have both common and conflicting interests that are most effectively governed through established liberal institutions. While societies can be relatively homogeneous racially, ethnically, and economically, most modern states are heterogeneous. Many groups form the **social pluralism** and diversity of liberal societies. People with common interests form associations to pursue these common interests, and the associations that are formed become the basis of human identity.[66] The best way to characterize a society is in terms of the associations that predominate within it, but associational arrangements will vary across societies. Countries like Great Britain, with a strong tradition of social classes, have developed strong parties and interest groups that reflect class divisions.[67] Countries like the Netherlands and Switzerland have evolved "consociational democracies," in which organizations representing the various ethnic groups in these societies play predominant political roles.[68] In Japan, corporations play key roles in social as well as economic life. In the United States, a wide variety of groups representing occupational, racial and ethnic, religious, and lifestyle interests have emerged, resulting in a "hyperpluralistic" society, one in which many people are simultaneously members of a variety of groups. Liberals doubt that any of these associational structures provides a model toward which liberal societies should seek to evolve.

Nevertheless, liberals believe that the social pluralism—the group and associational diversity—that exists within liberal societies is desirable and has several normative implications. First, individuals must be permitted to associate with others even if the purpose of their association is to oppose the existing authorities and policies of society.[69] Second, individuals should be encouraged to associate with a variety of groups in order to promote personal and

[66]According to Lowi in the *End of Liberalism*, p. 31–41, pluralists like Arthur Bentley and David Truman played a key role in the emergence of contemporary liberalism. Initially, such pluralists believed that groups are simply the product of the common interests of particular kinds of individuals, but recent pluralists recognize that ongoing associations play a large role in defining the interests and life plans of individuals. See, for example, Charles Anderson, "Pragmatic Liberalism: Uniting Theory and Practice," in *Liberals on Liberalism*, p. 210.

[67]Thus contemporary liberals acknowledge that Marxists and their ideological offspring are sometimes correct to point to classes as a fundamental characteristic of society. However, liberals stress that the importance of classes varies across communities and over time. For example, the importance of classes as a characteristic of British society may have declined in recent years. See Richard Rose and Ian McAllister, *The Loyalties of Voters* (Newbury Park, Calif.: Sage, 1990), chap. 3.

[68]Arend Lijphart, *Democracy in Plural Societies* (New Haven: Yale University Press, 1977).

[69]Liberals are less clear about extending toleration to groups which oppose liberal institutions and principles. Rawls suggests that intolerant groups, like fascist and communist organizations,

social stability.[70] Third, all groups have the right to seek power, and all legitimate interests should receive a fair hearing as issues are resolved. Fourth, while various groups need not have equal power, no group should be able to dominate other groups; existing inequalities in group power should reflect different groups' capacities to serve the public interest and the interests of justice.

In summary, contemporary liberals reject the idea of constructing political principles and institutions on the basis of some specific conception of society. Instead, they believe that a pluralistic society composed of many groups and associations should be promoted, as a means of providing multiple bases for individual attachment and identity. Such a pluralistic society should also disperse power broadly, in ways that prevent tyranny and authoritarianism and that promote freedom and democracy.

Epistemology

Most contemporary liberals have abandoned the Cartesian approach to the acquisition of political knowledge that formed the epistemological basis of classical liberalism. As we saw in Chapter 2, the purpose of Cartesian science was to discover indubitable truths about the physical and social worlds and about human psychology, so that humans could create economic and political arrangements conforming to the realities of the natural world. Contemporary liberals believe that this approach is fundamentally mistaken. There are no self-evident truths about the nature of the universe, society, and human beings from which the political principles of liberalism can be deduced. If liberalism is to be defended, it must be defended on some basis other than the Cartesian science used to defend classical liberalism. Contemporary liberals have provided a variety of alternative justifications for their political principles.

Perhaps the most influential defense of contemporary liberalism—at least among political theorists and philosophers—is the deontological justification offered by John Rawls. This approach is deontological because it gives "priority of the right over the good"[71]—it claims we can come to understandings about "what is right" without knowing "what constitutes the good." Like classical liberals, Rawls argues that conceptions of the good and the good life are subjective. No conception of the good merits special protection or promotion by the liberal state. Such a state must be neutral with respect to the various conceptions of the good life held by various individuals and groups. Indeed, governments must protect people's rights to be as free as possible in defining

should be tolerated if they are weak and liberal institutions are strong. But one of the primary obligations of a liberal citizen is to preserve and protect liberal institutions, and this can entail repressing those groups which become genuine threats to the persistence of liberalism. See, *A Theory of Justice*, pp. 216–221.

[70]Group attachments root individuals within society. Involvement in a variety of groups provides conflicting views on current issues, moderating political demands. Group involvement makes participants less susceptible to authoritarianism and the appeals of demagogues.

[71]Rawls, *A Theory of Justice*, p. 396.

and pursuing their own life plans based on their own views of the good life. If people agree that their highest concern is to secure their right to pursue their own (perhaps unique) idea of the good life with as few political, social, and economic constraints as possible, such people should also agree that others have the same concern, prompting them to the further agreement—or implicit social contract—to be governed by liberal principles, institutions, and practices promoting that right. According to this argument, a liberal society is the unique outcome of the rational choice of all individuals concerned with the right to pursue their real choices about the good life. While this argument has certain features in common with the defense of classical liberalism which is based on the idea of a social contract and grounded in Cartesian assumptions of universality, this justification is not Cartesian because it explicitly recognizes that citizens' agreement on liberal principles and institutions depends on their holding the ideas of equal respect, nonrisky rationality, mutual disinterestedness, and ignorance of their natural and social circumstances. (See discussion in the sidebar entitled, "John Rawls and His Liberal Theory of Justice.) Because liberal theorists understand that these ideas may not be consensually held, they recognize that the justification for liberalism which is based on deontological, social contractual arguments is not absolutely or universally compelling.

A second set of justifications for liberalism claims that liberal principles and institutions are better than rival principles and institutions because adoption of liberal principles produces positive outcomes. One such claim is that "it is only in a liberal society that human beings can fully flourish."[72] This argument asserts that liberal institutions best provide individuals the freedoms and opportunities to exercise self-determination, to take responsibility for their actions, to engage in collective deliberations about policy decisions, and to thus stimulate their moral and intellectual development. A second such claim is that liberal institutions promote social peace.[73] Unless groups with different conceptions of the good life accept the liberal idea of tolerating each other and develop institutions that ensure the fundamental rights of all individuals, they will continuously engage each other in "religious wars" and other such ideologically based conflicts, and live in fear that the strongest group will impose its vision of the good life on all others. A third such claim is that the adoption of liberal principles, institutions, and policies has contributed to social progress in many areas.[74] Such principles, institutions, and policies have reduced or eliminated many social and economic problems. They have brought about prolonged, stable economic growth. They have been able to regulate economic power, compelling businesses to pay attention to such public interests as protecting the environment. They have reduced income inequalities. They have

[72]Gray, *Liberalisms*, p. 254. Gray attributes this argument to John Stuart Mill, T. H. Green, K. W. von Humbolt, and Ernest Barker. He finds it wanting.

[73]Brian Barry, "How Not to Defend Liberal Institutions," *British Journal of Political Science* 20 (June 1990), pp. 4–5.

[74]See, for example, Schwarz, *The Hidden Success of American Politics.*

increased equal opportunities for minorities, women, and other disadvantaged groups. They have contributed to stable and democratic distributions of power. In short, the institutions, principles, and practices of contemporary liberalism are justified because they have produced many benefits for people in everyday life.[75]

A third defense of contemporary liberalism argues that it provides those principles and practices that are most suited to human fallibility and ignorance. In order to understand this argument, we must briefly consider the connection between science and liberal politics as presented by **pragmatists** from John Dewey to Charles Anderson. According to Dewey, it is a mistake to characterize science in Cartesian terms, as a dogmatic enterprise that seeks to establish absolute truths to govern human conduct. Instead, science is an open-ended activity in which humans who are ignorant of absolute truths and whose knowledge about life is a fallible attempt to improve their understanding through experimentation. Similarly, liberal politics—which is simply the "scientific method writ large"[76]—is not the assertion of absolute principles about how to govern, but an open-ended process in which people seek to solve the concrete problems that they experience. The liberal political process involves organizing people to produce increasingly accurate and useful information about these problems and employing "social intelligence" to solve these problems. Dewey's understanding of the link between science and liberalism was expanded upon by Karl Popper, who stressed that science could never verify a theory but could only falsify inadequate ideas and that all knowledge was thus tentative and subject to future revision. In *The Open Society and Its Enemies,* Popper argued that authoritarian, or closed, societies incorrectly presume that authorities can acquire absolute knowledge about the character of the good society and construct an all-powerful government having the knowledge to achieve such a society. In contrast, an "open," liberal society resembles a true scientific community, (1) because people recognize that their political programs can never be proven, (2) because alternative ideas are always tolerated, and (3) because institutions exist that provide for orderly social change. More recently, Charles Anderson has argued that contemporary liberalism provides a set of practices that is particularly well-suited to solving practical problems in ways that reform current practices and make them correspond more closely to various liberal ideals.[77] Contemporary liberals seldom begin with absolute principles—such as maximizing economic efficiency or promoting economic equality—and then construct policies and practices corresponding to these principles. Instead, contemporary liberals enter political life "in midstream." They become involved with particular projects—such as how to deal with toxic wastes or what courses should be required in a college

[75]While such consequentialist arguments are important to the defense of liberalism, they do not provide proof of its desirability, because they make empirical claims that are sometimes contentious and because they assume that everyone values the claimed consequences.

[76]David Ricci, *The Tragedy of Political Science* (New Haven: Yale University Press, 1984) p. 104.

[77]Charles A. Anderson, *Pragmatic Liberalism* (Chicago: University of Chicago Press, 1990).

curriculum. They assess the performance of current practices in the area against many criteria—for example, Are such practices economical? effective? fair? responsive to the preferences of interested parties? They consider new ways of doing things and, using various criteria, evaluate how these reforms affect performance. Because various proposed reforms affect various criteria in different ways, there can be no absolutely and objectively best reform. But through political deliberation in which people apply various kinds of rational judgments, people can come to reasonable decisions to experiment with reforms promising enhanced performances of ongoing practices. In addition, such experiments are subject to continual appraisal and reappraisal. Contemporary liberals believe that such processes provide for continuous social progress even in the absence of absolute liberal principles—despite our uncertainty about what the good society is like, and despite our tentative knowledge about the effectiveness of reforms.[78] In short, because human knowledge about the good society is always limited and tentative, the best society and government is a liberal one which guarantees human freedom and which continuously deliberates over how to reform problematic social and economic conditions.

SUMMARY AND CONCLUSIONS

Perhaps the principle of **tolerance** best summarizes the outlook of contemporary liberals, but their idea of toleration extends well beyond the religious toleration emphasized by John Locke and other founders of classical liberalism. Contemporary liberals are more tolerant than classical liberals, because they recognize the fragility of their own philosophical foundations. They understand that liberal principles cannot be proved on the basis of indubitable conceptions of how the universe, humans, or society works. They recognize that allegiance to liberal principles depends upon acceptance of certain liberal values that can be questioned by those who are attracted to other ideologies. While contemporary liberals have a low opinion of absolutist and intolerant ideologies like communism and fascism, such liberals regard democratic socialism and contemporary conservatism (and such emerging ideologies as feminism and environmentalism) as their "friends" as long as these ideologies remain tolerant and friendly toward liberalism.[79] Contemporary liberals share some principles with their friends. Like democratic socialists, they are committed to more equality. Like contemporary conservatives, they are committed to the maintenance of capitalism. Like feminists, they support equal rights and opportunities for women. Like environmentalists, they recognize the need to address our environmental problems. And all of these ideologies share with contemporary liberalism a commitment to constitutional and representative democracy. Such overlapping principles provide the bases for broad support for fundamental liberal institutions and for building temporary coalitions on specific policy issues.

In addition to being "externally" tolerant of other pluralist ideologies, contemporary liberals are "internally" tolerant of the diversity within liberal societies. Liberals tolerate life plans and lifestyles that differ from their own. They tolerate the expression

[78]Contemporary liberals may be contradictory on this point. How can liberals identify what constitutes social progress if they fail to have knowledge about what the good society is like?
[79]Bernard Crick, *In Defense of Politics* (Middlesex, England: Penguin Books, 1982).

of various viewpoints regarding religion and morality. Liberals disagree among themselves about many practical political issues. Which social and economic problems should rise to the top of the political agenda? Which reforms best address important problems? Which competing principles (e.g., efficiency or equality) should be stressed when dealing with a particular problem? Because answers to such questions cannot be deduced from the abstract principles of contemporary liberals, those who think of themselves as liberals are often in conflict with other liberals on these practical matters. Contemporary liberals tolerate other liberals who disagree with them on specific issues, hoping to reach accommodation through further deliberation and hoping to reconnect with their disagreeable liberal friends on future issues. However, the fact that internal disagreement on specific issues is implied by the principles of liberal ideology dashes any hope for a united and disciplined liberal party.

Currently, contemporary liberalism is both enjoying unprecedented success and experiencing an enormous crisis. On the one hand, the demise of communism has led some observers to argue that ideological conflict is at an end, because liberal principles and values now reign supreme over much of the world.[80] Capitalism is being introduced into Eastern Europe. Despite conservative attacks on the excesses of contemporary liberalism, liberal welfare states remain strong in much of the world. Constitutional and representative democratic regimes govern an increasing number of nations. Support for expanding citizen rights is widespread. And the secular and material values that accompany liberalism seem increasingly to dominate cultures throughout the world. On the other hand, liberalism is under attack, denigrated as the awful "L-word," and the "liberal" label is avoided by politicians (even politicians having liberal principles) because liberalism has become associated—at least in many American minds—with big and intrusive government, bureaucratic domination, excessive business regulations that strangle the economy, reverse discrimination, coddling of criminals, moral permissiveness, and (especially) higher taxes.[81] Perhaps contemporary liberalism is implicated in these problems, but solving such problems is what liberals like to do best. Given their commitment to and experience with reform, contemporary liberals may well be up to the task of reforming the society and politics they have created and, simultaneously, reforming their own political principles.

[80]Francis Fukuyama, *The End of History and the Last Man* (New York: Avon Books, 1992).

[81]R. Emmett Tyrrell, Jr., founder of *The American Spectator*, is perhaps the most caustic critic of contemporary liberalism. His criticisms are summarized in J. David Hoeveler, Jr., *Watch on the Right: Conservative Intellectuals in the Reagan Era* (Madison: University of Wisconsin Press, 1991), pp. 207–231. For a more academic discussion of how liberalism is currently regarded in America, see J. Roland Pennock, "Liberalism Under Attack," *The Political Science Teacher* 3 (winter 1990).

CHAPTER 9

Democratic Socialism

America is the only major industrialized democratic society without a significant democratic socialist party. Nevertheless, various types of radicals (and, to some extent, liberals) have brought to the American political conversation many democratic socialist ideas, such as the following. Although capitalist institutions, processes, and values can play legitimate roles in a good society, modern life is dominated by capitalism, resulting in economic inefficiencies, social injustices, and moral degradation. To curtail capitalist domination, private property and economic inequalities need not be abolished, but the public should control the use of property and make economic necessities equally available to all. To curtail capitalist domination, liberal values involving individual freedoms and rights need not be eliminated, but they must be complemented with other values emphasizing social solidarity, respect and concern for others, and individual responsibility to the community. Ending capitalist domination does not require revolutionary change but, rather, can and should take place slowly, through evolutionary processes by which citizens acquire socialist values, become empowered politically, and use democratic governments as primary vehicles for achieving a good and just society.

Socialist sentiments are probably nearly as old as human life, but the ideology of socialism is a reaction to capitalism. Thus, the precursors of socialism—people like Sir Thomas More (1478–1535),[1] Gerrard Winstanley (1609–1660?),[2] François-Noël (Gracchus) Babeuf (1760–1797),[3] and most impor-

[1]More published *Utopia* in 1516; in it he strongly criticized the acquisitive society that was emerging in Europe.

[2]Winstanley was the leading theoretician of the Diggers—a radical group within Cromwell's army during the English Civil War between 1651–1660. Winstanley called for communal ownership of and access to land. See George Shulman, *Radicalism and Reverence: The Political Thought of Gerrard Winstanley* (Berkeley: University of California Press, 1989).

[3]Babeuf sought to abolish private property during the French Revolution and advocated absolute equality. He wrote, "Let there be no other difference between people than that of age and sex. Since all have the same needs and same faculties, let them henceforth have the same education

Sidebar 9-1

Some Democratic Socialists and Their Main Writings

Eduard Bernstein (1850–1932)
Evolutionary Socialism (1899)

Sidney Webb (1859–1947) and
Beatrice Potter Webb (1858–1943)
Socialism in England (1890)

Richard H. Tawney (1880–1962)
Equality (1931)

George (G. D. H.) Cole
(1889–1959)
History of Socialism (1953–1960)

Erich Fromm (1900–1980)
Escape from Freedom (1941)
The Sane Society (1955)

Alec Nove*
The Economics of Feasible Socialism (1983)

Anthony (C. A. R.) Crosland
(1918–1977)
The Future of Socialism (1956)

Irving Howe (1920–1993)
Beyond the Welfare State (1982)
Socialism and America (1985)

Michael Harrington (1928–1989)
The Other America: Poverty in the United States (1962)
Twilight of Capitalism (1976)

Michael Walzer*
Spheres of Justice (1983)

*Living Author.

tantly Jean-Jacques Rousseau (1712–1778)[4]—wrote as capitalism began to emerge. Nevertheless, the term "socialism" did not appear until 1827, when it was introduced in the *Cooperative Magazine* by proponents of the ideas of Robert Owen (1771–1858). Owen suggested that the problems of capitalism could be overcome by inventing and developing new types of social communities that emphasized cooperation, sociability, and social control over private property and wealth.[5] Nevertheless, Owen and other early socialists were criticized by Marx and Engels as being **utopian socialists** because they thought that the truth of socialist principles could be shown by philosophy and science, that productive and harmonious communes would be developed by enlightened industrialists, true Christians, and social reformers, and that the success of these communes would prompt everyone to embrace them. Their belief that socialism would be embraced by everyone simply because it would ultimately benefit everyone was rejected by Marx. Perceiving that

and the same diet. They are content with the same sun and the same air for all; why should not the same portion and the quality of nourishment suffice for each of them?" For a discussion of Babeuf, see Steven Lukes, "Socialism and Equality," *Dissent* 22 (spring 1975), p. 155.

[4]Rousseau's anticipation of socialism includes his critique of the liberal bourgeois society that was emerging in Europe by the middle of the eighteenth century (in his *First Discourse* [1749]), his analysis of the evolution and causes of inequality (in his *Second Discourse* [1755]), and his vision of a communal society where people transcended self-interest and willed the good of all (in *The Social Contract* [1762]).

[5]Among the many interesting discussions of the utopian socialists is that of Robert Heilbroner, *The Worldly Philosophers* (New York: Simon and Schuster, 1953), chap. 5.

the immediate material interests of the upper classes would ensure their allegiance to capitalism, Marx theorized that socialism could only occur by means of a revolution by the working class. Under Marx's influence, socialism became a revolutionary ideology during most of the latter half the nineteen century. Despite its many precursors—from More to Marx—democratic socialism did not emerge as a distinct and complete ideology until radicals absorbed Marx's critical understanding of capitalism while they abandoned his theory that capitalism could only be superseded by socialism through revolutionary means. The Fabians in England and the Revisionists in Germany were instrumental in this regard and are thus the proper founders of democratic socialism.

In 1884, the Fabian Society was founded by a group of intellectuals led by Sidney Webb (1859–1947), his wife Beatrice Potter Webb (1858–1943), and the famous playwright George Bernard Shaw (1856–1950). The **Fabians** shared Marx's indictment of capitalism and were deeply committed to egalitarianism, humanism, and Christian morality. Nevertheless, they wanted to move away from capitalism and toward socialism gradually. Such an orientation was symbolized by their name, which they took from the Roman general Fabius. Just as Fabius defeated the stronger forces of Hannibal in 209 B.C.E. by his patient, cautious, and defensive strategies, the Fabians hoped to subdue the overwhelming power of capitalism by a patient, cautious, and defensive campaign demonstrating that socialism was economically, socially, and morally superior to capitalism. As support for socialism increased, the Fabians believed that socialists could be elected to Parliament, where they could introduce socialist reforms in the capitalist system. In 1901, the Fabians cooperated with leaders of the major British trade unions to form the Labour Party and, by 1906, they had secured twenty-nine seats in the House of Commons. Forty years later, following World War II, the Labour Party captured control of the House of Commons, and—under the rules of Britain's parliamentary system—it thus formed the government. While in power, the Labourites implemented a number of socialist policies—such as nationalizing the production of electricity, steel, and coal, and socializing the distribution of medical care. Throughout the century, the Fabian Society has continued to develop and defend socialism, and the Labour Party has been the principal competitor of the Conservative Party and a major force in British politics.

In continental Europe, a variety of socialist parties and movements formed toward the end of the nineteenth century, including the *Sozialistische Partei Deutschlands* (SPD) in Germany. By 1895, the SPD membership was divided between revolutionary (or orthodox) Marxists and Revisionists—Marxists whose views were influenced by the Fabians. The most prominent Revisionist, Eduard Bernstein (1850–1932), argued that orthodox Marxists had misinterpreted Marx, making his theory of change too deterministic. According to Bernstein, the orthodox Marxist doctrine of dialectical materialism—which claimed that capitalism would collapse and that socialism would arise when economic forces developed in predictable ways and produced an inevitable crisis—gave the SPD little to do but to sit around and await the revolution.[6] In 1899, Bernstein wrote *Evolutionary Socialism*, which argued that capitalism was not about to collapse, that the working class was becoming less revolutionary, and that increases in democratization permitted the SPD to achieve political power and institute reforms leading to socialism. However, Bernstein's aspiration to realize socialism through democratic means was thwarted at the turn of the century because Germany had an imperial system, headed by Kaiser Wilhelm II. Even though the SPD eventually won more popular votes in national legislative elections than any other party in Germany, it was unable to govern or enact socialist legislation during the Second Reich (1870–1918). The chaotic conditions of the Weimar Republic (1919–1933) and Hitler's totalitarian rule during the Third Reich (1933–1945) also provided few opportunities for the SPD to institute reforms. When the Federal Republic of Germany was created in West Germany following World War II, however, the SPD reemerged as a leading contender for power. During the 1970s, the SPD was the dominant party in a coalition that ruled West Germany, and its leader, Willy Brandt, became chancellor. Today, the SPD governs a variety of states and cities in a unified Germany and retains the potential to win control of the central government.

With the exception of the United States, all industrialized Western democracies have significant social democratic parties, and the ideology of democratic socialism remains a major voice in these nations. At one time or another since 1975, social democratic parties have ruled in Britain, France, West Germany, Greece, Spain, Portugal, Norway, Denmark, and other western European democracies. Social democratic parties have also formed governments in several provinces in Canada since the 1950s. Democratic socialism has been advanced by leaders of postcolonial Africa—such as Léopold Sédar Senghor of Senegal, Kwame Nkrumah of Ghana, and Gamel Abdel Nasser of Egypt—and socialists have effectively governed Tanzania, Algeria, and Guinea-Bissau.[7] Since 1989, many of the formerly communist nations in Eastern Europe have been guided by social democratic values and programs. However, social democracy's greatest success story has been in Sweden.

The Social Democratic Labor Party (SAP) first came to power in Sweden in 1932. By governing almost continuously since then, the SAP has helped transform Sweden from one of Europe's poorer nations to one of the world's most affluent. Simultaneously, Sweden has achieved one of the world's most equal distributions of income. In pursuit of economic prosperity and income equality, the SAP developed an extensive welfare state, but it eschewed public ownership of the means of production. Today about eighty-five percent of Swedish industry remains privately owned. While the SAP has thus aban-

[6]Bernstein's main opponent, Karl Kautsky (1854–1938), provided a basis for this interpretation by maintaining that "the task of Social Democracy consists, not in bringing about the inevitable catastrophe, but in delaying it as long as possible, that is to say, in avoiding with care anything that could resemble a provocation. . . ." This quote, along with an excellent summary of revisionism, is provided by David McLellan in *Marxism After Marx* (Boston: Houghton Mifflin, 1979), pp. 20–41.
[7]For a discussion of African socialism, see Crawford Young, *Ideology and Development in Africa* (New Haven: Yale University Press, 1982), pp 97–182.

doned one of the main programs of the Fabians and Revisionists, its successes have helped to reorient the focus of democratic socialism from economic production to economic distribution.[8]

In this chapter, we provide an account of democratic socialism, which we refer to as "socialism" for brevity. Our presentation is complicated by the fact there are several varieties of democratic socialism.[9] On the one hand, there is a relatively centralist vision—exemplified by the Fabians and the Revisionists and still often present in the rhetoric of socialist parties—stressing that economic production and distribution be managed by the national state. On the other hand, there is a relatively decentralist vision—exemplified by the utopian socialists and recent communitarian socialists and evident in the actual governing practices of socialists—stressing local attacks on capitalist domination, extensive citizen participation in workplaces and local communities, and a "socialized" (rather than "nationalized") approach to the just distribution of goods and services. The tensions between these different varieties of socialism ensure that when the term "evolution" is linked to socialism, it refers not only to the preferred means of change for achieving socialist values, but also to continuing development of the goals and principles of socialists.

THE POLITICAL BASES

Problems

For democratic socialists, most economic, social, and political problems result from the pervasive influence of capitalism. Because other ideologies also focus on the problematic aspects of capitalism, it is useful to compare and contrast the socialist critique of capitalism with those developed by contemporary liberals, fascists, and Marxists (and communists).

Like contemporary liberals, socialists believe that a pure capitalist system is plagued by various market failures. Recurring business cycles produce deep economic recessions that undermine economic productivity and prosperity. Free markets provide inadequate supplies of some goods (like housing) and services (like medical care) that the public needs but cannot afford. Market competition encourages businesses to externalize their costs of production onto the public (e.g., by dumping waste by-products into the environment). But socialists believe that a critique of capitalism that focuses solely on its economic shortcomings is superficial. They believe that liberals fail to see how the capitalist system dominates and undermines many other aspects of human life, as we shall see.

Like fascists, socialists believe that the individualistic and materialistic val-

[8]See Joanne Barkan in "Sweden: Not Yet Paradise, but. . . ." *Dissent* (spring 1989), pp. 147–151; Barkan, "The End of the Swedish Model?" *Dissent* (spring 1992), pp. 192–198; and Robert Heilbroner et al., "From Sweden to Socialism: A Small Symposium on a Big Question," *Dissent* (winter 1991), pp. 96–110.

[9]Anthony Wright, *Socialisms: Theory and Practice* (New York: Oxford University Press, 1986).

ues of capitalism undermine unity and service to the community. They believe that people take more pride in their work and obtain a greater sense of achievement from it when they are contributing to the broader society rather than merely toiling for the benefit of their private employers. However, socialists find the fascist alternative to capitalism to be worse than the original problem. The totalitarian state created by fascists to control capitalism has produced far more tyranny and far less liberty and equality than exist in capitalist societies.

Like Marxists and communists, socialists believe that capitalism leads to human alienation, economic vulnerability, and social injustice. They find offensive the extensive income inequalities that exist under capitalism and doubt that the large incomes that capitalists earn are justified, given the much smaller incomes that most men and women obtain from actually working. But socialists regard the communist solution to capitalism to be excessive. Instead of abolishing capitalism, they believe capitalism need only be kept in its proper place.

Keeping capitalism in its place, however, is difficult. While socialists disagree with the Marxist view that capitalism totally determines all aspects of social life, they agree that the institutions, processes, and morality of capitalism dominate—or extensively influence—modern societies.

First, capitalism dominates economic distributions. Socialists recognize that capitalism has a legitimate role to play in distributing the kind of commodities that people want to purchase downtown or in shopping malls, but in most liberal societies, necessities are illegitimately distributed through capitalist principles and institutions. In the United States, for example, the availability of health care is often dependent on the capacity of the afflicted to pay for it, and the willingness of some relatively wealthy people to pay extensively for various medical treatments prompts doctors and hospitals to set the costs of such treatments at levels beyond the reach of poor people. According to socialists, necessities like medical care should be allocated on the basis of need, not by market-based considerations, such as the ability to pay.[10]

Second, capitalism restricts human freedom by forcing people to do things in order to survive that they would not ordinarily choose to do. Because many necessities are distributed through capitalist markets, people are often required to make "desperate exchanges" and "trades of last resort."[11] In order to obtain basic food and shelter, poor people may have to engage in demeaning, dangerous, excessive, and alienating work. When people must accept such work to purchase necessities, it is fallacious to claim that they are truly free participants in market exchanges.

Third, capitalism dominates democratic governments by influencing who obtains power and by distorting governmental policies. Socialists stress that money illegitimately buys political influence in liberal democracies. Those with wealth (or access to wealth) are well positioned to win democratic elec-

[10]Bernard Williams, "The Idea of Equality," in *Philosophy, Politics, and Society,* edited by Peter Laslett and W. G. Runciman (Oxford: Basil Blackwell, 1962), p. 122.
[11]Michael Walzer, *Spheres of Justice* (New York: Basic Books, 1983), p. 102.

tions and influence officeholders. Additionally, the needs of capitalism are strongly reflected in the issues atop the agendas of democratic governments and in the policies these governments adopt. Issues that threaten the profitability of capitalists are usually dismissed. Policies that increase the power and material well-being of the disadvantaged at the expense of capitalists are seldom adopted. Because economic prosperity and full employment are dependent on the investment decisions of capitalists, democratic governments pursue policies that make private investments profitable.[12] In short, socialists recognize that a capitalist-dominated economy creates conditions under which governments inevitably pursue "trickle-down" economic policies, where benefits are targeted in the first instance to the wealthy—with the hope that their reinvested profits will eventually benefit labor and the poor.

Fourth, capitalism enables business (corporate) decisions to be made unilaterally by those who own and manage capital. A wide array of decisions having serious consequences for workers and the broader community—such as whether to adopt new laborsaving technologies and whether to relocate plants—are made without input from workers, consumers, and the public.[13] Many contemporary socialists are now willing to concede that capitalists can own and profit from private property, but they question whether ownership of capital gives capitalists a legitimate monopoly of power over important decisions regarding the use of capital. Just as the absence of political democracy leads to illegitimate domination of citizens by governmental authorities, so does the absence of industrial democracy lead to illegitimate domination of employees by capitalists.[14]

Fifth, capitalism dominates family life. Feminist socialists argue that capitalism encourages and supports patriarchal families. Fathers are empowered by their role as the primary revenue producers who pay for the goods that capitalism induces families to want. Mothers are relegated to a subordinate position as unpaid domestic servants, while also providing a flexible workforce, available for part-time and temporary jobs at reduced wage rates. Children are given little opportunity to explore their many potentialities but are instead socialized in the family to become productive and compliant men and women whose primary future function is to succeed in the capitalist system.[15]

Sixth, capitalism dominates our culture, determining the values we hold and pursue. Socialists recognize that capitalist practices manipulate citizen preferences—directly, by inducing people to want certain products through advertising, and indirectly, by maintaining a social system in which worth is

[12]Joshua Cohen and Joel Rogers, *On Democracy* (Hamondsworth Middlesex, England: Penguin Books, 1983), pp. 51–53.

[13]The tyranny of allowing capitalists to determine the fate of local communities through their plant relocation decisions is discussed by Barry Bluestone and Bennett Harrison, *The Deindustrialization of America: Plant Closings, Community Abandonment, and the Dismantling of Basic Industry* (New York: Basic Books, 1982).

[14]Walzer, *Spheres of Justice*, pp. 291–303.

[15]Alison Jagger's *Feminist Politics and Human Nature* (Totowa, N.J.: Rowman and Allenheld, 1983) is perhaps the most widely cited work in socialist feminism.

measured by economic exchange value. Socialists claim that the capitalist system induces everyone to seek material goods and economic advancement as their primary goals, but they argue that people who were truly in touch with their own needs—people whose goals had not been corrupted and who had not developed "false consciousness" because of the influence of capitalism—would recognize that their more important needs involve the expression of other values, such as engaging in meaningful and creative work, living in a healthy environment, living in harmony with others, and developing their intellectual and spiritual capacities. But such values are given far less emphasis than they deserve, because they have little economic value in capitalist societies.

Finally, capitalism dominates human psychology, undermining self-esteem and self-confidence. Capitalism breeds a corrupted sense of self—one that is strongly influenced by success and status in the economic marketplace. It is difficult for people to believe that they are important if they are in a subordinate position in the workplace and engaged in repetitive, meaningless work. When capitalist values and orientations dominate life, those who fail in economic competition are inclined to view themselves not only as economic losers, but as losers in life.[16]

In summary, socialists identify a wide range of problems in modern societies. By tracing the root or underlying cause of these problems to capitalism, socialism is the most radical of the pluralistic ideologies. Socialists "keep a weather eye on the nastier tendencies of capitalism,"[17] because they understand its deficiencies better than do contemporary liberals and conservatives. Still, socialism remains within the pluralist tradition because socialists tolerate capitalism and do not seek its abolition. Instead, they wish to limit its domination over economic, social, and political life. Rather than seeking to abolish private property, they wish to limit the benefits that accrue to those who own property. Rather than seeking to institute absolute economic equality, they wish to limit the excessive pride, luxury, and power that accompany the concentration of wealth.

Goals

To alleviate the problems of capitalism without eliminating capitalism, socialists seek a transformation of cultural values. Unlike Marxists, socialists believe that the basic values supported by democratic capitalism can be reformulated and extended in a socialist manner and incorporated into the culture of a society wherein capitalist institutions play an important role. When liberal values are transformed into socialist ones, broad popular support for curbing the abuses of capitalism and limiting its dominance can be develolped, and this popular support can form the basis for public and governmental control of capitalism.

[16]John Schaar, "Equal Opportunity and Beyond," *Equality: Nomos IX*, edited by J. Roland Pennock and John W. Chapman (New York: Atherton Press, 1967), pp. 238–239.

[17]Robert Kuttner, "Socialism, Liberalism, and Democracy," *The American Prospect* (spring 1992), p. 7.

The key to reformulating and extending liberal values into socialist ones involves rethinking individualism and placing a greater emphasis on community. Socialists do not want to abandon individualism, but rather than focusing on how solitary individuals can maximize their interests and freedoms, socialists want to focus on how people can cooperate with each other to attain a more satisfying communal life that will sustain their individuality and enhance their real freedom.

Socialists believe that both classical and contemporary liberals have a weak conception of **communal harmony**. For classical liberals, community (or civil society) is only an agreement among atomized individuals to refrain from trampling on each other's rights. Cooperation in such a liberal community is limited to engaging in mutually advantageous exchanges and to establishing a government with the capacity to secure individual rights. For contemporary liberals, community occurs when diverse groups tolerate each other, and cooperation is limited to solving problems and working toward social stability. Socialists agree that such cooperation is essential, but argue that a much deeper sense of community and fraternity is needed. When people live in a liberal culture and work in a capitalist economy stressing competition, rugged individualism, and materialism, they have no experience with, and thus no appreciation for, genuine community. Capitalism sustains only pseudo communities where people coexist by adhering to various norms and rules and where they are pleasant to each other as long as their relationships are mutually advantageous with respect to their individual interests. But genuine community can only occur when everyone is regarded as an equally valuable member of the community, when people feel that it is safe to express their individual differences, when people are committed to the mutual growth that occurs when they learn from the process of exploring their differences, and when people delight in the sense of belonging, concern, and mutuality that is imparted to the individual by his or her membership in the collectivity.[18]

Fraternity is not an abstract love of humanity or a total identification of the individual with the group. Instead, fraternity is an attitude of friendship, fellow feeling, mutual respect, support, empathy, sensitivity, and care.[19] But, more than simply an attitude of benevolence towards others, fraternity involves cooperative behavior whereby people treat each other with genuine respect. When people have genuine respect for others, they refrain from trying to control or dominate others and they do not flaunt their superior resources or successes before others. More than sustaining and enhancing individual rights, fraternity involves cooperative collective action to address common problems. More than tolerating each other, fraternity involves understanding each other's different needs and supporting each other's diverse goals.

[18]M. Scott Peck, *The Different Drum* (New York: Simon and Schuster, 1987), pp. 59–76.

[19]Bernard Crick suggests that these attitudes of "fraternity" may be most evident, paradoxically, in the "sisterhood" of the women's movement. See his *Socialism* (Minneapolis: University of Minnesota Press, 1987), pp. 102–103.

The development of more fraternal attitudes and cooperative behavior should not occur at the expense of individuality. Socialists believe that liberals have overemphasized the conflict between individuality and communal harmony. Achieving a sense of community and seeking common goals through cooperative action does not require that individuality be suppressed or that freedoms be reduced. Individual differences, with respect both to capabilities and to goals, are inevitable and desirable. Nothing can be gained by lamenting such individual differences and inequalities, and attempts to erase our individual differences would be both futile and monstrous.[20] Rather than aiming to suppress individuality, socialists want to stimulate the full blossoming of individuality, because they believe that individual differences are the source of social energy. Economic productivity and social progress can be maximized if everyone is allowed to utilize his or her particular capacities and strengths and to express his or her goals and understandings in an uninhibited and free manner. But liberal societies have not adequately removed the barriers to the full expression of individuality and to the maximization of individual freedom.

Socialists believe that the liberal concern with individual liberty should be extended in three ways. First, socialists want to increase the *range* of concrete freedom by extending the number of situations in which individuals have real choices among alternatives. For example, they believe that the abstract economic liberties and property rights emphasized by liberals do not ensure that people have a genuine choice to quit demeaning or exploitative jobs given that they may need the income to support their families. People cannot really choose to have beneficial medical treatments if they cannot afford them. Thus, socialists want to reduce the situations in which people cannot make choices that improve their well-being because of economic, social, or political constraints. Second, socialists want to increase the *domain* of freedom by extending freedom beyond the private realm to the public realm. Socialists agree with liberals that individuals should be free in choosing to do those private acts that don't affect others, but they believe that the liberal emphasis on liberty in the private realm gives insufficient attention to liberty in the public realm. They believe that individuals become more free when they are part of a public that makes public choices about their collective lives. For example, if a community is threatened by the decision of a private corporation to shut down a local plant and relocate it elsewhere, socialists believe that the affected citizens and workers should be able to make a public policy choice regarding the matter, for if corporate managers and owners can impose such decisions on people, the people are fundamentally unfree. Third, socialists want to increase the *scope* of freedom, extending the real choices that are available in both private and public life to as many people as possible. They believe that liberals place too great an emphasis on formal equal freedoms and ignore the fact that many people are nevertheless constrained by social barriers and economic inequalities from

[20]For a wonderful satire on attempts to erase human differences, see Kurt Vonnegut's "Harrison Bergeron" in *Welcome to the Monkey House* (New York: Dell, 1970).

making real choices. For example, even the presence of affirmative action programs and scholarships for the economically disadvantaged do not permit most blacks, women, and poor people to choose to enter a professional educational program and occupation, because their upbringing has left them unqualified. Public action to improve the social, economic, and cultural context in which all people are raised can allow individuals with natural ability to become qualified, and thus turn decisions about who can enter such professions into a matter of individual choice.

Socialists believe that extending individual freedom and developing communal harmony are, for the most part, compatible goals. When a genuine community exists, everyone encourages others to develop fully their unique capabilities so that they can most effectively contribute to the community. Nevertheless, socialists also recognize the liberal idea that there are some tensions between individuality and community. For example, individuals who pursue undisciplined and addictive lifestyles can be disruptive to the community. In such circumstances, the claims of individuality and those of social harmony must be balanced. Socialists also recognize that the liberties of some people will compete with the liberties of other people. For example, giving individual capitalists unlimited property rights undermines the freedoms of those whose lives are affected by how the property is employed. In such circumstances, the greater economic liberties of a few must be balanced with a more equal distribution of liberty.[21]

Thus, socialists want a more egalitarian society. For socialists, liberals have a weak conception of equality, since they are content when everyone has equal opportunities to achieve their individual goals. While agreeing that equal opportunity is important, socialists want to go beyond equal opportunity and attain more equal social and economic conditions for all. However, the socialist goal of an egalitarian society is nothing so simple as one having an equal distribution of all social and economic goods. Instead, an egalitarian society is one in which everyone is given equal respect as an individual and equal membership in the political community. As people acquire more respect for each other, they will make less-pronounced distinctions regarding the status of people, thereby reducing social inequality. As people deepen their sense of equal membership in political communities, they will identify their common material needs and provide certain necessities to everyone as basic entitlements, thereby reducing economic inequality. And as both equal respect and the sense of equal membership deepen, people will begin to question the legitimacy of extensive inequalities in political power. Socialists recognize that, because of their superior individual virtues and contributions to the community, some people will be more honored than others. Socialists also recognize that, because of their greater industriousness and skill, some people will be richer than others. And socialists recognize that, because of their greater leadership capacities and political interests, some people will acquire more power than others. The socialist goal is not to eliminate such inequalities, but to reduce them and

[21]Crick, *Socialism*, pp. 87–88.

make them more compatible with genuine community and extensive freedom for everyone. We will further develop the socialist goal of an egalitarian society in the section on justice, below.

Socialists also value political democracy. They believe that liberals—being satisfied with prevailing institutions of representative democracy—have a "thin" conception of democracy. While socialists disagree with the Marxist claim that representative democracy is completely dominated by capitalism, they believe that capitalists have disproportionate influence in representative institutions, and they want these institutions to be more responsive to the interests and needs of common people. While socialists agree with liberals that representative democracy is important, they believe that the institutions of such a system must be augmented with additional opportunities for citizen participation in decision making. We will further develop the socialist goal of augmenting representative democracy with participatory democracy in the section on rulers, below.

In summary, socialists believe that liberal values regarding fraternity, freedom, equality, and democracy can be given interpretations that transcend their liberal limitations. Fraternity involves more than tolerance; it demands genuine mutual respect and caring. Liberty involves more than formal political, economic, and social rights; it requires that everyone have genuine choices in as many situations as possible. Equality involves more than equal opportunity; it entails the reduction of existing inequalities in the distribution of social goods. And true democracy consists of more than just ensuring representative democracy; it requires broad citizen participation. Such socialist values can occasionally compete with each other, requiring that they be balanced. But socialists argue that these values are usually compatible with each other and that their realization will lead to the universal human values of peace and prosperity. Cooperating with each other involves supporting the individual strengths of others and promoting their individual freedoms. A regard for everyone's individuality and freedoms promotes a concern for inequalities in the distribution of social goods. Democratic participation provides opportunities for cooperation, for extending everyone's real liberties, and for reducing illegitimate inequalities. When people live within this cycle of compatible values, the sources of human friction—egotism, repression, injustice, and domination—can be eliminated, and conflict can be replaced by peace. And when people are motivated by these socialist values, the problem of scarcity can be solved by unleashing human energies that are currently restrained by alienation, poverty, and exploitation and by redirecting human energies away from unproductive competition and destructive conflicts.

While most socialists would accept this description of their fundamental goals, it must be augmented in two important ways. First, socialists understand that, beyond focusing on such value transformations, it is also important to articulate more concrete goals. Socialism is an ideology that wants to maximize public support so that socialist parties and candidates can win democratic elections. Thus, socialists propose a variety of specific measures—for example, increasing wages, shortening the work week, and making safer working conditions—that improve people's lives.[22] Second, socialists understand that their concrete goals and abstract values must continue to evolve. For example, Swedish Socialists are now focusing on two "new" goals for the twenty-first century.[23] While socialists have not previously been especially ecologically sensitive, there is an increasing realization that one of the foremost problems that must be resolved by cooperative action is the preservation of the natural environment. And while socialists have always been concerned with reducing the alienating aspects of work, they are now giving more attention to how work can be transformed into a genuinely pleasant aspect of life. "Quality work"—work that is cooperative and varied and results in products that are beautiful and enduring—may be just one of several emerging goals of socialism.

SUBSTANTIVE POLITICAL PRINCIPLES

Change

Although there is much overlap among Marxists, communists, and democratic socialists in their political bases—especially in their disdain for capitalism—democratic socialists depart from Marxists and communists in their principles regarding political change. While communists advocate revolutionary political change involving widespread rebellion by the working class, the seizure of political power by the dictatorship of the proletariat, and the sudden and forceful abolition of capitalism, socialists advocate evolutionary political change involving a broad transformation of values of all citizens, electoral victory by socialist and labor parties, and the adoption of political reforms and progressive public policies that tame the excesses of capitalism.

Eduard Bernstein provided several reasons for the socialist preference for evolutionary change over revolutionary change. First, Bernstein recognized that the objective conditions that Marx thought were necessary for a spontaneous revolution were nowhere in sight. European capitalism at the turn of the twentieth century was not about to collapse. Rather than producing massive unemployment, capitalism had created more jobs, as it became more diversified and specialized. Rather than impoverishing the working class, capitalism had produced a rapid rise in real wages. Rather than engaging in ruthless competition leading to the failure of many enterprises, capitalists had learned to cooperate among themselves and to regulate competition through the development of cartels, trusts, and joint-stock companies. And perhaps most importantly, the ownership of capital had become more diffused rather than more concentrated. All of these trends suggested that capitalism was

[22]Such "materialistic goals" have always been controversial within socialism, however, because some socialists believe that a focus on these practical issues will divert attention from socialism's more fundamental values and, thus, reduce socialism to "egalitarian liberalism."
[23]Barkan, "Sweden: Not Yet Paradise, But . . .", p. 151.

developing more harmoniously than had been predicted by Marx. Contemporary socialists agree that, instead of collapsing, capitalism has developed numerous mechanisms for averting an economic, social, and political crisis.

Second, Bernstein argued that the subjective conditions for a communist revolution were likewise fading. He argued that the working class was not becoming larger and more unified. It was not developing a "class consciousness" of its exploitation and alienation under capitalism, nor was it developing a commitment to revolutionary change. Contemporary socialists agree that the class structure of capitalism has become complex, diminishing revolutionary consciousness. Rather than being composed primarily of a small exploiting class of property-owning capitalists and a large exploited class of propertyless proletariat, mature capitalist societies have seen the evolution of several intermediate classes (e.g., the people who manage but do not own economic enterprises; white-collar salaried professionals like engineers, teachers, and civil servants; a "labor aristocracy" of highly skilled blue-collar workers who command high wages in the labor marketplace). Members of such classes are politically prominent but do not identify with the conditions and the revolutionary aims of the proletariat. However, such classes can support socialist organizations that merely hope to tame the excesses of capitalism and promote socialist values.

Third, Bernstein argued that Western industrial societies had become democratized in various ways—such as extending the vote to those without property—that facilitated the acquisition of power by socialist parties and their use of state authority to regulate capitalism, to exercise public control over property, and to distribute goods more fairly. Contemporary socialists point to continuing democratization throughout the world[24] and to the successful implementation of many socialist policies[25] to show that progress toward democracy can result in governmental reforms of capitalism and the evolution of the economy and society toward socialism.

Socialists also question whether revolutions actually produce enduring progressive change.[26] The French Revolution suggested to the Fabians and Revisionists that revolutions, although perhaps initiated in pursuit of noble ideals, inevitably become oppressive, as revolutionary leaders turn to coercion and violence to solidify their hold on power and to pursue their programs despite resistant populations. The Stalinist era following the Russian Revolution gave subsequent socialists additional evidence of the failures of revolutionaries to achieve their goals.

For socialists, reform can be much more enduring than revolutionary change. Sidney Webb argued that enduring change should be organic; it could

[24]Francisco Weffort, "The Future of Socialism," *Journal of Democracy* 3 (July 1992), pp. 90–99.

[25]Arnold J. Heidenheimer, Hugh Heclo, and Carolyn Teich Adams, *Comparative Public Policy*, 3d ed. (New York: St. Martin's Press, 1990).

[26]A landmark analysis of the repressive aftermath of revolutions remains Albert Camus's *The Rebel* (New York: Vintage Books, 1953).

not be imposed upon a society but must result from internal processes within society. Organic change had to be

> (1) Democratic, and thus acceptable to a majority of the people and prepared for in the minds of all; (2) gradual, and thus causing no dislocation, however rapid may be the rate of progress; (3) not regarded as immoral by the mass of people, and thus not subjectively demoralizing to them; and in this country, at any rate; (4) constitutional and peaceful.[27]

Recently, Bernard Crick has identified three time frames in the process of organic and evolutionary change. In the short run—which is the life of an existing administration or legislature—socialists must address immediate and particular abuses in the capitalist system and provide specific material benefits for citizens in order to build a political base for future socialist movements. Looking ahead twenty to twenty-five years, to the middle term, socialists must seek to change the enduring values of the next generation by demonstrating the deficiencies of existing institutions (such as private education and medicine) and the effectiveness and fairness of socialist practices (such as worker participation in corporate decision making). The long run, which is in the indefinite and faraway future, concerns the ideal socialist society. Socialists are little concerned with the achievement of a utopian final resting point, a time when socialism is achieved. They know that history is but a "long march" toward socialist ideals that will never be fully realized. Still, it is useful for socialists to refine and assert visions of a future ideal socialist society—not in a dogmatic manner but rather in a speculative manner—so that discussions of the good society are not limited to prevailing (liberal and conservative) values.[28] Such idealizations serve as reminders that socialism does not yet exist—even in those societies that have used democratic means to nationalize major industries or to create extensive welfare states. The limitations of such "socialist" institutions and policies ensure that they are only transitional stages in the slow and steady change toward the more full attainment of socialism.[29]

Finally, we should note that socialists—unlike Marxists—do not believe in the inevitability of the realization of socialist values or even of progress toward them. All that is inevitable is that the future will bring radical change. Capitalism, technology, and science—"our microbiology, phototonics, and superconductors"—are creating "epochal transformations of the very conditions of human life."[30] Such transformations could be regressive—promoting isolated individualism, reducing real freedom, increasing inequality, and being ultimately directed by a small number of political elites. Or such transformations could be progressive—leading toward socialist values. The task of socialist ideology is to clarify its principles in such a way as to inspire people to take as many small steps as they can down the road to socialism.

[27]Sidney Webb, *Socialism in England* (1890), quoted in Crick, *Socialism,* p. 68.
[28]Crick, *Socialism,* p. 113.
[29]Irving Howe, "The First 35 Years Were the Hardest," *Dissent* (spring 1989), p. 136.
[30]Michael Harrington, "Toward a New Socialism," *Dissent* (spring 1989), p. 163.

Structure

Being reformers, socialists are willing to move down the road to socialism using the political institutions that already exist within a given society. Constitutional and institutional arrangements that incorporate political rights and democratic principles offer socialists opportunities to pursue their values, win public support, and govern. Thus, rather than proposing fundamental constitutional changes, socialists focus on strengthening those existing institutions that facilitate the attainment of their goals. Hence, socialists want to enhance the role of political parties both in elections and in governance, because strong parties—especially strong socialist and labor parties—help organize and empower those with fewer economic resources. Socialists want to enhance the power of labor unions as an important countervailing force to corporate power in industry. In circumstances in which conservative and corporate interests are entrenched in state institutions, socialists may make proposals for "restructuring" and reorganization, but such proposals are limited and ad hoc. Because there are no clear socialist principles on how to structure government,[31] socialist proposals for institutional reform are, of necessity, opportunistic. Within contexts of particular problems and opportunities, socialists simply hope to make modest reforms in government structures that will allow working people to participate more readily in government and that seem likely to enhance the power of workers.

Rather than focusing on how to structure government, socialist theorists have focused on how to structure the broader political economy, but there is much disagreement here. On the one hand, centralists emphasize strong and disciplined political parties that control a strong state that owns most of the means of production and distributes many economic goods. On the other hand, decentralists emphasize face-to-face institutional arrangements in which political and economic power is dispersed among such organizations as industrial cooperatives, trade organizations and unions, local communities, and grassroots social movements. The term **market socialism** is often used to designate a mixed political economy having both the strong state institutions emphasized by centralists and the market institutions that are emphasized by decentralists.[32] Under market socialism, goods and services can be produced through at least six types of institutional arrangements:[33]

1. In **nationalized enterprises**, a centralized government owns the means of production, employs labor, and controls most decision making.
2. In **socialized enterprises**, the means of production are owned by various governments (and thus by the citizens of these governments) and these enterprises are accountable to the governments that own them. However,

[31]Crick, *Socialism*, p. 80.

[32]For a defense of market socialism, see John Roemer, *A Future for Socialism* (Cambridge: Harvard University Press, 1994).

[33]The following discussion draws extensively from Alex Nove, *The Economics of Feasible Socialism Revisited* (London: HarperCollins Academic, 1991), pp. 212–225.

workers of the plant directly or indirectly control most decision making and employ management to administer the enterprise. While nationalized enterprises normally have monopolistic control of a particular industry in a country, many socialized enterprises can compete with each other, developing different methods of production and product variations.

3. In **cooperatives**, the workforce owns the means of production and controls most decision making, subject to the regulations of various governments having jurisdiction over them.
4. In *private enterprise,* the means of production are owned by private stockholders and controlled by managers who are formally accountable to their stockholders and constrained by the agreements they make with other organizations (such as labor unions) and the regulations of those governments having jurisdiction over them.
5. In **worker-controlled private enterprises**, the means of production are owned by stockholders, but workers (and various affected publics) control decision making—either directly, or by selecting their managers, who are accountable to them.
6. In *individual entrepreneurial activity,* such unaffiliated persons as freelance writers, painters, and shopkeepers themselves own and control all the resources used in their businesses.

A political economy having some mix of these productive arrangements has many "market" characteristics. Many corporations are privately owned. The managers of the various types of enterprises must secure their resources in competitive markets; for example, even nationalized enterprises must attract workers from a labor market in which workers can try to secure higher wages and other benefits from the managers of other enterprises. Except for nationalized enterprises with monopoly control of their markets, enterprises must price their goods in ways that are competitive with those of other, similar enterprises (and even nationalized monopolies may have to consider international competition when setting prices). There is, for the most part, freedom of entry and exit throughout an economy of market socialism. Successful enterprises will encourage others to invest in the area, and unsuccessful enterprises will fail. Thus, market socialism encourages productivity and innovation.

This mix of productive arrangements also has many "public" characteristics. There is public ownership of some enterprises, especially those—like railroads and utilities—that are natural monopolies. The public can invest in certain industries by creating nationalized and socialized enterprises, and it can influence investment decisions elsewhere by having the state control credit and provide various financial incentives and disincentives for private investors. And the state can regulate production through labor, safety, environmental, trade, and other types of legislation.

In short, market socialism recognizes and exploits the benefits of economic markets. But extensive state participation in the political economy through public planning, regulation, and (at least occasional) ownership tempers competition and secures various public objectives.

Market socialism also has a mix of distributive organizational arrangements:

1. Individuals and organizations distribute commodities to other individuals and organizations based on the market principle of free exchange.
2. State agencies distribute many necessities to (potentially) everyone, as citizen rights.
3. Helping societies distribute some necessities and commodities to the poor, as mutual aid.

When thinking about distributive arrangements, socialists distinguish between commodities and necessities. "Commodities" are those goods (like luxury homes) and those services (like tennis lessons) that people often *want* but do not require. Socialists understand that people want a wide range of commodities, that such commodities are most efficiently distributed by the market, and that "market morality is a celebration of wanting, making, owning, and exchanging commodities."[34] In contrast, "necessities" are those goods (like minimal nutrition and basic housing) and those services (like police protection and essential medical care) that everyone needs in order to survive, to engage successfully in the pursuit of happiness, and to be free and contributing members of society.[35] Socialists with centralist perspectives have long maintained that necessities ought to be distributed by state agencies, because all citizens have a right to necessities, even if they cannot afford them in the marketplace. Such *nationalized distributions* are provided by state agencies that are merely acting as agents of the citizens of a nation, who are committed to providing for each other's essential needs and paying for these provisions through taxes. But socialists having more decentralist perspectives worry that the role played by state agencies in providing nationalized distributions undermines fraternal values; such distributions of necessities may be seen as "bureaucrats spending taxpayers' money" rather than as mutual aid. These socialists want to augment nationalized distributions with *socialized distributions*—which is aid to needy individuals provided directly by citizens through helping societies, rather than through the state. Helping societies are composed of citizens who, rather than being taxed on an involuntary basis to pay for assistance to others, give of their time, energy, and money on a voluntary and personal (face-to-face) basis.[36] Nevertheless, nationalized distributions—more than nationalized production—remain essential features of market socialism. To understand further the role of the state in a socialist political economy, we must consider socialist principles about governmental authority.

[34]Walzer, *Spheres of Justice* pp. 104–105.

[35]Mortimer Adler, *Six Great Ideas* (New York: Macmillan, 1981), pp. 164–173.

[36]This discussion of nationalized versus socialized distributions is drawn from Michael Walzer's "Socializing the Welfare State: Democracy in the Distributive Sector," *Dissent* (summer 1988), pp. 292–300. Walzer points out that helping societies should not be confused with more conservative philanthropic organizations that provide aid as charity. Conservative charities, like the United Way, are typically more bureaucratic and impersonal than socialist helping societies.

Authority

Like contemporary liberals, democratic socialists endorse a strong state; they believe that governmental authority should be expanded, as necessary, to deal with a variety of social problems. But socialists think that liberal governments usually fail to use their authority to attack the roots—or ultimate sources—of social problems, which lie in the capitalist system of production and distribution.

Consider, for example, the problem of crime. Liberals believe that crime is primarily caused by society's failure to provide poor and minority youths with adequate opportunities for social and economic advancement. Liberal governments thus hope to attack crime by using their authority to unblock opportunities—by improving education, providing job training, and so forth. In contrast, socialists believe that crime is inherent to capitalism. To ensure an adequate market for its products, capitalists stimulate acquisitive, materialistic appetites in all citizens, but the inequalities in wealth produced by capitalism leave the poor unable to satisfy these appetites through legal means. From a socialist perspective, crime can best be reduced by having government con-

Sidebar 9-2

The Socialist Perspective on Schools

It is instructive to contrast liberal and socialist perspectives on problems in education. An important educational problem for contemporary liberals occurs when rich white children attend better public schools than poor black ones do. In response, liberals in the United States have used governmental authority to desegregate schools, to equalize per-pupil expenditures among wealthy and poor school districts throughout a state, and to create special programs like Headstart and Upward Bound to help poor children catch up with their peers. While socialists do not reject such liberal approaches to educational problems, they believe they do not go far enough. The more fundamental problem is that the schools have not escaped capitalist domination. Socialists believe that schools teach the values and beliefs of conservative and liberal ideologies and mold children to accept passive roles in the prevailing political and economic systems. In the socialist perspective, the primary function of most schools in capitalist societies is to sort and label students, a process that ensures that the most advantaged children will be directed toward professional and managerial careers while the least advantaged children will be trained to perform and accept low-paying, unfulfilling jobs. For socialists, this educational problem can only be addressed by making schools completely autonomous from the existing political economy. Schools must enable students to be free and equal citizens of a democratic society instead of learning to be passive and unequal workers in a capitalist economy. To do this, governmental authority must be used to finance an equal basic education for all children in public schools and to protect such schools from pressure to use the curriculum as a means of advancing the goals of capitalism.

trol the ability of capitalism to generate excessive demands for its products (for example, by limiting advertising) and by redistributing wealth so that the poor have more resources with which to acquire goods legally.[37]

Because socialists believe that government authority should address various social problems and because they believe that such problems are ultimately rooted in capitalism, our discussion of socialist principles regarding governmental authority will focus on the role of government in producing and distributing economic goods. This discussion is complicated, however, by the fact that socialists agree only on the ends or purposes of governmental authority in the economy—they want government to curtail capitalist domination, to temper the spirit of competition with one of cooperation, to enhance real economic freedom, and to promote more equality. Socialists often disagree on whether specific governmental policies are likely to achieve these goals.

The founders of democratic socialism—the Revisionists and the Fabians—focused on economic production and supported the **nationalization of industry**. They wanted the state to own and manage most industries and thus employ most workers. They believed nationalization would promote communal harmony, as production could be based on rational assessments of social needs rather than on the basis of market competition. Nationalization would promote real freedom, because workers would no longer be dominated by private owners of the means of production. And nationalization would promote social equality because class distinctions between the bourgeoisie and the proletariat (and other classes or subclasses) would disappear when everyone worked for the state, and because the state could establish more equal wages than those that could be offered under capitalism.

For such reasons, many socialist parties, upon coming to power, have nationalized specific industries. For example, in Great Britain after World War II, the Labour Party nationalized the coal mines, the railroads, the utilities, and the iron and steel industries. In France in the early 1980s, the Socialist Party under François Mitterand nationalized almost all private banks, steel producers, a major armaments firm, and several multinational corporations. The Swedish Socialist Party (SAP) has created Statsforetag AB ("State Enterprise Ltd.") as a conglomerate of publicly owned industries, but Statsforetag accounts for only about five percent of Swedish productivity. Notice that in each of these cases nationalization has been limited to specific industries—particularly to those in which there were natural monopolies and extensive inefficiencies and where national priorities justified extensive investments by the national governments.

Wholesale nationalization of all private industry has never been seriously contemplated by socialists, for a variety of reasons. An initial constraint on large-scale nationalization is the cost of acquiring private enterprises. While communist regimes have been willing to confiscate private property by forceful means, socialist governments understand that capitalists are constitutionally and legally protected from confiscation of their property. Liberal laws

[37]Richard Quinney, *Criminology* (Boston: Little, Brown, 1979).

specify that the government can only acquire private property when such acquisitions serve compelling public purposes and when the owners of the property are fairly compensated. Providing just compensation to the owners of all private property is far beyond the means of any democratic government. Thus, socialists have had to be selective in choosing which industries they wish to purchase and manage.

In general, socialists have often concluded that nationalization of industry does not significantly enhance the achievement of socialist goals. Nationalized firms may have to compete with many other companies in an international marketplace, leading state authorities to treat workers in nationalized firms much like corporate managers of private companies treat their workers. As a result, there may be no greater degree of communal harmony, worker freedom, or economic equality in nationalized industries than exists in private ones. For example, nationalized firms in democratic societies have encountered two huge obstacles to promoting equality in wealth and income. First, the need to compensate the previous owners of private industries means that the actual act of nationalizing an industry results in little real change in the distribution of wealth. Second, the need to recruit skilled workers requires state authorities to base worker wages on market considerations. A petroleum engineer will command higher wages than a person who pumps gas at the local filling station, whether the employer is a nationalized firm like British Petroleum or a private firm like Amoco Oil.

Because of such difficulties, socialists have recently de-emphasized state ownership of the means of production and, instead, emphasized public control over economic production through **state planning**. Socialists differentiate three main levels of state planning: (1) comprehensive planning, as practiced by communists in the former Soviet Union, (2) partial socialist planning, as practiced by social democratic parties in Western Europe since World War II, and (3) minimal macroeconomic planning, as practiced by liberal governments in the United States. Socialists perceive many problems with comprehensive planning, in which central state authorities make all investment and production decisions for the economy: central planning promotes authoritarianism and discourages local initiatives; central planners are limited by inevitably imperfect foresight as they seek to predict changes in human tastes and technology; central planners focus on quantitative indicators of production performance, giving inadequate attention to the quality of goods produced; and central planners focus on achieving specified (minimal) goals, rather than taking risks that accompany innovation.[38] Such problems prompt socialists to reject comprehensive, or central, planning. In contrast, socialists accept the macroeconomic planning of the liberal state. Like liberals, socialists believe that governments should monitor the economy as a whole and introduce fiscal and monetary policies that stimulate stable growth, but socialists believe that governments should provide more explicit direction to, and extensive controls over, the economy than can be achieved by macroeconomic planning.

Socialists thus endorse a level of state planning that is intermediate in rela-

[38]Nove, *The Economics of Feasible Socialism Revisited*, pp. 73–85.

tion to comprehensive planning and macroeconomic planning. Under such partial socialist planning, the state normally directs and controls the economy in several ways.

First, planners project needs and preferences throughout the economy. To prevent bottlenecks in the production process—to avoid situations, for example, where production must slow down or cease because of inadequate energy supplies—state planners estimate the quantities of various resources (e.g., raw materials, component parts, and labor) that are necessary for production and develop plans to ensure their availability.

Second, the state controls major investment decisions, deciding where to build new plants and install new equipment in nationalized industries and influencing major private investments through control of banking and financing. The state determines those sectors of the economy that warrant new investments and those sectors that are no longer productive and successful, and thus require disinvestment.

Third, state planners monitor salaries, wages, and other compensation, establishing equitable compensation guidelines that reduce the huge and unjustified inequalities of an unregulated labor market.

Fourth, socialist planners seek to ensure job security for workers. However, rather than providing state subsidies to unproductive and failing industries to save jobs, the socialist state pursues job security by creating labor laws that protect workers from arbitrary dismissals and by facilitating worker mobility to more productive industries. For example, it provides vocational counseling, job retraining, job placement, and relocation subsidies for unemployed workers.

Fifth, the state monitors and regulates the products of both public and private enterprises. To protect consumer interests, it restrains excessive prices, it tests for the safety and reliability of goods, and it requires that companies adequately warrant and service their products. To guard against wasteful production and inefficiencies, it regulates such practices as pseudo product differentiation, garish packaging, and motivational rather than informative advertising.

Sixth, the state pursues foreign policy agreements that promote and secure the long-term economic interests of society. For example, the state may negotiate commodity agreements with other nations as a means of ensuring international markets for various goods for many years. Additionally, the socialist state is likely to seek cooperative agreements with underdeveloped nations that curtail the domination of northern countries over southern ones and that enhance global socialism. By providing international aid that transfers capital and technology to the southern hemisphere, socialists hope to reduce north-south hostilities, curtail such environmental problems as the deteriorating ozone layer and global warming, and enable southern nations to be prosperous consumers of northern products.[39]

Seventh, the state oversees the production of those goods that are distributed to citizens as rights. Most goods that are distributed to citizens as enti-

[39]Harrington, "Toward a New Socialism," p. 159–160.

tlements will be produced by the state. For example, public education and socialized medicine are publicly owned and controlled institutions, and teachers and doctors are employees of the state. Although socialists may allow certain entitlements to be produced by private firms—which are paid with public funds—they generally prefer state production of entitlements as the most effective way of ensuring adherence to state plans and goals, including the equal provision of entitlements to everyone.

The theoretical justification for extensive state planning rests on two related distinctions. First is the distinction between wants and needs. According to socialists, an unplanned, or market, system of production does a good job of responding to individual wants or preferences, but it does not do a good job of producing goods that respond to collective needs. When individuals want goods and can afford them, consumer demands are created that producers are motivated to satisfy by natural market forces, but some goods are needed by society as a whole or by individuals who are unable to pay for them. Socialist planning is needed to produce such goods. Second is the distinction between the short term and the long term. According to socialists, an unplanned economy responds well to short-term interests and forces but does not respond well to long-term interests and forces. The time horizons of producers, workers, and consumers are usually restricted. Enterprises are more concerned with short-term profits than long-term productivity. Workers are more concerned with annual wages than with the quality of their lives in the distant future. Consumers want to satisfy immediate gratifications rather than worry about tomorrow. State planners can better balance short-run goals with long-run goals than can actors in an unplanned and unregulated market. State planning to protect the environment, to enhance the education of all citizens, or to engage in research and development that can lead to cures of various illnesses are just some of the ways that state authority is used by socialists to give greater emphasis to long-term needs over short-term wants.

Socialists also claim that there is ample empirical evidence suggesting that socialist planning of the economy is superior to an unplanned economy. According to one socialist:

> The growth of the West European economies after 1945, with more extensive planning and much greater state intervention, was more rapid and stable than in any other period of modern history. . . . In the European socialist countries, the rate of growth was even higher, and in the face of great difficulties, most of these countries developed with remarkable speed the essential foundations of an advanced industrial society. . . . The success of planning may also be judged from the other side by observing that the two least-planned capitalist societies—Britain and the United States—are those which at present confront the greatest economic difficulties and show most clearly the symptoms of decline.[40]

Most socialists thus continue to favor an extensive role for government in the production of goods and services, but they put even greater emphasis, at least in recent years, on expanding the role of government in the distribution

[40]Tom B. Bottomore, *The Socialist Economy* (New York: Guilford Press, 1990), p. 48.

of goods and services. Socialists understand that most commodities—the goods that people prefer but don't need—should be distributed by the market. But socialists want the state to distribute as universal entitlements those goods that all need but are often unable to afford. While contemporary liberals also call for the state to distribute some goods as entitlements, the **social welfare state** is more expansive than the liberal welfare state in two respects. First, socialists think that people's needs are much more extensive than do liberals. Second, while liberals focus on the needs of the poor and the oppressed and often target entitlements to specific groups, socialists stress that certain needs are universal and thus claim that entitlements must be provided to everyone.

As one moves from classical liberalism to contemporary liberalism and then to socialism, there is a steady expansion of the concept of need and of the social contract to provide for needs. In classical liberalism, people are thought of as volitional beings—they are defined by their many wants and they are thought to have minimal needs. According to this ideology, people need the preservation of their natural individual rights (e.g., their right to own property), and the social contract is an agreement among citizens to form governmental authority that provides for the need of security. In contemporary liberalism, people are thought of as purposive beings—they want various kinds of lives, and certain goods (e.g., education, income, and power) are viewed as necessary means to the diverse ends that people want to pursue. According to this ideology, people need minimal amounts of these goods to have real opportunities to pursue their chosen lives, and the social contract is an agreement among citizens to have government provide baseline amounts of these goods. In socialism, people are considered to be social beings whose wants and needs are socially and culturally defined. According to this ideology, there is no particular list of goods that all people need. Instead, social, economic, and cultural conditions influence what people need in order to live individually fulfilling and socially productive lives within these conditions. In a socialist society, "the social contract is an agreement to reach decisions together about what goods are necessary to our common life, and then to provide those goods for one another."[41]

At least in an affluent and culturally sophisticated society, the goods that socialist citizens recognize as needed by everyone are likely to be much more extensive than those typically specified by liberals. Like classical liberals, socialists recognize the need for police and military protection. Like contemporary liberals, socialists perceive the need for basic education and the provision of minimal food and shelter for everyone. But socialists usually further recognize that contemporary societies have generated a large array of additional needs that could and should be available to everyone but that lower-income citizens cannot afford in the market. Major advances in medical treatments and capabilities, for example, have resulted in new conceptions of people's health needs, prompting socialists to argue that health is a needed good that ought to be socially (or communally) provided rather than distrib-

[41]Walzer, *Spheres of Justice*, p. 65.

uted by the market.[42] Vast changes in how cities are physically structured—with residential, industrial, and commercial areas often miles apart—have created new transportation needs, prompting socialists to call for the public provision of mass transport. Changes in family life and the economy have resulted in mothers joining fathers in the workplace, creating new needs in the areas of child care, prompting socialists to call for public day care facilities and family-leave policies allowing people to take time off work to deal with parental responsibilities. Such a list could be extended indefinitely, but there is no objective or natural list of human needs. Because all citizens have a reasonable understanding of what people need to thrive in their particular societies, an open, democratic process is the appropriate method of determining entitlements.

The socialist welfare state is also more universal than the liberal welfare state.[43] For socialists, socially recognized needs become **universal entitlements** that are provided to everyone based on their common citizenship rather than on some other criterion, such as destitution or prior contribution. Thus, the food stamp program in the United States is more consistent with liberal than socialist principles, because it provides for the nutritional needs of only those people living below the poverty level. Similarly, the Social Security program is more consistent with liberal than socialist principles, because it provides higher retirement payments to those who have made greater contributions to the program. In contrast, the fact that public schools are available to all children make them a universal and socialist entitlement. Socialized medicine provides specified medical care to all citizens regardless of how wealthy they are or how much (or little) they pay in taxes, unlike the market-based system in the United States. While liberals propose subsidies to poor families for child care, socialists argue that day care centers are a universal need and should be available to all families.

By targeting the poor for entitlements, it may appear that liberal welfare policies are more likely than social welfare policies to equalize conditions, which seems odd, because socialists value equality more than liberals. But socialists defend universal entitlements on a number of grounds. First, universal entitlements recognize the common needs that people have in response to their common problems. Wealthy working mothers as well as poor working mothers need quality day care. By providing universal entitlements, everyone makes a commitment to each other to provide for their common needs. Second, socialists view universal entitlements as an important antidote to middle- and upper-class hostility toward the liberal welfare state. The relatively well-off may view means-tested entitlements as redistributive, prompting

[42]Rashi Fein, "National Health Insurance," *Dissent* (spring 1992), pp. 157–163.

[43]Discussions of the importance of universal social provisions are found in William Julius Wilson, *The Truly Disadvantaged* (Chicago: University of Chicago Press, 1987), pp. 149–164; and Margaret Weir, Ann Schola Orloff, and Theda Skocpol, *The Politics of Social Policy in the United States* (Princeton: Princeton University Press, 1988), pp. 441–445. Skocpol links proposals for universal programs to democratic socialism in "Legacies of New Deal Liberalism," in *Liberalism Reconsidered,* edited by Douglas MacLean and Claudia Mills (Totowa, N.J.: Rowman and Allenheld, 1983), p. 102–103.

them to resent paying higher taxes for welfare benefits targeted toward those who, they believe, contribute little to society. Because universal entitlements benefit everyone, they help generate support for the welfare state, enhancing its long-term viability and prospects for expansion. Third, socialists believe that even universal entitlements promote equality of condition. While everyone may equally consume universal entitlements, such provisions constitute a relatively large share of all goods available to the poor and a relatively small share of all goods available to the rich. Thus, such entitlements provide a much greater increase in the quality of life of the poor than of the rich. Moreover, universal entitlements are normally paid for, in socialist states, by highly progressive taxes. Because the rich pay much more of the costs of entitlements than do the poor, the new social provisions lessen economic inequalities between the rich and the poor.

Most socialists regard nationalized distributions as being more successful than nationalized production.[44] By prompting people to recognize their common needs, the social welfare state promotes communal harmony. By making welfare a citizen right, it decreases the dependency of the poor on charity and thus increases their freedom. By linking the availability of some goods to equal citizenship rather than to unequal wealth, it fosters equality. But some socialists question the success of the social welfare state. Is communal harmony and fraternal fellow feeling better achieved by a fairly abstract social contract administered by the national government or by people coming to the aid of their neighbors? Are recipients of national welfare really free—or do they remain dependent on the state, incapable of shaping their own lives and of contributing to society?[45] Recognizing the limitations of the social welfare state, socialists regard it as one stage in the development of socialism and as only one element in the socialist program. Consequently, many socialists believe that the social welfare state must increasingly be complemented (and perhaps replaced) by helping associations in which people band together to contribute their time, energy, and resources to those with unmet needs. While such proposals have a distinctively "conservative" flavor, they well illustrate that the socialist commitment to a strong state is ultimately instrumental. It is not inherent in socialist ideology to seek a strong national government that controls many production and distribution decisions. Only commitment to socialist values is inherent in socialism, and socialist support of a strong state is dependent on the capacity of that state to promote social democratic values such as communal harmony, individual freedom, and social equality.

Justice

Socialists seek "social justice," but they are reluctant to describe any particular distribution of economic and other social goods as just. It is clear to socialists that the distribution of wealth produced under capitalism is unjust or

[44]Walzer, "Socializing the Welfare State," pp. 293–294.
[45]Walzer, "Socializing the Welfare State," p. 294.

unfair. They recognize that many fortunes have been gained by exploiting others (and the environment), and they recognize that the poor have been victims of many forms of oppression. They argue that people's incomes bear little relationship to how hard they work, to their contribution to society, or to their moral merit.

One reason why capitalism fails to distribute goods fairly, according to socialists, is that liberalism provides a faulty principle of justice. For liberals, justice is achieved if inequalities occur under conditions in which everyone has an *equal opportunity* of winning competitive races to get greater shares of those goods being sought. Formal equal opportunity ensures that everyone faces equal "hurdles"; the hurdles for minorities, women, and the poor are no higher than those for whites, men, and the wealthy. Fair equal opportunity ensures that social policies have been implemented that compensate socially disadvantaged competitors in ways that bring them to the same "starting line" as their more advantaged competitors. Socialists realize that formal and fair equal opportunities are important because they make unequal human rewards reflect differences in individual choices and efforts rather than undeserved differences in natural attributes and in social circumstances. Nevertheless, socialists see several limitations with this conception of justice. Equal opportunity encourages people to be preoccupied with being more successful than others—with rising to the top of the pyramids of education, wealth, status, and power—rather than encouraging them to attain satisfaction by simply acquiring knowledge, engaging in challenging work, and so forth. It prompts people to view others as competitors to be surpassed or defeated in the pursuit of scarce goods, rather than as companions with whom one can cooperate to achieve common goals. Equal opportunity justifies the victories and losses that occur in this struggle for scarce goods. The winners think they have won a fair fight under conditions of equal opportunity, and they see themselves—and are often seen by others—as better people. Meanwhile, the losers think they have lost a fair fight, and they see themselves—and are seen often by others—as inferior people. Such beliefs are wrong, because the winners may have merely been more ruthless or just more lucky than the losers. Because of these limitations, socialists believe that there should be a conception of social justice that goes beyond equal opportunity.[46]

For socialists, this more basic conception of justice is *not*—as is often believed—a simple **equality of condition**. Socialists recognize that a society in which everyone had absolutely equal amounts of education, wealth, power, or any other social good would be both undesirable and impossible. An equal distribution of any social good would restrict the liberty of those people who had the capacities and motivation to obtain more than the equal allotment. Unequal distributions of certain goods (such as advanced education for doctors and scientists or extensive political influence for elected officials) can benefit the public. Attempts to maintain equal distributions of such goods as wealth would necessitate a despotic government that continually meddled in

[46]Schaar, "Equal Opportunity and Beyond."

individual lives. And even such governments would inevitably fail to achieve equal conditions:

> We know that money equally distributed at twelve noon of a Sunday will have been unequally redistributed before the week is out. Some people will save it, and others will invest it, and still others will spend it (and they will do so in different ways).[47]

Seeking a society that provides more than merely equal opportunity, yet shy of static equal conditions, socialists want an **egalitarian society**, "one in which everybody would see each other as sister and brother, of equal worth and potential."[48] Socialists try to put such moral sentiments into practice in several ways.

First, explanations and justifications for inequalities are sought and assessed for validity. Inequalities reflecting individual choices and efforts are usually regarded as acceptable; discovering the legitimate bases for such inequalities helps reduce the social friction that they might otherwise spark. Inequalities arising from undeserved differences in social circumstances, however, are criticized, and public policies are sought to reduce such inequalities.[49]

Second, efforts are made to reduce inequalities in wealth, power, and other goods, even though legitimate and marginal differences in such goods remain. For example, material conditions are made more equal by collecting inheritance taxes and using the revenue from such taxes to provide more entitlements. Incomes can be made more equal by pursuing solidaristic wage policies providing equal pay for equivalent work across various industries nationwide.[50] Political power is made more equal through policies that encourage the organization and participation of groups of disadvantaged citizens.

Third, efforts can be made to contain deleterious effects of unequal distributions. Laws can block certain uses of money that permit the wealthy to have excessive options and opportunities that are unavailable to the less well-off.[51] For example, the capacity of money to buy better or more extensive education for the children of the rich could be reduced. Constitutional limitations and ethics laws can regulate the performance of public officials, constraining their ability to convert political power to personal gain.

Fourth, efforts could be made to make inequalities less permanent. For example, rather than giving some professors endowed chairs for the rest of their careers, economic bonuses and honors could be rotated among deserving professors on an annual (or other periodic) basis.

Finally, noncumulative inequalities would be promoted by efforts to have

[47]Walzer, *Spheres of Justice,* p. xi.

[48]Crick, *Socialism,* p. 90

[49]Determining what constitutes legitimate and illegitimate inequalities is a difficult problem that democratic socialists need to address more fully.

[50]In this area, socialists need to solve the problem posed by the apparent incommensurability of various kinds of work. It is unclear, for example, whether the work of a farmer is equal to that of a factory worker.

[51]Walzer, *Spheres of Justice,* pp. 100–102.

those with high levels of one good receive lower levels of other goods. In this regard, severing the link between having wealth and acquiring political power—for example, by having public financing of political campaigns—would be particularly important. As another example, those with the most education and the most prestigious jobs would not necessarily be given the highest wages and the longest vacations.

These principles show that the socialist goal of egalitarianism is nothing so simple as the equal distribution of all goods. Instead, it is a desire to move toward a society in which everyone is respected as a human being, and in which no human being is treated as a means to the good of others. No particular distribution of goods would conform to socialist ideals. Instead, the precise characterization of social justice "would remain perpetually ambiguous, open, flexible, debatable, a moving horizon that is never quite reached, irreducible to either economic formula or legislative final solution."[52]

Rulers

The socialist commitment to egalitarianism leads directly to a much more populist interpretation of democracy than those expressed by other ideologies. While conservatives, liberals, and Marxists support certain types of democracy, they also concentrate power in a ruling class that is considered to be more competent than ordinary citizens. But socialists believe that the ends of politics—communal harmony, individual freedom, and social justice—are not complex ideals, known only by an elite few. Instead, socialists believe that, potentially, everyone has the wisdom to grasp these ideals, the moral virtue to be guided by them, and the intelligence to make reasonable judgments about the particular policies and arrangements that will move society closer to the realization of these ideals.[53] Of course, socialists recognize that not everyone is guided by these ideals. Traditional prejudices and the material competitiveness of capitalism have hindered acceptance of socialist ideals among citizens. Socialists thus believe that democracy is an ideal that can be approached but never fully realized.

Rudimentary forms and institutions of democracy emergent in the nineteenth century encouraged socialists to believe that socialism could be pursued by democratic means. For example, the Fabians recognized that the **Chartist movement**, which was particularly influential between 1837 and 1848, gave impetus to many electoral reforms in England—such as universal manhood suffrage, equal electoral districts, the secret ballot, the abolition of property qualifications for candidates to Parliament, and payment of members of Parliament—which made it possible for the working class to be better represented in Parliament and which prompted all representatives to be more responsive

[52]Crick, *Socialism*, p. 90.

[53]Rousseau's *Social Contract* provides an enduring vision of such democratic ideals, making Rousseau one of the favorite classical philosophers of democratic socialists.

to the needs and values of the working class.[54] In short, electoral reforms that democratized British politics in the nineteenth century made it possible for a socialist party to seek the electoral support of the now enfranchised majority of Englishmen who were exploited and alienated under capitalism and thus enabled such a party to gain control of the English government through democratic elections.

Socialists recognize, however, that representative democracy is not a complete realization of democratic ideals, for two major reasons. First, socialist values may not be sufficiently dominant among citizens and representatives to guide the democratic process effectively. Even representatives who are socialists may emphasize the immediate economic concerns of their constituents rather than the longer-term realization of socialist values. Second, inequalities in ownership and control of the means of production create persistent and illegitimate political inequalities within the system of representative democracy. Rather than responding to grassroots concerns and preferences, representatives respond primarily to the needs of capitalists and to the preferences of those with disproportionate wealth and status. Representative democracy must, therefore, be continually reformed in ways that enhance the equality of influence between such capitalist interests as industrialists, bankers, and realtors and such countervailing actors as labor unions, environmentalists, and neighborhood groups.

Socialists also want to augment the institutions of representative democracy with those of populist democracy. While liberals are unconcerned even when most citizens choose to be inactive politically, socialists want citizens to be more actively involved in addressing and resolving community problems in many contexts.[55]

First, and most importantly, socialists support economic democracy, or **workplace democracy**. The workplace is a vital arena for democratic participation, because it is the place where people spend most of their lives and where relationships of authority and subordination are most pronounced. The importance of workplace democracy to socialism was emphasized by G. D. H. Cole (1889–1959), a British socialist professor who regarded the subordination of workers to their economic bosses as slavery and held it to be a greater evil than poverty.[56] Cole pointed to several positive effects of enhancing the involvement and influence of employees in industrial decision making. It would develop their appreciation of the socialist ideals of harmony, freedom,

[54]The Chartist movement emphasized radical democratic politics, but it did not embrace socialism. For example, the Chartists wanted unemployed workers to be provided with small holdings of land and capital in order to produce a more competitive market system of small proprietors.

[55]For an excellent analysis of the limitations of liberal democracy and a description of populist democracy, see Benjamin Barber's *Strong Democracy: Participatory Politics for a New Age* (Berkeley: University of California Press, 1984).

[56]G. H. D. Cole, *Self-Government in Industry* (London: G. Bell, 1919), p. 33. A more recent argument for workplace democracy is provided by Carole Pateman in *Participation and Democratic Theory* (New York: Cambridge University Press, 1970), pp. 67–84.

and justice; it would enhance their skills of participating in the democratic process; and thus, it would train workers for social democracy in the larger world. Workplace democracy would reduce workers' fear of authorities, instill in management an appreciation of the capacities of workers, and thus diminish social and class distinctions. And greater worker involvement would unleash the suppressed talents and energies of workers, enhancing economic productivity. Many recent experiments with worker participation in the governance of economic institutions provide encouragement to socialists (and even some liberals) about its effectiveness.[57]

Second, socialists support **grassroots democracy**. Just as socialists want citizens to exercise more power in their workplaces, they also want citizens to exercise more power in the other organizations and associations in which they live their daily lives: families, religious groups, schools, civic groups, ethnic associations, neighborhoods, and so forth.[58] Thus, socialists want to "democratize" the family, equalizing the power of husbands and wives and ensuring that the needs and interests of children will be heard and respected. They also want to democratize their local communities, employing neighborhood assemblies to provide opportunities for citizens to discuss their immediate problems and goals, using community boards and task forces to develop concrete policy proposals, and enacting policies through city councils made more representative by such devices as selection by lot and frequent rotation of office.[59] By practicing more democracy at the grassroots level, citizens should become more skilled at defending their rights and interests in national politics. By learning how to promote communal harmony, individual freedom, and social justice locally, they will incorporate such socialist values into their analysis of national issues.

Third, socialists often support **direct democracy**, in which citizens can bypass representative institutions and place certain issues on the national agenda through public initiatives and can resolve national issues by referendum. Because they recognize that the vast majority of issues must inevitably be resolved by full-time legislators, socialists do not wish to replace representative democracy with direct democracy. But allowing citizens to vote directly on some key issues has several advantages. First, direct democracy may be an antidote to the domination of representative legislatures by special interests, especially corporate power.[60] Second, the possibility that issues will be put to a public vote should encourage representatives to act as delegates of their constituents, thereby increasing their responsiveness and sense of accountability

[57]In *A Preface to Economic Democracy* (Berkeley: University of California Press, 1985), Robert Dahl argues that worker-controlled enterprises "are likely to tap the creativity, energies, and loyalties of workers to an extent that stockholder-owned corporations probably never can, even with profit-sharing schemes" (p. 132).

[58]Harry Boyte, *The Backyard Revolution: Understanding the New Citizen Movement* (Philadelphia: Temple University Press, 1980).

[59]Barber, *Strong Democracy*, pp. 267–278.

[60] It can be argued, however, that, corporate power may also influence citizens in referenda. See Thomas E. Cronin, *Direct Democracy* (Cambridge: Harvard University Press, 1989), pp. 99–116.

to the public. Third, providing for referenda and initiatives both acknowledges the wisdom, virtue, and judgment of citizens and encourages citizens to develop further these qualities. Contemporary liberals have exhausted the possibilities of quantitatively enlarging the franchise by extending the vote to everyone. By supporting direct democracy, socialists want to enlarge the franchise qualitatively, giving citizens not only a chance to select candidates who endorse socialist values but also opportunities to enact policies that can lead society down the road to socialism.

Citizenship

Socialists claim to have a much stronger sense of citizenship than do liberals. Their concern for communal harmony leads socialists to recognize that people are members of various groups and communities that offer them support and to which they give support in return. Their concern for individual liberty and their disdain for political domination leads socialists to emphasize the need for citizens to participate fully in the policy making of each such community. And their concern for social justice requires that socialists acknowledge the extensive obligations that this view of citizenship imposes.

While liberals emphasize one's citizenship within a particular nation, socialists acknowledge one's **multiple citizenships**. Socialists agree with liberals that a person is a citizen of a nation-state (and its various subnational governments), and their principles regarding the admission of newcomers as citizens to nation-states are similar to those of liberals. But socialists recognize that people are also citizens of supranational entities (e.g., the world community) and that this citizenship imposes certain moral obligations upon them. They also stress that people are citizens of nonstate communities (e.g., industrial enterprises, trade unions, minority groups, and women's groups) that make various demands on them. While contemporary liberals also recognize multiple memberships, they regard memberships in nonstate communities as elements of one's private life and as imposing moral obligations that can justify disobedience to the state and thus limit one's political obligations as a citizen. In contrast, socialists view multiple citizenships in states *and* in nonstate communities as essential parts of one's public life. Rather than limiting one's political obligations, citizenship in, say, a cooperative or a women's group extends one's need to participate in public life and to bear additional obligations to other members of these communities.

While liberals believe that citizens can be best served by limiting their participation, socialists call for extensive citizen participation. Citizen participation should begin locally, in families, schools, churches, neighborhood groups, and—most importantly—the workplaces of daily life. By actively participating in such local communities, citizens attain a greater sense of belonging, concern, and mutuality with others. Through such participation, they can use local groups as vehicles for solving common problems and thus exercise greater collective control over their lives. And a recognition that others should also participate in the decisions of local groups extends one's commitment to political equality. Greater participation in local communities and workplaces will also help to politicize the relatively disadvantaged who don't participate fully in national elections and policy-making processes. The resultant greater and more representative participation of the citizenry in politics at the national level can begin to rectify the limitations of representative democracy and thus approach the social democractic ideals of political equality and popular control of government.

Socialists want to extend citizen obligations beyond those stressed by liberals. At best, liberals connect citizen obligations to citizen rights, as liberal principles of political obligation are based on contract theories specifying that citizens get certain goods and rights in exchange for meeting various obligations. Socialists regard the liberal social contract as too individualistic and shortsighted. Before willingly meeting their obligations to pay taxes for welfare services or to serve in the military for national security, liberal citizens are inclined to ask, "Am I personally benefited by these services?" and, "What has the government done for me lately?" Socialists expect citizens to take a less individualistic and more farsighted approach to what the social contract and the obligations that it imposes mean. For socialists, the social contract is not so much an agreement among individuals about their individual rights as it is a common understanding among citizens about their common needs and their obligation to cooperate with one another to satisfy these needs. What people need is not just the provision of individual rights but community itself, and thus people are obligated to give each other the respect and support needed to sustain themselves as a community.[61] Additionally, citizens must participate in a collective decision-making process that enables them to identify what each individual needs in order to thrive in these communities. Once these needs—such as those for basic shelter, medical care, and transportation—have been identified, the socialist social contract calls on everyone to "pitch in" to satisfy these needs for all. Socialists do not try to provide a specific list of citizen obligations, because these obligations will depend on what each community regards as its common needs and universal obligations. Socialists would surely regard the communal provisions and accompanying obligations of American communities as inadequate.[62]

The difference between liberal and socialist views regarding citizen obligation can be illustrated by considering the issue of "public service." President Clinton's proposal to have youth work for one or two years in public service jobs in order to pay back college loans is an attempt by a contemporary liberal to extend the liberal conception of citizen obligation. Citizens—but only some citizens—are asked to serve, and their obligation to serve is directly tied to receiving a concrete and material personal benefit (student aid) that is otherwise unavailable to them. In contrast, socialists call for "a program of universal citizen service [that] would enlist every American citizen—male and female alike—in a service corps for one to two years of either military or non-

[61]Walzer, *Spheres of Justice*, pp. 64–65.
[62]Walzer, *Spheres of Justice*, p. 84.

military training and service."[63] Participants in the universal service programs of socialists would get some individual benefits, such as occupational training, but the greatest advantages garnered would be "fellowship and camaraderie, common activity, teamwork, service for and with others, and a sense of community . . . cooperation . . . and mutuality."[64] While extensive in comparison to liberal service—and mandatory instead of optional—socialist service is far less extensive and coercive than that conceived of by the fascist state, because socialist service covers only a brief period in the lives of youths and because people are provided choices as to where they will serve (e.g., in the military; in an international "peace corps"; in urban areas to aid the elderly, provide child care, or repair the infrastructure; in rural areas to work on ecological programs and flood control).

Liberals dislike such socialist proposals for extensive citizenship. Reflecting the liberal preference for private leisure over public participation, Oscar Wilde once commented that "the problem with socialism is that it takes too many evenings." And reflecting on the prospect of universal national service may prompt many students to believe that the problem with socialism is that it can take up too many years. Socialists reply that such criticisms embody the erroneous liberal belief that life can be segmented into a public life of citizenship and a private life of personal satisfaction. For the socialist, all life is necessarily social life. We are citizens even in the privacy of our homes, because our families (or other intimate associations) are de facto political associations involving collaborative problem solving, the identification of common needs, and the application of power. We are citizens at work, because our workplaces also involve collaborative problem solving, the identification of common needs, and the application of power. And the decisions of government and other public institutions profoundly affect how we live our "daily"—if not ever quite "private"—lives. Because it is impossible to distinguish public from private life, people are always citizens. By recognizing and acting upon the needs of people to participate in collective decision making and to accept their obligations as citizens, the socialist goals of communal harmony, individual freedom, social equality, and political democracy can be furthered.

THE PHILOSOPHICAL BASES

Ontology

As we have seen, socialists seek to change the world of capitalist domination by transforming liberal values into socialist ones and by pursuing socialist values through democratic applications of political power. Such a program is at odds with the Marxist ontology of economic determination. For orthodox

[63]Benjamin Barber, *Strong Democracy*, pp. 298–303. See also Walzer, "Socializing the Welfare State," pp. 298–299.
[64]Barber, *Strong Democracy*, p. 302.

Marxists, the economic infrastructure determines the social superstructure, which includes cultural values and the distribution of political power. Because capitalism requires and supports the liberal values of competition, rugged individualism, and equal opportunity, Marxist ontology asserts that socialist values cannot spread as long as capitalism persists. Because capitalism requires and supports the kind of representative democracy that empowers the capitalist class, Marxist ontology asserts that the development of more populist democratic institutions will inevitably be thwarted by capitalism. Eduard Bernstein viewed this orthodox Marxist ontology as being too materialist and too deterministic. Bernstein argued that orthodox Marxists are overly reductionist when they locate the source of all values and ideas in material and economic conditions.[65] In short, Bernstein claimed that ideology, ideas, and ethical considerations are important aspects of ultimate reality and that they are at least partly independent of economic factors.

While rejecting the materialism of Marx, the founders of democratic socialism did not, however, embrace the leading alternative ontology of the nineteenth century, Hegel's idealism, which claimed that ideas alone were real and that ideas determined historical progress. Instead, Bernstein turned to **neo-Kantianism** in order to synthesize these two ontologies.[66] In brief, Kant had distinguished between facts and values. For Kant, facts—like Marx's laws of economics and history—were part of the phenomenal world of appearance and could be known by humans through experience and reflection. But values and morality were part of a deeper ultimate reality (including God and immortality) that lay beyond the phenomenal world and was independent of factual and material considerations. Neo-Kantianism did not reject Marx's economic determinism but rather subordinated it to a deeper reality of morality and values. Neo-Kantianism permitted humans to will freely certain moralities—such as socialist values—simply because they were judged to be "right," rather than necessary.

Socialist ontology can also be understood by contrasting it with that of classical liberalism. As we have seen, classical liberals thought that historical progress was determined by natural laws; according to Herbert Spencer, for example, human progress requires the survival of the fittest, implying that progress is best served by letting the weak and unfit become extinct. But socialists refuse to be governed by such natural laws. According to T. H. Huxley, "social progress means a checking of the cosmic progress [of natural selection] at every step and the substitution for it of another, which may be called the ethical process."[67] In short, instead of submitting to a natural world of self-assertion, competition, and domination, humans can use their moral will to impose self-restraints, help their fellows, and create a just society.

Because they reject Marxist materialism and liberal naturalism, it can be

[65]Bernstein, *Evolutionary Socialism,* pp. 13–14.

[66]This discussion is based on McLellan, *Marxism After Marx,* pp. 33–38.

[67] T. H. Huxley, "Evolution and Ethics," in *Selections from the Essays of Huxley,* edited by Alburey Castell (Arlington Heights, Ill.: Crofts Classics, 1948 [1893]).

maintained that socialists do not ground their political ideology in any particular ontology. In one sense, this is true, because socialists do not claim to know ultimate reality and they believe that human history is neither determinate nor finite. In another sense, this is not true, because socialists do embrace certain ontological assumptions. Socialists believe that values are real, that they affect social life, and that they are at least partially independent of economic forces, natural laws, and other constraints on our freedom of choice. Socialists believe that humans—and human choices—can influence the course of evolution and history. Humans *should* choose democratic socialism, but humans *can* choose alternative ideologies. The choice is ours, and the course of history will reflect our choice.

Epistemology

Socialists do not believe that there is an independent epistemological basis for asserting the truth of socialist values. Their neo-Kantian ontology forces them to admit that humans cannot have certain knowledge that the values of communal harmony, individual freedom, social justice, and popular democracy should be pursued. Such values are chosen rather than known and accepted a priori. Because socialists recognize the subjectivity involved in choosing socialist values, they acknowledge that the values of their ideological competitors cannot be discounted. Socialists are thus willing to tolerate those ideologies that tolerate socialism, making socialism one of the "friends" of democratic pluralism.[68]

This does not mean that socialists doubt that there is an abundance of good reasons for choosing to pursue socialist ends. Indeed, they often employ arguments drawn from the epistemological orientations of their ideological competitors to justify socialist goals.

To persuade classical liberals to embrace various universal economic entitlements, for example, some socialists have employed natural-law arguments.[69] Such socialists maintain that human beings are, by nature, equal in their common humanity and in certain species-specific properties, including their biological need for subsistence to survive and their natural need for certain comforts to live humanly well. Given these natural and equal needs, socialists argue that each person has a right to "all due necessities: honorable and fitting work . . . decent surroundings. . . . and leisure."[70]

To persuade contemporary liberals, socialists have used utilitarianism to argue that more economic equality maximizes the aggregate sum of happiness for humans as a whole. Since the satisfaction experienced by a poor man from the gain of a given sum of money is greater than the dissatisfaction that a rich

[68]Bernard Crick, *In Defense of Politics* (Middlesex, England: Penguin Books, 1962).

[69]See Mortimer J. Adler, *Six Great Ideas* (New York: Macmillan, 1981), pp. 164–173. Most socialists argue, however, that needs are socially defined rather than defined by a determinate human nature.

[70]William Morris, in a lecture on Jan. 13, 1884. The full quote is provided in Crick, *Socialism*, p. 67.

man experiences from the loss of that same sum of money, overall happiness in society is increased by redistributing money from the rich to the poor.[71]

To persuade conservatives, socialists have drawn upon tradition in order to justify certain applications of socialist values. For example, in the United States, traditional patriotic and religious values may be used to justify the establishment of more national holidays and the enactment of more "blue laws" prohibiting work on the Sabbath as ways of increasing universal provision of leisure time.[72]

While socialist scholars hope that such justifications help convince people to accept the values of communal harmony, individual freedom, social equality, and popular democracy, they have been more concerned with showing deficiencies in the attainment of these values in existing capitalist societies. *Socialist social science* thus begins by describing departures from socialist ideals. Studies of "anomie"—a condition of personal detachment from the community and others in the community—reveal widespread and increasing departures from communal values.[73] Studies of "social control" reveal how the real liberties of individuals are compromised by capitalism and by even the most benevolent institutions of liberal governments.[74] Studies of the distribution of income and wealth reveal inequalities that shock the egalitarian spirit.[75] And studies of political power structures suggest illegitimate domination of democratic institutions by corporate chieftains.[76] By documenting departures from socialist and democratic ideals, social scientists with socialist orientations hope to awaken people to the need to pursue vigorously socialist alternatives.

Socialist social science also attempts to explain departures from socialist ideals. Of particular importance are the causes of economic and political inequalities. Inequalities of income might be acceptable if, for example, they were caused by such factors as natural differences in individual traits (e.g., IQ genotype) or in differences in individual effort (e.g., choosing to stay in school longer). But when research indicates that income differences are better

[71]Arthur Cecil Pigou, *The Economics of Welfare,* 4th ed. (London: Macmillan, 1948), p. 89.

[72]Walzer, *Spheres of Justice,* pp. 184–196. Socialists have long understood that leisure time is a fundamental human necessity and have complained that, under capitalism, the rich are able to buy much more of it than ordinary citizens. Observance of many holidays and of the Sabbath are conservative traditions while also being socialist measures to provide a baseline of leisure time to everyone.

[73]Steven Lukes, "Alienation and Anomie," in *Philosophy, Politics, and Society,* 3d ed., edited by Peter Laslett and W. G. Runciman (Oxford: Basil Blackman, 1967), pp. 140–156; and Herbert McClosky and John Schaar, "Psychological Dimensions of Anomy," *American Sociological Review* 30 (1965), pp. 14–40.

[74]Frances Fox Piven and Richard A. Cloward, *Regulating the Poor: The Functions of Public Welfare* (New York: Vintage Books, 1971).

[75]Harrell R. Rodgers, *Poverty Amid Plenty* (Reading, Mass.: Addison-Wesley, 1979); and E. Goffman, "The Income Gap and Its Causes," *Dissent* (winter 1990).

[76]C. Wright Mills, *The Power Elite* (New York: Oxford University Press, 1956); and G. William Domhoff, *The Power Elite and the State: How Policy is Made in America* (New York: A. DeGrayter, 1990).

Sidebar 9-3

*The Distribution of Household Income and Wealth in the United States**

Families, ranked by income (lowest to highest)	*% of total income* in 1947	in 1971	in 1991	% of total net worth in 1984	% of total financial assets in 1984
Lowest 20 percent	3.4	4.1	3.8	-1	-4
Middle 60 percent	51.1	52.4	49.7	34	14
Highest 20 percent	45.5	43.5	46.5	67	90

The above data on the distribution of income for 1947, 1971, and 1991 indicate the extent and degree of economic inequality in the United States. They suggest that the degree of income inequality has been fairly constant since 1945, though income inequality decreased slightly during the era of the "great society" and increased again during the Reagan era. These data also show that the richest 20 percent of all Americans have had over 10 times as much annual income as the poorest 20 percent of all Americans. While such inequalities may seem shocking in themselves, even more disturbing is the fact that such data significantly *underestimate* economic inequality. First, in arriving at these figures, the mean income of households with incomes greater than $100,000 was assumed to be $100,000 exactly. This assumption has the effect of making the shares of the highest income group about 20 percent smaller in the table than they actually were. Second, measures of the distribution of wealth for 1984 (reported in the last two columns) suggest the existence of much more inequality than is indicated by the measures of the distribution of income. When wealth is conceptualized as net worth—as the value of all family assets less any debts—survey samples show that the poorest families typically have more debts than assets and that the richest families have 67 percent of all net worth. Moreover, when wealth is conceptualized solely as net financial assets—a measure which excludes homes and vehicles and considers only those assets that are available for future transactions (like bank savings and holdings of stocks and bonds)—survey data suggest that about 90 percent of all such wealth is held by the richest 20 percent of all families.

*The data for the distribution of income for 1947 are drawn from Edward Budd, "Postwar Changes in the Size Distribution of Income in the U.S.," *American Economic Review, Papers and Proceedings* 60 (May 1970), p. 253. Data are aggregated by families and unrelated individuals. The data for the distribution of income in 1971 and 1991 are from the U.S. Bureau of the Census, "Money Income in 1991 of Households in the United States," *Current Population Reports,* P-60, no. 180 (Washington, D.C.: U.S. Government Printing Office, 1992), p. xv. Data are aggregated by household; this change in the unit of analysis has the effect of slightly decreasing the measured amount of inequality. Data on the distribution of net worth and financial assets in 1984 come from Melvin L. Oliver and Thomas Shapiro, "Wealth of a Nation: A Reassessment of Asset Inequality in America Shows at Least One-Third of Households Are Asset-Poor," *The American Journal of Economics and Sociology* 49 (Apr. 1990), p. 137.

humans. Countries constitute only one type of society—as local political communities, schools, churches, unions, workplaces, and other associations are also societies. Within and across these kinds of societies, two main differences should be analyzed. First, societies differ in the extent to which their members are committed to one another and seek a common life. Second, societies differ in terms of how power and privilege is distributed among the members of the community.

Societies may minimize or may emphasize the collective or common lives of their members. When societies minimize common lives, they may be little more than marketplaces in which individuals pursue their self-interest by exchanging goods with each other. In such societies, the prevailing question is, How should I live? In contrast, when societies emphasize their common lives, the prevailing question is, How should we live? In such societies, the members (or their representatives) assemble in order to define their collective goals. They decide what the people within that society need and how these needs should be provided. They decide what collective investments—goods that belong to society as a whole—should be pursued and protected. Most importantly, the individuals in such societies are willing to invest their time and commit their resources to improving their common lives. For socialists, societies that emphasize the common lives of their members are far more attractive than individualistic societies.[82]

Although societies can have more or less equal distributions of power and privilege, socialists recognize that there is no such thing as a classless society.[83] Individuals within all societies are stratified in various ways. Marx was right to emphasize stratification based on ownership of productive resources, as the class that owns most of society's productive resources normally dominates those classes with fewer productive resources. But inequalities in the distribution of power and privilege in a society can be based on other factors, such as occupational status, access to positions of authority, educational attainment, ethnicity, race, and gender. For example, even communist societies that abolish private property fail to become classless societies because they merely replace stratification based on property with stratification based on authoritative power or position. While all societies will have inequalities as the result of such factors, socialists prefer societies in which these inequalities are minimized and in which the inequalities that exist do not hinder or preclude the recognition that all individuals are equally members of society and entitled to equal respect as humans.

A socialist ethic of fraternity and equality helps to build societies in which there is a strong commitment by their members to building common lives and to minimizing the domination of some individuals by others. Socialist parties and socialist theorists can preach such an ethic, but the ethic must be lived on an everyday basis if a socialist society is to be built. Thus, local communities—like workplaces, neighborhoods, and schools—are places where people can

[82]Michael Walzer, "The Community," *The New Republic* (Mar. 31, 1982), pp. 11–14.

[83]Tom B. Bottomore, *Classes in Modern Society,* 2d ed. (London: HarperCollins Academic, 1991), p. 29.

actually work together to define common lives and treat each other with equal respect. As these local communities more closely approximate the communal and egalitarian associations that socialists prefer, it will be increasingly possible for national societies to evolve in socialist directions.

SUMMARY AND CONCLUSIONS

It is often observed that socialism is an endangered political ideology. In recent years, Western European societies (and the United States) have drifted toward more conservative outlooks. Socialist parties have lost political support. The demise of communism in the former Soviet empire is sometimes taken as additional evidence that socialism is unworkable as a set of ideas for governing nations. Democratic socialists, of course, deny that the collapse of communism signifies the weakness of socialism, because they regard communism as a distinct ideology, one they have always opposed because of its authoritarian and totalitarian tendencies. More troubling for democratic socialists is the ascension of the "ideology of selfishness" in both its contemporary conservative and liberal forms. They wonder about a "derangement of modern life" in which many people experience unprecedented levels of prosperity and erroneously believe that they have "made it on their own," ignoring that "we all prosper together or not at all" and retreating from the spirit of mutualism that lies at the heart of socialism.[84] Nevertheless, democratic socialists do not regard this movement away from socialist values as irreversible. The current period of retrenchment can be followed by fresh movements in socialist directions as people experience once again the economic and social problems and moral decay of capitalist domination and the evolution of its ideology of selfishness.

Perhaps the prospects for a democratic socialist resurgence are less favorable in the United States than they are elsewhere in the world. One commonplace in the study of ideologies is that the United States is exceptional because it is the only advanced industrial society where democratic socialist ideology and democratic socialist parties are dismissed as outside the realm of everyday politics. Students of **American exceptionalism** have proposed a number of explanations for this phenomenon.[85] Cultural explanations suggest that socialism in America is hindered by the ethos of rugged individualism, the dream of upward mobility, and the fear of equality. Economic explanations suggest that America's great natural resources, coupled with the development of industrialism, have permitted unusual economic expansion and have provided opportunities for the vast majority of Americans to succeed within capitalism and thus Americans are reluctant to oppose capitalism. Historical-political explanations suggest that the U.S. Constitution was specifically designed to reduce the capacity of any class-based faction—such as a socialist party—to dominate the political system. Sociological explanations suggest that American ethnic and racial heterogeneity have made it difficult for the working classes of various ethnic and racial groups to unify behind a socialist party that represents their common economic interests. While the thesis of American exceptionalism is certainly important—and discouraging to those who support democratic socialism—it may also be somewhat misleading.

Perhaps Americans are not exceptionally hostile to democratic socialist values and

[84]Walzer, "The Community," p. 11–12.

[85]A brief introduction to the literature on American exceptionalism is available in Irving Howe, *Socialism and America* (New York: Harcourt, Brace, Jovanovich, 1985), pp. 105–144.

policies. Perhaps what is remarkable about the United States is that "it practices middle-class socialism" through its extensive regulations of capitalism, its numerous social distributions, and its various uses of populist democratic processes, but "calls it something else."[86] Perhaps it is the term "socialism" that Americans dislike, even while they admire many of its values and ideals and put them into practice in many ways.

There are many ideas and ideals to admire in socialism. It provides provocative insights into problems with capitalism. Its goals regarding communal harmony, individual freedom, social justice, and popular democracy may simply constitute a logical, progressive extension of liberal values. It is difficult to dismiss as unreasonable socialist principles supporting a political economy of market socialism, endorsing governmental authority that acts as a counterforce to capitalist domination, seeking a more just distribution of economic goods and political power, and calling for a stronger sense of citizenship. Socialist strategies for achieving change, emphasizing evolutionary progress through democratic action and persuasion, certainly fall within the realm of acceptable pluralist politics.

What, then, are the deficiencies of socialism as a political outlook? Perhaps its criticisms of capitalism could lead to the dismantling of the world's most productive and prosperous economic system. Perhaps its goals—enhancing individual freedom, providing more equal conditions, and developing more communal harmony—are not as compatible with each other as socialists claim. Perhaps the changes sought by socialism threaten social stability. Perhaps its endorsement of strong government creates oppressive domination by a governmental elite. Perhaps socialist societies inevitably produce bureaucratic red tape, depersonalization, and inefficiency. Perhaps its ideas of social justice create false expectations about a more egalitarian society that is unachievable. Perhaps socialists seek too much democracy, forgetting that when citizens are overly empowered they end up electing charlatans and demagogues and pursuing policies that undermine the public good and the rights of minorities. Perhaps the whole socialist project is founded on naive and overly optimistic assumptions about human nature and society; while stressing the benevolent possibilities within humans and societies, socialists may ignore the inherent weakness of humans and the need to structure society to account for such weaknesses. Contemporary conservatives have found many such deficiencies in socialism (and its less radical friend, contemporary liberalism). Their ideas and arguments will be explored in the next chapter.

[86]Alan Ryan, "Socialism for the Nineties," *Dissent* (fall 1990), p. 438.

CHAPTER 10

Contemporary Conservatism

Contemporary conservatives—including such prominent political leaders as Ronald Reagan and Margaret Thatcher, such well-regarded academics as Thomas Sowell and Jeane Kirkpatrick, and such media pundits as Rush Limbaugh and Pat Buchanan—believe that communists, democratic socialists, and contemporary liberals create unrealistic expectations about what can be accomplished in political life. They assert that governments cannot solve a wide variety of human problems. While some governmental authority is needed to provide national security and social order, more expansive governmental power threatens individual liberty, the autonomy of civil society, and the economic prosperity provided by free markets. According to contemporary conservatives, most governmental programs intended to solve such problems must be regarded as failures, and they must be eliminated, reduced, and/or modified in ways that provide for greater individual incentives and choices. If there is to be progress, it will come about by the hard work of individuals who exhibit traditional virtues and who are motivated by the rewards available to them in the marketplace and from their involvements in voluntary associations.[1]

Contemporary conservatism is thus a reaction against communism, democratic socialism, and contemporary liberalism.[2] To criticize the "threats" posed to freedom and capitalism by these ideologies, contemporary conservatives rely on many of the ideas of classical liberalism. To condemn the assaults on traditional political practices and social customs by these ideologies, contem-

[1]A much more extensive list of ideas held by contemporary conservatives is provided by Rush Limbaugh, *The Way Things Ought to Be* (New York: Pocket Star Books, 1992), pp. 2–3. This best-seller by the popular talk show host is just the latest of a series of conservative books that have captivated Americans. Perhaps the first and most revered book in this tradition is Barry Goldwater's *The Conscience of a Conservative* (New York: Macfadden Books, 1960).

[2]Contemporary conservatives, such as England's Winston Churchill, have also been strong opponents of the totalitarian ideologies of fascism and nazism. However, because contemporary conservatism has been most fully developed since the heyday of these ideologies, its principles have been largely defined in reaction to those held by its opponents on the political left.

porary conservatives also draw on some of the ideas developed by traditional conservatives. Contemporary conservatism is a mix, then, of portions of two ideologies that were historically and philosophically antagonistic. Contemporary conservatism is able to overcome some of the contradictions and tensions between traditional conservatism and classical liberalism by focusing very sharply on the problems generated by communism, democratic socialism, and contemporary liberalism.

The rise of contemporary conservatism as a coherent ideology, especially in the United States, can be attributed to the publication of the first issues of *National Review* in 1955. William F. Buckley, Jr., the first editor of *National Review*, provided a magazine where intellectuals distressed about the advances made by contemporary liberals, socialists, and communists after World War II could air their grievances. Many of these intellectuals were uncomfortable with what they perceived to be the blatant contemporary liberal (and even radical) bias in journalism, in the entertainment industry, in government bureaucracies, and in universities. Buckley's magazine provided a forum where contemporary conservatives could articulate a more consistent critique of current affairs among colleagues with similar concerns.

Throughout the 1950s, conservatives prided themselves on their position as an intellectual elite outside the mainstream of academic and political affairs.

Sidebar 10-1

Some Contemporary Conservatives and Their Main Writings

William F. Buckley, Jr.*
- *McCarthy and His Enemies: The Record and Its Meaning* (1954)
- *Up From Liberalism* (1959)
- *Keeping the Tablets: Modern American Conservative Thought*, editor, with Charles R. Kesler (1988)

Milton Friedman*
- *Capitalism and Freedom* (1962)
- *Free to Choose: A Personal Statement*, with Rose Friedman (1980)

George Gilder*
- *Wealth and Poverty* (1981)

Friedrich von Hayek (1899–1992)
- *The Road to Serfdom* (1944)
- *The Constitution of Liberty* (1960)

Jeane J. Kirkpatrick*
- "Dictatorships and Double Standards" (1980)

Irving Kristol*
- *Two Cheers for Capitalism* (1978)

Thomas Sowell*
- *Preferential Policies: An International Perspective* (1990)
- *Inside American Education: The Decline, the Deception, and the Dogma* (1993)

George Will*
- *Statecraft as Soulcraft: What Government Does* (1982)
- *The Pursuit of Virtue and Other Tory Notions* (1983)

*Living author.

In the 1960s, conservatives began to deliver their criticisms to the public, and they launched political campaigns based on the conservative ideology that was developing. The conservatives associated with *National Review*—mostly intellectuals from the eastern United States—soon found allies among Republicans from the western states, who celebrated rugged individualism and the competition in free market economies. Many of these western conservatives were much more libertarian than were the eastern conservatives, but both were able to agree that communism abroad and big government at home were the most pressing problems facing American society after World War II.

During the 1960s, several developments in the United States gave momentum to the conservative movement. The growth of the welfare state, the free speech movement and antiwar demonstrations on college campuses, the women's movement, the civil rights movement, and the riots in urban areas were just some of the developments prompting many citizens to rethink their allegiance to contemporary liberalism. In the early 1970s, many intellectuals who had originally been supportive of contemporary liberal programs, especially the programs of President Lyndon Johnson's "Great Society initiative," joined the conservative movement because they considered these programs naive and dangerous failures. These intellectuals were dubbed the "neoconservatives," and they brought innovative ideas to conservatism by suggesting ways of using the market itself to achieve many of the goals that had previously been sought by governmental regulation of, and intervention in, the free market. The most important outlets for these ideas have been *The Public Interest* (first published in 1965) and the various publications of the American Enterprise Institute and the Heritage Foundation, two leading conservative think tanks.

The decade of the 1980s was marked by numerous victories by conservatives at the polls. The elections of Ronald Reagan and George Bush in the United States, Brian Mulrony in Canada, Margaret Thatcher (and, subsequently, John Major) in Great Britain, and Helmut Kohl in Germany are the most visible examples of the popularity of conservatism in recent years. Such politicians succeeded, in large part, because of their incisive criticisms of the failures of contemporary liberalism, socialism, and communism to deliver the good life for citizens. In the 1990s, conservatives have not always enjoyed the electoral successes of the previous decade, but over the past forty years, they have shaped an ideology that has mass appeal and that offers a constant counterpoint to communist, democratic socialist, and contemporary liberal ideologies.

THE POLITICAL BASES

Problems

Conservatives have identified four general problems facing Western Europe and the United States in recent years: (1) the failure of western foreign policy to promote the interests of the "free world"; (2) the promotion of socialist domestic policies by increasingly strong central governments; (3) the prominence and power of radical reformers, social engineers, and socialist utopians in educational institutions, especially at universities and colleges; and (4) a culture of permissiveness that combines a relativism of values with thoughtless uniformity of opinions and manners. Conservatives have not always agreed on solutions to these problems, but these areas of concern have served as rallying points for those holding a variety of perspectives within the conservative movement.

During the ten years following World War II, several international tragedies occurred, and conservatives attributed these tragedies to the growing **communist menace** and the failed foreign policies of Western democracies. The Soviet Union emerged as a world power, threatening western interests around the globe. Europe was divided by an "iron curtain" that separated a free west from Soviet-dominated totalitarian regimes in Eastern Europe. In Asia, China was lost to the Communists, and, despite a costly conflict, Korea remained a divided state, comprising the (pro-Soviet) North and (prowestern) South.[3] These communist advances in the international arena were certainly disturbing. However, even more troublesome for conservatives, especially those in the United States, was a sense that western leaders and policy makers were unwilling to acknowledge the profound threat posed by communism. Furthermore, conservatives suspected that communist spies and sympathizers had penetrated western governments and military research projects. The Soviet Union's rapid development of an atomic bomb in the 1950s was viewed as evidence by conservatives that a communist conspiracy existed within the national security systems of the United States.

Even those foreign policy makers who were anticommunist were, according to conservatives, much too willing to rely on international cooperation and international institutions as means of neutralizing the threat posed by communist advances. Conservatives in the United States have always been highly critical of the United Nations, arguing that such institutions deprive nations of their rightful sovereignty and pave the way for a single "world government." Such a world government would be controlled by nations and bureaucrats whose worldviews would be hostile to the best interests of the United States and her western allies.

Conservative criticisms of western foreign policy can be summarized by the four "C's." The west had accepted *capitulation,* by failing to respond vigorously to Soviet claims over spheres of influence in Eastern Europe and to Mao's communist forces when they overran mainland China. The United States had employed a policy of *containment* in which Soviet aggression around the world was contained but not counterattacked. In the west, there was a lack of vigilance against the spies and the *conspiracies* deployed by international

[3]The Korean conflict was waged between 1950 and 1953, and United States casualties reached thirty-five thousand. The boundary between North and South Korea remained the same, despite the fighting.

communism. Finally, the west had naively accepted international *cooperation* and the efforts of the United Nations as vehicles for conflict resolution, despite the dangers such an approach posed to national sovereignty.

The west, according to conservatives, must meet the communist menace with more moral zeal and greater military force. They hoped that the successful Republican presidential candidate in 1952, Dwight D. Eisenhower, would provide the requisite moral zeal and make use of greater military force. They were, however, disappointed when Eisenhower pursued a more moderate path of bipartisanship that accepted many of the policies criticized by conservatives. Indeed, not until Ronald Reagan was elected in 1980 did contemporary conservatives finally witness the moral rhetoric (e.g., Reagan's claim that the Soviet Union was an "evil empire") and the massive military buildup that they had sought for so long.

Strong anticommunism has been the "glue" binding contemporary conservatives throughout the "Cold War." The recent dismantling of the Soviet Union and its loss of power over Eastern European countries might weaken the anticommunist bond among contemporary conservatives in the 1990s. However, communism remains a powerful force. Communist regimes exist in Asia, and Castro remains in power in Cuba. Strong advocates of communism can be found in Central and South America, and in Africa. Communism may reappear in some of the regions of Eastern Europe and of the former Soviet Union. It is still too early to determine whether conservatism has lost a defining problem in its ideology. Continuing criticisms of Nicaragua, Cuba, China, and Vietnam by conservatives suggest that the fervent anticommunism of contemporary conservatism may still provide some ties that bind.

Contemporary conservatives view the pursuit of socialist policies that empower centralized bureaucracies as the most serious domestic problem. In Europe, conservatives have deplored the nationalization of industries and the development of elaborate welfare schemes. In the United States, Franklin D. Roosevelt's "New Deal" was seen not as an attempt to save capitalism during the great depression of the 1930s, but as an assault on business interests and on individual choice. The Social Security system in the United States, established by FDR in 1937, has long been a favorite target of conservatives because it creates a huge bureaucracy, compels citizens to participate, and (mildly) redistributes income from the rich to the working poor. Social Security socializes risk while reducing the need for individuals to make thoughtful and independent decisions about their futures. Although Social Security is now seen by most conservatives as too politically sensitive to be assaulted directly, it remains an indirect target, and conservatives continue to call for the privatization of retirement plans.

For conservatives in the United States, domestic policies from World War II until the 1980s were too antibusiness and too pro-union to foster the best in a capitalist economy. Government regulations are seen as costly, intrusive, and excessive. Support of union rights by FDR and subsequent Democratic presidents is seen as driving up wages beyond the market price for labor, thus contributing to inflation. Costly and unnecessary regulations on businesses, and high wages for workers, weaken U.S. businesses competing in the world economy. The antiregulatory views of conservatives have been received favorably by the owners of small and medium-sized businesses, and have helped broaden the appeal of contemporary conservative views beyond the eastern intellectuals mainly responsible for founding the conservative movement.

Especially after the government's turn in a socialist direction as a result of Lyndon Johnson's Great Society program, conservatives have been very critical of numerous programs expanding the size of central governments. They argue that many social and economic problems cannot be solved by governmental interventions and that, in fact, government interventions often compound or complicate the original problems. In *Wealth and Poverty,* George Gilder, reviewing the social programs of the American federal government during the 1970s, claimed that many of these programs had unanticipated and perverse consequences that he called **moral hazards**. Gilder explained, "Moral hazard is the danger that a policy will encourage the behavior—or promote the disasters—that it insures against."[4] Gilder's views on the failure of liberal social programs, widely shared by other contemporary conservatives, emphasized the counterproductive results of the programs:

> The moral hazards of current programs are clear. Unemployment compensation promotes unemployment. Aid for Families with Dependent Children (AFDC) makes more families dependent and fatherless. Disability insurance in all its multiple forms encourages the promotion of small ills into temporary disabilities and partial disabilities into total and permanent ones. Social security payments may discourage concern for the aged and dissolve the links between generations. Programs of insurance against low farm prices and high energy costs create a glut of agricultural commodities and a dearth of fuels. Comprehensive Employment and Training Act (CETA) subsidies for government make-work may enhance a feeling of dependence on the state without giving the sometimes bracing experience of genuine work. All means-tested programs (designed exclusively for the poor) promote the value of being "poor" (the credential of poverty), and thus perpetuate poverty. To the degree that the moral hazards exceed the welfare effects, all these programs should be modified, usually reducing the benefits.[5]

Gilder aimed his attacks at United States social policies, but his criticisms, and his views of the problems created by government subsidies, can also apply to the more vigorous welfare policies of many Western European countries.

Contemporary conservatives argue that liberal domestic policies are not only often counterproductive, they are often based on profoundly mistaken analyses of the roots of social problems. Conservatives claim that, too often, social problems are seen as the result of structural problems, rather than as the

[4]George Gilder, *Wealth and Poverty* (New York: Bantam Books, 1981), p. 132. The term "moral hazard" is taken from the language of the insurance business. For example, insurance companies must be careful not to overinsure for fire damages to property, because it may encourage policyholders to neglect safety procedures or, even worse, to resort to arson.
[5]Gilder, *Wealth and Poverty,* pp. 135–136.

result of a failure of individual character.[6] For example, drug use is a social problem that conservatives blame on the lack of individual character and the inability to "just say no," rather than on the poverty and powerlessness of the drug users. The willingness of liberal policy makers to place the blame for social problems on structural problems (like poverty) overextends government and ignores the crucial role that individual responsibility and virtue must play in a civil and well-ordered society.

According to contemporary conservatives, the increasing scope of government activity spawned by liberal policies creates both vast centralized bureaucracies and huge government expenditures. These massive expenditures have forced western governments to rely on high, and progressive, tax rates. High taxes stall general economic growth by diverting money from the private economy, and progressive rates discourage the wealthy from making more money and from investing in private ventures.

Conservatives hold some views on domestic politics, especially on government regulation and expenditures, that are very similar to the ideas held by Adam Smith and other classical liberals. Among these is the notion that government should keep its role in economic matters to a minimum and allow the economy to steer itself. The attempts by contemporary liberals to use Keynesian fiscal tools to steer the economy and avoid recessions have only created sluggish economies prone to inflation. Conservatives believe that, since the 1930s, liberal policy makers have had much too little faith in capitalist economies.

Conservatives point to the liberal and radical biases within higher education as one of the key sources for the lack of faith in capitalist economies. Western universities—at least since World War II—have been too sympathetic to liberal reforms and too critical of the workings of the private economy. Professors in the social sciences have encouraged the belief that social engineering is both necessary and easy, and have ignored the fact that vast structural reforms only enhance the power of national governments at the expense of local governments and private actors.

Contemporary conservatives are also critical of universities, because these institutions are seen as havens for socialist scholars and communist sympathizers who have little respect for western traditions and private economies. In the United States, conservative magazines, especially *National Review*, have complained that the universities have been, and are, hotbeds of subversive and radical thought. During the 1980s, Prime Minister Margaret Thatcher accused English universities of harboring socialists and communists, and of promoting antiwestern values. Her primary targets were sociology departments in publicly funded universities, which her Conservative Party tried to weaken, or eliminate, by underfunding.

Conservatives in the United States were particularly critical of the universities and colleges during the 1960s. The "free speech movement" in the early

[6]James Q. Wilson, "The Rediscovery of Character: Private Virtue and Public Policy," *The Public Interest* 81 (fall 1985), pp. 3–16.

1960s was seen as an assault on tradition and authority. Protests against the Vietnamese war often originated on college campuses during the late 1960s and were sometimes accompanied by verbal assaults on moderate and conservative professors.[7] Campuses also were the setting for "black pride" protests, "love-ins," ecology "teach-ins," women's rights demonstrations, and protests against traditional curricula. The universities were no longer institutions celebrating and transmitting the western tradition. Rather, universities had become a setting for unrelenting criticism of western beliefs and practices.

The universities and colleges were also blamed for creating a **culture of permissiveness** that permeated society during and after the 1970s. Too many professors, according to conservatives, were unwilling to defend (absolute) standards of conduct and a clear hierarchy of values. In the quest to develop independent critical thinkers sensitive to cultural differences, universities have produced, instead, spoiled children who consider all values to be relative.[8]

Indeed, according to conservatives, liberal reforms in education have fostered permissiveness in all public education, and have contributed to a general lack of respect for authority throughout society. This culture of permissiveness feeds on the relativism of liberalism, which will not, or cannot, provide a definition of "the good." For conservatives, many of the problems facing western societies are the result of liberal neglect of the importance of virtue and personal character. Crime, social disorder, single parents, large welfare rolls, and excessive public spending are traceable to this culture of permissiveness. James Q. Wilson has summarized clearly this contemporary conservative perspective:

> Conscience and character, naturally, are not enough. Rules and rewards must still be employed; indeed, given the irresistible appeal of certain courses of action—such as impoverishing future generations for the benefit of the present one—only some rather draconian rules may suffice. But for most social problems that deeply trouble us, the need is to explore, carefully and experimentally, ways of strengthening the formation of character among the very young. In the long run, the public interest depends on private virtue.[9]

Contemporary conservatives have identified a broad set of problems facing western societies. They have also articulated a variety of specific criticisms, many of which will be examined in the following sections.

[7]Not missing the irony, conservatives noted that former free speech protesters have recently become enforcers of "politically correct speech" in many of the elite universities in the United States. Conservatives coined the term "politically correct" to denigrate liberal approval of the agendas and language of militant minorities and feminists. To the extent that liberals have tried to curtail "insensitive" racial and sexist remarks, conservatives rightfully chide liberals for betraying their own free speech principles.

[8]See Allan Bloom, *The Closing of the American Mind* (New York: Simon and Schuster, 1987). Bloom's reverence for the ancient Greeks may have made him uncomfortable with being labeled a contemporary conservative, but his views on higher education in the United States clearly extend criticisms that have been launched by contemporary conservatives.

[9]Wilson, "The Rediscovery of Character," p. 16. Former Secretary of Education William Bennett has recently edited *The Book of Virtues,* an anthology of great literature depicting the character of virtuous men and women.

Goals

Like traditional conservatives, contemporary conservatives believe it is a mistake to articulate visionary and utopian goals. They believe that their ideological opponents have created unrealistic expectations by specifying such goals. For example, promising to create a more equal society only brings about demands for governmental programs that invariably fail to achieve equality and lead to frustration, distrust, and social instability. The goals of contemporary conservatives are more modest and, they believe, more realistic, involving the redirection of economic, moral, and social life. In this vein, three general goals seem to unite contemporary conservatives and, to some extent, set them apart from traditional conservatives. While traditional conservatives had some fears and reservations about capitalism, contemporary conservatives embrace the free market. Defending and extending free market capitalism has become the central goal of contemporary conservatives. While traditional conservatives emphasized a sacred morality that made reverence for God a core ethical value, contemporary conservatives emphasize a more secular morality that stresses a work ethic. Motivating people to forego immediate gratifications and instead become educated, skilled, and productive workers has become a central moral concern of contemporary conservatives. While traditional conservatives believed that many smaller voluntary associations must be sustained to have an organic society, contemporary conservatives have focused on the family as the most important social unit—one that gives people shelter in a society that is both increasingly individualistic and collectivist. Sustaining the family has become the central social goal of contemporary conservatives.

Contemporary conservatives agree with Adam Smith, the classical liberal economist, on two points—both regarding the desirability of capitalism.[10] First, minimal government intervention promotes dynamic domestic economies. When governments refrain from regulating economic activities, domestic economies are most efficient, they produce more economic growth, and national wealth is enhanced. Second, free markets among nations promote a harmonious international order. Free trade among nations produces maximum economic benefits (in the long run) for all parties to international trade and, thus, reduces tensions among nations.

After World War II, communism was viewed as the most fundamental threat to an international free market. Indeed, for most conservatives, the goal of an **international free market** was deemed so important that other political goals were clearly secondary. Conservatives defended many authoritarian and despotic third world governments, if they were also anticommunist and if they pursued favorable trade policies. Conservatives prefer that nations be run democratically, but they are much more critical of democratically elected gov-

[10]Milton Friedman's *Capitalism and Freedom* (Chicago: University of Chicago Press, 1962) is regarded by conservatives as the most important contemporary celebration of free market capitalism.

ernments that are communist (or socialist) than they are of undemocratic governments that are anticommunist and pro-free market.[11]

In defense of domestic free-market economies, contemporary conservatives champion **privatization**. In western Europe, conservatives have tried to reprivatize industries that have been nationalized. During the Thatcher years, for example, over half of the industrial assets that had been owned by the state were converted to private enterprises—including British Petroleum, Jaguar, Rolls Royce, and British Steel. According to conservatives, compared to nationalized industries, privatized industries are more competitive, more innovative, less bound by bureaucratic inertia, and less prone to labor disputes.

In the United States, where nationalization of industrial sectors is rare, conservatives have focused on the benefits of **deregulation**. Conservatives claim that governmental regulations reduce innovation, discourage investment, raise costs for consumers, and damage the international competitiveness of United States companies. Some regulations may be necessary, but most regulation is excessive, and all regulation creates frustrating and costly mounds of bureaucratic red tape. Domestic economies, then, are healthy when privately owned companies compete in markets in which they are unfettered by rigid regulations.

Conservatives believe an effective free market requires an educated, well-trained, and energetic workforce. Thus, they seek to reinvigorate the work ethic. According to conservatives, students in public schools are no longer challenged to develop academic and occupational skills that make them effective contributors to society. Conservatives fear that hard work has lost its luster in societies that are constantly increasing entitlements and welfare. Furthermore, taxes on the middle class, the working class, and small business owners dampen the work ethic and limit productivity. In particular, small business owners are "neglected heroes" to conservatives, because these entrepreneurs are willing to test their ideas, put their savings on the line, and work long hours in the face of excessive government taxes and bureaucratic red tape.

Conservatives want to strengthen the traditional family, which they regard as the most important mediating group in society.[12] According to one conservative group:

> Marriage and the family—husband, wife, and children joined by public recognition and legal bond—are the most effective institution for the rearing of children, for the directing of sexual passion, and for human flourishing in community. . . . It is necessary to discriminate between relationships; gay and lesbian "domestic partners," for example, should not be recognized as the moral equivalent of marriage. Marriage and family are institutions for our continual social well-being. In an individualistic society that tends to liberation

[11]Jeane Kirkpatrick, "Dictatorships and Double Standards," in *Keeping the Tablets: Modern American Conservative Thought*, edited by William F. Buckley, Jr., and Charles R. Kesler (New York: Harper and Row, 1988), pp. 392–414.

[12]The traditional (nuclear) family emerged in the eighteenth and nineteenth centuries and is thus a recent tradition.

from all constraints, they are fragile institutions in need of careful and continuing support.[13]

The traditional family, though, has been assaulted by government policy, schools, feminists, and children's rights advocates. Government welfare policy, which was designed to aid children without paternal support, has encouraged the emergence of female-headed single-parent households. Schools employ curricula and teach practices that undermine the role of the family in inculcating values in children. Liberal and radical feminists criticize the division of labor in the traditional family, and discourage women from playing their traditional domestic roles in the family. Children's rights advocates question (and limit) the authority traditionally exercised over children by their parents. Such assaults on the traditional family have led many conservative women—like Phyllis Schlafly and Bev LaHaye—to condemn contemporary liberals, and especially liberal feminists, as being "antifamily."[14]

Conservatives are far from unanimous in offering solutions to these threats facing the family. However, they believe public policy, culture, and institutions must all be reformed in ways that strengthen the family. The trend toward liberalized, "no-fault" divorce laws must be reversed. Children must be taught to respect the authority of their parents, and parents must recognize that their responsibilities include instilling proper moral values in their children. Schools must retreat from teaching liberal moral relativism to children and recognize that it is the parents' role to provide proper moral instruction.

Obviously, the goals of contemporary conservatives are close to the economic goals of classical liberals. Conservatives bring to these goals, though, concerns about family, tradition, and authority that echo some of the sentiments expressed by traditional conservatives.

SUBSTANTIVE POLITICAL PRINCIPLES

Authority

Conservatives want governmental authority to be limited, but within its limits it should be powerful. Governmental authority should not be used to solve every social problem. Indeed, labeling problems like the spread of AIDS and drug abuse as social problems, rather than as personal problems, is regarded by conservatives as a typical liberal tactic to invite governmental solutions to these allegedly social problems. Governmental authority should not be used to help every group seeking to realize its particular objective. Western governments have spread themselves thin, weakening the authority needed to fulfill the properly defined role of government.

[13]The Ramsey Colloquium, "Morality and Homosexuality," *The Wall Street Journal* (Feb. 24, 1994), p. A20. The authors of this article, which first appeared in *First Things* (Mar. 1994), were sponsored by the Institute for Religion and Public Life.

[14]Phyllis Schlafly, *Power of the Positive Woman* (New Rochelle, NY: Arlington House, 1977).

For contemporary conservatives, the most important tasks of government are to provide national security and domestic order. Governments must effectively pursue national interests in foreign policy and provide military forces strong enough to deter communist expansion, international terrorism, and nationalist aggression. Reducing military expenditures in order to finance the welfare state reflects a reversal of the proper governmental priorities. Governments must also focus on domestic disorder. Because of their great concern with the rights of criminals, liberals have shackled the police (and other law enforcement officers) and have been "soft" on crime. In contrast, conservatives want to expand police forces, reduce the "loopholes" in the law that allow the guilty to go free, make punishment more certain and severe, and reinstate the death penalty in cases of particularly heinous crimes.

Contemporary conservatives believe it important to use governmental authority to promote traditional cultural values and public virtue. Some conservatives, particularly those associated with the **new right**,[15] endorse governmental censorship of literature, movies, art, and music that they regard as offensive. Such conservatives also support laws prohibiting abortion, restricting the rights of homosexuals and lesbians, and curtailing other "objectionable" ideas and practices. More moderate conservatives, however, believe that government should simply not promote morally offensive ideas and practices. For example, they oppose governmental funding of "obscene" art shows and of abortions, and they oppose making homosexuals and lesbians a protected class in antidiscrimination legislation.

Contemporary conservatives also believe in some governmental intervention in the economy, though to a much lesser degree than do their ideological opponents on the left. They understand that a completely unregulated market may produce undesirable outcomes in some instances. Some governmental policies must be developed to deal with the problems of negative externalities, the provision of public goods, and poverty, but they must be much less heavy-handed and make better use of market incentives than do the policies of contemporary liberals and socialists.

Some governmental regulations of business practices may be necessary. For example, without governmental regulations concerning water pollution, it may well be in the best interest of a company to keep prices on products low by pouring the by-products (pollution) into a river. Pollution is a "negative externality" that imposes costs on third parties and that escapes the market mechanism. The polluter gains full advantage of disposing of the pollution, while it is the downstream residents who share the costs of foul water. For a company that is trying to maximize profit, there is thus little or no incentive to clean up the mess caused by its production processes.

Conservatives acknowledge the need for public action to correct market

[15]In American politics, "new right" is a term given to conservative populists who arose in the 1970s because of their disillusionment with the conservative establishment. Perhaps the best treatment of the "new right" remains Kevin Phillips, *Post-Conservative America* (New York: Random House, 1982).

deficiencies caused by externalities. They argue, though, that the approach to regulation taken by liberal policy makers is heavy-handed, excessively bureaucratic, *and* not attuned to the benefits of "marketlike" strategies for regulation. Following the arguments outlined in Charles L. Schultze's influential work, *The Public Use of Private Interest*, conservatives have argued against the almost exclusive reliance on "command and control" regulations by United States policy makers.[16] They contend, for example, that pollution regulations command industries to use the best available technology and to process their goods according to government controls and standards that must be written and enforced by large bureaucracies. These regulations do not encourage the development of innovative solutions by industries, and they provide no incentives for companies to reduce pollution to levels below the standards set by these bureaucracies.

Neoconservative economists have developed **marketlike incentives** to replace many command and control regulations. For example, pollution can also be reduced by creating situations in which polluters must pay for the pollution they produce. Government agencies would monitor pollution releases and set fees for units of pollution released. The costs of pollution would now be *internalized* by the polluting companies. Companies would be encouraged to reduce their pollution to keep the costs of their products low. Those companies with the most innovative pollution control techniques would be rewarded in the competitive market. Self-interest would be harnessed for a public good (e.g., clean waterways), and the size and scope of government bureaucracies could be reduced. Of course, some pollutants may be so toxic that no level of emissions is tolerable, and in these cases a command and control approach would still be necessary. Such cases should prove rare, though, and a "polluter pays" approach to the problem of negative externalities can take advantage of the market's ability to turn private interests into the public good.

Conservatives also seek to use market-like approaches to deliver public goods that are necessary and must be paid for by governmental expenditures. A public good has positive externalities that benefit others who do not consume or pay for them. Because inoculations help control the spread of diseases throughout society, governmental payment or subsidies for inoculations can serve the public interest. Because education helps create an informed and skilled citizenry and can disseminate important values, governmental expenditures for schools can serve the public good. But conservatives do not believe that public goods must necessarily be delivered by public bureaucracies that squelch innovation and raise the cost of goods. For example, instead of children receiving their education at designated public schools that are guaranteed students no matter how poorly (or well) the institutions perform, governments could provide parents with vouchers that they can use to send their

[16]Charles L. Schultze, *The Public Use of Private Interest* (Washington, D.C.: Brookings Institution, 1977); see also, Allen V. Kneese and Charles L. Schultze, *Pollution, Prices, and Public Policy* (Washington, D.C.: Brookings Institution, 1975).

children to the public or private schools of their choice.[17] Thus, the **voucher system** uses governmental authority to pay for (most of) the costs of education, ensuring its availability to the poor—who might be unable to afford private education without tax-subsidized vouchers—but it relies on a market-like mechanism to give incentives for schools to be innovative and effective, to be the parents' school of choice for their children. Bad schools, including public schools, that are unable to attract students would close, because they could not compete in the market created by the voucher system. But good schools would flourish, bringing a better delivery and quality of school services than that provided by the existing public school "monopolies."

Conservatives also recognize that poverty is a problem requiring some governmental response, but they oppose the massive welfare states created by contemporary liberals and socialists. Conservatives differ on their approaches to poverty, but all hope to reduce governmental spending on welfare, curtail bureaucratization in the delivery of welfare services, and encourage welfare recipients to acquire the education and job skills that will limit or eliminate their dependency on welfare. One conservative approach has been the negative income tax, a system that reduces the need for a welfare bureaucracy by having the Internal Revenue Service (IRS) simply issue checks to those whose incomes fall below a minimal level. Another conservative approach is to give tax breaks to businesses that locate in "urban enterprise zones" and employ the poor living in these depressed areas. Still another conservative approach is both to tighten eligibility requirements for welfare and to limit the time that persons can receive welfare benefits, thus reducing the number of recipients and encouraging recipients to work themselves off the "public dole." In general, conservatives doubt that the unequal distribution of income in society is unfair, and they reject the idea that it is governments' proper role to redistribute income. Rather than using government authority to achieve more income equality, income distributions are better left to the "impenetrable" workings of the free market.[18]

Contemporary conservatives argue that governmental authority is eroded when liberal legislatures provide too many programs and entitlements to too many groups and when liberal courts provide too many rights. Legislatures have created entitlement programs for the unemployed, the poor, and the elderly, and all of these groups now consider these entitlements part of their just desserts. Courts have expanded rights to groups and individuals, and these rights often conflict with public authority. Not only have the courts recognized the rights of welfare recipients, they have also granted rights to crim-

[17]The most thoughtful approach so far is by John E. Chubb and Terry M. Moe, *Politics, Markets and America's Schools* (Washington, D.C.: Brookings Institution, 1990). For a useful critique of school vouchers, see Jeffrey Henig, *Rethinking School Choice* (Princeton: Princeton University Press, 1994). Among the problems that the voucher system does not solve is that of providing or assuring special education for students having various learning disabilities and handicaps.

[18]Schultze, *The Public Use of Private Interest*, pp. 76–83. Schultze argues here that the market is preferable, because it is less accountable than government and because it tends to disguise equity issues.

inal suspects, prison inmates, asylum patients, refugees, children, and gays and lesbians. As these groups and individuals (or their advocates) press their rights-claims, they diminish governmental authority and limit the choices of public officials. For example, judges who find that overcrowded prisons violate prisoner rights can force state governments to change their budgets and, thus, limit the choices of elected officials. At the institutional level, judges can also weaken the authority of those in charge. For example, judges have ruled that asylum patients have the right to refuse certain medical treatments. The extension of rights diminishes both governmental authority and the authority of institutional officials who act in the name of public authority.

Public authority has also been diminished by the emergence of "interest group liberalism." Conservatives argue that liberals cater to almost every

Sidebar 10-2

Conservative Statism

Conservatives in the United States accept the need for (limited) governmental authority, but fear that excessive authority threatens individual liberties. Thus, while critical of liberal interpretations of the Bill of Rights that extend the freedom of speech to dancing, nudity, flag burning, and other forms of "nonpolitical" speech, conservatives generally value the protection against governmental power and majority tyranny that the Bill of Rights provides. Some conservatives, though, rely on the ideas of Thomas Hobbes (1588–1679) to defend the authority of the state against individual freedoms. Hobbes argued that individual rights must give way to the overpowering need to prevent anarchy and to enforce order. Only a powerful state free from constitutional restraints could prevent the natural chaos of human interaction. Hobbes rejected natural-rights claims and offered a defense of state power that can be interpreted to justify "might makes right" and "majority rule without restraints." The most vocal conservative supporter of Hobbes's statist position is William Rehnquist, chief justice of the U.S. Supreme Court.

Rhenquist, in his decisions on the Supreme Court as a Justice (1971–1986) and then as Chief Justice (1986–), rarely sides with individuals or minority groups in cases where governments are involved. In speeches and writings, Rhenquist argues that the U.S. Constitution was not designed to protect individual rights, but to create direct governmental authority over individuals.* The great danger facing modern society is not the tyranny of government, but the perils of anarchy. Rhenquist also is critical of the Bill of Rights for making no exceptions for curtailing political speech, and for protecting minorities against the "sovereign power" of the majority. Making claims very similar to those of Judge Robert Bork, Rhenquist argues that majority rule is too often hindered by the protections guaranteed by the Bill of Rights and the Fourteenth and Fifteenth Amendments to the Constitution.

*Samuel Blumenthal, "How Rhenquist Came Down in Hobbes v. Locke," *The Washington Post Weekly Edition* (Oct. 6, 1986) pp. 23–24.

group within society, resulting in the proliferation and empowerment of interest groups. Government has parceled out authority over public decisions to these groups, who look after their own interests rather than seeking the public good. Furthermore, these interest groups frustrate public authority by blocking policies which might erode benefits they have already achieved. Conservatives accuse the Democratic Party of being a party of interest group appeasement, rather than a party with firmly held principles. Democrats and liberals pander to interest groups for votes, without considering how this weakens the authority of government and limits the options available to government. This has been particularly evident in battles over the federal budget, where attempts to cut spending have been thwarted by interest groups seeking to preserve the economic benefits granted to them in previous years.

Governments have extended their reach throughout society since the 1940s, but they have lost authority as entitlements and rights have multiplied, and as interest groups have garnered power at the expense of the public good.

Justice

Contemporary conservatives' views on justice are very similar to those held by classical liberals. Indeed, the entitlement theory of Robert Nozick, which we discussed in our treatment of classical liberalism, has been embraced by most contemporary conservatives. According to Nozick, people are entitled to all of those goods they can acquire by means of any process of acquisition and exchange that does not infringe on the rights of others. Justice requires that people have the freedom to acquire and exchange goods. Given this freedom, the distribution of goods will be unequal, but not thereby unjust. The income and wealth that each individual attains will partially reflect his or her efforts and contributions to the marketplace, but will also reflect the degree of luck he or she has had. The role that luck plays in the market economy means that economic distributions will be, for the most part, unpredictable and unpatterned. However, economic inequalities are not unjust if all citizens are provided with an equal opportunity to apply their talents and to cope with their good and bad fortunes. Rather than seeking to redistribute wealth to attain more equality, a just society should provide individuals with equal treatment before the law and with equality of opportunity in education and employment. Government should protect the private property individuals accumulate and should refrain from legislating preferential treatment for individuals or groups.

Contemporary conservatives, then, are critical of ideologies which judge fairness by the final outcomes individuals achieve.[19] They reject the egalitar-

[19]According to Friedrich von Hayek, the market system is a spontaneous process where luck plays a significant role and whose results cannot be judged for their fairness. See Hayek's *Law, Legislation and Liberty,* Vol. II: *The Mirage of Social Justice* (London: Routledge, 1982). Irving Kristol, the longtime editor of *The Public Interest,* has been perhaps the most prolific opponent of egalitarian conceptions of justice. For a statement of his views, see *Two Cheers for Capitalism* (New York: Basic Books, 1978), esp. pp. 141–238.

ian notions of economic justice held by socialists, Marxists, and communists. They disapprove of the egalitarian tendencies in contemporary liberalism, and they are especially critical of contemporary liberals' attempts to "solve" inequalities by the use of affirmative action programs that specify demographic goals or quotas. If the market processes and opportunities are fair to all participants, economic inequalities are not unjust and, thus, do not require attention or social action.

This emphasis on the process, rather than the outcome, reveals an important difference between contemporary conservatism and traditional conservatism. Traditional conservatives defended hierarchies and inequalities as necessary components of complex organic societies. A just society produces a (fairly) predictable pattern of outcomes, and the good citizen accepts his allotted role within the (fairly) stable hierarchy created in each society. Different citizens will have different roles and responsibilities, and they will be treated differently according to their stations in society. Free market economies threaten the social stability by releasing citizens from traditional roles and by allowing competition among citizens that will lead to unpredictable economic outcomes. Traditional conservatives have always been wary of the consequences of a free market on a well-ordered, just, and stable society.

Contemporary conservatives also defend hierarchies and inequalities of outcome. However, positions within hierarchies and the distribution of wealth must be the unpredictable and dynamic results of competition among individuals who are treated equally before the law and given equal opportunity to pursue their educational and economic goals. Inequality will always exist, but each individual has an equal opportunity to compete for better positions and more income. The structures of hierarchies and the ranges of inequalities may be very stable in a society, but the individuals who occupy particular positions in those structures and ranges will be changing constantly. Government must avoid attempts to "correct" the outcome of this competition among individuals, and citizens must recognize that economic inequalities of outcome are not unjust if opportunities are equal. Government agencies or private organizations may aid those who compete unsuccessfully in the economic sphere, but such aid is an act of compassion, not a rendering of justice.

Contemporary conservatives have endorsed free markets and capitalism as mechanisms for distributing rewards and goods justly. The market produces and distributes goods efficiently, and free markets discourage discrimination on the basis of characteristics like race and gender because these traits are irrelevant to issues of economic productivity. Thus, markets encourage sellers and buyers to be "colorblind." Self-interested individuals will hire, promote, and deal with the most competent individuals—regardless of the race, ethnicity, religion, or gender of such individuals. According to these conservatives, discrimination against groups will ultimately hurt the discriminator by limiting his or her labor pool and his or her options to buy and sell.

While free markets should encourage colorblind behavior, contemporary conservatives believe that governments may have to enforce (what liberals call "formal") equal opportunity laws if discrimination persists. Governments must prohibit discrimination in the distribution of educational and job opportunities, outlaw discriminatory selling practices such as allowing realtors to discourage blacks from purchasing homes in white neighborhoods, and rescind any preferential policies that exist. Although some conservatives in the United States initially opposed the antidiscrimination reforms of the 1960s, they now accept such reforms as a necessary means of providing equal opportunities for minorities, especially African-Americans, who suffered from previous policies preferential toward whites.

Contemporary conservatives believe, however, that injustice results from policies (such as affirmative action and the establishment of quotas) that provide **preferential treatment** as compensation to victims of past discrimination. Conservatives point to the injustice of "reverse discrimination" policies such as those setting quotas for preferred-group students at universities. The insistence that freshmen classes mirror the general population often denies admission to qualified students, giving their places to underqualified preferred-group students in order to meet goals or quotas. This is unfair to both sets of students. The qualified students are denied the fairness of colorblindness, and the underqualified students are placed in settings where many are doomed to fail. Top-echelon universities in the United States, for example, accept African-American students with much lower Student Aptitude Test (SAT) scores than other students so that minority student quotas can be met. This not only leads to the failure of many African-American students at prestigious universities, it creates a "ratcheting effect," whereby second- and third-tier universities find that the better minority students have been placed in the top schools, and the second- and third-tier schools must now lower their standards to meet their minority recruitment quotas. Less-qualified minority students admitted in order to meet quotas, who might have done well at a second-tier school, face difficulties at the top schools, and minority students who might have been successful at third-tier schools suffer difficulties competing with students at the second-tier institutions. Quotas can result in the mismatching of students and institutions throughout all levels of the United States university system.

Economic and educational quotas may hurt non-preferred-group members more than they ever help preferred-group members, and thus create economic and educational losses for the entire system. The final economic and educational outcomes do not produce the justice or equality that liberal reformers promised, and the process of quota systems violates the conservative norm of market-produced colorblindness.

The conservative author writing most prolifically and thoughtfully about the dangers of preferential policies is Thomas Sowell. His criticisms of preferential treatment are provocative, because he marshals empirical evidence that challenges the basis for affirmative action policies and quotas. Most important in this regard is his argument that racism—while still an unfortunate aspect of American society—is not a significant cause of unfair economic outcomes. Sowell points out that not all minority groups which have encountered racism in the United States live under poor economic conditions. For example, Jews and Asians in the United States have average family incomes higher than the national average and higher than the Anglo-Saxon average.[20] Minority groups that do have average family incomes below the national average may have lower incomes as the result of factors other than racism. Advocates of preferential policies assume that racism is the most significant cause of different income levels between minorities and whites, but Sowell shows that the causal relations are more complex. While incomes are highest in the north and in urban areas, minorities are relatively concentrated in the south or in rural areas. While income levels rise with age, the median age for minorities tends to be younger and minority families tend to have more children. While income levels tend to rise with educational attainment, minorities tend not to place as high a cultural value on education as whites do. When such factors are incorporated into analyses of income differentials between minorities and whites, the impact of race per se—or racism—is rather small.

Sowell also argues that discrimination has historically been a transitory phenomenon, disappearing naturally over time—without the need for preferential governmental policies. In the American experience, immigrants such as the Irish, the Jews, Asians, and the Polish suffered deprivations upon arrival and only later caught up with (and often surpassed) the national family income average. Currently deprived groups—African-Americans, Hispanics, and Native Americans, as well as recent immigrants from such places as the West Indies—were making typical progress toward the national average before the development of preferential policies.[21]

Sowell also marshals empirical evidence describing and explaining the failures of moving from policies of colorblindness to "color awareness." When people are rewarded with positions and opportunities on the basis of their status as minorities (or women or other "victimized" demographic groupings) rather than on the basis of being the most qualified, several negative consequences are said to occur.

First, preferential policies demean the achievements of individuals in preferred groups and prompt the animosity of non-preferred-group members, who are resentful that they must pay for the errors of previous generations. Minority individuals who are successful must reap their rewards under the suspicion that they were granted privileges and opportunities unavailable to others. They and other minority members must also face the animosity and "new racism" which is directed against them by individuals who feel that they themselves have become members of an underprivileged group.[22] Preferential policies have spawned mass violence against preferred-group members in

[20]Thomas Sowell, *Ethnic America: A History* (New York: Basic Books, 1981), pp. 5–7.

[21]Sowell, *Ethnic America,* pp. 273–296.

[22]Sowell's discussion of "new racism" at U.S. universities is outlined in his *Inside American Education: The Decline, the Deception, and the Dogma* (New York: Free Press, 1993), pp. 132–173. Sowell neglects to mention that this "new racism" has also been aimed at Jews, Arabs, and Asians (and United States citizens with those religious, racial, and ethnic backgrounds), despite the lack of preferential treatment for members of these groups.

some countries and, in the United States, a rise in racism against African-Americans and Hispanics has been linked to affirmative action policies.[23]

Second, preferential policies have often harmed, rather than helped, members of the preferred group.[24] One of the reasons that affirmative action quotas have harmed members of the preferred groups is that hiring quotas create incentives for employers to practice "credentialism." Sowell argues that, in the United States, credentialism is the logical response by employers to quotas in the workplace.

> An employer who was once free to choose among job applicants on the basis of his own assessments of their ability to do the job must, because of preferential policies, consider how readily his decision can be justified to third parties (in terms that will be understood and accepted by those who are less knowledgeable about his business) who not only were not present at the interview but also would lack the pertinent experience on which such an assessment must be based. "Objective" criteria, in general—and educational credentials, in particular—are likely to gain more weight under these circumstances, because third parties can understand the use of such criteria, even if other qualities are in fact more important on the job.[25]

The employer is encouraged to hire members of preferred groups who are already experienced and who have had success in the workplace, and is discouraged from hiring those members who have not obtained adequate credentials or who have had no success in acquiring experience. Employers will be reluctant to hire members of preferred groups with limited credentials, because affirmative action procedural requirements can make firing such employees costly and time-consuming. Thus, quotas aid only the already successful members of the preferred groups, but hurt the opportunities of those members who are disadvantaged and who were supposed to be the beneficiaries of the quotas.

Third, because preferential policies are easily abused by democratic politics, these policies have often harmed the most deprived groups. Preferential policies are usually targeted initially for only a few groups, but more and more groups are included as protected groups when politicians respond to interest group demands. For example, affirmative action policies intended originally to benefit African-Americans, Hispanics, and Native Americans have often been modified to extend preferential treatment to women, then to veterans, then to the elderly, then to gays and lesbians, and so forth. According to Sowell, the extension of protected groups—combined with the growth of credentialism—results in "fewer job opportunities for less-educated black males" than would exist without affirmative action programs.[26] Further, because middle-class white women typically have more credentials in America than

[23]For an examination of the violent reactions against preferential policies, see Sowell's *Preferential Policies: An International Perspective* (New York: Quell, 1990), pp. 20–35.
[24]Sowell, *Preferential Policies,* p. 171.
[25]Sowell, *Preferential Policies,* p. 171.
[26]Sowell, *Preferential Policies,* p. 171.

black males, employers often fill their affirmative action quotas with women who possess the requisite credentials, and otherwise qualified black males remain unemployed. While colorblind equal opportunity policies allow deprived groups to progress over time, "coloraware" affirmative action policies become permanent features of the political economy that curtail the advancement of the most deprived groups. As preferential treatment is expanded to more groups, the leaders of these groups seek to ensure that their members continue to receive protected status under affirmative action laws. Preferential policies, which were announced as "temporary" remedies to address past injustices, have become permanent features of liberal government, and its replacement with a policy of colorblindness has been pushed off to some future date that is never specified. Unequal treatment based on "color awareness" becomes a permanent injustice of liberal regimes.

Structure

Contemporary conservatives accept the institutions of representative democracy as legitimate. In Western Europe, conservatives have worked within parliamentary systems and, in the United States, conservatives have supported our presidential system, including the separation of powers and federalism.

Rather than embracing universal structural principles, contemporary conservatives have sought to retain, and sometimes return to, the institutions that define the particular historical identities of their nations. Canadian politics during the past twenty-five years has been preoccupied with the efforts of Pierre Trudeau, the former Liberal Prime Minister, to build a stronger national Canadian government and of the Parti Quebecois and the recently formed Bloc Quebecois to create a sovereign Quebec. Canadian conservatives have sought to position themselves between these forces by developing and endorsing various accords (e.g., Meech Lake and Charlottetown) that provide greater power and autonomy to the provinces and territories while retaining a unified, multiethnic state of Canada. British politics has addressed the issue of integrating England into the European Community, a proposal that has been strongly opposed by Margaret Thatcher, the former Conservative Prime Minister, on the grounds that England's sovereignty and cultural identity may be endangered by joining the Common Market. Germany has, of course, had to deal with issues regarding the reunification of West and East Germany. In this instance, conservative Chancellor Kohl has been a strong supporter of unification, as he attempts to reclaim a German community under a constitution that retains the principles of representative democracy.

In the United States, the structural issue of greatest concern to conservatives deals with the character of American federalism. Conservatives generally support states' rights and local governmental power, and accuse liberals of expanding excessively the size, range, and power of the federal government. Conservatives support the decentralization of political power because state and local governments provide a defense against a powerful national government and promote regional and local values and responsibilities. Local governments have local knowledge and, thus, can best determine the proper cultural values to be reflected in law and policies. Libertarian conservatives—that is, those conservatives most committed to extensive economic and social liberties and to minimal government—are not always comfortable with this idea of enforcing community standards, because it violates their commitment to personal freedom. However, they do agree with other conservatives that local control over many policies forces citizens to recognize that public programs are expensive. President Reagan's purpose in decentralizing some federal programs in the 1980s was to awaken citizens to the costs of the many responsibilities governments had assumed. Awakened citizens, Reagan hoped, would be willing to prune these programs.

Indeed, Republican presidents since 1968 have regularly promised a new division of responsibilities among the three levels of the federal system. Both Nixon and Reagan announced "New Federalism" approaches that would reduce the size of the federal government and provide local governments with increased discretion for spending in some policy areas. Nixon's plans were more specific about the distribution of responsibilities than were Reagan's, but his plans were not implemented. Reagan's approach was guided less by concerns about proper spheres of responsibility than by the desire to transfer spending from the national to the local level.[27]

Rulers

Conservatives embrace popular sovereignty and representative institutions. Rulers should be selected by citizens, although mechanisms (e.g., the electoral college) that distance the rulers from popular passions are reasonable. While critical of "professional politicians," conservatives expect those who hold positions of power in legislatures and executive offices to be talented individuals. Good rulers should be able to listen to the people, and yet still provide guidance and direction for the country. In particular, good leaders should be able to avoid being captured by interest groups which seek their own good, rather than the public good.

Conservatives believe that there have been several threats to the proper functioning of representative democracy, particularly in the United States. One threat is that provided by the "**new class**"—an elite of liberal professionals, intellectuals, journalists, public bureaucrats, and cultural megastars who are committed to various abstract liberal values like egalitarianism and absolute human rights. While committed to abstract economic equality, the "new class" betrays a political elitism. According to Jeane Kirkpatrick, the "new class" believes in utopian possibilities, ideas arrived at by intellectual speculation and artistic imagination, and it forgets the real limits of human nature and economic scarcity.[28] Although the "new class" advocates values and ideas that are often at odds with popular beliefs, it nevertheless is portrayed in the media as

[27]For a discussion of the idea that guided Nixon's "New Federalism," see Robert P. Nathan, *The Plot That Failed: Nixon and the Administrative Presidency* (New York: John Wiley, 1975), esp. pp. 13–34.
[28]Jeane Kirkpatrick, "Politics and the 'New Class'," *Society* 16 (Jan./Feb. 1979), pp. 42–48.

speaking for American ideals, and it eventually influences popular thinking on many concrete issues. Because the realities of political life cannot live up to "new class" ideals, it breeds cynicism and despair about political life. In short, the "new class" has power over the public and in representative institutions that is unwarranted and undemocratic. Members of the "new class" have great influence in education, in the media, in culture, and in government—influence that is not subject to democratic control and that is unrepresentative of the views of the "silent majority" of conservative Americans.

Another danger to representative democracy is posed by what James Payne calls **autonarchy**. While "democracy" refers to a system where government is controlled by the people (and "oligarchy" refers to a system where government is controlled by the rich), "autonarchy" refers to a system "of circular government-by-itself [where] those working for and paid by government dominate the decision-making process themselves."[29] According to Payne, almost all those who testify at congressional hearings support new governmental initiatives and spending. Most of these people are federal bureaucrats who administer programs in the area of interest, state and local officials who seek funding for their initiatives, other congressmen with interests in the program, and lobbyists for groups benefited by the programs. In short, government is dominated by those who are part of the political system and understand that the political system can be used to target benefits for specific groups; taxpayers who must pay for these programs or future generations that must deal with the resulting national debt are in no position to control "government by itself."[30]

While the concepts of the "new class" and autonarchy address conservative concerns about democratically elected leaders being "outgunned" by idealistic elites and self-interested insiders, some conservatives also fear that representatives can be overwhelmed by populist forces. In fact, U.S. conservatives have battled among themselves over how much democratization is healthy in representative government. The libertarian conservatives of the western United States have populist tendencies that eastern conservatives find, at the least, unnerving. Eastern conservatives endorse republican structures and processes that distance the rulers from the ruled. They believe that Congress should be above the fray of passionate democracy. Eastern conservatives have always displayed an almost traditional conservative reverence for the Senate and its elitist moment in representative politics. George Will has even argued the C-SPAN 2 coverage of the Senate deprives the institution of the requisite distance and isolation from the public.[31] Western conservatives, on the other

[29]James Payne, "The Congressional Brainwashing of Congress," *The Public Interest* (summer 1990), p. 12.

[30]A more theoretical discussion of this problem is provided by William Mitchell, "Efficiency, Responsibility, and Democratic Politics," in *Liberal Democracy: Nomos XXV*, edited by Roland Pennock and John Chapman (New York: New York University Press, 1983), pp. 343–373.

[31]Will's views on U.S. history and political institutions are presented clearly in J. David Hoeveler, Jr., *Watch on the Right: Conservative Intellectuals in the Reagan Era* (Madison: University of Wisconsin Press, 1991), pp. 53–80. Hoeveler presents the views of many leading conservatives in the United States in this thoughtful and well-researched work.

hand, have endorsed and used the populist mechanisms of recall, referendum, and initiative. Eastern conservatives view such democratic devices as unnecessary contrivances that reduce the distance between thoughtful representation and the passions of constituencies. Neoconservatives are critical of western populism and have sided with eastern conservatives in this debate.

Libertarian conservatives have favored term limit legislation, arguing that term limits will make elected representatives more attentive to their constituents and less likely to be influenced by national interest groups. Eastern conservatives have been reluctant to endorse term limits because such restrictions would limit the opportunities for talented and prudent politicians to participate in legislative politics. George Will, though normally associated with eastern conservatives, now supports term limits, arguing that they would free politicians from reelection concerns and provide them with the distance from the electorate needed to make wise national decisions.[32] Thus, most conservatives now find themselves in agreement over the desirability of term limits, although they still differ over the nature of the consequences that term limits will have on the connection between elected officials and their constituents.

Finally, conservatives have had to address themselves to the issue of the executive power in modern democracies. In the United States, conservatives were critical of the growth in presidential power achieved during Franklin Roosevelt's four terms as president and of his use of direct appeals to the populace as a means of gaining popular support in his battles with Congress. FDR created what has been termed the **imperial-plebiscitarian presidency**.[33] Wary of concentrated power and of power too closely linked to a passionate public, conservatives have defended congressional power and warned against the dangers of populist impulses. Despite these concerns, conservatives in the 1980s could safely endorse the strong and plebiscitarian presidency of Ronald Reagan. Only a strong and popular president seemed capable of slowing the growth of federal government and of shaking up politics in the insulated and liberal world of Washington, D.C. Reagan, who developed into a conservative in the more populist environs of the western United States, was adept at deploying popular support in his legislative battles with Congress and was an open admirer of FDR's presidential style.

There remains a tension, then, in contemporary conservative thought. On the one hand, there is the fear of strong executive leadership and of a populist politics that promotes passion and reduces the requisite distance leaders must have to rule thoughtfully. On the other hand, at times conservative goals may only be achievable when there is a strong populist president who can be an effective counterforce against the "new class" and who can rally the public against an autonarchic government. Republican principles about rulers clash with prag-

[32]George F. Will, *Restoration: Congress, Term Limits, and the Recovery of Deliberative Democracy* (New York: Macmillan, 1992).

[33]For the best discussion of the plebiscitarian element, in the context of United States presidential history, see James W. Ceaser, *Presidential Selection: Theory and Development* (Princeton: Princeton University Press, 1979).

matic concerns about goals for United States conservatives, making conservatives inconsistent in their commentary on leadership in the United States.

Citizenship

The issue of citizen participation has divided contemporary conservatives. The populists in the "new right" have called for the empowerment of "average Americans." They have developed sophisticated techniques for identifying and mobilizing conservative voters. They have called on their troops to become active in local politics, especially in demanding that prayer be allowed in the schools, in forcing removal of "scandalous" books from the libraries, and in blocking access to abortion clinics. They have developed a broad network of national lobbies to further conservative causes on Capitol Hill. Jack Kemp, Barry Goldwater, Phil Gramm, Howard Jarvis, and Pat Buchanan are just some of the most prominent conservatives who support *Initiative America*, a proposal to allow national initiatives, thus giving citizens an opportunity to participate

Sidebar 10-3

Contemporary Conservatives and the Working Class

By the 1980s, conservatives in the United States and Britain had gained a new ally, the working class. Many working-class voters who had long been supporters of socialist and liberal parties shifted their allegiance to conservative parties. Partly because of this new climate, Ronald Reagan and Margaret Thatcher were successful in cultivating working-class voters. Reagan, in particular, was successful in making conservatism folksy and populist.

In the 1980 election, Reagan won 44 percent of the union household vote. In 1984, Reagan captured 48 percent of these voters. Reagan succeeded in breaking a weakening bond that had existed between the working class and the Democratic Party since Franklin D. Roosevelt's election to the presidency in 1932. Reagan's personal qualities helped deliver working-class votes to the Republican Party, but many working-class voters appear to have left the Democratic Party permanently. Recent Democratic nominees for the presidency have not fared very well with working-class voters. In 1988, Michael Dukakis received only 57 percent of the union household vote and, in 1992, Bill Clinton only managed to secure 55 percent of this vote. The Democratic Party can no longer count on receiving overwhelming support from union households.

Thatcher was able to attract working-class support through appeals to nationalism. She was also able to recruit future Conservative Party leaders from the working class. When John Majors became the prime minister in 1990, he became the first Conservative Prime Minister with a working-class background.

Contemporary conservatism has cut across class lines in its appeal to voters in western countries. This marks a major shift in the national politics of these countries. A historic dividing line in electoral politics has been erased, and socialist and liberal parties have lost their old base of support.

directly in policy making. According to Kemp, a constitutional amendment to enable national initiatives would "allow you to vote yes or no on such issues as a balanced budget, reducing your income taxes, tax limitations, and much more."[34]

Nevertheless, most conservatives in the eastern United States have rejected calls for greater citizen involvement, questioning whether the citizens have the wisdom, technical knowledge, and virtue to support appropriate policy choices. In his classic work, *Capitalism, Socialism, and Democracy,* Joseph Schumpeter developed a "realistic" theory of democracy that claimed that the proper role of citizens is limited to choosing a government among competing parties.[35] According to Schumpeter, greater citizen involvement in politics should be discouraged because citizens tend to be motivated by irrational mob impulses and because their preferences (or "will") can be manufactured and manipulated by demagogues. More recently, neoconservatives have also warned against a **democratic distemper**, in which too much citizen participation is a disruptive force in politics.[36] According to Samuel Huntington, a professor of government at Harvard, citizen participation is, for the most part, citizen demand-making. The needs and wishes of various groups of citizens—minorities, women, the poor, children, students, the elderly, and so forth—become demands for "rights" and lead to claims on the public purse that involve an expansion of governmental activity. But government cannot and should not satisfy all of the competing demands made on it. When citizen participants fail to have their demands for rights satisfied, they become cynical and disrespectful of government, leading to a crisis of governmental authority. Thus, except for voting, citizen participation in governance should be discouraged.

While conservatives disagree about citizen participation in policy making, they agree that citizens ought to become more involved in community life, especially through involvement in voluntary associations. Rather than demanding that government be expanded to provide assistance to various needy populations, citizens ought to form various local charitable and service organizations that provide help to the disadvantaged and that build character and a sense of community in those who volunteer. George Bush described such voluntary groups as a "thousand points of light," and he believed that citizen involvement in such groups evoked the true spirit of American citizenship described by Tocqueville in his classic work, *Democracy in America,* written in the 1830s.

Conservatives also agree that liberal societies have done far too little to

[34]Quoted in Thomas Cronin, *Direct Democracy* (Cambridge: Harvard University Press, 1989), p. 173. Allowing national initiatives and referenda would require a constitutional amendment because Article 1, Section 1 of the United States Constitution vests all legislative power of the United States in the Congress.

[35]Joseph Schumpeter, *Capitalism, Socialism, and Democracy* (New York: Harper and Row, 1942). Schumpeter had been the Conservative minister of finance in the Austrian government and a professor at the University of Berlin before Hitler rose to power, prompting him to move to the United States.

[36]Samuel P. Huntington, "The Democratic Distemper," *The Public Interest* 41 (fall 1975), pp. 9–38.

cultivate the virtue of citizens. Governments have provided too few incentives to keep intact the nuclear family, and public schools have not provided students the guidance they need if they are to become virtuous citizens. Liberals (and their institutions) have preached an ethic of self-expression, when what is needed is an ethic of self-control. The good citizen should have self-discipline and a good character. James Q. Wilson has described the conservative view of the good citizen as follows:

> By virtue, I mean the habits of moderate action; more specifically, acting with due restraint on one's impulses, due regard for the rights of others, and reasonable concern for distant consequences.[37]

Conservatives believe that governments have only a limited role to play in developing the virtue and character of citizens. Legislatures can pass laws regulating the most obvious vices—prostitution, drug abuse, pornography, and so forth. Legislatures can reform or eliminate those public policies and programs, such as Aid to Families of Dependent Children (AFDC), that provide incentives for persons to abandon responsible behavior. Schools can promote good character in children by emphasizing academic achievement, by instilling discipline through homework, and by praising conduct that conforms to agreed-upon standards of human virtue.[38] The police can apprehend and the courts can punish those who violate the rights of others and who undermine social order. Conservatives believe that liberals have only exacerbated the decline of citizen virtue by giving undue attention to the "root causes of crime."[39] Even if some criminal acts are the results of poverty, broken homes, abuse, and substance dependency, it still may well be in the best interest of society to act "as if crime is the result of individuals freely choosing among competing alternatives . . ."[40] Stiffer sentences for crimes, fewer opportunities for parole, and larger police forces may be the best ways to deter criminal activity, and should produce results that are much more cost-effective than the current attempts to solve root problems.

Nevertheless, conservatives are wary of "moral imperialism" by the state, as they believe that individual liberty and social order can be threatened when state power is used for moral crusades.[41] According to William F. Buckley, Jr., for example, government ought not legislate against smoking; however, it may legitimately try to alert the public to dangers of the habit. Ultimately, the individual must choose.[42] James Q. Wilson argues that citizens do not require government to instruct them on the moral virtues, as most people have deep intuitions about the requirements of sympathy, fairness, self-control, and duty. What is required is that citizens confidently acknowledge their "moral sense," repudiate the unwarranted skepticism and exaggerated tolerance that have

[37]Wilson, "The Rediscovery of Character," p. 15.
[38]Wilson, "The Rediscovery of Character," pp. 5–9.
[39]Wilson, "The Rediscovery of Character," p. 13.
[40]Wilson, "The Rediscovery of Character," p. 14.
[41]Hoeveler, *Watch on the Right,* p. 37.
[42]William F. Buckley, Jr., *The Jeweler's Eye: A Book of Irresistible Political Reflection* (New York: Putnam, 1968), pp. 257–259.

been promoted by liberals, speak out against immoral behavior, and reinforce virtue through robust civil institutions encompassing family life, churches, schools, and other voluntary institutions committed to instilling character in the citizenry.[43]

Change

Conservatives are suspicious of changes in the practices of society. They draw on traditional conservative ideas about the dangers and unanticipated consequences of social engineering in complex societies. However, contemporary conservatives' view of change differs from that held by traditional conservatives in three important ways. First, contemporary conservatives are much more tolerant of the changes that free-market economies create. Traditional conservatives were critical of the new technologies, changing social relations, and unexpected developments that markets produce. In contrast, contemporary conservatives, especially libertarians and neoconservatives, are even willing to celebrate the dynamic and creative features of capitalism. According to Michael Novak, the free market encourages beneficial social and economic change by reinforcing self-discipline and creativity.[44]

Second, compared to traditional conservatives, contemporary conservatives are much more confident in their ability to undo existing, long-standing liberal reforms which interfere with market relations. In the 1980s, contemporary conservatives in elected offices took the opportunity to reverse liberal reforms that had long histories. For example, in England, Prime Minister Thatcher rapidly reprivatized industries and privatized much public housing, despite the length of time these socialist reforms had been in practice. In the United States, President Reagan deregulated industries that had operated within regulatory structures for many years—in some cases, for up to ninety years. Indeed, Reagan had, in the 1970s, called for an end to Social Security, as he considered it an unnecessary government infringement on citizens' rights to choose their own retirement programs in a free market. A traditional conservative would be very wary of ending a program that began in 1937 and has shaped the expectations and practices of several generations of citizens.

Third, contemporary conservatives are much more willing than traditional conservatives to experiment with new reforms. Traditional conservatives cautiously endorsed some social reforms—if problems were persistent and costly and if institutions were clearly broken. But such conservatives were wary that reforms often had costly unintended consequences. Contemporary conservatives sometimes invoke this traditional conservative view, but they have been willing to push reforms that are quite wide in scope and that may produce a broad range of unanticipated consequences. Contemporary conservatives are

[43]James Q. Wilson, *The Moral Sense* (New York: Free Press, 1993).
[44]Michael Novak, *Freedom with Justice: Catholic Social Thought and Liberal Institutions* (San Francisco: Harper and Row, 1984) and *Will It Liberate? Questions about Liberation Theology* (Mahwah, N.J.: Paulist Press, 1987).

Sidebar 10-4

From Protest to Governance
Conservative Ascendance in the 1994 U.S. Midterm Elections

As a result of the 1994 midterm elections, Republicans won more than 50 Congressional seats previously held by Democrats and gained control of the United States House of Representatives for the first time in 40 years. Republicans—mostly those holding conservative or New Right views—also gained eight seats and became the majority party in the United States Senate. In addition, Republicans wrested control of eleven governorships from Democrats. Such gains mean that the role of conservative lawmakers will no longer be limited to criticizing liberal initiatives and programs, but rather will include new opportunities to govern on the basis of their conservative ideals.

Conservative ascendance to a governing role is indicated not only by this increase in the number of Republican legislators and governors but in the ideological leanings of the new legislative leaders. The new Speaker of the House for the 104th Congress is "Newt" Gingrich, the leader of the more-conservative forces in the Republican Party and a highly vocal opponent of the liberal programs established during FDR's New Deal and LBJ's Great Society. The new majority whip, the second most-powerful position in the Senate, is Trent Lott, who is aligned with Gingrich on many issues and who won his position over a more moderate candidate preferred by Senate Majority Leader Bob Dole. Dole, a long-standing, acidic critic of liberal Democrats, is widely regarded as the most moderate Republican leader in Congress—suggesting just how far to the right the ideological pendulum has swung.

Gingrich was the architect of a ten-point "Contract with America" that promised voters speedy enactment of laws embodying conservative principles in return for their electoral support. Conservative Republicans—as well as many commentators—interpret the electoral results as constituting a mandate to make policy changes in the following areas:

1. Enacting a constitutional amendment requiring a balanced budget
2. Reducing crime (e.g., through funding additional law enforcement personnel and imposing stiffer sentences, including the death penalty)
3. Reducing welfare spending and imposing two-year benefits limitations and work requirements on welfare recipients
4. Reinforcing family values (e.g., by encouraging adoptions and giving parents greater control over their children's education)
5. Providing tax relief for the middle class
6. Strengthening national defense
7. Changing Social Security laws in ways that benefit senior citizens
8. Stimulating economic growth by reducing capital gains taxes and business regulations
9. Stemming the "endless tide of litigation"
10. Enacting laws that limit the terms of elected officials

In order to achieve these changes, conservatives will have to cut, eliminate, and/or turn over to the states many federal programs that liberals regard as important responses to social, economic, and environmental problems. The members of the 104th Congress can be expected to hold vigorous debates between contemporary conservatives and contemporary liberals as they consider these initiatives.

generally supportive of school choice or voucher approaches to public education. Attempts to make education more marketlike may well change the education system and the larger community dramatically. For example, a choice system—where parents can send their children to school in any of a variety of locations in a large city—might produce new community groups of concerned parents, but it might erode the sense of community within neighborhoods by eliminating local schools. Contemporary conservative support for term limits would also strike the traditional conservative as overly enthusiastic. Term limits could produce a variety of consequences that are difficult to foresee. Some conservatives support term limits in the belief that such limits will produce legislators whose ideals are closer to those held by their constituents, but other conservatives support term limits in the belief that such limits will help distance legislators from their constituents. In contrast to contemporary conservatives, traditional conservatives would be wary of term limits because the major outcomes of this reform are so uncertain.

Contemporary conservatives, then, are more comfortable with change than are traditional conservatives. They do resist change, though, especially the egalitarian reforms sought by liberal and socialist social engineers. They are particularly resistant to liberal reforms that demand changes in behavior before citizens have been persuaded that such changes are necessary. Wilmoore Kendall stated, most forcefully, the contemporary conservative resistance to politically mandated changes when he wrote the following in 1971:

> The Conservatives *do* drag their feet—let the Liberals take note that I concede the point. When a Conservative reads in his newspaper that nearly 90% of the Southern schools are still segregated, and that the rate at which Southern schools are being desegregated is tapering off, he does not—unlike the Liberal—feel moved to the condemnation of the White Southerners for their allegedly wicked ways. . . . When the Conservative finds himself up against proof that the kids in the public schools of Middletown, Connecticut—which is 90 percent Catholic—recite "Hail Marys" in the classrooms and even the corridors, he does *not* feel that liberty has died in America. . . . And when the Liberal hammers the Conservative over the head with the awful fact that the good folk of New Haven and Hartford . . . do not have the voice in the state legislature to which their numbers might seem to entitle them—when the Liberal hammers the Conservative over the head with that awful fact, I say, he feels no temptation to order a couple of divisions of the U.S. Army to Connecticut to restore its republican form of government. I repeat: I concede the point that the Conservatives do drag their feet on what are fashionably called civil liberties, equal representation, desegregation.[45]

Kendall's defense of foot-dragging is even too forceful for some conservatives, but it captures the conservative resistance to liberal reforms designed to enhance egalitarianism.[46]

[45]Wilmoore Kendall, "Equality and the American Political Tradition," in *Keeping the Tablets,* p. 81.
[46]Harry V. Jaffa criticizes Kendall's views on equality in his *How to Think About the American Revolution* (Durham, N.C.: Carolina Academic Press, 1978).

Contemporary conservatives view change as inevitable, given their defense of the dynamism of capitalism. Change should, however, rarely be instigated by government unless it is designed to undo the damage of liberal reformers.

THE PHILOSOPHICAL BASES

For the most part, contemporary conservatives have eschewed deep philosophical issues. They believe that socialists and liberals have used philosophy to develop ideals about what human nature and society should be like, but these ideals are often naive fantasies. They accept the idea of limits on human and social possibilities, and, like George Bush, they have problems with "the vision thing." Contemporary conservatives pride themselves on their **realism**. They accept the world, humans, and societies as they are—in all their wonder and with all their deficiencies. They doubt the existence of some epistemology that will provide sure knowledge about how to solve all human problems and lead the way to a perfect world. Conservatives point to the works of such political philosophers as Eric Voegelin and Leo Strauss as providing a conservative philosophy, but specific instances of conservatives drawing on these works are rare.[47]

Ontology

Questions about the nature of reality have not been of much interest to conservatives. Conservatives usually avoid metaphysical explanations and treat reality as a material world in which people can draw on common sense and science to help guide them in their activities.

Religion is important to conservatives, but for most conservatives, it does not serve as an essential guide to understanding the material world. Religion promotes values that improve the social order, and religious institutions provide local sites for solidarity and for charitable work. Religion can help define and shape the good life for individuals, but conservatives do not invoke religious explanations of how the world is ordered.

In the United States, much of the conflict between mainstream conservatives and the "new right" grows out of efforts by the latter to invoke religious explanations. For example, some leaders of the "new right" originally claimed that AIDS was a disease sent by God as a punishment for homosexuality, but most conservatives distance themselves from such an interpretation. Most con-

[47]In *Keeping the Tablets,* edited by Buckley, the following works by Voegelin and Strauss are included: Eric Voegelin, "Gnosticism—The Nature of Modernity," pp. 181–197; and Leo Strauss, "The New Political Science," pp. 198–216. These essays, though, are rarely mentioned in any of the other essays. In Hoeveler's *Watch on the Right,* Voegelin and Strauss are given their due as important political thinkers for conservatism, but the conservative thinkers examined in the text rarely draw on Voegelin and Strauss. While Voegelin and Strauss have influenced such conservative scholars as Harry Jaffa and Herbert Storing, their influence on the more popular literature of conservatism is hard to detect.

servatives have also been unsupportive of "new right" attempts to introduce creationism into the curricula of public schools, acknowledging that creationism relies on a particular, untestable reading of the Bible. Conservatives argue that contemporary liberalism has not been supportive of religious life, but conservatives are unwilling to join the "new right" in seeking religious explanations of reality. For conservatives the world is well-ordered, and speculation over ultimate design is not fruitful.

According to contemporary conservatives, the natural world is a source of beauty that is extremely resistant to human abuses, and should remain "open" for human uses. Conservatives, thus, are very critical of the environmental movement. To conservatives, the doomsday prophecies of environmentalists on such issues as global warming underestimate the resilience of nature, and the attempts by environmentalists to "protect" nature from human uses prevent the sustained management of natural resources. Nature is there for us to use, and, with careful management, both nature and humans can benefit. The proper approach to nature, according to conservatives, includes conservation and managed use. It is based on common sense, and does not rely on any metaphysical assumptions.

Human Nature

For conservatives, people are neither naturally good nor naturally bad. People have a moral sense that propels them to virtue, but this can be undermined by the excessive egoism and relativism of liberal society. The good society encourages virtuous action and uses disincentives to discourage vices. Individuals generally possess sufficient rationality to respond appropriately to incentive structures. Rationality is limited by passion, but rational action should prevail in a well-structured society.

Contemporary conservatives assume a level of rationality in individuals far beyond that considered to exist by traditional conservatives. Contemporary conservatives believe that individuals are capable, in general, of pursuing their own interests intelligently. Indeed, in justifying free markets, contemporary conservatives often point to the market as a place where rational decision making, patience, and self-control are rewarded.[48]

Contemporary conservatives are divided on the issue of how much control must be exercised over the decisions of individuals, but they all assume that individuals are capable of a broad range of decision making in political, social, economic, and private life. Thus, even when contemporary conservatives differ on the freedom of choices that ought to be available to citizens, their arguments bear little resemblence to the concerns expressed by traditional conservatives on this subject.

Among contemporary conservatives, the more libertarian conservatives are willing to allow individuals a very wide range of choices in their lives, if

[48]This has been a theme in Michael Novak's attempts to reconcile Catholicism with capitalism; see *The Spirit of Democratic Capitalism* (New York: Simon and Schuster, 1982).

no one else is harmed unwillingly. Libertarian conservatives, sharing the views of classical liberals, believe that attempts to control behavior limit freedom and expand the tyrannical force of government. Most conservatives, though, are not persuaded that the libertarian approach to freedom can work. Individuals should be free to make a wide range of choices, and government regulation should not be expansive, but activities that are self-destructive or that violate established norms can be regulated. Conservatives will, for example, prohibit drug use, pornography, and prostitution, because such activities are bad even for consenting adults and because they incur social costs. The toleration of vice creates an environment in which the worst in people can prevail, but a virtuous society can promote virtuous citizens.

Attempts to encourage virtue and discourage vice are not the result of conservatives' entertaining utopian ideals. Conservatives do not think human nature can be perfected, and they accept **human imperfection**. There will always exist the industrious and the lazy, the wise and the foolish, the multitalented and the ungifted, and the witty and the banal. No reforms by egalitarian dreamers can alter the broad differences in proclivities and abilities of individuals without denying freedom and enforcing mediocrity. Conservatives seek to limit bad behavior, but they do not seek to mold the perfect individual.

Conservatives also believe that men and women have essential differences that sometimes justify different treatment before the law. For example, conservatives in the United States oppose drafting women into the military, claiming that most women lack the strength and ferocity characteristic of male soldiers. Conservatives especially oppose the use of female soldiers in combat, because the mix of women and men in a highly charged and dangerous setting will lead to tensions and emotions among soldiers that could harm combat morale. Conservatives also argue that women are less likely than men to be career-driven and more likely to leave jobs for marriage and childrearing, thus justifying some inequalities between men and women concerning wages and promotions. While conservatives generally believe that men and women should be equal under the law and question traditional laws that have denied women basic economic rights, they oppose egalitarian reforms that ignore substantial differences between the sexes. For example, conservatives in the United States opposed the Equal Rights Amendment on the grounds that it would generate egalitarian reforms blind to gender differences.

Society

Conservatives view society as a complicated mechanism that must be treated delicately. They reject traditional conservatism's organic metaphor of the "body politic." However, contemporary conservatives see society and its components as so complicated and interconnected that they often draw conclusions about social life similar to those of traditional conservatives. Both contemporary and traditional conservatives fear that reforms will produce unanticipated consequences that will shred the social fabric. Both also support mediating institutions, such as families and churches, that bind people to local communities and offer protection against centralized government. Contemporary conservatives, though, endorse a dynamic market economy that traditional conservatives viewed with distrust because of the unhealthy effects it would have on a stable society. For contemporary conservatives, the well-structured society must foster the dynamic qualities of the market, without allowing the economic sphere to upset the more stable relations conservatives value in the political, cultural, and private spheres of social life.

The good society, for conservatives, then, must be a mechanism that runs at different speeds in different spheres of life. In the economic sphere, technological changes and social mobility will generate fairly rapid changes in the ways people live and interact. In the political sphere, change should be much slower and should be the result of careful and prudent consideration. In the cultural sphere, the pace of change must be slower still, so that religion and traditional values can curb the unsettling changes generated by the economic sphere. Conservative criticisms of the avant-garde in literature and the arts, especially when publicly funded, and conservative endorsements of "solid middle-class values" reveal the conservative concern over the "new" in cultural life. In the private sphere of individual and family life, change must be very slow, so that individuals can enjoy the certain and expect the expected. The **metaphor of a "delicate watch"** is useful for describing a society that is authoritatively tuned.[49] The second hand is economics, the minute hand is politics, and the hour hand is both culture and private life.

Maintaining the different speeds for different spheres of life in society is a difficult task for conservatives, and one that is made more difficult by the recent liberal embrace of the policies of **multiculturalism**, such as endorsing bilingual education. Society is delicate, even fragile, according to conservatives. Shared values and a shared respect for political and cultural traditions keep society from flying apart. Multiculturalism, which celebrates the diversity of worldviews and the richness of various cultures, does not promote the shared set of understandings and values required for social cohesion. It encourages excessive skepticism about the values needed for social stability. It invites a cultural relativism which refuses to recognize the superiority of western, middle-class values. Bilingual education promotes permanent cultural separateness and discourages immigrant groups from conforming to mainstream values necessary for educational and economic success. Liberals may think they are assisting minorities and illustrating respect for other cultures by advocating bilingual education, but conservatives insist liberals are in

[49]The metaphor of the "delicate watch" has been used by classical liberals. They emphasized the delicate qualities to point out that interference with the economy should be carried out carefully and precisely, and only when the economy is not accurately "keeping its own time." Conservatives here, once again, take up part of the classical liberal program, but such liberals were not concerned about different spheres of life moving at different paces. A discussion of the watch as a metaphor in the history of classical liberal political economy can be found in Albert O. Hirschman, *The Passions and the Interests: Political Arguments for Capitalism Before Its Triumph* (Princeton: Princeton University Press, 1977), esp. pp. 81–93.

fact ignoring the normal patterns of cultural adaptation that all immigrants must face and are thus harming the futures of immigrant and minority groups.

In the United States, conservatives have never objected to citizens of similar racial, ethnic, or religious backgrounds living together in their own neighborhoods instead of rapidly becoming assimilated into the "melting pot" of an integrated community. These conservatives, relying on nineteenth- and twentieth-century experiences in the United States, argue that separate communities are but a temporary feature and disappear as groups are slowly integrated into the dominant culture.[50] Multicultural and bilingual education threaten to turn temporary preferences for separation into permanent arrangements. The permanent "balkanization" of society makes impossible the shared cultural norms that conservatives desire and makes probable the disintegration of social norms.[51]

This vision of society as a complicated mechanism whose components must be held together while they move at different speeds in different spheres requires conservatives to embrace a rather difficult account of social harmony. Social harmony is not created by the egalitarianism of socialists and communists, nor is it fostered by the organic stability of traditional conservatives. Social harmony is the result of careful tending of the interactions between different spheres as they move along at their respective speeds. The dynamics of a market economy must be nurtured, but the pace of cultural change must be protected from the rapid innovations generated in the economy. It is far from obvious how culture can be sheltered from the innovations of the economy. The conservative can respond that there exists a natural proclivity to embrace the familiar and the traditional, but the conservative cannot push this claim too far, or else he or she cannot explain the success of entrepreneurs who have acted creatively and innovately in the economic sphere. What the conservative can endorse in public policy matters, though, is that government should not put added pressure on the cultural and private spheres to meet the pace of economic transformation. Furthermore, the conservative can wage battles against the liberal reformers who refuse to see the complicated relations among spheres of life that exist in society.

Epistemology

Rather than developing epistemological theories, conservatives employ four forms of reason to guide understanding and action. These four forms of reasoning—examination of tradition, reliance on historical knowledge, use of common sense, and development of science—provide insights into the world, but alone, or in combination, they do not result in perfect knowledge. Our knowledge about the world can be improved, but it will always be limited.

[50]Sowell, *Ethnic America,* pp. 277–280.

[51]Conservatives have not addressed how this problem of shared norms will be answered by school choice or voucher systems. School choice may encourage a wide variety of educational and cultural norms, and fail to provide social cohesion.

Conservatives rely on reason (broadly understood), but they do so without the optimism of liberal social reformers or of utopian social engineers.

Contemporary conservatives draw on some of the views on reason expressed by traditional conservatives. Traditional conservatives argued that tradition was the accumulated reason of previous generations, and thus it deserved respect and deference. Contemporary conservatives do not desire to recreate the past that traditional conservatives revered, but they agree with traditional conservatives that traditional beliefs and practices are the result of reason being tested over time. For contemporary conservatives, tradition distills some knowledge of the social world, but it does not reveal certainties about social life, nor does it create a foundation for an unchangeable social order. Indeed, the social, economic, and political traditions defended by contemporary conservatives are rarely older than two hundred years. The traditions that contemporary conservatives respect are the beliefs and practices that emerged during and after the traditional conservative defense of tradition.

Paying attention to the "lessons of history" is a second form of reason. Reliance on historical knowledge as a means of determining appropriate actions should prevent the repetition of errors and highlight effective practices. For example, the "lesson of Munich"—where the Western Allies permitted Hitler to incorporate parts of Czechoslovakia into Germany in return for a promise that he would curtail further expansionary efforts—teaches that democracies must never attempt to appease aggressors. And the "lesson of Watergate" teaches that cover-ups rarely succeed and that immediate disclosure of mistakes is the best policy. Historical knowledge is far from perfect, though, because different lessons can be drawn from the same events and previous events may bear little resemblance to current conditions. History is a guide that only charts general directions.

Conservative reliance on common sense as a form of reason provides both an acknowledgment of the value of everyday experience and a counterweight to the abstract and theoretical tendencies in scientific thought. For example, common sense argued that the Soviet Union was not to be trusted concerning nuclear weapons, that the best policy was therefore to be able to deter nuclear attack, and that it was foolish to pursue arms limitation treaties and, worse, unilateral disarmament policies that depended on theories about Soviet goodwill. Just as tradition has withstood the test of time, common sense is the result of reason and action put to the test. Common sense is a form of reason that works without theoretical elaboration, and one which is centered on the everyday needs of people. Common sense resists the utopian ideas of abstract thinkers.

Contemporary conservatives are not as critical of science as are traditional conservatives. Traditional conservatives called into question the very foundations of the scientific approach to knowledge by challenging the idea of causality. Contemporary conservatives have serious reservations about science as a form of reason, but they do not challenge the idea of causality, nor do they challenge the ability of science to render explanations about behavior in the natural and social worlds.

Contemporary conservatives employ scientific methods in their studies and call upon scientific results to strengthen their arguments and interpretations. Many conservatives, especially the neoconservatives, have been trained in the social sciences and are familiar with the techniques and methods used for describing and explaining social activity. According to Albert Hirschman, the findings of neoconservatives can be summarized in terms of three basic theses.[52] First is the **perversity thesis**: conservative social science suggests that well-intended social policies often produce perverse effects that are precisely the opposite of those intended. For example, the crosstown busing of children was a liberal attempt to integrate schools, but the policy prompted white flight away from inner-city public schools to private schools and the suburbs, resulting in increasingly segregated schools.[53] Second is the **futility thesis**: conservative social science shows that liberal reformers are oblivious to deep social laws that resist attempts at social improvement. For example, George Stigler argued that the distribution of income has a natural character that cannot be significantly changed by redistributive federal policies.[54] Third is the **jeopardy thesis**: conservative social science shows that naive attempts to expand prior reforms only undercuts the gains that these reforms produced. For example, the equal opportunity laws of the 1960s succeeded in breaking down many barriers to minority employment, but when radicals attempted to expand equality through affirmative action, the unintended results included increased white resistance to minority advancement and a reduction in minority employment opportunities. (Our discussion of Thomas Sowell in the section on justice further illustrates the jeopardy thesis.)

Despite employing social science to demonstrate the failures of liberal programs, conservatives generally regard science with skepticism. Science—without the addition of tradition, historical knowledge, and common sense—encourages scholars to assume the world is much more pliable, and much more amenable to reform, than it actually is. Dependence upon science must be tempered by the prudence that reliance on tradition, historical knowledge, and common sense provides.

Science is missing more, though, than just prudence. Conservatives view science as missing the proper grounding in the quest for knowledge. The natural sciences should be driven by the quest to improve the living standards of citizens. The agricultural researcher improving the quality and quantity of crops provides more valuable information than does the astronomer seeking to explain black holes or the anthropologist seeking the remains of human ancestors. Research that does not have practical applications is not regarded highly by conservatives. Most conservatives in the United States were not particularly supportive of funding a space program unless it illustrated United States superiority over the communists' space programs or unless it could be

[52]Albert Hirschman, *The Rhetoric of Reaction: Perversity, Futility, and Jeopardy* (Cambridge, Mass.: Belknap Press, 1991).

[53]James Coleman and Sara Kelly, "Education," in *The Urban Predicament,* edited by William Gorham and Nathan Glazer (Washington, D.C.: Urban Institute, 1976).

[54]George Stigler, "Director's Law of Public Income Distribution," *Journal of Law and Economics* 13 (Apr. 1970), pp. 1–10.

deployed for nuclear defense systems. The search for theoretical insights that have little foreseeable application is not opposed by conservatives, but they see little reason for the government to support such research.

Conservatives draw on the works of Eric Voegelin and Leo Strauss to question the concerns of the social sciences. Voegelin and Strauss argued that classical political thought sought to understand the social world in order to improve political life and to nourish the qualities of the good citizen. The modern social sciences have forsaken the quest for the good citizen in the good polity in order to provide an "objective" explanation of how social life works. The social sciences now explain behavior, but that behavior is not judged in relation to any model of the best behavior, because social scientists seek neutrality in their presentations. The modern social sciences are thus distanced from the concerns of the good political life and have lost the classical ability to criticize political life.[55]

Social sciences that only explain, but that cannot judge, have a disastrous effect on society. Neutrality in scholarship leads to relativism in the classroom. Since standards of the good citizen in the good polity are not used, all forms of political life are deemed worthy of attention and respect. Universities promote a multicultural tolerance that leaves the critical abilities of students impaired and that fails to win the allegiance of citizens to the best in the western tradition.[56] Conservatives claim that modern knowledge of the social world is too often simply the explanation and prediction of behavior, without the evaluation of human action.

Conservatives employ reason, but they recognize the limitations of all forms of reason in understanding a natural world and a social world that are too complex for human mastery. The best understandings of the human condition will blend the four forms of reasoning that conservatives employ. These understandings will be rich and multifaceted, but they will not approach the richness and complexity of our lives.

SUMMARY AND CONCLUSIONS

Contemporary conservatism has achieved dramatic and rapid success as an ideology. Conservatives have scored electoral successes in many western nations, especially since the 1980s. Conservatives, once highly critical of the media—from which they felt excluded—now command much space on the editorial pages of newspapers and magazines, and control much time on the radio and on television. Conservative ideas on policy issues are taken seriously by policy makers, including those who would never describe themselves as conservatives. Possibly the most telling aspect of conservative success is the unwillingness of nonconservative politicians to describe themselves as liberals. Conservatives have effectively turned liberalism into a ten-letter "four-letter word."

[55]For detailed and explicit criticisms of this type applied to political science research, see *Essays on the Scientific Study of Politics*, edited by Herbert J. Storing (New York: Holt, Rinehart and Winston, 1962).

[56]Sowell, *Inside American Education*, esp. pp. 70–74.

This, of course, does not mean that conservatism is without difficulties as an ideology. Conservatives still confront the challenge posed by their defense of dynamic market economies *and* their desire for stable social and private relationships. Can communities be cohesive and stable when markets create innovation and dislocation? Are market approaches to education dangerous to neighborhoods, which have been a source of community valued by conservatives? Can the nuclear family survive when economic conditions in many western countries force or, at least, encourage, both spouses to work? Can the self-discipline that conservatives applaud be generated in market economies that often laud immediate gratification? These are questions that cannot be answered by merely criticizing liberal and radical reforms.

In the foreign policy arena, conservatives must respond to a world in which their archenemy, communism, is no longer as powerful or as threatening. Conservative reluctance to embrace international organizations makes the future of conservative foreign policy difficult to predict. Conservatives are now arguing among themselves over how much internationalism to embrace, and how to carry out foreign policy objectives.

In the domestic policy arena, conservatives must start to illustrate the effectiveness of their approaches to domestic issues. Conservatives cannot simply point to the failure of previous liberal regimes after conservatives too have had the opportunity to wield national power. Marketlike approaches to pollution and education seem likely to be pursued by western governments in the 1990s, and the results of these attempts may provide conservatism with the positive agenda needed for continuing its electoral success. Conservatives must also illustrate that they can cut taxes without engaging in the deficit spending that they so often criticized when they were not in power.

In the electoral arena, conservatives also face tough questions and decisions. Were the electoral successes in the 1980s the result of broad ideological changes in the populace of western nations, or were they the result of the charisma and forcefulness of such leaders as Reagan and Thatcher? Can conservatives win elections without procuring the allegiance of "new right" and neofascist groups? In the United States, the 1992 campaign of George Bush was damaged when he alienated the "new right," but it was also hurt when Bush then allowed the "new right" to dominate the first night of the Republican National Convention—its adherents scared many voters with their strident and mean-spirited oratory. In France and Germany, conservative politicians must decide how much anti-immigrant rhetoric and policy they will borrow from neofascist groups and parties.

Conservatives must also decide whether, without diluting their ideology, they can broaden their appeal in western nations. The environmental concerns of young people are not met by conservative ideas about nature, and conservatives may have to reassess their utilitarian and "managed-conservation" approaches to the environment. Conservatives must also confront the lack of support for their ideology among women and minorities. Conservatism has some adherents among women and minorities, but its strongest support is from white males. Conservative leaders have not been very effective so far in making their ideology more inclusive. Can they do so, without threatening the base of conservative support?

Conservatism, despite its many challenges, remains a potent ideology. The defense of the economic ideas of classical liberalism will continue to find adherents in a world in which planned economies have rarely proved dynamic or successful. The search for stable social and personal relations is unlikely to disappear from the modern agenda. How conservatives will handle the tension between these two powerful sources of support will shape the future successes (or failures) of contemporary conservatism.

PART FOUR

Nascent Ideologies

My ground is the Bible. Yes. I am a Bible-bigot. I follow it in all things, both great and small.

—John Wesley

It isn't necessary to imagine the world ending in fire or ice—there are two other possibilities: one is paperwork, and the other is nostalgia.

—Frank Zappa

We abuse land because we regard it as a commodity belonging to us. When we see land as a community to which we belong, we may begin to use it with love and respect.

—Aldo Leopold

How to be green? Many people have asked us this important question. It's really very simple and requires no expert knowledge or complex skill. Here's the answer: Consume less. Share more. Enjoy life.

—Penny Kemp and Derek Wall

The true Republic: men, their rights and nothing more; women, their rights and nothing less.

—Susan B. Anthony

Feminism is an entire world view or gestalt, not just a laundry list of women's issues.

—Charlotte Bunch

CHAPTER 11

Fundamentalism

Strong fundamentalist movements emerged in Judaism, Christianity, and Islam after World War II. All three types of fundamentalism had origins in earlier orthodox movements, but all three developed specific criticisms aimed at contemporary liberalism and secular humanism—"western" ideas that are seen as threatening religious belief and destroying the moral fabric of communities. Fundamentalists rely on the sacred texts of their religions to offer criticisms of, and alternatives to, established ideologies. While fundamentalist movements in the past often retreated from the world to build isolated and pure communities of believers, contemporary fundamentalists wage political battles, and some even employ violent tactics.[1]

Fundamentalists are also critical of the "mainstreams" of their own religions. Fundamentalists argue that the mainstream believers have made too many compromises with modern social and political practices, and thus have strayed from the path of orthodoxy. Throughout their histories, Judaism, Christianity, and Islam have faced criticisms from believers who assert that fundamental beliefs have been abandoned and traditional practices have lapsed. The books of the Old Testament can be read as the story of a series of lapses by the Hebrews, punctuated by dramatic returns to the true faith.[2] In Christian history, St. Francis and Martin Luther are just two of the most prominent figures to seek a return to the original form of Christianity as lived by Jesus and as outlined by the Apostle Paul in the New Testament. Shiite Muslims have historically opposed the mainstream (Sunni) Muslims on the grounds that Sunnis have erred fundamentally in accepting distinctions

[1]Some Islamic and Jewish radicals have engaged in armed attacks on their opponents. Radical antiabortion opponents—mostly Christian fundamentalists—have, although very rarely, committed violent acts against doctors who perform abortions.

[2]All three faiths venerate the Old Testament, in which special individuals deliver messages of warning from God about lapses in belief and conduct. Mohammed, for example, asserted that, despite having been abused by scribes and translators, both the Old and New Testaments were divinely inspired.

Sidebar 11-1

Some Fundamentalists and Their Main Writings

JEWISH FUNDAMENTALISTS

Rabbi Meir Kahane
Listen World, Listen Jew (1978)

Rabbi Zvi Yehuda Kook*
In the Pathways of Israel (1968)

CHRISTIAN FUNDAMENTALISTS

Jerry Falwell*
The Fundamentalist Phenomenon (1981)

Tim LaHaye*
The Battle for the Mind (1980)

Pat Robertson*
The Secret Kingdom (with Robert Slosser)

ISLAMIC FUNDAMENTALISTS

Ayatollah Ruhollah Khomeini (1900–1989)
Islam and Revolution (1981)

*Living author.

between the public and private spheres.[3] In all three religions, then, fundamentalism has a rich history. Contemporary fundamentalists draw on this history, but they have also had to respond to some very specific developments of the twentieth century.

Contemporary Jewish fundamentalism emerged after the Holocaust in Europe and the creation of the state of Israel in 1948. Many ultraorthodox Jewish groups were not very supportive of Israel, because many of its early leaders were secular Zionists. However, a few ultraorthodox rabbis, especially Rabbi Avraham Itshak Hacohen Kook and his son, Rabbi Zvi Yehuda Kook, viewed the creation of modern Israel as a sign that all of the original Promised Land would be returned to create a **greater Israel**. Such a state would be a spiritual beacon for the coming of the Messiah, which will signal an age of plenty and happiness for all true believers. Kookist followers—a group of bright, energetic, and devout Israelis—interpreted the Six-Day War of 1967 as a miracle that revealed the truth of their messianic message. The Kookists considered the Six-Day War a miracle because Israel gained many of the lands promised to Abraham by God four thousand years before and did so by crushing very large and heavily armed Arab armies. After 1967, Kookist followers became central figures in Jewish fundamentalism and formed the first, and most powerful, fundamentalist political organization in Israel, *Gush Emunim* (the "Bloc of the Faithful").[4]

[3]Both Shiite and Sunni Muslims have been involved in orthodox criticism of "mainstream" Islam, but Shiites generally have most often carried the banner of fundamentalism against the Sunnis. The common theme in Shiite criticism has been Sunni acceptance of the separation of religious and political leadership. Fundamentalist Shiites believe that the separation of church and state is forbidden by the Koran, and that a Muslim country should be guided by a religious leader.

[4]An excellent discussion of the Kooks and the rise of Gush Emunim is provided by Ehun Sprinzak, *The Ascendance of Israel's Radical Right* (New York: Oxford University Press, 1991).

Gush Emunim and other ultraorthodox Jewish sects insist that Israel enforce strict observance of traditional religious beliefs as detailed in the Torah and the Halakah.[5] However, they are most adamant that Israel maintain and enlarge the settlements of Jews in the Gaza Strip and the occupied West Bank.[6] They oppose any peace accord with Arab countries in which land from greater Israel is exchanged for peace. Jewish fundamentalists have engaged in protest and party politics in Israel but have not fared well at the polls. Nevertheless, they often have some influence in the coalition governments common under Israel's parliamentary system, and their views are often respected by many nonorthodox Jewish leaders. Israeli fundamentalists also draw strength from their ability to raise funds, especially from fundamentalist Jews in the United States, who share their opposition to any peace plan that would compromise greater Israel.

Contemporary Christian fundamentalists emerged in the early twentieth century; they are committed to, among other things, the **inerrancy** of the Bible. "Inerrancy" is the doctrine that claims that the Bible is literally and absolutely correct in all of its claims. This doctrine was spelled out in a twelve-volume series, *The Fundamentals*, published between 1910 and 1915. Criticizing the mainstream churches for becoming involved in politics and social policy, *The Fundamentals* called for an emphasis on personal salvation and the power of faith. The early fundamentalists believed that Jesus Christ would return, conquer evil, and begin a thousand-year reign of peace. The millennium of peace would be followed by the end of the material universe and the "day of judgment." Fundamentalists argued that the best preparation for the future was to concentrate on personal salvation, rather than on social improvements. Most Christian fundamentalists, therefore, withdrew from political activities.[7]

In the United States, Christian fundamentalist attention to politics was first generated in the 1950s and 1960s by moderate evangelicals, like Billy Graham, who expressed concerns about the expansion of communism and its atheistic teachings. More important in politicizing these fundamentalists, however, was the 1973 ruling on abortion by the U.S. Supreme Court in *Roe v. Wade*. Profoundly disturbed by what they perceived as the Court's decision to license "murder" of the unborn, fundamentalist ministers felt compelled to speak out on political issues and to become involved in political campaigns. Fundamentalists gradually joined forces with ultraconservatives in the Republican Party to establish the "new right," an avowedly political movement.[8] Although some

[5]The Torah is the Pentateuch, comprising the first five books of the Old Testament, and is the central source of Jewish religious law. The Halakah, or legal part of the Talmud, provides thousands of rules to guide the daily life of the devout and orthodox.

[6]These areas, occupied by Israel after the 1967 Arab-Israeli War, remain disputed territories.

[7]A final political blow to those Christian fundamentalists who had not wished to retreat from public life was delivered in 1925 by the famous Scopes trial. Fundamentalists sought to prevent the teaching of evolution in Tennessee's public schools. Clarence Darrow, the lawyer for the fundamentalist side, won the court battle in this highly publicized trial but lost the public relations war. Fundamentalist rejection of evolutionary theory was widely perceived as reactionary and "parochial."

[8]For an insider's account of these developments, see Richard Vigurie, *The New Right: We're Ready to Lead* (Falls Church, Va.: Vigurie, 1980).

Sidebar 11-2

Evangelical Religions and Fundamentalism

Evangelical religions in the United States trace their origins to the "Great Awakening" that took place from the 1730s to the 1750s. During the "Great Awakening," evangelical preachers stirred religious enthusiasm and nationalistic fervor in the rural areas of New England and in the mid-Atlantic colonies. Rejecting the rationalism of the mainstream Protestant religions on the urban coast, evangelicals spoke of both the joys of salvation and the eternal pain of damnation. Evangelicals emphasized the depravity of humans, but also the possibility of salvation through the free choice of faith. For evangelicals, then, the most important sacrament was adult baptism. Evangelicals also offered a millennialist vision of the future where America would be the "new Israel," the site of the return of the Messiah and the beneficiary of a thousand years of peace and plenty. The evangelical fervor of the Great Awakening, when thousands would gather in small towns to hear local and itinerant preachers deliver an emotional message of justification by faith, expired long before the American Revolution began. However, the Great Awakening stirred political and religious ideas that are still powerful.

Evangelical religions were an important source of nationalism in areas settled during the western expansion of the early eighteenth century. This nationalism helped create among the colonists the solidarity that was necessary during the Revolutionary War and the creation of the Union. (Contemporary fundamentalists continue to espouse the special role of the United States in their millennialist messages. Some of the nationalism of the "new right" draws on this view that the United States is the chosen country.) Evangelical religions also promoted social and economic discipline in

fundamentalist ministers endorsed Jimmy Carter during the 1976 presidential campaign because of his "born-again" religious affiliations, fundamentalists have been most supportive of the brand of conservatism espoused by Ronald Reagan during the 1980s. Opposition to contemporary liberalism unites Christian fundamentalists, because liberal ideas and policies are regarded as being responsible for the moral decay of the country. Most Christian fundamentalists now seek their political goals by working in coalitions with other conservatives within the Republican Party.[9]

Contemporary Islamic fundamentalism emerged as a response to the decolonization of the Middle East before and after World War II, the creation

[9]The political power of the Christian fundamentalists in the United States is probably greater than their numbers alone would suggest. They have formed many effective interest groups and political action committees. Fundamentalists have been effective in registering previously nonpolitical Christians and in organizing voters for elections, especially at the local level. Their fundraising has also been very successful. Most dramatically, fundamentalist television ministries reach millions of homes to deliver their religious and political messages. The continuing public clashes over abortion give fundamentalists access to the media, and these confrontations are a source of solidarity among the various denominations that are active in the Christian fundamentalist movement.

the frontier towns, where traditional practices and norms were not established.

Although evangelical religious fervor died out in the 1750s, evangelical religious ideas prospered. Many Congregationalists, Presbyterians, Baptists, and, later, Methodists would adopt evangelical ideas and practices. Evangelical ideas would also be active in a wide variety of independent churches that accepted the evangelical ideas on baptism and on the inerrancy of the Bible, but that embraced somewhat different liturgical practices. Evangelical beliefs inspired the formation of many Protestant denominations in the United States, some of which manifested the evangelical belief in an active Holy Ghost by "speaking in tongues" and by "healing." Such evangelicals are termed "charismatic," and they practice an enthusiastic form of evangelical belief, which many evangelicals and some fundamentalists reject.

The long tradition of evangelical religions in the United States has led to a situation where some evangelical churches, such as the Presbyterians, now are considered by other evangelicals to be mainstream churches that have lost the fundamental beliefs which guide traditional evangelical thought. Contemporary fundamentalists are evangelicals who argue that mainstream Christians, including mainstream evangelicals, have lost their way. For fundamentalists, too few of the mainstream churches insist on the inerrancy of the Bible and on the nonrationalist joy of religious faith. Evangelicals are all "born-again" Christians, because they have freely chosen their faith, many expressing this in adult baptism. Between one-third and one-half of United States adults consider themselves evangelical or born-again Christians, but fundamentalists constitute only between one-tenth and one-fifth of the adult U.S. population.

of Israel, and the continuing influence of Western ideas and practices on Islamic countries. For many Arabs, fundamentalism is also a voice for Arab pan-nationalism. The boundaries established during decolonization were largely imposed by Western imperialist states, and many Arabs desired an Arab nation that would dissolve these artificial borders. Islamic fundamentalism, however, found its greatest source of support in non-Arabic Iran, where Iranian Shiites staged a fundamentalist revolution in 1979.

Iran (and, earlier, Persia) has been a historical stronghold for radical Shiites. After World War II, and with the aid of Western countries, Iran was established as an independent country having a "constitutional" monarchy. Opposition to the Shah, the monarch of Iran, was fueled by fundamentalist criticism of him, his westernization of Iran, the brutality of his police and security forces, and the economic inequalities in Iran. The most sustained and vocal criticism of the Shah's government was delivered by the Shiite fundamentalist leader, Ayatollah Khomeini (1900–1989), whom Shiites widely respected as a learned and brilliant religious scholar. Shiite fundamentalists expect religious leaders to assume political power. With the support of many Iranian citizens, Khomeini returned to Iran from exile in France and established himself as the religious and political leader of Iran in 1979.

The revolution in Iran stirred fundamentalist sentiments throughout the Muslim world. In Arab countries, support for fundamentalism was further increased when Egypt and Israel signed the Camp David Peace Accords in 1979. Many Arabs asserted that Egyptian President Sadat (1918–1981) had betrayed the Palestinians and the Arab world by recognizing Israel's right to exist.[10] Fundamentalists accused the "secular" governments of Arab countries of failing to rid the Middle East of Israel and of assuming too many of the trappings of Western countries. Islamic fundamentalism also appeals to Muslim citizens in non-Arab countries such as Pakistan, who have not benefited from the westernization of their countries.[11]

THE POLITICAL BASES

Problems

Fundamentalists from all three religions identify many similar problems in contemporary societies. They believe that the most dangerous threat is the continuing power of **secular humanism**. Secular humanists, who often embrace contemporary liberalism, regard questions of faith as being a private matter and view science and reason as the sources of knowledge for practices, decisions, and activities in the public sphere. Secular humanists endorse human rights and individual liberties on the basis of a shared humanitarianism that does not seek its foundations in religion. They subscribe to liberal ideas about individual autonomy and the separation of church and state. They not only tolerate a plurality of ideas and practices in society, they follow John Stuart Mill in valuing the benefits that cultural pluralism confers on thoughtful individuals and on social discourse. Secular humanism is, for fundamentalists, a competing ideology that compartmentalizes religious life, replaces faith with science, and encourages an individualism that is always prone to hedonism.

Fundamentalists object to the public/private split in liberal societies and the banishing of religion to the private sphere; they wish to retain religious influence on public institutions, political decisions, and social practices. They refer to their respective sacred texts for guidance regarding public and private decisions and actions. Although Jewish and Islamic guidelines in such matters as dietary restrictions, for example, are much more detailed and specific than Christian guidelines, fundamentalists from all three religions believe certain personal behaviors should be prohibited by law. As another example, these fundamentalists are opposed to homosexuality because it is forbidden in each of their sacred texts. Hence, fundamentalists argue that many private actions

[10]President Sadat was assassinated by Islamic fundamentalists in 1981. Many Arabs who do not consider themselves fundamentalists approved of the assassination.

[11]For a more detailed account of the development of Christian and Islamic fundamentalism, see Martin Riesebroat, *Pious Passion: The Emergence of Modern Fundamentalism in the U.S. and Iran* (Berkeley: University of California Press, 1993), and *Fundamentalism in Comparative Perspective,* edited by Lawrence Kaplan (Minneapolis: University of Minnesota Press, 1992).

between consenting adults are not, in fact, private, but are public concerns that should be regulated.

While Christian fundamentalists in the United States do not seek to dissolve entirely the boundary between public and private, they argue that the separation of the church and state has been misinterpreted by the Supreme Court in ways that limit religious expression and diminish the role of religion in social life.[12] They believe that the founders of the country intended a limited separation of church and state that would allow for religious toleration by forbidding governmental establishment of a single religion. The Founding Fathers, in this interpretation, did not want to discourage religious belief, restrict religious speech at public events, or remove religious symbols from public buildings. Fundamentalists view the United States as a Christian nation that must pursue Christian values while tolerating non-Christian religions. A limited separation can promote religious freedom without rejecting the role of religion in public life. Unlike Jewish and Islamic fundamentalists, Christian fundamentalists do not seek to restrict the rights of citizens who do not share the Christian faith. They reluctantly acknowledge the religious freedom and full citizenship of persons who do not practice Christianity.

All fundamentalists remain skeptical of the contributions made by Enlightenment science, especially those that threaten the ontology revealed in their sacred texts. Science is problematic for fundamentalists, because it offers material explanations of the universe and calls into question the claims about the origins of life made in sacred texts. In the United States, fundamentalists advocate the teaching of "creationism" in public schools as an alternative explanation to evolution. **Creationism** is an explanation of the beginning of the world and of man which is drawn directly from a literal reading of the account of the creation of the world by God in the book of Genesis.[13]

Secular humanism is also responsible, according to fundamentalists, for glorifying individualism. Thus, fundamentalists share many of the concerns about individualism that have been expressed by traditional and contemporary conservatives. They view individualism as a threat to the family, the community, and the Christian (evangelical) faith. Individualism encourages people to seek personal rights and immediate happiness, and discourages them from acknowledging their duties to family and community. It denies people the sustained pleasure obtainable through dedicating one's life to God. For fundamentalists, individualism promotes a drive for immediate gratification. Hedonistic behavior and the disregard of traditional moral rules are results of individualism.

Relativism and cultural pluralism are also problems that fundamentalists hope to attack. Relativism is understood as the viewpoint that all beliefs and

[12]Many Christian fundamentalists and contemporary conservatives rely on the interpretation of the Founding Fathers' religious views as they were expressed by Robert L. Cord in *Separation of Church and State: Historical Fact and Current Fiction* (New York: Lambeth Press, 1982).

[13]This does not mean that fundamentalists reject all scientific understanding nor does it imply that they reject, or deny, the advances in technology achieved through Enlightenment science.

practices, including those of fundamentalists, are simply matters of individual tastes. Relativists assert that no belief or practice is objectively correct. Relativism, combined with hedonism, produces the lack of morality and loss of community that fundamentalists deplore. For example, cultural pluralism teaches schoolchildren to appreciate a wide variety of cultures and traditions. In the southern United States, fundamentalists have gone to court to prevent their children from reading multicultural materials that favorably portray people of various cultures.[14] Fundamentalists claim that multicultural approaches confuse children and encourage relativist ideas. For fundamentalists, education should make clear the superiority of the specific culture and religion of the fundamentalists. Other cultures and religions can be tolerated, but they are not recognized as equal to those of the fundamentalists.

For Islamic fundamentalists, the hedonism promoted by secular humanism is abetted by capitalist practices. Islamic fundamentalists criticize capitalism, because it encourages greed, competition, and self-interest. Islamic fundamentalists are not, however, sympathetic to communism.[15] Like other fundamentalists, they reject the atheism of communism and the lack of opportunities for individual entrepreneurship. Jewish fundamentalists are wary of some of the effects on community—especially, the rapid changes in lifestyle—that capitalism can cause, but they are much less critical of capitalism than are the Islamic fundamentalists. Christian fundamentalists in the United States support capitalism as a system that is fair and that secures some freedom from the secular state. They are much more concerned about the dangers of government regulation of the economy than they are about the dangers of capitalism. They espouse a free market vision, with the exception that they believe government should prohibit the sales of services and goods—such as prostitution, pornography, and drugs—that promote vice.

For fundamentalists, a political economy that is not guided by at least some moral concerns produces a society that promotes relativism and the sins of individualism. Thus, all three types of fundamentalism are critical of contemporary liberal views on freedom of speech and on the marketplace of ideas. Islamic fundamentalists are willing to ban books, and to place bounties on the lives of Muslim authors who have published works criticizing Islamic beliefs. Jewish fundamentalists are also willing to prohibit the publication and distribution of texts that they find sacrilegious. Christian fundamentalists are willing to tolerate a broader range of texts in the marketplace, but they are very critical of the liberals' willingness to protect—under the banner of "freedom of political speech"—such activities as burning the flag, dancing in a suggestive manner, and displaying obscene art.[16] Christian funda-

[14]*Mozert v. Hawkins*, U.S. District Court for Eastern District of Tennessee, 24 Oct. 1986. For a brief and interesting discussion of the issues in this case, see Amy Gutmann, "Undemocratic Education," in *Liberalism and the Moral Life*, edited by Nancy Rosenblum (Cambridge: Harvard University Press, 1989), pp. 81–83.

[15]A constant theme in Ayatollah Khomeini's speeches after the revolution in Iran was the danger of being seduced by either the West (capitalism) or the East (communism).

[16]Christian fundamentalists have been very active in trying to ban many books from the shelves of public schools.

mentalists make the same distinction as contemporary conservatives between political speech, which deserves the full protections of the right to free speech, and nonpolitical speech, which deserves fewer protections. In the United States, Christian fundamentalists have been supportive of religious free speech, including the religious free speech of sects whose views diverge sharply from theirs. Christian fundamentalists have not always been treated kindly by mainstream denominations or by the U.S. government, and they would like to prevent precedents that might later be aimed at themselves. Christian fundamentalists accept the plurality of religions that coexist in the United States as "incurable," and, thus, religious speech must be protected so that the fundamentalists can deliver their message to all who will receive it. Nevertheless, all fundamentalists question the assumption that a system which allows competition among ideas will be intellectually healthy and will promote progress. They see no need for a competition among many ideas, especially religious ones, because the correct ideas are available in their sacred texts.

For fundamentalists, the world is unprepared for the apocalypse—the end of the material world—that is at hand. If there has been material and technological progress under secular humanism, it has been overwhelmed by moral decay. Secular humanism bears much of the responsibility for the current immorality and loss of faith evident in all societies. The individualism celebrated by secular humanism separates people from each other, from their families and communities, and from God. Given this moral breakdown, only the faithful will be saved.

Goals

Fundamentalists seek to create a community of believers wherein religious ideas will be integrated completely into political and public life. They expect such a community to prepare for the future, a future in which the material world will end. All three fundamentalisms share millenialist visions. It is the role of the fundamentalists to prepare the population of believers for this future by maintaining correct or orthodox religious beliefs and practices.

While all fundamentalists seek to create a community of believers, they have differing views on its scope. Jewish fundamentalists are not interested in expanding their community to include non-Jewish peoples. Christian fundamentalists are much more inclusive. They believe they are obligated to evangelize, preaching the Gospel throughout the world. They are not, however, seeking a world community of believers that would replace nation-states. Rather, they accept the development of nation-states, and hope that communities of believers will develop in each country. Ideally, there would be a relationship of brotherhood among all Christians, but it would be a spiritual brotherhood that would not threaten national boundaries.

Islamic fundamentalists seek to convert the entire population of the world, as do Christian fundamentalists, but they envision a community of believers that abolishes the boundaries of the nation-state. According to the fundamentalists, Muslims are not required to convert Jews or Christians, but they consider all others to be pagans who need conversion into the world community of believers.

All fundamentalists want to establish a community of believers that will be conducive to the purification of the faithful as they prepare for a meeting with God.

PHILOSOPHICAL BASES

Ontology and Epistemology

For fundamentalists, the world is a creation of God, and God is an active force in the world. Materialistic accounts of the universe fail to acknowledge the active role He plays in worldly affairs. Only a spiritual understanding of the world can grasp at least part of the divine handiwork. The real is not just material, but spiritual. Science may explain the way that things work in the world, but science can never explain why things are.

All fundamentalists view the creation story in Genesis as an accurate rendering of the spiritual force behind material creation. After the creation, God did not remove himself from the world to watch his handiwork, as some classical liberal deists maintain. Rather, God continues to play an active role in the lives of individuals and the fortunes of people and nations. Fundamentalists insist that the world is still filled with miracles performed by God and that the devout are able to work the will of God in this world. Fundamentalists have faith that they can and will persevere against overwhelming odds, because miraculous intervention is always possible.

All fundamentalists also share a belief that the end of the world is near. God will act to punish those who have strayed from the path of devotion and will reward those who have remained devout. Fundamentalists have a role to play in preparing the world and fellow believers for the final years of this material world.

All fundamentalists rely on the absolute authority of their **sacred texts**. For the fundamentalist, holy words written in sacred texts are the words of God and, thus, cannot be in error. Fundamentalist reliance on sacred texts leads to an epistemology of faith and to extensive textual scholarship. Faith is necessary because complete comprehension of God and God's handiwork is beyond the capability of humans. Textual scholarship is necessary in order to understand the sacred texts and to grasp the ideas and practices delineated in the texts.

The fundamentalists' claim that their sacred texts are never in error produces obvious conflicts with "scientific" evidence that frequently calls into question the histories provided by these texts. Fundamentalists may initially deny such evidence because of their faith, but in the Jewish and Christian world, at least, serious, theologically conservative scholars have also mounted significant arguments supporting their views of these texts. Fundamentalists claim absolute knowledge on many questions that are viewed by many other contemporary ideologies as open questions that require ongoing study.

Human Nature

For all Islamic fundamentalists—and for many Christian fundamentalists—human nature is depraved. Humans need the constant spiritual guidance of God, as provided by religious leaders, lest they lapse into the sins of the ego and the temptations of the flesh. The wall between church and state in liberal societies is a symptom of an egoism that claims some human interests are beyond religious control. Jewish fundamentalists have been, and remain, more skeptical about human nature than are mainstream believers in Judaism, but these fundamentalists are generally less concerned about human depravity than they are in encouraging the righteousness that is a potential within humans.

For all fundamentalists, humans are by nature social beings who can only realize their potential within the structures of the family and of the religious community. Fundamentalists emphasize the importance of personal decision making, but the "good" human is aided in this activity by family and community.

All fundamentalists agree that men and women have different roles within society. Fundamentalists reject perspectives (especially liberal and feminist ones) that claim that gender-based differences are not a central issue in understanding human nature and social practices. For many fundamentalists, women have private roles within the family that are important, but they should not have full access to the realms of religious and political authority. The sacred texts and the traditions that have developed in their societies make distinctions between male and female roles that must be maintained. Women must remain in the private sphere of the family, bearing and raising children.[17]

Society

The family is the basic unit in society for fundamentalists. According to fundamentalists, individual responsibility is necessary but individuals can only be fully responsible when they are bound to their families and their religious community. The religious community is not so much a community of individual believers as it is a community of religious families.[18]

The structure of Islamic families can be very different from that typical of Jewish and of Christian families, because Muslim males may take as many as four wives legitimately. However, fundamentalists agree that social policy should support the maintenance of their traditional family units. In the United States, Christian fundamentalists have emphasized "family values" in their political programs, and they have traced the decay of morality in society to

[17]Some Christian fundamentalist women have taken active political and religious roles, but they have not received much support from fundamentalist male preachers. At the 1994 annual convention of the Southern Baptists, for example, Jerry Falwell spoke out against female leadership of fundamentalist denominations.

[18]It should be noted that fundamentalists are not necessarily speaking about the liberal conception of an isolated, nuclear family.

the breakdown of the traditional family and the increase in single-parent families. Indeed, Christian fundamentalists and "new right" politicians often point to a revitalization of the traditional family as the essential ingredient in a moral rebirth of the nation.

SUBSTANTIVE POLITICAL PRINCIPLES

For fundamentalists, this section should properly be entitled, "Substantive Principles." Fundamentalists reject the western and liberal assumptions that political principles can be separated from other principles.

Authority

While "mainstream" versions of Judaism, Christianity, and Islam have accepted a variety of secular governments, fundamentalists endorse a version of authority that transcends or eliminates boundaries erected among religion, society, and the state. In Jewish and Christian fundamentalism, religious authorities should have significant influence over political authorities. In Islamic fundamentalism, religious authorities should be political authorities. In any fundamentalist state, however, governmental authority should be exercised to foster a community of believers and the moral conduct required of such believers. Rather than prohibiting the expression of religious beliefs, governmental authorities should facilitate the free display of dominant religious orientations. Rather than teaching secular humanism, relativism, and cultural pluralism, public education should make clear the superiority of the cultures and religions of the fundamentalists. Rather than permitting unabated capitalism, governments should prohibit free markets in goods and services that promote vice. Rather than permitting complete freedom of speech, governmental authority should regulate nonpolitical "speech" that denigrates sacred values and accepted morality. In short, while fundamentalists accept individual freedoms, they want governmental and religious authority to promote the moral values and actions emphasized in their particular religious beliefs.

Rulers

With the exception of some Christian fundamentalists who accept women in positions of authority, rulers should be males steeped in religious learning who can speak authoritatively on the sacred texts of their religions. Some Jewish fundamentalists insist ". . . on the restoration of the Sanhedrin—the council of seventy sages that was the Jewish Supreme Court and the final Halakic authority before the destruction of the Second Temple."[19]

Most Shiite Muslims believe that public authority can reside in a single

[19]Sprinzak, *The Ascendance of Israel's Radical Right*, p. 278.

religious-political leader. In Iran, Khomeini demanded that political leadership rest in the hands of religious leaders. Thus, the religious leader speaks with complete authority on all political issues.[20]

In the United States, Christian fundamentalists have accepted secular rulers, but they have expressed clear preferences for evangelical candidates and have voiced support for Christian leadership at all levels of the federal system. Tim LaHaye, a Christian fundamentalist, has taken the position that

> . . . no humanist is qualified to hold any governmental office in America—United States senator, congressman, cabinet member, State Department employee, or any other position that requires him to think in the best interest of America.[21]

Citizenship

For Jewish, Christian, and Islamic fundamentalists, discussions of citizenship emphasize obligations and duties rather than rights and privileges. The idea of *submitting oneself to God* informs the idea of citizenship within a fundamentalist community.[22] One gives up individualism and seeks the path of righteous living. The idea of submission involves the rejection of any individual desires that will harm the moral well-being of the religious community and an acceptance of individual responsibility for living a moral life within the community.

For many Jewish fundamentalists, Israel is the territorial space in which the fullest realization of the self as citizen and Jew can take place. Jewish fundamentalists envision a future in which Israel is a theocratic state where gentiles will have personal rights and very limited property rights, but no political rights. For radical Jewish fundamentalists, gentiles have no basis on which to claim rights in the land of Israel. The most radical fundamentalists advocate the removal from Israel of all gentiles.

Christian fundamentalist discussions of citizenship have focused on the need to promote the development of religious and patriotic citizens by instilling these values in children as a part of their education. They have been very critical of public schools, because they argue that religious history and moral values have been eliminated from the curricula. Furthermore, public schools endorse a multiculturalism that undermines patriotism and moral development. When the courts declared that prayer in public schools was unconstitutional, this was further evidence that schools could no longer be trusted to prepare future citizens. Fundamentalists have been one of the most active groups

[20]This view is regarded by some as a radical departure from Islamic teachings. Mangol Bayat, "Shi'a Islam as a Functioning Ideology in Iran: The Cult of the Hidden Imam," in *Iran Since the Revolution*, edited by Barry M. Rosen (New York: Columbia University Press, 1985), pp. 21–29.
[21]Tim LaHaye, *The Battle for the Mind* (Old Tappan, N.J.: Revell, 1980), p. 78. Quoted in A. James Richly, *Religion in American Public Life* (Washington, D.C.: Brookings Institution), p. 331.
[22]"Islam" means "to submit."

in the "home schooling" movement. They see home schooling as one of the prerequisites to creating citizens who understand the Christian heritage of the United States and who can fulfill the obligations of responsible citizenship.

Islamic fundamentalists view citizenship within the confines of nation-states as a temporary situation that will eventually give way to a world community of believers, the *ummah*. The rights of citizens are not the product of contractual relations among people, but are delineated in the Koran.

Structure

Given their belief in the authority of their sacred texts, fundamentalists are not always comfortable with those structures of government that draw on the democratic tradition of Western countries. Almost all fundamentalists make concessions to representative structures of governance, but fundamentalists do not believe that the majority has special insights into legislative matters.

There is considerable disagreement among Jewish fundamentalists over the proper structure of government for Israel. Many fundamentalists in the Gush Emunim accept the parliamentary structure of the Israeli Knesset. The Knesset, acting within the confines of the Torah and the Halakah, is an acceptable intermediary between God and the people of Israel. In recent years, however, more radical fundamentalists have criticized the Knesset and other representative institutions. For these fundamentalists, the proper structure of government is the structure that existed during the rule of King David. Representative institutions are seen as Western ideas that have no relevance for the chosen nation of Israel.

Fundamentalists in the United States accept the general structure of the present government, usually targeting their criticisms at its personnel or specific policies rather than at its structures. Fundamentalists have been critical of the Supreme Court's use of judicial review, but these criticisms subside when judicial rejection of legislation favors positions taken by the "new right." Christian fundamentalists are willing, then, to abide by the existing governmental structures in the United States, but they insist on their ability and right to determine which man-made laws violate the laws of God and, thus, to determine which laws of earthly governments must be rejected and resisted.

Justice

Jewish and Christian fundamentalists generally accept the concepts of justice that prevail in Israel and in the United States. Jewish fundamentalists think that the Israeli government should be more attentive to religious law and traditions, but they see no injustice in the disparities of wealth and income that characterize Israeli society. For Jewish fundamentalists, the poor should not be supported by expansive governmental welfare programs. Instead, religious convictions about caring for others result in obligations toward the poor that good Jews discharge voluntarily. In the United States, Christian fundamentalists, drawing on the arguments developed by contemporary conservatives, regard capitalist distributions as fair, and they criticize "welfarism" and affirmative action. Both Jewish and Christian fundamentalists accept the unequal distribution of goods that results from competition in the marketplace.

Islamic fundamentalists are highly critical of capitalist practices, the inequalities that result from competition in the marketplace, and the exploitation of Middle East resources by multinational corporations. Khomeini never disguised his disgust for capitalist practices, especially what he saw as the ravaging of Iran during the Shah's years by imperialist forces:

> Whenever our oppressive anti-national rulers enter in agreements with foreign states or companies, they pocket huge amounts of our people's money and lavish additional huge sums on their foreign masters. It is a veritable flood of forbidden consumption that sweeps past us, right before our eyes. All this misappropriation of wealth goes on and on: in our foreign trade and in the contacts made for the exploitation of our mineral wealth, the utilization of our forests and other natural resources, construction work, road building, and the purchase of arms from imperialists, both Western and communist. We must end all this plundering and usurpation of wealth.[23]

In Iran, Khomeini sought an economic path that would be neither capitalist nor communist. Citizens are free to engage in a variety of economic activities, and differences in income and wealth are acceptable. Certain industries, especially energy and transportation, were nationalized, and banks were nationalized in order to provide the interest-free loans that Iranian leaders assert are demanded by Islamic teachings. These nationalized sectors are operated with attention to their consequences on society in general, and the most economically deprived in particular. The state has an obligation to provide for the poor and disadvantaged and it levies taxes that are used to provide for the unfortunate. Extreme inequalities in income and wealth are not to be tolerated, and entrepreneurs should be sensitive to community needs. The state will redistribute land and goods if it determines that such redistribution would serve the greater good of society.

Change

Fundamentalists—Christian, Muslim, or Jewish—have not reached agreement among themselves on acceptable approaches to changing society. Some fundamentalists work within the existing system of governance, others engage in protest politics, including civil disobedience, and still others employ acts of violence.

Most Christian fundamentalists work within the political system. They rely on endorsing candidates, voting, lobbying, and taking issues before the courts. Abortion, however, has caused controversy within the fundamentalist movement over the desirability or effectiveness of working within the system. Some prolife fundamentalists, frustrated by the failure to achieve legislative or

[23]Ayatollah Khomeini, *Islam and Revolution: Writings and Declarations of Iman Khomeini*, translated by Hamid Algar (Berkeley: Mizan Press, 1981), p. 116.

judicial prohibition of abortion, have engaged in civil disobedience during protests at medical clinics. The most common form of such disobedience is to blockade the entrances to clinics that perform abortions. Some prolife fundamentalists, probably far fewer than a thousand, engage in the tactics of harassing, intimidating, and stalking medical personnel and their families. These types of activities move well beyond traditional norms of civil disobedience. A very few prolife fundamentalists have advocated or used violence against doctors who perform abortions. Many, but not all, fundamentalists have criticized or condemned the use of violence.

All three types of fundamentalism include the idea of "**holy war**" or "holy struggle." In a holy war, acts of violence are sanctioned by God, and casualties among the fundamentalists are regarded as martyrs. In their spiritual battle for a remoralized United States, Christian fundamentalists often do invoke the idea of a holy war, but they do so carefully. Similarly, because wars can have unholy consequences, Jewish and Islamic fundamentalists have engaged in lengthy debates over the question of holy wars and the ethics of violent action.

Jewish fundamentalists, particularly members of Gush Emunim, originally opposed the use of violence. Gush Emunim decided to employ standard political tactics. Indeed, in the early 1970s, Gush Emunism criticized Rabbi Meir Kahane's advocacy of Jewish terrorism to combat Arab terrorist attacks. Kahane, the U.S.-born founder of the Jewish Defense League (JDL), endorsed vigilante attacks before and after his arrival in Israel in 1971. Kahane's extreme anti-Arab rhetoric was well received by some fundamentalists, but nearly all continued to reject his violent tactics until the Camp David Peace Accords in 1978.

Camp David was a devastating blow to the territorial maximalists in Gush Emunim. Since 1968, Gush Emunim has actively, and sometimes illegally, supported settlements on land occupied after the Six-Day War in 1967. The Camp David Peace Accords included the return to Egypt of lands that had substantial Jewish settlements. Fundamentalists viewed the trading of land for peace as illegitimate and a retreat from the goal of a "greater Israel" that would prepare the way for the Messiah. Angered by Arab violence that followed the accords and frustrated over the failure to progress toward creation of a greater Israel, some members of Gush Emunim joined with other fundamentalists to form a "Jewish underground" that planned and engaged in vigilante acts. Illustrative of the underground's approach to change was their planned destruction of the Dome of the Rock, a Muslim mosque that sits on the Temple Mount, the site of Israel's First and Second Temples. One of the leaders of the underground, Yehuda Etzion, argued that progress toward a "greater Israel" was being blocked, because Israel had not reclaimed the Temple Mount and had not started building the Third Temple. The destruction of the Dome of the Rock would please God and awaken Israel to its responsibilities.[24] Israeli authorities thwarted the underground's plan, but Etzion argued that such

[24]Sprinzak, *The Ascendance of Israel's Radical Right*, pp. 94–99, 252–269.

actions were justified, because Jews are ruled by "laws of destiny" that mandate the realization of God's plan and allow them to break the "laws of existence" of nation-states.[25]

While many Jewish fundamentalists reject terrorist operations and the idea of "laws of destiny," they are willing to struggle against government movement of settlers in occupied territories. Furthermore, many of the fundamentalists who are settlers view violence against Arabs as necessary to combat Arab violence aimed at settlements. Settlers have also threatened violence against government troops should the soldiers try to remove them from their settlements. These fundamentalist attitudes toward violence will be tested if the peace process continues in the Middle East.

Many Islamic fundamentalists, but not all, believe violence is necessary to create Islamic states. Terrorist activities are condoned by some Islamic religious leaders and, in some cases, violent actions are declared sacred under the idea of a "jihad." A jihad is a holy war or struggle. "Jihad" can refer to the individual struggle to achieve devoutness, to spiritual struggles by groups of individuals to achieve religious goals, to terrorist struggles against Arab secular leaders and Israel, and to military actions by Islamic soldiers (including defensive actions). For Khomeini, it was the responsibility of religious leaders to lead a jihad against the anti-Islamic forces in the Middle East. Not all Islamic fundamentalists agree with Khomeini's frequent use of "jihad" to describe Islamic struggles. These scholars argue that a jihad can only be called by the "lost Imam" and that this will occur when the Apocalypse is at hand. Khomeini's version of jihad, however, has been accepted by many fundamentalists who see no other possibility for the creation of Islamic states.

SUMMARY AND CONCLUSIONS

Jewish fundamentalism may be the most short-lived of the fundamentalisms. The steps taken toward peace in the Middle East have continued to include "land for peace" agreements. The goal of a "greater Israel" may become more and more distant, and this would dampen the appeal of Jewish fundamentalism. The settlers in occupied territories will remain an important force in Israel, though, even if they are resettled. The question is: Will they remain politically active or will they retreat into orthodox communities that withdraw from political life?

Christian fundamentalists are likely to remain a powerful political force, especially in the United States. Although they have, in most cases, joined the Republican Party, it does not seem that they will be swallowed up in the "large tent" of political party inclusiveness. Given their access to television, it is difficult to believe that Christian fundamentalists will simply slide back into mainstream conservatism. If they elect fellow believers to positions of political power, Christian fundamentalists may sharpen their ideological perspective, particularly on substantive political principles. However, they may find that politics is more complicated than they suspect. There is always the possibility that the acquisition of power will lead to disillusionment.

[25]Sprinzak, *The Ascendance of Israel's Radical Right*, pp. 257–258.

Islamic fundamentalism may profoundly shape the future of some Middle Eastern and Asian countries. Islamic fundamentalists must, however, confront the problems of political leadership and political decision making. Without the charismatic leadership of Khomeini, they must give more attention to the structures of political life and to political accountability. Islamic fundamentalism nevertheless continues to appeal to many Arabs, regardless of developments in Iran.

Fundamentalist approaches to Judaism, Christianity, and Islam will always be appealing to some individuals who are frustrated by what they see as excessive cooperation by mainstream religions with the secular world. What marks the fundamentalist movements of the last thirty years is the willingness of fundamentalists to engage in political activity rather than retreating into religious enclaves. The future of contemporary religious fundamentalism may depend on the willingness of fundamentalists to "dirty their hands" in the messy world of politics.

CHAPTER 12

Environmentalism

During the 1960s and 1970s, new and radical voices emerged in the environmental movements in western Europe and the United States. Dissatisfied with the "shallow" conservationism of existing environmental groups, these new environmentalists demanded a "deep" ecological movement that would focus on revealing the fundamental flaws in contemporary ideas and actions. **Deep ecologists**, or "**greens**," argue that traditional environmental groups fail to grasp the primary causes of environmental degradation and simply protect ". . . the health and affluence of people in developed countries."[1] For greens, the prevailing ideologies in developed countries all rely on flawed views on production, consumption, and technological development. A new ethic is necessary to avoid the antienvironmental assumptions and practices embedded within existing western ideologies.

The greens, then, have been very self-conscious in their attempts to provide an alternative to contemporary ideologies. Greens have sometimes been reluctant to call their alternative an ideology, but they are certainly engaged in trying to create a comprehensive and cohesive worldview. As in most nascent ideologies, there is much greater agreement among greens about the problems that must be solved than there is agreement about the principles, procedures, and institutions required to solve them.

THE POLITICAL BASES

Problems

Greens agree with the older conservation groups that pollution, resource depletion, and the inhumane treatment of animals are pressing problems. Greens, though, see these problems as symptoms of two more basic, and inter-

[1]Arne Naess, *Ecology, Community, and Lifestyle: Outline for an Ecosophy* (Cambridge: Cambridge University Press, 1984), p. 28. Naess first developed these points in "The Shallow and the Deep, Long-

Bizarro

The "Bizarro" cartoon by Dan Piraro is reprinted by permission of Chronicle Features; San Francisco, California.

related, problems. The first of these basic problems is the **homocentric perspective** in western and developed countries. This perspective views nature as something that exists for humans to use, control, and master. Rather than living in and with nature, people in developed countries seek to exploit and dominate the environment. Rather than appreciating the intrinsic value of nature, people in developed countries see the environment as a warehouse that has value only in human use. Failing to understand the complexity of ecological systems and the present limits of science, individuals in developed countries rearrange and try to dominate nature only to create environmental devastation. According to greens, merely limiting pollution, preserving a wetland, or protecting a rare animal is, then, insufficient. Greens demand that the relationship between humans and nature be rethought.

The second basic problem is that developed countries, regardless of their dominant ideology or ideologies, have recklessly pursued economic growth at the expense of the environment. Nature is plundered in the quest for affluence. In the pursuit of economic growth, developed countries make the production of goods a fetish. Countries evaluate their quality of life by referring to productivity measurements, such as the GDP (gross domestic product),

Range Ecology Movement: A Summary," *Inquiry* 16 (1973), pp. 95–99. For a useful overview of the political theory of environmentalism, see Robyn Eckersley, *Environmentalism and Political Theory: Toward an Ecocentric Approach* (Albany: State University of New York Press, 1992).

rather than considering the quality of their natural environment and the physical, mental, and spiritual health of the people inhabiting that environment. The consumption of goods also becomes a fetish in developed countries. Consumerism seems to have no limit, and the luxuries of yesterday become the necessities of today. The excessive consumption of goods and energy in developed countries scars the developed countries own landscapes and threatens the environment of developing countries. The developing countries damage their own environments by emulating the wasteful western societies that are the gauge of progress.

Pollution, resource depletion, and the loss of ecological diversity, then, are caused by an arrogance toward nature combined with the never-ending crusade for greater economic growth. For greens, the specific battles fought over preservation issues are necessary in the greater war against homocentrism and rampant economic growth. Without changes in the basic human orientations, though, environmental movements will simply be fighting rearguard actions against the overwhelming forces of "progress."

Goals

Green goals involve major restructuring of how humans think and act. Human arrogance toward nature must be replaced by a reverence for the environment. The intrinsic value of nature must be realized by all. The "deepest" greens even suggest that the earth itself must be viewed as a living entity to be cherished as the life-giving mother. These greens come very close to advocating a virtual pantheism, where the gods, or moments of the sacred, are found in all natural things. A proper appreciation of nature should result in new practices, the most important being the reshaping of the economies of developed countries into "no-growth" economies, or **steady-state economies**. Only steady-

Sidebar 12-1

Some Environmentalists and their Writings

Aldo Leopold (1886–1948)
A Sand County Almanac; and Sketches Here and There (1949)

Rachel Carson (1907–1964)
Silent Spring (1963)

Barry Commoner*
Science and Survival (1966)
The Closing Circle: Nature, Man and Technology (1974)
The Poverty of Power: Energy and the Economic Crisis (1977)

E. F. Schumacher (1911–1977)
Small Is Beautiful (1973)

James Lovelock*
Gaia: A New Look at Life on Earth (1979)

Petra Kelly (1947–1992)
Fighting for Hope (1984)

Arne Naess*
Ecology, Community, and Lifestyle: Outline for an Ecosophy (1984)

Tom Regan*
The Case for Animal Rights (1983)

*Living author.

Sidebar 12-2

Conservationism, Environmentalism, and the Greens

Two distinct environmental movements preceded the deep ecologists, or greens, in the United States. In the late nineteenth century, concern over resource depletion—especially the loss of forests and trees—fueled **conservationism**. Conservationists view nature as a renewable resource of material for human consumption but insist that rational planning and management must be instituted in order to provide for human benefits from nature now and in the future. Early conservationists, such as Gifford Pinchot (1865–1946), were critical of the chaotic and ruthless exploitation of forests by a few large, well-organized special interests. Pinchot, who was the chief forester during Teddy Roosevelt's two terms as President (1901–1909), argued that natural resources had to be managed so that all citizens would have fair access to the bounty.

During the first decades of the twentieth century, early conservationists were responsible for creating national parks and wildlife refuges, and for placing environmental issues on the public agenda. Conservationists also formed interest groups that fought to protect animal resources from environmental degradation. Fishing and hunting groups have, since the founding of the Izaak Walton League in 1922, lobbied government to protect the environment so that humans will continue to have natural resources for their benefit.

A competing view of nature was offered by **environmentalists**, who argued that aesthetic values should be included in resource protection and that nature is valuable in itself. Unlike conservationists, who relied on utilitarian calculations about future material benefits to justify environmental protection, environmentalists sought the protection of pristine areas from human impact. Some of the early environmentalists, such as John Muir (1838–1914), regarded nature with a religious awe that has much in common with "green" thought. Muir preached a preservationist ethic, which valued nature for itself and for the spiritual benefits it granted humans. Muir was the first president of the Sierra Club, founded in 1892, and he was one of the first environmental lobbyists. His keen appreciation for nature, honed during long periods spent studying remote areas in North America, convinced him that all things in nature were interrelated. He moved environmental sciences toward a holistic conception of nature.

Conservationists and environmentalists have fought over issues of development, especially over the benefits of the vast damming of western waterways in the United States. Conservationists generally argue that the total benefits accrued by damming outweigh the benefits of maintaining the pristine wilderness that environmentalists value. Nevertheless, conservationists and environmentalists have often worked together on many ecological issues. Each movement has been successful in raising consciousness about nature and in protecting some of nature from the most ruthless aspects of exploitation by humans.

Greens owe much to the actions and ideas of conservationists and environmentalists, but feel a far greater affinity for environmentalists than they do toward conservationists. Both, of course, are too "shallow" for greens because both fail to question the fundamental patterns of life in liberal capitalist societies and fail to grasp the global consequences of the exploitation of nature.

state economies can stop the excessive energy consumption and the resource depletion that damage the environment.

A steady-state economy would rely on small or intermediate technologies to provide transportation, utilities, and consumer goods. Many greens endorse the ideas in E. F. Schumacher's *Small Is Beautiful*.[2] Schumacher (1911–1977) argued that the finite resources on this planet must be protected by replacing large-scale production (and unending consumption) with local, clean, and appropriate technology. For example, food production should be local, should require minimal energy consumption, and should forego the use of pesticides and herbicides. The shipment of exotic foods over long distances, the farming of single crops for cash, and the packaging of prepared meals are all ecologically detrimental and should be eliminated. Organic farming should be practiced, and the appropriate method for most farm labor is the use of animal power. People should eat simply from the local bounty.

The production of consumer goods should also be local, when this is feasible. Production facilities should not be large, and they should rely on renewable sources of power such as the wind, water, and geothermal and solar energy. The goods produced should be easy to repair, durable, and recyclable. The diversity of goods available will be reduced, but the goods produced will be high quality products.

Approaches to transportation and utilities will also need to be dramatically altered. Use of the automobile—and other forms of transportation that require vast amounts of (irreplaceable) fossil fuels—should be limited or eliminated. Energy consumption in homes should be reduced substantially. New buildings must be designed that limit the need for expensive heating and cooling devices, and new "soft" technologies (that don't rely on nonrenewable sources of energy) that make many homes energy independent must be developed.

Most greens view large metropolitan areas as environmentally unsound. Large cities require high levels of energy consumption and resource depletion to maintain the quality of urban life. Some greens contend that large urban areas—even with recycling, more careful attention to energy expenditure, and a massive restructuring of landscapes—will always maintain an environmentally fatal pace of life and reliance on imported goods.

Greens view all contemporary developed societies as a threat to the natural environment. Greens share three goals in protecting the earth and its creatures from human abuse. First, greens want to preserve diverse ecosystems. They argue that diverse ecosystems are complex entities that deserve to be protected, because they have intrinsic value that cannot be measured by human use values. For example, greens desire the protection of tropical rain forests, not because such forests may hold possible cures for cancer or other human diseases, but because the forests are part of the natural life on the planet—life which is to be valued because it exists. Rain forests may produce medicines and they may temper global warming, but their value exists independent of

[2]E. F. Schumacher, *Small Is Beautiful* (New York: Harper and Row, 1973).

utilitarian concerns. The richness of life on earth is something that, for greens, transcends the values of homocentric societies.

Greens argue that ecosystems have been poorly understood by western science. By emphasizing linear causation in its understanding of the natural world, science has blinded scientists to the complexities and interdependencies of ecological systems. Greens argue that science must attempt to comprehend the whole set of relations that exist in ecosystems. Only a **holistic approach** to understanding how ecological systems maintain and change themselves can provide an accurate appreciation of nature. This holistic view of nature leads greens to be very skeptical of scientific attempts to engineer and manipulate nature. Sounding very much like traditional conservatives, greens fear that scientific tampering with nature is sure to produce unanticipated consequences and unexpected disasters. The protection of ecological diversity has as its premise the intrinsic value of nature, but it also promotes the development of human understanding about the complex relations that exist in nature.

A second goal of greens, related very closely to the goal of protecting ecological diversity, is the preservation of pristine wildernesses. Greens reject the idea that all of nature is ours for consumption and use. Greens will accept some instances of "managed conservation," but they argue that nature must generally be protected from all human incursion.

A third goal of greens is to stop the use of animals in scientific and commercial research. In the 1970s, greens placed the issue of animal experimentation on the political agenda by revealing the poor conditions in which many laboratory animals were kept and by detailing the unnecessary pain inflicted on them.[3] In the 1980s, greens began demanding the abolition of all experimentation on animals. Greens reject utilitarian arguments that some animal experimentation is necessary and proper because of the benefits to human health and human understanding gained thereby. Criticizing utilitarian arguments for animal experimentation, Tom Regan presents a green "**animal rights**" perspective:

> No one, whether human or animal, is ever to be treated as if she were a mere receptacle, or as if her value were reducible to her possible utility for others. We are, that is, never to harm the individual merely on the grounds that this will or just might produce "the best" aggregate consequences. To do so is to violate the rights of the individual. That is why the harm done to animals in pursuit of scientific purposes is wrong. The benefits derived are real enough; but some gains are ill-gotten, and all gains are ill-gotten when secured unjustly.
>
> *. . . Those who accept the rights view . . . will not be satisfied with anything less than the total abolition of the harmful use of animals in science—in education, in toxicity testing, in basic research.*[4]

Green objectives for human interaction with the environment call for rejecting the utilitarian outlook on nature that dominates almost all western

[3]Peter Singer, *Animal Liberation* (New York: Avon Books, 1975).

[4]Tom Regan, *The Case for Animal Rights* (Berkeley: University of California Press, 1983), p. 393.

ideologies and practices. The utilitarian perspective, based on human-use values, views nature as a "standing reserve." A standing reserve is a stock of goods that humans are free to appropriate, mix with their labor, and consume. The utilitarian sees forests as warehouses of lumber, mountains as repositories of minerals, rain forests as medical chests, valleys as grazing sites for domestic animals, domestic animals as food units, and wild animals as recreational objects.

Greens demand a major change in our views toward the natural world. They demand not just changes in practices, but fundamental changes in the ways in which people value the world.

THE PHILOSOPHICAL BASES

Greens, despite their call for a revaluation of values with regard to the environment, have not articulated clear philosophical foundations for such a revaluation. On questions of ontology and epistemology, greens hold such a wide variety of views that it is difficult to discern a shared foundation. On questions of human nature and society, greens have only begun to explore possible understandings. This is, of course, not unusual in the development of ideologies, and some greens argue that demands for philosophical bases require them to adhere to standards of ideological "precision" held by post-Enlightenment ideologies that are exploitive and antiecological.[5]

Ontology and Epistemology

Green ontological views cover a wide range of beliefs and claims. "Deep" ecologists have relied on materialistic explanations, on spiritual understandings, and on mystical intuitions. Greens hold various religious views. Some greens are atheists, others are members of the major world faiths, some rely on Native American (or other indigenous) spiritual beliefs, and some worship Mother Earth, or *Gaia*, as a living entity.

Greens, thus, rely on many sources to support their claims that nature is valuable and/or sacred. It is not clear that this diversity of views is ultimately compatible with their goal of establishing respect for and promoting care of the environment. Greens, though, are not especially troubled by the very broad range of beliefs that prompt them to make nature a valued entity with which to live, rather than exploit. The sources that lead them to acknowledge the sacredness of nature or that instill in them a reverence for nature are less important to most greens than the existence of beliefs that value nature for itself. Most greens presently hold a broad ecumenical view in terms of ontological beliefs.

The diversity of green ontological thought supports a variety of views

[5]David Ehrenfeld, *The Arrogance of Humanism* (New York: Oxford University Press, 1978); Vandana Shiva, *Staying Alive* (London: Zed Books, 1988).

Sidebar 12-3

Gaia and the Greens

In 1979, James Lovelock published *Gaia: A New Look at Life on Earth.* He used the word **Gaia**, the ancient Greek term for "Mother Earth," to describe the life-nourishing properties of the earth's environment. Lovelock's book generated two movements in the wide array of green ontological views. First, *Gaia* provided a scientific and materialistic perspective that focused on the interactions among plant life, animal life, the atmosphere, soil, and water. Lovelock argued that the "biosphere," the sphere of plant and animal life that covers the earth, has self-regulatory capabilities. The climate and the atmosphere of earth have remained quite stable for the 3,500 million years of life on earth. The earth may not be alive, but it is covered and regulated by a living biosphere. Lovelock uses the metaphor of a huge one-celled organism to describe the biosphere. The biosphere has many parts that function interrelatedly in the same complex ways observed in the interior of a single cell. Animals, plants, and the gases they produce regulate the climate and atmosphere to make possible the continuing conditions for life. The biosphere does not protect specific species, but it does regulate against climatic and atmospheric changes that are so great as to threaten life itself.

Lovelock's views have been criticized by some greens and by mainstream scientists. Some greens doubt the degree of resiliency of the biosphere that is implied by its adaptive and regulatory capabilities. An adaptive biosphere suggests that regardless of human activities, nature will make the requisite adjustments. Lovelock counters this criticism by pointing out that the biosphere will protect the conditions for life in general, but that human abuse may make life for some animals (including humans) impossible. Mainstream scientists have criticized Lovelock for implying a purpose to nature and have noted that Lovelock has identified only a few regulatory mechanisms. Lovelock responds that a purpose is not needed for nature to have regulatory mechanisms, and he concedes that it is difficult to reveal adaptive and regulatory mechanisms. Lovelock claims that he is simply presenting a "*Gaia* hypothesis" and that he offers this hypothesis to the scientific community for testing.

The second movement spawned by Lovelock's account of *Gaia* is an increasingly popular spiritual belief that the earth, or the biosphere, is a living entity. The belief in a living earth provides some greens with a foundational sacredness for human interaction with the environment. Humans are just some of the many actors in the living organism of earth, and humans should treat this living mystery with respect and awe. The belief in a sacred Mother Earth is, of course, not new. Many premodern religions contain an idea of a sacred Mother Earth; Native American spiritual beliefs are often centered on the idea of the environment as a living deity. Lovelock's claim about a living biosphere was greeted enthusiastically by "New Age" advocates and by some ecofeminists. The latter endorsed the idea of a female deity and hoped that reference to an image of a caring Mother Earth would encourage people to place limits on the exploitation of humans and nature.

on epistemology. Greens rely on science, awe, and/or faith to understand, and to act in, the world. Despite this ecumenicism, greens share an epistemological criticism of Enlightenment science. For greens, the science of the Enlightenment assumed that linear causality could explain the relations among things in the world. It assumed that there were series or combinations of events that could explain results. Thus, a series of events (seen as independent variables) is specified that cause a result (that is seen as a dependent variable). For greens, the assumption of linear causality is flawed. Linear causality emphasizes a single direction, or chain of events, thus ignoring the complex interactions that may occur among variables. Linear causality also portrays objects in the world as mechanical and assumes that mechanisms can be broken down into discrete parts that have singular functions. Greens reject a mechanistic understanding of natural systems and emphasize the organic properties of ecosystems. They claim that a mechanical view of nature misses the dynamics of ecosystems and disregards their interdependencies. A mechanical view of nature also encourages an "engineering attitude" towards the earth. Humans dredge, drain, dam, level, burn, and consume nature with little regard for the consequences to its complex ecosystems.

The greens' criticisms of science are similar to the criticisms that traditional conservatives made of Enlightenment science when it was applied to political, economic, and social change. Both greens and traditional conservatives fear the unanticipated consequences of mechanistic interventions on complex organic systems by scientists intent on progress. Traditional conservatives viewed the body politic as a complex system to be protected from *social* engineers. Greens view nature as a complex organism that must be protected from *civil* engineers. However, greens do not always extend their organic perspective to society, the economy, and political institutions. Often, greens assume that nature is organic, but that political institutions, society, and the economy are artificial constructions that can be reformed within a mechanistic perspective.

Human Nature and Society

Green writings on society and human nature are not extensive or detailed. Most greens assume that society and human nature are amenable to rather extensive changes. Certainly human nature is not viewed as rigid or given, because greens expect dramatic changes in the way people value and act in the world. Green views on society are difficult to discern. Greens reject the atomistic and egoistic individualism that liberal societies engender, but it is not clear what they will suggest to serve as the social glue for a less competitive and more communitarian social life. Neither is it clear whether humans will be willing (and able) to forego the luxuries and conveniences of consumer societies. Green attempts to respond to these issues can best be presented by turning briefly to green views on political principles.

SUBSTANTIVE POLITICAL PRINCIPLES

Authority

Greens hold a wide variety of political views, including diverse views on authority. Some of the early environmentalists, such as Garret Hardin, argued that the only way to prevent individual self-interest and democratic politics from ravaging nature was to place scientific experts in control of natural resource use.[6] Hardin argued that only powerful technocrats freed from the burdens of elections could make the sensible decisions necessary to protect the environment from capitalism and consumerism. Hardin viewed individuals as naturally self-interested, and thus he argued that a Hobbesian solution—a strongly controlling sovereign power—was the only political alternative. Most greens accept Hardin's view that governmental authority is necessary to protect the environment from the unregulated self-interest allowed by libertarian ideologies. However, they understand that ecological problems cannot be solved entirely by an authoritative government. To induce widespread citizen compliance with the environmental regulations of government and to instill in all citizens an environmental ethic, governmental controls must be formulated and implemented democratically, not authoritatively.

Structure

Drawing loosely on the thought of Jean-Jacques Rousseau (1712–1778), greens such as Petra Kelly and Arne Naess in Europe and Wes Jackson in the United States criticize the centralized governments and representative politics of western societies.[7] Kelly, Naess, and Jackson envision a future with many small, self-sufficient communities that will provide for direct, participatory democracy. Government in these participatory democracies would be decentralized and, in each community, authority would derive from participatory decision making. The unwieldy structure of parliamentary and republican governments would disappear, replaced by democratic city-states.

Rulers and Citizens

In such small, democratic city-states, rulers and citizens would rotate in holding the few public offices necessary. Nation-states would disappear, and any regional authorities would be concerned with protecting shared ecosystems.

Many greens would not be willing to endorse changes as substantial as those advocated by Kelly, Naess, and Jackson, but many are sympathetic to

[6]Garrett Hardin, "The Tragedy of the Commons," in *Managing the Commons*, edited by Garrett Hardin and John Baden (San Francisco: W. H. Freeman, 1977), pp. 16–30. This important article was originally published in *Science* in 1968.

[7]Petra Kelly, *Fighting for Hope* (Boston: South End Press, 1984); Naess, *Ecology, Community, and Lifestyle*, esp. pp. 204–212.

this vision of a more communitarian future with a much slower pace of both production and consumption. This vision is also attractive, because it might promote ideas about justice that many greens seek.

Justice

Greens are generally skeptical of the validity of liberal capitalism's ideas about justice because these ideas promote excessive economic inequality and deny ecological values. In small communities, economic differences would exist, but they would not be great. Communities based on mutual concern would replace huge marketplaces of competition. Ecological values would be included within a green concept of justice. This might involve the extension of liberal rights to animals, plants, and the earth, or it might involve recognizing some fundamental values that simply cannot be translated into monetary units. Justice must include justice for the earth, and for the flora and fauna of the earth. Justice is not, for greens, simply the fair treatment of citizens.[8]

Change

The issue of how to bring about change is highly contested among greens. Greens acknowledge that major changes in the way people value nature are necessary, but they disagree about how much change is necessary and how that change can be achieved. Almost all greens reject violent revolution as an acceptable means of change. Violence against humans is another form of violence against life and earth. However, greens are not always willing to work within the established legal frameworks of western countries. Obviously, those legal frameworks dismiss values considered crucial by greens. Some greens thus recommend fighting against environmental degradation by engaging in small-scale and highly decentralized guerrilla warfare. Groups such as "Earth First!" advocate the destruction of roads, surveying equipment, and construction vehicles. From the greens' perspective, these types of **monkeywrenching** activities must avoid injury to humans while increasing the costs of "development." Monkeywrenching is not simply vandalism; it is, according to its proponents, thoughtful, planned, ethical interference with the thoughtless and unethical exploitation of nature.[9]

Greenpeace, another deep ecology group, engages in more public and confrontational tactics. For example, Greenpeace vessels have interfered with whale hunts and have followed French ships suspected to be engaged in nuclear testing activities. Greenpeace's objective is not just to make the use of

[8]For a recent attempt to provide a more comprehensive green view of justice, see Eric T. Freyfogle, *Justice and the Earth: Images of Our Planetary Survival* (New York: Free Press, 1993).

[9]Earth First! has been very careful to distance itself from the few groups that are willing to protect the environment with actions that pose risks to or threaten human life. Earth First! has produced a manual for the prudent monkeywrencher, *Ecodefense: A Field Guide to Monkeywrenching*, 2d ed., edited by Dave Foreman and Bill Haywood (Tucson, Ariz.: Ned Ludd Books, 1989).

nature more expensive, but to publicize activities that harm nature. Greenpeace plans and carries out actions that it believes will stop the destruction of nature and raise consciousness among observers.

These tactical approaches to change do not claim to answer the question of how to reform the larger political arena. In the United States, greens and "shallow" environmental groups have relied largely on interest group politics to influence public policy. Only in 1980 was there an attempt at a national green party, and it failed.[10] In Europe, there has been much more controversy over the benefits of green political parties. The parliamentary systems of European countries, especially Germany, are more open to new and minority parties than is the republican system in the United States. Greens in Germany have formed a political party and have had some success in elections, and greens have served in the German parliament. Limited electoral success, though, has not brought harmony to the German Green Party. Some greens have abandoned party politics, because party politics inevitably involves compromise and negotiation on issues and values that these greens consider inviolable. German greens are now split between those who wish to pursue party politics and those who reject party politics in favor of public actions not sanctioned or legitimized by public authorities.[11]

Greens continue to debate the appropriate avenues of change on both tactical and strategic levels. Of course, the most profound change that greens seek is in people's basic attitudes toward nature. Greens certainly can point to some signs that attitudes towards nature are changing, in both developed and developing countries.[12] In the developed countries, environmental issues have a high priority among many voters, and environmental concerns do not seem likely to disappear. Many governments now require the preparation of environmental impact statements for both public and private development projects. Ecological values are considered in these assessments. Older (shallow) environmental groups, which were once seen as clubs for bird-watchers and as peripheral political actors, are now seen as legitimate players in public policy making. In the United States, environmental educational packages have been incorporated into the curricula of elementary and secondary public schools, and universities award degrees in environmental sciences and environmental engineering. Children's television programming is filled with cartoons and documentaries that extol green values. In short, there has been a "greening" of the educational system in the United States. These changes have

[10]The Citizens Party, with a green focus, was led by Barry Commoner, who could garner no more than one percent of the vote as the party's presidential candidate. Commoner has authored several important works on the environment. His most influential book in the United States is *The Closing Circle: Nature, Man and Technology* (New York: Bantam Books, 1974).

[11]For a brief review of the debate between German Greens on party politics, see the selections from Petra Kelly, *Fighting for Hope*, and Rudolph Bahro, "Building the Green Movement," in *The Green Reader: Essays toward a Sustainable Society*, edited by Andrew Dobson (San Francisco: Mercury House, 1991), pp. 192–198.

[12]These attitude changes are described and analyzed in Ronald Inglehart, *Culture Shift* (Princeton: Princeton University Press, 1989).

largely gone unchallenged, even by ideologies criticized by greens. Some contemporary conservatives do warn about the limits imposed on private property rights by environmental regulations and criticize the antigrowth positions of greens. However, many contemporary conservative politicians are sensitive to the environmental concerns of their constituents and try to avoid conflict with environmental groups.

Environmental activism is appearing in developing countries, and it sometimes has promoted green ideals. For example, in 1974, women in rural India formed a circle around a small forest to prevent loggers from removing the trees. This "Chipko" movement (*Chipko* means "to hug" in Hindi) involved "tree hugging" that protected the environment for its own sake. In Kenya, a Greenbelt movement has been organized by women to restore trees to the landscape. The Greenbelt movement has promoted an appreciation of nature and provided members with an environmental education.[13]

These changes are too shallow to satisfy greens that sufficient change is taking place. However, even the shallow level of raised global consciousness about ecology is impressive. Less than twenty-five years after the first Earth Day, there have been major changes in the environmental values and practices of individuals and societies. Environmental concerns do not seem limited to industrialized countries nor to wealthy individuals. Clearly there is the potential for green concerns to have a universal appeal.

SUMMARY AND CONCLUSIONS

While greens have been assembling the foundations for a green ideology, more work remains for its full and coherent rendering. Some continuing and important differences can exist within an ideology, but greens' differences on many significant political and philosophical issues are presently too diverse to allow green thought to be considered as more than a nascent ideology.

If greens should decide to pursue party politics, they must broaden their appeal and clarify their economic proposals. Greens have often been more sensitive to the environmental hazards posed to animals than to the environmental hazards that humans confront in the workplace and in urban settings. Greens need an environmental approach that includes workers and urbanites. Greens have not been clear about how industrialized societies could deindustrialize into small, self-sufficient agrarian and low-technology communities. Furthermore, it is far from obvious what type of economic system would be appropriate for a green future. Would communities produce only enough goods for use and not for exchange? How would the "greedy" producer who sought to exchange goods for sustained and planned profits be sanctioned? Is the slower pace of life envisioned by greens a pace that modern individuals could endure and enjoy? Are individuals who have been raised to be good consumers willing to forego the delights of consumption that capitalism provides? Can the self-interested individuals in capitalist societies be easily changed into communitarians in harmony with nature?

[13]V. Spike Peterson and Anne Sisson Runyan, *Global Gender Issues* (Boulder, Colo.: Westview Press, 1993), pp. 142–147.

The idea of being in harmony with nature raises some difficult issues for greens. What are the relative values of humans, fauna, and flora? Is an animal life equal to a human life? Are some animals and plants more valuable than others? Should native animals and plants be protected against nonnative species? If so, what should be done when nonnative species encroach "naturally" (without human intervention)? How should animal and plant populations be managed?[14] What ethic should guide the managed conservation and use of natural resources?

Greens do not have to provide specific answers to all of these questions in order to be taken seriously, but they do have to tackle tough questions for which nature provides no obvious answers if they are to realize their goals. In exploring these questions, greens may come to greater agreement not only on how to value the environment, but also on why we should value nature at all. If greens are to replace utilitarian calculations with ecologically sensitive approaches, they must provide a convincing argument that human-use values are not the appropriate guide for human ideas and actions.

[14]For an excellent brief discussion of the controversy surrounding the protection of African elephants, see Elisabeth Marshall Thomas, "Of Ivory and the Survival of Elephants," *The New York Review of Books* 41 (Mar. 24, 1994), pp. 3–6.

CHAPTER 13

Feminism

Most of the contributors to the ideologies that we have thus far examined have been men, and we, too, are men. Historically, political activists, theorists, and philosophers have been predominately men. Feminists question this marginalization and near exclusion of women's voices from the political world. Feminists ask whether the questions that men ask and the problems that men address reflect a peculiarly male view of human life and give inadequate attention to the concerns of women. They ask whether the ideas that men provide in answer to these questions reflect male experiences and understandings, rather than reflecting human experiences and understandings that include those of women. Feminists ask whether men have structured social, economic, and political life in ways that undermine the rights and interests of women—and, perhaps, of men too.[1] In short, just as environmentalists accuse political thought to date of reflecting a *homocentric* bias, feminists accuse such thought of reflecting an **androcentric bias**.

The idea that women should have "equal rights" with men dates at least to the birth of ideologies. In 1792, Mary Wollstonecraft (1759–1797) wrote *A Vindication of the Rights of Women,* in which she reminded the founders of classical liberalism that women, too, could reason, and thus should be equal participants in the liberal project. Throughout the past two centuries, other women have made and extended these claims, but in the past twenty-five years there has been an explosion of female voices, both in the world of political theory and in the concrete world of political activity. These contributors have not spoken in a single voice. Consequently, feminism—understood as the voices of women expressing the experiences, concerns, and interests of

[1]Among the many recent works in the history of political thought that raise these sorts of questions are Susan Moller Okin, *Women in Western Political Thought* (Princeton: Princeton University Press, 1979), and Jean Bethke Elshtain, *Meditations on Modern Political Thought* (New York: Praeger, 1986).

women[2]—is not a single cohesive ideology. Perhaps women have (marginally) contributed—in ways that reflect women's perspectives—to most of the other ideologies we have examined. Perhaps such contributions imply the existence of different versions of feminism—liberal, conservative, anarchist, Marxist, socialist, among others.[3] Yet, many feminists resist such classifications, and the boundaries among these various feminist groupings remain unclear. In an attempt to capture some of the diversity within feminism without aspiring to present a comprehensive account of this diversity, we distinguish three main forms of feminism.

Liberal feminists are primarily concerned with providing women the same rights that men already possess. They assert the intrinsic equality of men and women, and they argue that women's interests, needs, and preferences should be given consideration equal to that given men's interests, needs, and preferences. Liberal feminists rely on legal reform and electoral victories to bring about change. Thus, they accept the basic institutions of liberal society—its representative democracy, its capitalist economy, and the basic structure of social life—including the primacy of the nuclear family. The goals of liberal feminists are to have women share political power equally with men, to have opportunities for economic advancement for women that parallel those of men, and to reform the patriarchal family so that mothers and fathers share parental authority and household responsibilities more equally.

In contrast, **radical feminists** often reject the basic institutions of liberal society. Drawing from anarchists, they question the kind of power structures that exist in representative democracies, and they search for alternative forms of political decision making in which power is conceptualized and exercised in a different, less controlling manner than has been the case in male-dominated liberal societies. Drawing from Marxists and democratic socialists, radical feminists often believe that capitalism creates environments hostile to women's (and men's) interests. For them, major restructuring of politics and economics is necessary to eliminate the gender biases in modern societies. Some radical feminists assert that all western social institutions, including marriage, undermine the freedom of all and abet the oppression of women. The most radical feminists claim that the oppression of women is inherent in female/male relationships. For these feminists, only separate women's communities can provide women the freedom, cooperation, and mutual affection that fully tap the potential of women.

As both liberal and radical feminists have criticized the political and social practices of liberal and other modern societies, many female scholars have begun to question the epistemological bases of the ideologies that sustain these practices. Many of these scholars have argued that the foundations of all

[2]By adopting this as our initial definition of feminism, we intentionally express our belief that women should *define* the ideas of feminism. Nevertheless, we think that men can understand, interpret, and support feminism. Charlene Stinard, Marisa Kelly, and Cryss Brunner have been particularly helpful in defining feminism for us, but all errors of interpretation are, of course, ours.

[3]A good summary of different types of feminism is presented by Rosemarie Tong, *Feminist Thought* (Boulder, Colo.: Westview Press, 1989).

Sidebar 13-1

Some Feminists and their Writings

LIBERAL FEMINISTS

Mary Wollstonecraft (1759–1797)
A Vindication of the Rights of Women (1792)

Betty Friedan*
The Feminine Mystique (1963)
The Second Stage (1981)

Gloria Steinem*
Outrageous Acts and Everyday Rebellions (1983)

Susan Moller Okin
Justice, Gender, and the Family (1989)

RADICAL AND SOCIALIST FEMINISTS

Kate Millet*
Sexual Politics (1970)

Catherine MacKinnon*
Feminism Unmodified (1977)
Toward a Feminist Theory of the State (1989)

Juliet Mitchell*
Women's Estate (1971)

Lise Vogel*
Marxism and the Oppression of Women: Towards a Unitary Theory (1983)

Marilyn French*
Beyond Power: On Women, Men and Morals (1985)

POSTMODERN FEMINISTS

Mary Daly*
Gyn/Ecology: The Metaethics of Radical Feminism (1978)
Pure Lust: Elemental Feminist Philosophy (1984)

Nancy Hartsock*
Money, Sex, and Power: Toward a Feminist Historical Materialism (1983)

Lorraine Code*
What Can She Know? (1991)

Sandra Harding*
The Science Question in Feminism (1986)

*Living author.

human knowledge are seriously flawed. They question the abstractness and "objectivity" of the scientific and philosophical modes of thinking characteristic of political ideologies (and other intellectual constructions) that men have provided to understand the natural and social worlds. Such **postmodern feminists** argue that we must first "deconstruct" our understandings of the world, as such understandings are based on male experiences. They argue for quite different ways of thinking and knowing that give equal—and perhaps greater—attention to the more immediate, concrete, and relational ways that women experience the world. Postmodern feminists thereby challenge not only the ideas that other ideologies have provided but the very process of developing any ideology.[4]

[4]These forms of feminism are not distinct, as some women are simultaneously and without contradiction both radical and postmodern feminists. However, not all postmodern feminists are radical.

THE POLITICAL BASES

Problems and Goals

All feminists identify common problems facing women, criticize the deficiencies of classical liberalism, and share some specific policy goals. All feminists agree that women are discriminated against and oppressed by current practices and laws. While such oppression is particularly acute in eastern, traditional, and underdeveloped countries, feminists claim that extensive discrimination against and oppression of women remains in Western liberal (and socialist) societies, too. Women are treated as second-class citizens by public institutions, are treated unequally in the economic sphere, and are denied autonomy in the private sphere of family and marriage. Women are targets of various forms of male violence, including verbal abuse, sexual harassment, physical assault, rape, and murder.

Feminists argue that the source of such discrimination and oppression is that the freedoms and rights sought by classical liberals were only partially, and grudgingly, extended to women. In securing natural rights for (some) men, classical liberalism revolutionized political and economic life, but maintained traditional ideas and practices in the private sphere of the household. Women were to inhabit a private sphere, men to act in public arenas.[5] Women were deemed incapable of exercising the reasoning powers necessary for participation in political activities and for interaction in economic competition. Classical liberals viewed women as insufficiently autonomous to own property and sufficiently dependent to warrant their becoming the property of their husbands. Classical liberals, including the early utilitarians, were little concerned with the freedoms and rights of women. John Stuart Mill, writing in the 1860s, was one of the first prominent male liberals to advocate the rights of women. Mill, however, supposed that few women would seek access to public activities, because he shared the basic male assumption that the natural inclination of most women would be to devote themselves to child-raising and household activities.[6] Classical liberalism, despite the universal moments in natural rights claims and despite public demands for suffrage made by women as early as the 1660s, excluded women from the liberal project.

In some respects, women were more restricted from public life in the eighteenth and nineteenth centuries than they had been in premodern Europe. Women in seventeenth-century England had contributed to the arts and had been active in the more radical Protestant sects. In the eighteenth and nineteenth centuries, women's voices were largely ignored by liberals, and liberal regimes denied women property rights that had been traditionally granted to them in premodern Europe, when economic activity was still centered in the home. Enlightenment science contributed to the view that women lacked ade-

[5]For an insightful discussion of this distinction, see Jean Bethke Elshtain, *Public Man, Private Woman* (Princeton: Princeton University Press, 1981).

[6]See Carole Pateman, "Feminism and Democracy," in *Democratic Theory and Practice*, edited by Graeme Duncan (Cambridge: Cambridge University Press, 1986), pp. 209–214.

quate ability to reason by "illustrating" that women had smaller brains than men and that women suffered from diseases, such as hysteria, that were unique to their emotional nature.[7]

Developments in family life after 1700 also created conditions under which women were often less independent than they had been in premodern Europe. The emergence of the nuclear family, encouraged after the Reformation, deprived women of sources of child care and of the economic support available through the extended family. In the nuclear family there was a promise of equality in the reciprocity of romantic love, but in practice, the nuclear family made the wife a subordinate of the husband and the primary, if not sole, child-care provider and home maintainer. The idea of romantic love celebrated those "characteristics" of women—emotionalism, passivity, compassion, selflessness—that were viewed as less appropriate to the public spheres of activity than to the private sphere (that of the home and family). Women were thus admired and praised for qualities that excluded them from public life. Indeed, women needed to be protected from exposure to the public realm, given women's lack of the required reason and competitiveness. Women were placed on a pedestal, but it was a **debilitating pedestal**, one that protected their special qualities by barring them from the freedom and equality sought by classical liberals for men.

Most feminists agree that the public/private distinction in liberal societies has not benefited women, and they agree on some public policies that should help free women from relegation to the private sphere and thus enable them to engage in public life. Feminists generally agree that women must have control over their bodies. They must be free to choose whether they will bear children, how many children they will bear, and when they will bear them. Thus, public policies should protect women from marital rape, provide women access to contraception, and allow them to choose abortion. Only when women have **reproductive freedom** can they control their futures. Feminists also agree that public child care should be available in order to free women from their traditional role of primary caregiver for children. Reproductive freedom and public child care should provide women with opportunities to pursue activities outside the family.

Feminists also agree that stopping the violence against women, inside and outside the family, must be a public policy goal. Tougher laws and longer sentences for those convicted of violence against women must be implemented. Laws that prohibit sexual harassment, domestic violence, stalking, and marital and other types of rape should be enforced strictly, and those who violate these laws should be punished severely. For much too long, they argue, crimes against women have not been treated seriously.

Beyond these general areas of agreement, liberal and radical feminists emphasize quite different economic and social goals. Liberal feminists have focused on attaining equality of rights under the law, and were thus promi-

[7] For a discussion of the problems of the pseudoscience of linking brain size and intelligence, see Stephen J. Gould, *The Mismeasure of Man* (New York: W. W. Norton, 1983).

nent in the effort to establish the Equal Rights Amendment.[8] Liberal feminists have also focused on acquiring more economic and political equality for women. For example, they have raised the issue of "comparable worth," arguing that salaries in such fields as teaching and nursing, where women have traditionally been employed, should be equal to salaries in comparable fields where men have most often worked. Such goals are regarded as too modest by radical feminists. In order to overcome the limitations on women that are deeply embedded in our culture and institutions, radical feminists may call for such things as the abolition of private ownership of the means of production—which they argue are mostly owned and controlled by men—and the abolition of the conjugal family—which they argue virtually imprisons women by saddling them with child-rearing responsibilities.[9] Such feminists want new communal arrangements that would free women from the sole responsibility of bringing up children. Others—like Shulamith Firestone—want to see women relieved of the burdens of pregnancy by exploiting new developments in medical technology allowing for in vitro fertilization. Although most feminists do not seek such extensive modifications to human life, radical feminists believe that it is important to think about the deepest causes of women's repression—the productive and reproductive roles that women have been required to assume in capitalist and sexist societies—and to envision institutional arrangements that offer escape from these roles.

The goals of postmodern feminists are even more extensive. They call for a complete deconstruction of human knowledge. They want a reevaluation of all ideas—especially social, economic, and political ideas—that are presumed to be generally valid, but that reflect a male viewpoint. They then want to reconstruct knowledge in a way that includes—and perhaps gives prominence to—the voices of women.

PHILOSOPHICAL BASES

Epistemology and Ontology

While liberal feminists have given scant attention to epistemological and ontological issues, radical feminists have stimulated a fundamental rethinking of human conceptions about the universe and how we know things about our natural and social worlds. Radical feminists often argue that the analytical methods developed by men do not allow for an adequate understanding of

[8]For an interesting account of the history of the ERA movement, see Jane Mansbridge, *Why We Lost the ERA* (Chicago: University of Chicago Press, 1986). In the early 1980s, the ERA amendment failed to be ratified in three-fourths of the states, and thus, as required by the U.S. Constitution, it could not become law.

[9]See, for example, Shulamith Firestone, *The Dialectic of Sex: The Case for Feminist Revolution* (New York: Morrow, 1970). See Marge Piercy, *Women on the Edge of Time* (New York: Knopf Publishing, 1976) for an interesting depiction of the world envisioned by Firestone.

women's lives—or, for that matter, men's lives. They argue that existing methodologies and philosophies of science that emphasize basic dichotomies (for example, between reason and intuition and between "objective" and "subjective" knowledge) demean and ignore ways of knowing that women experience as valuable. In response to this "male bias" in existing epistemologies, women scholars have sought to develop a **feminist epistemology** that is highly critical of the compartmentalization, rigidity, and instrumentalism that characterize the epistemologies used by other, male-oriented, ideologies. Mary Daly, for example, argues that traditional philosophical categories of epistemology and ontology assume a fixedness or stability that does not reflect reality, but rather is the result of men's attempted domination of women and nature. In her recent writings, such as *Pure Lust: Elemental Feminist Philosophy*, Daly rejects the instrumental mentality of traditional philosophy and the static categories of male books by producing poetic and affective literature abounding with new words, strange connections, and the redefinition of established meanings. Daly's books are carnivals in which the world is turned upside down to expose "gentle" violence and to reinterpret words that have been used to oppress women.[10] Daly doesn't avoid words that have been used to denigrate women; she endorses the words while changing their meaning. Thus, "hags" and "witches" become positive descriptions of women, and "lust," freed from its patriarchal bonds, becomes a rich thirst for living, "being," and "be-coming" by women with women.

In addition to celebrating more artistic and poetic modes of understanding than are normally displayed in political philosophy, postmodern feminists have also emphasized a more open and inclusive social science. They question the assumption that there is a "real" and "natural" world that can be described by unambiguous scientific concepts and categories, by the measurement of human activity in terms of these concepts, and by the assertion of universal scientific laws. To correct the distortions in understanding the social world that have been created by such methods of analysis, radical feminists call for new approaches to social inquiry that question the possibility of "objective" scientific truths. By including in social and political discourse the voices of women and other marginalized groups, radical feminists seek to replace the artificial categories of understanding that represent masculine worldviews with other human representations. They believe that political truth—if there is such a thing—will be better grasped by hearing the subjective realities of everyone than by conducting various "scientific" tests to determine which view is most valid.[11]

Nancy Hartsock has provided one of the most intriguing postmodern

[10]Mary Daly, *Pure Lust: Elemental Feminist Philosophy* (Boston: Beacon Press, 1984). Also, see *Gyn/Ecology: The Metaethics of Radical Feminism* (Boston: Beacon Press, 1978).

[11]Feminist epistemology is presented by Patti Lather, *Getting Smart: Feminist Research and Pedagogy with/in the Postmodern* (New York: Routledge, 1991), chap. 3; Carol A. B. Warren, *Gender Issues and Field Research* (Newbury Park, Calif.: Sage Publications, 1988); and Chris Weedon, *Feminist Practice and Post-Structural Theory* (New York: Basil Blackwell, 1987), chaps. 3–5.

approaches to political knowledge.[12] Like Karl Marx and Karl Mannheim, Hartsock contends that human understandings of life are inevitably shaped by our "standpoint." If material life is structured differently for two different groups—as it was for the bourgeoisie and proletariat in Marx's analysis—then these groups will experience life differently. Because men experience life differently from women, their visions of life reflect only those aspects of reality that they have experienced—and the way in which they have experienced them. In patriarchal and capitalist societies, the experiences of men have focused on the production of goods for exchange in a competitive arena and an open market, and men have generated their ideas about politics from these experiences. While women have had some experiences in this arena, they have also experienced much more profoundly the production of goods for immediate use (rather than exchange) and, more importantly, they have been more involved in reproduction. As a result, women experience the world in less competitive terms, in a more concrete manner, in a way that fosters understanding of nurturing relationships, and so forth. Women have made their daughters aware of these aspects of social life, because mothers have long modeled their concrete realities for their daughters. Sons, however, have little understanding of this "world of women" because they have been raised as "abstracted" men. Because fathers have been engaged in productive labor outside of the home, they have not been present as concrete models for their sons. As a result, the standpoint of men is a partial, abstracted one, compared to that of women. Yet, perversely, it is the abstractions of men—their science and their philosophy—that are regarded as the higher forms of knowing. Hartsock suggests that to better understand the world it is necessary to include the standpoint of women. Indeed, it may be necessary to give the standpoint of women a privileged position relative to that of men.

Society

Just as Marxists normally focus on dominant and subordinate classes when they think about the nature of society, feminists usually focus on the distinction between the **public and private spheres of social life**. Just as Marxists view the class structures of society as oppressive, feminists view the public/private distinction within society as oppressive. For liberal feminists, however, the public/private split in liberal societies does not need to be abolished. Rather, women must be accorded equal rights in, and fair access to, the public sphere, with increasing calls for men to take more responsibility in the private sphere. Women must have equal political rights, equal standing before the law, and equal opportunities in the economy. Liberal feminists object to the gendered distinctions that are practiced within the public/private framework of liberal societies, but they do not reject the framework itself.

[12]Nancy Hartsock, *Money, Sex, and Power: Toward a Feminist Historical Materialism* (New York: Longman, 1983).

Sidebar 13-2

Pornography: Radical and Liberal Views

For radical feminists—such as Katherine MacKinnon and Andrea Dworkin—pornography is both a symptom and a cause of the constant demand by men to control and exploit women. In *Feminism Unmodified,* McKinnon argued that pornography celebrates the existing exploitation of women and provides examples for the continuing oppression of women. In *Pornography: Men Possessing Women,* Dworkin claimed that pornography objectifies women, makes them targets of violence, and perpetuates a culture of contempt in which women must constantly face the threat of sexual abuse and rape.

Radical feminists make a distinction between pornography and erotica. Both include the graphic depiction of sexual relations or acts, but erotica portrays relations of mutual respect based upon affection. Pornography portrays acts of domination, violence, and pain in which women (usually) are objects of male pleasure. Radical feminists seek legal prohibition of pornography because of the violence it represents and promulgates.

In contrast, liberal feminists may find pornographic material objectionable, but they are not confident that a clear line can be drawn between pornography and erotica. Different individuals may have radically different views on what constitutes pornography. Furthermore, if women (or others) are not coerced into pornographic activities and if citizens are not forced to view pornography, then it is not obvious why pornography should be banned. As long as there is no direct harm from pornography, liberals will support free speech protection for pornography and/or erotica. Only if there is certain evidence that pornography leads to acts of violence, should legal prohibitions be invoked.

Radical feminists view liberal feminists as trapped within a liberal understanding of voluntary action and free speech that serves patriarchal interests. Just as Marxists assert that workers do not freely contract their labor in capitalist societies, radical feminists assert that women who "consent" to pornographic activities are far from free in these encounters. The women who consent to pornographic activities have fallen victim to the false consciousness nurtured in patriarchal societies. These women have accepted their objectification and their exploitation. Free speech in a society that is dominated by male values and interests makes little sense to radical feminists, since what is protected is the right of the dominant group to demean women and to tolerate practices that further enhance the power of males over women. Radical feminists reject the liberal claim that public action can only be taken if there is a certain statistical link between the consumption of pornography and acts of violence against women. Radical feminists point to specific instances where pornographic material does seem to have encouraged mimicked acts of violence, and they emphasize how pornography represents a general view of women as objects of male power. Pornography is simply the most graphic expression of a culture that continually assaults women and denies them avenues for expression of their own autonomy and their own sexuality.

Radical feminists, however, reject the public/private distinction by claiming that "the personal is the political." They argue that men have developed and maintained the idea of distinct public and private spheres in order for them to dominate public life by relegating women to the private sphere. Male domination over women in public life is revealed by the overrepresentation of men in positions of power in business and government, by the demeaning treatment of women in the boardrooms of corporations and in legislatures, and by the exploitive treatment of women in the press and by the media more generally. Male domination in the public sphere has, inevitably, spilled over into the private sphere. Although the private sphere was intended as a place where women's interests would be valued and women could exercise autonomy, the fact that women have fewer economic resources, less power, and lower status than men in public life has required women to submit to male desires in the private sphere. Thus, women are dominated in the bedroom as well as in the boardroom.

Some radical feminists also argue that the public/private split encourages the exploitation of women and creates advantages for capitalists. Work in the private sphere is undervalued and not rewarded fairly. Women are a cheap source of labor in the home and in the economy. Women, cast as home caretakers, but not family providers, have rarely gained access to jobs or professions that provide a paycheck sufficient to support a family. Women also serve as a reserve labor pool that can be hired cheaply during economic booms and sent back to the private sphere during economic downturns.

While liberal feminists seek only to allow women equal access to the public spheres of life, radical feminists seek to end distinctions between the public and private spheres and simply attack male domination over women wherever it exists in society. Radical feminists regard liberal feminists as naive, because they fail to appreciate how male values that dominate public life oppress women in all aspects of social life. For example, liberal feminism has accepted the liberal idea that there must be free speech in public life, and they therefore tolerate pornography. Radical feminists argue that this has the effect of promoting violence against women as they live their everyday lives in both the public and the private spheres of society.

Postmodern feminists regard the public/private dichotomy as a male construction that distorts reality. From the male viewpoint, the public is the sphere of economic competition and power, and the private is the sphere of intimate family life. From the female viewpoint, however, the private sphere is infused with power relations and economic domination. As long as the male viewpoint prevails, questions of power and domination can be confined to the public arena and ignored in the family.

Human Nature

Feminists view human nature as malleable. Some feminists claim that many of the differences in personal characteristics between the sexes that have traditionally been ascribed to biological differences are the result of cultural values and socialization. Accordingly, feminists have engaged in wide-ranging debates over the relative importance of nature and nurture in the shaping of personality.

Many liberal feminists acknowledge that biological differences do exist between the sexes, but they assert that these differences are irrelevant in political, social, and economic domains. They seek a future in which the rights and privileges of males will be extended to women in a "gender-blind" fashion.

Some feminists have suggested that there are few natural differences between men and women; as a consequence, both men and women can be nurtured so as to move beyond gendered characteristics by creating an androgynous future. The goal of **androgyny** is for individuals to combine the best of both sexes' traits and qualities.[13] For example, rather than accepting such characterizations as "men are more analytical and women are more intuitive," those who seek androgyny believe both men and women can develop fully the analytical and intuitive potentialities that reside in all humans, but that are often undeveloped in men or women because of differences in their socialization.

Some radical feminists, such as Shulamith Firestone, argue that differences between men and women are the result of women's biological role in reproducing human communities and men's traditional roles in producing goods within those communities. Women's biological role emphasizes the nurturing, compassionate, and passive qualities of females, while men's productive roles emphasize the instrumental, abstract, and aggressive qualities of males. For Firestone, these gendered characteristics can be overcome by renouncing the gendered division of reproductive and productive labor. In order for women to experience their full human potential, they must be freed from the burdens of pregnancy, birth, and child rearing.[14]

The most radical feminists insist that the oppression of women is so embedded within the gendered division of labor that women must remove themselves from contact with males altogether. They argue that even if the burdens of pregnancy, birth, and child rearing were removed from women, they could not explore their full human potential, because men would still oppress them politically, personally, and physically. Male dominance has been built into the religious, philosophical, political, and linguistic understandings of patriarchal societies. Radical feminists, such as Mary Daly, insist that women must separate themselves from men to escape the patriarchal "construction" of women by men. Feminist separatists often endorse a lesbian separatism that rejects heterosexual relations. Men will always be violent, possessive, instrumental, and competitive. If sexual relations are the source of sexism, then lesbian relations can avoid the very starting place of sexist prac-

[13]For examples, see Kate Millet, *Sexual Politics* (Garden City, N.Y.: Doubleday, 1970); Marilyn French, *Beyond Power: On Women, Men and Morals* (New York: Summit Books, 1985).
[14]Firestone, *The Dialectic of Sex*.

tices. Lesbian separatists can begin to articulate new definitions of women's qualities and women's powers by avoiding or undermining the language of oppression in patriarchies. Women can build worlds of affection that celebrate women's bodies, women's abilities, and women's relationships.

Still other feminists, like Jean Bethke Elshtain, warn against overestimating the malleability of human nature and ignoring the possibility of important biological differences between the sexes. Elshtain believes that women have communitarian values that are a valuable asset in warding off the overdevelopment of individualism and the loss of community experienced in liberal societies. For Elshtain, women who choose the role of mother and homemaker are not necessarily deluded by culture; they are seeking modes of experience that they rightfully find fulfilling. Elshtain suggests that the traditional characteristics ascribed to women—such as compassion and an ethic of care—are encoded in the biology of women, and that these characteristics should be accepted and valued.[15]

SUBSTANTIVE POLITICAL PRINCIPLES

Authority

Most feminists see a need for state activities to enhance women's status and are willing to use the power of the state to achieve some of their policy goals. Liberal feminists generally support legislation that prohibits discrimination, protects women from violence, and provides women with easier access into the political and economic spheres. They believe that the state should play a larger role in providing day care facilities to relieve women from some part of their child-rearing responsibilities. Radical feminists generally support these uses of governmental authority, but they often want the state to go further. Some radical feminists, for example, call on the state to appropriate (predominately male-owned) private property. Other radical feminists may want the state to become involved in the development and dissemination of reproductive technologies.

Feminists realize, however, that there are limits to legislative reform and what the state can accomplish. Legislation will not eliminate all discrimination, and it will not erode the private prejudices of some citizens. State involvement in the productive and reproductive processes will not liberate women if men continue to dominate government and if the ideas of men are typically the bases for public policy. Thus, feminists, and especially postmodern feminists, are opposed to establishing any fixed principles about what governmental authority should look like and what its role should be.

[15]Jean Bethke Elshtain, "Feminism, Family and Community," *Dissent* 29 (fall 1982), and *Power Trips and Other Journeys* (Madison: University of Wisconsin Press, 1990). Elshtain argues that acceptance of the biological qualities of women does not preclude them from developing other parts of themselves through broader participation in public life.

The Evolution Of Authority...

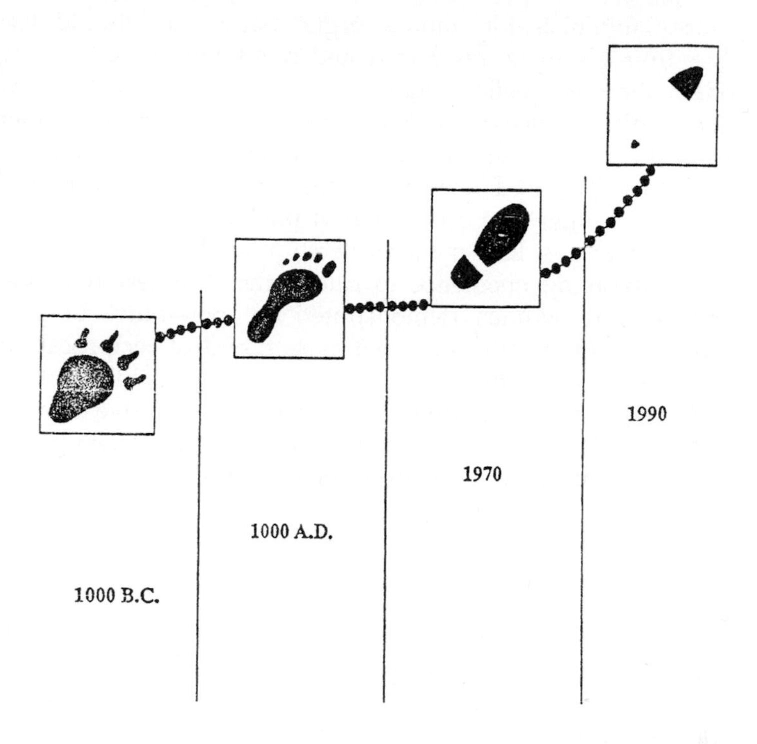

Rulers and Citizens

One of the central goals of liberal feminists during the nineteenth century was the extension of suffrage to women. Feminists viewed suffrage as essential for gaining liberal political and economic rights. Throughout this century, liberal feminists have waged battles to secure for women the citizenship rights granted to men in western democracies. Having gained equality with men regarding most formal political rights, liberal feminists increasingly focus on attaining more equal power. In addition to having more women in the administrative, legislative, and judicial branches of government, feminists have sought to empower women in economic and family life.[16] In addition to women having equal opportunities to participate in political life, feminists have sought to make women's participation as influential in the policy-making process as that of men.[17]

Most radical feminists accept the goals and achievements of liberal femi-

[16]Ann Bookman and Sandra Morgen, *Women and the Politics of Empowerment* (Philadelphia: Temple University Press, 1989).

[17]Barbara J. Nelson and Najma Chowdhury, *Women and Politics Worldwide* (New Haven, CT: Yale University Press, 1994).

nists regarding the political rights and power of women. But many question whether reforms giving more power to women and extending women's rights within liberal society can provide enough meaningful change for women. Some "separatist" feminists, for example, argue that women should disassociate themselves from the male community and rule themselves.

Postmodern feminists believe that our conceptions of ruling and citizenship are too limited, reflecting male perspectives on the need for hierarchy and control and on the importance of individual rights over affective relationships among people. For example, they note that the very question, "Who should rule?" suggests a conception of power as the capacity of some people to rule over others. Rather than rulership involving *power over* others and citizenship involving obedience to rulers, they suggest that the organizational practices of women demonstrate "the possibility of power as the provision of energy to others as well as self, and of reciprocal empowerment."[18] In other words, they wonder about the possibility of redefining ruling as the *power to* accomplish things in collaborative relationships with others, where all gain both from the nurturing relationships that can emerge by working with others and from the accomplishment of community goals.

Structure

Liberal feminists normally support the social, economic, and political structures that exist in modern society; they have not offered detailed critiques of the structures of modern governments. However, some have argued that levels of participation in modern societies are inadequate for developing democratic and communitarian values.[19] Governmental and economic institutions that allow higher levels of participation may encourage the more deliberative and less conflictual politics that some feminists seek.

Radical feminists, however, question the adequacy of liberal institutions. While they have often criticized the capitalist economy and representative democracy, their attacks mainly focus on the structure of family life. Alternatives to the nuclear, patriarchal family are still a matter of contention among radical feminists, however. Some simply want the nuclear family to become more democratic and less restrictive of women's needs for involvement in public life outside of the home. Some call for more communal living arrangements, where small communities of men and women share various child-raising and homemaking responsibilities. But some call for separate communities of women.

[18]Sandra Harding, *The Science Question in Feminism* (Ithaca, N.Y.: Cornell University Press, 1986), p. 149.

[19]Amy Gutmann "Undemocratic Education" in *Liberalism and the Moral Life*, edited by Nancy Rosenblum (Cambridge: Harvard University Press, 1989), pp. 71–88; Carole Pateman, "Feminism and Democracy," pp. 204–217; and Iris Marion Young, *Justice and the Politics of Difference* (Princeton: Princeton University Press, 1990).

Justice

All feminists believe that women have not received their fair share of economic opportunities and social rewards in modern societies. Historically, women have generally been subjected to sexual discrimination in pursuing economic and educational opportunities. In the United States, liberal feminists were instrumental in the passage of the Equal Pay Act of 1963, which required that men and women who did the same work would also receive the same pay. They were also instrumental in passage of the Civil Rights Act of 1964, which prohibited other forms of discrimination based on race and sex. Subsequent laws have extended women's opportunities in education and made them a protected class in affirmative action policies. Nevertheless, liberal feminists note that women still are paid, on average, wages about 20 percent lower than are paid to men doing comparable work. Thus, they continue to seek laws that advance the economic position of women, such as public provision of child care facilities, maternity leave policies that prevent employers from firing women while they are caring for their infants at home, and alimony payment laws that allow for garnishing the wages of "deadbeat dads."

Some liberal feminists also argue that women will never achieve justice in the public sphere unless they attain justice in the family.[20] If women are rendered to be subservient to men in the private sphere, they will never acquire the sense of personal empowerment that is necessary to pursue their interests in business and government. If women must bear the lion's share of child rearing and housekeeping responsibilities, they will not have the same opportunity as men to succeed outside of the home. When liberal feminists suggest that justice must begin at home, they remain liberals, because they accept the basic framework of liberal institutions. But this understanding of the roots of injustice against women approaches radical feminism, because it suggests the need to eliminate the patriarchal family.

For radical feminists, **patriarchy** is an important root cause of injustices.[21] "Patriarchy," moreover, refers not only to the domination of husbands over wives; it also refers to the domination by men over women that extends to all spheres of political, social, and economic life. Romance, marriage, child rearing, school, work, play, and political life are organized in ways that demean women, undervalue their contributions, and reward male attitudes and interests. In order to address the injustices due to patriarchy, it is necessary to question the celebration of masculine values and to offer a revaluation of the qualities ascribed to women. Radical feminists view the politics of sexuality as central to a critique of patriarchy. Men desire control of women's bodies, and they dominate women through political and economic means and through

[20]Susan Moller Okin, *Justice, Gender, and the Family* (New York: Basic Books, 1989).

[21]For examples, see Juliet Mitchell, *Women's Estate* (New York: Pantheon Books, 1991); and Heidi Hartmann, "The Unhappy Marriage of Marxism and Feminism: Towards a More Progressive Union," in *Women and Revolution: A Discussion of the Unhappy Marriage of Marxism and Feminism*, edited by Lydia Sargent (Boston: South End Press, 1981), pp. 1–41.

physical and verbal violence and intimidation. Legal and economic practices force women to rely on men, condemning them to lives of dependence. Cultural practices objectify women, making them targets of sexual exploitation and violence. Unless cultural and social practices change, women will always be treated unjustly.

While recognizing the inequalities and injustices that women suffer, feminists have not endorsed or developed a particular theory of justice containing principles of fair distribution. Indeed, postmodern feminists question the basis

Sidebar 13-3

Women's Movements and Feminism

Since the 1960s there have been many women's movements in both western and nonwestern countries. Some women's movements aim at providing women with greater rights and tie reforms to issues of gender equality. Other movements aim, instead, at addressing particular grievances that women have, without tying reforms to broader concerns about gender. The former movements seek "strategic gender interests," while the latter movements are concerned with "practical gender interests."

Movements guided by practical gender interests have had many different and particular aims. Women have generally been very active in peace movements, in part because their children have been the victims of warfare. Women in Argentina organized the Mothers of Plaza de Mayo to protest the brutality of the government and the "disappearance" of their children. Women have often organized protests over economic conditions when a lack of food or economic opportunities have denied them the ability to provide satisfactory nutrition for their families. Women have also been involved in some ecological reform movements, often to protect economic interests, but also to nurture their environment.

When women seek practical gender interests, they are not necessarily criticizing the gender roles they occupy. Indeed, they are protesting their inability to fulfill traditional roles of mothering, caring, and nurturing. Some women's movements, then, may actually reinforce, rather than question, the traditional roles of women.

Women's movements that begin by asserting practical gender interests may, however, start to seek strategic gender interests. Practical women's movements may foster raised consciousness about the general and systemic problems facing women. In *Global Gender Issues,* V. Spike Peterson and Anne Sosson Runyon suggest that

> When women participate in political movements as a result of their practical gender interests, they may develop an awareness of strategic gender interests by self-consciously confronting their subordination as women. In the process, they come to the understanding that their practical gender interests are not being satisfied because their strategic gender interests are being thwarted. This insight enables them to link gender inequality and the problems—often of sheer survival—that they face in their daily lives.*

Simply put, bread riots may be the source of later protests over rights.

*V. Spike Peterson and Anne Sosson, *Global Gender Issues* (Boulder, CO: Westview Press, 1993), p. 122.

for, and value of, abstract theories of justice, such as theories of "just deserts" that link one's rewards to one's contributions. Carol Gilligan questions the assumption of most ideologies that moral development demands allegiance to abstract and universal claims about just treatment. While contemporary liberals—such as John Dewey and Lawrence Kohlberg—have argued that the ability to generate universal and abstract rules of fairness is central to moral development, Gilligan argues that such abstract rules are simply unimportant and irrelevant to women's understanding of the treatment of self and of others. For Gilligan, the liberal fascination with theories of justice is a male fetish, and she proposes an **ethic of care** as an alternative to (or at least as a complement to) theories of justice. In an analysis that reflects the "natural justice" sought by anarchists, Gilligan argues that women see justice as particular acts of caring that are not amenable to theorizing or abstraction.[22] Rather than learning abstract principles of justice, women develop a disposition to care for the particular people in their communities. Rather than attend to abstract rights, women seek to act responsibly toward others and to nurture relationships. Women respond to the particulars of ethical dilemmas, and this is not an indication of mental weakness but an alternative and thoughtful way to respond to questions of justice.

Change

All feminists want social, economic, and political change, but—as indicated by their diverse principles—they differ greatly on how extensive and of what kind these changes should be. Nor have feminists reached agreement on strategies for bringing about change. Some seek to work within existing institutions to bring about incremental changes in public policies, while others want revolutionary changes. Most feminists, however, have relied on nonviolent forms of action to encourage change. The most radical separatist feminists have given up on the possibility of change within patriarchal societies and have opted to engage in change within their own communities. Postmodern feminists believe that the key to real change is to begin the slow process of rethinking everything we know about the world and social life.

SUMMARY AND CONCLUSIONS

The issues that link feminists together have not disappeared. Women still face many of the same problems that motivated early feminists to action. Liberal states have made some legislative reforms that address women's issues, but inequities remain. Socialist and communist countries have also addressed some women's issues, but in doing so they have revealed the deep cultural habits and perspectives that limit women's access to social activities and to equal treatment.

[22]Carol Gilligan, *In a Different Voice* (Cambridge: Harvard University Press, 1982). For a recent defense of the ethic of care, see Joan C. Tronto, *Moral Boundaries: A Political Argument for an Ethic of Care* (New York: Routledge, 1993).

Feminists have opened a dialogue that calls into question many traditional activities and understandings. Even those who don't consider themselves feminists have been forced to refocus their personal and political lenses because of the critiques generated by feminists. Feminists may continue to disagree on a wide range of political and philosophical issues, but the dialogue they have initiated will not be dampened by these disagreements.

Feminists have not (yet) created a single cohesive ideology to redress the grievances of women, but they have generated many insights that demand respect. They have forced theorists to consider that the differences between men and women may be both minimal—in terms of their fundamental rights—and profound—in terms of their different perspectives on social life. They have illustrated that what occurs in the intimacy of family relationships can be as politically important as the activities of the state. Most importantly, they have been successful in bringing women's voices to the conversation about how humans can live peaceful and prosperous lives.

Conclusions

Art and ideology often interact on each other; but the plain fact is that both spring from a common source. Both draw on human experience to explain mankind to itself; both attempt, in very different ways, to assemble coherence from seemingly unrelated phenomena; both stand guard for us against chaos.

—Kenneth Tynan

Our blight is ideologies—they are the long-expected Antichrist.

—Carl Jung

Science may be described as the art of systematic over-simplification.

—Karl Popper

Philosophy is like trying to open a safe with a combination lock: each little adjustment of the dials seems to achieve nothing; only when everything is in place does the door open.

—Ludwig Wittgenstein

CHAPTER 14

Beyond Ideologies

Recently there has been considerable discussion about the "end of ideology." At times, the intent of this discussion has been to prescribe eliminating ideological concepts and debate from political life. From this perspective, the rhetoric employed by liberals and conservatives (or other ideologues) only obfuscates the issues that face political communities and leads to unnecessary division and deadlock.[1] In this view, our pressing problems are clear enough, and pragmatic, "businesslike" solutions to these problems are needed. Rather than a conservative or a liberal approach to crime (or health care or education or any other problem), we need workable and effective approaches developed by competent experts who transcend ideological preconceptions and biases. Such a technocratic prescription reflects a perennial aspiration to reduce political conflict, but it forgets that problems need to be recognized and prioritized, and that ideologies play a major role in this regard. It also forgets that experts, too, disagree about solutions to problems precisely because the most workable and effective solutions to political problems remain unknown.

At other times, the intent of pointing to the end of ideology has been to argue that ideologies have lost their relevance for understanding political life. From this perspective, such factors as the interests and powers of political actors have become much more important determinants of political actions and public policies than are ideological motivations and concerns. According to Theodore Lowi, after both liberals and conservatives embraced positive government during the New Deal:

> The basis for the liberal-conservative dialogue did die. Liberalism-conservatism as the source of public philosophy no longer made any sense. . . .
>
> [Now] the most important difference between liberals and conservatives,

[1]See, for example, E. J. Dione, *Why Americans Hate Politics* (New York: Simon and Schuster, 1991), pp. 9–28; and Alexander Shtromas, *The End of ISMs?* (Cambridge: Harvard University Press, 1994).

Republicans and Democrats, is to be found in the interest groups they identify with.[2]

Such claims deserve serious consideration, because ideological rhetoric can serve to deflect attention from the actual motivations and activities of political actors. Nevertheless, the actions and behavior of people are clearly influenced by the ideas that they hold, and ideologies continue to influence people's thoughts.[3] Lowi's observation, moreover, is directed only at the American polity at a particular point in time. Even if his remarks are accurate, they do not reflect a global situation.

Most often, however, discussions of the end of ideology have focused on the perception that ideological conflict is ending worldwide. From this perspective, the winding down of the cold war and the apparent decline in the appeal of communism as an ideology has been interpreted as indicating that a consensus is forming that democracy and capitalism—the ideas of liberal democracy—best achieve peace and prosperity.[4] The claim that ideological conflict is ending may be an attractive idea, but such claims have been made before and have proven rather misleading, at best.

The relatively peaceful and prosperous 1950s witnessed the first claim that ideological conflict was ceasing. The formulators of this **end-of-ideology thesis** adopted a critical conception of ideologies as simplified ideas packaged in a manner that appeal to human emotion rather than to reason; in this conception, ideologies were viewed as "weapons" used to arouse people to take often fanatical actions in the false, chiliastic hope that such actions would lead to human and social perfection.[5] They then claimed that such ideologies were "exhausted," because their "truth" was no longer credible. Few serious minds could believe that the "blueprints" of ideologies like fascism and communism could bring about the new utopias they proclaimed when they were instead responsible for "such calamities as the Moscow Trials, the Nazi-Soviet pact, the concentration camps, the suppression of the Hungarian workers," and so forth.[6] The initial formulators of the end-of-ideology thesis also claimed that ideological struggle over the perennial issues of politics had ceased to characterize domestic politics. Conservatives no longer regarded every increase in state power as an intrusion on personal and political liberty. Socialists no longer advocated the abolition of private property.[7] Instead, a "rough consensus" had emerged that accepted the welfare state, preferred decentralized to centralized power, advocated a mixed economy rather

[2]Theodore J. Lowi, *The End of Liberalism: The Second Republic of the United States,* 2d ed. (New York: Norton, 1979), pp. 43, 51. For a more recent claim about the declining relevance of the differences between liberalism and conservatism, see Christopher Lasch, *The True and Only Heaven* (New York: Norton, 1991).

[3]Lawrence J. R. Herson, *The Politics of Ideas: Political Theory and American Public Policy* (Homewood, Ill.: Dorsey Press, 1984), esp. pp. 279–294.

[4]Francis Fukuyama, *The End of History and the Last Man* (New York: Avon Books, 1992).

[5]Daniel Bell, *The End of Ideology* (New York: Collier Books, 1960), pp. 393–396.

[6]Bell, *The End of Ideology,* p. 397.

[7]Seymour Martin Lipset, *Political Man* (Garden City, N.Y.: Doubleday, 1960), p. 404.

than pure capitalism or pure socialism, and supported political pluralism—understood as the existence and toleration of many groups having diverse ideas and interests and pursuing their interests in competitive electoral and legislative arenas.[8] Within this broad consensus, political conflict was reduced to questions regarding the need for a little more or a little less governmental welfare, ownership, regulation, and planning in particular policy areas.[9]

Perhaps domestic politics during the 1950s did approach such an ideological consensus, but, in retrospect, it is hard to understand how the end-of-ideology thesis could be seriously entertained in a world that was increasingly divided by the capitalist-communist split. In any event, the turbulent 1960s made the end-of-ideology notion rather short-lived domestically. Sharp ideological differences were most clearly evident in the Goldwater-Johnson Presidential elections in 1964 and in the Nixon-McGovern race in 1972. Not only did conservative principles clash significantly with liberal and socialist principles in most Western democracies during the 1970s and 1980s, but these decades saw a rise in new ideological perspectives such as feminism, black nationalism, environmentalism, and various types of religious fundamentalism. As the 1990s approached, few political analysts believed that ideological differences had waned.

But the decline of communism has renewed discussion of the end-of-ideology thesis, and in a perhaps more profound form than that espoused during the 1950s. The most notable expression of the idea that ideological differences are evaporating as we approach the "**end-of-history**" is that presented by Francis Fukuyama in *The End of History and the Last Man.* According to Fukuyama, the transformation of communist regimes in Eastern Europe into democratic countries bent on establishing market economies is simply the most visible event in a trend that has been evident since the dawn of the age of ideology almost two hundred years ago. According to Fukuyama, the superiority of capitalism and democracy became evident as early as 1806, when Napoleon defeated the Prussian monarchy at the Battle of Jena.[10] Drawing on the work of Hegel as interpreted by Alexandre Kojeve, Fukuyama argues that the ideals of classical liberalism—"the twin principles of liberty and equality"—cannot be improved upon. Societies that are governed by modern technocratic and bureaucratic states that are based on these ideas satisfy mankind's "deepest and most fundamental longings,"[11] making impossible the further historical development of the ideas that should govern political communities. Capitalism is the system of economic organization that best embodies the principle of liberty while it also provides the economic development that satisfies human desires for security and the accumulation of wealth. Democracy is the system of political organization that best embodies the principle of equality,

[8]Bell, *The End of Ideology,* p. 397.
[9]Lipset, *Political Man,* pp. 404–405.
[10]Fukuyama, "The End of History?" *The National Interest* (summer 1989), p. 5.
[11]Fukuyama, *The End of History and the Last Man,* p. xi.

assuring the equal recognition of everyone as a human being and as a citizen with equal basic rights.

By claiming that the triumph of democratic capitalism implies an "end of history," Fukuyama does not deny that there have been—and will continue to be—very important historical events. Instead, he claims that there has not been—and there will not be—any further historical "development of underlying principles and institutions, because all of the big questions have been settled."[12] Since the development of classical liberalism, there has been no credible denial of the idea that states must be based upon, and must act upon, the principles of liberty and equality. From this perspective, Marxism and communism simply had mistaken notions of how to achieve liberty and equality, and these flaws would inevitably be discovered and corrected. From this perspective, the horrors of fascism and nazism simply taught humans of the incredible evils achievable by capitalist technology when it is employed in opposition to the principles of liberty and equality. Of course, the principles of liberty and equality are not fully realized in any political community. But today even illiberal and undemocratic regimes give lip service to the principles of liberty and equality, because these ideas are so universally acknowledged that no regime can long survive if it denies allegiance to them. In time, however, the internal contradictions of regimes that violate these principles become apparent, leading to the demise of illiberal and undemocratic regimes and to the universal realization of capitalist and democratic communities.

Fukuyama does not argue that the end of history—or the end of ideological conflict—is a good thing. The formal equalities (such as equal political and legal rights to all) and extensive economic and social liberties within the (private) sphere of civil society provided by democratic capitalism are interpreted as "freedom," but such equal freedom is directed toward the fulfillment of material desires rather than toward encouraging deeper spiritual pursuits. At the "end of history," in Fukuyama's interpretation, politics no longer involves moral or ethical debate about such great ideas as the appropriate principles of justice. Without such fundamental conflict over the meaning of existence, the differences among political communities wane, and a boring sameness characterizes human life. Think of it this way: Every good story has a plot that involves conflict between a protagonist and an antagonist. This conflict may be within a single individual, between individuals or groups, between an individual and nature, and so on. Without some form of conflict, there is no story. If all serious conflict among ideological, religious, and philosophical points of view has been resolved by liberalism, then there is no story left to tell. History has ended, and boredom ensues.

There is much to admire in Fukuyama's analysis. Political communities do appear to be losing their unique identities as they become more homogeneous. Certainly there is much recent movement toward more democratic political systems and more capitalist economies. Perhaps the ideals of equality and liberty are fundamental to contemporary political communities. But, to para-

[12]Fukuyama, *The End of History and the Last Man*, p. xii.

phrase Mark Twain, the rumors of the demise of ideological conflict may be greatly exaggerated. Two considerations lead us to question Fukuyama's end-of-history thesis. First, the broad global trends toward democratic capitalism should not obscure the viability of regimes that practice neither democracy nor capitalism. Various brands of authoritarianism, nationalism, tribalism, and fundamentalism cannot be disregarded as ideological alternatives to democratic capitalism in today's world or in the world of the future. Second, within democratic capitalism the ideals of liberty and equality continue to be given quite different interpretations, yielding very different political principles. Even if there should be agreement that the basic ideas of capitalism should be adopted, large ideological disagreements would persist about where to limit or override pure capitalist processes. Even if there should be agreement that democracy is better than nondemocratic regimes, significant ideological differences would remain about the requirements of democracy. Even if people should accept the highly abstract ideas of liberty and equality, fundamental questions would remain about authority, justice, and citizenship. In short, even at the "end of history," ideological differences would persist. Such differences imply an escape from boredom, as individuals and communities will continue to have different ideas and practices about how best to constitute political life. Such differences also impose a responsibility that we think clearly about the ideas and practices that should govern our political lives.

LEVELS OF INTELLECTUAL UNDERSTANDING ABOUT POLITICS

Few people, however, seem to think clearly and deeply about politics and, according to the conventional wisdom in American political science, the few people who are most sophisticated in their political thinking are "ideologues." In a classical study of the political ideas of Americans, Philip Converse suggested that there were five levels of sophistication in political thinking. As a principal investigator in the National Election Surveys, Converse drew upon interview data collected from thousands of American citizens during the 1956, 1958, and 1960 national elections to describe these "political belief systems."[13] According to Converse, at level one—the lowest level of political understanding and thinking—are 22.5 percent of the public who are largely without political ideas; they are generally uninformed about political issues and attribute no significance to political matters. At level two, 24 percent of the public simply evaluates parties and candidates in terms of the "nature of the times" (giving them credit and praise for peace and prosperity or blame for war and economic difficulties), or in terms of how they stand on a narrow issue. At level three, 42 percent of the public understand politics as involving conflicting group interests, and they orient themselves toward particular issues and can-

[13]Philip E. Converse, "The Nature of Belief Systems in Mass Publics," in *Ideology and Discontent*, edited by David E. Apter (New York: Free Press, 1964).

didates based on their chosen leaders' assessments of how those issues (or electoral outcomes) affect the interests of the groups with whom they identify. Thus, according to Converse, the 88 percent of the public comprising levels one through three are therefore "innocent" of ideology because they fail to make much use of abstract ideas or principles when orienting themselves toward politics. At level four are people who make some use of the abstract ideas that characterize ideologies, but they do not understand such abstractions very well nor do they apply them to current issues very much; such "near ideologues" constitute another 9 percent of the public. Only at level five, comprising just 2.5 percent of the public, are there "ideologues" who are adept at employing abstract concepts and whose ideas are coherently structured.

Converse's findings have been viewed with alarm by most students of American democracy because they indicate that the political ideas of most American citizens have no foundation in broader principles, are inconsistent with each other, are unstable over time, and are generally ill-considered and ill-informed.[14] Moreover, these findings suggest that the political thinking of the general public is markedly different from and inferior to that of political elites. While ideologies play a very important role in the political thinking of elites, the general public is largely innocent of ideologies. When political leaders and activists discuss political and policy choices, they draw upon the abstract and well-organized principles that ideologies provide. But most citizens do not hold or make use of the abstract political ideas that are central to political ideologies. Thus, the lack of facility with ideological thinking among citizens may hinder their active and effective participation in politics.

These findings and considerations suggest that citizens need to develop abstract principles and general political beliefs, such as those provided by ideologies, in order to become active and effective participants in politics. They suggest that large numbers of citizens need to become ideological in order to

[14]There are least two major rebuttals to this conventional wisdom in political science. First, Converse's findings may reflect the particularly nonideological period in American history in which his data were collected. According to Norman Nie, Sidney Verba, and John Petrocik, in their study, *The Changing American Voter* (Cambridge: Harvard University Press, 1979), the public is more ideological when elections are ideologically polarized. However, others have found that such elections seem to enhance ideological sophistication only minimally, bringing about only a small increase in "the nonideological use of ideological terminology." Second, Converse's findings may reflect certain preconceptions about how ideas should be patterned and may fail to take into account the ways in which citizens reach reasonably sophisticated conclusions through "often unique patterning of ideas in their own terms." According to Robert Lane in his *Political Ideology* (New York: Free Press, 1962), the public can achieve a fairly high level of sophistication in political thinking by "morselizing" (by thinking about political events in isolation from one another) rather than by "contextualizing" (by placing events in ideological and historical perspective). Such challenges to the conventional wisdom have resulted in a general recognition that the American mind is not completely empty of political ideas, but that "such ideas defy parsimonious description. Some beliefs are classically liberal, some classically conservative. There are some authentic opinions, tenaciously held; there are some nonattitudes, casually expressed. There are patches of knowledge and expanses of ignorance." For an excellent summary of this literature, see Donald Kinder, "Diversity and Complexity in American Public Opinion," in *Political Science: The State of the Discipline*, edited by Ada Finifter (Washington, D.C.: American Political Science Association, 1983), p. 401.

close the gap between elites and the masses and thereby move political communities towards more genuine democracy. Developing broad principles about how political communities are and should be governed and applying these principles to current issues would, according to this argument, increase political sophistication for those whose political thinking is at or below the level of "near ideologues" in Converse's scale of political sophistication. But are ideologues the most sophisticated political thinkers? Is there not some kind of political thinking that improves on the ideas held by ideologues?

QUESTIONING ONE'S IDEOLOGICAL PRECONCEPTIONS

In Converse's analysis, an "ideologue" is someone who understands and applies to the real world a coherent system of abstract political beliefs and ideals. If there is some form of political understanding that transcends ideological orientations toward politics, it calls into question the ideas that the ideologue readily accepts and searches for better ideas than any particular ideology provides. Questioning one's current ideology is the first step a person should take in order to move beyond being merely an ideologue who accepts an entire ideological system to becoming a political theorist and philosopher who seeks better beliefs and ideals. Why do you hold certain political beliefs and ideals? Unless the ideas that one holds are based on fairly extensive self-reflection, it is entirely possible that one should discard these ideas as products of a previous "false consciousness." At least four major sources of our ideological preconceptions can be identified; people seeking to transcend ideological thinking might profit from asking themselves whether their current beliefs and values simply reflect (1) various socialization experiences, (2) psychological strains that they have experienced, (3) control needs that they possess, or (4) an unquestioning assimilation of the ideas of the most powerful interests in society.

Many social institutions can obviously play important roles in influencing our ideological preconceptions. Parents and other family members can express certain ideas and principles that shape people's political principles for years to come. Both in the content of what they teach and in the procedures they employ, schools and churches can influence people's political beliefs and values. Various social organizations—ranging from fraternities and sororities to various community service groups—espouse political ideas that can be assimilated into one's basic political outlook. Workplace organizations—the companies that employ people and the unions that organize them—stress certain ideas that can be perhaps too easily accepted. Governmental and party leaders peddle ideas continually, and we presumably assimilate some of them. In short, our ideological predispositions are often influenced by a variety of **agents of socialization.** As a first step in questioning our allegiance to a particular ideology, it may be helpful simply to recall those agents whose views we have trusted, and to ask whether our trust has been well-founded. However, the impact of such socialization agents is often complex and subtle, and we must consider other determinants of our ideological predispositions.

Sigmund Freud (1856–1939) argued that our political beliefs and values (as well as religious and other ideas) are based on psychological strains. When people feel insecure and anxious, they seek comfort by developing beliefs in the benevolence of powerful authorities—in God or in some wise and virtuous political rulers. Freud's analysis gave rise to **strain theory** as an explanation for our ideological predispositions.[15] According to strain theory, ideologies are the psychological responses of people living under troubled and stressful social conditions. Societies and the secondary associations within societies put multiple and conflicting demands on people, causing similar stresses on people having similar roles in society. For example, white men who have developed some expertise and seniority in their particular jobs are likely to feel that their economic "rights" (e.g., that promotions should go to the most qualified and senior workers) are jeopardized by affirmative action (e.g., that special consideration be given to minorities and women for those promotions that are "rightfully" theirs). Strain theory claims that such people will develop an ideology that allows them to integrate the tension between their concerns as workers and their status as citizens who are expected to obey the just laws of government. Rather than viewing affirmative action policies as legitimate efforts by governments to rectify past injustices to minorities and women, they will define such policies as "reverse discrimination." Rather than viewing such policies as the result of a democratic process, they will see these policies as the work of a small group of African-American extremists, radical feminists, and bungling bureaucrats. And they may conclude that their government has been taken over by such illegitimate factions, necessitating a political (nonviolent) "counterrevolution" by "the silent majority." As an alternative example, strain theory might recognize that comfortable white men with secure jobs may also belong to organizations that proclaim the historical mistreatment of minorities and women. Such circumstances may lead them to feel "white man's guilt," facilitating their ready acceptance of affirmative action and other aspects of the more egalitarian strand of contemporary liberalism. In short, strain theory maintains that particular ideologies are developed to accommodate the tensions felt by people living in similar social positions and experiencing similar value conflicts. The ideas of the ideology are then tenaciously maintained in order to allow those experiencing such stress to cope both intellectually and emotionally with the frustrations, anxieties, or guilt that they feel.

A third basis for our ideological thinking may be found in the concept of the **libido dominandi**, or "lust for ruling," presented by St. Augustine (354–430) long before ideologies per se had been created. In this interpretation, ideological thinking is the product of a desire to rule over nature, history, other human beings, or the world, even though we cannot, in fact, completely exer-

[15]"Strain theory" is discussed by Clifford Geertz in "Ideology as a Cultural System" in *Ideology and Discontent*, pp. 52–57.

cise such control. An ideology gives us the illusion of control by providing a coherent or consistent set of principles about the world, nature, history, or human beings and by providing prescriptions about the manner in which we can control them. Thus, we develop ideologies because of a need for control or power. Augustine underscored the often arbitrary control and violent power that emerges from this "lust" to rule, and recognized that such control and power may bring a kind of satisfaction and enjoyment.[16] In a manner somewhat similar to that described by Freud's "strain theory," this satisfaction of the *libido dominandi* arises in part from a relief from fear. The fear of death, the fear of not being in complete control of one's destiny, and the anxiety of not being completely certain about the meaning of one's existence—all of which everyone experiences from time to time—may be relieved by adherence to a satisfying ideology that provides extended and morally certain answers addressing these fears. If, moreover, those who espouse a satisfying ideology come to hold political power, they can make the world over in conformity to the requirements of their ideology, as communists and nazis have attempted to do. For good or ill, most people desire a release from existential anxiety and uncertainty, but the perilous qualities of the *libido dominandi* have been revealed several times in this century when various ideological "makeovers" have resulted in the deaths of millions of human beings.

Karl Marx suggested a fourth basis for our ideological preconceptions, asserting that widespread acceptance of classical liberal ideology emerges from the interests and power of the ruling class. Because capitalists control the major economic resources of society, they have an interest in generating and disseminating certain ideas that legitimate democratic capitalism—such as the ideas that the inequalities derived from market exchanges are just, that representative democracy empowers average citizens more than it empowers business interests, and that minimal regulation of the economy improves everyone's condition. Moreover, Marx contended that capitalists' control over economic resources gives them control over "mental production," enabling them to create "false consciousness" in the working class; contrary to their real interests, many workers are falsely persuaded that the ideology of capitalists provides natural truths about social and economic life and serves the interests of the working class as well as those of the capitalists.

Marx's analysis has given rise to **interest theory** as an explanation for our ideological preconceptions. According to interest theory, ideologies are the political weapons of everyone—not just of capitalists, as Marx had contended. Every ideology is developed in order to further the interests of a particular class or group of people, and each ideology attempts to persuade others to support its political objectives by claiming a universal validity and benevolence. An ideology claiming that inequality produces freedom and prosperity for all is rooted in the interests of the wealthy. An ideology claiming that economic equality will deliver humans from alienation and exploitation is rooted

[16]John Milbank, *Theology and Social Theory: Beyond Secular Reason* (Oxford and Cambridge: Blackwell Publishers, 1990), p. 390. Cf. St. Augustine, *The City of God,* Book XIV, 15 and 28; Book XV, 7.

in the interests of the economically disadvantaged. An ideology that looks to divine supremacy as the source of political guidance is rooted in the interests of those who claim to know the word of God. In short, interest theory asserts that humans are primarily motivated to further their own economic well-being, power, and status, and that they do so by developing and articulating the ideological principles that are said to be true and beneficial to all, but of which primary effect is to enhance the position of a particular set of people.

Interest theory thus suggests that we should examine two possible sources of our ideological preconceptions. First, we should consider the most powerful interests in our society and their capacity to mold our political beliefs and ideals. Do capitalists dominate our society, and have they used their power to induce unquestioned allegiance to the principles of classical liberalism? Does a "new class" dominate our society, and have its members used their power to bring about widespread acceptance of the ideas of contemporary liberalism or democratic socialism? Or does some other interest dominate society, bringing about another sort of ideological hegemony?

Second, interest theory suggests that we consider our own interests as a source of our ideological preconceptions. Perhaps, because we are professors at public universities, we have an interest in supporting the strong state endorsed by contemporary liberals that is given the authority to invest more money in education (including faculty salaries!) to solve various social problems. Perhaps you or your family are effective entrepreneurs who have the skills and resources to succeed in capitalist competition, predisposing you to support classical liberalism or contemporary conservatism. One's political ideas naturally *seem* more thoughtfully grounded when they reflect one's own interests, rather than the views of the dominant interests of society, but it is doubtful that principles should be grounded in self-interest. Contemporary political philosophers generally argue that people should choose their principles in an *impartial* manner that ignores their own talents, capacities, resources, and backgrounds.[17] When we adopt and hold "principles" that merely reflect our interests and capacities, we are subject to the charge by others that our principles are but rationalizations for our actions and weapons for "forcing" others to conform to our interests. Although it may be impossible for us to assume a completely impartial position that enables us to put aside our interests and capacities, it may be desirable for us to employ various intellectual

[17]The "veil of ignorance" has been proposed by John Rawls as a device for requiring people to choose their principles in a manner that overlooks their talents and backgrounds. Rawls suggests that people should choose principles without considering their own class or status in society, their own natural talents, intelligence, strength and so forth. According to Rawls, the veil of ignorance helps people to choose principles that they are prepared to live with whatever their circumstances turn out to be. Rawls claims that it is a basic presumption of morality and justice that people not design their principles to coincide with their known interests. See his *A Theory of Justice* (Cambridge: Harvard University Press, 1971), pp. 136–142. Brian Barry agrees with Rawls on the importance of impartiality, but he believes impartiality can be achieved without such devices as the veil of ignorance; according to Barry, it is part of human nature to seek to justify one's actions to others without appealing to self-interest. See Barry's *A Treatise on Social Justice,* Vol. 1, *Theories of Justice* (Berkeley: University of California Press, 1989), p. 364.

methodologies and devices that curtail the influence of self-interest when we assess competing political ideas and become committed to certain political principles.

POLITICAL SCIENCE

As a scholarly discipline, political science aspires to achieve impartiality, or "objectivity," regarding political beliefs. In general, political science serves to provide methods for guarding against the influence of various biases in determining the validity of our ideas that describe and explain the workings of actual political communities, and its scientific procedures are usually thought to have little or no efficacy in the assessment of "value-laden" or "subjective" normative ideals. Nevertheless, the capacity of the scientific method to overcome ideological predispositions about how the political world functions has often been questioned.[18] For example, our ideological orientations are alleged to shape the questions we ask about the empirical world, the hypotheses we form about it, and the observations we make about it. Such allegations suggest that we cannot transcend ideology in forming political beliefs because ideologies are particular and narrow lenses that channel our thoughts and perceptions about the empirical world, and these lenses necessarily distort our thinking and perceptions in ways that make objectivity impossible.

Ideologies undoubtedly do shape the questions we ask about how the political world actually works. For example, many contemporary liberals and conservatives, who recognize that their Marxist and socialist rivals emphasize the importance of classes and class conflict, have raised the question, "Are social classes dying?" in the hope of undermining the current relevance of Marxist and socialist ideas.[19] As another example, a Marxist who holds the idea that democratic governments are merely "the executive committee for the capitalist class" is likely to raise questions about the distribution of power in communities that are formally democratic: Who really rules? Who really has predominant power in American cities and other political communities? Thus, if ideologies influence the subject matters of scientific investigations, this is probably an asset rather than a liability. Insofar as science often focuses on rather trivial questions, ideologies can redirect political scientific research back to bigger issues, such as the importance of classes and the distribution of power in contemporary communities.

Ideologies may also influence the hypotheses that one chooses to investigate. In response to the question of whether classes are losing their importance, conservatives and liberals are predisposed to suggest that the political signif-

[18]See, for example, Eugene Miller, "Positivism, Historicism, and Political Inquiry," and the rejoinders to his argument in the *American Political Science Review* 66 (Sept. 1972), pp. 796–873.

[19]Robert Nisbet, "The Decline and Fall of Social Class," *Pacific Sociological Review* 2 (1959), pp. 11–17, and Terry Clark and Seymour Martin Lipset, "Are Social Classes Dying?" *International Sociology* 6 (Dec. 1991), pp. 397–410.

icance of classes has declined because capitalism has brought increasing affluence to everyone, reducing the most fundamental differences in the life chances of the rich and the poor.[20] In contrast, Marxists and socialists are predisposed to claim that classes are still important because inequalities in wealth and income persist and have even increased significantly since 1980, and that social class continues to be the main determinant of people's life chances and political behavior.[21] In response to the question of who really rules, liberals normally suppose that democratically authorized elected representatives are the actual rulers in a democratic society, but Marxists hypothesize that various business interests—members of the capitalist class—have extensive power over such officials,[22] while contemporary conservatives suggest that a "new class" of intellectuals and bureaucrats may be the real rulers. Thus, ideological predispositions often result in the formulation of not only one hypothesis regarding an important topic, but alternative or rival hypotheses. At least in principle, these rival hypotheses can be tested scientifically, resulting in more precise and valid descriptions and explanations about the (un)importance of class, the actual distribution of power within communities, and other contrasting beliefs held by persons of different ideological orientations.

Ideological preconceptions may, however, affect the evidence that people marshal on behalf of their hypotheses and theories. Marxists allege, for example, that the authors of the death-of-class thesis "neglect evidence which shows the continuing—and even rising—importance of class."[23] Meanwhile, conservatives contend that Marxists obfuscate the declining importance of class by pointing to the few occasions when class is an important factor in giving rise to collective actions and fail to consider the greater number of instances when political and social movements are based on nonclass (ethnic, religious, racial, and regional) cleavages.[24] Similarly, it is claimed that those Marxists who believe that capitalists really rule in liberal democratic communities employ research methods that reinforce the perception of capitalist dominance, but that fail to distinguish adequately between a perception of capitalist influence and the actual and very significant limits on the power of capitalists.[25] Meanwhile, Marxists argue that liberals, who believe that elected representatives rule, use methods that do not reveal the hidden control that wealthy busi-

[20]Terry Nichols Clark, Seymour Martin Lipset, and Michael Rempel, "The Declining Political Significance of Social Class," *International Sociology* 8 (Sept. 1993), pp. 293–316.

[21]Mike Hout, Clem Brooks, and Jeff Manza, "The Persistence of Classes in Post-Industrial Societies," *International Sociology* 8 (Sept. 1993), pp. 259–276.

[22]This Marxist hypothesis is developed by G. William Domhoff in *Who Really Rules?* (Santa Monica, Calif.: Goodyear Publishing, 1978), in response to the more liberal characterization of the distribution of power in American cities provided by Robert Dahl in *Who Governs?* (New Haven: Yale University Press, 1961).

[23]Hout, Brooks, and Manza, "The Persistence of Classes," p. 261.

[24]Jan Pakulski, "The Dying of Class or of Marxist Class Theory?" *International Sociology* 8 (Sept. 1993), p. 283.

[25]Raymond Wolfinger, "Reputation and Reality in the Study of Community Power," *American Sociological Review* 25 (Oct. 1960), pp. 636–644.

nessmen exercise over representatives.[26] Such arguments about the biases of the "scientific" methods used to collect evidence in support of rival hypotheses about the distribution of power have led some observers to conclude that there is little likelihood of attaining objective answers to "Who really rules?," because the field of study is hopelessly muddied by ideological preconceptions and biases.[27]

Despite such difficulties, the **scientific method** is designed to overcome ideological biases. While ideological positions may influence the evidence that is brought to bear on such hypotheses, science has developed many procedures—such as insisting on the replicability of findings—to winnow out questionable empirical claims and to increase our confidence in the validity of these scientific findings. When ideologically derived beliefs are subjected to scientific examination, the controversy that usually ensues about the adequacy of the methods employed often leads to the development of more complicated—though ultimately more adequate—answers to such questions as, "Are classes dying?" and "Who rules?"

The ideologically based argument about the decline of classes has led to the reworking of the concept of class and to many findings about the causes and consequences of class conflict that have been accepted by both Marxist and non-Marxist analysts.[28] For example, even neo-Marxists acknowledge that Marx's simple differentiation between the bourgeoisie and proletariat must be modified because of the increasing complexity of people's relationships to the means of production. According to Erik Wright, the bourgeoisie must be differentiated into large-scale employers, small-scale employers, and the petty bourgeoisie who own their own property but do not employ others, and the working class should be differentiated into various "expert," "semicredentialed," and "uncredentialed" workers. Such more complex typologies of social classes allow Marxists and non-Marxists to agree that persons in different classes tend to have significant differences in values, lifestyles, and resources. While Marxists still insist that "the underlying logic of class is unchanged," they agree with non-Marxists that "the political consequences of class may remain latent" in specific circumstances.[29] Both Marxists and non-Marxists now seem to agree that, in order for different class interests to be brought to bear on politics, political organizations (like parties) must actively organize around class themes. To the extent that political organizations stress class-based political beliefs and ideals, people vote and participate in social movements on the basis of their social class.[30] In short, ideological disputes about the declining or remaining importance of social classes have not thwarted sci-

[26]Domhoff, *Who Really Rules?*

[27]David Ricci, "Receiving Ideas in Political Analysis: The Case of Community Power Studies, 1950–1970," *Western Political Quarterly* 33 (Dec. 1980), pp. 451–475.

[28]The following distinctions are drawn from Pakulski, "The Dying of Class?" pp. 280–282.

[29]Hout, Brooks, and Manza, "The Persistence of Classes," p. 268.

[30]Adam Przeworski and John Sprague, *Stone Papers: A History of Electoral Socialism* (Chicago: University of Chicago Press, 1986).

entific progress toward discerning the role of classes in contemporary societies. Better understandings of the nature of social classes, the causes of class conflict, and the consequences of such conflict have emerged as more complex ideas about this phenomenon have undergone scientific development and analysis.

Perhaps the issue of whether elected representatives or capitalists really rule democratic communities has never been resolved, but ideas about the distribution of power have also evolved significantly because of the scientific research that has been generated by the ideological controversy in this area. First, more adequate understandings of the concept of power have emerged. Rather than simply conceptualizing and measuring political power in terms of who holds office in governmental institutions, persons from different ideological perspectives now acknowledge that power has several, more subtle, faces or dimensions. There is a "first face" of power that appears when some people are able to get other people to defer to their preferences when policy decisions are made. There is a "second face" of power that appears when some people are able to establish and control the agenda of issues that come before a community, providing a context in which the first face of power can be effective. And there is a "third face" of power that appears when some people are able to shape the preferences of other people so that those whose preferences have been shaped will use their power to help secure the goals of those who shaped their preferences.[31] Perhaps liberals developed the concept of the first face of power—and methods for analyzing the first face—because they anticipated that these methods would support their claim that elected officials have more such power than do capitalists. And perhaps neo-Marxists developed the concepts of the second and third faces of power because they anticipated that analyses would reveal that capitalists usually set the agenda to which elected officials respond and that the ideological hegemony of capitalist values shapes the preferences that elected officials (and even the working class) pursue in the policy-making process. While ideological motivations perhaps gave rise to the conceptualizations of these different dimensions of power, both liberals and neo-Marxists now acknowledge that power is multidimensional, involving at least these three separate facets.[32] Additionally, the ideological debate over who rules has led to a scientific consensus that neither elected representatives nor capitalists rule entirely, but rather that the distribution of power varies across communities and even within communities, depending on the kinds of issues that are being addressed. Business interests do predominate in some communities that are formally democratic, but interests that oppose business predominate in other communities. Indeed, scientific investigations suggest that business interests are particularly likely to predominate under spe-

[31]These three faces of power are discussed in more detail in Paul Schumaker, "Estimating the First and (Some of) the Third Faces of Power," *Urban Affairs Quarterly* 28 (Mar. 1993), pp. 441–461.

[32]For a neo-Marxist acknowledgment of these three dimensions of power, see Steven Lukes, *Power: A Radical View* (London: Macmillan, 1974). For a liberal acknowledgment of these three dimensions of power, see Robert Dahl, *Democracy and Its Critics* (New Haven: Yale University Press, 1989), pp. 111–114.

cific conditions—such as when communities employ institutions that depoliticize government (e.g., by having nonpartisan elections for office).[33] Such investigations also suggest that business interests are likely to predominate on economic development issues, but have much less influence on "allocation" issues concerned with the provision of governmental services.[34]

In summary, scientific analyses of ideologically motivated debates over "Are social classes dying?" and "Who rules?" show the inadequacy of the simple answers provided by various ideological perspectives. While some ideologues in the debate have resisted more complex scientific advances in our ideas about social classes and the distribution of power, ideological blinders have not prevented the development of more sophisticated and more accurate beliefs. These examples suggest that more adequate political beliefs can be attained by asking the suggested questions about political reality within the framework for studying ideologies that we presented in the first chapter, by entertaining as rival hypotheses the contrasting beliefs held by those from different ideological perspectives, and by analyzing these hypotheses using normal scientific methods. This is not to claim that such scientific investigations will be free of ideological biases and, thus, "objective." Nor is this to claim that scientific progress in analyzing particular questions will result in "true" answers to these questions. Instead, our claim is that the examination of the rival hypotheses provided by different ideologies through the most adequate scientific methods available leads to progressively better descriptions and explanations of political reality.

POLITICAL PHILOSOPHY

Scientific methods are of little help in overcoming prejudice when we are choosing normative political ideals (or principles for governing a good political community), because such methods are intended to detect biased beliefs rather than biased ideals. According to ancient philosophers like Socrates and Plato, the best method for informing our political ideals is the dialectical method, and this method still has its defenders.[35]

Most simply, the **dialectical method** involves submitting one's principles of how political communities ought to be governed to the critical inspection of others. When the dialectical method is employed, the goal is not simply to win a debate against those having opposing views; instead, the goal is to attain bet-

[33]Willis Hawley, *Nonpartisan Elections and the Case for Party Politics* (New York: John Wiley, 1973). For a discussion of those factors that result in more concentration of power among business interests, see Philip Trounstine and Terry Christensen, *Movers and Shakers* (New York: St. Martin's Press 1982), pp. 40–47.

[34]Paul Peterson, *City Limits* (Chicago: University of Chicago Press, 1981). The idea that power arrangements vary according to policy area was first proposed by Theodore J. Lowi, "American Business and Public Policy, Case Studies, and Political Theory," *World Politics* (July 1964).

[35]Interesting recent uses of the dialectical method are found in the various conversations between democrats and their opponents in Robert Dahl, *Democracy and Its Critics*.

ter ideas, even if this entails modifying one's initial position. The Socratic dialogues, particularly Plato's *Republic,* illustrate the application of the dialectical method to the question, "What is justice?" Here, conventional Athenian ideas, the Sophistic views of Thrasymachus, and Socrates's vision of just citizens and just cities are presented and subjected to critical examination by others. Having learned the justice ideals held by people of various ideological perspectives, we might regard this dialogue as an unsatisfactory attempt to discover unbiased principles of justice. By initially conceiving justice as being the whole of human and social virtue, rather than as being a concept specifically directed at the best distribution of social goods, the dialogue seems poorly focused on contemporary concerns about justice. The principles of justice held in various modern ideological perspectives do not seem to be considered by Plato. And, although there is the appearance of critical analysis of the various positions presented by his interlocutors, Socrates's own views seem to be rather meekly accepted. Thus, employing the dialectical method in a contemporary attempt to resolve the issue of "What is justice?" might be a much more demanding enterprise than that depicted by Plato.

What is involved in moving beyond holding ideologically derived ideals of justice (or other great issues regarding political authority, rulers, citizenship, structure, and change) to choosing justice ideals on the basis of philosophical inquiry employing the dialectical method? According to David Ricci, this method involves engaging in the "**great conversation**."[36]

> What this requires, in effect, is a great conversation, larger than any small conversations that members of particular social groups, such as professions, or learned disciplines, are accustomed to conducting among themselves. The goal of this large-scale dialogue is, in fact, for various groups to express diverse aesthetic, moral, and scientific opinions and somehow thrash them out on common grounds, in intelligible terms, so that a slowly moving consensus on truth and decency can be worked out and maintained over the generations, to serve as a framework of social cement binding members of the community to one another and enabling them to live good lives together. Withal, it is an intellectual enterprise intent on examining a great many facts by comparing them to canons of right and wrong, good and evil, sin and virtue, rights and obligations.

To conduct the "great conversation," we can imagine "various groups" holding diverse beliefs and ideals—in short, representatives of various ideological perspectives—assembling with the intention of somehow achieving "consensus" about the requirements of justice (or authority or citizenship or any of the other fundamental political issues). We would expect proponents of each ideology to express clearly their principles on the issue. We would expect proponents to explain, as fully as possible, the philosophical bases for their principles and to show the implications of the principle for the overall structure and governance of community life. We would expect proponents to explain how these principles would solve (or reduce) various social, economic, and political problems, achieve (or approach) various political goals, and reflect

[36]David Ricci, *The Tragedy of Political Science* (New Haven: Yale University Press, 1984), pp. 300–301.

various moral concerns. Each of these arguments would, of course, be subjected to the critical scrutiny of persons from all other ideological perspectives gathered at the assembly, leading to lengthy debates about the adequacy of each argument. Given the many ideological perspectives at the assembly, the conversation would not only be "great" in terms of the importance of the issues being discussed or in terms of the diversity of views under consideration, it would certainly be of very great—perhaps endless—duration.

To help move the "great conversation" toward consensus, it would certainly help if there were some prior agreement among all those assembled regarding the "common grounds"to be used to evaluate the various principles being expressed. We can imagine the following evaluative criteria being proposed as such common grounds:

1. *Non-violence.* We should reject those ideas that justify the use of violence by some groups against others or that legitimate governmental murder of innocent people. Conversely, we should accept those ideas that are most likely to produce a society that resolves its conflicts through nonviolent means.
2. *Social stability.* We should reject those ideas that lead to social disorder, rancorous conflict among citizens, and personal insecurity. Conversely, we should accept those ideas that are most likely to lead to a stable and peaceful society where citizens are confident that their lives, liberties, and possessions will not be violated by others.
3. *Human perfection.* We should reject those ideas that lead to human ignorance, slovenliness, and moral decay. Conversely, we should accept those ideas that stimulate the intellectual and moral development of citizens and that promote communities where citizens exhibit the greatest virtue in relationship to each other.
4. *Human liberty.* We should reject those ideas that allow some humans to be dominated by others or that restrict the choices available to humans. Conversely, we should accept those ideas that minimize political, social, economic, and environmental constraints on individual freedom.
5. *Human equality.* We should reject those ideas that assign different individuals to different social positions and that discriminate among individuals on the basis of their social positions. Conversely, we should accept those ideas that promote a basic equality of being, that insist that everyone's happiness is of equal worth, and that accept the principle that each individual can rightfully claim that his or her life, liberty, and happiness is as important as the life, liberty, and happiness of any other individual.

We doubt that any of these criteria, or any other such criteria, would be readily agreed upon as the "common grounds" from which the great conversation could be conducted. Communists, nazis, and at least some anarchists would recognize that the nonviolence criterion would undermine acceptance of many of their principles. Marxists, social democrats, and feminists might recognize that the social-stability criterion would ensure the continuation of the oppressive regimes they abhor. Classical and contemporary liberals would view the human-perfection criterion as an invitation to limit individual choices and build a nonneutral and intolerant state. Traditional conservatives, nazis, and fascists would view the human-freedom criterion as giving too much weight to individual rights and desires at the expense of the greater good of society or the nation.

Perhaps the human-equality criterion would be most readily accepted by proponents of many ideologies, but such a criterion would not be consensually embraced. The commitment of fascists to elitism and of nazis to racism and anti-Semitism clearly violate the ideal of treating people as equals. Similarly, the commitment of traditional conservatives to maintaining natural hierarchies and to providing different rights and duties for people in different roles within these hierarchies would appear to violate the human-equality standard. While communists are theoretically committed to developing social, economic, and political conditions that promote human equality, they also proclaim the necessity of a "vanguard" having superior political and ethical understanding and judgment, and they subordinate the rest of the population to this vanguard, at least temporarily. To the extent that communists would sacrifice the liberties and interests of some people (or generations of people) for the well-being of others (or some future golden age), they have political principles that would violate the human-equality criterion. Thus, this criterion does not constitute a prior, universally embraced common ground for evaluating the principles of various ideologies.

Because some ideologies do not accept nonviolence, social stability, human perfection, human freedom, or human equality, we might conclude that their proponents should be excluded from those conversations focusing on these criteria. Clearly the prospects for achieving consensus would be enhanced by excluding those who fail to recognize such moral standards, but political philosophy is, by its nature, an open-ended inquiry into the best principles of community life, and excluding any voices from the dialogue seems antithetical to the entire enterprise. Despite reservations among some people regarding these criteria, it is worth discussing which political principles are most consistent with each of them.

Which ideology, for example, has principles that best correspond to the human-equality criterion? The answer is not obvious. According to Ronald Dworkin:

> We might say that individuals have a right to equal concern and respect in the design and administration of the political institutions that govern them. This is a highly abstract right. Someone might argue, for example, that it is satisfied by political arrangements that provide equal opportunity for office and position on the basis of merit. Someone else might argue, to the contrary, that it is satisfied only by a system that guarantees absolute equality of income and status, without regard to merit. A third man might argue that equal concern and respect is provided by that system, whatever it is, that improves the average welfare of all citizens, counting the welfare of each on the same scale. A fourth might argue, in the name of this fundamental equality, for the priority of liberty, and for other apparent inequalities.[37]

[37]Ronald Dworkin, *Taking Rights Seriously* (Cambridge: Harvard University Press), pp. 180–181.

Various democratic ideologies claim a great concern for human equality, broadly defined, but they propose competing political principles as being consistent with this human-equality criterion. Classical liberals insist on equality of being, that everyone's happiness is of equal worth, and that each individual can rightfully claim that his life, liberty, and happiness is as important as the life, liberty, and happiness of any other individual. As we have seen, classical liberals believe that such equality requires minimal governments that protect property rights and permit the inequalities of economic wealth that flow from such rights. Anarchists, too, accept a basic equality of being and the moral idea of respecting the dignity of all people, but they believe that equal liberty requires complete freedom from governmental control. Contemporary liberals also accept equal liberty and interpret it to mean that the real opportunities of all people to choose and achieve their life goals should be made more equal, and that this requires strong governments that regulate and redistribute economic resources. For democratic socialists, a commitment to human equality requires reductions in most inequalities of status, power, and wealth, or at least those inequalities that cannot be justified in terms of extending the range and domain of liberties for all. And contemporary conservatives, too, have an egalitarian core, as they stress the equal opportunity of everyone to use and profit from his or her differing natural talents and social advantages; as a consequence, governments should ensure formal equal opportunity but not seek equal conditions. As we have seen, how different ideologies interpret the abstract ideal of human equality has much broader implications for their political principles than these basic differences. We only want to underscore the conclusion that the principles of several democratic ideologies *appear* to be consistent with the human-equality criterion. Determining whether this appearance is accurate—or whether a more rigorous examination of the human-equality criterion reveals the greater merit of the principles of a particular ideology—is one of the tasks to be undertaken during the great conversation.[38]

In addition to engaging in the "great conversation," it is also important that people engage in *many smaller conversations* addressing the perennial

[38]For an application of the human-equality criteria to the evaluation of competing principles of justice, see Will Kymlicka, *Contemporary Political Philosophy* (New York: Oxford University Press, 1990). Kymlicka argues that the principles of justice of John Rawls (or contemporary liberals) are most consistent with this standard, but his arguments have not necessarily prevailed. Kymlicka's analysis is, however, an excellent reminder that the notion of a "great conversation" is a metaphor for the kind of analyses that characterize contemporary political philosophy. To conduct the great conversation or to engage in the dialectical method, people need not actually assemble in one place or present their arguments orally. Indeed, because of the complexity of the "great ideas," precision is surely enhanced by writing down one's arguments in a manner that clarifies ambiguous terms and lines of argumentation, and that allows one's audience ample opportunities to reflect upon and analyze these arguments. In short, the great conversation best occurs through books and articles where someone presents and defends her ideas, where others respond to perceived shortcomings, and where authors then rework their claims. Such a process broadly characterizes the practices of contemporary political philosophy, as exemplified by Rawls' initial presentation of his *A Theory of Justice,* the enormous response that his views received from both his liberal "friends" and his ideological opponents, and by his recent reformulation of his ideas in *Political Liberalism* (New York: Columbia University Press, 1993). Of course, this response of Rawls to his critics does not end the great conversation; it only continues it.

issues of politics. The great conversation aspires to discover the ideals that are *generally* best for governing political communities, but perhaps there are important variations in the ideals that are best for particular communities in particular circumstances.[39] We might recognize, for example, that certain countries might have political cultures that make democratic institutions undesirable for them, even though we are convinced that, generally and ideally, democratic institutions are best. The recognition that different principles may be best for different communities suggests that the members of each community should conduct their own "smaller conversation" about what principles are best for them. Because people are members of many communities (such as their families, their churches, their workplaces, their cities, and their nations), they should be engaged in several ongoing conversations about the principles that are best for each of their communities. We see no reason for assuming that people will conclude from these conversations that the same principles should apply to each of their communities. For example, the members of particular workplaces might conclude that participatory democracy is the best method for governing their community, even though these same people would prefer representative democracy to participatory democracy in the larger-scale communities to which they belong.[40] Members of particular cities might conclude that their local governments should not apply more redistributive principles of justice even though these same people prefer a more egalitarian welfare state at the national level.[41] Smaller conversations about the principles that should govern particular communities should, of course, use such abstract criteria as those employed in the great conversation to evaluate the desirability of alternative principles, but information about specific contextual conditions may be especially important in thinking about what is best for the particular community. Members of particular workplaces, for example, might conclude that direct participation in decision making would impair the quality of the products they produce or the efficiency of production, and such considerations might be decisive. Members of particular economically distressed cities might conclude that their redistributive policies have attracted many poor people to their communities and driven away many wealthy citizens and businesses, making less egalitarian principles necessary for their future economic viability. Specific contextual conditions thus can influence people's thinking about the ideals that are right for their community, but contextual conditions change, requiring that smaller conversations—like the great conversation—be ongoing affairs. Specific contextual conditions can also influence people's thinking

[39]Aristotle is usually credited with developing a form of political analysis that recognizes that different principles may be appropriate in different circumstances. For Aristotle, political philosophy addresses four types of questions: (1) What is ideal? (2) What is generally best in practice? (3) What is best under the circumstances? and (4) What is best under the worst possible circumstances?

[40]See Jane J. Mansbridge, "The Limits of Friendship," in *Nomos XVI: Participation in Politics*, edited by J. Roland Pennock and John W. Chapman (New York: New York University Press, 1977), pp. 246–266.

[41]See Paul Peterson, *City Limits*.

about the ideals that are right for the different communities to which they belong. Thus people might discover that the principles of some ideology seem best in a particular time and place while principles of another ideology seem best in other circumstances. People move beyond ideology—understood as a complete commitment to a particular ideological perspective—when the principles they adopt are drawn from different ideologies in a manner that reflects the different circumstances in which they find themselves.[42]

Although great and smaller conversations about various big political ideas have been conducted over the centuries, it is difficult to point to occasions when such conversations have resulted in consensus about the best political principles. Does this mean that the dialectical method as a means for overcoming personal bias in informing one's political ideals is inferior to the scientific method as a means for overcoming bias in informing one's political beliefs? The historical record suggests that science has been more successful in producing agreement (if not consensus) on ideas describing and explaining the political world than philosophy has been at producing agreement about our political ideals, but the differences should not be overdrawn. Among thoughtful and perceptive people, much disagreement remains about empirical, as well as normative, theories of politics. Perhaps the dialectical method cannot produce "truth" about political ideals, but the scientific method has not produced "truth" about political beliefs. Just as the scientific method helps produce better descriptions and explanations of politics, so does the dialectical method help produce better political goals, prescriptions, and evaluations. With respect to all political ideas, the transcendence of ideological thinking does not involve the attainment of objective truth but the search for better ideas that one can defend in the company of others.

POLITICAL EVALUATION

While political philosophy involves a "great conversation" that is enhanced by the inclusion of all of the many distinct voices, particular ideologies dominate the discussion of how particular political communities ought to be governed. In the United States, for example, the main debate occurs between contemporary liberals and contemporary conservatives, and though environmentalists, feminists, fundamentalists, and other less dominant voices add distinct concerns when specific issues are raised, they often accept certain ideals embraced

[42]This discussion suggests the need to distinguish two types of "relativism." One type of relativism asserts that there are no objectively best political principles, that judgments about best principles are imbedded in subjective tastes and values. Such relativism is antithetical to political philosophy because it implies that the search for the best principles is a hopeless enterprise. The second type of relativism is the kind that can emerge from many little conversations. Such relativism asserts that our judgments about the best principles depend on specific circumstances. When evaluating alternative principles, people in particular communities attempt to determine which principles are most likely to achieve such ends as human equality, freedom, and perfection, but specific circumstances may influence their judgments about the principles that are likely to achieve these ends.

by the central ideologies within the particular culture. As a result, particular communities often have a rough consensus on certain "great ideas" about politics. Few Americans, for example, question the ideas that citizens should have a right to acquire private property, that wages should be determined by a free labor market, that all citizens should be equal under the law and receive equal treatment by the courts, and that governmental power should be distributed and limited according to the principles of representative and constitutional democracy. The presence of such consensus provides the opportunity for another kind of political thinking and analysis that transcends ideology. Political evaluation involves thinking about whether the ideals that are consensually embraced within a political culture are realized in practice. Political evaluation is a particularly attractive form of political thinking for those individuals and communities having commitments to the particular ideals of an ideology (or to particular ideals that are shared by partially overlapping ideologies), but who are uncertain about what to believe regarding the realization of these ideals.

Political evaluation involves determining the gaps between the ideals embraced by dominant particular cultures and the actual practices within political communities. Because the extent of the gaps between ideals and practices can vary over time or across subcommunities within the culture, political evaluation also involves generating ideas about how to narrow such gaps and improve political life—at least as improvement is regarded within the ideological traditions that dominant the particular culture. In other words, political evaluation involves providing **immanent** (or internal) **critiques** of the failures of political practices, developing and testing theories about the factors that account for variations in the gaps between ideals and practices, and proposing reforms that mitigate or eliminate those factors producing such gaps or that enhance those factors the close the gaps between ideals and practices. Political evaluation thus facilitates ideological transformation, or the introduction of new ideas into an ideology.

For example, both contemporary liberals and contemporary conservatives (and most other voices) in America are committed to equal legal justice, but many studies of the court system reveal significant differences in the justice received by the rich and the poor and by whites and minorities. Blacks, for example, are much more likely than whites to receive the death penalty.[43] Such studies are, however, only the first step in evaluating the legal justice in America. Conservatives claim that such disparities in sentencing, while real, are the result of legitimate legal factors, such as the seriousness of the crime and the defendant's prior record. If such factors are taken into account (i.e., adjusted for in statistical analyses), the relationship between race and sentencing proves spurious; no discrimination based on race or class occurs. Liberals respond that

[43]For a review of the extensive research on discrimination in U.S. courts, see David W. Neubauer, *America's Courts and the Criminal Justice System*, 4th ed. (Belmont, Calif.: Wadsworth Publishing, 1992), pp. 379–398.

such conservative evaluations are unconvincing. Judgments about the seriousness of crimes involve subjective values; conservative analysts seem to assume that when black men rape white women the crime is more serious than when white men rape black women or when white men embezzle millions of dollars, but such judgments only sustain the unequal treatment of poor black men. Consideration of a defendant's prior records also contributes unfairly to unequal treatment of black men as prior records often reflect previous unequal treatment by police and other actors in the criminal justice process. For liberals, then, racial, ethnic, and class differences in sentencing reflect unjustified discriminatory treatment. Such controversies serve to heighten awareness of (potential) deficiencies in the attainment of equal legal justice, and heighten receptivity among most participants in the legal justice system to reforms that can remove possible causes of discrimination. For example, liberals have emphasized an expanded public defender system to aid the poor, and they have sought to curtail the capacity of state prosecutors to exclude potential jurors on racial or ethnic grounds. Conservatives have emphasized the development of sentencing guidelines that limit the court's discretion in imposing penalties. While such reforms seem to have reduced racial, ethnic, and class differences in sentencing, they have more significantly contributed to the conservative goal of enhancing the certainty and severity of punishment. Such ideological differences are obviously much more focused than the ideological differences that can occur on the "great issues" of politics, but they illustrate the ideological conflict that can persist even when competing ideologies agree on larger ideals that may remain unrealized in practice.

As a final example, contemporary liberals and conservatives (and most other voices) in America are committed to representative democracy. They believe that governmental decisions should reflect the judgments of elected representatives, whose policy-making authority has been constitutionally authorized by elections, and whose judgments are normally expected to reflect the preferences of those citizens who voted them into office and to whom they are accountable at the next election.[44] However, critical assessments suggest that elected representatives are often overwhelmed by the pressures applied by "big business"[45] and governmental bureaucrats.[46] Because of their more critical attitudes toward capitalism and "big business," contemporary liberals have emphasized the need for reforms that restrict corporate lobbying and corporate and special-interest campaign contributions to curtail "domination by

[44]For a discussion of the ideals of representative democracy, see Hanna Pitkin, *The Concept of Representation* (Berkeley: University of California Press, 1972). For an evaluation of the extent to which such ideals have been realized in one American community and of the factors that influence the gap between democratic ideals and democratic performance, see Paul Schumaker, *Critical Pluralism, Democratic Performance, and Community Power* (Lawrence: University Press of Kansas, 1991), esp. pp. 23–30, 141–172.

[45]See, for example, Charles E. Lindblom, *Politics and Markets* (New York: Basic Books, 1977), esp. pp. 170–188.

[46]Theodore Lowi and Benjamin Ginsberg, *Poliscide* (New York: Macmillan, 1976).

economic elites" in the practices of representative democracy. Because of their more critical beliefs about the overextension of governmental authority, contemporary conservatives have emphasized the need for reforms—such as term limitations and "sunset laws"—that lessen the likelihood that cozy relationships will develop between bureaucrats and legislators, and that curtail "bureaucratic domination" in the practices of representative democracy. Thus, ideological consensus on the ideals of representative democracy has not prevented either contemporary liberals or contemporary conservatives from perceiving deficiencies in the realization of these ideals in their communities or from generating significant ideological conflict over how to correct these deficiencies. Ideological conflict may be relatively muted, because the conflict is not over the "great idea" of who should govern but rather over the more narrow question of how best to attain agreed-upon democratic ideals. Nevertheless, significant ideological differences persist.

SUMMARY AND CONCLUSIONS

Political leaders and activists usually have an ideology—understood as an extensive, well-organized, logically consistent set of political principles—that helps define the problems they seek to address and the goals they seek to attain through political action. In contrast, most citizens are innocent of ideology, and this may undermine their awareness of politics, their ability to make sustained political commitments, and their effectiveness and influence as political actors. Wherever people have relatively undeveloped sets of generalized beliefs and abstract ideals about political life, it would seem desirable that they become more ideological. Becoming more ideological, however, does not necessarily entail choosing among the ideologies or nascent ideologies presented in this text, as thoughtful citizens can develop many unique ideas addressing those particular big issues of politics that represent their own commitments and understandings. Insofar as people resist being entrapped by the most prominent ideologies but are willing to work out their own beliefs and ideals, we think it is entirely possible and desirable that the world is experiencing not the end of ideologies but a great explosion or proliferation of ideologies.

However, developing one's own ideological perspective cannot be a completely individualized or autonomous endeavor. Political ideas concern political communities, and because one's political ideas concern others, they must be worked out in conjunction with others. It seems to us that politically aware citizens will examine their current beliefs and ideals and question the validity of those ideas that seem to have questionable foundations. It seems to us that thoughtful citizens will work out principles that further nonviolence, social stability, and the paths to human perfection, human liberty, and human equality. They will be willing to state their political beliefs and subject these beliefs to evaluation by various scientific methods, revising them as the evidence points to more complex and more defensible ideas. They will be willing to defend their ideals in conversations with others having different ideological perspectives, and they will be willing to revise those ideals that cannot withstand critical scrutiny. They will have certain particular political commitments, evaluate whether their political communities practice the ideals reflected in these commitments, and continue to search for new ideas that further the realization of these ideals.

It may be pleasant to dream that ideal political communities will emerge from such processes. It may be important to hope that political truth will be discovered from these processes. While the history of the past two hundred years teaches that such hopes and dreams are likely to remain unrealized, the future remains uncharted. We think that the appropriate aspiration for the twenty-first century is not that political truth will be attained or that utopian communities will be achieved, but that the "great conversation," and many smaller conversations, will continue in a peaceful fashion.

Glossary

abolition of private property In the Marxist socialist state, there would be no private ownership of the means of production (such as factories, banks, and land), since this would continue to create inequalities in power. Only personal property (food, clothing, shelter, leisure goods) would remain privately owned, and not in excessive amounts.

abstract rights Rights divorced from history and tradition. Traditional conservatives defend those rights that have been historically developed in particular countries. They have thus been critical of classical liberal arguments that natural rights are guaranteed to all regardless of specific and concrete circumstances. Traditional conservatives criticize these liberal views on rights by calling them abstract rights.

accountability The principle of allowing other people to review the actions of those empowered to act in certain areas and to remove those whose actions are deemed ineffective, unfair, or otherwise undesirable.

affirmative action Policies that attempt to help members of numerically underrepresented groups—such as minorities, women, and handicapped persons—to attain desired positions in society.

agents of socialization Those social institutions—like our families, schools, churches, workplaces, and the media—that shape our ideological predispositions.

alienation An estrangement of our potential condition from our actual condition. According to Marx, the division of labor in all historical societies leads to four kinds of alienation: from ourselves, from each other, from our laboring activity, and from the products of our labor.

American exceptionalism Strong socialist parties and the principles of democratic socialism are prominent in all advanced industrial societies except the United States. Theories of American exceptionalism attempt to explain the absence of socialism and the socialist movement in America.

anarchism The belief that all governments are coercive and unnecessary. This ideology holds that if all oppressive institutions are destroyed, more natural and voluntary social arrangements can come into existence.

androcentric bias Feminists argue that males have so dominated social, political, and economic arenas of life that a male-centered, or androcentric, bias pervades our thoughts and actions.

androgyny The synthesis of traditionally distinct masculine and feminine characteristics. Some feminists have argued that a goal for the future should be the development of individuals who are androgynous in the sense that they combine the best characteristics and qualities that are now ascribed separately to either males or females.

animal rights In the 1970s and 1980s, many environmentalists began to argue for the extension of many human rights to animals. Most animal rights advocates not only want animals protected from abuse and from painful laboratory tests, they want animals protected from being used in any research, regardless of the benefits of that research to humans.

antithesis A theory or a set of material conditions that stands in opposition to a dominant factor, or thesis, in society. *See* thesis and synthesis below.

antitrust agencies Governmental bodies that investigate corrupt business practices and scrutinize proposed business mergers to ensure that such practices or mergers do not significantly reduce competition in a sector of the economy.

apartheid The former South African racial policy of keeping its various races completely separated.

Aryan supremacy The nazi doctrine that their definition of the Aryan race (of which the Germans are a representative) is the culturally, intellectually, and technologically most developed race and the naturally strongest, so that it should subjugate or destroy all the others.

ascribed social status A stratification system in medieval Europe and in some traditional societies of the present day in which a person's rank depends on birth rather than achievement. In most societies having ascribed social status, people have little or no capacity to advance their social standing.

ascriptive principles of justice The idea held by traditional conservatives that power, status, and other goods should be distributed on the basis of such inborn, circumstantial, and hereditary traits as class, race, ethnicity, and gender.

authoritarianism The belief that the leaders of communities should exercise predominant and even unlimited power over their followers and that these subjects should accept the claims and obey the commands of their leaders.

autonarchy Contemporary conservatives have coined this term to describe a situation in which government programs and laws are designed solely by and for those who are part of the government.

Bayreuth Circle A group of artists, musicians, and intellectuals gathered around Richard Wagner in Bayreuth. Wagner was a composer and essayist, as well as a German Romantic and nationalist who attracted to himself a coterie of German nationalists and European racists.

bicameral legislatures Legislative institutions that have two chambers or two legislative bodies representing different constituencies and that require that laws be approved by both bodies.

bourgeois hegemony According to Antonio Gramsci, an Italian communist, the bourgeoisie rules not by force, but through a widely proliferated ideology that legitimizes its rule through processes of education, socialization, and mass communication in a variety of institutions, thereby destroying proletarian class-consciousness and the possibility for genuine revolutionary change.

bourgeoisie A term that originally referred to "those who dwell in the city" (and were middle class). Karl Marx used it to refer to that socioeconomic class in capitalist society that owns the means of production (land, banks, factories, natural resources, etc.).

budget deficits The increasing debt that governments incur when their expenditures are greater than their revenues.

capitalism An economic system in which productive property such as land and factories is privately owned and in which individuals have extensive liberties to work, invest, trade, and consume as they like, constrained only by their natural capacities and economic resources.

Cartesian method The belief that the first step in acquiring sure knowledge is to doubt all propositions except clear and distinct ideas. Such self-evident ideas then form the basis for deducing more complex ideas.

centralization Focusing authority in a particular institution or in particular leaders. While many political systems practice some centralization, the nazis and fascists have most rigorously designed central government hubs to control multiple institutions of power, thereby enabling them to concentrate on the national will and achieve national goals, rather than accommodating factional interests.

centralized proletarian state In Marx's conception, the proletariat would temporarily have to centralize all instruments of political and economic power in the state as means for destroying capitalism. As socialism matured, however, central control would be unnecessary, and the state would "wither away."

charismatic leadership A broad term that refers generally to the ability of some leaders to sway private and public opinion by the power of their personality.

Chartist movement A group of reformers who sought further to democratize English politics during the nineteenth century. Among their goals were less restrictive voting rights (approaching universal suffrage), equal electoral districts, and abolition of property qualifications for holding office.

citizen (or welfare) rights The rights—such as particular rights to food, shelter, and medical care—that contemporary liberal and socialist societies extend to all citizens to foster their positive liberty. In contrast to natural rights, the contents of these citizen rights are politically determined.

citizen mobilization The nazi notion that whereas elites (led by the Fuehrer) should rule, the people must also be activated and directed en masse toward the realization of national goals. Such activation would, in particular, demand loyalty and obedience.

civil disobedience The public disregard or violation of a law in order to point out its injustice and to promote social change. Such acts are premeditated, done for a limited purpose, carried out nonviolently, and understood to be illegal. Those who engage in such acts are prepared to accept penalties for violating the unjust law, but they believe their defiance can educate the public about its injustice.

classical liberalism Often called "nineteenth-century liberalism" to distinguish it from contemporary liberalism, this worldview emphasizes individual liberty, free-market or capitalist economies, limited government, and representative democracy.

classless society Marx's vision of the posthistorical society in which there will be no distinguishable socioeconomic classes, because the division of labor that establishes such classes will no longer exist. Every person will be free to labor in the creative, nonalienated manner that Marx envisions as the natural, desirable state for human beings.

collectivist Soviet state Refers to the state Joseph Stalin established in 1929 in the Soviet Union, in which all industrial property was nationalized, all agricultural activities collectivized, and the national economy was controlled by a powerful, centralized bureaucracy.

colorblind Contemporary conservatives believe that even without government intervention or intense social pressure, businesses in their quest for profits will not discriminate against buyers or employees. Accordingly, there is no systematic discrimination with regard to race and ethnicity in a free-market economy.

commensurate rights and obligations A traditional conservative justification for the unequal distribution of rights in a hierarchical society. Those who receive the greatest rights must bear the greatest social and political obligations. Those at the bottom of the hierarchy have few rights, but they also have few responsibilities.

communal harmony In contrast to liberals, who believe that social stability is achieved when individuals tolerate each other and don't trample upon one another's rights, socialists believe that social harmony requires a much deeper sense of belonging, concern, and mutuality among the citizens in a community.

communism A twentieth-century ideology that encourages the fomenting of revolutions in underdeveloped societies, such as Russia and China. It justifies state ownership and control of the economy, authoritarian rule by the communist party, and extensive citizen sacrifices as necessary but temporary measures toward creating future utopian societies.

communist menace The danger posed to the Western world by communist countries, especially the Soviet Union. Under this slogan, communist expansion and "wars of liberation" were portrayed as the major external threats to the West, but the lack of internal vigilance against communism and communist sympathizers was considered equally dangerous.

conflict between authority and autonomy Political authority imposes a duty on citizens to obey governmental commands. Individual autonomy is the right of all persons to use their capacities to reach their own moral judgments. According to anarchists like R. P. Wolff, whenever governments command individuals to do something that conflicts with their own moral judgment, their moral capacities require that they disobey government. Anarchists conclude that governmental authority is thus unjustified.

conservationism Conservationism is a homocentric approach to the environment that emphasizes the rational management and use of natural resources. Wilderness, for example, is to be protected, because it provides enjoyment, employment, and resources for humans.

constitutional democracies Political systems in which leaders are constrained by constitutional provisions that supersede statutory laws. Such constraints include the requirement that top leaders stand for (re)election.

constitutions The "bylaws" of political communities. They contain general principles specifying the legitimate powers or authority of governments, the institutions that are empowered to make and implement specific laws and policies, and the processes for selecting policy makers and enacting legislation.

contemporary conservatism A prominent ideology that emerged after World War II and that is defined, in large part, by its opposition to communism, democratic socialism, and contemporary liberalism. It believes that strong liberal and socialist governments fail to solve the problems they address and, instead, create new economic and social problems—such as economic stagnation, bureaucratic red tape, a loss of individual initiative, and moral decay.

contemporary liberalism A political outlook that both retains and modifies the ideals of classical liberalism. It celebrates certain older liberal values and goals such as individual freedom, an expanding economy based largely on private initiatives, and a democratic political system. However, it departs from the classical liberal principle of limited government by believing that an active, problem-solving government can stimulate economic well-being for all citizens and enhance individual liberty. It also asserts that democratic institutions should represent the diversity of group interests that prevails in modern pluralist societies.

continuous revolution Mao Zedong's doctrine, according to which prolonged political activities of violence, reformation, and social transformation are required in order to keep people in a continual state of dislocation so that their natures may be reshaped in accordance with the needs of the postrevolutionary society.

contribution principle In the transition to a socialist egalitarian society, Marx believed that this principle of rewarding people unequally for unequal labor would be *temporarily* maintained until material scarcity had been eliminated. At that point, all such inequalities of reward would disappear.

cooperatives Businesses that are owned and operated by workers and consumers.

corporatism The Italian fascist unification of broad sectors of the economy into large corporations by means of which the rulers could control and coordinate workers and managers (and the economy as a whole), directing them toward predetermined national goals.

creationism The belief that the version of the creation of the world as presented in the sacred texts of Christianity, Judaism, or Islam is accurate literally. It usually rejects contemporary natural-scientific theories of the origins and development of life, such as spontaneous generation and evolution through natural selection.

creative laborers According to Marx, every human being has the potential to transform nature by his or her creative laboring activity, but current material and economic conditions (capitalism) prevent most people from realizing that potential. Creative laborers will be the norm in the ideal communist society.

Cuban model A paradigm for exporting communist revolutionary activity that was first developed by Fidel Castro and Che Guevara. In contradistinction to Lenin's belief, it de-emphasizes the role of a centralist communist party and advocates popular insurrection and the use of many small revolutionary cells.

cult of the primitive Because anarchists call for simpler and more natural lifestyles than conventional societies provide, they have sometimes been accused of championing more primitive societies.

culture of permissiveness A critical appraisal of western culture during and after the 1960s by contemporary conservatives, who assert that contemporary liberalism has destroyed morality and authority by failing to assert an absolute standard of the good.

debilitating pedestal Women have often been praised for having, as a gender, the very characteristics—such as compassion, selflessness, and emotionalism—that may reduce their chances to succeed in the political and economic spheres, where competitiveness, abstract thought, and stoicism are stressed.

decentralism Institutions that are organized from the bottom up, rather than from the top down.

deep ecologists Many radical environmentalists argue that traditional environmental groups are "shallow," because they ignore the fundamental sources of environmental degradation, especially the exploitative approaches of industrialized nations. To distance themselves from "shallow environmentalists," radical environmentalists in the 1970s dubbed themselves "deep ecologists."

deism The belief—common among classical liberals—that God exists, that He created the universe and the laws governing the universe, and that He no longer interferes with the operation of these natural laws.

democracy (1) Processes for resolving political disagreements in which all members of a community are treated as political equals. When democratic processes exist, all qualified citizens have equal basic political rights and their diverse interests and ideas are given impartial consideration. (2) Processes by which leaders of political communities are selected by free, competitive, and fair elections.

democratic capitalism A term that is synonymous with "classical liberalism," it emphasizes the individual freedom that occurs when the economy is structured by the principles of free enterprise and when governments are based on political rights, including the right to vote and the right to oppose existing policies and regimes.

democratic centralism This term refers to a set of principles for organizing parties and states, and these principles were embraced by the Communist Party in the Soviet Union. These principles (developed by Lenin) called for open debate—democracy—but also emphasized the need for subordination to duly constituted authorities within the party once a decision had been made—hence, centralism.

democratic distemper Contemporary conservatives have been critical of attempts to expand citizen participation. They argue that such attempts will not succeed and will produce frustration and cynicism, the democratic distemper.

democratic socialism A prominent twentieth-century ideology that believes that a more egalitarian society can be achieved, not by revolution as Marx specified, but by evolutionary means. Socialists call for citizens to acquire "deeper" understandings than liberalism provides of individuality, equality, democracy, and communal harmony; to elect politicians committed to these values; and for popularly elected socialist governments to then tame the worst aspects of capitalism.

deontology The general idea that it is fruitless to try to define the true natures of the universe, societies, or humans. More particularly, many liberals believe that there is no objective knowledge of "the good" or "the good life" other than the subjective understandings of individuals. A deontological approach to political theory attempts to define what people's rights are independently of any conception of what constitutes the good.

dependency theory A theory of international relations that accounts for many phenomena in the international system by means of Marxist concepts. It suggests that the majority of states suffer underdevelopment as the result of the economic and technological dominance of a few powerful states in the international system.

deregulation The removal or reduction of laws and administrative rules that regulate private economic actors. Contemporary conservatives argue that it would increase competitiveness, reduce costs to consumers, decrease the costs of government administration, and lower the expenses of businesses, especially paperwork costs.

dialectical materialism Marx's term for the historical changes in economic or material conditions of life that lead to class conflicts that, in turn, lead to new social, political, and ideological conditions.

dialectical method Procedures employed by philosophers to examine ideas about how political communities ought to be governed. Such procedures involve submitting one's ideas to the critical inspection of others.

dictatorship of the proletariat In Marxist doctrine, a brief period of time after the revolution in which the proletariat would have to suppress the attempts of the bourgeoisie to reestablish capitalism. Once all such attempts and goals had been suppressed, everyone would accede to universal communism.

difference principle The claim by John Rawls that, in a liberal society, social goods should be distributed equally unless unequal distributions normally advantage the poor and unless all members of society have equal prospects for acquiring greater-than-average shares of such goods.

differentiated world-system Communists argue against Marx that capitalism is not a universally uniform economic system, but that there are structural variations between capitalist societies that distinguish them from one another and that determine their behavior in the international system in important ways.

direct democracy Arrangements allowing citizens to resolve controversial issues and to participate directly in the decision-making process, often through public referenda.

disciplined Bolshevik Party According to Lenin, a successful transition to communism required a small, trained group of (middle-class) intellectuals (the disciplined Bolshevik Party) that would lead the proletariat in developing and implementing the appropriate strategy and activities. This notion implies a degree of human voluntarism in historical affairs not foreseen by Marx.

distributions according to one's deeds or needs When goods are distributed according to deeds, those who have made the greatest contribution deserve larger shares. When goods are distributed according to needs, individuals' contributions to the community are overlooked, and goods are distributed to those who most need them. Anarchists maintain that the members of local associations should agree among themselves which of these principles of justice should be adopted. Marxists maintain that distribution according to one's deeds should prevail during the transition to an ideal communist society while distributions according to one's needs can occur only when an affluent and classless society has been achieved.

dominant protective agencies Libertarians maintain that, without governments, individuals would hire agents to protect their rights; in fact, to ensure that they would win any dispute over rights, everyone would hire the strongest agent. Consequently, one protective agency would become dominant in society and its powers would approach that of a government. Libertarians use such reasoning to argue that minimal governments—but only minimal governments—are necessary.

economic and social indicators Periodic measurements of various aspects of the state of the economy (such as the levels of unemployment and inflation) and of such social and environmental problems as the crime rate and levels of water pollution.

economic determinism Also called "historical materialism," orthodox Marxists attribute this doctrine to Marx. It claims that the ultimate realities in human life, and the basic causes of change and conflict, are not intellectual or spiritual, but economic and material, and that they are essentially beyond intentional human control.

egalitarian ethic The belief among many anarchists and socialists that, while justice does not require a strict equality of social goods, it does entail recognition that all people deserve many goods that are only available to the few and that the needs of everyone are equally important.

egalitarian society A group of people who are committed to the idea of intrinsic equality among themselves, who question the legitimacy of existing inequalities, and who seek to redress unjustified inequalities.

elite theorists A prominent school of Italian social scientists at the beginning of the twentieth century who were very critical of democratic rule and advocated the rule of political or economic elites. Contemporary elite theorists usually believe that democratic procedures mask elite domination in contemporary societies, but they do not advocate such elite rule.

elitism The belief that political power is, or should be, concentrated in the hands of a few most-qualified leaders and that ordinary citizens are, or should be, without significant political power. Some ideologies—like democratic socialism—make the empirical claim that power is concentrated among a few elites while stressing the normative claim that such concentration of power should be eliminated. Other ideologies—like fascism—make the empirical claims that concentration of power is widespread and perhaps an inevitable feature of all social groups while also making the normative claim that the resulting leadership is good for society and human progress.

empirical theory Generalized descriptions and explanations of politics as it in fact occurs. Empirical theory focuses on actual political behavior and events rather than making claims about how to achieve more ideal conditions.

end-of-history thesis The Hegelian claim—by Francis Fukuyama—that ideological conflict is ending, because democratic capitalism is everywhere emerging triumphant at the end of the twentieth century. According to this thesis, the big questions about politics have been settled and there can be no further significant historical evolution in political thinking.

end-of-ideology thesis The claim that ideological conflict is ending. The claim was first made at the end of the 1950s to suggest that both right-wing and left-wing ideologies were moving toward the center, and that a "rough consensus" on big political issues could be reached.

enlightened self-interest The idea that individuals should not simply maximize immediate personal and sensual pleasure but rather should maximize their higher (intellectual and spiritual) pleasures over the course of a lifetime in a society where other individuals are likewise satisfied.

Enlightenment An intellectual movement during the eighteenth century in Europe that sought to free humans from ignorance and superstition and to develop understandings of the universe, society, and humans based on reason and scientific applications of reason.

entitlement theory The libertarian idea that unequal distributions of wealth are fair if they arise from processes of production and exchange that violate no one's rights. Libertarians acknowledge that freedom to produce and exchange goods often results in distributions that reflect neither one's deserts nor one's needs, but they assert that such unpatterned distributions are not thereby unjust, because they are the result of freedom.

entitlements The provisions in liberal and socialist societies of certain essential goods and services to all members of society, regardless of their ability to pay. When governments make laws calling for such provisions, citizens who qualify for these benefits have "welfare rights" provided to them.

environmentalism A nascent ideology claiming that humans must stop treating the natural environment, including other animals, as a warehouse of resources whose value depends solely on their use to humans. It calls for a deeper appreciation of ecological systems and diversity, and for restraint in the pursuit of economic growth, in order to attain a healthier environment. Environmentalists share with conservationists the desire to conserve natural resources, but they are uncomfortable with the utilitarian views of conservationists, who want to protect and manage nature only as a means of assuring its availability for further human use.

epistemology The branch of philosophy dealing with the nature and origins of knowledge.

equal liberty principle The claim by John Rawls that all members of liberal society are guaranteed equal political liberties, liberties of conscience, property rights, and legal rights.

equality of being The classical liberal belief that beyond the many differences in individual capacities and interests, all humans are fundamentally equal in the sense that everyone's life, liberty, and happiness are equally important.

equality of condition In the public imagination, this concept refers to a situation in which everyone has equal amounts of education, wealth, power, and other social goods; in some fantasies, efforts would be made to eradicate even natural inequalities. When socialists speak of equality of conditions, they usually envision something much less equal than this, but something more equal than what presently exists.

established religion A religion that is endorsed and supported by the state. Traditional conservatives supported the establishment of religion, because it provided moral authority for society. Most classical liberals attacked established religions as enemies of the freedom of conscience and of religious toleration.

ethic of care In most contemporary liberal discussions of justice, it is assumed that the most sophisticated and most mature understandings of justice are built on abstract rules. Some feminists have questioned the idea that abstract justice is superior to concrete and particular thinking about justice, which they call an "ethic of care." They argue that many women respond to concrete, particularistic cases of need, rather than to abstract rules, and that caring dispositions and actions should complement or replace more abstract notions of justice.

ethnographic studies Ethnography is the study of ethnically distinct groups. It attempts to explain certain behaviors of such groups on the basis of their physiological characteristics or the environments in which they live. In nineteenth-century Europe, such studies were often tied to questionable assumptions concerning the biological ("racial") characteristics of various ethnic groups.

executive-centered and bureaucratic government The idea that strong governmental executives and expanded governmental administrative agencies are necessary to solve social problems.

exploitation Using other persons for one's selfish purposes. Marxists argue that capitalists as a class unfairly and selfishly profit from the labor of the proletariat and provide the working class inadequate compensation.

externalities The effects on third parties or the public as a whole that sometimes arise from the transactions between two parties in a free market. Because such effects are often harmful, liberals emphasize that governments should regulate such actions as cutting production costs by using manufacturing processes that pollute the environment.

Fabians British intellectuals who organized as a society in 1884 to educate the public about the desirability of moving slowly away from capitalism and toward democratic socialism.

fair equal opportunity A condition that might exist if governments compensated those having undeserved social disadvantages (like being raised in poverty) or deficiencies in natural talents (such as being less intelligent) so that these individuals could compete for desired positions on a more equal basis with those having undeserved social and natural advantages.

fascism An ideology most clearly articulated by the Fascist Party in Italy under Mussolini between 1920 and 1945. It emphasized an extreme form of nationalism, calling for a totalitarian state to control all aspects of social and individual life in order to achieve state goals and demanding the complete obedience of citizens to the dictates of an authoritative central leader.

fascist conception of liberty In contradistinction to liberalism, fascism holds that the freedom of the individual is found in compliance with the will of state authority, thus empowering the state to act on behalf of society as a whole.

federalism A method of dividing and limiting governmental authority by granting certain governmental powers to national governments, other governmental powers to state or provincial governments, and still other governmental powers to local governments.

felicific calculus The utilitarian method by which governments may estimate the net happiness (pleasure minus pain) that accrues to each individual because of existing laws and the net happiness that would accrue to each individual under proposed changes. These individual utilities are then aggregated to determine whether proposed reforms would increase or reduce the "greatest good for the greatest number."

feminism An outlook deploring the dominance of men and the underrepresentation of women in public life. While all feminists call for women to have "equal rights" with men, more radical feminists call for eliminating many social and economic practices that they believe contribute to male domination in both the public and private aspects of life.

feminist epistemology Some feminist scholars argue that existing theories of knowledge and ways of knowing (epistemologies) are too rigid in category construction and too narrow in defining what is authentic. They argue that other ways of understanding the world are necessary in order to include the insights and voices of those marginalized (e.g., women) by previous social thought.

Final Solution A term for the nazi policy of killing all the Jews, Gypsies, and other "undesirable" races of the world, beginning in Europe, as a way of resolving the mortal conflict between these races on the one hand and the "Aryan" race on the other.

finance capitalism According to Lenin, this form of capitalism historically followed the industrial capitalism that Karl Marx had analyzed. Under this new form of capitalism, large banks and other financial institutions lend capital to corporations. They make capitalists increasingly dependent on such loans, until these lending institutions actually come to control the corporations to which they have been lending money. This concentration of power and wealth eventually leads the financiers and banks to look for new venues in which to invest their capital. One such market is the industrially underdeveloped colonies of imperialist nations.

fiscal policies An approach developed by contemporary liberals such as John Maynard Keynes to address the problems associated with business cycles. To reduce unemployment, governments should increase spending and cut taxes. To reduce inflation, governments should cut spending and increase taxes.

forces of production In Marxist theory, the way in which activities of production are socially organized and the materials and technologies that are used in such activities.

formal equal opportunity A condition that exists when laws prohibit discrimination against people on the basis of their race, gender, or other social characteristics.

French Revolution An upheaval that began in France in 1789. Its leaders set out to abolish aristocratic and clerical privileges and limit the power of the monarchy. For the most part, the revolution was based on liberal and democratic principles, although some radical ideas were pursued. Few lasting reforms were achieved, as the revolution was marked by terror and bloodshed, and led to Napoleonic domination in 1799. In large part, the principles of traditional conservatives were given clear expression by Edmund Burke in opposition to it.

Fuehrerprinzip The nazi doctrines that the national leader (the "Fuehrer") has the right to unlimited authority and that his immediate subordinates speak for him and command the obedience that the Fuehrer himself requires.

fundamentalism An outlook common to many devout Jews, Christians, and Muslims proclaiming that the will of God is plainly revealed in sacred texts. It rejects those secular ideologies that ignore divine truth and calls on humans to submit to God's will.

futility thesis Contemporary conservatives believe that many liberal reforms are attempts to change outcomes that cannot be changed. They view many liberal attempts to reduce income inequality, for example, as futile, because inequality is natural.

Gaia The ancient Greek term for the goddess, "Mother Earth," that greens use to remind us that the earth is a living planet. James Lovelock has tried to illustrate how the earth has self-regulating capacities that promote the conditions necessary for life, which makes it a quasi-living being.

German Romanticism Romanticism was a nineteenth-century European philosophical movement that emphasized the emotional, intuitive, and irrational forces of human life in reaction to what it saw as the excessive rationalism, positivism, scientism, and utilitarianism of the eighteenth-century European Enlightenment. Its German form often took on nationalist or even racist connotations.

Gleichschaltung The nazi policy of using the state to synchronize all private, social, and political institutions or activities for the purpose of fulfilling nazi goals most effectively and efficiently.

grassroots democracy Extensive citizen participation and influence in "institutions of daily life," such as schools, civic groups, religious organizations, neighborhoods, and families.

Great Chain of Being A conception of a hierarchical universe in which all things are linked ultimately to the highest, to God. The hierarchy descends from God to angels, to humans, to beasts, to flora, to microcosms. This conception was widely held during the Middle Ages and remained popular through the early nineteenth century. Traditional conservatives pointed to this hierarchy as evidence that society should also be arranged hierarchically.

"great conversation" A metaphor for the kinds of analyses that take place in political philosophy. In this metaphor, each viewpoint on a big issue is presented, and these viewpoints are then criticized, defended, debated, and modified at great length and in great depth. In the metaphor, these exchanges are conversational; in philosophical practice, they occur largely through books and articles.

greater Israel All the land promised to the Hebrews by God after their exodus from Egypt, including lands now held by several Arab states. Modern advocates of recovering "greater Israel" for the Jews include many Jewish fundamentalists.

greens Greens are "deep ecologists." The use of "greens" as a term was promoted by environmental-issue-based political party activists who called their new organizations "green" parties.

guardianship The claims that communities are best ruled by the most capable and virtuous persons in the community and that such leaders should be selected by those who are already members of the most qualified guardian class. When guardianship principles persist, political leaders are not accountable to ordinary citizens, who are deemed unqualified to judge their performances.

guerrilla warfare A type of rural, populace-based military strategy whose basic doctrines were first developed by Mao Zedong.

historicism In Marxist theory, the claim that history is composed of major events that mark the beginnings and endings of successive historical stages. These events are strongly influenced by material conditions and processes that are beyond intentional human control.

holistic approach Greens favor this way of understanding the environment, which emphasizes the interconnections in ecosystems and appreciates how the whole of the ecological picture must be understood. Greens contrast this approach with what they see as the limited, linear approach of modern science.

Holocaust Generally refers to an extensive destruction of life, especially by fire. Capitalized, it refers specifically to the nazi "Final Solution" to the race struggle between Jews and Aryans, namely the murder of six million European Jews and millions of others between 1938 and 1945.

holy war Religious fundamentalists sometimes assert that they must engage in wars and violent acts to cleanse the world of evil and to return communities to the correct moral path. Such conflicts are "holy wars," in which violence can be sanctioned by religious leaders. The faithful who are killed are considered martyrs.

homocentric perspective A view of nature as something that is valuable only in its use for humans. This perspective is criticized by environmentalists, who argue that it is the dominant outlook in industrialized nations, and at the root of many problems.

human imperfection Contemporary conservatives often point to human vices and shortcomings as a source of many of the problems that liberals try to solve with structural changes. Recognition of such human imperfection should lead one to be careful about overstating or overestimating the possibilities of reforms.

human malleability The belief that fundamental human characteristics and motivations are not fixed by some biological or natural human essence but, rather, change as environmental conditions change. According to this doctrine, which is prominent among most left-wing ideologies, including anarchism and Marxism, such frailties as selfishness and laziness are a result of living under repressive conditions rather than being fixed human traits.

ideologies of irrationality Fascism and nazism have sometimes been given this label because of their appeal to human will, which they stress is not always rational, and because of their emphasis on a strong leader's emotional appeals as a means of motivating people in large numbers.

ideologies Interrelated political ideas constituting a comprehensive political worldview. The logically connected ideas within such worldviews provide descriptions and explanations about political life and prescriptions for how political communities should be structured and perform in the near future. The ideas within these worldviews often have deep philosophical foundations and are expressed as abstract generalizations, but these ideas nevertheless provide a basis for understanding and evaluating concrete political events and conditions and for acting in the everyday world of politics. Because the ideas of ideologies serve political purposes, their validity is problematic.

Ideologues (1) A group of French philosophers who were most active between 1795 and 1815, who sought to develop a "science of ideas," and who coined the term "ideology." They sought to reveal the biases and inadequacies of traditional ideas and replace these ideas with the new, "more rational" ideas that became known as classical liberalism. (2) According to Philip Converse, those few people who have the most sophisticated intellectual understanding of politics, because they understand and effectively apply abstract concepts drawn from ideologies.

immanent critiques A type of political evaluation in which the actual practices of a community are investigated to see if they live up to the ideals that people claim to hold and seek.

immiseration of the proletariat Marx's prediction that capitalist competition and economic cycles would cause extensive downward economic mobility, as unsuccessful capitalists would fall into lower classes and workers would become unemployed and impoverished. This process would lead people to question the desirability of capitalism, and this questioning would eventually lead them to revolt against capitalism and to transform the system into a socialist society.

imperial-plebiscitarian presidency Scholars of the executive branch have developed this term to describe twentieth-century U.S. presidents, who have substantial (imperial) power and who must rely on mass (plebiscitarian) approval for the effective use of that power.

imperialism The nineteenth-century practice of various European powers of colonizing less technologically and politically developed territories in Africa, Asia, and Latin America for purposes of economic exploitation. Lenin saw this practice as a means of extending the life of capitalism, which, he thought, would otherwise have already been doomed by its internal contradictions.

incrementalism Making many small adjustments in programs and policies over time. Liberals believe that such changes can eventually result in extensive and desirable progress.

independent judiciaries Court systems that adjudicate conflicts without interference from the legislature or the executive branch of government.

individualist image of society The classical liberal view that societies are simply associations of individuals—that societies have no emergent properties beyond those of the individuals that compose them. Liberals proposed this "weak" conception of society to deflate traditional conservative claims that social requirements are more important than individual rights.

industrial capitalism According to Lenin, this was the form of capitalism that Karl Marx studied, in which market competition led increasingly to monopolies as corporations were either destroyed or merged with their competitors.

inerrancy Theologically, the doctrine that the sacred text of a religion is divinely inspired and is without error.

infrastructure Marx's term for the various material, economic conditions of a particular historical era (the means and modes of production).

instrumental reason While ancient political theorists emphasized the capacity of humans to know "the good," classical liberals claim that the good is a matter of subjective preference, and that human reason consists not in knowledge of the good itself, but in the means by which subjective understandings of the good can be attained.

interest theory The hypothesis that our ideological beliefs reflect the interests of the most powerful groups in society, who use their control of "mental production" to get people to believe what they want them to believe.

international free market The removal of trade and tariff barriers among all nations. Classical liberals, and many contemporary conservatives, argue that such an arrangement will promote global economic growth and reduce hostilities among countries.

intrinsic equality The idea that, despite obvious differences in human values and capacities, the life of each person is equally valuable.

intuitionism A philosophical doctrine opposing scientism and positivism. It claims that we can know more about reality than merely what is reflected in the surface phenomena, with which science is concerned, by looking to intuition—the emotional and spiritual dimensions of human experience—to tell us of the "real" world behind the appearances that science studies.

jeopardy thesis Contemporary conservatives believe that, too often, liberal reformers try to expand on the limited success of previous reforms and that the expanded reforms destroy the limited successes that have been achieved.

judicial activism The contemporary liberal idea that judges should interpret vague and abstract constitutional language in ways that expand the rights of disadvantaged citizens and the powers of government to address social and economic problems.

juridical democracy Policy-making processes that are more consistent with constitutional requirements. In particular, Theodore Lowi has called for legislatures to write clear and specific laws rather than passing bills asserting the desirability of achieving certain values and directing administrative agencies to solve particular problems.

labor theory of value John Locke's argument that people are the owners of their labor, that the value of property comes from the labor that people put into it, and that those who mix their labor with nature are thus the legitimate owners of that property.

laissez faire, laissez passer "Let it alone, leave it be." A slogan developed by classical liberals calling for an unregulated economy.

laws of supply and demand As the supply of a good or service increases, the price that must be paid to secure it decreases. As the demand for a good or service increases, the price that must be paid to secure it increases. The laws of supply and demand encourage people to move their resources into those areas where there are opportunities to earn profits, because there is greater demand for goods than there is supply of them.

legislative oversight The practice of having legislators and their staffs evaluate the legality, effectiveness, and fairness of bureaucratic programs and activities.

liberal conception of liberty The idea that each person should choose and pursue his or her self-defined conception of a good life and that the state should constrain self-chosen acts only when such action is required to prevent harm to others.

liberal feminism An outlook that accepts liberal values, practices, and institutions, but claims that women have been excluded from public life. Proponents seek reforms that will make women equal citizens in liberal societies.

liberal science of politics The belief of early liberals like John Locke that deductions from indubitable assumptions about humans and societies could yield clear political principles giving individuals specific rights and liberties and limiting governmental authority to the securing of these rights.

liberation theology A movement among Roman Catholic theologians that emerged in Latin America during the 1950s. It expresses the traditional Christian concern for the poor and disenfranchised in recognizably Marxist terms, and advocates political (and sometimes revolutionary) action on their behalf.

libertarianism A contemporary antistatist viewpoint that draws heavily on classical liberalism. Libertarians seek extensive economic and social freedoms for individuals, an unregulated free market, and the decriminalization of individual behaviors that offend dominant moral sensibilities but do not cause significant injuries to others.

libido dominandi "A lust for ruling." One hypothesis for the existence of ideological beliefs is that they help satisfy our desires to rule over nature, other human beings, the world, and history. According to this idea, ideologies give us a sense—or perhaps an illusion—of control in a disorderly and unpredictable world.

limited government The idea that governments should perform only a small number of functions, mostly to provide security for their citizens. When people call for limited government, they usually object to governmental regulations on economic activity and governmental redistribution of wealth.

macro-level planning A contemporary liberal approach to addressing problems. Rather than micromanaging the economy or individual behavior, liberals create a broad framework of incentives and disincentives to induce organizations and individuals to act in ways that reduce problems.

maximizer of utilities The assumption of classical liberals that humans are self-interested, seeking to maximize personal pleasure and minimize personal pain.

market failures Various economic problems—such as an inadequate supply of public goods and business cycles—that can arise from an unregulated free-market system.

market justice The idea that the unimpeded workings of the free market reward people on the basis of their contribution to the supply of demanded goods and services, and that the earnings that people receive in a free market are therefore fair.

market socialism An economy containing a mix of publicly owned and privately owned businesses, in which workers and the public exercise significant control over business decisions, but in which market forces greatly influence such things as the goods that are produced, the prices of these goods, and the wages of employees.

marketlike incentives Economic motivations that can be administratively developed to encourage individuals and businesses to engage in behavior that they normally would avoid. Contemporary conservatives have endorsed marketlike incentives to replace the government rules and regulations that they see as too costly and intrusive.

Marxism The ideas of Karl Marx and his followers that have been interpreted both as a science predicting an inevitable downfall of capitalism and the subsequent emergence of a communist society and as an ideology protesting private ownership of productive property and other liberal ideas, institutions, and practices.

Marxist-Leninism The version of communist ideology that guided the Soviet Union and many of its client states following the Russian Revolution of 1917 and during the cold war. It emphasized V. I. Lenin's reinterpretation of Marx's doctrines to allow revolutionary activities in underdeveloped industrial nations and to justify strong rule by communist parties in such nations after successful revolutions

means of production In Marxist theory, the physical materials and technologies that human beings use to produce material things. Marx focused on changes in these factors and on the impact of these changes on social, cultural, and political life.

metaphor of a "delicate watch" Classical liberals developed this metaphor to describe society and, especially, the workings of the economy. It emphasizes that, while government may make some adjustments, government should be careful not to interfere excessively or crudely in the complex interactions of the marketplace. With some expansion, this metaphor is useful for describing contemporary conservative images of society.

metaphor of the "ship of state" A classical liberal metaphor for the governance of society. The term "ship" implies that government and society are made by man and not by God. It also implies that society may steadily progress toward some destination, that the "passengers" (the citizens) should decide this destination, and that the "captains" (qualified officials) should decide the best means of getting there.

midrange theories Generalizations that focus on one (or, at most, a few) important political ideas, but that are not part of a comprehensive political worldview.

mixed economy An economy that is largely privately owned and operates according to free-market forces, but in which governments augment, stimulate, and regulate the activities of investors, workers, and consumers.

modes of appropriation In Marxist theory, a description of who owns what and the basis for ownership.

modes of exchange In Marxist theory, a term that refers to the social mechanisms that determine how goods are transferred among people and classes.

modes of production In Marxist theory, the ways in which the activities of producing material things are socially and politically organized. Such organizations may include households, factories, guilds, labor unions, business corporations, and the like. This term may also include more subtle forms of tacit organization and discipline within these formally recognized social structures.

monkeywrenching "Monkeywrenching" is green guerrilla warfare against ecological degradation. It targets machinery and other physical infrastructures for destruction, but it must not include humans. Opponents of monkeywrenching claim it is simply vandalism against developers, but proponents consider it to be ethical action to protect nature from thoughtless exploitation.

moral autonomy The right of individuals to make rational and ethical judgments about their conduct and its effects on others. Anarchists are particularly adamant that individuals should never surrender any capacity to make moral judgments to governmental authority.

moral hazards The danger that government programs will produce the very consequences they were supposed to prevent. For example, a generous welfare program—intended to remove people from poverty—may discourage the work ethic and encourage people to get welfare benefits, stay on welfare, and thus live in perpetual poverty.

multiculturalism Multiculturalism is an approach to education, mainly found in the United States, that focuses on the diversity and richness of the component cultures in a society. Contemporary liberals generally support this approach, because they believe it teaches respect and tolerance for cultural differences. Many contemporary conservatives reject this approach, because they view it as relativistic and unpatriotic.

multiple citizenships The socialist understanding that people are simultaneously members of many "political communities" encompassing not only the nation-state, but also business enterprises, labor unions, neighborhoods, and ethnic groups, among others. In contrast to liberals, socialists regard such "nonstate citizenships" as part of one's public life, and they argue that these citizenships extend one's political obligations.

mutual aid A biological urge present in all humans to help other humans in need or distress. Anarchists believe that all humans have both egoistic and social instincts, but that the social instinct that inclines us to help each other can be suppressed by repressive institutions like governments and by competitive arrangements like capitalism.

mutualism Social relations based on voluntary, mutually agreeable, and mutually beneficial agreements among the parties involved. Anarchists believe that all coercive relationships are bad and that only those based on mutualism are good.

national solidarity The nazi and fascist policy of ending all competition between classes and individuals within a state for the purpose of consolidating, preserving, and expanding state power against other states. Nazis, unlike fascists, thought that racial purity was necessary to attain national solidarity.

nationalism The fervent belief among a group of people having similar ethnic, cultural, linguistic, and/or historical backgrounds that they are entitled to form an independent political community.

nationalization of industry The process by which socialist governments acquire ownership and control of industries that have been previously owned by private persons. In totalitarian communist regimes, nationalization occurred by confiscation of property. In social democratic regimes, nationalization only occurs when owners are compensated for their property.

nationalized enterprises State-owned and controlled businesses.

natural aristocracy The views of traditional conservatives that society is inherently hierarchical, that some members of society are born with special talents to fulfill leadership roles, and that such roles come with much greater power, privileges, and responsibilities than others.

natural communities Associations among individuals based on bilateral, face-to-face agreements and understandings and on genuine mutual respect and support. Anarchists regard such communities as reconciling people's desire for freedom with their need for social order.

natural rights The idea that nature bestows on each individual ownership of his or her own life and that each person is thus entitled to pursue his or her own understanding of happiness using the resources (mind and body) that nature has bestowed upon him or her. Classical liberals argue that the natural entitlements of life, liberty, and the fruits of one's own labor cannot be curtailed by government except to secure or protect similar rights for other individuals.

nazism An ideology most clearly articulated by the German National Socialist Party (Nazis) under Adolf Hitler between 1920 and 1945. It proclaimed the racial superiority of the "Aryan race," sought to create a "greater Germany" composed of such people, and pursued this goal through policies of military domination and genocide—particularly of the Jewish people.

negative liberty The type of freedom that a person has when he or she is left alone and is unrestrained by government. Classical liberals emphasized the importance of this type of freedom.

neo-Kantianism A synthesis of Marxist materialism and Hegelian idealism. Social democrats acknowledge that economic conditions influence historical developments, but they insist that ideas also matter. Drawing on neo-Kantianism, they thus argue that people can freely choose socialist values, even though their choices are likely to be influenced by economic circumstances.

neo-Marxism The use and modification of a variety of Marx's concepts and theories for the purpose of providing a critique of contemporary societies and international affairs, without necessarily accepting fully Marx's dialectical materialism or his prognosis of the coming revolution.

neoliberals Contemporary liberals who believe government should focus less on the problems of the poor and more on achieving economic prosperity.

new class A term by contemporary conservatives for a new elite of liberal professionals, journalists, bureaucrats, educators, and cultural megastars (among others) who advocate abstract economic equality.

new left A political movement that was especially prominent on American campuses during the 1960s and that drew significantly on anarchist principles in questioning all authority and in criticizing many conventional arrangements. The "new left" was particularly critical of capitalism, militarism, and representative democracy.

new right In the 1970s, a coalition of ultraconservatives and Christian fundamentalists emerged with the self-proclaimed label of the "new right." This coalition has emphasized family and moral issues, and has been successful in using the media to project and promote its message.

noblesse oblige "Nobility obligates." In medieval society, the nobility were granted special privileges, but these were balanced by special obligations. The nobility were expected to give generously to the poor, and to provide conditions for serfs and commoners that were better than mere subsistence levels. Traditional conservatives relied on this idea to help justify a hierarchical society.

normative theory Generalized ideas about politics that criticize existing conditions and practices, that advocate a more ideal political world, or that justify particular political principles.

ontological materialism The liberal doctrine that the world is composed only of "matter in motion."

ontology The branch of philosophy dealing with being and the ultimate causes of historical events.

organic conception of society A view held by traditional conservatives that society is like a living body, not like an inanimate machine, as implied by liberals. Society is a living, evolving entity; it has some parts that are more crucial than others; but all parts are important, and the well-being of the whole can suffer if any part is neglected or severed from the body. Because the complexity of this living, highly interdependent entity is not easily grasped, even minor changes must be introduced cautiously, because they can have widespread and unanticipated consequences.

organic evolution The view of traditional conservatives that societies should change slowly, in ways that allow for adjustments for the consequences of change.

orthodox Marxists Those followers of Karl Marx who interpret his writings as indicating that historical events are determined by economic conditions. They insist that revolutions against capitalism can only occur when economic conditions are "ripe"—when countries are highly industrialized but experience severe economic depressions resulting in widespread economic unemployment and deprivation, prompting workers to revolt.

pantheism The belief, common among anarchists, that God is not a supernatural force that dominates humans, but rather, is a vital natural force within human beings connecting man to man and man to nature.

paradigms Comprehensive theories describing and explaining the most important features of the existing political world and the basic processes of political change as they have occurred historically.

patriarchy The dominance of men over the women in their households. For many feminists, however, such dominance often extends to most other arenas of public and social life.

peasantry Persons of low education and status who till the soil. According to Mao Zedong, this "preproletarian" class could play a significant role in the revolution to bring about communism. Such a role was not foreseen by Marx or orthodox Marxists.

perestroika A Russian term (literally, "turning around"). It refers to a set of reforms instituted by the last Soviet premier, Mikhail Gorbachev, that were intended to reduce the centralized power of the Soviet bureaucracy and to introduce privatization of the means of production.

permanent revolution In communist theory, this involves a continuous process of transforming a feudal or colonial society to a communist one, without establishing a distinct capitalist society for any prolonged period.

perversity thesis The contemporary conservative belief that many liberal reforms produce consequences that are precisely the opposite of those desired by liberal reformers.

political absolutism Political systems in which the power of the leader—usually the monarch—is uncontested, unshared, and unquestioned.

political culture The beliefs and values regarding governance that predominate within particular communities.

political obligations The responsibilities that members of a political community have to one another. Such obligations may include the duty to obey just laws, to engage in public service, and to pay necessary taxes.

political reform Modifying the policies, laws, and programs of a government without altering in any fundamental way its constitutional and institutional arrangements.

political revolution Dissolving or overthrowing a government. For political revolutions to occur, the constitutional and institutional arrangements of governments must be significantly altered, as wholesale changes in governmental leaders or policies are not revolutions. Moreover, political revolutions may not be "social revolutions," since significant changes in governmental regimes can occur without having great effects on the social order or the economic system.

political theory Generalized descriptions, explanations, and evaluations of how humans live in communities and how they govern these communities.

politics The process in which humans express, debate, and resolve their often conflicting ideas and interests as they consider how to govern their communities.

polyarchy A form of democracy for large and heterogeneous societies that makes elected officials responsible for the policies and activities of government, that allows all citizens to participate in choosing their elected officials and in holding them accountable to the electorate, and that gives citizens various rights to oppose governmental institutions, authorities, and policies.

popular sovereignty The idea that government derives its authority from the people and that citizens can dissolve governments that abuse their powers.

positive liberty The capacity to make real choices. Contemporary liberals believe that such things as poverty, racism, and disease restrict the choices of many people, and that governments can play a role in overcoming such restraints on human choices.

postmodern feminists Those feminists who most question the fundamental assumptions and categories of Western thought. They believe that gender biases are so pervasive that the very structure and bases of ontological and epistemological thought are suspect.

pragmatism The idea that neither science nor politics is engaged in a search for absolute truth, but that both are instead interested in making improvements, through experimentation, on what we know and on what exists. Pragmatists do not ask, "Is this true or is this best?" but rather ask, "Does this serve better than what we already know or have?"

preferential treatment Contemporary conservatives argue that affirmative action and the use of hiring quotas favor the traditionally disadvantaged groups they target in ways that amount to reverse discrimination. Such favoring is preferential (and unfair) treatment.

prejudice The influence on thought produced by one's particularity. In contrast to liberals, who decry prejudice, traditional conservatives believe that one's history, society, social position, family, and so forth, inform one's ideas in a positive manner.

privatization The removal of companies and conglomerates from public or semipublic control. By returning nationalized companies to the private economy, European governments during the 1970s sought to increase efficiency and reduce government expenditures. In the 1990s, formerly communist countries have implemented this same policy in their transition to market economies.

proletariat The working class who, along with the bourgeoisie, constitute a significant socioeconomic class in capitalist society, according to Marx. Members of the proletariat do not own any of the means of production in capitalist society (land, factories, banks, natural resources), and so they must sell their labor to the owners of these means (the bourgeoisie).

property Goods that a person possesses and can use for his or her enjoyment. The right to possess and control various forms of property is contested by competing ideologies. In general, liberals and conservatives recognize extensive rights to property. Marxists decry ownership of productive property (property such as factories that produce other property) but do not object to personal property.

property is robbery A slogan of the anarchist Pierre Proudhon, criticizing those who use their control of productive property to dominate other people or who use their power over others to claim private ownership of the products of joint labor.

proportional representation The characteristic of an electoral system such that different interests or political parties are represented in a legislative body in approximately the same proportion that these different interests or political parties are advocated among voters.

protest movements Relatively unorganized collections of people seeking major extensions of rights to excluded groups (such as to racial or ethnic minorities, women, and gays) or seeking major transformations of public beliefs and values (such as protesting American involvement in Vietnam, insufficient protection of the natural environment, or inadequate concern for the unborn).

public and private spheres of life The public sphere of life concerns those activities in which a person's conduct can harm others, while the private sphere of life concerns those activities in which a person's conduct harms only himself. Classical liberals like John Stuart Mill believed that government should only regulate actions in the public sphere. Some feminists believe that this distinction has been (mis)used to define the family and other nonstate associations as private and then to justify noninterference with male actions that harm women at home.

public goods A good, like national defense, whose benefits are indivisible. If a public good is provided to one member of the community, other members of the community benefit by its provision, even if they do not pay for it.

racial struggle The nazi notion that all of history—and, especially, the problems of Germany in the post-World War I era—could be understood as the result of a struggle between races, especially the Jewish and the "Aryan."

radical feminists Those feminists who are most critical of liberal societies. Some promote socialism as a remedy for the inequalities facing men and women in liberal capitalist nations. Others insist that women must separate themselves from males if they are to discover the full potential of being women.

reactionary A somewhat pejorative term for ideas, actions, or persons that resist new and emerging forces and defend previous conditions.

realism Believing that liberals and socialists view the world through optimistic lenses that distort accurate perceptions of it, contemporary conservatives claim that the world must be seen as it really is. Conservative "realists" claim to describe the world in a way that accepts its deficiencies as they are given, rather than falsely envisioning the world as that which liberals and radicals want it to be.

rebellion The refusal to submit to the commands of governmental authorities and the desire to destroy institutions of domination without any provision for their replacement. While Marxists call for revolution—in which the power relations among classes are inverted—anarchists seek rebellion, because they believe that revolutions simply trade one oppressive arrangement for another.

relations of production In Marxist theory, a description of material (economic) and social (power) interactions between the different socioeconomic classes of a society. These relations are based on class distinctions, which are, in turn, based on a division of labor in the productive activities of that society.

representative democracy A system of selecting the most powerful political officeholders through popular elections. According to the principles of representative democracy, winning elections authorizes the elected to participate directly in policy making, and it requires those who have made policy and who wish to remain in office to be accountable to voters at the next election.

reproductive freedom Feminists insist that if women are to achieve freedom and equality with men, they must have control over their ability to bear children. Reproductive freedom includes the right of women to choose whether or not they will have children, and—should they choose to have children—how many they will bear, and when they will bear them. For almost all feminists, reproductive freedom includes the right to contraceptives and the right to abortions.

republican structures Governmental institutions that are designed to prevent any faction or self-interested group from controlling all governmental power. According to republican theory, the common good is most likely to emerge through enlightened representatives who rise above the passions of narrow interests and when structures ensure that no faction is able to dominate all governmental institutions.

Revisionist Marxists These socialists accept the authority of Marx's writings, but they interpret them less literally and deterministically than orthodox Marxists. They believe that Marx did not foresee the political, economic, and social changes that enabled capitalists to resist the predicted overthrow of capitalism. They also believe that a socialist, egalitarian society could be approached through democratic, rather than revolutionary, means.

revolution A process that brings about profound and rapid changes in political, economic, and/or social institutions. While traditional conservatives opposed revolutionary change, those allegiant to other ideologies usually support such fundamental changes, at least in certain areas. *See* political revolution, above.

sacred texts The most influential and authoritative writings within particular ideological traditions. Thus, certain writings of John Locke and John Stuart Mill are the sacred texts of classical liberals. Certain writings of Edmund Burke are the sacred texts of conservatives. And certain writings of Karl Marx are sacred texts for neo-Marxists, communists, and some democratic socialists. For fundamentalists, sacred texts are the divinely inspired holy texts of their religions.

science of politics The belief that the scientific revolution could yield indubitable laws regarding humans, social life, and government, just as science had provided such indubitable laws about the universe and physical environment. This belief was especially prominent among early classical liberals, but it is seldom asserted in the postmodern age characterized by uncertainty and relativism.

scientific method Various procedures employed by the academic community to guard against biases and distortions in the theories and ideas that describe and explain the operations of natural and human phenomena.

scientific socialism Engel's term for a study of the economic laws of history that shows that a socialist, egalitarian society is not a question of moral goodness or desirability, but of historical inevitability.

Scottish Enlightenment An intellectual movement in eighteenth-century Scotland. Its proponents shared the views of French Enlightenment thinkers that a science of human behavior was possible and might contribute to human progress. However, they did not believe in the reliance on unabashed reason alone, arguing that the usefulness of both reason and passion must be acknowledged.

secular humanism The this-worldly view that human rights, individual liberties, and shared concerns can be articulated and safeguarded without reference to, or worship of, the spiritual.

self-managed workers' councils Tito's method of transforming human consciousness, in which the alienation of workers is ameliorated by giving them control of factories at the local level.

separation of church and state A tenet of liberalism that calls for governments to focus on secular matters and not to promote particular spiritual beliefs and for churches to focus on spiritual matters and to leave worldly matters to the state.

separation of powers The ideas that legislative, executive, and judicial powers of government should be distinguished and relegated to different institutions, that positions within these different institutions should be held by different people representing different interests, and that officials in each institution should be given devices to resist usurpations of powers by officials in other institutions. In classical liberal theory, the separation of powers helps to limit and check governmental power.

social contract A hypothetical or implicit agreement among individuals in a state of nature, according to which each person agrees to obey government, if it secures her or his basic rights. This concept has been employed by liberal theorists to legitimate liberal democratic government.

social goods Those things—like wealth, honor, and influence—that most people value, that are scarce, and that can be had only by associating with others.

social laws In contrast to the regulations on humans imposed by governments, social laws are norms about how citizens ought to treat one another that arise from natural understandings and social customs. Anarchists believe social laws, enforced by informal arrangements and social pressure, can better produce social order than can governmental laws.

social pluralism The beliefs that human social life is enriched by the presence of many economic, social, cultural, religious, and local political associations, and that such associations must be independent of government.

social welfare state The welfare programs and policies provided by social democratic governments. Such programs are typically more extensive than those provided by liberal governments and often provide universal welfare rights to all citizens, in contrast to programs targeted exclusively at the most needy.

socialized enterprises Public ownership and worker control of the means of production.

state of nature A concept often employed by liberals and anarchists to depict a condition in which there are no political or social institutions or cultural practices that shape human behavior. This concept was formulated to try to convey how people would behave naturally, if they were unconstrained by conventional institutions and practices.

state planning A term for control and guidance (to varying degrees) of the economy by governments. Comprehensive, "Soviet-style" planning involves governmental control of most economic decisions. Minimal, "U.S.-style" planning involves the government's providing some incentives and disincentives for private actors to act in ways supported by governmental leaders. An intermediate level of planning—that is practiced by social democratic governments—includes extensive state influence over private investment decisions.

steady-state economies A conception of economic well-being in which production and consumption levels are regarded as satisfactory if they remain stable. Greens argue that a contrary emphasis on always achieving higher levels of production and consumption threatens natural resources and the earth's ecology. The solution to the problem of environmental degradation is to move to more modest levels of technology and to end the quest for constant economic growth.

strain theory The hypothesis that our ideological orientations are based on emotional considerations—such as our fears, our frustrations, and our sense of guilt.

subgovernments Arenas of policy making and implementation that are dominated by those who specialize in the policy area and who have particular interests at stake in these areas.

subsistence wage According to Marx, this is the wage the capitalist pays to the worker for his labor. It is just enough to permit the laborer to survive and perhaps to support a family (in order to generate new laborers), but it does not represent the value of the total contribution of the laborer to the production process.

superstructure Marx's term for the ideas the members of a society have about religion, morality, law, and politics. Marx claimed that these ideas were determined by the infrastructure of a society (the means and the modes of production).

surplus value In Marxist theory, surplus value is the difference between the actual value of what the laborer produces and what the capitalist owner of the means of production pays the laborer for his labor. This difference, minus the costs of equipment and raw materials, is the profit the capitalist makes from the production process.

synthesis The resolution of competing forces or ideas by dialectically combining these forces or ideas into a higher form or truth. *See* thesis, antithesis, and synthesis below.

telescoping the revolution This is the theory of communists like Trotsky and Lenin that a socialist revolution could perhaps be most easily accomplished at capitalism's "weakest link"—namely, in nonindustrialized, noncapitalist countries. The transformation from a primitive society to a postcapitalist one could, therefore, be accomplished in one giant step—(i.e., "telescoped") rather than in an extended historical process in which capitalism had to mature and develop internal contradictions, as Marx had suggested.

thesis, antithesis, synthesis Marx borrowed these terms from Hegel's theory of the historical dialectic to describe the three basic elements of dialectical materialism. The "thesis" embodies the existing dominant material and social conditions of a society (e.g., capitalism and the bourgeoisie class). The "antithesis" includes those material forces and social classes that stand in opposition to the thesis (e.g., the proletariat). The conflict between these two eventually results in a revolution to some new social form, a "synthesis," which is a kind of temporary resolution of the conflict. This resulting synthesis, in turn, becomes a new "thesis," opposed and complemented by a new, contradicting "antithesis."

tolerance The liberal ideas that different individuals have different conceptions of the good life, that each individual is the best judge of his or her own good, and that neither other individuals nor governments should impose their conceptions of the good on others.

total obedience The nazi and fascist notion that complete compliance with the will of state authority is the true freedom of every citizen.

totalitarianism The claim that governmental leaders should be given "total control" over all aspects of society—including the economy, religion, the arts, and even family life—in order to achieve great transformations in social and human life.

trade unionism The belief, held by Lenin and other communists, that the development of organizations (trade unions) by workers to engage in collective bargaining with capitalists undermines the proletariat's revolutionary consciousness, because unions are preoccupied with improving working conditions and remuneration *within* the capitalist system, rather than encouraging workers to overthrow the system entirely.

trade-off between efficiency and equality The idea that societies must choose between seeking a "larger pie" (more total goods) and a more equal "cutting of the pie." Efforts to achieve equality are said to reduce economic efficiency and growth.

traditional conservatism A political outlook that dominated Europe before the French Revolution and that strongly opposed the liberal and radical aspects of that upheaval. The central ideas of this outlook—the greater emphasis on society rather than on the individuals constituting it, the natural inequalities among people, the need to allow the most talented leaders to govern, and the importance of following traditional wisdom rather than "abstract reason"—were best expressed by Edmund Burke.

trusteeship The view expressed by Burke that representatives should be guided in their voting by their own understandings of the best outcomes for the entire country. According to traditional conservatives, representatives should act as trustees who act to secure what is good for all members of society, not merely do what their local constituents demand.

tyranny of the majority A fear among classical liberals that unlimited majority rule could result in the passage of laws that would violate the property rights of the wealthy or the civil rights of unpopular minorities.

unanimous direct democracy A process in which every member of a community participates directly in making community decisions and in which every member concurs in the decisions that are made.

universal entitlements Goods—such as education, health care, public transportation, and child care—that are provided to all members of a (socialist) society at very low or no cost because of the citizens' common need and rights to such goods because of their citizenship.

utilitarianism The liberal view that government should act to maximize public welfare or happiness. According to Jeremy Bentham, government should promote "the greatest good for the greatest number."

utopian socialists The term that Marx and Engels used to describe early nineteenth-century social reformers who sought to replace capitalism with more cooperative and decentralized communities having social control over private property and wealth.

utopias Comprehensive depictions of idealized communities. The concept comes from the Greek word meaning "nowhere," suggesting that these portrayals may help envision political possibilities, but are ultimately unattainable in their idealized forms.

validity A concern with ensuring that one's political ideas are well grounded. Because political theorists believe that many ideas are based on emotion, self-interest, and indoctrination, they seek methods for testing the "objective" truth of these ideas.

vanguard of the proletariat In Lenin's doctrine, this is the small group of intellectuals that understands the "historical moment"—namely, the appropriate time and circumstances for the communist revolution to take place—and that directs the proletariat accordingly. It implies a significant degree of human voluntarism in historical events that Marx's own thought does not seem to have allowed.

virtual representation The traditional conservative idea that those who did not elect representatives to a legislature could nevertheless be (virtually) represented in the legislature as long as legislators acted as trustees for the entire country. According to this doctrine, for example, American colonists could be represented in the British Parliament even if they were not given the power to elect representatives, as long as sitting legislators acted in the interests of the British empire, including the colonies.

Volk A German term and a cognate of the English, "folk"; it means "people," but the Nazis gave it Romantic connotations of national unity, historical determinacy, and racial identity.

voucher system This contemporary conservative approach to educational reform would provide students with vouchers to use in securing elementary and secondary education. Parents and students could purchase education from either a public or a private school with funds (vouchers) provided by government. Advocates believe this system will create a healthy competition among schools, producing better and safer schools.

worker-controlled private enterprises Privately owned businesses that are controlled directly or indirectly by the workers.

working-class consciousness Marx believed that one's consciousness—one's interpretation of the world, awareness of problems and solutions, and very sense of self—was determined by one's activities of production, which are a combination of the resources with which one produces and on which one labors, and one's social location in the productive process. One's consciousness could make one aware of one's real interests or not, depending on the historical situation. Members of the working class must overcome those factors that distort awareness of their real class interests before a revolution can occur.

workplace democracy The application of democratic principles to industrial enterprises, giving workers the right to participate in corporate decision making in ways that parallel the right of citizens to participate in state decision making.

young Marx Karl Marx's early writings contain philosophical and humanistic aspects that his later, more economically deterministic writings do not. Some interpreters prefer to emphasize the philosophical and idealist themes of these writings of the "young Marx," rather than the "more scientific" and "materialistic" strains of his later work.

References

ADAMS, JOHN, "Discourses on Divila," in *The Portable Conservative Reader,* edited by Russell Kirk (New York: Penguin, 1982 [1814]).
ADAMS, HENRY, *Democracy: An American Novel* (New York: Harcourt Brace Jovanovich, 1973 [1880]).
———, *History of the United States of America,* edited by Herbert Agar (Westport, Conn.: Greenwood Press, 1974 [1889]).
ADLER, MORTIMER, *Six Great Ideas* (New York: Macmillan, 1981).
AIKEN, HENRY, *The Age of Ideology: The Nineteenth Century Philosophers* (New York: George Braziller, 1957).
ALFORD, ROBERT and ROGER FRIEDLAND, *Powers of Theory: Capitalism, the State, and Democracy* (Cambridge: Cambridge University Press, 1985).
ALMOND, GABRIEL A., *A Discipline Divided: Schools and Sects in Political Science* (Newbury Park, Calif.: Sage, 1990).
ALTHUSSER, LOUIS, *Essays in Ideology* (London: Verso Press, 1984).
———, "Ideology and Ideological State Apparatuses," in *Lenin and Philosophy* (London: Monthly Review Press, 1972).
ANDERSON, CHARLES, *Pragmatic Liberalism* (Chicago: University of Chicago Press 1990).
———, "Pragmatic Liberalism: Uniting Theory and Practice," in *Liberals on Liberalism,* edited by Alfonso J. Damico (Totowa, N.J.: Rowman and Littlefield, 1986).
ARENDT, HANNAH, *Eichmann in Jerusalem* (New York: Penguin, 1963).
———, *The Human Condition* (Chicago: University of Chicago Press, 1958).
———, *The Origins of Totalitarianism* (New York and London: Harcourt Brace Jovanovich, 1951).
BAHRO, RUDOLPH, "Building the Green Movement" in *The Green Reader: Essays Toward a Sustainable Society,* edited by Andrew Dobson (San Francisco: Mercury House, 1991).
BAKUNIN, MIKHAIL "Letter to La Liberte" in *Bakunin on Authority,* edited by Sam Dolgoff (New York: Alfred A. Knopf, 1972 [1872]).
———, *The Political Philosophy of Bakunin: Scientific Anarchism,* compiled and edited by G. P. Maximoff (New York: Free Press of Glencoe, 1953).
BARBER, BENJAMIN, *Strong Democracy* (Berkeley: University of California Press, 1984).
BARKAN, JOANNE, "Sweden: Not Yet Paradise, but. . . ." *Dissent* (spring 1989): 147–151.
———, "The End of the Swedish Model?" *Dissent* (spring 1992): 92–98.

BARRY, BRIAN, "How Not to Defend Liberal Institutions," *British Journal of Political Science* 20 (June 1990): 1–14.

———, *A Treatise on Social Justice, Volume One: Theories of Justice* (Berkeley: University of California Press, 1989).

BAY, CHRISTIAN, "Civil Disobedience: Prerequisite for Democracy in Mass Society," in *Political Theory and Social Change,* edited by David Spitz (New York: Atherton Press, 1967).

BAYAT, MANGOL, "Hi'a Islam as a Functioning Ideology in Iran: The Cult of the Hidden Imam," in *Iran Since the Revolution,* edited by Barry M. Rosen (New York: Columbia University Press, 1985).

BEECHER, JONATHAN, and RICHARD BIENVENU, *The Utopian Vision of Charles Fourier* (Boston: Beacon Press, 1971).

BELL, DANIEL, *The End of Ideology* (New York: Collier, 1960).

BELLAH, ROBERT, et al., *Habits of the Heart* (New York: Harper and Row, 1985).

BENNETT, WILLIAM, J. (ed.), *The Book of Virtues* (New York: Simon and Schuster, 1993).

BENTHAM, JEREMY, "Fragment on Government," in *A Bentham Reader,* edited by Mary Peter Mack (New York: Pegasus, 1969 [1776]).

———, *An Introduction to the Principles of Morals and Legislation,* edited by Wilfred Harrison (Oxford: Basil Blackwell, 1967 [1789]).

BERGSON, HENRI, *The Two Sources of Morality and Religion,* translated by R. Ashley Audra and Cloudesley Brereton (Garden City, N.Y.: Doubleday 1954 [1935]).

BERLIN, ISAIAH, *Four Essays on Liberty* (London: Oxford University Press, 1969).

BERNSTEIN, EDUARD, *Evolutionary Socialism* (New York: Schocken, 1961 [1899]).

BLOOM, ALLAN, *The Closing of the American Mind* (New York: Simon and Schuster, 1987).

BLUESTONE, BARRY and BENNETT HARRISON, *The Deindustrialization of America: Plant Closings, Community Abandonment, and the Dismantling of Basic Industry* (New York: Basic, 1982).

BLUMENTHAL, SAMUEL, "How Rhenquist Came Down in Hobbes v. Locke," *The Washington Post Weekly Edition* 6 (Oct. 1986): 23–24.

BOOKMAN, ANN, and SANDRA MORGEN, *Women and the Politics of Empowerment* (Philadelphia: Temple University Press, 1989).

BOTTOMORE, TOM, *Classes in Modern Society,* 2d ed. (London: HarperCollins Academic, 1991).

———, *The Socialist Economy* (New York: Guilford Press, 1990).

BOYTE, HARRY, *The Backyard Revolution: Understanding the New Citizen Movement* (Philadelphia: Temple University Press, 1980).

BRADER, KARL DIETRICH, *The German Dictatorship* (New York: Praeger, 1970).

BRAYBROOKE, DAVID, and CHARLES LINDBLOM, *A Strategy of Decision* (New York: Free Press, 1963).

BROOKER, PAUL, "The Nazi Fuehrerprinzip: A Weberian Analysis" in *Political Ideologies and Political Philosophies,* edited by H. B. McCullough (Toronto: Wall and Thompson, 1989).

BROWN, LESTER R. HAL KANE, and DAVID MALIN BOODMAN, *Vital Signs* (Washington, D.C.: Worldwatch Institute, 1994).

BUCKLEY, WILLIAM F., JR., *The Jeweler's Eye: A Book of Irresistible Political Reflection* (New York: Putnam, 1968).

———, *McCarthy and His Enemies: The Record and Its Meaning* (Chicago: H. Regney, 1954).

———, *Up from Liberalism* (New York: McDowell, Obolensky, 1959).

BURKE, EDMUND, "An Appeal from the New to the Old Whigs," in *The Political Philosophy of Edmund Burke,* edited by Iain Hampshire-Monk (London: Longman, 1987 [1791]).

———, *Burke's Politics: Selected Writings and Speeches of Edmund Burke on Reform, Revolution and War,* edited by Ross J. Hoffman and Paul Levack (New York: Alfred A. Knopf, 1967).

———, *Reflections on the Revolution in France* (New York: Liberal Arts Library Press, 1955 [1790]).

BURNS, JAMES MACGREGOR, *Leadership* (New York: Harper and Row, 1978).

CAMUS, ALBERT, *The Rebel* (New York: Vintage Books, 1953).

CARENS, JOSEPH H., "Aliens and Citizens: The Case for Open Borders, *Review of Politics* 49 (spring 1987): 251–273.

CARSON, RACHEL, *Silent Spring* (Greenwich, Conn.: Fawcett Publications, 1962).

CASTRO, FIDEL, *Fidel Castro Speaks,* edited by Martin Kenner and James Petras (New York: Grove Press, 1969).

CEASER, JAMES W., *Presidential Selection: Theory and Development* (Princeton: Princeton University Press, 1979).

CHALMERS, JOHNSON, *Autopsy on People's War* (Berkeley: University of California Press, 1973).

CHAMBERLAIN, HOUSTON S., *Foundations of the Nineteenth Century,* translated by George L. Mosse (New York: H. Fertig, 1968 [1899]).

CHENERY, HOLLIS, et al., *Redistribution with Growth* (New York: Oxford University Press, 1974).

CHUBB, JOHN E., and TERRY M. MOE, *Politics, Markets and America's Schools* (Washington, D.C.: Brookings Institution, 1990).

CLARK, TERRY N., and SEYMOUR MARTIN LIPSET, "Are Social Classes Dying?" *International Sociology* 6 (Dec. 1991): 397–410.

———, ———, and MICHAEL REMPEL, "The Declining Political Significance of Social Class," *International Sociology* 8 (Sept. 1993): 293–316.

CODE, LORRAINE, *What Can She Know?* (Ithaca, N.Y.: Cornell University Press, 1991).

COHEN, G. A., *History, Labour, and Freedom: Themes from Marx* (Oxford: Oxford University Press, 1988).

COHEN, JOSHUA, and JOEL ROGERS, *On Democracy* (Hamondsworth Middlesex, England: Penguin, 1983).

COHN, NORMAN, *The Pursuit of the Millennium* (New York: Oxford University Press, 1970).

COLE, G. D. H., *History of Socialism* (London: Macmillan, 1953–1960).

———, *Self-Government in Industry* (London: G. Bell, 1919).

———, *Worker's Control and Self-Government in Industry* (Nendelin, England: Kraus Reprint, 1979 [1933]).

COLEMAN, JAMES, and SARA KELLY, "Education," in *The Urban Predicament,* edited by William Gorham and Nathan Glazer (Washington, D.C.: Urban Institute, 1976).

COMMONER, BARRY, *Science and Survival* (New York: Viking, 1966).

———, *The Closing Circle: Nature, Man and Technology* (New York: Bantam Books, 1974).

———, *The Poverty of Power: Energy and the Economic Crisis* (New York: Knopf, 1977).

CONRADT, DAVID P., *The German Polity,* 5th ed. (New York: Longman, 1993).

CONVERSE, PHILIP E., "The Nature of Belief Systems in Mass Publics," in *Ideology and Discontent,* edited by David E. Apter (New York: Free Press, 1964).

COOPER, BARRY, *The End of History: An Essay on Modern Hegelianism* (Toronto: University of Toronto Press, 1984).

CORD, ROBERT L., *Separation of Church and State: Historical Fact and Current Fiction* (New York: Lambeth Press, 1982).

CRAWFORD, ALAN, *Thunder on the Right* (New York: Pantheon, 1980).

CRICK, BERNARD, *In Defence of Politics* (New York: Penguin, 1962).

———, *Socialism* (Minneapolis: University of Minnesota Press, 1987).

CRONIN, THOMAS E., *Direct Democracy* (Cambridge: Harvard University Press, 1989).

CROPSEY, JOSEPH, *Political Philosophy and the Issues of Politics* (Chicago: University of Chicago Press, 1977).

CROSLAND, C. A. R., *The Future of Socialism* (London: Cape, 1956).

DAHL, ROBERT A., *Democracy and Its Critics* (New Haven: Yale University Press, 1989).

———, *A Preface to Economic Democracy* (Berkeley: University of California Press, 1985).

———, *Who Governs?* (New Haven: Yale University Press, 1961).

DALY, MARY, *Gyn/Ecology: The Metaethics of Radical Feminism* (Boston: Beacon Press, 1978).

———, *Pure Lust: Elemental Feminist Philosophy* (Boston: Beacon Press, 1984).

DE LEON, DAVID, *The American Anarchist* (Baltimore: Johns Hopkins University Press, 1971).

DESCARTES, RENE, *Discourse on Method,* translated by Donald A. Cress (Indianapolis: Hackett, 1980 [1637]).

———, *Meditation on First Philosophy,* translated by Donald A. Cress (Indianapolis: Hackett, 1980 [1641]).

DEUTSCH, KARL, "On Political Theory and Political Action," *American Political Science Review* 65 (Mar. 1971): 11–27.

DEWEY, JOHN, *Liberalism and Social Action* (New York: Capricorn, 1935).

———, *The Public and Its Problems* (New York: Henry Holt, 1927).

DICKERSON, MARK O., and THOMAS FLANAGAN, *An Introduction to Government and Politics: A Conceptual Approach* (Toronto: Methuen, 1982).

DIONE, E. J., *Why Americans Hate Politics* (New York: Simon and Schuster, 1991).

DJILAS, MILOVAN, *The New Class: An Analysis of the Communist System* (New York: Praeger, 1957).

DOLGOFF, SAM, *Bakunin on Authority* (New York: Alfred A. Knopf, 1972).

DOMHOFF, G. WILLIAM, *The Power Elite and the State: How Policy Is Made in America* (New York: A. DeGrayter, 1990).

———, *Who Really Rules?* (Santa Monica, Calif.: Goodyear, 1978).

DRUCKER, H. M., *The Political Uses of Ideology* (London: Macmillan Press, 1974).

DURKHEIM, EMILE, *Suicide: A Study in Sociology,* edited by George Simpson (New York: Free Press, 1966 [1897]).

DWORKIN, ANDREA, *Pornography: Men Possessing Women* (New York: Perigee, 1981).

DWORKIN, RONALD, *Law's Empire* (Cambridge, Mass.: Belknap, 1986).

———, *Taking Rights Seriously* (Cambridge, Mass.: Harvard University Press, 1977).

ECKERSLEY, ROBYN, *Environmentalism and Political Theory: Toward an Ecocentric Approach* (Albany, N.Y.: State University of New York Press, 1992).

ECKSTEIN, HARRY, "Case Study and Theory in Political Science," in *Handbook of Political Science,* vol. 7., edited by Fred I. Greenstein and Nelson Polsby (Reading, Mass.: Addison-Wesley, 1975).

EHRENFELD, DAVID, *The Arrogance of Humanism* (New York: Oxford University Press, 1978).

ELSHTAIN, JEAN BETHKE, "Feminism, Family and Community," *Dissent* 29 (fall 1982): 442–449.

———, *Mediations on Modern Political Thought* (New York: Praeger, 1986).

———, *Power Trips and Other Journeys* (Madison: University of Wisconsin Press, 1990).
———, *Public Man, Private Woman* (Princeton: Princeton University Press, 1981).
ENGELS, FRIEDRICH, *Socialism: Utopian and Scientific,* in *The Marx-Engels Reader,* 2d ed., edited by Robert C. Tucker (New York: W. W. Norton, 1978 [1880]).
FALWELL, JERRY (ed.), *The Fundamentalist Phenomenon* (Garden City, N.Y.: Doubleday, 1981).
FECHER, CHARLES A., *The Philosophy of Jacques Maritain* (New York: Greenwood Press, 1953).
FEIN, RASHI, "National Health Insurance," *Dissent* (spring 1992): 157–163.
FEUERBACH, LUDWIG, *The Essence of Christianity,* translated by Marian Evans (London: John Chapman, 1854 [1845]).
FIRESTONE, SHULAMITH, *The Dialectic of Sex: The Case for Feminist Revolution* (New York: Morrow, 1970).
FLATHMAN, RICHARD, *Toward a Liberalism* (Ithaca, N.Y.: Cornell University Press, 1992).
FOREMAN, DAVID, and BILL HAYWOOD (eds.), *Ecodefense: A Field Guide to Monkeywrenching,* 2d ed. (Tucson, Ariz.: Ned Ludd, 1989).
FORMAN, JAMES D., *Fascism: The Meaning and the Experience of Reactionary Revolution* (New York: Dell, 1974).
FOWLER, ROBERT BOOTH, "The Anarchist Tradition of Political Thought," *Western Political Quarterly* (Dec. 1973): 738–752.
FRENCH, MARILYN, *Beyond Power: On Women, Men and Morals* (New York: Summit, 1985).
FREYFOGLE, ERIC T., *Justice and the Earth: Images of Our Planetary Survival* (New York: Free Press, 1993).
FRIEDAN, BETTY, *The Feminine Mystique* (New York: W. W. Norton, 1963).
———, *The Second Stage* (New York: Summit, 1981).
FRIEDMAN, MILTON, *Capitalism and Freedom* (Chicago: University of Chicago Press, 1962).
———, and ROSE FRIEDMAN, *Free to Choose: A Personal Statement* (New York: Harcourt Brace Jovanovich, 1980).
FROMM, ERICH, *Escape from Freedom* (London: Routledge and Kegan Paul, 1960 [1941]).
———, *The Sane Society* (New York: Rinehart, 1955).
FUKUYAMA, FRANCIS, *The End of History and the Last Man* (New York: Avon, 1992).
———, "The End of History?," *The National Interest* 16 (summer 1989): 3–18.
GALBRAITH, JOHN KENNETH, *The Affluent Society* (Boston: Houghton Mifflin, 1958).
———, *Economics and Public Purpose* (New York: Houghton Mifflin, 1973).
———, *The New Industrial State* (New York: Signet, 1972).
GALSTON, WILLIAM, "Civic Education in a Liberal State," in *Liberalism and the Moral Life,* edited by Nancy L. Rosenblum (Cambridge: Harvard University Press, 1989).
———, "Liberalism and Public Morality," in *Liberals on Liberalism,* edited by Alfonso J. Damico (Totowa, N.J.: Rowman and Littlefield, 1986).
GASSET, JOSE ORTEGA Y, *The Revolt of the Masses* (New York: W. W. Norton, 1957 [1930]).
GEERTZ, CLIFFORD, "Ideology as a Cultural System," in *Ideology and Discontent,* edited by David E. Apter (New York: Free Press, 1964).
GENTILE, GIOVANNI, "The Philosophical Basis of Fascism," in *Readings on Fascism and National Socialism* (Chicago: Swallow Press, 1952 [1928]).
GILDER, GEORGE, *Wealth and Poverty* (New York: Bantam, 1981).
GILL, EMILY, "Goods, Virtues, and the Constitution of the Self," in *Liberals on Liberalism,* edited by Alfonso J. Damico (Totowa, N.J.: Rowman and Littlefield, 1986).
GILLIGAN, CAROL, *In a Different Voice* (Cambridge: Harvard University Press, 1982).
GLENDON, MARY ANN, *Abortion and Divorce in Western Law* (Cambridge: Harvard University Press, 1987).

———, *Rights Talk: The Impoverishment of Political Discourse* (New York: Free Press, 1991).
GOBINEAU, JOSEPH ARTHUR DE, *Essay on the Inequality of Human Races* (New York: Garland, 1984 [1854]).
GODWIN, WILLIAM, *Enquiry Concerning Political Justice* (Middlesex, England: Penguin Classics, 1985 [1793]).
GOFFMAN, E., "The Income Gap and Its Causes," *Dissent* (winter 1990): 8.
GOLDMAN, EMMA, "Anarchism: What It Really Stands For," in *Anarchism and Other Essays* (New York: Dover, 1969 [1911]).
GOLDWATER, BARRY, *The Conscience of a Conservative* (New York: Macfadden, 1960).
GOODMAN, PAUL, and PERCIVAL GOODMAN, *Communitas* (New York: Vintage, 1960).
GORBACHEV, MIKHAIL, "The Socialist Idea and Revolutionary Perestroika," *National Affairs* (Nov. 17, 1989): 70–80.
GOULD, STEPHEN J., *The Mismeasure of Man* (New York: W. W. Norton, 1983).
GRAMSCI, ANTONIO, "The Study of Philosophy," in *Selections from the Prison Notebooks of Antonio Gramsci,* edited and translated by Quinton Hoare and Geoffrey Nowell Smith (New York: International, 1971).
GRAY, JOHN, *Liberalisms: Essays in Political Philosophy* (London: Routledge, 1989).
GREEN, THOMAS HILL, *Lectures on the Principles of Political Obligation* (London: Longmans, Green, 1907 [1886]).
GUEVARA, ERNESTO, *Che Guevara Speaks,* edited by George Lavan (New York: Pathfinder Press, 1983).
———, *Guerrilla Warfare* (New York: Vintage, 1969).
———, *Reminiscences of the Cuban Revolutionary War,* translated by Victoria Ortiz (New York: Monthly Review Press, 1968).
GUTMANN, AMY, "Undemocratic Education," in *Liberalism and the Moral Life,* edited by Nancy Rosenblum (Cambridge: Harvard University Press, 1989).
HABERMAS, JÜRGEN, *Legitimation Crisis,* translated by Thomas McCarthy (Boston: Beacon Press, 1975).
HARDIN, GARRETT, "The Tragedy of the Commons," in *Managing the Commons,* edited by Garrett Hardin and John Baden (San Francisco: W. H. Freeman, 1977).
HARDING, SANDRA, *The Science Question* (Ithaca, N.Y.: Cornell University Press, 1986).
HARRINGTON, MICHAEL, *The Other America: Poverty in the United States* (New York: Macmillan, 1961).
———, "Toward a New Socialism," *Dissent* (spring 1989): 153–163.
———, *Twilight of Capitalism* (New York: Simon and Schuster, 1976).
HARTMANN, HEIDI, "The Unhappy Marriage of Marxism and Feminism: Towards a More Progressive Union," in *Women and Revolution: A Discussion of the Unhappy Marriage of Marxism and Feminism,* edited by Lydia Sargent (Boston: South End Press, 1981).
HARTSOCK, NANCY, *Money, Sex, and Power: Toward a Feminist Historical Materialism* (New York: Longman, 1983).
HARTZ, LOUIS, *The Liberal Tradition in America* (New York: Harcourt, Brace, and World, 1955).
HAWLEY, WILLIS, *Nonpartisan Elections and the Case for Party Politics* (New York: John Wiley, 1973).
HAYEK, FRIEDRICH VON, *The Constitution of Liberty* (Chicago: University of Chicago Press, 1960).
———, *The Road to Serfdom* (Chicago: University of Chicago Press, 1944).
HEGEL, G. W. F., *Phaenomenologie des Geistes* (Frankfurt: Verlag Ullstein, 1970).
HEIDENHEIMER, ARNOLD J., HUGH HECLO, and CAROLYN TEICH ADAMS, *Comparative Public Policy,* 3d ed. (New York: St. Martin's Press, 1990).

HEILBRONER, ROBERT L., *The Worldly Philosophers* (New York: Simon and Schuster, 1953).
———, et al., "From Sweden to Socialism: A Small Symposium on a Big Question," *Dissent* (winter, 1991): 96–110.
HENIG, JEFFREY, *Public Policy and Federalism* (New York: St. Martin's Press, 1985).
———, *Rethinking School Choice* (Princeton, N.J.: Princeton University Press, 1994).
HERSON, LAWRENCE J. P., *The Politics of Ideas: Political Theory and American Public Policy* (Homewood, Ill.: Dorsey Press, 1984).
HERZEN, ALEXANDER, *From the Other Shore,* translated by Moura Budberg (London: Weidenfeld and Nicolson, 1956 [1850]).
HIRSCHMAN, ALBERT O., *The Passions and the Interests: Political Arguments for Capitalism Before Its Triumph* (Princeton: Princeton University, 1977).
———, *The Rhetoric of Reaction: Perversity, Futility, and Jeopardy* (Cambridge, Mass.: Belknap Press, 1991).
HITLER, ADOLF, *Mein Kampf,* translated by Ralph Mannheim (Boston: Houghton Mifflin, 1971 [1925–6]).
HOBBES, THOMAS, *Leviathan,* edited by Herbert Schneider (Indianapolis: Bobbs-Merrill Liberal Arts Library, 1958 [1651]).
HOCHSCHILD, JENNIFER, *What's Fair?* (Cambridge: Harvard University Press, 1981).
HOEVELER, DAVID, JR., *Watch on the Right: Conservative Intellectuals in the Reagan Era* (Madison: University of Wisconsin Press, 1991).
HOLMES, STEPHEN, "The Liberal Idea," *The American Prospect* 7 (fall 1991): 81–96.
HOOVER, KENNETH, *Ideology and Political Life,* 2d ed. (Belmont, Calif.: Wadsworth, 1993).
HOUT, MIKE, CLEM BROOKS, and JEFF MANZA, "The Persistence of Classes in Post-Industrial Societies," *International Sociology* 8 (Sept., 1993): 259–276.
HOWE, IRVING, *Beyond the Welfare State* (New York: Schocken, 1982).
———, "The First 35 Years Were the Hardest," *Dissent* (spring 1989): 133–136.
———, *Socialism and America* (New York: Harcourt Brace Jovanovich, 1977).
HUBER, RUDOLF, *Constitutional Law of the Greater German Reich,* in *Communism, Fascism, and Democracy: Theoretical Foundations,* edited by Carl Cohen (New York: Random House, 1962 [1939]).
HUME, DAVID, *A Treatise of Human Nature,* edited by L. A. Selby Bigge (Oxford: Clarendon Press, 1975 [1739]).
HUNTINGTON, SAMUEL P., "The Democratic Distemper," *The Public Interest* 41 (fall 1975): 9–38.
HUXLEY, T. H., "Evolution and Ethics," in *Selections from the Essays of Huxley,* edited by Alburey Castell (Arlington Heights, Ill.: Crofts Classics, 1948 [1893]).
INGERSOL, DAVID E., and RICHARD K. MATTHEWS, *The Philosophic Roots of Modern Ideology: Liberalism, Communism, Fascism,* 2d ed. (Englewood Cliffs, N.J.: Prentice Hall, 1991).
INGLEHART, RONALD, *Culture Shift* (Princeton: Princeton University Press, 1989).
JAFFA, HARRY V., *How to Think About the American Revolution* (Durham, N.C.: Carolina Academic Press, 1978).
JAGGER, ALISON, *Feminist Politics and Human Nature* (Totowa, N.J.: Rowman and Allenheld, 1983).
JENCKS, CHRISTOPHER, *Inequality* (New York: Harper Colophon, 1972).
JOLL, JAMES, *The Anarchists* (New York: Grosset and Dunlop, 1964).
JOUVENAL, BERTRAND DE, *The Pure Theory of Politics* (Cambridge: Cambridge University Press, 1963).
KAHANE, RABBI MEIR, *Listen World, Listen Jew* (Jerusalem and Brooklyn, N.Y.: Institute of the Jewish Idea, 1978).

KAPLAN, LAWRENCE (ed.), *Fundamentalism in Comparative Perspective* (Minneapolis: University of Minnesota Press, 1992).

KARIEL, HENRY, "Creating Political Reality," *American Political Science Review* 64 (Dec. 1970): 1088–1098.

KELLY, PETRA, *Fighting for Hope* (Boston: South End Press, 1984).

KENDALL, WILMOORE, "Equality and the American Political tradition," in *Keeping the Tablets: Modern American Conservative Thought,* edited by William F. Buckley, Jr., and Charles R. Kesler (New York: Harper and Row, 1988).

KEY, V. O. JR., *The Responsible Electorate* (Cambridge: Harvard University Press, 1966).

KEYNES, JOHN MAYNARD, *The Collected Writings of John Maynard Keynes,* edited by Donald Moggridge (London: Macmillan, 1980).

KHOMEINI, IMAM, *Islam and Revolution: Writings and Declarations of Imam Khomeini,* translated by Hamid Algar (Berkeley: Mizan Press, 1981).

KINDER, DONALD, "Diversity and Complexity in American Public Opinion," in *Political Science: The State of the Discipline,* edited by Ada Finifter (Washington, D.C.: American Political Science Association, 1983).

KING, MARTIN LUTHER, JR., "Letter from Birmingham Jail," in *Why We Can't Wait* (New York: Harper and Row, 1963).

KIRK, RUSSELL, *A Program for Conservatives* (Chicago: Henry Regnery, 1954).

KIRKPATRICK, JEAN, "Dictatorships and Double Standards," in *Keeping the Tablets: Modern American Conservative Thought,* edited by William F. Buckley, Jr., and Charles R. Kesler (New York: Harper and Row, 1988 [1980]).

———, "Politics and the 'New Class'," *Society* 16 (Jan./Feb. 1979): 42–48.

KNEESE, ALLEN V., and CHARLES L. SCHULTZE, *Pollution, Prices, and Public Policy* (Washington, D.C.: Brookings Institution, 1975).

KOESTLER, ARTHUR, *Darkness at Noon,* translated by Daphne Hardy (New York: Macmillan, 1941).

KOLAKOWSKI, LESZEK, *Main Currents of Marxism,* translated by P. S. Falla (Oxford: Oxford University Press, 1978).

KORNHAUSER, WILLIAM, *The Politics of Mass Society* (Glencoe, Ill.: Free Press, 1959).

KRISTOL, IRVING, *Two Cheers for Capitalism* (New York: Basic, 1978).

KROPOTKIN, PETER, "Anarchist Communism: Its Basis and Principles," in *Revolutionary Pamphlets* (New York: Vanguard Press, 1927).

———, *Conquest of Bread* (New York: Vanguard Press, 1926 [1892]).

———, *Memoirs of a Revolutionist* (New York: Horizon Press, 1968 [1899]).

———, *Mutual Aid: A Factor in Evolution* (New York: New York University Press, 1972 [1907]).

KUENNE, ROBERT, *Economic Justice in American Society* (Princeton: Princeton University Press, 1993).

KUHN, THOMAS, *The Structure of Scientific Revolutions* (Chicago: University of Chicago Press, 1962).

KUTTNER, ROBERT, "Socialism, Liberalism, and Democracy," *The American Prospect* (spring 1992): 7–12.

KYMLICKA, WILL, *Contemporary Political Philosophy* (New York: Oxford University Press, 1990).

———, "Liberalism and Communitarianism," *Canadian Journal of Philosophy* 118 (June 1988): 181–203.

LAHAYE, TIM, *The Battle for the Mind* (Old Tappan, N.J.: Revell, 1980).

LANE, ROBERT, *Political Ideology* (New York: Free Press, 1962).

LASCH, CHRISTOPHER, *The True and Only Heaven* (New York: Norton, 1991).
LATHER, PATTI, *Getting Smart: Feminist Research and Pedagogy with/in the Postmodern* (New York: Routledge, 1991).
LENIN, V. I., "Foreign Communist Parties and the Russian Spirit," in *The Lenin Anthology,* edited by Robert C. Tucker (New York: W. W. Norton, 1975 [1920]).
———, "Introducing the New Economic Policy," in The *Lenin Anthology,* edited by Robert C. Tucker (New York: W. W. Norton, 1975 [1921]).
———, " 'Left-Wing' Communism: An Infantile Disorder," in *The Lenin Anthology,* edited by Robert C. Tucker (New York: W. W. Norton, 1975 [1920]).
———, *Imperialism: The Highest Stage of Capitalism* (New York: International, 1939 [1917]).
———, "The State and Revolution," in *The Lenin Anthology,* edited by Robert C. Tucker (New York: W. W. Norton, 1975 [1917]).
———, "What Is to Be Done?," in *The Lenin Anthology,* edited by Robert C. Tucker (New York: W. W. Norton, 1975 [1902]).
LEOPOLD, ALDO, *The Sand County Almanac* (New York: Oxford University Press, 1947).
LERNER, DANIEL, *The Passing of the Traditional Society* (Glencoe, Ill.: Free Press, 1959).
LIFTON, JAY, *The Nazi Doctors: Medical Killing and the Psychology of Genocide* (New York: Basic, 1986).
LIJPHART, AREND, *Democracy in Plural Societies* (New Haven: Yale University Press, 1977).
LIMBAUGH, RUSH, *The Way Things Ought to Be* (New York: Pocket Star, 1992).
LINDBLOM, CHARLES E., *Politics and Markets* (New York: Basic, 1977).
LIPSET, SEYMOUR MARTIN, *Political Man* (Garden City, N.Y.: Doubleday, 1960).
LIPSON, LESLIE, *The Great Issues of Politics,* 8th ed. (Englewood Cliffs, N.J.: Prentice-Hall, 1989).
LOCKE, JOHN, *Essay on Human Understanding,* edited by Peter H. Nidditch (Oxford: Clarendon Press, 1975 [1690]).
———, *Letter Concerning Toleration,* edited by Patrick Romanell (Indianapolis: Bobbs-Merrill, 1950 [1689]).
———, *Two Treatises of Government,* edited by Peter Laslett (New York: Mentor, 1960 [1690]).
LOVELOCK, JAMES, *Gaia: A New Look at Life on Earth* (New York: Oxford University Press, 1979).
LOWI, THEODORE J., "American Business and Public Policy, Case Studies, and Political Theory," *World Politics* (July 1964).
———, *The End of Liberalism: The Second Republic of the United States* (New York: W. W. Norton, 1979).
———, and BENJAMIN GINSBERG, *Poliscide* (New York: Macmillan, 1976).
LUKES, STEVEN, "Alienation and Anomie," in *Philosophy, Politics, and Society,* 3d ed., edited by Peter Laslett and W. G. Runciman (Oxford: Basil Blackman, 1967): 140–156.
———, "Socialism and Equality," *Dissent* 22 (spring 1975): 154–168.
———, *Marxism and Morality* (Oxford: Oxford University Press, 1987).
———, *Power: A Radical View* (London: Macmillan, 1974).
LUSTIG, R. JEFFREY, *Corporate Liberalism* (Berkeley: University of California Press, 1982).
LUXEMBURG, ROSA, *The Accumulation of Capital,* translated by Rudolf Wichmann (New York: Monthly Review, 1973 [1913]).
MACHAN, TIBOR R., *The Main Debate: Communism versus Capitalism* (New York: Random House, 1987).
MACKINNON, CATHERINE, *Feminism Unmodified* (Cambridge: Harvard University Press, 1977).

———, *Toward a Feminist Theory of the State* (Cambridge: Harvard University Press, 1989).

MACPHERSON, C. B., *The Life and Times of Liberal Democracy* (New York: Oxford University Press, 1977).

MADISON, JAMES, ALEXANDER HAMILTON, and JOHN JAY, *Federal Papers,* edited by Isaac Kramnick (New York: Penguin, 1987 [1788]).

MAISTRE, JOSEPH DE, "Considerations on France," in *The Works of Joseph de Maistre,* edited by Jack Lively (New York: Macmillan, 1965 [1797]).

MANNHEIM, KARL, *Ideology and Utopia* (London: Routledge and Kegan, 1936).

MANSBRIDGE, JANE J., "The Limits of Friendship," in *Nomos XVI: Participation in Politics,* edited by J. Roland Pennock and John W. Chapman (New York: New York University Press, 1977): 246–266.

———, *Why We Lost the ERA* (Chicago: University of Chicago Press, 1986).

MANUEL, FRANK E., and FRITZIE P. MANUEL, *Utopian Thought in the Western World* (Cambridge: Harvard University Press, Belknap Press, 1979).

MAO ZEDONG, *The Collected Works of Mao Tse-tung* (Arlington, Va.: Joint Publication Research Service, 1978).

MARSH, MARGARET S., *Anarchist Women, 1870–1920* (Philadelphia: Temple University Press, 1981).

MARX, KARL, "Amsterdam Speech of 1872," in *Karl Marx, Selected Writings,* edited by David McClellan (Oxford: Oxford University Press, 1977).

———, *The Civil War in France,* in *The Marx-Engels Reader,* 2d ed., edited by Robert C. Tucker (New York: W. W. Norton, 1978 [1871]).

———, *Critique of the Gotha Program,* in *The Marx-Engels Reader,* 2d ed., edited by Robert C. Tucker (New York: W. W. Norton, 1978 [1875]).

———, *The German Ideology,* in *The Marx-Engels Reader,* 2d ed., edited by Robert C. Tucker (New York: W. W. Norton, 1978 [1846]).

———, *On The Jewish Question,* in *The Marx-Engels Reader,* 2d ed., edited by Robert C. Tucker (New York: W. W. Norton, 1978 [1843]).

———, *Philosophical and Economic Manuscripts,* in *The Marx-Engels Reader,* 2d ed., edited by Robert C. Tucker (New York: W. W. Norton, 1978 [1844]).

———, *Theses on Feuerbach,* in *The Marx-Engels Reader,* 2d ed., edited by Robert C. Tucker (New York: W. W. Norton, 1978 [1845]).

———, and FRIEDRICH ENGELS, *The Manifesto of the Communist Party,* in *The Marx-Engels Reader,* 2d ed., edited by Robert C. Tucker (New York: W. W. Norton, 1978 [1848]).

MARZORATI, GERALD, et al., "Who Owes What to Whom?," *Harper's Magazine* 282 (Feb. 1991): 44–54.

MAZZINI, GUISEPPE, "The Duties of Man," in *Dogma and Dreams,* edited by Nancy Love (New York: Chatham House, 1991 [1875]).

MCCLOSKY, HERBERT, and JOHN SCHAAR, "Psychological Dimensions of Anomy," *American Sociological Review* 30 (1965): 14–40.

MCCOY, CHARLES, *Contemporary ISMS: A Political Economy Perspective* (New York: Franklin Watts, 1982).

MCLELLAN, DAVID, *Ideology* (Minneapolis: University of Minnesota Press, 1986).

———, *Karl Marx: His Life and Thought* (New York: Harper and Row, 1973).

———, *Marxism After Marx* (Boston: Houghton Mifflin, 1979).

MEHRING, FRANZ, *Karl Marx: The Story of His Life,* translated by Edward Fitzgerald (Ann Arbor: University of Michigan Press, 1962).

MILBANK, JOHN, *Theology and Social Theory: Beyond Secular Reason* (Oxford and Cambridge: Blackwell, 1990).

MILL, JAMES, *Essay on Government,* edited by Jack Lively and John Rees (Oxford: Clarendon Press, 1978 [1820]).
MILL, JOHN STUART, *Considerations on Representative Government* (Oxford: Blackwell, 1946 [1861]).
———, *On Liberty,* edited by Elizabeth Rapaport (Indianapolis: Hackett, 1978 [1859]).
———, *Principles of Political Economy* (New York: Penguin, 1985 [1846]).
———, *Utilitarianism* (New York: Bobbs-Merrill, 1957 [1861]).
———, and HARRIET TAYLOR, *The Subjection of Women* (London: Virago, 1983 [1869]).
MILLER, EUGENE, "Positivism, Historicism, and Political Inquiry," *American Political Science Review* 66 (Sept. 1972): 796–873.
MILLET, KATE, *Sexual Politics* (Garden City, N.Y.: Doubleday, 1970).
MILLS, C. WRIGHT, *The Power Elite* (New York: Oxford University Press, 1956).
MITCHELL, JULIET, *Women's Estate* (New York: Pantheon, 1991).
MITCHELL, WILLIAM, "Efficiency, Responsibility, and Democratic Politics," in *Liberal Democracy,* NOMOS XXV, edited by J. Roland Pennock and John W. Chapman (New York: New York University Press, 1983): 343–373.
MONTESQUIEU, CHARLES-LOUIS DE SECONDAT, BARON DE, *The Spirit of Laws,* translated by Anne M. Cohler, Basia C. Miller, and Harold Stone (New York: Cambridge University Press, 1989 [1750]).
MORE, THOMAS, *Utopia,* edited by Robert M. Adams (New York: Norton, 1992 [1516]).
MOSCA, GAETANO, *The Ruling Class,* translated by H. D. Kahn (New York: McGraw-Hill, 1939 [1896]).
MUELLER, INGO, *Hitler's Justice* (Cambridge: University of Harvard Press, 1991).
MUSSOLINI, BENITO, "The Doctrine of Fascism," in *Readings on Fascism and National Socialism* (Chicago: Swallow Press, 1952 [1928]).
NAESS, ARNE, *Ecology, Community, and Lifestyle: Outline for an Ecosophy* (Cambridge: Cambridge University Press, 1984).
———, "The Shallow and the Deep, Long-Range Ecology Movement: A Summary," *Inquiry* 16 (1973): 95–99.
NAKANE, CHIE, *Japanese Society* (Berkeley: University of California Press, 1970).
NATHAN, ROBERT P., *The Plot That Failed: Nixon and the Administrative Presidency* (New York: John Wiley, 1975).
NELSON, BARBARA J., and NAJMA CHOWDHURY, *Women and Politics Worldwide* (New Haven: Yale University Press, 1994).
NEUBAUER, DAVID W., *America's Courts and the Criminal Justice System,* 4th ed. (Belmont, Calif.: Wadsworth, 1992).
NIE, NORMAN, SIDNEY VERBA, and JOHN PETROCIK, *The Changing American Voter* (Cambridge, Mass.: Harvard University Press, 1979).
NIETZSCHE, FRIEDRICH, *The Genealogy of Morals,* translated by Carol Diethe (New York: Cambridge University Press, 1994 [1887]).
NISBET, ROBERT, *Conservatism: Dream and Reality* (Minneapolis: University of Minnesota Press, 1986).
———, "The Decline and Fall of Social Class," *Pacific Sociological Review* 2 (winter 1959): 1–17.
NOVAK, MICHAEL, *Freedom with Justice: Catholic Social Thought and Liberal Institutions* (San Francisco: Harper and Row, 1984).
———, The *Spirit of Democratic Capitalism* (New York: Simon and Schuster, 1982).
———, *Will It Liberate? Questions about Liberation Theology* (Mahwah, N.J.: Paulist Press, 1987).

NOVE, ALEC, *The Economics of Feasible Socialism Revisited* (London: HarperCollins, 1991).
NOZICK, ROBERT, *Anarchy, State, and Utopia* (New York: Basic, 1974).
OAKESHOTT, MICHAEL, "On Being Conservative," in *Rationalism and Politics and Other Essays* (New York: Basic, 1962).
OKIN, SUSAN MOLLER, *Justice, Gender, and Family* (New York: Basic, 1989).
———, *Women in Western Political Thought* (Princeton: Princeton University Press, 1979).
OKUN, ARTHUR M., *Equality and Efficiency: The Big Tradeoff* (Washington, D.C.: Brookings Institution, 1975).
OLLMAN, BERTIL, "Marx's Vision of Communism: A Reconstruction," *Critique* 8 (1978).
OLSON, MANCUR, "Rapid Growth as a Destabilizing Force," *Journal of Economic History* 23 (1963).
PAINE, THOMAS, *The Rights of Man* (New York: Penguin, 1984 [1791]).
PAKULSKI, JAN, "The Dying of Class or of Marxist Class Theory?" *International Sociology* 8 (Sept. 1993).
PARETO, VILFREDO, *The Mind and Society*, edited by A. Livingston (New York: Harcourt, Brace, 1937 [1916]).
PATEMAN, CAROLE, "Feminism and Democracy," in *Democratic Theory and Practice*, edited by Graeme Duncan (Cambridge: Cambridge University Press, 1986): 209–214.
———, *Participation and Democratic Theory* (New York: Cambridge University Press, 1970).
PAYNE, JAMES, "The Congressional Brainwashing of Congress," *The Public Interest* (summer 1990): 3–13.
PECK, M. SCOTT, *The Different Drum* (New York: Simon and Schuster, 1987).
PEFFLEY, MARK, and JON HURWITZ, "A Hierarchical Model of Attitude Constraint," *American Journal of Political Science* 29 (1985): 871–890.
PENNOCK, J. ROLAND, "Liberalism Under Attack," *The Political Science Teacher* 3 (winter 1990): 6–9.
PETERS, CHARLES, "The Neoliberal Manifesto," *The Washington Monthly* (May 1983): 9–18.
PETERSON, PAUL, *City Limits* (Chicago: University of Chicago Press, 1981).
PETERSON, V. SPIKE, and ANNE SISSON RUNYAN, *Global Gender Issues* (Boulder, Colo.: Westview Press, 1993).
PHILLIPS, KEVIN, *Post-Conservative America* (New York: Random House, 1982).
PIERCY, MARGE, *Women on the Edge of Time* (New York: Knopf, 1976).
PIGOU, ARTHUR CECIL, *The Economics of Welfare*, 4th ed. (London: Macmillan, 1948).
PITKIN, HANNA, *The Concept of Representation* (Berkeley: University of California Press, 1972).
PIVEN, FRANCIS FOX, and RICHARD A. CLOWARD, *Regulating the Poor: The Functions of Public Welfare* (New York: Vintage, 1971).
POLANYI, KARL, *The Great Transformation: The Political and Economic Origins of Our Time* (Boston: Beacon Press, 1944).
POPPER, KARL, *The Open Society and Its Enemies*, 4th ed. (New York: Harper and Row, 1963 [1945]).
PROUDHON, PIERRE, *The General Idea of the Revolution in the Nineteenth Century*, translated by John B. Robinson (New York: Haskell House, 1923 [1851]).
———, *What Is Property?* translated by B. R. Tucker (London: William Reeves, n.d. [1840]).
PRZEWORSKI, ADAM, and HENRY TEUNE, *The Logic of Comparative Social Inquiry* (New York: Wiley Interscience, 1970).
———, and JOHN SPRAGUE, *Stone Papers: A History of Electoral Socialism* (Chicago: University of Chicago Press, 1986).

PUTNAM, ROBERT, "Studying Elite Political Culture: The Case of Ideology," *American Political Science Review* 65 (Sept., 1971): 651–681.

QUINNEY, RICHARD, *Criminology* (Boston: Little, Brown, 1979).

RAE, DOUGLAS, *Equalities* (Cambridge: Harvard University Press, 1981).

RAMSEY COLLOQUIUM, THE, "Morality and Homosexuality," *Wall Street Journal* (Feb. 24, 1994): A20.

RAND, AYN, *Atlas Shrugged* (New York: New American Library, 1957).

———, *Capitalism: The Unknown Ideal* (New York: New American Library, 1966).

———, *The Fountainhead* (New York: Bobbs-Merrill, 1943).

———, *The Virtue of Selfishness* (New York: New American Library, 1961).

RAWLS, JOHN, *A Theory of Justice* (Cambridge, Mass.: Harvard University Press, 1971).

———, "Justice as Fairness: Political Not Metaphysical," *Philosophy and Public Affairs* 14 (1985): 223–251.

———, *Political Liberalism* (New York: Columbia University Press, 1993).

REGAN, TOM, *The Case for Animal Rights* (Berkeley: University of California Press, 1983).

REICH, ROBERT, *The Next American Frontier* (New York: Times, 1983).

———, *The Work of Nations: Preparing Ourselves for the 21st Century* (New York: Knopf, 1991).

REIMAN, JEFFREY H., *In Defense of Political Philosophy: A Reply to Robert Paul Wolff's In Defense of Anarchism* (New York: Harper Torchbacks, 1972).

RICCI, DAVID, "Receiving Ideas in Political Analysis: The Case of Community Power Studies, 1950–1970," *Western Political Quarterly* 33 (Dec. 1980): 451–475.

———, *The Tragedy of Political Science: Politics, Scholarship, and Democracy* (New Haven: Yale University Press, 1984).

RIESEBROAT, MARTIN, *Pious Passion: The Emergence of Modern Fundamentalism in the U.S. and Iran,* translated by Don Reneau (Berkeley: University of California Press, 1993).

RIKER, WILLIAM, *Liberalism Against Populism* (San Francisco: W. H. Freeman, 1982).

ROBERTSON, PAT, with ROBERT SLOSSER, *The Secret Kingdom* (Nashville, Tenn.: T. Nelson, 1982).

ROCCO, ALFREDO, "The Political Doctrine of Fascism," in *Readings on Fascism and National Socialism* (Chicago: Swallow Press, 1952).

RODGERS, HARRELL R., JR., *Poverty Amid Plenty* (Reading, Mass.: Addison-Wesley, 1979).

ROEMER, JOHN, *Free to Lose: An Introduction to Marxist Economic Philosophy* (Cambridge: Harvard University Press, 1988).

———, *A Future for Socialism* (Cambridge: Harvard University Press, 1994).

ROSE, RICHARD, and IAN MCALLISTER, *The Loyalties of Voters* (Newbury Park, Calif.: Sage, 1990).

ROSEN, STANLEY, *The Limits of Analysis* (New Haven: Yale University Press, 1980).

ROTHBARD, MURRAY N., "Society Without a State," in *NOMOS XIX: Anarchism,* edited by J. Roland Pennock and John W. Chapman (New York: New York University Press, 1978).

ROTHENBERG, RANDALL, *The Neoliberals* (New York: Simon and Schuster, 1984).

ROUSSEAU, JEAN-JACQUES, *The First and Second Discourses,* edited and translated by Roger D. Masters and Judith R. Masters (New York: St. Martin's Press, 1969 [1949 and 1755]).

———, *On the Social Contract,* edited by Roger D. Masters and translated by Judith R. Masters (New York: St. Martin's Press, 1969 [1762]).

RYAN, ALAN, "Socialism for the Nineties," *Dissent* (fall 1990): 436–442.

SCHAAR, JOHN, "Equal Opportunity and Beyond," *NOMOS IX: Equality,* edited by J. Roland Pennock and John W. Chapman (New York: Atherton Press, 1967).

SCHLAFLY, PHYLLIS, *Power of the Positive Woman* (New Rochelle, N.Y.: Arlington House, 1977).

SCHOPENHAUER, ARTHUR, *World as Will and Idea,* translated by R. B. Haldane and J. Kemp (London: Kegan, Paul, Trench, Trubner, 1883 [1818]).

SCHRAM, STUART R., *The Political Thought of Mao Tse-Tung,* rev. ed. (New York: Praeger, 1969).

SCHUCK, PAUL H., "The Great Immigration Debate," in *The American Prospect* 3 (fall 1990): 100–117.

SCHULTZE, CHARLES L., *The Public Use of Private Interest* (Washington, D.C.: Brookings Institution, 1977).

SCHUMACHER, E. F., *Small Is Beautiful* (New York: Harper and Row, 1973).

SCHUMAKER, PAUL, *Critical Pluralism, Democratic Performance, and Community Power* (Lawrence: University Press of Kansas, 1991).

———, "Estimating the First and (Some of) the Third Faces of Power," *Urban Affairs Quarterly* 28 (Mar. 1993): 441–461.

SCHUMPETER, JOSEPH, *Capitalism, Socialism, and Democracy* (New York: Harper and Row, 1942).

SCHWARZ, JOHN, *America's Hidden Success* (New York: W. W. Norton, 1983).

SELIGER, M., *Ideology and Politics* (New York: Free Press, 1976).

SHIVA, VANDANA, *Staying Alive* (London: Zed Books, 1988).

SHKLAR, JUDITH, *After Utopia: The Decline of Political Faith* (Princeton: Princeton University Press, 1957).

SHTROMAS, ALEXANDER, *The End of ISMs?* (Cambridge: Harvard University Press, 1994).

SHULMAN, GEORGE, *Radicalism and Reverence: The Political Thought of Gerrard Winstanley* (Berkeley: University of California Press, 1989).

SIBLEY, MULFORD Q., *Political Ideas and Ideologies: A History of Political Thought* (New York: Harper and Row, 1970).

SINGER, PETER, *Animal Liberation* (New York: Avon, 1975).

SKOCPOL, THEDA, "Legacies of New Deal Liberalism," in *Liberalism Reconsidered,* edited by Douglas MacLean and Claudia Mills (Totowa, N.J.: Rowman and Allenheld, 1983).

SMITH, ADAM, *The Wealth of Nations,* in *Adam Smith's Moral and Political Philosophy,* edited by Herbert W. Schneider (New York: Hafner, 1948 [1776]).

SMITH, TONY, *Thinking Like a Communist: State and Legitimacy in the Soviet Union, China, and Cuba* (New York: W. W. Norton, 1987).

SOREL, GEORGES, *Reflections on Violence,* translated by T. E. Hulme (London: Allen, 1915 [1906]).

SOWELL, THOMAS, *Ethnic America: A History* (New York: Basic, 1981).

———, *Inside American Education: The Decline, the Deception, and the Dogma* (New York: Free Press, 1993).

———, *Preferential Policies: An International Perspective* (New York: Quell, 1990).

SPEER, ALBERT, *Inside the Third Reich: Memoirs,* translated by Richard and Clara Winston (New York: Macmillan, 1970).

SPENCER, HERBERT, *The Man Versus The State* (Caldwell, Idaho: Caxton Press, 1969 [1892]).

———, "The Survival of the Fittest," in *Social Statics* (New York: D. Appleton, 1851).

SPITZ, ELAINE, "Citizenship and Liberal Institutions" in *Liberals on Liberalism,* edited by Alfonso J. Damico (Totowa, N.J.: Rowman and Littlefield, 1986).

SPRAGENS, THOMAS, "Reconstructing Liberal Theory," in *Liberals on Liberalism,* edited by Alfonso J. Damico (Totowa, N.J.: Rowman and Littlefield, 1986).

———, *The Irony of Liberal Reason* (Chicago: University of Chicago Press, 1981).

SPRINZAK, EHUN, *The Ascendance of Israel's Radical Right* (New York: Oxford University Press, 1991).

STALIN, JOSEPH, *Dialectical and Historical Materialism* (Tirana: "8 Nentori," 1979 [1938]).

———, *Economic Problems of Socialism in the USSR* (Moscow: Foreign Language Publishing House, 1953).

STARR, PAUL, "Liberalism After Socialism," in *The American Prospect* (fall 1991): 70–80.

STEINEM, GLORIA, *Outrageous Acts and Everyday Rebellions* (New York: Holt, Rinehart and Winston, 1983).

STIGLER, GEORGE, "Director's Law of Public Income Distribution," *Journal of Law and Economics* 13 (Apr. 1970): 1–10.

STIRNER, MAX (JOHANN KASPAR SCHMIDT), *The Ego and His Own,* translated by S. T. Byllington (London: Jonathan Cape, 1921 [1843]).

STONE, ALAN, "Justifying Regulation," in *The Liberal Future in America,* edited by Philip Abbot and Michael B. Levy (Westport, Conn.: Greenwood Press, 1985).

STONE, CLARENCE, *Regime Politics* (Lawrence: University Press of Kansas, 1989).

STONE, DEBORAH A., "Why the States Can't Solve the Health Care Crisis," *American Prospect* (spring 1982): 51–60.

STONE, LAWRENCE, *The Family, Sex, and Marriage: In England 1500–1800* (London: Widenfelf Nicolson, 1977).

STORING, HERBERT J. (ed.), *Essays on the Scientific Study of Politics* (New York: Holt, Rinehart, and Winston, 1962).

STRAUSS, LEO, "The New Political Science," in *Keeping the Tablets: Modern American Conservative Thought,* edited by William F. Buckley, Jr., and Charles R. Kesler (New York: Harper and Row, 1988).

SUNDQUIST, JAMES, *Policies and Politics: The Eisenhower, Kennedy, and Johnson Years* (Washington, D.C.: Brookings Institution, 1968).

TANNENBAUM, EDUARD, *The Fascist Experience: Italian Society and Culture, 1922–1945* (New York: Basic, 1972).

TAWNEY, RICHARD, *Equality* (London: Allen and Unwin, 1964 [1931]).

TERCHEK, RONALD, "The Fruits of Success and the Crisis of Liberalism" in *Liberals on Liberalism,* edited by Alfonso J. Damico (Totowa, N.J.: Rowman and Littlefield, 1986).

THOMAS, ELIZABETH MARSHALL, "Of Ivory and the Survival of Elephants," *The New York Review of Books* 41 (Mar. 24, 1994): 3–6.

THOMPSON, JOHN B., *Studies in the Theory of Ideology* (Cambridge, England: Polity Press, 1984).

THOREAU, HENRY DAVID, *Walden* and *On the Duty of Civil Disobedience* (New York: Collier, 1962 [1854, 1849]).

THORSON, THOMAS, *The Logic of Democracy* (New York: Holt, Rinehart, and Winston, 1962).

THUROW, LESTER, *The Zero Sum Society* (New York: Penguin, 1980).

TINDER, GLENN, *Political Thinking: The Perennial Questions,* 5th ed. (New York: HarperCollins, 1991).

TOLSTOY, LEO, *The Kingdom of God Is Within You,* translated by Leo Wiener (New York: Farrar, Straus, and Giroux, Noonday Press, 1961 [1905]).

TONG, ROSEMARIE, *Feminist Thought* (Boulder, Colo.: Westview Press, 1989).

TRACY, ANTOINE LOUIS CLAUDE DESTUTT DE, *Elements of Ideology,* translated and edited by John Morris (Detroit: Center for Public Health, 1973).

TRIBE, LAWRENCE, "Ways Not to Think About Plastic Trees: New Foundations for Environmental Laws," *Yale Law Review* 83 (fall 1974): 1314–1348.

TROTSKY, LEON, *History of the Russian Revolution,* translated by Max Eastman (New York: Simon and Schuster, 1933).

———, "The Defense of Terrorism," in *Basic Writings of Trotsky,* edited by Irving Howe (New York: Random House, 1963 [1920]).

TROUNSTINE, PHILIP, and TERRY CHRISTENSEN, *Movers and Shakers* (New York: St. Martin's Press, 1982), pp. 40–47.

TSONGAS, PAUL, *The Road from Here: Liberalism and Realities in the 1980's* (New York: Knopf, 1981).

VERBA, SIDNEY, and GARY ORREN, *Equality in America* (Cambridge: Harvard University Press, 1985).

VIGURIE, RICHARD, *The New Right: We're Ready to Lead* (Falls Church, Va.: Vigurie, 1980).

VOEGELIN, ERIC, "Gnosticism—The Nature of Modernity," in *Keeping the Tablets: Modern American Conservative Thought,* edited by William F. Buckley, Jr., and Charles R. Kesler (New York: Harper and Row, 1988).

VOGEL, LISE, *Marxism and the Oppression of Women: Toward a Unitary Theory* (New Brunswick, N.J.: Rutgers University Press, 1983).

VOLTAIRE (FRANCOIS-MARIE ARGUET), "Lettres Philosophiques," in *The Selected Letters of Voltaire,* edited by Richard A. Brooks (New York: New York University Press, 1973 [1734]).

VONNEGUT, KURT, "Harrison Bergeron" in *Welcome to the Monkey House* (New York: Dell, 1970).

WALZER, MICHAEL, "A Day in the Life of a Socialist Citizen" in *Obligations: Essays on Disobedience, War, and Citizenship* (Cambridge: Harvard University Press, 1970).

———, "Socializing the Welfare State," *Dissent* (summer 1988): 292–300.

———, "The Community," *The New Republic* (Mar. 31, 1982): 11–14.

———, *Spheres of Justice* (New York: Basic, 1983).

WARREN, CAROL A. B. (ed.), *Gender Issues and Field Research* (Newbury Park, Calif.: Sage, 1988).

WEBB, SIDNEY, *Socialism in England* (London: Sonnenschein, 1890).

WEEDON, CHRIS, *Feminist Practice and Post-Structural Theory* (New York: Basil Blackwell, 1987).

WEFFORT, FRANCISCO, "The Future of Socialism," *Journal of Democracy* 3 (July 1992): 90–99.

WEINSTEIN, JAMES, *The Corporate Ideal and the Liberal State* (Boston: Beacon Press, 1966).

WEIR, MARGARET, ANN SCHOLA ORLOFF, and THEDA SKOCPOL, *The Politics of Social Policy in the United States* (Princeton: Princeton University Press, 1988).

WELCH, SUSAN, and TIMOTHY BLEDSOE, *Urban Reform and Its Consequences: A Study in Representation* (Chicago: University of Chicago Press, 1988).

WILL, GEORGE F., *Restoration: Congress, Term Limits, and the Recovery of Deliberative Democracy* (New York: Macmillan, 1992).

———, *Statecraft as Soulcraft: What Government Does* (New York: Simon and Schuster, 1982).

———, *The Pursuit of Virtue and Other Tory Notions* (New York: Simon and Schuster, 1983).

WILLIAMS, BERNARD, "The Idea of Equality," in *Philosophy, Politics, and Society* edited by Peter Laslett and W. G. Runciman (Oxford: Basil Blackwell, 1962).

WILSON, EDMUND, *To the Finland Station* (London: Macmillan, 1972).

WILSON, JAMES Q., *The Moral Sense* (New York: Free Press, 1993).

———, "The Rediscovery of Character: Private Virtue and Public Policy," *The Public Interest* 81 (fall 1985): 3–16.

WILSON, WILLIAM JULIUS, *The Truly Disadvantaged* (Chicago: University of Chicago Press, 1987).

WOLFF, ROBERT PAUL, *In Defense of Anarchism* (New York: Harper and Row, 1970).

WOLFINGER, RAYMOND, "Reputation and Reality in the Study of Community Power," *American Sociological Review* 25 (Oct. 1960): 636–644.

WOLLSTONECRAFT, MARY, *A Vindication of the Rights of Women*, 2d ed., edited by Carol H. Poston (New York: W. W. Norton, 1988 [1792]).

WOODCOCK, GEORGE, *Anarchism: A History of Libertarian Ideas and Movements* (Cleveland: World, 1962).

WRIGHT, ANTHONY, *Socialisms: Theory and Practice* (New York: Oxford University Press, 1986).

YOUNG, CRAWFORD, *Ideology and Development in Africa* (New Haven: Yale University Press, 1982).

YOUNG, IRIS MARION, *Justice and the Politics of Difference* (Princeton: Princeton University Press, 1990).

Z (an anonymous observer of the Soviet Scene), "To the Stalin Mausoleum," *Daedalus* (winter 1990): 295–342

ZIMMERMAN, EKKART, "Macro-comparative Research on Political Protest," in *Handbook of Political Conflict*, edited by Ted Gurr (New York: Free Press, 1980).

Index